REAL ESTATE PRINCIPLES

SEVENTH EDITION

Charles F. Floyd
Marcus T. Allen

Dearborn™
Real Estate Education

Senior Vice President & General Manager: Roy Lipner
Publisher: Evan Butterfield
Development Editor: David Cirillo
Development Editor: Amanda Rahn
Production Manager: Bryan Samolinski
Senior Typesetter: Janet Schroeder
Creative Director: Lucy Jenkins

Published by Dearborn™ Real Estate Education,
a division of Dearborn Financial Publishing, Inc.®
155 N. Wacker Drive
Chicago, IL 60606-1719
(312) 836-4400
http://www.dearbornRE.com

Printed in the United States of America.

02 03 04 10 9 8 7 6 5 4 3 2 1

Library of Congress Cataloging-in-Publication Data

Floyd, Charles F.
    Real estate principles/Charles F. Floyd, Marcus T. Allen—7th ed.
        p. cm.
    Includes bibliographical references and index.
    ISBN 0-7931-4183-4
        1. Real estate business—United States.   I. Allen, Marcus T.   II. Title.

HD255.F57   2002
333.33'0973–dc21   2001048859

DEDICATION

This book is dedicated to
R. W. Barber
a man of the land
and
C. O. Floyd
a man of business.

—Charles F. Floyd

This book is dedicated to
Rhonda, Melanie, and Issabella.

—Marcus T. Allen

CONTENTS

PART THREE

Real Estate Service Industries   197

CHAPTER 20
Home Purchase Decisions   426

Welcome to the 7th edition of *Real Estate Principles!* As one of the most popular and well-respected texts in college-level real estate education, this book has served as the framework for a practical and rigorous learning experience for introductory real estate students at schools across the nation since its first edition was published in 1981. This 7th edition continues that tradition by incorporating the latest industry advances and education technologies into a comprehensive, student-friendly presentation of the real estate "body of knowledge." We are absolutely convinced that students who master the material presented in this text will become better-informed real estate market participants whether their primary real estate interests lie in consumption, investment, brokerage, appraisal, law, property and asset management, or any combination of these disciplines.

In addition to an overall updating of the material from previous editions, readers will find substantive application of many cutting-edge topics in the real estate realm, including residential and commercial property financing, Wall Street's influence, innovative land-use control measures, and recent trends in real estate development, brokerage, property management and appraisal.

■ PEDAGOGICAL DEVICES

For students, the book contains numerous pedagogical devices designed to enhance their learning experience.

- ■ Each chapter begins with a "Chapter Preview" that clearly sets forth the learning objectives.

- ■ The key terms discussed in each chapter appear in boldface for emphasis. These terms are succinctly defined in the end-of-book Glossary.

- ■ Many tables, figures, and photographs are provided throughout the text to help readers visualize the topics and incorporate them in their knowledge base.

- ■ Each chapter ends with a "Chapter Review" that concisely summarizes the key concepts.

- ■ Thought-provoking review exercises are provided at the end of each chapter.

- ■ Suggested reading lists for each chapter are included to direct students who wish to learn more about specific concepts to additional sources of information, including books, academic journals, practitioner journals, newspapers, magazines, and Internet sites.

■ INSTRUCTOR SUPPORT

For instructors, we have developed an extensive collection of support materials that can be easily downloaded (with the proper password) from the publisher's web pages at *www.dearbornRE.com.* The materials include

- detailed lecture notes in Microsoft PowerPoint and Microsoft Word format for each chapter (for use with a computer display projector or as transparency slides);
- assignment exercises for each chapter (with answers);
- an extensive multiple-choice, true-false, and short-answer test bank for creating customized assignments and examinations; and
- ready-made examinations for each part of the text, including

    - real estate legal analysis,
    - real estate market analysis,
    - real estate services analysis, and
    - real estate finance and investment analysis.

Readers familiar with previous editions of this text will be pleased to find that this edition continues to incorporate many of the special features from previous editions that enhance the students' learning experiences. Close-Ups, Legal Highlights, People Profiles, and Case Studies are liberally sprinkled throughout the book to demonstrate how real estate principles can be observed and applied in the "real world."

■ FLEXIBLE PATHWAYS THROUGH THE TEXT

Because real estate is such a dynamic and diverse discipline, we have purposefully designed this edition of *Real Estate Principles* in such a way that instructors who wish to approach the material from their own preferred direction can do so with relative ease. Each chapter can be treated as a stand-alone learning module within the real estate body of knowledge. While we recommend presenting the material in the chapter order provided for general business students, an instructor who wishes to focus on finance and investment analysis issues can easily shift Chapters 13 through 17 to the beginning of the semester (after Chapter 1) to allow adequate time for in-depth coverage. Or an instructor who wishes to focus on real estate economics might consider following the first chapter with Chapters 8 and 9. We would be pleased to get feedback from instructors describing how they choose to sequence the chapters in their courses.

■ ACKNOWLEDGMENTS

No project of the magnitude of this book can be accomplished without a spirit of teamwork and mutual respect between all the parties involved. We wish to sincerely thank all of the people who provided comments, suggestions, and other invaluable forms of support in the research, writing, and production process. Our reviewers included

Gayle H. Boudousquie, Tulane University
Nancy Campiglia, Chief Attorney, Department of Business and Professional Regulation, Division of Real Estate
Gloria M. Iverson, Educational Seminars for Professionals, Inc.
John W. O'Neill, MAI, CHE, Ph.D., Johnson & Wales University
Jeff Rymaszewski, School of Business Administration, University of Wisconsin-Milwaukee
V. Carlos Slawson, Jr., Louisiana State University
Robert William Young, Associate Professor, University of Nebraska at Kearney

In addition, special thanks are due to the students in our classrooms who served as guinea pigs for the new material.

Finally, we hope that everyone who reads this book will be able to use the lessons contained herein to improve their real estate decision-making skills and, ultimately, to enrich their lives with respect to real estate resources.

Charles F. Floyd, Ph.D.
University of Georgia

Marcus T. Allen, Ph.D.
Florida Atlantic University

CHAPTER

1

The Market for Real Estate Knowledge

The decision to acquire real property requires the consideration of a variety of factors, including location, demographics, financing, and the environment.

What is **real estate** and why do we study it at the college and university level? The answer to the first question is, simply put, "land and things attached to it." We study real estate because people who understand the intricacies of real estate assets and the markets in which they are traded are better able to make informed decisions regarding real estate for either personal or business use. In short, the more we know about real estate, the better our decisions will be.

Some people may benefit from knowing about real estate when faced with personal and business decisions relating to housing, investment portfolios, and other business activities. Other people may benefit from real estate knowledge by offering their skills to others in the marketplace as real estate professionals: brokers, appraisers, developers, market analysts, investment advisers, financing specialists, real estate attorneys, property managers, and many other real estate service specialists. This book presents the general principles of real estate that are necessary for effective decision making from the perspective of real estate consumers, investors, and professionals. This text serves as a starting point for more advanced study of the concepts and issues facing real estate market participants.

In this introductory chapter, we will discuss the components of the **real estate body of knowledge** and evaluate the market for this knowledge. After reading this chapter, you will have a good understanding of the body of knowledge that underlies real estate decisions.

The objectives of this chapter are to

■ define the real estate body of knowledge,

■ describe the market for real estate knowledge, and

■ familiarize the reader with the organization of this book.

■ DEFINING THE REAL ESTATE BODY OF KNOWLEDGE

Every field of study (chemistry, mathematics, history, art, engineering, etc.) is defined by the collection of concepts, skills, and ideas that form that discipline's "body of knowledge." As with other disciplines, we can define the real estate discipline or field of study in terms of the component parts of its body of knowledge. While there are many individual components within the real estate discipline, these concepts can be categorized along the following dimensions:

- Legal Analysis Concepts
- Market Analysis Concepts
- Real Estate Service Industry Concepts
- Financial and Investment Analysis Concepts

In the next several paragraphs, we discuss each of these major dimensions of the real estate discipline and describe how this book is organized around them. After that, we discuss some of the characteristics of the market that exists for real estate knowledge and some recent statistics regarding employment and wages for real estate service industry professionals.

Legal Analysis Concepts

Legal analysis concepts in real estate include property rights, restrictions on property rights, deeds, leases, contracts, and title transfer issues. Real estate market participants (consumers, investors, and real estate professionals) must be familiar with these concepts in order to use them effectively in their decision-making processes. Chapter 2 describes several different collections or bundles of rights an owner or tenant can hold regarding a particular parcel of real estate. These bundles of rights are called **estates in land.** In addition, we consider the methods by which individual parcels of real estate are legally described to distinguish them from all other parcels. Chapters 3 and 4 examine private and public restrictions that can be imposed on the property rights held by owners and tenants. Examples of these restrictions include liens, easements, zoning ordinances, and other land-use control measures. In Chapters 5, 6, and 7 we consider the role of deeds and leases as legal documents that convey property rights from one party to another, contracts that are used to bind parties together in the transaction process, and the procedures used to finalize real estate transactions.

Market Analysis Concepts

Because real estate assets trade in localized markets, we spend considerable time in Chapters 8 and 9 of this text describing and evaluating real estate market dynamics and several theories that help explain the reasons why urban areas grow and change the way they do. In particular, we distinguish between the real estate "space" and "asset" markets and show how the development industry ties these markets together. We also review several theories that help us understand urban area land-use and value patterns. These theories include central place theory, economic base theory, highest and best use theory, the neighborhood life cycle model, and the concentric circle, axial growth, sector growth, and multinuclei growth models of urban form.

Real Estate Service Industry Concepts

People who develop expertise in certain aspects of the real estate body of knowledge may be able to offer their services to other real estate market participants for compensation. The most obvious example of a real estate service professional is a real estate broker. In a general sense, a broker serves as an intermediary between a buyer and seller of an asset and works to facilitate the transfer of ownership of the asset from the seller to the buyer. Thus, real estate brokers help buyers and sellers negotiate real estate transactions. The real estate brokerage industry is regulated by state governments with the objective of protecting the public from incompetent and/or unscrupulous actions by brokers. All states require that real estate brokers complete specialized training courses and pass competency examinations before granting them a license. We consider the details of the real estate brokerage industry in Chapter 10. Other examples of real estate service professions include appraisal (Chapter 11) and property management (Chapter 12).

Financial and Investment Analysis Concepts

A major component of the real estate body of knowledge concerns the application of financial economic theories and concepts to real estate decision-making situations. Successful real estate market participants should be familiar with the procedures and mechanisms used to finance residential and commercial real estate (Chapter 13); the relationship between risk, return, and the time value of money (Chapter 14); basic mortgage mechanics (Chapter 15); investment property analysis (Chapter 16); and development project analysis (Chapters 17 and 18).

Special Topics

In addition to the major components of the real estate body of knowledge described above, there are several special topics that we will address in an effort to make the learning experience as comprehensive as possible. Specifically, we discuss property insurance in Chapter 19 and the home purchase decision in Chapter 20. Together, the topics considered in this text form a solid foundation of knowledge for real estate investors, real estate consumers, and real estate service professionals. This knowledge is quite specialized and, as we will see in the next section, quite valuable.

■ DEFINING AND ANALYZING THE MARKET FOR REAL ESTATE KNOWLEDGE

At its most general level, a **market** is a set of circumstances and arrangements through which buyers and sellers exchange goods and services. When the good involved is real estate knowledge, the buyers are the people and entities who are willing to pay the sellers (the knowledgeable participants) for their skills and expertise in real estate. In the remainder of this chapter, we use a simple supply and demand model to examine the dynamics of the market for real estate knowledge. We begin by discussing the characteristics of the demand and supply sides of this market.

The Demand for Real Estate Knowledge

On the *demand* side of the market for real estate knowledge, all households and businesses need some type of real estate from which to conduct their affairs. These market participants can be thought of as the "consumers" of real estate. To make effective real estate decisions, real estate consumers must be personally familiar with the characteristics of real estate assets and markets or they must obtain the services of someone who is familiar with real estate assets and markets. Consumers, especially those who do not engage in real estate transactions frequently enough to gain a sufficiently high personal level of knowledge in the field, often seek the services of a real estate broker when they wish to buy or sell a home, lease an apartment, add income-producing real estate to their investment portfolios, or acquire or dispose of business facilities. Similarly, real estate consumers may be willing to purchase the services of other real estate professionals in their real estate transactions, including appraisers, who prepare formal estimates of property value; financing specialists, who assist in obtaining funding for transactions; and title agents, who finalize the legal documents in real estate transactions.

The Supply of Real Estate Knowledge

The *supply* of real estate knowledge comes from a variety of sources, including college and university degree programs, proprietary school programs, and, perhaps most important, on-the-job training in the real estate industry and other industries. Many colleges and universities offer undergraduate and graduate degree programs in real estate, including such prestigious schools as Massachusetts Institute of Technology, Harvard University, University of Pennsylvania, New York University, University of Connecticut, University of Georgia, Louisiana State University, and the University of Wisconsin. In addition to teaching students about the existing real estate body of knowledge, many of these colleges and universities require that their faculty conduct research studies on real estate topics and publish their results in academic journals. Ultimately, the purpose of academic real estate research is to expand the amount of knowledge in the discipline.

Industry-related trade groups and organizations are other important suppliers of real estate knowledge. Organizations such as the National Association of REALTORS® and the Appraisal Institute require that their members abide by a code of ethics and encourage them to continuously update their real estate knowledge. As members progress through the training courses and seminars, they are awarded designations that convey the level of their knowledge to the marketplace. For example, an appraiser who has completed the rigorous requirements of the Appraisal Institute earns the much coveted designation "MAI," which stands for "Member of the Appraisal Institute." Similarly, some real estate agents join the National Association of REALTORS® and work diligently to obtain designations offered by that trade association for completing training in various specialty areas as indicators of their professionalism.

There are a large number of proprietary (for-profit) real estate schools around the nation that offer real estate training courses designed to assist students in complying with state-level licensing requirements. For example, most states require that applicants for a real estate broker's license complete a minimum number of classroom hours of real estate education before sitting for a general competency examination. Some proprietary training programs cater to entrepreneurial individuals who are seeking advice on how to get started in real estate investing and who have little or no interest in licensing requirements. These programs are often marketed with more emphasis on personal motivation and less emphasis on professional real estate education.

In addition to formal real estate education and training, an important source of real estate knowledge is, of course, the real world. Experience is an excellent teacher in all disciplines. Consequently, one of the best ways to acquire real estate knowledge is to become active in the local real estate market. People who have a business background are often quick to gain the specialized knowledge needed for success in the real estate industry. In fact, many students report that some of the facts and concepts they learn in the classroom do not really "sink in" until they crop up in the real world. For some people, the authors of this book notwithstanding, the best way to accumulate real estate knowledge is through a combination of a formal real estate education program and a few hard-learned lessons from the "School of Life's Hard Knocks!"

Equilibrium in the Market for Real Estate Knowledge

Theoretically speaking, if there were a way to collect accurate and timely information from all participants in the market for real estate knowledge, we could use this information to create a graphic image of the market's supply and demand conditions. **Supply** refers to the amount of a good or service (real estate knowledge, in this case) available in a market at various prices. **Demand** refers to the amount of a good or service (real estate knowledge) desired in a market at various prices. As with most "normal" goods and services, the quantity of real estate knowledge desired by consumers decreases as the price of acquiring the knowledge increases, resulting in a downward-sloping demand function. Similarly,

FIGURE 1.1 Supply and Demand Graph

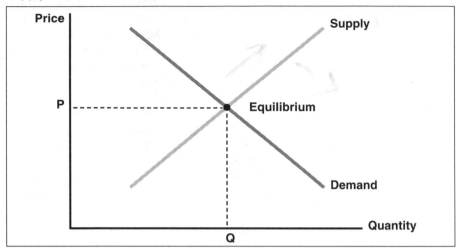

the supply function would most likely increase as prices increase, resulting in an upward-sloping supply function. When plotted together, the intersection of the supply and demand functions indicates the point of **equilibrium** between the quantity and price of real estate knowledge (see Figure 1.1).

Drawing on this familiar economic model, the **principle of supply and demand** states that the equilibrium price in a market is directly related to changes in demand and inversely related to changes in supply. The interaction of supply and demand determines the value of real estate knowledge at any given point in time. An *increase in demand* (that is, a shift to the right of the demand function) with supply held constant will result in an increase in equilibrium price. But an *increase in supply* with demand held constant will result in a decrease in equilibrium price. *Decreases in the supply* result in price increases, while *decreases in demand* result in price decreases if other factors remain constant.

Of course, the supply and demand model is a theoretical construct used to depict market dynamics in a simplified fashion. Even so, the model is useful for considering how the value of real estate knowledge is determined in the marketplace. Keep the supply and demand model and its equilibrium point in mind as we discuss real estate employment and wage statistics in the next several paragraphs. While we cannot put a precise dollar value on real estate knowledge, examining nationwide real estate employment and wage statistics gives us a broad-brush view of the value of real estate knowledge for those who choose to use it to earn a living providing real estate services to others.

Figure 1.2 shows annual U.S. Bureau of Labor Statistics (www.bls.gov) data for total employment in the real estate industry from 1972 to 2001. Overall, the total number of persons working in the industry has nearly doubled over this time

FIGURE 1.2 Total Real Estate Industry Employment

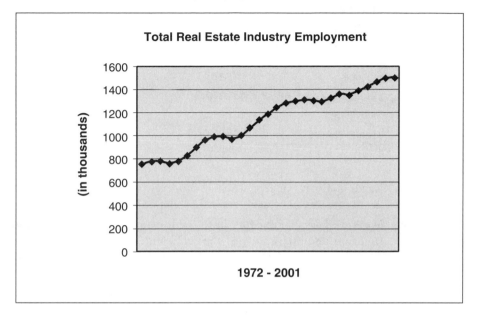

period, with slightly more than 1.5 million people employed in various aspects of the real estate industry as of 2001. This trend suggests that the equilibrium quantity of real estate knowledge has consistently and dramatically increased over the last three decades in the United States.

Additional data collected by the U.S. Bureau of Labor Statistics via a mail survey of more than 400,000 establishments each year are a good indicator of average earnings of real estate professionals around the nation. Table 1.1 shows the national average annual wage for real estate brokers, salespersons, appraisers, title examiners, and property managers for the most recent two years of data availability. Of course, people in each of these occupations may earn much more (or less) than the average wage. The top ten percent of real estate brokers in the United States earned at least $145,600 each in 1999. Similarly, real estate salespersons in the top ten percent earned at least $78,340 each in 1999. Overall, these wage estimates suggest that real estate knowledge is a valuable resource in the United States, though the value of this resource varies over time as supply and demand forces change.

■ CHAPTER REVIEW

■ The real estate body of knowledge can be divided into four primary divisions: legal analysis concepts, market analysis concepts, real estate service industry concepts, and finance and investment analysis concepts.

| TABLE 1.1 | Occupational Employment Statistics Survey Results Published by U.S. Bureau of Labor Statistics, 1998 and 1999 | |

	1998	1999
Brokers	$54,220	$62,190
Salespersons	$37,270	$36,990
Appraisers	$44,340	$41,670
Title Examiners	$31,850	$30,880
Property Managers	$35,960	$40,940

- Legal analysis concepts include property rights, restrictions on property rights, deeds, leases, contracts, and title transfer issues.

- Market analysis concepts in the real estate body of knowledge focus on the function and operations of the real estate space market, the real estate asset market, the development industry, and the forces that shape urban areas and influence their growth.

- Real estate service industry concepts focus on the specialized skills and knowledge provided by real estate professionals (brokers, salespersons, appraisers, etc.) to real estate consumers for compensation.

- Real estate finance and investment analysis concepts address the application of financial economic theories and concepts to real estate decision-making situations, including how to structure the financing for residential and commercial properties and how to analyze income-producing properties and development projects.

- Real estate knowledge trades in a market similar to the markets for other goods and services.

- The demand for real estate knowledge comes from real estate consumers (households, investors, and businesses).

- The supply of real estate knowledge comes from those who acquire knowledge through college and university degree programs, proprietary schools, and on-the-job training in real estate and other industries.

- The value of real estate knowledge is determined by the interaction of supply and demand forces in the marketplace.

■ KEY TERMS

demand	principle of supply and	real estate body of
estates in land	demand	knowledge
equilibrium	real estate	supply
market		

■ STUDY EXERCISES

1. Visit the website for the U.S. Bureau of Labor Statistics (www.bls.gov) and research the mean and median annual wages for real estate brokers, salespersons, title examiners, property managers, and appraisers in your state for the most recent two years based on the occupational employment statistics. Present the data graphically and comment on the direction and amount of any significant changes in wages from the previous year. Which of these three occupations do you think has the greatest year-to-year volatility in income *for an individual* working in that occupation? Why?

2. Identify three colleges or universities around the United States that offer real estate degree programs for undergraduate and/or master's level students. List the real estate courses required for each program and discuss how the courses "fit" into the real estate body of knowledge as discussed in the text.

3. List and describe the four main dimensions of the real estate body of knowledge.

4. If the number of knowledgeable real estate brokers in a metropolitan area stays constant and the number of people wishing to hire brokers to assist in real estate transactions increases dramatically, what does the supply and demand model say will happen to the value of brokers' knowledge? Show your answer with a simple graph similar to Figure 1.1.

5. A significant component of the demand for real estate appraisals comes from lending institutions. Because lenders want to minimize the risk of the loan, they frequently hire appraisers to provide an independent estimate of the value of the collateral being pledged by the borrower as security for the debt. Suppose the lending industry decides that appraisers' estimates of value are not effective in assessing the risk exposure of real estate loans. What does the supply and demand model predict will happen to the value of real estate appraisal knowledge?

■ FURTHER READINGS

REALTOR® *Magazine,* National Association of REALTORS®, Chicago, Ill. (monthly periodical)

WWW.REALTOR.COM, National Association of REALTORS®, Chicago, Ill. (Internet site)

The Appraisal Journal, Appraisal Institute, Chicago, Ill. (quarterly periodical)

WWW.APPRAISALINSTITUTE.ORG, Appraisal Institute, Chicago, Ill. (Internet site)

PART ONE

Real Estate Legal Analysis

CHAPTER

2 Property Rights and Legal Descriptions

The St. Louis Arch, a monument rising high above the city, holds rights not only to the land on which it is located but also to the air space that it occupies.

Perhaps you own or lease some real estate. What exactly are the rights that come with owning or leasing this property? These can be difficult questions because real property rights associated with real estate can be quite complex. Real property rights can be divided in many ways, with one party owning the right to use the surface of the land, another holding the right to subsurface minerals, and a third party another holding the right to use the water that flows across or under the land. Or two or more owners may hold unique and specific rights to exactly the same parcel of real estate, perhaps jointly, perhaps separately. This chapter examines these and other "property rights" issues that every market participant should know to ensure effective real estate decisions.

After reading this chapter, you should be familiar with how property rights are divided among various claimholders. The objectives of this chapter are to

- Define the concepts of real property and personal property;

- Demonstrate how property rights are physically divided;

- Consider how property rights are bundled into "estates in land";

- Describe how properties can be owned jointly by two or more owners; and

- Examine the three methods for legally and uniquely identifying each parcel of real estate.

■ REAL VS. PERSONAL PROPERTY

In the previous chapter, we defined **real estate** as the land and things attached to the land. Another important term real estate market participants need to understand is **property.** Although the term *property* can be used in several ways, we generally think of it as objects that can be owned or possessed—buildings, boats, books, or bonds, for example. Legally, the concept of property can be divided into two broad classes: real property and personal property. **Real property** consists of legal interests in land and things permanently attached to the land, such as buildings. **Personal property** includes legal interests in all other types of property. Stated simply, real property refers to real estate—land and things attached to that land—while personal property refers to movable property such as automobiles, furniture, clothing and business equipment.

There is an important distinction between the two types of property, particularly when ownership is transferred. The requirements for transfer of personal property are much less complex than are those for real property. Most personal property is exchanged or sold informally, and a bill of sale may or may not be given to conclude the transaction. But with only a few exceptions (such as short-term leases in a few states), whenever rights in real property change hands, a written agreement signed by both buyer and seller is required.

When ownership rights to real property (often called **title**) are transferred, the document used to convey the rights from one party to another is called a **deed.** When a tenant acquires property rights to leased property, the document used to convey the rights from the property owner to the tenant is called a **lease.** Leases merely convey the rights of use and possession under the agreed-on terms, not ownership rights. Both deeds and leases are considered in detail in a later chapter.

■ FIXTURES

Whether a particular item of property is considered real or personal property cannot always be readily determined. For example, an air-conditioning unit clearly is movable personal property at the time it is purchased. However, when it becomes attached to land as part of a building, it is treated as part of the real estate and is considered real property. Personal property that becomes part of the real property when it is attached to the land or a building is termed a **fixture.**

For example, the antique chandelier you inherited from Aunt Matilda and hung in your dining room is a fixture and part of your house. Unless it is specifically excluded when the house is sold, the new buyer becomes the proud owner of the chandelier along with the rest of the real estate. Other items generally considered fixtures include landscaping, appliances installed in the house (such as built-in dishwashers and central air conditioners), and television antennas. It is important to remember that if you are selling a home and want to retain ownership of Aunt Matilda's chandelier or your prized rose bushes, you must specifically exclude them from the transaction in the contract. Other important aspects of real estate sales contracts are discussed in a later chapter.

Tests for Fixture Status

Whether an item of personal property has become a fixture can be critically important in determining (1) the value of real property for tax purposes, (2) whether a real estate sale includes the item, (3) whether the item is part of the security given to the mortgagee (lender), and (4) whether the item remains with the landlord or can be removed by the tenant when the lease terminates.

Intent of the Parties

The most crucial test used to determine whether something is a fixture or personal property is the parties' intent. The best way to indicate this, of course, is by a written agreement at the time of sale or lease that states clearly which items are to remain as part of the real estate and which are personal property. For instance, a sales contract for a house might specify that the satellite television antenna may be removed by the seller; a lease agreement for a factory or warehouse building might state that the tenant may attach such **trade fixtures** (personal property used in a trade or business) as machinery, office equipment, and counters to the building without losing the right to remove these items at the termination of the lease. As long as the intent of the parties is made clear, there should be no confusion about whether the item in question is considered a fixture or personal property.

Other Tests of Fixture Status

Unfortunately, the intent of the parties often is unclear, so other tests of fixture status must be applied. If an item of personal property becomes attached to the real estate, it usually is considered a fixture, and the damage caused to the land or building by the item's removal is a crucial element in the **test of attachment.** For example, while a window air conditioner would be personal property, one built into a wall would be considered a fixture because the building would be damaged if the air conditioner was removed. Another method for determining whether an item is a fixture is the **test of adaptability.** Under this test, items that have been specifically adapted to the real estate are generally considered fixtures. The issue considered in this test is whether removal of the item would substantially alter the usefulness of the remaining real estate. For example, kitchen cabinets and a built-in entertainment center would probably be considered fixtures, while free-standing, noncustom cabinets would be classified as personal property.

Because these last two tests for fixtures do not necessarily provide clear-cut distinctions between real and personal property, the parties involved always should indicate their clear intent by a written agreement. This, of course, helps avoid disputes in *all* business matters.

■ MINERAL AND AIR RIGHTS

Real property rights are not limited to the surface of the earth; they also include the space above the earth's surface **(air rights)** and the space below it **(mineral rights).** Originally, a landowner's real property interests were conceptualized as pie-shaped, beginning at the earth's center and extending through the surface indefinitely into outer space. In modern thought, the property rights associated with the surface of the land, minerals that exist under the land, and airspace above the land are often separated among several different owners. Similarly, the rights to water that may flow over the land or adjacent to the land are sometimes considered separately from the land itself.

Today, ownership of airspace is limited to a reasonable distance above the earth's surface. Obviously, an airplane flying over a property at an altitude of several thousand feet rarely interferes with the owner's use or enjoyment of the land. But when aircraft fly so low that a reasonable use of the land is prevented (for example, near a lengthened airport runway), the owner of the land may be entitled to compensation on the basis that the plane is interfering with the owner's property rights.

Mineral rights and air rights may be owned by someone other than the owner of the surface of the land. It is common, for example, for a surface owner to sell to a third party the rights to any oil, gas, coal, and other minerals that may be located below the surface. The air rights, likewise, may be transferred to persons other than the owner of the surface. For example, office buildings and parking decks have been constructed over the tracks of railroads, with the owner of the building owning only the air rights.

A developing area of real estate law concerns a landowner's right to sunlight. This right has become especially important to those who depend on solar energy. People have questioned the legality of building a tall structure on a parcel of land if that building will partially or totally block the adjoining landowner's use of sunlight. This matter is currently unresolved and, in many jurisdictions, undoubtedly will be the subject of future litigation and legislative attention.

■ WATER RIGHTS

Water rights—who has the right to withdraw water from the land—is a question of considerable importance, particularly in the more arid western states, and increasingly in the eastern states. These rights vary from state to state and depend primarily on what type of water the land touches.

Rights Relating to Navigable Bodies of Water

The owner whose land joins a navigable body of water, such as an ocean, a sea, or certain rivers, generally owns the land to the high-water mark (the government owns the water and the land underneath). The owners of such adjoining lands are called **littoral proprietors.** Disputes regarding the use of water from these waterways seldom occur because there usually is sufficient water to be shared. The principal issue involving navigable waters has been pollution. Laws regulating the pollution of these waters exist at both the federal and state levels.

Rights to Nonnavigable Bodies of Water

The rights of a landowner to use water from a nonnavigable lake or stream that flows across the land are more complex. If an upstream owner uses too much water, for example, there may be none left for landowners downstream. How should these waters be allocated? The laws that answer this question have developed in a way that reflects the abundance or scarcity of water within the geographic area. The two dominant theories with regard to an owner's rights to nonnavigable bodies of water are the **riparian rights doctrine** and the **prior appropriation doctrine.** In the eastern United States, the dominant theory is the riparian rights doctrine. Under this theory, all owners whose land underlies or borders the water have equal rights to the water. This concept allows all riparian landowners to use all the water needed as long as the use does not deprive other landowners who are also entitled to some of the water.

In contrast, many states west of the Mississippi are extremely arid and, consequently, have rejected the theory of riparian rights and adopted the *prior appropriation doctrine.* Under this concept, the first person to use a body of water for some beneficial economic purpose has a right to use all the water needed, even if landowners who later find a use for the water may be precluded from using it. This "first-come, first-served" concept is based on the premise that there is an insufficient supply of water to satisfy everyone's needs; therefore, the first landowner(s) who uses the water for some worthwhile purpose should be allowed to use all of the water. Prior appropriation states usually establish a permit system whereby a governing authority can control the water's use.

Underground Water

There are two types of underground water. Water that flows in a defined channel is called an *underground* or *subterranean stream,* while water in pockets not clearly located is known as *percolating water.* Issues involving underground streams generally are resolved by applying the same principles that would be used if the body of water existed on the earth's surface. In the case of percolating waters, states generally apply a reasonable use test: A landowner may use the water beneath the land for industrial, agricultural, or other purposes necessary to the beneficial use of the land. However, if withdrawing the water depletes the underground water supply of adjoining landowners, the courts may restrict such action.

■ ESTATES IN LAND

Collections or bundles of ownership interests in real property often are described as **estates in land.** These are divided into two basic types: **freehold**

FIGURE 2.1   Types of Estates in Land

Freehold Estates ✓

Freehold estates are separated into presently possessed interests and those that may be possessed in the future. Presently possessed interests are classified as fee simple absolute estates, qualified fee estates, or life estates. Future interests that accompany qualified fee and life estates include reversion and remainder interests. We discuss each of these ownership interests starting below.

estates, or ownership, and **leasehold estates,** or the right to use and possess (but not own) a property owned by someone else. Homebuyers normally purchase a freehold; renters have a leasehold. Figure 2.1 summarizes the different types of estates. When discussing estates in land, the terms *grantor* and *grantee* often are used. The **grantor** is the party who transfers (by sale or gift) a real property interest; the **grantee** is the party who receives the interest. In the case of leasehold estates, the landlord is known as the **lessor,** and the tenant is known as the **lessee.** Deeds and leases are considered in detail in Chapter 5.

Freehold Estates ✓

Freehold estates are separated into presently possessed interests and those that may be possessed in the future. Presently possessed interests are classified as fee simple absolute estates, qualified fee estates, or life estates. Future interests that accompany qualified fee and life estates include reversion and remainder interests. We discuss each of these ownership interests starting below.

Fee Simple Absolute Estates ✓

The **fee simple absolute estate** is the fullest and most complete set of ownership rights one can possess in real property. Also known as a *fee estate* or a *fee simple estate,* this estate is the one most commonly associated with "owning real estate" and is the type of estate acquired in a typical residential transaction.

The property owner receiving a fee simple absolute title has an unlimited right to transfer the property to another during his or her lifetime or at death. Legally stated, the fee simple absolute estate is alienable, devisable, and descendible. **Alienable** means the owner can transfer any interest in the property while living. **Devisable** means interests can be transferred by a will on the death of the owner. **Descendible** means the interest passes to the owner's legal heirs if he or she dies without a valid will.

In addition to the ability to transfer a fee simple absolute estate without restriction, the owner has the right of unlimited use and even abuse of the land, constrained only by liens and other encumbrances, public land-use controls, and restrictive covenants. These restrictions are discussed in Chapters 3 and 4.

Qualified Estates

In a **qualified** (or **defeasible**) **estate,** the owner's rights can be "defeased" or lost in the future, should a stated event or condition come to pass. For example, the University of Georgia holds a qualified estate in an old rock house located on the campus in the midst of its modern buildings. Many years ago, the Lumpkin family donated a large tract of land to the university with the qualification in the deed that the family house had to be "forever maintained." If the university were to destroy the building or let it fall to ruin, a large portion of the campus (with many modern buildings) would revert to the donor's heirs.

Although qualified estates are present interests in real property, each qualified estate must also be accompanied by a future interest in the property. The future interests that follow qualified fee estates are known as **reversion interests,** or *reversion estates.* If the condition specified is ever violated (for example, removal of the Lumpkin house), ownership in the property automatically reverts to the grantor (or the grantor's heirs). In *a qualified fee conditional estate,* the grantor (or the grantor's heirs) must seek a court order to terminate the qualified estate if the condition is ever violated.

Many qualified estates are set up to protect a seller's or donor's wishes. A will might state that a parcel will transfer to Al, provided he marries before he is 25 years old; if not, then to Bob. If Al wants the property, he had better marry before 25 candles come up on the cake. In this case, Al holds a qualified estate in the property, while Bob holds a future interest in the property, which may or may not become a present interest.

Life Estates

The noninheritable estate, or **life estate,** is an ownership interest of indeterminable length that normally ends on the death of a named person but may be terminated by some other stated condition. In most cases, the person who receives the life estate is the named person, but life estates also can be held by someone other than the person whose death terminates the estate. In the latter situation, the estate is known as an **estate pur autre vie** (estate for the life of another). The future interests associated with life estates include *reversion* and **remainder interests.**

Suppose, for example, that a woman remarries after the death of her husband and wants to ensure that in the event of her death the new spouse will have a home to live in for the rest of his life. On the other hand, she wants the home ultimately to pass to her four children. In this case, her will might state that the home would be transferred to "my husband Alan for life." Alan has a life estate in the property, which gives him the right to possess the property until his death. During his lifetime, he can sell, lease, or mortgage his life estate (if the grantee, lessee, and lender agree), but at his death the property reverts back to the grantor. The future interest retained by the grantor is known as *reversion,* just as we saw in the case of qualified fee estates. Because the grantor is deceased when the reversion occurs, the property would pass to her four children.

Alternately, the grantor could give Alan a life estate and name only two of her children, Ivy and Nell, as **remaindermen.** In this case, the future interest is known as a **vested remainder.** On Alan's death, Ivy and Nell automatically become the owners of the property. Future interests following a life estate can also take the form of a **contingent remainder.** Suppose the original grantor's will states that the home would be Alan's "for life, then to my daughter Ivy provided she is married at the time of his death, otherwise to Nell." In this case, both Ivy and Nell hold a contingent remainder. If Ivy is married when Alan dies, she receives the property, and Nell's future interest is terminated. If Ivy is not married, Nell receives the property.

The life estate is a very useful technique in estate planning. John might, for example, put the family home and farm in trust for his children Sue and Sally but give his wife Mary a life estate. Estate taxes have to be paid upon John's death. Mary may use the property during the remainder of her lifetime, but at her death, no additional taxes are due because she possessed only a life estate. This often can reduce taxes greatly, particularly if the property has risen appreciably in value since John's death.

Leasehold Estates   - NON freehold

A *leasehold estate* is a possessory interest created by the establishment of a landlord-tenant relationship. These estates may last for a definite time period or for as long as the parties are willing to continue their relationship. For the duration of a lease, the tenant possesses or occupies the land or building with the understanding that the landlord retains full ownership of the real property. In other words, the landlord has a reversionary interest, often referred to as the *right of reentry.*

Leases, or tenancies, can be divided into the following four categories:

1. Tenancy for a stated period
2. Tenancy from period to period
3. Tenancy at will
4. Tenancy at sufferance

A **tenancy for a stated period** occurs when a landlord and a tenant enter into an agreement for a specified term. The stated period may be six months, a year, ten years, or any mutually acceptable time. In most states, leases that exceed one year must be written and signed by the parties. Of course, it is advisable always to have a written agreement even if the law does not require one.

A **tenancy from period to period** is created when landlord and tenant agree to continue their relationship from year to year or month to month. The agreement may establish an original term of one year, for example, with the provision that the lease is to continue yearly unless terminated with proper notice by either party. The method of giving proper notice should be set forth in the lease agreement. It is common to require notice of termination 30 to 60 days prior to the expiration of a period, depending on state law.

Should a lease term be unspecified, it is likely that the parties have entered into a **tenancy at will.** As the name implies, this lease lasts as long as both tenant and landlord desire. The tenancy at will can be treated as a *lease from month to month.* The required termination notice is provided by state statute. A 30-day notice is most typical for the tenant; some states require, however, that the *landlord* give 60 days' advance notice of termination. Although the tenancy at will might last more than one year, the original agreement does not have to be in writing, as there is the possibility that it will end within one year. Generally, it is unwise to enter into any type of tenancy without a written agreement.

A **tenancy at sufferance** occurs when a tenant refuses to re-lease the premises at the termination of the lease but continues to reside in the property. The landlord must decide whether to evict the holdover tenant or negotiate a new lease agreement. A tenancy at sufferance also might occur when a homeowner's existing mortgage is foreclosed and sold at public auction. Until the original borrower moves out, a tenancy at sufferance is established, and the purchaser at the foreclosure sale is considered the landlord.

■ CONCURRENT ESTATES   *more than one person*

The preceding discussion of property interests was based on the assumption that only one person owns each interest. These interests are known as **estates in severalty,** that is, estates "standing alone." Nevertheless, most of the real property interests discussed above may be owned simultaneously by more than one person. Perhaps you want to buy a house with your spouse, another relative, or even an unrelated person; perhaps your Aunt Matilda left you and your sister Bess a farm to be owned jointly; perhaps you want to make a real estate investment with business associates. All these situations involve the ownership of property simultaneously by two or more persons or entities and are examples of **concurrent estates** or, more simply, joint ownership. The most common types of concurrent estates are

■ tenancy in common,

■ joint tenancy,

■ tenancy by the entirety, and

■ community property.

Note that although the word *tenancy* is used here, it should not be confused with the tenant's relationship with a landlord.

Tenancy in Common

The traditional form of concurrent ownership is **tenancy in common.** Each of the joint owners holds an undivided, proportional interest in the entire property. For example, if Jack and Bob own a warehouse as tenants in common, each owns a portion of the entire property, but neither knows which portion is his. Each owner can dispose of his or her portion of ownership through sale or will.

Tenants in common who become unhappy with the joint relationship can demand a *partition* of the property. Voluntary partitions result when cotenants agree how to divide the property. If they cannot agree, however, a court may order a compulsory partition.

Joint Tenancy

Joint tenancy is similar to tenancy in common except it carries with it the **right of survivorship.** If a co-owner should die, the other owner or owners automatically divide the share owned by the deceased. This type of ownership often is used to ensure the continued operation of an investment property should one of the owners die. The joint tenancy ends if any tenant sells his or her share of the property to a third party. The joint tenancy then converts to a tenancy in common.

Historically, to establish a valid joint tenancy, the four unities of time, title, interest, and possession had to be present. To satisfy the *unity of time,* the joint tenants' ownership had to be created at the same time by the same conveyance. The *unity of title* exists when the owners have the same estate in the land, such as a fee simple estate, a life estate, or another estate discussed in this chapter.

Joint tenants meet the *unity of interest* requirement only when they have the same percentage interest in the real estate. For example, two joint tenants must each own 50 percent of the undivided property, three must own 33.3 percent each, four must own 25 percent each, and so forth. Finally, joint tenants have *unity of possession* only when each owner has the right to possess all of the real estate subject to the other owners' rights of possession.

Originally, due to the unity of time requirement, a grantor who was the sole owner of real estate could not create a joint tenancy with the right of survivorship between himself and another person. To get around this problem, the grantor had to deed the property to a friendly third party, known as a "straw man," who would then transfer that property to the grantor and the other party as joint tenants.

Some states have abolished the need to use a straw man in the above situation. In other words, these states have relaxed the unity of time requirement under these particular circumstances.

Tenancy by the Entirety

A **tenancy by the entirety** is a specialized type of joint tenancy that can be created only between husbands and wives. The spouses share ownership equally, shares automatically pass to the surviving spouse, and individual interests cannot be sold without the consent of the other spouse or without division by a court in case of divorce. Many states do not recognize tenancy by the entirety.

Community Property

Nine states (Arizona, California, Idaho, Louisiana, Nevada, New Mexico, Texas, Washington, and Wisconsin) recognize a system of property rights between husbands and wives generally called **community property.** In these states, all property acquired during the marriage, whether real or personal, is considered property of the "marital community." In other words, property ownership is divided equally between husband and wife. This division disregards the financial contribution each spouse actually made to the property's acquisition. Real property in community-property states cannot be transferred without the consent of both parties. Thus, a purchaser of real community property must obtain the signatures of both husband and wife on the sales contract and deed.

It is possible for married couples in one of these community-property states to acquire property not subject to a spouse's interest. Examples of this separate property include property owned prior to the marriage or property received by one of the spouses as a gift or an inheritance. Generally, any income derived from a spouse's separate property also is separate income.

■ CONDOMINIUM OWNERSHIP

In addition to the traditional forms of concurrent ownership, the condominium and cooperative are two other ways to own real estate jointly. In a **condominium** (condo) all owners have fee simple titles to their personal units, while common areas such as sidewalks, yards, entrances, hallways, pools, tennis courts, and other recreational facilities are jointly owned in a tenancy in common. (If the condominium is built on land that is leased with a ground lease, the unit owners hold a leasehold interest in the land rather than a fee interest.) A condominium association maintains these common areas, and each unit pays a mandatory association fee for this purpose.

All states have laws governing the formation of condominiums. These statutes require that three basic documents be filed—the condominium declaration, the bylaws, and deeds conveying the individual units. The purchase of a condominium interest is legally more complex and potentially more demanding than the typical single-family home purchase. In most states, this complexity and past abuses have led to more rigorous disclosure of information to prospective buyers of condominium homes. In Florida, for example, where condos abound, condo developers are required to give potential buyers 15 days to rescind a contract to purchase a new condo. Sales of existing condos require a rescission period of 3 days. The clock for these rescission periods starts ticking when the buyer is given copies of condominium documents to examine rather than the effective date of the contract, so most developers and sellers give such documents to potential buyers in advance of signing a contract.

Condominium Declaration

The condominium declaration describes the individual units and all common areas, assigns a specific share of the common areas to each unit, creates an association to govern the project and maintain the common areas, and sets forth restrictions on use. These restrictions usually are quite extensive and often deal with such details as the color of curtains in the windows and whether pets must be kept on a leash.

The declaration also may grant the association the *right of first refusal* to help it screen prospective purchasers. If an individual property owner locates a willing buyer, the association has a limited time either to approve of the purchaser or to purchase the unit under the same terms. This right of first refusal cannot be used to exclude prospective purchasers on the basis of race, creed, color, or national origin, although this type of discrimination often is hard to prove.

Bylaws

The bylaws represent a private contract among property owners regarding the operation of the condominium. They provide for the selection of the board of directors, the powers and duties of the directors, meetings, regulations for the common areas, assessment and collection of association fees, and other relevant matters.

Individual Unit Deed

Deeds for condominium units are similar to other deeds conveying real property. These deeds are described in Chapter 5.

■ COOPERATIVE OWNERSHIP

In the **cooperative** form of ownership, the land and building usually are owned by a nonprofit corporation; individual residents own stock in the corporation and have the right to live in a particular unit. Rather than a fee simple ownership, residents have a *leasehold interest* in a specific unit. The tenants run the cooperative through their stock interest in the corporation. They are assessed a periodic amount (according to their proportionate interest) for mortgage payments, maintenance, repairs, taxes, and other operating costs.

Cooperatives, the majority of which are located in New York City and Florida, are often accused of being the last bastions of housing discrimination. A tenant usually needs approval from the board of directors to sell to a new tenant, and approval has sometimes been withheld for reasons that appear to have a racial or religious motivation. Or the directors may withhold approval because they simply feel the buyer is incompatible for some reason. For example, former President Nixon was turned down as a tenant in an expensive New York cooperative because the board members felt he would attract too much attention to their building.

■ TIME-SHARES

Time-shares, or interval ownership, is a type of concurrent estate that splits ownership further by time. Most of the activity in the time-share is vacation oriented, with several large companies such as Disney and Marriot expanding into this market. There are two basic categories of time-sharing interests, a fee interest and a right-to-use. A **fee interest time-share** divides the ownership of a unit, usually a resort condominium, into 52 separate, weekly intervals. Owners receive a fee simple title to their particular ownership period. A **right-to-use time-share,** on the other hand, basically is a lease arrangement with a leasehold interest for a specific period of time and often with more restrictions regarding resale.

Whether or not it is deserved, the time-share industry is sometimes regarded as having a less than stellar reputation because of the high-pressure sales tactics used by some developers and promoters. Potential buyers often are lured to the property on the pretense of a free vacation, only to find that the time they planned to lie in the sun by the pool is eaten up with relentless sales seminars and guilt-laden pitches from aggressive sales agents. The entry into the time-share market by larger, more stable companies may be a signal that the reputation of the time-share industry is poised for improvement.

■ LEGAL DESCRIPTIONS

A proper legal description of the property involved is essential in all documents that affect title to real estate. When it comes to the actual transfer of title to real estate through a deed, for example, a precise legal description is necessary. Specification of the exact boundaries of the land being conveyed is essential for a valid transfer. In the United States, three methods commonly are used to obtain a precise legal description of land—the metes-and-bounds system, the rectangular survey system, and reference to recorded plats. Each property has a unique legal description.

Preparing the Legal Description

For existing properties, a proper legal description of a property often can be obtained from the tax office or other public records. A new, original legal description will be needed, however, for a property that is being subdivided from an existing parcel or created by combining multiple existing parcels. New, original

FIGURE 2.2	Angles in a Circle

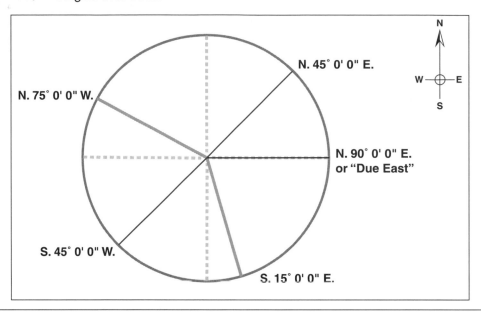

legal descriptions should probably be prepared by an attorney and a certified land surveyor. This avoids potential risks for buyer, seller, and real estate professional (broker, appraiser, etc.) that can result from an improperly drafted legal description. A correctly drafted legal description is important, particularly in deeds, mortgages, and other instruments directly affecting title to land.

Metes and Bounds

The original way to achieve a formal legal description of the exact boundaries of any piece of land was to refer to **metes and bounds.** *Metes* are the distances used in a description, and *bounds* are the directions of the boundaries that enclose a piece of land. A metes-and-bounds description starts at a designated point of beginning and, through specific distances, directions, and reference points, locates the boundary lines of the parcel of land. When a surveyor uses the legal description to identify the exact boundaries of a parcel of land, he or she usually drives an iron pin or stake deep into the ground at each corner of the property. These pins serve as the reference points in the legal description and can easily be located (perhaps with a metal detector) many years after they are placed in the ground.

In modern metes-and-bounds descriptions, distances are measured in feet to the nearest one-tenth or one-hundredth of a foot, and the angles are measured in degrees, minutes, and seconds. Recall that there are 360 degrees in a circle and that a circle can be divided into four quadrants: northeast, southeast, southwest,

FIGURE 2.3 Metes-and-Bounds Description

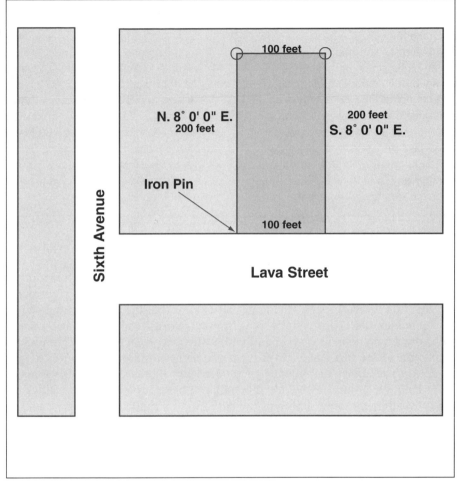

and northwest. Each quadrant contains 90 degrees, each degree contains 60 minutes, and each minute contains 60 seconds. Figure 2.2 demonstrates various angles using this system.

The following metes-and-bounds description describes the property depicted in Figure 2.3.

Beginning at an iron pin on the northern side of Lava Street 95.0 feet due east of the northeastern corner of the intersection of Sixth Avenue and Lava Street, as measured along the northern side of Lava Street; running thence N. 8º 0' 0" E. 200.0 feet to an iron pin; running thence due east 100.0 feet to an iron pin; running thence S. 8º 0' 0" W. 200.0 feet to an iron pin; running thence due West 100.0 feet to the point of beginning.

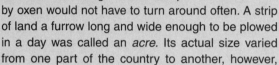

REAL ESTATE TODAY

How Did an Acre Get To Be an Acre?

Legal Highlight

Unlike the national metric system, the English system of land measurement that the United States inherited does not seem to make much sense. It does, however, but only if related to experience rather than to mathematics. Village farmland in medieval England was laid out in long rows so that plows drawn by oxen would not have to turn around often. A strip of land a furrow long and wide enough to be plowed in a day was called an *acre.* Its actual size varied from one part of the country to another, however, until a standard measure was introduced by one Edmond Gunter during the time of King James I. Gunter defined a *chain* as 66 feet and a *furlong* (the length of furrow for an ox-drawn plow) as ten chains. An acre was defined as the length of a furlong by the width of one chain (660 feet by 66 feet, or 43,560 square feet). Eight furlongs stretch 5,280 feet, or one mile, and 640 rectangular acres fit in a square mile. It is all very logical, but only if your frame of reference is medieval England.

While a metes-and-bounds description may look a bit cryptic at first glance, it simply describes the boundary lines and corners of the parcel of land being described. Each metes-and-bounds description must start with a point of beginning (POB). Thereafter, each boundary is detailed—its length, its direction, and the points where it begins and ends. It is vital that the boundaries described actually enclose the property involved. In other words, each boundary must begin at the preceding boundary's end and end at the next boundary's beginning. The description of the last side always must conclude at the original point of beginning.

The metes-and-bounds method easily addresses irregular shaped parcels of land, even those with curved boundary lines. Curved boundary lines are described by referring to the length of the curve and its radius. With this system, land surveyors can accurately identify the corners of a parcel of real estate and the boundary lines that connect them.

By now, it should be obvious that reference points are crucial to the metes-and-bounds description. Before developers began to use iron pins to mark these points, natural monuments often were used. Such a monument might be "the large oak tree," "the spring-fed stream," or "the old Indian rock mound." Although reference to such natural objects could cause some confusion because they are subject to change over time, they still are used today to describe some rural land. The following land description, found in an old deed in North Carolina, demonstrates an interesting use of natural monuments as reference points in a standard metes-and-bounds description.

Beginning at an ash bush on the North bank of Withrow's Creek above the bridge, corner to the lands of R. N. Barber, and running thence North 14 degrees West 17.50 chains [one chain equals 66 feet] to a stone pile, in the line of Mrs. E. M. Summerell; running thence North 68 degrees East 6.56 chains to a post oak, corner to the lands of Elias Barber; running thence South 27 degrees East 8.80 chains to a hickory on the North bank of Withrow's

| FIGURE 2.4 | Principle Meridians and Base Lines in the United States |

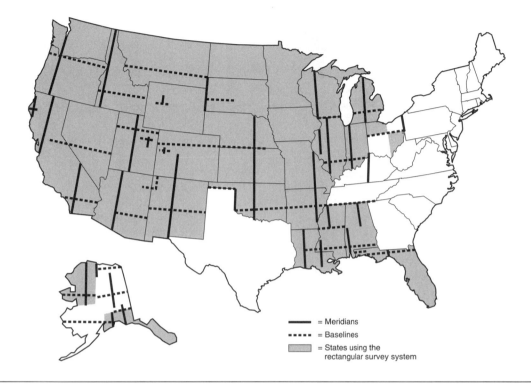

= Meridians
= Baselines
= States using the rectangular survey system

Creek, corner to the lands of Jane Barber; running thence Southwesterly up said creek 13.75 chains to the point of beginning, containing 12$\frac{1}{10}$ acres, more or less.

Legal descriptions do not describe "the side of the hill"; they define a flat plane that may or may not have a mountain in it. In mountain states, many sellers will tell you they have, say, 20 fenced acres, thinking they are really selling 20 acres—not their actual smaller number of surveyed acres. For example, suppose a tract of land measures 1,000 feet by 1,000 feet, or approximately 23 acres. If the property contains a steeply sloped hill within its boundaries, the actual ground area of this tract could be much more than 23 acres.

Rectangular Survey System

Shortly after the end of the Revolutionary War, when the westward movement from the original states began, a method of describing wilderness land was required. The U.S. Congress approved a description method known as the **rectangular survey system.** With the exception of Texas, land descriptions in all states

| FIGURE 2.5 | Quadrangles Divided into Townships |

		SECOND STANDARD PARALLEL NORTH			
	T.8N. R.2 W.				T.8N. R.4 E.
		T.7N. R.1 W.			
	T.6N. R.3 W.				
			T.5N. R.1 E.		
		FIRST STANDARD PARALLEL NORTH			
T.4N. R.4 W.	T.4N. R.3 W.	T.4N. R.2 W.	T.4N. R.1 W.	←6mi→	T.4N. R.3 E.
T.3N. R.4 W.	T.3N. R.3 W.	T.3N. R.2 W.	T.3N. R.1 W.	T.3N. R.2 E.	
T.2N. R.4 W.	T.2N. R.3 W.	T.2N. R.2 W.	T.2N. R.1 W.		T.2N. R.4 E.
T.1N. R.4 W.	T.1N. R.3 W.	T.1N. R.2 W.	T.1N. R.1 W.		
		BASELINE			

FIRST GUIDE MERIDIAN WEST — PRINCIPAL MERIDIAN — FIRST GUIDE MERIDIAN EAST

west of the Mississippi; the five states formed from the Northwest Territory; and most of Alabama, Florida, and Mississippi are based on this method.

Principal Meridians and Base Lines

The rectangular survey system is based first on **principal meridians** running north and south and **base lines** running east and west. Placement of these meridians and base lines generally coincides with an established landmark, such as the mouth of the Ohio River. The principal meridian was drawn north-south through the river's mouth, and the base line was drawn east-west to intersect the meridian at the landmark. The principal meridians and base lines around the United States are shown in Figure 2.4. Because the earth is round, lines that are drawn to run north and south eventually converge at the north and south poles. Surveyors use reference points created by "guide meridians" and "standard parallels" to account for this convergence when locating the corners of a property using the rectangular survey method.

Townships

The land on each side of the principal meridian is divided into six-mile-wide strips known as **ranges,** which are numbered consecutively east or west of the

FIGURE 2.6   A Township Divided into Sections

principal meridian. Lines running east and west parallel with the base line and six miles apart are called **township lines.** The range and township lines form the basic unit of the rectangular survey, the **township,** an area of land six miles square.

To identify a specific township, reference is made to the intersection of the principal meridian and the base line. For example, the shaded township in Figure 2.5 is Township 3 North, Range 2 West, indicated as T.3N.,R.2W.

Townships are not only the basic unit of the rectangular survey system, they often are the basis of political subdivisions as well. Somewhat confusingly, however, the term is also used to describe political subdivisions in states that were not surveyed under the rectangular system.

Sections

The rectangular survey system divides each township into 36 equal-sized **sections.** Within any given township, sections were numbered beginning in the northeast corner, moving westerly, then southerly one section, and back easterly. The

| FIGURE 2.7 | Subdivision of a Section (640 Acres) |

5,280 FEET
(1 MILE)

process continued until all sections were numbered. Figure 2.6 demonstrates this numbering process. Each section consists of one square mile, or 640 acres.

In the states covered by the rectangular survey, rural land is generally sold in patchwork pieces. Of course, farms in these states may be smaller than the sectional size of 640 acres. For example, farms claimed under the Homestead Act were one-quarter section, or 160 acres. As another example, a buyer might purchase the land indicated in the shaded portion of Figure 2.7, the northwest quarter of the southeast quarter of the northeast quarter of the Section. How many acres did the buyer purchase? The answer is ten.

Aerial photographs clearly show the effect a particular method of land survey has on rural areas. Under the metes-and-bounds survey system, farmlands are laid out in the random pattern illustrated in Figure 2.8, a photograph of farmland in the eastern United States. A comparable rural area that was surveyed under the rectangular system, with its even patchwork pattern, is shown in Figure 2.9. This photograph of land in Kansas is typical of the midwestern and western United States.

FIGURE 2.8   Aerial Photograph of Land Surveyed under the Metes-and-Bounds System

Combined Use of Metes-and-Bounds and Rectangular Survey Systems

The rectangular survey system describes very accurately the extensive acreage involved in farmland. It becomes difficult to use, however, when one wishes to describe the small subdivision lots found in most communities. Subdividing a section of 640 acres into lots of one-half acre or less is an all but endless task. Therefore, metes-and-bounds descriptions become vital to clear legal descriptions. Many properties are described by some combination of the metes-and-bounds and rectangular survey methods. For example, a combined description might appear as follows:

> Part of SW¼ of the SE¼ of Section 14, T.43S.,R.34E., Tallahassee Principal Meridian, Hendry County, State of Florida, beginning at a point being 202 feet East of the SW corner of the SE¼ of said Section 14; running thence North 8 degrees East 200 feet to an iron pin; running thence due East 100 feet to an iron pin; running thence South 8 degrees West 200 feet to an iron pin; running thence due West 100 feet to the point of beginning.

FIGURE 2.9   Aerial Photograph of Land Surveyed under the Rectangular Survey System

Figure 2.10 represents the southwestern quarter of the southeastern quarter of Section 14 in Township 43 South, Range 34 East of the Tallahassee Principal Meridian. The parcel in question is located near the southwest corner of the section.

Figure 2.11 shows a residential development that has grown up in and around farmland that was surveyed under the rectangular survey system. Here, we see the combined use of the metes-and-bounds system applied on the rectangular survey system. Notice that the undeveloped tracts still appear rectangular, but the newer subdivided tracts reflect irregularly shaped lots on curving streets.

References to Recorded Plats

A common alternative and supplement to these methods of legally describing real estate is to refer to engineers' drawings of parcels of real estate, called **plats,** that have been recorded as part of the official public record. Plats or similar documents show the streets, blocks, and lots as they actually exist. A plat of a subdivision appears in Figure 2.12. Land can be described simply by reference to the number of the lot as it appears in the plat of the block of the subdivision in

FIGURE 2.10   Location of the Stewarts' Lot in Southwestern Quarter of the Southeastern Quarter of the Section of the Township

which the lot is located. For example, we could identify the parcel highlighted in Figure 2.12 as "Lot 4 of Block G" of this subdivision as recorded in the public records of the county where the subdivision is located.

In the case of a condominium, each individual unit of the complex is described separately by referring to a previously recorded plat of the complex. In addition, a condominium description includes a reference to the fractional share (based on the number of units) of the common areas within the complex.

A different problem of legal description arises when the property does not actually touch the ground—for example, an apartment condominium on the 32nd floor, air rights above a railroad line, or subsurface mining rights below the surface of the earth. In these cases, vertical distances are measured from a point of known vertical height called a **datum.** The most common vertical reference is mean sea level, but official **bench marks** have been established all over the United States by the Coast and Geodetic Survey that can be used as reference points for both horizontal and vertical distances. Thus, the air lot of the 32nd-floor condo-

---

FIGURE 2.11   Aerial Photograph of Land Surveyed by the Combined
Metes-and-Bounds and Rectangular Systems

---

minium might be described by identifying the parcel of land underneath and the
vertical measurements of the airspace above this ground lot.

■ CHAPTER REVIEW

■ Real estate refers to land and things attached to it. Real property refers to the
legal interests associated with real estate. Personal property refers to all movable items (not real estate) and the rights associated with them.

■ Items that were once considered personal property but have become part of
the real property are called *fixtures.*

■ Real estate can be physically divided into surface rights, mineral rights, air
rights, and water rights.

FIGURE 2.12   Plat of a Subdivision

- Real property can be divided into different bundles of property rights called *estates in land.*
- Estates in land can be divided into freehold (ownership) and leasehold estates.
- Freehold estates include the fee simple absolute estate, qualified fee estates, life estates, and reversion and remainder interests.
- Leasehold estates include tenancy for a stated period, tenancy from period to period, tenancy at will, and tenancy at sufferance.
- Freehold estates are generally transferred by a legal document called a *deed.* Leasehold estates are transferred by a legal document called a *lease.*
- When more than one owner has rights to the same real estate, the ownership is referred to as *concurrent ownership.*
- Examples of concurrent ownership include tenancy in common, joint tenancy, and tenancy by the entirety.

■ Other ways the rights to real property can be divided among multiple owners include condominiums, cooperatives, and time-shares.

■ Three different methods are used to describe individual parcels of real estate: metes and bounds, rectangular survey, and references to recorded plats.

■ KEY TERMS

air rights	grantor	remainderman
alienable	joint tenancy	reversion interest
base line	lease	right of survivorship
bench mark	leasehold estates	right-to-use time-share
community property	lessee	riparian rights doctrine
concurrent estate	lessor	section
condominium	life estate	tenancy at sufferance
contingent remainder	littoral proprietor	tenancy at will
cooperative	metes and bounds	tenancy by the entirety
datum	mineral rights	tenancy for a stated period
deed	personal property	
defeasible estate	plat	tenancy from period to period
descendible	principal meridian	
devisable	prior appropriation doctrine	tenancy in common
estate in severalty		test of adaptability
estate pur autre vie	property	test of attachment
estates in land	qualified estate	time-share
fee interest time-share	range	title
fee simple absolute estate	real estate	township
	real property	township line
fixture	rectangular survey method	trade fixture
freehold estates		vested remainder
grantee	remainder interest	water rights

■ STUDY EXERCISES

1. What is the difference between the terms *real estate* and *real property?*
2. What are "fixtures" and why is it important to be able to identify them?
3. What are the three general physical divisions of property rights?

4. Fred leases a building from George for his new restaurant. To increase his business, Fred installs an antique bar in the center of the restaurant, complete with water and drain lines. A year later, Fred's business is so successful he decides to move to a larger building. He plans to remove the bar and take it to the new location, but George protests, claiming the bar is a fixture and cannot be removed. Does Fred have the right to remove the bar? Why or why not?

5. Distinguish between the reasonable use theory and the prior appropriation doctrine of water rights.

6. If Bob buys a parcel of land from Sarah, who is the grantor and who is the grantee?

7. What do each of the following terms mean with respect to the fee simple estate: *alienable, devisable, descendible.*

8. What is the primary difference between a fee simple absolute estate and a qualified fee estate?

9. What is the difference between a life estate and an estate pur autre vie?

10. Mabel, a senior citizen, has a life estate in the home in which she lives that was willed to her by her husband. She wishes to move to a warmer climate, so she offers her interest in the house to a neighbor for $10,000. The house has a total value of $100,000. Under what circumstances would the neighbor buy Mabel's interest?

11. If the neighbor declines to purchase her property, Mabel will offer it to her grandson, who has the remainder interest. Would he be likely to buy her estate?

12. If Mabel's grandson declines to purchase her property, Mabel plans to leave it to her friend Betty in her will. What interest will Betty have upon Mabel's death?

13. Lisa and Anne were business partners who owned real estate as joint tenants, not as tenants in common. At the time of Lisa's death, a dispute arose between Lisa's heirs and Anne as to who was the rightful owner of Lisa's one-half interest in the property. Who is entitled to the property interest that Lisa owned?

14. Madeline has an opportunity to invest in either a cooperative or a condominium. What are the differences between these types of ownership?

15. Dick agrees to rent a two-bedroom house from Larry for a two-year period. What type of leasehold interest is involved in this transaction?

16. Charles rents a home from Woodley on a month-to-month basis. On June 15, he gives notice that his new home will be ready on July 15, and he will move at that time. On July 22, he still has not moved. Under what kind of tenancy is Charles now holding possession?

17. According to the rectangular survey, if a buyer purchases the south half of the northeast quarter of a section of land, how many acres has he or she purchased?

18. How many square feet are in an acre? How many acres are in a section? How many sections are in a township?

19. Use a simple sketch to show the location of T.5S.,R.6E. Label the principal meridian, base line, and each of the range and township lines appropriately.

20. Use a simple sketch to show the location of section 17 in a township.

21. Use a simple sketch to show the location of the parcel described as "the NW 1/4 of the NE 1/4 of the SE 1/4 of the SE 1/4" of a section. How many square feet does the parcel contain?

22. Use a simple sketch to show the boundaries and reference points of a property described as follows

"Beginning at a point 200 feet due North of the southwest corner of Section 11; running thence 100 feet N. 45º E to an iron pin; running thence 100 feet S. 45º E. to an iron pin; running thence 100 feet S. 45º W. to an iron pin; running thence 100 N. 45º W. to the point of beginning."

■ FURTHER READINGS

McCormak, Jack C. *Surveying,* 4th ed. New York: John Wiley and Sons, 1999.

Jennings, Marianne Moody. *Real Estate Law,* 5th ed. Cincinnati, Ohio: West Publishing Co., 1999.

3 Private Restrictions on Ownership

Property ownership does not necessarily mean total control. Historic business districts, such as this one in New Orleans, often require that property owners preserve the architectural style of their buildings.

CHAPTER PREVIEW

Even though someone owns the entire fee simple ownership rights in a piece of real estate, this interest is limited by certain restrictions placed on the property by other private entities or by a government. These restrictions and limitations, known collectively as **encumbrances,** generally run with the land; in other words, they are binding on anyone who gains a subsequent interest in the property. In some cases, encumbrances may adversely affect both the use and the value of the property. In extreme cases, the land may be so encumbered that it would be valueless for a potential purchaser. Conversely, some public or private land-use restrictions may enhance the value of a property by protecting it from detrimental actions by others.

Several forms of private restrictions on ownership are discussed in this chapter. These include

■ liens,

■ casements,

■ licenses,

■ adverse possession,

■ encroachments, and

■ restrictive covenants.

The next chapter examines public restrictions on ownership, including

■ the property tax,

■ tax liens,

■ eminent domain,

■ zoning and other land-use controls under the police power, and

■ escheat.

Legal Highlight
Prescriptive
Easement

Legal Highlight
Adverse
Possession

Close-Up
Meadow Brook
Ranch Use
Covenants

Legal Highlight
Validity of
Restrictive
Covenants

■ LIENS

A **lien** is a claim on a property as either security for a debt or fulfillment of some monetary charge or obligation. For example, an owner might give a mortgage on a property in order to borrow money, thus creating a lien on the property. The lien does not represent right of ownership for the creditor; rather, it amounts to a **financial security** interest in the property, a claim the creditor holds against the property to help make sure the debt will be repaid. If the creditor is a private individual or business, the mortgage lien creates a private restriction on ownership; when the property is sold, the creditor receives payment before any money is turned over to the seller. If the creditor is a government, the resulting encumbrance is a public restriction on ownership. The property tax lien is a common example of a public restriction.

Real estate liens may be either voluntary or involuntary. Voluntary liens are those placed on property by the owner, usually in the form of a mortgage to secure repayment of long-term debt. Involuntary liens protect the interest of persons who have valid claims against the owner of real property—such as those resulting from a judgment in a lawsuit, from not being paid for some service, or from unpaid taxes.

Liens are also classified as special or general. A **special lien** is created to secure debts that are associated with a particular parcel of real estate. A *general lien*—for example, a judgment lien or an income tax lien—is placed on all the property that might be owned by an individual, including any real estate.

Special Liens

The two types of special liens that are created specifically to protect creditors using real estate as their security for repayment of debts are mortgages and mechanics' liens.

Mortgages

Because few people choose to buy real estate without borrowing money, a **mortgage** is the most common encumbrance on an owner's title. In return for a loan to buy real property, purchasers normally mortgage their property. They create a lien in favor of the lender, and the mortgage represents a limitation on their ownership interest. The borrower who gives real estate as security or collateral against a loan is the **mortgagor;** the lender that receives the benefits of this lien is the **mortgagee.** (A helpful hint for keeping the "ors" and "ees" straight in all real estate terms: the "ors" give and the "ees" receive.) Although mortgage liens put a restriction on a mortgagor's ownership interest, they make it possible for a purchaser to obtain long-term financing for a relatively large real estate purchase.

A mortgage lien acts as a private restriction to ownership in that if the loan is not repaid on schedule, or if other requirements of the loan contract are not met, the mortgagee may instigate **foreclosure** proceedings. By satisfying the legal requirements of foreclosure, the mortgagee can have the encumbered property sold to the highest bidder at a public auction to satisfy the debt. Mortgage lending and the foreclosure process will be discussed more fully in Chapter 13.

Mechanics' Liens

A **mechanic's lien** protects those who provide labor or materials for real estate improvements, including suppliers, architects, engineers, landscapers, carpenters, plumbers, and similar workers. Any such suppliers of materials and labor who are not paid can file a mechanic's lien on the property. If payment still is not made, foreclosure proceedings can result, with the property being sold to satisfy the debt.

Mechanics' liens are not just a concern to persons who fail to pay for work done to their real property; they also can create problems for subsequent purchasers. Suppose, for example, that Marty and Carole Teem purchase a home from Potts Development. Some weeks after closing on the house they are dismayed to learn that several subcontractors have filed mechanics' liens on their home because they were not paid by the general contractor. Even though the Teems have already paid for the house, they may have to pay twice for the same work if the claims are valid. Needless to say, it is vital to see that all suppliers of material and labor are paid before the general contractor is fully paid or the house purchase completed.

General Liens

Like special liens, general liens do not represent property ownership; they are, however, creditors' claims against a property owner's title. Unlike special liens, general liens normally may be filed on either personal or real property.

A common general lien is a **judgment lien.** The winner in a lawsuit who has not been paid may collect the debt by claiming an interest in the loser's property, including any real estate. If the judgment debt still is not paid, the real estate can be sold to satisfy the creditor's claim. Such a sale, commonly referred to as a **judicial sale,** is conducted as an auction by a sheriff or another legal authority. In some states, the debtor-owner of the real property may redeem ownership interest within a year of the sale by reimbursing the purchaser for the sales price and paying all of the costs of the sale.

Other general liens that could result in similar ownership limitations are public liens for delinquent taxes: federal income, federal estate, state income, and state estate or inheritance. As in a court-awarded judgment, such unpaid tax debts can be levied on real property. Ultimately, if the lien is not satisfied and removed, the land can be sold at public auction.

■ EASEMENTS

An **easement** is a right given to one party by a landowner to use the land in a specified manner. The landowner does not have to give up his land, but rather coexists with the holder of the easement. For example, property owners may grant

FIGURE 3.1   Easement Appurtenant Created by a Joint Driveway

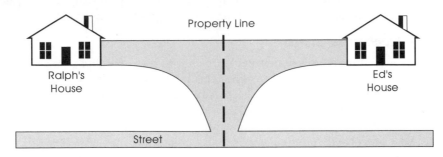

a utility company the right to run a power line across their land, or one landowner may allow an adjoining owner to build a driveway across her property.

Types of Easements

There are two types of traditional easements: an easement appurtenant and an easement in gross. An **easement appurtenant** exists when an easement is legally connected to an adjoining property. Suppose, for example, that Bill pays Susan to grant him an easement to run a sewer line from his house across her property to the city's trunk sewer line. In this case, Bill's land is being served or benefited by the easement and is known as the **dominant estate.** Susan's land, on the other hand, is burdened by the easement and is known as the **servient estate.** Susan can continue to use her land, but cannot do anything that would interfere with Bill's use of the sewer line.

As with almost all easements, this easement "runs with the land;" in other words, it continues when ownership changes. Even though the new owners of Susan's land may not want Bill's sewer line to remain on their property, they have no choice in the matter.

In some cases, adjoining properties are both dominant and servient. Suppose that Ralph and Ed are neighbors, and each wants a paved driveway. To save money, they decide to share the building costs of one driveway that will serve both lots, as shown in Figure 3.1. Each grants the other an easement appurtenant to use the portion of the driveway on each other's land. Both lots are simultaneously the servient estate and the dominant estate.

With an **easement in gross** there is no dominant estate, only a servient estate. For example, a utility company that acquires an easement to run its power line or pipeline across a property or the highway department that acquires an easement for a road right-of-way has acquired an easement in gross. The easements have been granted to the utility company or the highway department, not to parcels of land. The land over which the utility line or road crosses is the servient estate, and the easement binds all future owners of the property.

FIGURE 3.2   Easement Created by Express Grant

Creation of Easements

Both easements appurtenant and easements in gross may be established in a number of ways. The most common method is by an express grant or reservation, but easements also may be established by implication and by prescription.

Express Grant or Reservation

Most easements are created by either **express grant** or express reservation. Suppose Scott sells half of his ten-acre lot to Darlene. If the property Darlene is purchasing has no road frontage, Scott may expressly grant her the right to use a portion of his remaining property for a driveway. In this case, Scott owns the servient estate, and Darlene owns the dominant estate. The deed Scott gives Darlene should specify the easement appurtenant that has been created. This easement is shown in Figure 3.2.

An easement also may be established by an **express reservation.** If Sam were to sell the front half of his land to Bob, the remainder of Sam's property would be landlocked because it does not front on a public road. In the deed that transferred ownership of the frontage land to Bob, Sam could reserve a right of passageway through Bob's newly acquired land. Sam owns the dominant estate, and Bob owns the burdened (servient) estate. By this express reservation in the sale of land, an easement appurtenant has been created, as shown in Figure 3.3.

Implication

Sometimes, when one or more parcels are severed from a larger tract under common ownership, the right to use the land may be implied from the factual circumstances even when an easement is not created expressly. The easement supposedly reflects the intentions of the parties and is called an *easement by implication.*

Suppose no mention of an easement was made in the previous examples. If Scott sold the land illustrated in Figure 3.2 to Darlene, and he allowed her to use the road on the property he retained, an easement by **implied grant** probably would be established. Likewise, as depicted in Figure 3.3, Sam's continued use of

| FIGURE 3.3 | Easement Created by Implied Reservation |

the passageway over the land granted to Bob would create an easement by **implied reservation.**

In both of these situations, the implied easement is called an **easement by necessity**—that is, a court-ordered easement that permits the owner of a landlocked parcel to continue crossing a portion of land of which the easement formerly was a part. In the absence of the easements, the properties would have no access and virtually no value. Of course, even when an easement can be implied, it is best that all easements be stated expressly in writing.

Prescription

An **easement by prescription** may be created when someone other than the owner uses the land "openly, hostilely, and continuously" for a statutory time period. To use the land openly means that the user comes onto the land and acts entitled to be there. Such a user does not use the land secretly, as if to hide the use. Hostile use means the user treats the land as if he or she is the true owner of an easement. If the landowner has given specific permission for the use of land, hostility does not exist. To be continuous, the use must be uninterrupted for the time period provided by the applicable statute, usually between 7 and 20 years. These elements of prescription are very similar to those required for gaining title by adverse possession, a topic discussed later in this chapter.

Suppose, for example, that college students begin driving across kindly farmer Wilhelm's land to reach a swimming hole on the river. Being a good fellow, he says nothing about it, and the use continues for many years. Later, when Mr. Wilhelm attempts to close the road, he is sued successfully to keep it open because of the prescriptive easement. This may seem to be unfair, but it is the law.

The lesson of all this for property owners is clear: they should not allow anyone to use their property without specific permission, and they should make certain the use is interrupted at intervals. Otherwise, these property owners may find that a prescriptive easement has been created.

REAL ESTATE TODAY

Prescriptive Easement

Not all disputes about prescriptive easements involve roads across relatively undeveloped lands; some involve very valuable urban properties. Such was the case in a dispute between the owners of two abutting commercial properties, the Powers Ferry Square Shopping Center and the Boston Sea Party restaurant.

The shopping center had a main parking lot and a little-used north parking lot that was reached by using a one-lane drive around one corner of the building. There was no clearly defined dividing line between the shopping center and restaurant property, and the center actually paved the disputed small part of the restaurant's land in 1986.

There was no conflict until 1994 when Harry's in a Hurry moved into the corner space in the shopping center, shifting its main entrance to the north parking lot. To provide better access, the center extended the sidewalk alongside the building between the two parking lots and widened the driveway to two lanes. The Boston Sea Party restaurant's owners pointed out that the driveway was crossing their land and

Legal Highlight

threatened to put a fence across it unless they were paid for the land by the shopping center's owner, Metropolitan Life. Metropolitan sued, claiming it had used the disputed property as a driveway for more than the required seven years and was entitled to a prescriptive easement. It lost.

Not only did the court hear witnesses regarding the use or nonuse as a driveway of the disputed land, the court actually inspected the site. It found that although old pavement markings had been painted over after the construction for Harry's, the old markings were still visible. The markings clearly showed that two parking spaces for the center blocked cars from traveling over the disputed restaurant land, and other markings directed traffic to the north lot by way of the narrow driveway on the shopping center property. Thus, the land had not been used for the requisite seven years as a driveway, and the center was not entitled to a prescriptive driveway easement.

Source: *Metropolitan Life Insurance Company v. Popescu,* 172 Bankr. 691 (1994).

Nature of Easements

Easements are considered to be permanent in nature. That is, easements "run with the land" from owner to owner. Under an easement appurtenant, both the benefit to the dominant estate and the burden on the servient estate are transferred to the new owner if either of the properties is transferred. Owners Scott and Bob represented in Figures 3.2 and 3.3 own their respective lots subject to an easement of passageway over the their land. If ownership of these lots were to change, the easement would still exist, as the passageway continues to be necessary for both Darlene and Sam to have access to the highway.

The burden on the servient estate also runs with the land in easements in gross. If Susan grants a utility company an easement to use her land for its electrical lines, then sells her land to Wilbur, the transfer does not destroy the utility company's right to use the land. The easement, therefore, is just as valid under

Wilbur's ownership as it is under Susan's. In some states, the utility company normally could pass this right to another organization as long as the burden on the servient estate is not increased. For example, an electric company could permit a cable television company to run its cable alongside those of the utility. In other states, additional users would have to negotiate their own easements with the landowner.

Termination of Easements

Even though easements are considered permanent and pass from owner to owner, the rights and restrictions of an easement may be terminated under certain circumstances. Methods of terminating an easement include agreement, merger, and abandonment.

Agreement

Parties affected by the easement may expressly agree to terminate their respective rights in the easement. Such an agreement should be written and recorded so that notice is given to everyone interested that a prior easement no longer exists. Because easements are valuable, convincing the owner of the dominant estate can be quite expensive. If an easement is created by an express grant or reservation that specifies it will last for a limited term only, the easement automatically ceases at the end of that term.

Merger

An easement can also be terminated by the merger of the dominant and servient estates. If Bill's land is burdened by an easement that permits Sarah, the adjoining landowner, to travel across a portion of his property, Bill could persuade Sarah to sell him the land and thereby terminate the easement. Bill could then sell the land to another party without granting an easement, provided the property has another access route. Such a strategy is used when an agreement to terminate an easement cannot be reached.

Abandonment

A third method of terminating an easement is abandonment. If the benefited party does not exercise his or her rights to use the servient estate over an extended period of time, the easement may be terminated. The length of time an easement may remain in effect without being used varies from state to state and from case to case. Some states require that the holder of a servient estate perform some act to block the easement's use before any abandonment is possible. In essence, these states say that the easement must be terminated by the burdened owner's prescriptive use or adverse possession.

■ LICENSES

A **license** is a revocable personal privilege to use land for a particular purpose. Whereas easements are created by express grants, prescription, or implication, licenses are established by verbal or written grants of permission. A landowner might, for example, rent parking spaces by the hour, with the right to park evidenced only by a ticket stub. Licenses can generally be revoked at will by the owner. The benefits under a license and the burdens to the grantor's land are temporary in nature and do not pass to successive owners.

■ PROFIT A PRENDRE

A *profit,* more correctly known as a **profit a prendre,** is a nonpossessory interest in real property that permits the holder to remove part of the soil or produce of the land. It is similar to an easement, although the holder of a profit has the right to remove specified resources, such as soil, produce, wild animals, coal or other minerals, or timber, while the holder of an easement does not.

■ ADVERSE POSSESSION

Perhaps nothing in real estate law is so upsetting to property owners as **adverse possession,** which allows individuals to acquire title to land they do not own because they have openly possessed it for a statutory period of time, usually 7 to 20 years.

For title to be transferred by adverse possession, such possession must be "actual and exclusive, open and notorious, hostile, and continuous" for a statutory period of time. The phrase actual and exclusive does not require that the adverse possessor physically occupy the land at all times. Improving the land with a residence would constitute actual possession. So would clearing the land, building a fence along its boundaries, or farming it. Allowing other people to use the land without express permission would prove that the possession was not exclusive. The possessor must maintain possession in the manner of a reasonable owner. The terms *open and notorious, hostile,* and *continuous* have the same meaning in the case of adverse possession as they do in the case of a prescriptive easement.

Another important prerequisite for adverse possession in some states is that the possessor be under a "claim of right." This means that the adverse possessor must have a basis for believing he or she owns the real estate claimed. A tenant who takes possession of a house while acknowledging the landlord's ownership cannot adversely possess the leased property. If a claim of right is based on a written document, such as an invalid deed, the claim is said to be made under "color of title." Some states require that the possessor have color of title to possess land adversely, while other states reduce the number of years required for continuous possession if written color of title is present. Still other states treat all claims of right in the same manner, whether or not they are based on documents.

REAL ESTATE TODAY

Adverse Possession

The Cappuccios purchased a lot in the town of Narragansett, Rhode Island, for the purpose of building a home. Unfortunately, they did not have the lot surveyed before completing the purchase, and when they finally did, they received quite a shock.

Legal Highlight

Twenty-five years earlier, the Fortunes had purchased the adjoining lot. They also did not have their lot surveyed but cleared it to what they believed were the side pro-perty lines perpendicular to Win-terber-ry Road. The Fortunes then built a house with a septic tank and drainage field in the back of the lot, and also constructed a driveway along what they thought was the side lot line.

The Fortunes lived in the house for five years. It then passed through a succession of owners and renters, who maintained the same area, cutting the grass and even planting a garden along the assumed side boundary. According to his later testimony, when James Walsh purchased the property the real estate agent told him the side lot line was marked by a line of rocks, and he cut the grass to the apparent property line established many years earlier.

The Cappuccio survey revealed that the platted lots were laid out at a 57-degree angle to the road, not a perpendicular angle, as the Fortunes had assumed 13 years earlier. Because of the Fortunes' mistake, a portion of Walsh's home and most of the rear yard, including the septic system, encroached on a substantial portion of the Cappuccios' lot. In fact, the encroachment occupied approximately half of the land.

Walsh sued to have the disputed portion of the Cappuccios' lot de-clared his property through adverse posses-sion. He won. The court ruled that possession by Walsh and his predecessors was "actual, open, notorious, hostile, under claim of right, continuous, and exclu-sive" for a period in excess of the statutory ten years, clearly establishing adverse possession of the property.

The Cappuccios then sued the seller for indemnification. The result of that dispute is not yet settled, but obviously the Cappuccios are now much sadder and hopefully wiser.

The lesson of this saga is quite clear. One should never purchase property without having it surveyed before closing. It also shows why lenders usually require a survey before loaning mortgage monies.

Source: *Walsh v. Cappuccio, Supreme Court of Rhode Island,* 602 A.2d 927.

Diagram labels:
- Assumed Lot Lines
- Land acquired by Walsh by Adverse Possession
- Actual Lot Lines
- Walsh House
- 57°
- Cappuccio
- Walsh
- Winterberry Road

At times, it is hard to imagine how anyone could become confused about land ownership unless a mistake has been made in the legal description in the deed. Adverse possession today is much more common in connection with boundary disputes than with possession of entire tracts. Boundary disputes involving adverse possession are of particular importance in residential areas, as can be seen in the Legal Highlight on page 52.

■ ENCROACHMENTS

An **encroachment** is an unauthorized invasion or intrusion of a fixture, a building, or other improvement onto another person's property. Examples are a fence that strays across the property line and a driveway or patio that is constructed partially on the adjoining property. Although most of these intrusions are the result of carelessness or poor planning rather than intent, they should not be taken lightly. The owner of the property being encroached on has the right to force the removal of the encroachment; however, if that owner fails to force removal, the other party may claim the legal right to continue encroaching by adverse possession or easement.

Before making a loan, almost all lending institutions require a survey of the property primarily to reveal any encroachments, as they can adversely affect the value of a home or other real estate.

■ RESTRICTIVE COVENANTS

Restrictive covenants, also called *deed restrictions,* are promises made by a landowner or predecessor in title that the land will or will not be used in certain ways. These covenants are found in the deeds or plats (plans or maps) of real property and are recorded as part of the deed or plat in the public records. For example, the developer of a single-family residential subdivision wants to establish an aesthetically pleasing neighborhood that will increase the value of all owners' property, and he or she wants to be able to assure purchasers that they will be protected in the future. Protection against many property abuses can be achieved through restrictive covenants.

Typical covenants restrict property to single-family uses, require that a house be a certain minimum size, and prohibit business enterprises, domestic animals, or large antennas. Covenants also can be much more specific, requiring the approval by an architectural committee of all buildings and landscaping plans, prohibiting the use of certain building materials, and even mandating the painting of a home at regular intervals and approval of paint colors. The Real Estate Close-Up on page 54 shows some of the covenants that restrict use of property in a rural subdivision called Meadow Brook Ranch.

Covenants cannot create unreasonable or unlawful limitations on an owner's use of land. For example, restrictions preventing the sale of property to a person of a particular ethnic or racial group clearly are unenforceable because they violate the laws and Constitution of the United States.

REAL ESTATE TODAY

Meadow Brook Ranch Use Covenants

1. All lots in Meadow Brook Ranch are restricted to use for residential purposes only. No signs shall be placed on any part of these residential lots indicating a commercial or nonresidential use thereof.

Close-Up

2. No animals or fowl shall be permitted other than those types of animals or fowl normally found on rural property that are raised for personal family use and/or pleasure on a strictly noncommercial basis. Permitted types of animals shall include horses, chickens, and household pets. No swine shall be permitted. A maximum of two (2) dogs per lot shall be permitted. Exotic Game shall be allowed upon the property, with the exception of those that would affect the health, safety, and/or welfare of any of the landowners within the subdivision. Any and all animals, including household pets, require appropriate fencing to confine them to their lot. No animal shall be permitted until this appropriate fencing is completed.

3. No junk or junkyards of any kind or character shall be permitted, nor shall accumulation of scrap, used materials, inoperative automobiles, or machinery, or other unsightly storage of personal property be permitted.

4. No portion of the property shall be used in a manner that adversely affects adjoining property owners or creates an annoyance or nuisance to other property owners. This shall include noise pollution such as barking dogs, loud music, or any animal or fowl that causes a nuisance.

5. No hunting with firearms shall be permitted on any lot. Bowhunting shall be allowed on lots of at least 10 acres. No discharging of any firearms or fireworks shall be permitted on any lot.

6. No residence shall be erected on any part of said property or building site having less than 1,700 square feet of floor space livable area in the main building with one-half (1/2) thereof of masonry construction, with the exception of log homes, which will not require one-half (1/2) masonry construction.

7 All buildings erected on the premises shall be of new construction and materials. No buildings or portion of buildings of old material may be moved into said subdivision.

8. It is the intent of the undersigned that all dwellings and other structures have a neat and attractive appearance. No metal walls or walls of temporary sheeting will be allowed. The entire exterior walls of all dwelling units or other buildings hereafter constructed must be completed within one year after the commencement of work thereon or the placing of materials therefor on said property, whichever occurs the earliest, and in connection therewith it is understood that the use of the word "completed" also means the finishing of all such exterior walls.

9. No more than one residence shall be erected per each two and one-half (2.5) acres.

10. No outside toilets, privies, or cesspools will be permitted, and no installation of any type of sewage disposal device shall be allowed that would result in raw or untreated or unsanitary sewage being carried into any water body; all septic tanks must conform to the regulations of the State and County concerning septic systems.

11. No tents, campers, or trailers shall be used on any of the property for residential purposes, on a temporary or permanent basis. No premanufactured, modular, trailer, or any other structure not built on the site shall be permitted.

12. All tracts shall be kept in a clean and orderly condition at all times, and all trash, garbage, and other waste shall be kept in sanitary containers. Waste placed by the roadway for pickup shall be in disposable containers.

13. No structures used for storage purposes shall be erected or placed upon any parcel that will be visible from any roadway, unless placed within the most rear one-third (1/3) of the parcel, that being such portion farthest away from any road-way. All such structures shall be neatly maintained.

14. No resubdivision of any tract of less than two and one-half (2.5) acres shall be permitted.

REAL ESTATE TODAY

Validity of Restrictive Covenants

Legal Highlight

Salima Worthington purchased a home in the Mains Farm subdivision near Sequim, Washington, for the purpose of establishing an adult-care facility. She knew restrictive covenants limited land use in the subdivision to "single-family residential purposes only," but contended that the proposed use did not violate the covenants. She and her daughter moved into the home, along with four elderly residents. The homeowners' association sued to enforce the deed restrictions. The association won.

The court held that Worthington's use of her home was not for "single-family residential purposes only" because of the business elements involved. Since Worthington provided 24-hour care for fees of $500 to $1,000 per person per month, the property's use was essentially commercial, a use that was inconsistent with a residential purpose.

Worthington also contended that even if her use violated the restrictive covenants, the covenants could not prevent a home-care facility because the state legislature had adopted legislation permitting such facilities in all areas zoned for residential or commercial purposes, including areas zoned for single-family dwellings. She contended that this enactment established the fact that maintaining disabled persons outside institutions is of greater value to the public than is the right to restrict the use of land through restrictive covenants.

Again, the court disagreed, holding that unlike covenants that might attempt to restrict ownership by race, creed, color, national origin, or handicap, the covenants in question served the legitimate public purpose of protecting residential neighborhoods from the effect of business uses. Although the legislature had restricted local governments from zoning adult family homes out of residential areas, it did not limit the right of private homeowners to adopt restrictive covenants that prohibit certain uses of land in residential areas.

Source: *Mains Farm Homeowners Association v. Worthington,* 824 P. 2d 495.

Restrictive covenants are particularly important to the owners of attached condominium dwellings. Suppose, for example, that the owners of a town house paint their unit in their college's colors—a brilliant orange and green. Or suppose they decide that plastic flamingos would be just the thing for the front yard. Not only would these actions have definite detrimental aesthetic impacts, they would have economic impacts on fellow property owners and, therefore, could be prevented through restrictive covenants (stating, for instance, that outside paint colors must meet the approval of a homeowners' committee and that no statuary or other furniture can be placed in front yards).

Because a restrictive covenant is a type of contractual agreement, parties to the original agreement may enforce it. To recover damages or obtain an injunction, the nonbreaching party must be able to show that some damage has been suffered. In other words, to be justified in enforcing a covenant, the party must be able to show how the intended benefit has been denied.

Suppose, for example, that Mary violates the covenants in the deed to her home by erecting a 12-foot satellite dish antenna in her front yard. Either the developer or other property owners could secure a court injunction to force the removal of the offending antenna. If the covenant violation were even more severe, they could seek monetary damages.

Covenants generally run with the land, from owner to owner. They may exist only for a stated period of time—say, 20 years—or they can be terminated by the agreement of all affected parties should the right of enforcement be waived or abandoned or if the restricted land is condemned for a public use. Alternatively, an owner could place a permanent restriction on the land. Restrictive covenants can supersede zoning regulations if they are more restrictive, and such covenants generally offer more protection to property owners, as the Legal Highlight on page 55 illustrates.

■ CHAPTER REVIEW

■ Restrictions and limitations on ownership interests in real property take many forms. A private restriction is a claim on the owner's title by some private individual or business. An encumbrance created by a governing body or public authority is a public restriction.

■ A common ownership restriction is the lien. A lien is a claim on property held by a creditor as security for repayment of a debt or other obligation. It does not represent an ownership interest in the property. Some liens are created to secure debts that arise out of real estate ownership. Mortgages and mechanics' liens are examples of special liens. Other claims, such as judgment liens, are more general in that they can be attached to real or personal property. If a debtor fails to satisfy a specific or general lien, his or her property may be auctioned at a judicial sale, and the title will then pass to the highest bidder.

■ Easements and licenses are restrictions on a landowner's title. They also represent ownership interests in real property held by another person. An easement is one person's right to use someone else's land. When an easement is granted, the land where the easement is located becomes the servient estate. An easement appurtenant exists when the easement's benefits are tied to another piece of property—the dominant estate. If such benefits are held by an individual or a business without regard to the location of that individual or business, an easement in gross exists. A license is created by the landowner's grant of permission to use his or her property. Generally, licenses can be revoked at the landowner's whim; therefore, they are less permanent than easements.

■ Restrictive covenants, also called deed restrictions, are restrictions in the deed for a property that restrict how it may be used. Restrictive covenants in residential subdivisions and condominiums protect and enhance property values by preventing uses that would be incompatible with other properties.

■ KEY TERMS

adverse possession	express reservation	mechanic's lien
dominant estate	foreclosure	mortgage
easement	general lien	mortgagee
easement appurtenant	implied grant	mortgagor
easement in gross	implied reservation	profit a prendre
easement by prescription	judgment lien	restrictive covenant
encroachment	judicial sale	security instrument
encumbrance	license	servient estate
express grant	lien	special lien

■ STUDY EXERCISES

1. What is the difference between a general lien and a special lien?

2. Suppose that Charlie decides that he is going to cheat Harry out of the money he owes Harry for installing a new air-conditioning system in Charlie's house. What steps might Harry take to collect the debt? (Do not include breaking Charlie's legs.)

3. Why would someone voluntarily allow a mortgage lien on their property?

4. Define the following terms: *easement, license,* and *encroachment.*

5. What is the difference between an easement appurtenant and an easement in gross?

6. Suppose that David sells Joan an easement to run a water line across his property to her property. Who has the dominant estate and who has the servient estate? Explain your answer. Is this an easement appurtenant or an easement in gross?

7. Suppose that David sells the above property to Tamara. She tells Joan to remove the water line from her property. Can she force Joan to remove the line?

8. What is the difference in creating an easement by grant, by reservation, or by implication?

9. Describe an easement by necessity. Describe an easement by prescription.

10. List three methods for terminating an easement.

11. What is the difference between an easement and a license? Between an easement and a profit a prendre?

12. Suppose that Cindy purchases a house and discovers that her neighbor Eleanor has several rose bushes that encroach on her lot. When Cindy asks Eleanor

to move the bushes, Eleanor becomes indignant and accuses Cindy of being unfriendly and a poor neighbor. Can Cindy legally insist that the bushes be moved? Why or why not?

13. Suppose that Jack inherits his grandmother's house. He finds that the deed granted many years ago contains a restriction that the property can only be sold to someone of the Caucasian race. Could this restriction be enforced? Why or why not?

14. When Claudia decides to sell her house, she discovers that there is a restriction in her deed that prohibits putting up a For Sale sign in her yard. "This violates my free speech," she fumes. "I'm going to sue the community association." Will she win? Why or why not?

15. Tim makes the following argument: "Even though restrictive covenants limit what a property owner can do with his land, they may increase property values." Is Tim right? Why or why not?

16. Suppose a new homeowner in the Meadow Brook Ranch development is upset because his neighbor is keeping a horse on her property. Based on the covenants for this development discussed in the Real Estate Close-Up on page 54, can the upset owner demand that the horse be removed?

4 Public Restrictions on Ownership

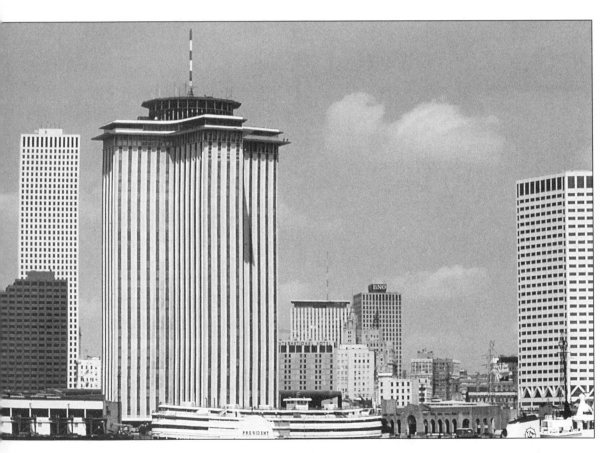

Local governments can control the density, height, and appearance of property through the enforcement of zoning laws.

CHAPTER PREVIEW

In addition to the private restrictions on property rights discussed in the previous chapter, governments also have the power to create limitations on the ownership of real estate. These powers include

■ the power of taxation,

■ the power of escheat,

■ the power of eminent domain, and

■ zoning and other land-use controls under the police power.

After reviewing the four powers governments have over real property, this chapter discusses some of the techniques and tools of public land-use control and examines a few of the controversies surrounding land-use policy issues. The specific topics covered are

■ the history of land-use controls,

■ the public land-use planning process,

■ zoning and other land-use control methods, and

■ the takings issue.

■ THE PROPERTY TAX

The first power of government over private property to be considered is the **power of taxation.** The government exercises this power by levying both property taxes and income taxes. We will consider the impact of income taxes later in this text and focus our attention on the property tax in this chapter.

The property tax is an important source of revenue for state and local governments. On average, property taxes account for about 75 percent of state and local government tax revenues in the United States. These revenues are used to fund education, police and fire protection, and other government services. Governments often find that property taxation provides a stable source of revenue that is not greatly affected by short-term fluctuations in business activity. And because it is tied to property that is largely immobile, the property tax is relatively easy to administer and very difficult to evade.

The Property Taxation Process

The property tax is an **ad valorem tax;** that is, it is levied as a percentage of value. It is a tax on the *value of the property,* as opposed to a tax on the *income earned from the property.* Property taxes are often expressed in **millage rates** rather than percentage rates. One mill is equal to one dollar of tax for every one thousand dollars of value. One percent is equal to one dollar of tax for every one hundred dollars of value. Stated another way, one *mill* equals $.001, or 1/1,000 of $1. In some jurisdictions, only a portion of the market value of the property is subject to taxation, where **market value** is defined as the price that the property probably would bring in the market, given knowledgeable and willing buyers and sellers who act under no unusual pressures and who have a reasonable time to complete the transaction. The portion of market value subject to taxation is called the **assessed value.** The fraction used to determine assessed value from market value is called the **assessment ratio.** Furthermore, some jurisdictions exempt certain amounts of a property's assessed value to provide tax relief for certain types of property owners (full-time residents, disabled persons, elderly, etc.). Subtracting the amounts of **exemptions** from assessed value gives the property's **taxable value.**

To see how property taxes are calculated, consider a property with a market value of $120,000 in a jurisdiction that applies an assessment ratio of 40 percent. For this property, the assessed value is $48,000 ($120,000 × .40 = 48,000). Suppose the property qualifies for a tax exemption of $2,500 because it is a homestead. The taxable value of this property is thus $45,500 ($48,000 − $2,500 = $45,500). If the tax rate in this jurisdiction is 25 mills (or 2.5 percent), then the property tax amount is $1,137.50 (45,500 ÷ 1,000 × 25 = $1,137.50). The following framework shows how the property tax bill is calculated:

Market Value	$120,000
multiplied by Assessment Ratio	× .40
equals Assessed Value	$48,000
minus Exemptions (if any)	−$2,500
equals Taxable Value	$45,500
divided by 1,000	÷1,000
times Millage Rate	× 2 5
equals Property Tax	$1,137.50

Administering the Property Tax

From the government's perspective, the steps involved in administering the property tax are

1. property value assessment,
2. development of the budget and tax rate, and
3. tax billing and collection.

Property Value Assessment

The first step in the property taxation process is to estimate the market value for all properties within the jurisdiction, a process known as **assessment.** The government official responsible for doing so, usually called the **assessor** or **property assessor,** must identify, list, and value all taxable properties. An efficient assessor needs a complete set of maps that show each parcel of real estate and its features, as well as a system of continuing inspection of deeds and building permits in order to keep up with new construction and changes in property ownership.

After all properties have been identified, the assessor must accomplish the most difficult part of the job, that of estimating the market value of the properties within the jurisdiction. Many states use mass appraisal techniques, or statistical models, to assess the value of all properties in a jurisdiction each year. After estimating the property's market value and applying the assessment ratio, the assessor arrives at the property's *assessed value.* This value is subject to review, and the results of the review process may be appealed by the taxpayer before an appeal board or court.

Certain properties may qualify for exemption amounts designed to reduce the tax burden. Many jurisdictions, for example, exempt a stated dollar amount of assessed value from taxation if the property is used as a homestead (a permanent residence of the property owner). Exemptions, often described as "circuit breakers," provide property tax relief for certain types of properties. In addition to the **homestead exemption,** some jurisdictions offer exemptions for properties that are owned by a low-income owner, a disabled person, or a widow or widower. The total amount of all exemptions is subtracted from the assessed value to arrive at the property's taxable value.

Development of a Budget and Tax Rate

The next step in the property taxation process is the development of a budget and tax rate by the city council, the county commission, or other government body. The amount of revenue coming from other taxes and from nontax sources is subtracted from the total budget; the remainder must be collected in property taxes. This amount then is divided by the total of the taxable values of all properties in the jurisdiction to determine the tax rate.

For example, suppose that the local government needs to raise $10 million in property taxes, and the total taxable value of all properties in the jurisdiction, known as the *tax digest,* is $500 million. The tax rate needed to raise these revenues is:

$$\frac{\$10,000,000}{\$500,000,000} = .02$$

The tax rate usually is expressed as the rate per thousand dollars of assessed value—the millage rate, where one mill equals $.001, or 1/1,000 of $1. In the example above, 20 mills equal $20 tax per $1,000 assessed valuation, or 2 percent.

As a matter of practice, of course, the local governing body does not merely decide what it would like to spend and then set a corresponding tax rate. It may feel constrained not to raise the present tax rate at all, to raise it only slightly, or even to lower it. In many areas, tax rate adjustments require a vote on the issue by the people in the jurisdiction.

After the tax rate is set, the taxable values are multiplied by the tax rate to obtain individual tax bills. If a house in our hypothetical locality has a taxable value of $50,000, for example, the property tax would be $1,000 (20 mills × $50,000).

Tax Billing and Collection

Tax billing and collection procedures vary widely among the states. In some, property tax bills are payable annually; in others, taxes are payable semiannually or quarterly. Some states have special taxing districts that send their tax bills at different times of the year.

If property taxes are not paid when due, the government to which the taxes are owed can place a lien on the real estate for the unpaid taxes, plus a penalty and interest. If the taxes remain unpaid for a certain period of time, which varies from state to state, the property may ultimately be sold at public auction to satisfy the tax lien. In essence, the tax sale is similar to a foreclosure sale that follows default on either a mortgage or a mechanic's lien. The Real Estate Legal Highlight on page 65 demonstrates how one state enforces property tax payments through the use of "delinquent tax certificates."

■ ESCHEAT

The second power governments have over private property is known as the power of **escheat.** In the event a landowner dying without leaving either a valid

REAL ESTATE TODAY

Mechanics of the Property Tax Certificate Market in Florida

**Legal
Highlight**

This legal highlight describes how property taxes in Florida are collected from delinquent property owners. In essence, the state's laws allow counties to auction off any unpaid tax bill to the highest bidder. The highest bidder (usually an investment group formed for just this purpose) pays the taxes on behalf of the property owner in exchange for a "tax certificate" that represents a lien against the property and entitles the holder to receive interest on the amount paid on the owner's behalf. If the interest and taxes are not repaid to the certificate holder within two years, the holder can force the sale of the property at public auction to recover the investment and interest due. The details of this process are described below.

Under Chapter 197 of the Florida Statutes, all property taxes represent a first lien, superior to all other liens, as of January 1 of each year. Taxes are due and payable in November of the same year and are considered delinquent if unpaid on April 1 of the following year. After proper notice is provided by mail to the property owner and any lien holder of record who has previously requested notification, the tax collector is required to advertise a public sale of tax certificates on all properties in the county with delinquent taxes. This advertisement must appear in a locally circulated newspaper within 45 days of April 1 and must list each parcel for which taxes are delinquent, including owner's name, delinquent tax amount, and a property identification number. The sale is scheduled to begin on or about June 1. Prior to the sale, a property owner can preempt the sale of the certificate for the property by paying all taxes due plus 18 percent annual interest to date and proportional share of any advertising costs.

On the day advertised, the tax collector begins the sale of certificates in the order listed in the advertisement and continues day to day until each certificate is sold. Rather than bidding a dollar amount, bidders bid the interest rate they are willing to accept in exchange for paying the property taxes for the property owner. Bids start at 18 percent and go down in

1/4-point increments until a low bid is determined. In the event no bidder bids on a certificate, the certificate is issued to the county with an interest rate of 18 percent. Certificates are fully transferable on payment of a nominal fee to the tax collector. In 2000, more than 21,000 such certificates were sold to investors in Palm Beach County, Florida, for a total of more than $41 million. The average interest rate on these certificates was 12.68%.

After the sale, a property owner can redeem the certificate by paying the taxes and interest due to the tax collector. The tax collector then cancels the certificate and remits the funds to the certificate holder. If the certificate is not redeemed within 2 years of issuance, the holder may apply for a tax deed to be issued by the Clerk of the Circuit Court. The tax deed applicant must pay for a title search and must pay the amount required for redemption of all other outstanding tax certificates, interest, omitted taxes, and current taxes. A completed application forces the sale of the property at public auction.

At the tax deed auction, the Clerk of the Circuit Court issues a tax deed to the highest bidder. The opening bid must cover all the costs paid by the tax deed applicant plus all other costs for conducting the sale. If the property involved is a homestead property (the permanent residence of a full-time Florida citizen), the minimum bid at the tax deed auction is increased by one half of the assessed value of the property. Anyone may bid at the tax deed auction, including the property owner and the tax deed applicant. The proceeds from the sale are used to repay the tax certificate holder, with any excess proceeds being returned to the property owner. The title granted to the winning bidder at a tax deed auction is subject only to other government liens, easements, and usual restrictions and covenants. In particular, no liens for a private debt (including mortgages) survive a tax deed sale. The winning bidder is entitled to immediate possession of the property.

Fifth Amendment of the Constitution of the United States
Rights of Persons

No person shall be held to answer for a capital, or otherwise infamous crime, unless on a presentment or indictment of a Grand Jury, except in cases arising in the land or naval forces, or in the Militia, when in actual service in time of War or public danger; nor shall any person be subject for the same offence to be twice put in jeopardy of life or limb; nor shall be compelled in any criminal case to be a witness against himself, **nor be deprived of life, liberty, or property, without due process of law; nor shall private property be taken for public use, without just compensation.** [emphasis added]

Fourteenth Amendment of the Constitution of the United States
Rights Guaranteed

All persons born or naturalized in the United States, and subject to the jurisdiction thereof, are citizens of the United States and the State wherein they reside. No State shall make or enforce any law which shall abridge the privileges or immunities of citizens of the United States; nor shall any State deprive any person of life, liberty, or property, without due process of law; nor deny to any person within its jurisdiction the equal protection of the laws.

ill or living relatives, the state government becomes the new owner of the property. This power prevents real estate from simply becoming "unowned." The right of the government to the land under these limited circumstances is called *escheat,* a concept that dates back to the medieval feudal system. The king gave land to his barons, but if they died without surviving sons, the king would reclaim the land. If a knight or servant had no male heirs, that person's land would escheat to the next higher tier in the feudal order. Today, of course, the presence of any heir, even if not a relative of the deceased landowner, will prevent the state from asserting its right of escheat.

■ POWER OF EMINENT DOMAIN

Under the power of **eminent domain,** a government can acquire property for a public use, even if the owner doesn't want to sell, when it pays **just compensation.** This power comes from the Fifth Amendment to the U.S. Constitution, which, among other things, states that property shall not be taken from any person for public uses without the payment of just compensation. Although this provision applies specifically to the federal government, it has been extended to the states through the due process clause of the Constitution's Fourteenth Amendment.

In an eminent domain proceeding, also known as a *condemnation proceeding,* the government must establish that the land is needed for a public use or benefit and that the amount of money offered to the landowner is the reasonable value of the land being taken. The concept of public use is quite broad. It has been extended to include the condemnation of private land for resale to other private individuals or firms for urban renewal, as well as the enforced breakup of old Hawaiian estates to extend land ownership more widely. The concept also has been extended to include quasi-public organizations, such as utility companies, railroads, and pipelines.

Whether the taking is for a public use is generally not the major issue, however. Of utmost concern is the question of adequate compensation. If the condemning authority and the owner fail to agree on the property's value, the owner can request a jury trial to determine the amount of just compensation. If property is condemned for a highway, a school, a utility plant, or another similar public purpose, the government will, of course, take complete fee simple absolute title to the land. Certain situations, however, require that only an easement be acquired. For example, consider VORTAC stations, which transmit radio signals that airplanes use to track their positions. Although such stations physically take up only a portion of an acre, the area around the stations must not contain any object more than six feet high for a radius of approximately one-half mile. In other words, the government has no need for the actual land surrounding VORTAC stations; it needs only the assurance that no physical obstructions will be constructed. In this situation, the government would condemn both the title to the station's physical location and an easement surrounding the building. The landowner could continue to use the land for farming purposes right up to the VORTAC building. Of course, the owner is entitled to just compensation for both the easement restriction and the land that is taken completely.

Inverse condemnation occurs when a property owner, seeking to force the purchase of the property, starts condemnation proceedings against the government, contending that a government action has destroyed or reduced the value of the property. For example, suppose a highway department announces plans for a new road but delays purchasing the necessary rights-of-way. A property owner in the path of the proposed road could sue to force the highway department to purchase the land, contending that the announced plans have made it impossible to sell the land for private purposes. Or a property owner near an airport might bring legal action to force a condemnation and collect payment for damages caused by the noise of low-flying aircraft.

■ POLICE POWER

Under **police power,** governments have the power of regulation, which gives them the ability to protect the public health, safety, morals, and general welfare. In addition to obvious actions such as protecting against crime and health hazards, governments have also relied on these police powers to enact a variety of controls over the way landowners can use their properties.

The use of a particular parcel of land is affected greatly by other nearby land uses and depends heavily on public investments and the economic vitality of the surrounding neighborhood and community. It is this interdependence of land uses that creates the need for public land-use controls. Generally speaking, the use of

The Impact of Environmental Hazards on Real Estate Values

Environmental legislation can have a significant effect on real estate values, but perhaps no piece of environmental legislation had a greater or more general impact than the Comprehensive Environmental Response, Compensation, and Liability Act of 1980 (CERCLA), commonly called the *Superfund Act*. In contrast to almost all other environmental legislation that seeks to prevent harmful acts in the future, the purpose of CERCLA is to clean up environmental pollution that occurred in the past.

Under CERCLA, the current owner of a contaminated property may be held responsible for the costs of cleanup even though that owner did not cause the contamination and had no knowledge of it when he or she purchased the site. Even financial institutions have been held liable when they have become the "owners" of contaminated properties through foreclosure. The cost of the cleanup may far exceed the cost of the property. For example, one purchaser bought a property at a tax sale

Close-Up

for $200, but was later forced to spend over $250,000 in cleanup costs.

Because of the potential liability, lenders and insurers, as well as many purchasers, require an environmental site assessment when there is possible environmental contamination. A Phase I environmental assessment is performed by an environmental professional to determine if there may be potential environmental hazards on the site. If so, it may be necessary to move to a Phase II assessment, which involves soil, water, and other testing. If these tests confirm contamination, an extensive Phase III environmental assessment will be required to determine the horizontal and vertical extent of the contamination. If it is determined that there is major site contamination, the cleanup costs may either greatly reduce the property's value or make it worthless.

Source: Robert V. Colangelo and Ronald D. Miller. *Environmental Site Assessments and Their Impact on Property Value: The Appraiser's Role*. Chicago: Appraisal Institute, 1995.

land affects the owners of other nearby properties more than the use of any other type of private property. Conversely, financial returns for the real estate developer or investor may be greatly affected by the land uses that are permitted by governments or by the allowable intensity of land use. Consequently, the issue of public land-use controls is of vital importance to all who are concerned with real property.

The concept of planning and control of land use is not new. In fact, in this country, it dates back to the colonial era. Many early American cities were carefully planned and developed under a variety of land-use controls. One of the early controls still valid today is the English common-law concept of **nuisance law,** laws relating to the use of property in such a way as to harm the property of others. Most of the prohibited land uses were hazardous or noxious practices, such as the operation of a slaughterhouse or the manufacture of bricks near a residential area. In these cases, the offending activity might be declared a nuisance. The injured parties could seek an injunction to force the polluter to stop the offending activity, or they could seek monetary damages.

Nuisance laws provided some relief to individual property owners from the worst types of injurious land uses, but it was not well suited for public land-use control because a substantial injury had to be proved before any relief could be given. As the United States rapidly urbanized around the turn of the century, municipalities increasingly turned to police power controls to regulate land uses. Most cities have found that a comprehensive general plan is necessary to effectively implement land-use controls.

■ THE COMPREHENSIVE GENERAL PLAN

To ensure that urban areas develop in an orderly fashion, many local governments have formulated and adopted a **comprehensive general plan** that serves as a statement of policies for the future development of the community. These policies provide a basis for the land-use control methods employed by the municipality.   The policies should reflect a long-range plan that examines closely the community's predicted physical needs for 15 to 25 years in the future. It usually contains the following elements:

- ■ An analysis of projected economic development and population change
- ■ A transportation plan to provide for necessary circulation
- ■ A public-facilities plan that identifies such needed facilities as schools, parks, civic centers, and water and sewage-disposal plants
- ■ A land-use plan
- ■ An official map

The comprehensive plan may also include other elements, such as housing, redevelopment, and historic preservation. It should not be a static document but must be revised continually as conditions change.

Implementing the Comprehensive Plan

The comprehensive plan and its land-use component are implemented through several tools of land-use control. The most prominent of these is comprehensive zoning, but they also include building codes, mandatory dedication, impact fees, zoning for planned unit development, performance or impact zoning, incentive zoning, and transfer of development rights. We will consider each of these methods in turn.

■ COMPREHENSIVE ZONING

Comprehensive zoning divides a community's land into districts to regulate the use of land and buildings and the intensity of various uses. The first comprehensive zoning ordinance was passed in New York City in 1916 to restrict the use and height of buildings in various districts of Manhattan. Zoning gained increasing acceptance during the 1920s, and after the constitutionality of the

Shaping the Skyscrapers of Manhattan

Close-Up

Although the office skyscraper has become symbolic of New York City, it was not until almost the turn of this century that a secular building rose above Manhattan's church steeples. Then, within a few years, a number of monumental towers were constructed, climaxed by the 792-foot Woolworth Building. Although tall, all of these early skyscrapers featured relatively slender towers rather than tremendous bulk. All this changed with the construction of the Equitable Building at 120 Broadway, a 1.2-million-square-foot, 42-story monolith that rose 340 feet straight up from the lot lines. The building was overpowering, casting a huge shadow that denied direct sunlight to both the street and the building's neighbors. The city's 1916 zoning law, the United States' first comprehensive zoning, was largely a response to the excesses of this building.

The zoning law established height and setback regulations that led to "wedding-cake" architecture, which stacked buildings in layers, like those on wedding cakes. Instead of a happy couple perched on the top, however, towers shot up from the tops of these buildings. These towers often were rather short and dumpy, but sometimes, as in the case of the Empire State Building, the towers fairly soared to the heavens.

By the late 1950s, reaction to the wedding-cake style led to changes in the zoning law to promote "towers in a plaza." This movement was fostered by the completion of the landmark Seagram Building, which consisted of an elegant 38-story tower that was situated in a large plaza.

Thus, New York turned enthusiastically to incentive zoning in 1961. A "sky exposure plane" standard replaced height districts to govern establishment of setbacks, while the floor-area-ratio (FAR) concept was introduced to govern bulk. To promote the construction of plazas and other amenities, a 20 percent floor-area bonus was offered if these features were included in a new building. It also was possible for a developer to increase density by acquiring air rights. Through the compounding of bonuses and air rights, it was possible to construct buildings that made a mockery of the regulations designed to protect the openness of the streets. The incentive system also led to an era of zoning negotiations for almost every major new building and to a maze of special districts and zoning amendments.

The zoning law recently was modified with two strategic goals. The first was to simplify the zoning process and give it more certainty and predictability. The number and amount of development bonuses were reduced in the new regulations and made less subject to negotiation. New bulk regulations provide for daylight and openness while offering architectural latitude without the necessity of obtaining variances or entering into other zoning negotiations. Second, the new zoning law attempts to shift growth from the overheated East Side to the West Side and the south through higher allowable floor-area ratios in the growth-incentive areas.

Will the new zoning ordinance achieve the desired effects? The regulations definitely are simplified, and the bulk regulations provide greater flexibility in design. Some observers have expressed fears that a multitude of "ski-slope" buildings will result from the daylight requirements and will supplant wedding-cake architecture as the new standard of urban banality. Hopefully, these fears will not materialize. It is comforting to note that the highly acclaimed Citicorp Center, for example, scores quite well under the new daylight requirements.

The second goal of the modified zoning law is the more difficult. Although strong market forces still favor the East Side, the zoning and tax incentives have steered a much greater percentage of recent growth toward the west and south.

concept was upheld in 1926, zoning ordinances and related land-use controls were adopted in most urban areas and many rural communities of the United States. The Real Estate Today Close-Up on page 70 describes how the zoning ordinance in New York City helped shape the city's skyline.

Zoning

The most widely employed method of regulating the use of land is zoning, which divides land within the local jurisdiction into zones and prescribes regulations relating to the type and intensity of use. Provisions also are made to deal with changes in zoning and the phasing out of nonconforming uses.

Type of Use

The three main kinds of districts classified by use are residential, commercial, and industrial. Each such district usually is divided into several subcategories. For example, there generally are several single-family districts with varying minimum sizes of lot and house. Other residential districts may permit multifamily housing. Similarly, commercial and industrial districts usually are subcategorized as neighborhood shopping districts, highway commercial districts, light industrial districts, and so on. Most zoning ordinances contain, in addition to the three main categories, such special-purpose districts as agricultural, floodplain, and historic preservation.

Intensity of Use

Intensity of use, also referred to as *developmental density,* is the extent to which the land within a given district may be used for its permitted purposes. The government can regulate intensity of use in several ways, including placing restrictions on building height and bulk, specifying minimum lot sizes, and establishing setback requirements.

Height and Bulk Limitations.   Height limitations regulate the maximum height of buildings in feet or stories. Bulk regulations control the percentage of the lot area that may be occupied by buildings. Both serve to control the volume of a structure on the land and, therefore, the intensity of use.

Floor-Area Ratio.   Another measure by which building volume may be controlled is the floor-area ratio (FAR). The FAR is the relationship between the total floor area of a building and the total land area of the site. For example, an allowable ratio of four to one would permit a four-story building to occupy the entire area of its lot; an eight-story building would be permitted to occupy only half of the site's surface area; a 16-story building could occupy only one-fourth of the land area. Other FARs are illustrated in Figure 4.1.

| FIGURE 4.1 | Examples of Floor-Area Ratios |

Minimum Lot Size and Setback Regulations.   The most common method of regulating development density is through provisions for a minimum lot size. Relatively large lots may be necessary for public health reasons if public sewer and water systems are not provided. However, requirements of very large minimum lot sizes may run into court challenges on the basis that they deprive the owner of reasonable use or are designed to exclude various groups.

Zoning ordinances generally provide for setback of buildings from the street and minimum size of side yards in residential districts. Such restrictions also may be applied to commercial and industrial districts, but this is less common. The way intensity of use regulations have been used to regulate building in Manhattan is covered in the Close-Up on page 70.

Zoning Changes

For various reasons, a property owner may seek a change in zoning or relief from some provision of the zoning ordinance. This can be accomplished through legislative, administrative, or judicial means.

Legislative Relief

If a property owner seeks a change in the property's use, he or she can request a change in zoning use classification from the local zoning authority, usually the city council or county commission. Zoning amendments generally require review by a planning commission, an advertised public hearing, and some type of justification from the applicant demonstrating that changed conditions justify the zoning change. Because zoning changes often are quite controversial, so are the hearings, with spirited and sometimes acrimonious public debate.

Administrative Relief

If a property owner seeks a relatively minor change, it sometimes can be accomplished administratively through a variance or special-use permit granted by a board of adjustments, a zoning appeals board, or some similar body. A **variance** permits use to deviate slightly from a strict interpretation of the zoning ordinance to avoid placing undue hardship on an owner. For example, for a house to be constructed on an oddly shaped lot, some relief from minimum side-yard requirements may be needed.

A zoning ordinance often permits special uses within certain districts if certain conditions are met. For example, a public utility substation, church, school, or recreational facility may be permitted in a residential district if the board determines that the required conditions have been satisfied.

Variances and special-use permits can make a zoning ordinance much more reasonable and less burdensome to property owners. If not carefully controlled, however, these permits also can completely undermine the community's land-use planning efforts. Variances that change the essential character of land use within a district often are granted with little justification. The powers of the board must be spelled out carefully to prevent such happenings.

Judicial Relief

If property owners are unhappy because the legislative or administrative relief they sought is not granted, they may appeal to the courts. An appeal is based on a contention that the zoning regulations are in some way unconstitutional or that owners were deprived of the property without due process of law because a decision was arbitrary, unreasonable, or capricious. Even with the increased aggressiveness of the judicial branch, courts are generally reluctant to substitute their judgment for that of legislative bodies, and zoning ordinances usually are upheld unless they involve clear abuses of power or are unduly restrictive.

Zoning restrictions are of great importance to real estate developers. Those who disregard them do so at their peril, as the developer in the Legal Highlight on page 74 found to his chagrin and financial loss.

Nonconforming Uses

A **nonconforming use** is a continuing use that was legal before a zoning ordinance was passed but that no longer complies with the current zoning regulation. Such a use generally is allowed to continue for some period of time unless the nonconforming structure is substantially destroyed or abandoned. Regulations concerning nonconforming use usually do not permit the existing structure to be enlarged or substantially changed in use. They also may require that the nonconforming use be discontinued after a stated period of time, a process that is known as *amortization*. Most amortization periods for buildings are relatively long, perhaps 50 years. Most controversy has centered around more minor uses, such as nonconforming signs and billboards.

Although the courts have not been unanimous in their approval of the amortization concept, most have regarded relatively long phase-out periods, such as three to seven years, as reasonable compensation for nonconforming signs.

The Strange Case of the Incredible Shrinking Building

In New York City, developer Laurence Ginsberg applied for a building permit to construct a 31-story apartment building on Park Avenue at 96th Street. The city had established a special zoning district 150 feet on each side of Park Avenue that limited new buildings to 210 feet (18 floors), but Ginsberg based his application on a zoning map that erroneously showed the special district to extend only 100 feet from Park Avenue. He received the building permit and began construction. Later, however, the city discovered the error, canceled the permit, and issued a stop-work order on the top 12 floors. Ginsberg appealed the order and kept on building—all the way to the 31st floor.

New York's highest court turned down Ginsberg's appeal, ruling that "reasonable diligence would have readily uncovered for a good-faith inquir-

Legal Highlight

er the existence of the unequivocal limitations of 150 feet in the original binding metes and bounds description of the enabling legislation, and that this boundary has never been changed by the [City]." The court ordered the top 12 floors removed. Ginsberg then applied, after the fact, to the city for a variance for the additional height, but this was also denied.

Finally, eight years after construction began, a 7,000-pound, hammer-wielding robot began pounding away, reducing the 31-story apartment building to 18 stories, at an estimated cost of $1 million. The developer's total losses were approximately $14 million.

Source: *Parkview Associates v. City of New York*, 519 N.E.2d 1372 (1988).

Building Codes

Another tool used in implementing a comprehensive land-use plan is the set of ordinances known as *building codes*. Such codes establish detailed standards for the construction of new buildings and the alteration of existing ones. Their primary purpose is to protect health and provide safety, and they are related primarily to fire prevention, quality and safety of construction, and public health safeguards.

Building codes also may be used to promote energy conservation and other public purposes. A building permit is required before construction can begin. This procedure enables local officials to ascertain that the site plan has been approved and the proposed construction complies with applicable building codes, zoning regulations, and subdivision regulations.

Property owners who choose to ignore building code requirements do so at their peril, as the owner of the rental property in the Legal Highlight on page 75 discovered.

REAL ESTATE TODAY

The Case of the Costly Permit

Legal Highlight

In 1990, the Boynton Beach, Florida, building code inspector observed Mr. Andre St. Juste performing extensive repairs to the roof of a residential rental house he owned. The inspector ordered Mr. St. Juste to stop work until he obtained a permit, and later sent him an official notice that he was violating city codes.

Mr. St. Juste ignored the notice, and several weeks later the Code Enforcement Board began fining him $200 per day. Four months later St. Juste finally applied for a building permit, but when he told the building department that the repairs would cost only $21.80, they told him he didn't need a permit because the repairs cost less than $500. When the code inspectors learned that the repairs would actually cover more than 25 percent of the roof and cost considerably more than $500, they again ordered St. Juste to get a permit. Again, he ignored them.

In 1992, the city made Mr. St. Juste an offer: get a permit, fix the roof, and ask the Code Enforcement Board to reduce the fines. He refused.

In 1994, the circuit court ruled that the city had made every effort to help Mr. St. Juste pass the building code, and that he owed $316,000 in fines and $20,000 in court costs. St. Juste attempted to declare bankruptcy to avoid the fines, but the judge refused to approve the bankruptcy.

Finally, in 1995 the city commissioners voted unanimously to auction off the St. Juste house to pay the fines. It was sold on the courthouse steps.

Subdivision Regulations

Subdivision regulations, another tool for implementing the community planning process, establish the standards and procedures for regulating the subdivision of land for development and sale. Their purpose is to protect both the community and future residents from poorly planned and executed developments.

The local planning board or another planning agency determines the standards that must be met for subdivision approval. Standards are provided for the design and construction of new streets, utilities, and drainage systems. The planning board also establishes an approval procedure, usually consisting of three distinct steps: a preapplication conference, approval of the preliminary plat, and approval of the final plat.

Preapplication Conference

The purpose of the preapplication conference is to allow the developer to meet informally with the planning board before going to the expense of preparing a formal plat. Working with a sketch plan, the planning staff can review the proposal with the developer and make suggestions for changes that may be necessary to meet the subdivision regulations. The developer also may benefit from general planning efforts of the board that may affect the development.

FIGURE 4.2   A Preliminary Plat

The Preliminary Plat Shall Show:

Name, location, owner and designer

Date, north point, and graphic scale

Location of property lines, roads, existing utilities, etc.

Present zoning classification

Names of adjoining properties

Proposed utility system

Names of new streets

Dimensions, lot lines, and building setbacks

Location of proposed culverts

Contours at 5' intervals

Acreage of land subdivided

Approval of the Preliminary Plat

The next step is for the developer to prepare and submit a preliminary plat for approval. The term *preliminary plat* is misleading because all construction and mapping of the lots will be done on the basis of this plat. Detailed information is required, therefore, usually including topographic data regarding existing boundary lines, utilities, and ground elevations. Also required is the layout of the proposed subdivision, including streets, other rights-of-way or easements, lot lines and numbers, sites of special uses, and minimum building setback lines. A preliminary plat is shown in Figure 4.2.

Approval of the Final Plat

After receiving approval of the preliminary plat, the developer can stake the lots and construct streets and other required improvements. After these tasks are completed, or with the posting of a certified check or bond to guarantee completion, the developer can prepare a final plat and related documents.

The final plat is intended to be filed in the registry of deeds and must contain all information necessary for land titles, such as exact lot lines, street rights-of-way, utility easements, and surveying monuments. A final plat is shown in Figure 4.3. The required accompanying documents usually include a certification by a licensed engineer or surveyor regarding the accuracy of the details of the plat, plans concerning utility improvements within the subdivision, and certification that the improvements have been constructed in accordance with the approved plans.

After approval by the planning board, the final plat will be recorded, and the developer then will be permitted to sell the lots in the subdivision.

Mandatory Dedication

Another method used to shape city growth is referred to as **mandatory dedication.** To obtain approval for a project, the developer often is required to dedicate parts of the property to such public purposes as rights-of-way for streets, utilities, and drainage. In some communities, developers also may be required to dedicate land for parks, open space, and schools. If the development is small, payments in lieu of dedication sometimes are required.

The mandatory dedication of land for parks and schools understandably is controversial. One view is that the need for such facilities is created by the new subdivision, while the opposing view holds that parks and schools are a general government responsibility that should be borne by the public at large. The courts are divided on the issue as well. In some cases they have upheld mandatory dedication of land for such purposes, and in other cases they have held that the denial of the right to subdivide land on the condition that the developer donate land for parks and schools is a violation of due process. In some jurisdictions, the developer is required to reserve the land for only a stated period of time, during which the municipality may purchase the property. If the land has not been purchased by the end of the period, the developer no longer is bound by the reservation.

FIGURE 4.3   A Final Plat

The Final Plat Shall Show:

Streets, lots, setback lines, lot numbers, etc.

Sufficient engineering data to reproduce any line on the ground

Dimensions, angles, and bearings

Monuments

Name of adjoining properties

Date, title, name, and location of subdivision

Graphic scale and true north point

Impact Fees

In addition to mandatory dedications, a community may also enact **impact fees** on new development to help raise the funds necessary for the expansion of public facilities. These fees are specific assessments on development; for example, $2,500 per dwelling unit or $2,000 for each 1,000 square feet of new commercial or office space. As might be expected, these fees are quite controversial, but their use by local governments is spreading rapidly.

Recent court decisions and legislation in many states have made it a necessity for governments that impose impact fees to tie them directly to the need created by the development. Otherwise, the fees may be regarded as extortion.

■ INNOVATIVE LAND-USE CONTROL METHODS

Traditional zoning has been criticized for being inefficient, for being subject to poor administration and even corruption, and for having little relationship to planning goals. Some attack it for its flexibility, charging that true separation of uses seldom is achieved because zoning boards submit to developer pressure to grant extensive rezonings. Others attack zoning for its rigidity, charging that its inflexible requirements stifle good design and foster inefficiency and rising costs. A few have come to the conclusion that zoning controls should be abolished, while others have attempted to improve the zoning process. The latter movement has led to some innovative techniques, including zoning for planned unit development, performance or impact zoning, incentive zoning, and transfer of development rights.

Planned Unit Development

Zoning for planned unit development (PUD) can avoid some of the failings of traditional zoning practices. Generally, many bulk and use regulations may be waived to permit greater flexibility of design. For example, lot sizes may be reduced to permit greater densities, and setback and side-yard requirements may be waived to permit attached housing. Convenience shopping also may be permitted within the development. In return, the community should receive the advantages of preservation of natural features, community recreation and open space, greater housing choice, safer streets and pedestrian ways, reduced need for automobile travel, and lower costs.

Performance Zoning

Performance zoning, often known as **impact zoning,** is a technique to relate permitted uses of land to certain performance standards, usually to protect the environment. Such performance standards, particularly industrial-use standards related to noise, smoke, smell, and the like, sometimes are quite detailed.

Adoption of performance zoning generally results in simplified land-use controls. The performance standards relate land-use demands to land-use capacity, and they can be used to achieve better design and to reduce the cost of regulation, as well as to protect the environment. The standards used are often related to density, open-space ratio, impervious-surface ratio (surface-water runoff), and the number of vehicle trips generated by the site.

During the past several decades, a number of municipalities in Bucks County, Pennsylvania, have adopted performance zoning ordinances that reduce the number of residential zoning districts to only one or two. A variety of housing densities is possible, however, because the number of units permitted is related to the environmental carrying capacity of each site. Although at first glance these rules seem somewhat complex, developers generally have favored the innovation because the performance standards are not subject to varying administrative interpretation and permit much greater variety in design.

Breckenridge, Colorado, has abolished zoning altogether and regulates all development through a comprehensive permit system based on performance standards. A small Victorian-era mining community in the Rocky Mountains, Breckenridge has become a major ski area in recent years, with attendant development pressure. The performance standards establish architectural guidelines to ensure that new development is compatible with the existing Victorian character of the town, prohibit certain features in a development and require others, and assign positive or negative scores for other features related to environmental impact. The development must achieve a total score of zero or better to receive a permit but can receive significant density bonuses if it achieves higher scores. As in Bucks County, developers generally have been pleased with the permit system because its structured nature reduces uncertainty and processing time.

Performance zoning also can aid redevelopment of an area. For example, South Pointe, a deteriorated, 250-acre, multifamily residential district on the southern tip of Miami Beach, was originally platted in small, 50-by-100-foot lots sold to individual buyers in the 1920s. Attempts to redevelop the area had met with little success until a new performance zoning ordinance was enacted that increased the minimum lot size and minimum width of lots, required 60 to 70 percent open space, yet increased the allowable FAR. These changes have encouraged the aggregation of the small lots and already have led to substantial development.

Incentive Zoning

Closely related to performance zoning is **incentive zoning,** which encourages developers to provide certain publicly desired features in return for various incentives. For example, the San Francisco City Planning Code permits increased floor area if the developer provides a pedestrian plaza or arcade. New York City has provided similar incentives, although they have been reduced in the new zoning code. Other communities permit higher densities for residential developments that provide such features as open space.

Transfer of Development Rights

Another creative technique of land-use regulation that has received increasing attention involves transfer of **development rights.** Under a transfer system, landowners can sell part of their bundle of rights to develop their property to other landowners, who then can use their own land more intensively. For example, suppose that Mrs. Johnson owns a ten-acre wooded tract that she wishes to preserve as it is. Nearby, Mr. Hite owns another ten-acre tract that he wishes to develop. Existing regulations require minimum one-acre lots in the area, so Mr. Hite could build only ten houses on his land. Mrs. Johnson, having no interest in developing her property, could sell her development rights to Mr. Hite, who then could build 20 houses on his ten acres, while Mrs. Johnson's land remained in its wooded state. Proponents of this system contend that it is more equitable than one that does not permit such transfer of development rights; it enables communities to preserve floodplains, open space, and historic structures without wiping out their property values because development rights can be sold to other property owners.

The use of transfer of development rights still is limited but is growing in application. Several communities in New Jersey and California are experimenting with the system in their efforts to preserve open space. A number of cities, including New York, Chicago, Denver, and Washington, are using the transfer mechanism as a means to preserve historic landmarks. FARs on such properties can be transferred to other properties to allow denser development on those sites. For example, Tiffany sold development rights over their Fifth Avenue building to Donald Trump to enable him to add more space to his Trump Tower development.

■ THE TAKINGS ISSUE

If a governmental unit acquires property for public use under the power of eminent domain, this action is a *taking* which requires the payment of compensation, whether it involves acquisition in fee simple or only partial property rights, such as an easement. Regulation of land use under police power, on the other hand, normally does not constitute a taking. The courts have ruled, however, that if the regulation is so severe that it deprives owners of any beneficial use of their property, it may then constitute a taking and, thus, be invalid. The problem is that the courts have never defined the exact point at which regulation goes too far and becomes a taking. The increasing magnitude of land-use regulation has made this a very real issue for many property owners.

Land-use regulation generally is not ruled unconstitutional simply because it reduces the value of a parcel of land. It is only when a regulation deprives the landowner of the entire use and value of the property, or does not allow a reasonable return, that regulation is held unconstitutional as applied to that particular parcel. As discussed in the Legal Highlight on pages 83-86, exactly how far regulation can go without becoming a taking, however, has not been fully resolved by the U.S. Supreme Court. Some states have passed property rights laws that entitle landowners to compensation if government regulations significantly reduce their property values. The question of whether a property owner is entitled to compensation as a result of a government regulation undoubtedly will continue to be debated for many years.

■ CHAPTER REVIEW

■ Government has four basic powers that affect real estate owners. These powers are (1) the power of taxation, (2) the power of escheat, (3) the power of eminent domain, and (4) police power.

■ Property taxes are an important source of revenues for state and local governments. They provide a relatively stable source of revenue that is not subject to wide fluctuations in short-term business activity, and they are very difficult to evade because they are tied to property that is largely immobile.

■ The steps involved in the property taxation process are (1) property value assessment, (2) development of the budget and a tax rate, and (3) tax billing and collection.

■ In the event that a property owner dies without heirs or a valid will, the government, through the power of escheat, becomes the owner of the property.

■ The government's right to condemn land is founded on the power of eminent domain, as granted by the Fifth Amendment to the U.S. Constitution. Once the government establishes the right to take title to or place an easement on property for society's needs, the major issue of concern is the determination of just compensation.

■ The police power is the power of government to regulate activities to promote the public health, safety, and general welfare.

■ The interdependence of land uses—that is, the impact that the use of land has on other property and on the public as a whole—leads to land-use controls.

■ A comprehensive general plan is a statement of a community's long-range policies covering its predicted physical needs for 15 to 25 years in the future. It usually contains the following elements: (a) an analysis of projected economic and population developments, (b) a transportation plan, (c) a public facilities plan, (d) a land-use plan, and (e) an official map.

■ The most widely employed method of regulating the use of land is comprehensive zoning. This divides land into zones and prescribes regulations relating to the type and intensity of use. Relief from zoning regulations can be sought through legislative rezoning, through administrative variance or special-use permit, or through the courts.

REAL ESTATE TODAY

The Supreme Court Grapples with the "Takings" Issue

Although the general rule is that actual or potential losses resulting from police power regulations do not require compensation, the U.S. Supreme Court has ruled that if a restriction goes "too far," it will be considered a taking. Unfortunately, the court has provided little guidance as to how far is "too far." Some recent decisions offer some guidance, however.

Legal Highlight

The *Euclid* Decision

Sometimes, the Supreme Court issues a decision that is truly momentous in a particular area. *Village of Euclid v. Ambler Realty Company* (1926) was such a case, upholding the constitutionality of comprehensive zoning regulations.

Euclid, a suburb of Cleveland, adopted a comprehensive zoning ordinance in 1922. The Ambler Realty Company owned a 68-acre tract of land that it hoped to sell for industrial development. Because industrial use was precluded by the ordinance, which zoned part of the tract for single-family residential use only, Ambler Realty attacked the ordinance on the ground that it was a taking of the company's property without compensation. The district court agreed and declared the ordinance null and void.

The village appealed to the U.S. Supreme Court, which reversed the lower court by a five-to-four decision. The victory was a narrow one, with one justice changing his mind in favor of upholding the ordinance after an opinion striking down the principle of zoning had been written but not made public. In its final decision, the court ruled that the community was not taking or destroying Ambler Realty's property for public use but was invoking a general power over private property, which was necessary for the orderly development of the community.

For better or worse, the *Euclid* decision changed the course of urban development in the United States. The zoning ordinances of more than 400 municipalities were upheld, and hundreds of others were soon passed. Now, almost every city of more than 10,000 population has enacted a comprehensive zoning ordinance, as have many smaller municipalities and counties. It is interesting to speculate what might have happened to the course of urban development in the United States if the one justice had not changed his vote.

Upholding Historic Preservation Regulations

Following the *Euclid* decision and two related cases in the 1920s, the U.S. Supreme Court did not accept another zoning case for 50 years, when the Court upheld New York City's landmarks preservation law. Not only was this an important victory for preservationists; it was also a landmark takings decision.

New York enacted a landmarks preservation law in 1965 to establish a citywide program of identification and preservation of historic structures and sites. Designation barred any construction or alteration of a building's exterior appearance without the approval of the Landmarks Preservation Commission. Grand Central Terminal, a monumental building in the Beaux-Arts style that was completed in 1913, was designated as a landmark under the law. Later, the Penn Central Railroad leased air rights over the terminal for a proposed skyscraper. The Landmarks Preservation Commission rejected the plan, reasoning: "To balance a 55-story office tower above a flamboyant Beaux-Arts facade seems nothing more than an aesthetic joke which would reduce the Landmark itself to the status of a curiosity."

Penn Central challenged the constitutionality of the landmarks law, contending it resulted in the taking of private property without compensation. The Court disagreed, concluding that:

The Supreme Court Grapples with the "Takings" Issue (continued)

The submission that appellants may establish a taking simply by showing that they have been denied the ability to exploit a property interest that they heretofore had believed was available for development is quite simply untenable.

Legal Highlight

Even so, the Court made it clear that preservation laws could not deprive the owner of a reasonable return from the property but that the return need not be the highest possible return.

Preservation of Open Space

In 1980, the Court upheld Tiburon, California's, open-space zoning ordinance against a takings claim. The Agins owned five acres of unimproved land overlooking San Francisco Bay that they considered "the most valuable land in California." The city subsequently enacted a zoning ordinance that restricted density on the tract to between one and five single-family residences. The Agins sued, asserting that the city had effectively taken the property, preventing its development for residential use and completely destroying "the value of the property for any purpose or use whatever." They also sought $2 million in damages for inverse condemnation—the taking of private property by a governmental unit through an inference of property rights without actually seizing the property. In other words, the Agins felt the rezoning was a taking that required compensation. The U.S. Supreme Court did not agree.

In upholding the ordinance, the Court held that a zoning ordinance would constitute an unconstitutional taking only if (1) legitimate governmental interests are not substantially advanced or (2) the landowner is denied any economically viable use of the property. The Court considered the preservation of open space and the promotion of orderly development to be legitimate state interests and noted

that the effects of the ordinance fell on numerous property owners, not just on the Agins. It also found that although the ordinance restricted the density of development, it did not deny the Agins "economically viable use" of the land because it could still be developed for residential purposes, though perhaps not at the density they desired.

Limits on Mandatory Dedications

Property owners commonly are required to dedicate land or make infrastructure improvements as a condition to obtaining developmental approvals. Another Supreme Court decision dealt with the question of how far these developmental regulations can go in requiring such exactions—to the question of the limits and relevance of "legitimate state interests."

The Nollans wanted to replace a small bungalow on their beachfront lot with a larger house. As a condition to granting a building permit, the California Coastal Commission required the donation of a ten-foot walkway easement along the beach in front of the Nollan property. The commission contended that the easement was necessary to offset the reduced "visual access" caused by the construction and to help prevent congestion of the public beaches. The Nollans contended the exaction was not related to any need to which their project contributed directly and was, therefore, a taking.

The Supreme Court reaffirmed the constitutionality of developmental controls and exactions, stating that the commission could have legitimately imposed conditions to protect the public's ability to see the beach, such as height and width restrictions or a ban on fences; could have required the dedication of a "public viewing spot" on the Nollans' property; or even could have prohibited the new construction altogether. however, the Court agreed with the Nollans that the requirement to dedicate the public walkway

REAL ESTATE TODAY

The Supreme Court Grapples with the "Takings" Issue (continued)

easement was not sufficiently related to the problems supposedly created by the new construction:

> [T]he lack of nexus between the condition and the original purpose of the building restriction converts that purpose to something other than what it was. The purpose then becomes, quite simply, the obtaining of an easement to serve some valid governmental purpose, but without payment of compensation. . . . Unless the permit condition serves the same governmental purpose as the development ban, the building restriction is not a valid regulation of land use but an out-and-out plan of extortion.

This need to tie any dedication requirements more closely to the actual impact of the proposed development was made clearer in the Supreme Court's 1994 decision in the case of *Dolan v. Tigard.* The Dolans owned a plumbing and electrical supply store in the City of Tigard, Oregon. They wanted to double the size of their building and add parking spaces. The Planning Commission approved the plans with the requirement that the Dolans dedicate about a tenth of their land for flood control for the adjacent creek, and about an additional 15 feet for a bike path.

The Dolans challenged the dedication requirement. The Supreme Court decided, by a five-to-four vote, that requiring a dedicated easement as a condition of permission to build or expand was an unconstitutional taking unless the government can show "a rough proportionality" between the regulation and impact of the development.

Do these decisions mean that local governments can no longer require mandatory dedications from developers? No, but the Court has

Legal Highlight

made it clear that any required dedications must be closely related to the regulatory objective.

The *Lucas* Decision

In another important land-use decision, the Supreme Court made it clear that regulation that rendered land virtually valueless definitely went "too far." Lucas had bought two residential lots in 1986 on the Isle of Palms, a South Carolina barrier island, for $975,000. He intended to build single-family homes on the lots, as the owners of adjacent lots had already done. To his dismay, however, the South Carolina legislature passed the Beachfront Management Act in 1988, which prohibited building on Lucas's lots. He sued, contending that the regulation had taken his property because he was left with no economically viable use of his land. The Supreme Court agreed and ruled as follows: "Total deprivation of beneficial use is, from the landowner's point of view, the equivalent of a physical appropriation. . . . We think, in short, that there are good reasons for our frequently expressed belief that when the owner of real property has been called upon to sacrifice all economically beneficial uses in the name of the common good, that is, to leave his property economically idle, he has suffered a taking."

Although this ruling seems to settle the issue for extreme cases—a property owner must be left with some economic use of his property unless the use constitutes a public nuisance—the Court still has not adequately defined the dividing line between a regulation that reduces property value but does not result in a taking and one that does result in a taking, requiring compensation. Uncertainty will still be the rule for all involved in land-use development and planning until the Supreme Court more clearly defines exactly what is permissible in land-use regulation and what is not.

The Supreme Court Grapples with the "Takings" Issue (continued)

The Takings Battle in the Legislatures

Recently, the takings battle has moved into the legislatures and the Congress, with takings assessment bills and compensation laws being introduced in many states. The takings assessment laws would require that an assessment be made for land-use regulations that would assess their impact on private property values. The compensation bills would require that private property owners be compensated if regulations reduced the value of their property by some percentage, often 25 percent. At this writing the fate of these bills remains uncertain, as they will undoubtedly be challenged through the court system.

Legal Highlight

The Takings Issue

The takings controversy boils down to the basic question of the nature of private property rights. Do private parties own property subject to regulations, or do they have the unlimited right to use their property as they choose? Where is the proper middle ground? This is an issue that promises to be a lively one for many, many years to come.

Sources: Village of Euclid, Ohio v. Ambler Realty Co., 272 U.S. 365, 47 S.Ct. 114 (1926); Penn Central Transportation Co. v. City of New York, 438 U.S. 104 (1978); Agins v. Tiburon, 447 U.S. 255 (1980); Nollan v. California Coastal Commission, 483 U.S. 825 (1987); Lucas v. South Carolina Coastal Council, 112 S.Ct. 2886 (1992); Dolan v. Tigard, 114 S.Ct. 2309 (1994); John Tibbetts, "Everybody's Taking the Fifth," *Planning*, January 1995, personal property. 4–9.

- Developers often are required to dedicate rights-of-way for public streets, utility, and drainage, and in some communities, they also may be required to dedicate parks, open space, and schools.

- Building codes establish detailed standards for the construction of new buildings and the alteration of existing ones.

- Under a system of planned unit development (PUD), many regulations are waived to permit greater flexibility of design. Lot sizes may be reduced, for example, if community open spaces are provided.

- Performance zoning is a technique that relates permitted uses of land to certain performance standards. Such standards usually are intended to protect the environment.

- Incentive zoning, which is closely related to performance zoning, is any type of zoning provision that encourages developers to provide certain publicly desired features in return for such incentives as increased density of land use.

- Under the concept of transfer of development rights, a landowner is able to sell part of his or her bundle of rights to another landowner, who then can use his or her own land more intensively.

■ Regulation of land use under the police power normally does not constitute a taking unless the regulation is so severe as to deprive the owner of any beneficial use of the property. Land-use regulation generally is not held to be unconstitutional simply because it reduces the value of a parcel of land.

■ KEY TERMS

ad valorem tax	escheat	millage rate
assessment	exemption	nonconforming use
assessed value	homestead exemption	nuisance laws
assessment ratio	impact fees	performance zoning
assessor (property assessor)	incentive zoning	planned unit development
comprehensive general plan	inverse condemnation	police power
	just compensation	power of taxation
comprehensive zoning	mandatory dedication	subdivision regulations
development rights	market value	taxable value
eminent domain	mill	variance

■ STUDY EXERCISES

1. What are the desirable features of the property tax for local governments?
2. What is the tax digest?
3. Suppose a local government has a tax digest of $500 million and feels it must raise $15 million for the operation of its schools and general government. What would be the millage rate?
4. Why is the government's power of escheat so seldom used?
5. By what authority does the government have the power of eminent domain?
6. What is meant by "public use"?
7. What characteristic of real estate leads to the need for public land-use controls?
8. Contrast police power and the power of eminent domain.
9. Discuss the history of the takings issue.
10. Describe the elements usually contained in a comprehensive general plan.
11. How is zoning used to control land use and intensity of use?
12. What are mandatory dedications?
13. What is incentive zoning? Performance zoning?

14. Describe the transfer of development rights process.

15. Suppose that Mack owns 25 acres of land on the edge of town on a major road that is now zoned for residential use. He decides he would like to develop this land as an office park and shopping center. What steps would he have to take to secure approval of his project?

16. Suppose Mary owns a lot on which she wishes to build her dream house. To her consternation, she finds that if the house is placed on her rather narrow lot, it will fail to meet the sideyard setback requirements by three feet. What can she do?

 Go to the Student Study Guide CD-ROM and work through Case 1.

■ FURTHER READINGS

Callies, D. L., ed. *Takings: Land-Development Conditions and Regulatory Takings after Dolan and Lucas.* Chicago: American Bar Association, Section of State and Local Government Law, 1996.

Platt, R. H., *Land Use Control: Geography, Law and Public Policy.* Englewood Cliffs, N.J.: Prentice Hall, 1996.

Stein, J. M., ed. *Classic Readings in Real Estate and Development.* Washington, D.C.: Urban Land Institute, 1996.

Wright, R. R., *Land Use in a Nutshell,* 3rd ed. St. Paul, Minn.: West Publishing Company, 1994.

5 Deeds and Leases

In order to transfer ownership of any parcel of property, a deed containing the exact legal description of the property must be conveyed. This description involves much more specific information than property name or street address.

CHAPTER PREVIEW

The previous chapters in this section have described the concept of real estate ownership, including the legal rights held by real estate owners and the public and private limitations on those ownership rights. In this chapter, we consider deeds, which are the legal documents used to convey ownership from one party to another, and leases, which are the legal agreements used to convey leasehold interests in property from one party to another.

Under the topic of deeds, we examine the necessary elements of a deed and

■ types of deeds, including the (1) general warranty deed, (2) special warranty deed, (3) bargain and sale deed, and (4) quitclaim deed.

Under the topic of leases we consider

■ the recommended elements of a lease,

■ specific clauses in lease agreements, and

■ duties of the lessor and lessee.

■ DEEDS

Centuries ago in England, any person who possessed land generally was considered to be the legal owner, as possession and ownership essentially were synonymous. In the presence of witnesses, an owner could transfer his title, or legal ownership, to another person simply by going on the land and handing the new owner a clod of earth while announcing that title was transferred. This symbolic transfer of title by delivery caused great confusion because there were no written records. The potential for fraud or forcible seizure was limitless. Therefore, in 1677, Parliament enacted a statute of frauds, which required that all title transfers of real property be in writing. This provision has been adopted by every state in the United States with the goal of limiting the opportunities for fraudulent transactions. Thus, when title to real estate is to be transferred today, a written document called a deed must be given by the grantor to the new owner, the grantee.

Once the deed is written, title to real property is transferred by delivery of the deed to and its acceptance by the buyer. The delivery can be made by the seller or a person acting on behalf of the seller. Delivery of a signed deed can even be made after the seller's death if that was the seller's intent. When ownership is to be transferred, a deed must be drafted, signed by the grantor, and delivered to and accepted by the new owner.

Several elements are necessary for a deed to be valid. In addition to the basic requirement that a deed must be in writing, a valid deed must include

- designation of the parties,
- consideration given for the conveyed interest,
- legal description of the property,
- specification of the interests conveyed, and
- signatures of the proper parties.

After the deed has been written properly, it must be delivered to and accepted by the new owner.

Necessary Elements of a Deed

All deeds begin by identifying the parties involved in the transfer of title. In general, the seller is the grantor and the buyer is the grantee. The grantee must give up something in return for the interest conveyed, generally the purchase price. Sometimes the exact amount of this consideration is stated, but often a nominal amount (such as $10) is mentioned in the deed as the consideration paid. This tends to keep the actual purchase price a secret known only to the parties involved in the transaction.

Next, the property being transferred must be described accurately so that the precise boundaries can be determined. A mere street address is an insufficient description in the deed because the address does not establish the exact property boundaries and is subject to change. Buyers frequently discover that the street number by which their new property is known (and where mail is delivered) is not the number stated in other documents; at some time in the past, the number was changed. To describe the real property's precise location, the metes-and-bounds method, the rectangular survey method, and/or a reference to plats should be used. We considered each of these methods in Chapter 2.

The legal description is followed by the words that actually convey the property interest. The words of conveyance should make it clear what rights are being transferred. The grantor then must sign the deed. Before a deed can be recorded, most states require that the grantor sign in the presence of one or more witnesses (who also sign the document). Notice that the grantee's signature is not required on the deed in some states.

Once the deed is properly signed, it can be said to have been executed, or subjected to all requirements that establish its validity.

Finally, the deed must be delivered to the grantee. Title to the property is not actually transferred from the grantor to the grantee until delivery has been completed. Of course, it is assumed for the purposes of this discussion that the grantee accepts the deed. Refusal to accept the deed results in an ineffective delivery. Although a transfer of title need not be recorded in the public records to be valid, the grantee must record the new deed in the county's record or deed office to be assured of protection against claims that the grantor later transferred his or her title to someone else. The public records system will be discussed in more detail in Chapter 7.

Additional Elements

Although the elements just described are the only ones essential to a valid deed, the most common types of deeds contain additional elements called covenants and warranties. A covenant is any agreement or promise, and a warranty is a guarantee that the statements made are true. Traditionally, there are four covenants and one warranty: (1) covenant against encumbrances, (2) covenant of seisin or ownership, (3) covenant of quiet enjoyment, (4) covenant of further assurances, and (5) warranty forever. Whether all, some or none of these items exists in a deed depends on the type of deed the grantor is required to give. In some states the five items are not expressly stated in the deed, but are incorporated by reference to statute.

Degree of Protection

It is important to understand the degree of protection each type of deed gives to the grantee. The order in which these types of deeds will be discussed is also the order of the amount of protection provided. The general warranty deed contains the greatest assurances by the grantor that the grantee will have security for nearly all potential claims. The special warranty deed (and the grant deed) limits the grantor's liability to title defects that occurred during the grantor's ownership. The bargain-and-sale deed simply states that the grantor has the right to convey the title involved, but all other assurances are missing. Finally, the grantor who gives a quitclaim deed does not even promise that he or she has any rights in the land at all.

Types of Deeds

There are many kinds of deeds, each having its own special characteristics. The more common types are general warranty deeds, special warranty deeds, bargain and sale deeds and quitclaim deeds.

General Warranty Deed

The warranty deed is the broadest type of all deeds. In a **general warranty deed,** the grantor makes promises that cover the traditional covenants and warranty. The grantor assures the grantee that no liens or encumbrances other than those on public record exist against the property **(covenant against encumbrances),** that the grantor has a fee simple interest in the property, and that he or she is in full possession of the interest being conveyed and, thus, has the right to convey it **(covenant of seisin).** (The covenant against encumbrances does not mean that there are no encumbrances on the property but rather that if there are encumbrances, they will be listed in the deed or in public records. In many states, encumbrances that are open and visible and that benefit the land are also excluded.) The grantor also promises that the grantee's enjoyment of the property will not be disturbed by some party claiming to own or to have a lien on it (covenant of quiet enjoyment). These covenants relate to the present condition of the grantor's title.

A general warranty deed further assures the grantee that the grantor will execute any future documents needed to perfect the grantor's title (covenant of further assurances). Finally, the grantor promises to always defend the title conveyed (warranty forever). These latter two items relate to the grantor's duties as they might arise in the future.

In the typical residential sales transaction, the buyer should insist that the sales contract require that the seller transfer title by warranty deed. Figure 5.1 presents a sample warranty deed for a single-family home transaction.

The traditional warranty deed is not divided by section headings, as shown in Figure 5.1. The roman numerals are used only to facilitate the explanation that follows. Section I identifies the parties as "Grantors" and "Grantees." Section II discloses the consideration paid in return for the deed, states that the property is being conveyed, and describes the property's boundaries. Section III actually indicates that the grantees now hold the property in a fee simple absolute estate. These first three sections plus the grantors' signatures satisfy the necessary elements of a deed.

Because Figure 5.1 is a general warranty deed, the remaining paragraphs contain the covenants and warranty previously discussed. For example, Section IV provides the grantors' promise that no encumbrances exist against the property other than those clearly stated. Section V includes the grantors' statement that they have a fee simple interest and the right to convey this interest to another person. This provision also contains the covenant of quiet enjoyment. Section VI includes the covenant of further assurances and the warranty forever. This latter covenant and warranty create the grantors' duty to provide any documents of title needed in the future to give the grantees clear title. For example, the grantors have

---

FIGURE 5.1   General Warranty Deed*

I. THIS DEED, made this 20th day of December, 1998, between Harold J. Stewart and Gladys Atwater Stewart, husband and wife, of St. Joseph, Missouri, hereinafter referred to as "Grantors," and Frank L. Barr and Elizabeth McKenna Barr, husband and wife, St. Joseph, Missouri, hereinafter referred to as "Grantees."

II. WITNESSETH, that Grantors, in consideration of the sum of ten dollars ($10.00), receipt whereof is hereby acknowledged, do grant, sell and convey unto Grantees, their heirs and assigns, all that tract or parcel of land with improvements thereon located in Buchanan County, Missouri, described as follows:

Part of SW ¼ of the SE ¼ Section 14, T. 57 N., R. 35 W., of the 5th P.M., Buchanan County, State of Missouri, beginning at a point being 202 feet East of the SW corner of the SE ¼ of said Section 14; running thence North 8 degrees East 200 feet to an iron pin; running thence due East 100 feet to an iron pin; running thence South 8 degrees West 200 feet to an iron pin; running thence due East 100 feet to the point of beginning. This property is that described as Lot 3, Block G, of the Harris Billups Estate, as recorded in Plat Book 8, page 37, in the Office of the Clerk of the Circuit Court of Buchanan County, Missouri.

III. TO HAVE AND TO HOLD the premises hereby granted to Grantees, their heirs and assigns in fee simple forever.

IV The Grantors warrant that the premises are free from all encumbrances except for the following:.

   (a) The underground gas line easement running along the eastern boundary within five feet thereof

   (b) All other restrictions of record

V. The Grantors, having a fee simple interest and the right to convey such interest, warrant that Grantees, their heirs and assigns shall enjoy quietly and peaceably possession of the premises.

VI. It is further warranted that Grantors shall procure and execute any further assurances of the title to the premises and that Grantors will forever defend the title to the premises against all claims.

IN WITNESS WHEREOF, Grantors have set their signatures and seals, the day and year first written above.

                  _____ (Seal)

                              Harold J. Stewart

                  _____ (Seal)

                            Gladys Atwater Stewart

Signed, sealed and delivered in the presence of

_____

_____

Notary Public, Buchanan County, Missouri

_____

*This form is intended for instructional purposes only and should not be relied on in practice, as it may not satisfy all existing circumstances.

---

promised that if this deed is defective for any reason, they will sign a new deed free of all defects.

When the deed has been signed, or executed, by the grantors and the witnesses, it is ready to be delivered to the grantees. Remember that title to real property actually passes only when the deed is delivered and accepted.

A warranty deed provides some protection to the purchaser concerning the acquisition of "good title." This protection, however, may not extend to "marketability" of the title. If, for example, a neighbor has obtained an unrecorded easement by prescription (as described in Chapter 3) over the land being transferred, the grantee under a warranty deed can successfully sue the grantor for the amount by which this encumbrance has diminished the property. In this situation, the grantor would have breached the covenant of quiet enjoyment and the covenant against encumbrances. Some states have interpreted the covenants and warranties of a deed as being breached only if the grantee loses possession to another party. Obviously, under this interpretation, the existence of a prescriptive easement would not be a breach of the covenant of quiet enjoyment or the covenant against encumbrances.

Special Warranty Deed

A **special warranty deed** limits the extent of the seller's warranties to events that occurred during the seller's period of ownership. It does not protect the grantee against encumbrances that may have arisen before the grantor took title. The grantor's warrants cover only title defects that occurred during the grantor's ownership. For example, a corporation might give a special warranty deed to protect itself against any potential liabilities resulting from a foreclosure that happened before it owned the property. This type of deed is similar to the grant deed that is commonly used in California.

Bargain and Sale Deed

A deed that implies the grantor has title to the property and the right to convey it but does not contain any express covenants as to the title's validity is called a **bargain and sale deed.** This deed is also called a **warranty deed without covenants.**

In essence, the bargain and sale deed simply specifies that the grantor "does hereby grant, sell, and convey" some interest in real property to the grantee. If the sales contract fails to specify what type of deed must be delivered, the bargain and sale deed may be the only one required. If the buyers want to make certain they receive a warranty deed, this must be clearly stated in the sales contract.

Quitclaim Deed

A **quitclaim deed** transfers any interest that the grantor may have in the property described but does not imply that the grantor has any valid interest in it. The quitclaim deed is most commonly used to clear defects in the title to property. For example, suppose Bob wished to sell land he allegedly owned to David, but Clare, Bob's sister, claimed to own a one-fourth interest in the land. Before David would be willing to purchase the land, he would want a quitclaim deed from Clare. That deed would indicate that Clare had relinquished her claim to her one-fourth interest, but she would not be liable for any defects in the title.

FIGURE 5.2	Language of a Quitclaim Deed*

I. THIS DEED, made this 20th day of December, 2001, between Harold J. Stewart and Gladys Atwater Stewart, husband and wife, of St. Joseph, Missouri, hereinafter referred to as "Grantors," and Frank L. Barr and Elizabeth McKenna Barr, husband and wife, St. Joseph, Missouri, hereinafter referred to as "Grantees."

II. WITNESSETH, that Grantors, in consideration of the sum of ten dollars ($10.00), receipt whereof is hereby acknowledged, do grant, sell and convey unto Grantees, their heirs and assigns, all that tract or parcel of land with improvements thereon located in Buchanan County, Missouri, described as follows:

Part of SW Z\v of the SE Z\v Section 14, T. 57 N., R. 35 W., of the 5th P.M., Buchanan County, State of Missouri, beginning at a point being 202 feet East of the SW corner of the SE Z\v of said Section 14; running thence North 8 degrees East 200 feet to an iron pin; running thence due East 100 feet to an iron pin; running thence South 8 degrees West 200 feet to an iron pin; running thence due East 100 feet to the point of beginning. This property is that described as Lot 3, Block G, of the Harris Billups Estate, as recorded in Plat Book 8, page 37, in the Office of the Clerk of the Circuit Court of Buchanan County, Missouri.

III. The Grantors, their heirs and assigns hereby grant and convey all the interests, if any, they might have in the premises to the Grantees, their heirs and assigns in fee simple forever. The Grantors, their heirs and assigns shall not hereafter claim or demand any right or title to the aforesaid premises or any part thereof, but they and every one of them shall be excluded and forever barred.

IN WITNESS WHEREOF, Grantors have set their signatures and seals, the day and year first written above.

_____(seal)
Harold J. Stewart

_____(seal)
Gladys Atwater Stewart

Signed, sealed and delivered in the presence of:

_____

_____
Notary Public, Buchanan County, Missouri

_____

*This form is intended for instructional purposes only and should not be relied on in practice, as it may not satisfy all existing circumstances.

If David wished to get full clear title to the land, he typically would insist on receiving a general warranty deed from Bob, as well as the quitclaim deed from Clare.

Similarly, a quitclaim deed is also used to release marital interests in a property. If Bob and Jane divorce, and Jane is awarded ownership of the family home, then Bob may be required to sign a quitclaim deed that releases any interest he may have in the property to Jane. The quitclaim deed would serve as evidence that Bob no longer held an interest in the property after the divorce.

The grantee who takes property under a quitclaim deed must understand that he may be receiving nothing at all of value. A person could give a quitclaim deed describing a neighbor's land, or even a university's football stadium for that matter. Under a quitclaim deed, the grantor conveys all the interests possessed with out any assurances that any rights of ownership exist. If the grantor has no rights in the property, then nothing is transferred.

A sample of the language used in a quitclaim deed is shown in Figure 5.2.

Deeds for Special Uses

There are several other kinds of deeds that have specific purposes. Each of these specialized deeds is named for the signer, and the warranties given, if any, depend on that signer's capacity. An executor's deed is an example. An executor of an estate seldom will be willing to promise that the title being transferred is free of all defects. Therefore, the executor covenants only that he or she is conveying the title held by the deceased person and that he or she has not encumbered the property in his or her capacity as executor. A grantee taking property under any such special deed must be aware that the grantor's covenants and warranties are very limited or nonexistent.

■ LEASES

When a property owner agrees to transfer rights of use and possession (but not ownership) of the property to a tenant in exchange for rent payments, the agreement is called a **lease.** Leases divide estates in land into two components: a leased fee and a leasehold.

Although some leases need not be put into written form (short-term residential leases, for example), most prudent real estate market participants know the importance of making sure the agreement between parties is clearly stated in writing to minimize misunderstandings and disputes.

A lease is a type of contract, and its basic requirements are the same as the general requirements for contracts. Through the lease contract, the landlord conveys use and possession of the property in return for the tenant's agreement to pay rent. The lease also defines the rights, duties, and liabilities of both landlord and tenant and should contain the following elements:

- Names of the **lessor** (landlord) and **lessee** (tenant), both of whom must have contractual capacity to enter into the lease agreement
- Identification of the premises
- Conveyance of the premises
- Term or duration of the lease
- Amount of rent and manner of payment
- Duties and obligations of the parties
- Signatures of the parties

As in all contracts, a lease becomes valid when it is delivered and accepted. If the lease is for a term of one year or longer, it must be in writing to be enforceable in court.

Classification of Leases

Leases can be classified in several ways. Generally, they are classified by duration of term, type of use, and method of rental payment.

Duration of Term

The duration of the term of a leasehold determines whether it is a tenancy for a stated period, a tenancy from period to period, a tenancy at will, or a tenancy at sufferance.

A **tenancy for a stated period** conveys the property to the tenant for a stated period of time, sometimes called the **term.** The term may be for any length of time from one month to many years, although in most states a lease for longer than 99 years is regarded as a fee simple transaction. Possession of the property reverts to the landlord at the end of the term, subject to any right of renewal set forth in the lease. Many states require that long-term leases, usually for more than one to three years, be recorded in the public record to be enforceable as a contract.

A **tenancy from period to period** is of indefinite duration. The tenancy does not terminate until proper notice is given by either party. It commonly exists from month to month and is renewed automatically at the end of each month, provided the tenant has paid the rent.

A **tenancy at will** may be terminated by either party at any time. Tenant-protection statutes, however, generally require reasonable notice on the part of the landlord—usually 30 days.

A **tenancy at sufferance** is created when a tenant continues to occupy property after the expiration of the lease period. The tenant has no right to the property and remains there at the sufferance of the landlord. Even so, many states require that the tenant be given notice to quit the premises before eviction proceedings can be instituted.

Type of Use

Leaseholds are used for either commercial or residential purposes. A commercial lease permits the tenant to use the property for income-producing retail, manufacturing, or office activities. The purpose of the residential lease is to provide housing for the lessee, not to produce income. A commercial lease is generally of longer duration and more complicated in its terms than is a residential lease.

A **ground lease** is a long-term (usually 50 years or longer) lease involving unimproved land. The leased land is usually developed by the tenant for commercial, residential, or agricultural purposes. At the end of the lease, the land and any improvements revert to the landowner. Because such a lease makes it possible to separate the ownership of the land from the ownership of the improvements, the ground lease frequently is used as a financing device in the development of major office buildings.

For example, many Manhattan office buildings are built on leased land. Because the land often constitutes 30 to 40 percent of the cost of such projects, a ground lease can greatly reduce the amount of money the developer must raise. The ground lease can also offer substantial tax advantages to the lessee because lease payments are fully deductible from taxable income as an ordinary expense, whereas the cost of land cannot be depreciated—that is, the owners cannot reduce their taxes by stating on their tax return an amount by which the value of the land has decreased with age, as one can do in the case of buildings.

Methods of Rent Payment or Adjustment

Arrangements for rental payments between tenant and landlord can take many forms, and rental arrangements are far from uniform. Two factors that determine the form of the lease are the degree of overhead cost that is assumed by the tenant and whether the amount of rent is fixed or variable.

Under a **gross lease,** the landlord agrees to pay the real estate taxes, utilities, insurance, and all other operating expenses in connection with use of the prem-ises.

Under a **net lease,** the tenant pays the operating expenses in addition to rent. Such a lease transfers uncertainty regarding the future cost of operating expenses to the tenant and leaves the landlord with a more definite net return. Occasionally, the tenant assumes responsibility for other costs as well, so there are net net leases and net net net leases. Under a **net net lease,** the lessee pays not only operating expenses but insurance premiums as well. Under a **net net net lease,** also known as the *triple net lease,* the lessee pays operating expenses, insurance premiums, and real estate taxes.

Under a **fixed-rent lease,** the amount of the rental payment is fixed for the term of the lease. This type of rental payment is most common for short-term residential leases.

In the **graduated-rent lease,** or **step-up rent lease,** the rental payment is fixed for the initial term of the lease and then is increased by specified percentages at designated intervals. This type of lease provides some protection against inflation for the landlord and also may be used for a new business or property whose income-producing ability is expected to increase in the future. This type of lease is seldom used for rental terms longer than ten years.

The **reappraisal lease** is similar to the graduated-rent lease except that the level of each rent increase is determined by a reappraisal of the property. Such leases are used most often for the long-term rental of entire buildings. For example, if a tenant leases an entire warehouse for $10 per square foot, and the property value increases by 10 percent, the rent in the following year would be $11 per square foot.

The **percentage lease** is a lease of a property used for commercial purposes under which the rent payments are based on some percentage of sales made on the premises. Usually, the stated percentage of gross sales is combined with a flat minimum rent. Such leases are found predominantly in shopping centers, particularly in the larger malls. For example, a toy store in a mall may be charged a base rent of $1,500 per month, plus 2 percent of gross sales over $50,000. If the store's December sales are $90,000, the rent will be $1,500 plus 2 percent of $40,000, for a total of $2,300. If January's sales are only $25,000, the store will pay only the base rent of $1,500.

The percentage of gross sales charged as rent will vary, depending on whether the store is a low-margin/high-volume or high-margin/low-volume outlet and on its relative importance to the shopping center. For example, an "anchor" department store almost always can negotiate more favorable lease terms than can a small merchant.

Another type of lease is known as the **index lease.** In this arrangement, lease payments are "indexed" to some measure of the cost of living, such as the Consumer Price Index. Rents are adjusted periodically to account for changes in the value of the dollar. The adjustments provide protection for the landlord against inflation and rapidly changing prices in the economy.

■ THE LANDLORD-TENANT RELATIONSHIP IN A RESIDENTIAL LEASE

Much of the above information regarding lease terms relates to commercial leases. A residential lease can be on a month-to-month or fixed-term basis. On a month-to-month basis, either the landlord or the tenant has the right to terminate the lease after giving the other party 30 days' notice. With a tenancy for a stated period, the tenant has the right to occupy the property for a specific period of time, such as six months or two years. At the end of that time, the tenant can move out, the lease can be renewed for another stated period, or the parties can agree to continue the relationship as a tenancy from period to period.

Many leases contain a **renewal option,** a provision that protects the tenant against large increases in rent. The renewal option specifies what the rent will be if the lease is renewed, usually at a higher level to protect the landlord against rising costs. Without the renewal option, the landlord can raise the rent to any level desired. The tenant then has the option of paying the higher rent or moving out.

Expenses

The lease should state clearly who pays for expenses in connection with the property, including maintenance, property taxes, insurance, and utilities. Generally, the landlord is responsible for normal maintenance to the building and for taxes and insurance on the real estate. Utilities usually are the responsibility of the tenant, as is breakage or other damage caused by the actions of the tenant. Some commercial leases include **expense stops** that set the maximum amount of operating expenses the landlord will pay. Above the stop, the tenants will be charged for all operating expenses that exceed the stop in proportion to the amount of space each tenant has as a percentage of the total space available in the property.

Assignment and Subleasing

It often is desirable to a tenant to be able to assign a lease or sublease to another tenant if plans change before the end of the lease term. **Assignment** means that all of the tenant's rights under lease are transferred to the new tenant, although the lessee still is liable unless released by the landlord. **Subleasing** means transferring a portion of rights under a lease. For example, a tenant could sublease an apartment for only six months of a two-year lease term. Under a sublease clause, the landlord may reserve the right to approve of any sublessee, generally for reasons of creditworthiness. Unless the landlord consents, the tenant is not relieved of his or her obligation to pay the rent.

If rents are rising, it may be possible to sublease to another tenant at a profit, receiving rent from the sublessee and then paying the required rent under the original lease to the landlord. In a long-term commercial lease, this "leasehold interest" may be worth literally millions of dollars. If the lease contains a clause against subleasing, then subleasing is a violation of the lease agreement and can result in eviction.

Security Deposits

The lease may require that the tenant provide a **security deposit** prior to occupancy. Security deposits are intended to give the landlord protection if the tenant damages the property, moves out early, or fails to pay the rent. The landlord may also require that the tenant pay a cleaning fee at the termination of the lease, which is usually withheld from the security deposit owed to the tenant. Deposits make it essential that both landlord and tenant inspect the property *before* occupancy and note any damages that may exist.

Improvements

If a tenant makes improvements to a rented dwelling, the tenant must recognize that unless they can be removed easily, these improvements normally become part of the real estate (fixtures) and remain with the property when the lease expires. If built-in bookcases were added, for example, these would become a fixture and part of the property. Before making any improvements, it is wise to reach an agreement with the landlord, preferably written, as to who will own them at the termination of the lease.

The following Case Study on pages 103-104 illustrates the provisions of a typical residential lease.

After identifying the parties and the property, the agreement states that the property is rented only for the purpose of a single-family residence. If Jill should open some type of business in the apartment, for example, she would be in default, and Virginia Wells would have the right to terminate the lease agreement. Jill also agrees to pay $850 per month rent in advance and to pay a late-payment fee if the rent is not paid on time. This agreement does not allow subletting or assignment of the apartment without the consent of Virginia.

Jill needs to be certain the apartment is in good repair before signing the agreement because she is agreeing to accept the premises in their present

REAL ESTATE TODAY

Jill Rents an Apartment

Jill Jewell had just graduated from college and moved to Charlotte, North Carolina, to take a job with Amalgamated Whitzadiddle Corporation. She needed a place to live and decided to rent a duplex apartment in a nearby suburb. Let's look at the rental agreement to see what Jill agreed to do and what was promised by the landlord, Virginia Wells.

Case Study

Rental Agreement

(Underlined portions are entered on standard rental agreement form.)

STATE OF NORTH CAROLINA, MECKLENBURG COUNTY.

This agreement, made the <u>21st day of May, 2001,</u> between <u>Virginia M. Wells</u> of the County of Mecklenburg, hereinafter known as Lessor, and <u>Jill J. Jewell</u>, of said county, hereinafter known as Lessee:

WITNESSETH; That the said Lessor has this day rented to said Lessee the following: <u>two-bedroom duplex apartment</u> situated on <u>the easterly side of Harden Mill Road between High Shoals Road and U.S. 21 Highway</u> in <u>High Shoals, Mecklenburg County, North Carolina,</u> and known as <u>149 Jarnigan Drive</u> for the purpose of single-family residence and for no other purpose.

The duration of said rental shall be <u>12 months</u> commencing on the <u>1st</u> day of <u>June, 2001</u>, and ending on the <u>31st</u> day of <u>May, 2002.</u>

PAYMENT OF RENT

For the rental of said premises said Lessee is to pay the sum of <u>$850.00, Eight Hundred Fifty and 00/100,</u> Dollars per month, payable in advance; rent payments are due promptly on the first day of each month, and a late fee of 5 percent of rent for 5 days late and 10 percent of rent for 10 days late shall be paid.

SUBLETTING AND ASSIGNMENT

Should said Lessee fail to pay said rent promptly when due, or sublet said premises or assign this lease without the consent of the Lessor in writing, or use said rented premises for any other purpose than that specified, or otherwise violate any of the terms of this contract, then the Lessor may at her option terminate this contract, cancel the same and take immediate possession of the rented premises, without waiving any rent that may have accrued at the time of cancellation, or any claim for damages for breach of the contract on the part of the Lessee.

INSPECTION AND REPAIRS

Said Lessee hereby certifies that said premises have been examined by Lessee and agrees to accept them as they now stand, and agrees that said Lessor shall make only such repairs to said premises during the term of this contract as seem to the Lessor advisable, but the Lessor reserves the right to enter upon said premises for the purpose of making repairs or improvement upon the same or upon adjoining property of Lessor.

UTILITIES AND DAMAGES

Lessee agrees to repair at her own expense any damage to the plumbing on said premises caused by freezing, and to pay the water, gas and electric expenses on said premises, and to deliver said premises to the Lessor at the expiration of the term of rental in as good order as when received, ordinary wear and tear with careful usage excepted. Said Lessee further agrees to pay for all breakage or loss occurring to said premises.

HABITABILITY

Said Lessor agrees that if the premises should be destroyed by fire or act of God or so damaged as to become untenable, due not to the fault or neglect

Jill Rents an Apartment (continued)

of Lessee or her employees or family or guests or other persons on said premises with Lessee's consent or knowledge, the rent on said premises shall cease until the same are restored to tenable conditions, the Lessor having the option to rebuild, repair or make any other disposition of said premises that she may deem proper.

Case Study

CLAIMS FOR DAMAGES

No claims for damages shall be made by Lessee nor delay in payment of rent for the want of repair in these premises or any other premises of Lessor.

FOR RENT SIGNS

Lessor reserves the right to place a "For Rent" or "For Sale" sign on the premises at any time within 60 days prior to the termination of this contract of rent.

RENEWAL

It is agreed between the parties to this contract that neither shall be bound by any verbal statement or agreement or any subsequent contract relating to the above described property during the period covered by this contract unless endorsed hereon and signed by the parties hereto.

KEYS

Upon termination of this agreement, Lessee agrees to leave floors of the premises broom clean, close all windows, lock all outside doors and return all keys to the Lessor or her agent.

SPECIAL STIPULATIONS

1. Lessor acknowledges receipt of a $850.00 security deposit.

2. Lessee agrees that no pets are allowed in the apartment.

_____   _____
Jill J. Jewell   Virginia M. Wells

Date_____   Date _____

condition. If she thinks the apartment needs painting, for example, it is too late after the agreement is signed unless a written notation is made on the agreement that Virginia will paint the apartment. Jill also is agreeing to keep the premises in good repair; to pay for damages, including repair to plumbing caused by freezing; and to pay all utility bills on the property. The agreement contains no renewal provisions. If Jill wants to renew the lease after the first year, she must agree on new terms with Virginia. Because this leaves her vulnerable to future price increases or other changes in lease conditions, she might seek the inclusion of a renewal provision that would specify renewal terms.

The Rights and Obligations of Tenant and Landlord

The fundamental right of the landlord is to receive rents, while that of the tenant is to use, enjoy, occupy, and possess the leasehold premises. The tenant has the right of exclusive possession of the property during the period of the lease, known as the *covenant of quiet enjoyment,* and can use the property in any legal manner that is agreed to in the lease document. Unless exceptions are made in the lease, the landlord cannot enter the property except to abate some nuisance or prevent destruction of the property. For example, a landlord could enter a tenant's apartment without securing permission to repair a burst water pipe but not to make alterations or improvements without the tenant's prior consent. Conversely, the tenant cannot alter the leasehold premises without the permission of the landlord. The tenant has the obligation to pay the rent when due and not violate any of the lease provisions. If the tenant fails to pay the rent or violates other provisions of the lease, the landlord can move to have the tenant evicted from the premises.

Under the implied **warranty of habitability** principle, the landlord also has the obligation to maintain the premises in reasonable condition. Should a landlord fail to do so, many states have granted tenants of residential property the right to repair minor defects and deduct the cost of such repairs from rent payments. Local ordinances also require that landlords meet city and county health and safety codes.

Landlords also have the obligation to maintain common areas, such as elevators, hallways, and grounds, in a safe condition. If they do not, they may be liable for injuries that result from any defects or lapses in security.

The landlord's responsibility to protect tenants against criminal acts committed by third parties is still a murky area; nevertheless, courts are increasingly awarding tenants damages when landlords are held partially responsible because of some type of negligence (such as not repairing locks, etc.).

Many leases contain provisions giving the tenant the option of renewing the lease before its expiration. As mentioned above, this does not necessarily mean, however, that the lease can be renewed with the same terms as in the old lease, and rental rates often are raised at this time.

A lease may contain one or two distinct types of renewal clauses. If, by its terms, a lease is renewed automatically if neither party gives notice of termination, a negative renewal clause is involved. A lease that provides for renewal only when the tenant gives notice to the landlord that renewal is desired contains a positive renewal clause. In accordance with this latter provision, if no notice of renewal is given properly, the landlord-tenant relationship terminates at the end of the original lease period.

Most leases have a specific time period within which notice to terminate (under a negative renewal clause) or notice to renew (under a positive renewal clause) must be given. Although the landlord and tenant always may agree to whatever time period they desire, one to two months prior to the expiration of the lease is very common.

State Statutes Affecting the Landlord-Tenant Relationship

In addition to the agreed-on lease terms, the relationship between a landlord and tenant may be further defined by state laws that regulate the relationship. For example, state laws dictate the eviction process that landlords must follow for removing tenants who have violated the lease agreement, including the nonpayment of rent. Similarly, state laws may specify how long the landlord has to return any security deposit at the end of a lease, assuming the tenant has not damaged the landlord's property. Laws such as these vary dramatically from state to state. The table below provides a listing of the specific laws affecting the landlord-tenant relationship in all fifty states. To view the actual statutes, visit the website for www.nolo.com and follow the links to your state.

■ CHAPTER REVIEW

- A deed is a legal document that conveys title, or ownership, from one party to another. A valid deed must be written formally to include (a) identification of the parties, (b) a legal description of the property, (c) language of conveyance in return for the consideration named, and (d) signature of the grantor. It then must be (e) delivered to and accepted by the grantee.

- Deeds are differentiated by the covenants and warranties that the grantor makes regarding the title being transferred. Such assurances may include (a) covenant against encumbrances, (b) covenant of seisin, (c) covenant of quiet enjoyment, (d) covenant of further assurances, and (e) warranty forever. The general warranty deed, special warranty deed, grant deed, bargain and sale deed, and quitclaim deed are the most common deeds used in real estate transactions. Each has a special purpose, with which the parties involved should be familiar.

- A lease is a contract that conveys use and possession of a property from the landlord to the tenant in return for the tenant's agreement to pay rent.

- The four types of leasehold estates in regard to duration of term are (a) tenancy for a stated period, (b) tenancy from period to period, (c) tenancy at will, and (d) tenancy at sufferance.

- A ground lease is a lease of land to the exclusion of any improvements. Such leases frequently are used as a financial device in the development of major office buildings.

- In a gross lease, the landlord agrees to pay the overhead expenses that arise in connection with the use of the premises. In a net lease, the tenant pays the operating expenses.

- Rental payments can be fixed or variable under a lease. In a graduated-rent lease, the payment is increased by specified percentages at stated intervals, while under a reappraisal lease, the level of each rent increase is determined by a reappraisal of the property. A percentage lease is a lease of property used for commercial purposes under which the rental payments are based on some percentage of sales made on the premises.

TABLE 5.1	State Real Estate Statutes
Alabama	Ala. Code §§ 35-9-1 to -100
Alaska	Alaska Stat. §§ 34.03.010 to .380
Arizona	Ariz. Rev. Stat. Ann. §§ 12-1171 to -1183; §§ 33-1301 to -1381
Arkansas	Ark. Code Ann. §§ 18-16-101 to -306
California	Cal. [Civ.] Code §§ 1925-1954, 1961-1962.7, 1995.010-1997.270
Colorado	Colo. Rev. Stat. §§ 38-12-101 to -104, -301 to -302
Connecticut	Conn. Gen. Stat. Ann. §§ 47a-1 to -50a
Delaware	Del. Code. Ann. tit. 25, §§ 5101-7013
District of Columbia	D.C. Code Ann. §§ 45-1401 to -1597, -2501 to -2593
Florida	Fla. Stat. Ann. §§ 83.40-.66
Georgia	Ga. Code Ann. §§ 44-7-1 to -81
Hawaii	Haw. Rev. Stat. §§ 521-1 to -78
Idaho	Idaho Code §§ 6-301 to -324 and §§ 55-201 to -313
Illinois	Ill. Comp. Stat. Ch. 765 para. 705/0.01-740/5
Indiana	Ind. Code Ann. §§ 32-7-1-1 to 37-7-19
Iowa	Iowa Code Ann. §§ 562A.1-.36
Kansas	Kan. Stat. Ann. §§ 58-2501 to -2573
Kentucky	Ky. Rev. Stat. Ann. §§ 383.010-.715
Louisiana	La. Rev. Stat. Ann. §§ 9:3201-:3259; La. Civ. Code Ann. art. 2669-2742
Maine	Me. Rev. Stat. Ann. Tit. 14, §§ 6001-6045
Maryland	Md. Real Prop. Code Ann., §§ 8-101 to -604
Massachusetts	Mass. Gen. Laws Ann. ch. 186 §§ 1-21
Michigan	Mich. Comp. Laws Ann. § 554.601-.640
Minnesota	Minn. Stat. Ann. §§ 504B.01 to 504B.471
Mississippi	Miss. Code Ann. §§ 89-8-1 to -27
Missouri	Mo. Ann. Stat. §§ 441.010-.650; and §§ 535.150-.300
Montana	Mont. Code Ann. §§ 70-24-101 to -25-206
Nebraska	Neb. Rev. Stat. §§ 76-1401 to -1449
Nevada	Nev. Rev. Stat. Ann. §§ 118A.010-.520
New Hampshire	N.H. Rev. Stat. Ann. §§ 540:1 to 540:29; 540-A:1-540-A:8
New Jersey	N.J. Stat. Ann. §§ 46:8-1 to-49
New Mexico	N.M. Stat. Ann. §§ 47-8-1 to -51
New York	N.Y. Real Property Law ("RPL") §§ 220-338; Real Property Actions and Proceedings Law ("RPAPL")§§ 701-853; Multiple Dwelling Law ("MDL") all; multiple Residence Law ("MRL") all; General Obligation Law ("GOL") §§ 7-103-108
North Carolina	N.C. Gen. Stat. §§ 42-1 to 42-14.2; 42-25-6 to 42-76
North Dakota	N.D. Cent. Code §§ 47-16-01 to -41
Ohio	Ohio Rev. Code Ann. §§ 5321.01-.19
Oklahoma	Okla. Stat. Ann. tit. 41, §§ 1-136
Oregon	Or. Rev. Stat. §§ 90.100-.450
Pennsylvania	Pa. Stat. Ann. tit. 68, §§ 250.101-.510-B
Rhode Island	R.I. Gen. Laws §§ 34-18-1 to -57
South Carolina	S.C. Code Ann. §§ 27-40-10 to -910
South Dakota	S.D. Codified Laws Ann. §§ 43-32-1 to -29
Tennessee	Tenn. Code Ann. §§ 66-28-101 to -520
Texas	Tex. Prop. Code Ann. §§ 91.001-92.354
Utah	Utah Code Ann. §§ 57-17-1 to -5, -22-1 to -6
Vermont	Vt. Stat Ann. tit. 9, §§ 4451-4468
Virginia	Va. Code Ann. §§ 55-218.1 to -248.40
Washington	Wash. Rev. Code Ann. §§ 59.04.010-.900, .18.010-.910
West Virginia	W. Va. Code §§ 37-6-1 to -30
Wisconsin	Wis. Stat. Ann. §§ 704.01-.45
Wyoming	Wyo. Stat. §§ 1-2-12-1 to 1-21-1211; 34-2-128 to -129

■ KEY TERMS

assignment	gross lease	security deposit
bargain and sale deed	ground lease	special warranty deed
covenant	index lease	step-up rent lease
covenant against	lease	subleasing
encumbrances	lessee	tenancy at sufferance
covenant of further	lessor	tenancy at will
assurances	negative renewal clause	tenancy for a stated peri-
covenant of quiet	net lease	od
enjoyment	net net lease	tenancy from period to
covenant of seisin	net net net lease	period
deed	percentage lease	term
executor's deed	positive renewal clause	title
expense stop	quitclaim deed	warranty
fixed-rent lease	reappraisal lease	warranty forever
general warranty deed	renewal option	warranty of habitability
graduated-rent lease		

■ STUDY EXERCISES

1. What are the essential elements of a deed?

2. Describe the covenants and warranty contained in a general warranty deed.

3. What are the differences between

    a. a general warranty deed and a special warranty deed?

    b. a general warranty deed and a bargain and sale deed?

4. What is a quitclaim deed and when might it be used?

5. Define the following terms: lease, lessor, lessee, tenancy for a stated period, tenancy from period to period, tenancy at will, tenancy at sufferance.

6. What is the difference between a gross lease and a net lease?

7. Define the following terms: percentage lease, graduated-rent lease, ground lease, reappraisal lease, and index lease.

8. What is the difference between subleasing and assignment? When is subleasing desirable for the existing tenant?

9. What do the terms *covenant of quiet enjoyment* and *warranty of habitability* mean?

10. What purpose do security deposits serve from the lessor's perspective?

11. What is the difference between a negative renewal clause and a positive renewal clause?

12. Al's Shoe Store has a percentage lease that requires a base rent of $2,000 per month, plus 2 percent of gross sales over $10,000. What will the rent be when the monthly gross sales are $18,000?

■ FURTHER READINGS

Alexander, A. A., and Muhlebach, R. F., *Managing and Leasing Commercial Properties.* New York: Wiley, 1994.

Banning, K. B., *Residential Property Management Handbook.* New York: McGraw-Hill, 1992.

Irwin, Robert, *The Landlord's Troubleshooter,* 2nd ed. Chicago: Dearborn Financial Publishing, Inc., 1999.

Lapides, P.D. and Miller, E. R., *Managing and Leasing Residential Properties.* New York: Wiley, 1993.

6 Contracts in Real Estate Transactions

The real estate sales contract is a detailed and complex document that establishes the terms under which ownership of a property will be transferred.

CHAPTER PREVIEW

A *contract* is the legal device used by two or more parties to indicate they have reached an agreement. In essence, a **contract** is an exchange of promises between parties, conditioned on certain events and enforceable by law. Leases, as we saw in the previous chapter, are contracts that transfer the rights of use and possession, but not ownership, of real estate between a landlord and tenant. The deeds we discussed in the previous chapter are legal documents, but they are more accurately classified as *documents of conveyance* rather than contracts. Recall that deeds are used to convey ownership in real property from one party to another. Before title is transferred by a deed, however, the parties must negotiate and agree on the details of the transaction. Thus, deeds are typically preceded in time by a contract that reflects the agreement between the parties regarding the pending transaction.

Real estate contract negotiations can be quite involved because there are often many details to be agreed on by the parties. The issues to be resolved in a real estate contract negotiation include the consideration (price) to be given by the grantee to the grantor for the property, the date for the transfer, the type of deed to be delivered by the grantor, the conditions by which either party could withdraw from the agreement, who is obligated to pay for the various expenses of the transaction, the penalties for failing to comply with the contract terms, and many other factors.

This chapter focuses on three specific types of contracts that define the agreement between parties to eventually transfer ownership in real property: sales contracts, option-to-buy contracts, and contracts for deed. Each of these types of contracts provide the rules governing the parties' rights and duties during the time between the agreement to transfer real property and the actual transfer of title using a deed. As we will see, the real estate sales contract is a bilateral contract because it requires the seller to sell and the buyer to buy the property in accordance with the con-

Legal Highlight
Validity of an Oral Contract

ditions and terms of the contract. On the other hand, the option contract is considered to be a unilateral contract because the buyer is not required to buy the property unless he so chooses before the expiration date of the contract. The seller, however, is obligated to sell if the buyer chooses to buy within the agreed-on time period. The contract for deed is essentially an installment sales contract, binding on both parties, in which the seller holds legal title to the property while the buyer makes payments to the seller over time. The buyer has possession of the property while making payments, but the seller does not give the buyer a deed until the agreed-on amount has been paid.

Specifically, we will examine

- the necessary elements of a contract,

- performance and breach of contract,

- the purpose and structure of the real estate sales contract,

- the purpose and structure of option-to-buy contracts,

- the purpose and structure of contracts for deed, and

- some contract negotiation tips and strategies.

■ NECESSARY ELEMENTS OF A CONTRACT

The required elements of any valid contract consist of (1) an offer, (2) an acceptance, (3) consideration, (4) parties with capacity, and (5) a lawful purpose. When contracts involve real estate, there is an additional requirement that the agreement be expressed in writing to be enforceable by the court system (one exception is a lease for one year or less).

Offer and Acceptance

Before any contract can be created, one person must make an offer to another. In essence, an **offer** is a statement that specifies the position of the maker of the offer (who is called **offeror).** The offeror states implicitly in an offer that he or she is willing to be bound by the stated position. An offer becomes a valid contract when it is accepted by the party who receives it. The receiving party is called an **offeree,** and his or her acceptance should create a contract.

An **acceptance,** which expresses satisfaction with an offer, must mirror the precise terms and conditions stated in the offer. If the terms in the purported acceptance differ from those of the offer, no contract is formed. Indeed, such an attempted acceptance becomes a **counteroffer.** With a counteroffer, the original offeror and offeree switch legal positions, and a contract may result when a counteroffer is accepted.

Consideration

The law requires that an exchange of consideration occurs before a contract is enforceable. **Consideration** often is described as anything that incurs a legal detriment or the forgoing of a legal benefit. What that means, in simple terms, is that each party to a contract must give up something. In a typical real estate contract, the seller promises to give up title to the land in return for money; the buyer promises to give up the right to the money in return for title to the land.

Capacity of Parties

To have a valid contract, all parties involved must have contractual capacity. The law insists that all parties have the mental capability to know what the contract represents and to understand its terms. Most commonly, two categories of people are said to lack *capacity to contract.* First, those who have been declared mentally incompetent are protected from people who attempt to take advantage of their mental condition. Because the law cannot distinguish people with unjust intent from those with good intentions, insane persons cannot be held to the terms and conditions of a contract. Therefore, such contracts, although binding on the competent party, are voidable, or can be rescinded, at the election of the incompetent party's guardian.

The second category of people who lack contractual capacity consists of minors—that is, those who have not reached the age of majority, usually 18 or 21. Although some minors (typically defined as people under 18 years of age) have the intelligence to comprehend even the most complex transactions, the law provides them with protection.

Any time before a person reaches the age of majority and within a reasonable period thereafter, nearly all contracts that the minor has entered into may be voided by the minor. Certain types of contracts involving a minor's purchase of necessities—such items as food, clothing, and medical care, essential for the preservation and reasonable enjoyment of life—cannot be voided. Because real estate is seldom considered a necessity, however, minors generally lack the capacity to purchase or sell it. Therefore, when one party to a contract involving the transfer of real estate is a minor, that contract is voidable at the minor's (or his guardian's) option.

If a contract is voided, the minor and adult parties must return any consideration that was previously exchanged. Therefore, an adult must beware of buying real estate from or selling it to a minor, as such a transaction subsequently may be undone.

Lawful Purpose

A valid contract must have as its ultimate purpose some legal act or function. For example, a contract for the delivery of illegal drugs is not enforceable—at least not in the courts. Although people sometimes subsequently put real estate to an illegal use, the sale or lease of real estate seldom directly involves illegal intentions; therefore, this element of a valid contract generally is less crucial than the other elements.

Even so, both buyers and sellers should be aware that any illegal purpose in the contract may make it void. For example, suppose a sales contract specifies the buyer's intent to utilize the property in violation of current zoning provisions. This clause may give the buyer an "out" that the seller may not recognize.

Writing Requirement

Contracts may be either implied or expressed, and expressed contracts may be oral or written. All contracts involving land or items attached to it, however, must be in writing before a court will enforce them. Contracts involving the sale of timber and crops may be oral and remain binding. The rules governing contracts for personal property are found in each state's version of the Uniform Commercial Code, a collection of laws that govern business transactions. Each state's law should be consulted regarding the requisites of such contracts.

The requirement that real estate contracts be in writing to be enforceable by the legal system is found in each state's **statute of frauds,** a law designed to prevent fraudulent practices by requiring that certain contracts, including those involving real property, be in writing and signed. Real estate contracts must be written to reduce the possibility that a court may be defrauded or tricked into ruling improperly when the subject matter is valuable real estate. The required writing does not have to be a formally drafted document. Indeed, any written words that indicate the parties' positions and that are signed by the parties involved satisfy the statute of frauds. For example, the words "I agree to sell my farm to Robert Harris for $50,000," written on a paper napkin, are enforceable by Harris if they are signed by the farm owner. Of course, it is assumed that the owner has only one farm; otherwise, the property designated as "my farm" is not adequately described. An adequate written description of the real property being sold is essential. Methods of legal description were discussed in a previous chapter.

Although the statute of frauds requires that contracts involving real estate be in writing, there are exceptions to this rule. Courts may, for instance, enforce an oral contract if the parties have partially performed their agreement. **Partial performance** is the fulfillment of the terms of an agreement to such an extent that the existence of the agreement may be reasonably inferred, even though no written contract exists. If a court can determine from the parties' actions what their intentions were, it may hold that a contract exists despite the lack of a written document. Generally, mere payment of some money by the buyer is not sufficient to replace a written contract.

Payment plus possession by the buyer and physical improvements made to the property, however, point to the existence of some kind of contractual understanding, and the courts often will rule in favor of such a buyer—but not always, as the buyers found in the Connecticut case described in the Legal Highlight on page 115.

REAL ESTATE TODAY

Validity of an Oral Contract

Legal Highlight

The statute of frauds requires that contracts for the sale of real estate be written in order to be enforceable. Richard and Mary Kelly learned this to their sorrow.

The Kellys reached an oral agreement with William Ryan to purchase his residential waterfront property in Greenwich, Connecticut, for $2,125,000 in cash. The sale was subject to securing approval from the Coastal Area Management Commission for construction on the property that would double the size of the existing house and add a tennis court. The Kellys had a wetlands survey made and site plans prepared for submission of the application. A few days later, their attorney submitted a contract to Ryan's attorney, which essentially put the oral agreement into writing. Ryan refused to sign, and the next day, he contracted to sell the property to a third party. The Kellys sued, seeking specific performance by Ryan of the oral contract. They lost.

The court ruled that:

> However plain and complete the terms of an oral contract for the sale

and purchase of real estate, it cannot be enforced against a party thereto unless he, or his agent, has signed a written memorandum which recited the essential elements of the contract with reasonable certainty.

Even though the Kellys had a definite oral agreement with Ryan, as the Hollywood producer Sam Goldwyn used to say, "An oral agreement isn't worth the paper it's written on." The Kellys also argued that they had made "substantial improvements" to the property on the basis of the oral agreement, thus defeating the written requirement in the statute of frauds. The court did not agree, holding that the survey and site plans, at a cost of less than $5,000, were not "substantial" to a property with a value of more than $2 million. The lesson is clear: *Never, never, never* rely on an oral contract in the sale or purchase of anything of value, particularly not in the sale or purchase of real estate.

Source: *Kelly v. Ryan,* Nos. CV 91 011 53 81, CV 91 011 54 38 S. (Connecticut Superior Court, 1991).

■ BREACH OF CONTRACT

Failure to perform a required contractual obligation is called a *breach* of the contract. If a party to an agreement breaches its terms, the other party has a choice of remedies, either outlined in the contract or provided by law. Let's assume the seller, who has signed a valid real estate sales contract, refuses to transfer title to the buyer. The buyer may then sue for **specific performance;** that is, ask the court to order the breaching party to perform the terms of the contract.

A suit for specific performance is possible only if the contract concerns a unique item. Because land and improvements on land are considered one-of-a-kind items, a buyer probably will be successful in obtaining an order of specific performance. As an alternative, a buyer may seek payment for any damages that result from the seller's breach. Such damages could include compensation for the buyer's loss of time and the buyer's expenses related to the sale, such as legal fees for a title search, a land survey, and a building inspection.

If the buyer refuses to perform the duties under a valid contract, the seller also has the right to sue. In many states, however, the seller's rights are limited to recovering monetary damages, including any earnest money that may have been paid by the buyer. Usually, a seller cannot seek specific performance because courts do not feel that a ready, willing, and able buyer is a unique commodity. Eventually, the courts presume, some other purchaser will be found.

■ CONTRACT CONTINGENCIES

The preceding discussion of remedies for a breached contract is based on the presumption that the party's nonperformance is not excused. A well-drafted contract provides that the parties will be discharged from performance in the event of certain conditions. These conditions are called *contingencies.* A common clause in residential real estate sales contracts is a *financing contingency* that allows a buyer who is not able to arrange the necessary financing within a certain time period to cancel the contract and recover any earnest money paid without further obligation. Similarly, real estate sales contracts often contain a *title contingency* that allows either party to cancel a contract if the title search reveals a problem with the seller's legal title to the property that cannot be resolved within a certain time period. Another common component of real estate sales contracts is the *inspection and repair contingency.* This clause permits the buyer to have a qualified inspector examine the property for any physical defects. If defects are found, the seller may be obligated to make repairs up to an agreed-on amount. If the cost of repairs exceeds this amount, the buyer may elect to cancel the contract. Almost any condition can be added to an agreement, as long as it does not create a contract for an unlawful purpose. Also, most courts would consider a contract that included an "unconscionable" condition (one that is shockingly unfair) to be invalid.

■ REAL ESTATE SALES CONTRACTS

Now that we understand the fundamental concepts behind the theory of contracts, let's consider some specific examples of contracts used in real estate transactions. Frequently encountered contracts in real estate transactions include sales contracts, option-to-buy contracts, contracts for deed, leases, listing agreements, buyer representation agreements, and property management agreements. Our focus in this section is on the real estate sales contract. Sales contracts provide for the eventual transfer of title to real property. **Title,** or the legal right to ownership of land, is passed by use of a deed and does not change hands until the transaction actually is closed, or brought to a successful conclusion. The sales contract's purpose is to provide the rules governing the parties' rights and duties during the time between the agreement to transfer real property and the actual transfer of title. A reasonable time period generally is necessary to allow the buyer to secure financing, check the seller's title, and obtain property insurance.

Negotiating a Sales Contract

In most real estate markets, property owners who wish to sell their properties will advertise them at a specified price through a local real estate broker or as a for-sale-by-owner deal (**FSBO,** sometimes pronounced "fizbo"). Potential buyers examine the property and decide if they are interested in purchasing it. Preliminary negotiations between buyers and sellers are very often oral, but, because the ultimate agreement must be in written form, sincere negotiations usually begin with one party (either the buyer or the seller) writing his or her offer, signing it, and presenting it to the other party for review. If the other party accepts the offer and signs it, then a contract is formed as specified in the document. If the other party, however, suggests a change to the first party's offer, then the second party has essentially rejected the offer and presented a counteroffer. Perhaps the first party will accept this change and thus a deal is struck, or the other party may choose to make yet another counteroffer to the second party's counteroffer. The negotiations continue in this fashion until the parties either reach an agreement or discontinue negotiations. Keep in mind that one party must make an offer, or a counteroffer, that the other party accepts in the exact form in which it was offered before a final agreement is reached.

Sales Contract Example

Parties to a real estate transaction are free to negotiate any legal and conscionable agreement they can reduce to written form. To ease the process of negotiating a real estate sales contract "from scratch," most states allow real estate brokers to fill in the blanks on contract forms that have been drafted by an attorney and/or approved by the state bar association. An example of such a contract form is shown in Figure 6.1. This "contract for sale and purchase" of real estate has been jointly adopted by the Florida Association of REALTORS® and the Florida Bar for use by real estate agents who are assisting buyers and sellers to negotiate transactions in that state. Most other states have a similar contract form that reflects any state-specific requirements for valid real estate contracts. This type of contract form often serves as the framework for the negotiation between the parties, as well as the final agreement.

Let's consider an example to understand how this contract is used in a real estate transaction. Suppose Clay Williams is purchasing a house listed with Rodriguez Realty Company and owned by Sarah Howell. Sarah was asking $194,900 for the home, but the parties have agreed on a price of $189,000, as shown on line 15. Clay paid $5,000 as an earnest money deposit to Julio Rodriguez, the real estate agent assisting the parties in the transaction. In his capacity as the escrow agent Julio must safeguard the deposit according to the terms of the contract and state laws regulating escrow account management. Clay will borrow $150,000 from a mortgage lender and will need an additional $34,000 as the balance to close this transaction ($189,000 − $5,000 − $150,000 = $34,000). Let's consider some of the key points of this contract.

FIGURE 6.1 Sales Contract

THIS FORM HAS BEEN APPROVED BY THE FLORIDA ASSOCIATION OF REALTORS® AND THE FLORIDA BAR.

Contract for Sale and Purchase
FLORIDA ASSOCIATION OF REALTORS® AND THE FLORIDA BAR

*1 PARTIES: __Sarah Howell_____ ("Seller"),

2 of _____ (Phone) _____,

*3 and __Clay Williams_____ ("Buyer"),

4 of _____ (Phone) _____,

5 hereby agree that Seller shall sell and Buyer shall buy the following described real property and personal property (collectively "Property") pursuant to the terms and conditions of this Contract
6 for Sale and Purchase and any riders and addenda ("Contract"):

7 I.   **DESCRIPTION:**

*8   (a) Legal description of the Real Property located in __Hendry_____ County, Florida: __Lot 1, Block A of Ridgeview__

9   __Subdivision_____

10   _____

*11 (b) Street address, city, zip, of the Property is: __1000 Banyan Street Suburb Florida 33323__

*12 (c) Personal Property: _____

13   _____

14   _____

*15 II. **PURCHASE PRICE:** .... $ __189,000__

16   **PAYMENT:**

*17 (a) Deposit held in escrow by __Julio Rodriguez_____ (Escrow Agent) in the amount of .... $ __5,000__

*18 (b) Additional escrow deposit to be made to Escrow Agent within _____ days after Effective Date (see Paragraph III) in the amount of............ $ _____

*19 (c) Subject to AND assumption of existing mortgage in good standing in favor of _____

20   _____ having an approximate present principal balance of .... $ _____

*21 (d) New mortgage financing with a Lender (see Paragraph IV) in the amount of _____ $ __150,000__

*22 (e) Purchase money mortgage and note to Seller (see rider for terms) in the amount of _____ $ _____

*23 (f) Other: _____ $ _____

*24 (g) Balance to close by U.S. cash or LOCALLY DRAWN cashier's or official bank check(s), subject to adjustments or prorations................. $ __34,000__

25 III. **TIME FOR ACCEPTANCE OF OFFER; EFFECTIVE DATE; FACSIMILE:** If this offer is not executed by and delivered to all parties OR FACT OF EXECUTION communicated in writing
*26 between the parties on or before ___June 13,2001___, the deposit(s) will, at Buyer's option, be returned and this offer withdrawn. For purposes of delivery or notice of
27 execution, parties include Buyer and Seller or each of the respective brokers or attorneys. The date of Contract ("Effective Date") will be the date when the last one of the Buyer and Seller
28 has signed this offer. A facsimile copy of this Contract and any signatures hereon shall be considered for all purposes as an original.

29 IV. **FINANCING:**

*30   ☐ (a) This is a cash transaction with no contingencies for financing;

*31   ☒ (b) This Contract is conditioned on Buyer obtaining a written loan commitment within __15__ days after Effective Date for (CHECK ONLY ONE): ☒ a fixed; ☐ an adjustable; or ☐ a
*32   fixed or adjustable rate loan in the principal amount of $ __150,000__, at an initial interest rate not to exceed __9__%, discount and origination fees not to exceed __0__% of
*33   principal amount, and for a term of __20__ years. Buyer will make application within _____ days (5 days if left blank) after Effective Date and use reasonable diligence to obtain a loan
34   commitment and, thereafter, to satisfy terms and conditions of the commitment and close the loan. Buyer shall pay all loan expenses. If Buyer fails to obtain a commitment or fails to waive
35   Buyer's rights under this subparagraph within the time for obtaining a commitment or, after diligent effort, fails to meet the terms and conditions of the commitment by the closing date,
36   then either party thereafter, by written notice to the other, may cancel this Contract and Buyer shall be refunded the deposit(s); or
*37   ☐ (c) The existing mortgage, described in Paragraph II(c) above, has: ☐ a variable interest rate; or ☐ a fixed interest rate of _____% per annum. At time of title transfer, some fixed
*38   interest rates are subject to increase; if increased, the rate shall not exceed _____% per annum. Seller shall furnish a statement from each mortgagee stating the principal balance,
39   method of payment, interest rate and status of mortgage or authorize Buyer or Closing Agent to obtain the same. If Buyer has agreed to assume a mortgage which requires approval
40   of Buyer by the mortgagee for assumption, then Buyer shall promptly obtain the necessary application and diligently complete and return it to the mortgagee. Any mortgagee charge(s),
*41   not to exceed $ _____ (1% of amount assumed if left blank), shall be paid by Buyer. If Buyer is not accepted by mortgagee or the requirements for assumption
42   are not in accordance with the terms of this Contract or mortgage makes a charge in excess of the stated amount, Seller or Buyer may rescind this Contract by written notice to the
43   other party unless either elects to pay the increase in interest rate or excess mortgage charges.

*44 V.   **TITLE EVIDENCE:** At least __3__ days before closing date, (CHECK ONLY ONE): ☒ Seller shall, at Seller's expense, deliver to Buyer or Buyer's attorney; or ☐ Buyer shall at Buyer's
*45 expense obtain (CHECK ONLY ONE): ☐ abstract of title; or ☒ title insurance commitment (with legible copies of instruments listed as exceptions attached thereto) and, after closing, an
46 owner's policy of title insurance.

*47 VI. **CLOSING DATE:** This transaction shall be closed and the closing documents delivered on __August 4, 2001__, unless modified by other provisions of this Contract.

48 VII. **RESTRICTIONS; EASEMENTS; LIMITATIONS:** Buyer shall take title subject to: comprehensive land use plans, zoning, restrictions, prohibitions and other requirements imposed by
49 governmental authority; restrictions and matters appearing on the plat or otherwise common to the subdivision; outstanding oil, gas and mineral rights of record without right of entry; public
50 utility easements of record (easements are to be located contiguous to real property lines and not more than 10 feet in width as to the rear or front lines and 7 1/2 feet in width as to the side
51 lines, **unless otherwise stated herein**); taxes for year of closing and subsequent years; assumed mortgages and purchase money mortgages, if any (if additional items, see addendum);
*52 provided, that there exists at closing no violation of the foregoing and none prevent use of the Property for _____ purpose(s).

53 VIII. **OCCUPANCY:** Seller warrants that there are no parties in occupancy other than Seller; but if Property is intended to be rented or occupied beyond closing, the fact and terms thereof
54 and the tenant(s) or occupants shall be disclosed pursuant to Standard F. Seller shall deliver occupancy of Property to Buyer at time of closing unless otherwise stated herein. If occupancy
55 is to be delivered before closing, Buyer assumes all risks of loss to Property from date of occupancy, shall be responsible and liable for maintenance from that date, and shall be deemed
56 to have accepted Property in its existing condition as of time of taking occupancy unless otherwise stated herein.

FIGURE 6.1   Sales Contract (continued)

57 **IX. TYPEWRITTEN OR HANDWRITTEN PROVISIONS:** Typewritten or handwritten provisions, riders and addenda shall control all printed provisions of this Contract in conflict with them.
58 **X.   RIDERS:** (CHECK those riders which are applicable AND are attached to this Contract):
*59   ☐ **COMPREHENSIVE RIDER**   ☐ HOMEOWNERS' ASSN.   ☐ COASTAL CONSTRUCTION CONTROL LINE
*60   ☐ **CONDOMINIUM**   ☐ "AS IS"   ☐ INSULATION
*61   ☐ **VA/FHA**   ☐ LEAD-BASED PAINT   ☐ _____

*62 **XI. ASSIGNABILITY:** (CHECK ONLY ONE): Buyer ☐ may assign and thereby be released from any further liability under this Contract; ☐ may assign but not be released from liability
*63 under this Contract; or ☒ may not assign this Contract.

64 **XII. DISCLOSURES:**
65   (a) Radon is a naturally occurring radioactive gas that when accumulated in a building in sufficient quantities may present health risks to persons who are exposed to it over time. Levels of radon
66   that exceed federal and state guidelines have been found in buildings in Florida. Additional information regarding Radon or Radon testing may be obtained from your County Public Health unit.
67   (b) Buyer acknowledges receipt of the Florida Building Energy-Efficiency Rating System Brochure.
68   (c) If the real property includes pre-1978 residential housing then a lead-based paint rider is mandatory.
69   (d) If Seller is a "foreign person" as defined by the Foreign Investment in Real Property Tax Act, the parties shall comply with that Act.
70   (e) If Buyer will be obligated to be a member of a homeowners' association, **BUYER SHOULD NOT EXECUTE THIS CONTRACT UNTIL BUYER HAS RECEIVED AND READ THE**
71   **HOMEOWNERS' ASSOCIATION DISCLOSURE.**

72 **XIII. MAXIMUM REPAIR COSTS:** Seller shall not be responsible for payments in excess of:
*73   (a) $ __5,000__ for treatment and repair under Standard D (if blank, then 2% of the Purchase Price).
*74   (b) $ _____ for repair and replacement under Standard N (if blank, then 3% of the Purchase Price).

*75 **XIV. SPECIAL CLAUSES; ADDENDA:** If additional terms are to be provided, attach addendum and CHECK HERE ☐.
76 **XV.   STANDARDS FOR REAL ESTATE TRANSACTIONS:** Standards A through W on the reverse side or attached are incorporated as a part of this Contract.

77   **THIS IS INTENDED TO BE A LEGALLY BINDING CONTRACT. IF NOT FULLY UNDERSTOOD, SEEK THE ADVICE OF AN ATTORNEY PRIOR TO SIGNING.**
78   THIS FORM HAS BEEN APPROVED BY THE FLORIDA ASSOCIATION OF REALTORS AND THE FLORIDA BAR.
79 *Approval does not constitute an opinion that any of the terms and conditions in this Contract should be accepted by the parties in a particular transaction. Terms and conditions should*
80   *be negotiated based upon the respective interests, objectives and bargaining positions of all interested persons.*
81   COPYRIGHT 1998 BY THE FLORIDA BAR AND THE FLORIDA ASSOCIATION OF REALTORS

*82 *Clay Williams*   June 6, 2001   *Sarah Howell*   6/11/01
83   (Buyer)   (Date)   (Seller)   (Date)

*84 Social Security or Tax I.D. # _____   Social Security or Tax I.D. # _____

*85 _____   _____   _____   _____
86   (Buyer)   (Date)   (Seller)   (Date)

*87 Social Security or Tax I.D. # _____   Social Security or Tax I.D. # _____

*88 Deposit under Paragraph II (a) received; IF OTHER THAN CASH, THEN SUBJECT TO CLEARANCE. _____ (Escrow Agent)
89 **BROKER'S FEE:** The brokers named below, including listing and cooperating brokers, are the only brokers entitled to compensation in connection with this Contract:

*90 Name: _____   _____
91   **Cooperating Brokers, if any**   **Listing Broker**

   FAR/BAR-5a Revised 8/98   RIDERS CAN BE OBTAINED FROM THE FLORIDA ASSOCIATION OF REALTORS® OR THE FLORIDA BAR

Lines 25-26: We see that when Clay made this offer to Sarah, he allowed her until June 13, 2001, to consider it. Looking ahead to line 82, we can see that Clay signed the offer on June 6, 2001, implying that he gave her one week from that date to consider it. Obviously, the time allowed to consider the offer can be important in the negotiation strategy. If she had not accepted the offer before the date specified, his offer would have been automatically withdrawn and his deposit would have been returned to him. Until his offer is withdrawn (either by Clay or automatically by time expiration), Sarah could create a binding contract by accepting the outstanding offer. Note that Sarah signed the contract (again, line 82) on June 11, 2001. Once it is accepted, an offer cannot be withdrawn because an accepted offer is a binding contract.

Lines 31-36: Clay and Sarah have agreed that Clay will apply for a mortgage loan for $150,000 that has a fixed interest rate of no more than 9 percent and a term of 30 years. Notice that if Clay's loan application is denied, he is entitled to a refund of his earnest money deposit.

Lines 44-46: Clay and Sarah have agreed that Sarah will be responsible for obtaining a title insurance policy to protect Clay's property rights from any undiscovered defects in the title. Title insurance will be addressed in a later chapter.

Line 47: The parties have set the closing date for August 4, 2001.

Lines 62-63: Clay may not assign this contract (transfer his right under this contract) to another buyer.

Lines 73-74: Sarah has agreed to pay up to $5,000 to treat and repair any termite or wood-destroying organism damage and up to 3 percent of the purchase price amount for any functional defects identified by qualified inspectors. To see the full impact of these clauses, refer to Standard D on line 118 and Standard N on line 155. The contract specifically states who must pay for the inspections (the buyer) and what the buyer's choices are if the cost of treating and repairing the property due to termite or wood-destroying organism damage exceeds $5,000 or the cost of repairing functional defects exceeds 3 percent of the purchase price. Termite damage and hidden functional defects often require an expert to detect and can be quite expensive to correct. Lenders are concerned about the loss of value of the loan collateral and typically require certifications from appropriately qualified inspectors stating that the property is free of termites or functional defects before final loan approval. These clauses limit the seller's exposure to the agreed-on amounts in each case and give the buyer a choice of paying any additional costs of treatment and repairs or canceling the contract and having any earnest money refunded.

As you can see, the contract form addresses many more details than we have outlined here. Before signing this document, Sarah and Clay should each ensure that all of the terms and conditions are acceptable. The fine print is crucial in any contract and should be read carefully. Whether the real estate sales contract is drafted by an attorney or completed by a broker, it should provide answers to any questions that arise during the time between the signing of the agreement and the closing, and the obligations of both buyer and seller. For example, a close reading of this contract will answer each of the following questions.

- When does the buyer get occupancy of the premises? (line 53)
- What actions can the buyer take if the seller's title proves to be unmarketable? (line 100)
- Whose responsibility is it to obtain and pay for a survey to detect any encroachments? (line 115)
- If an encroachment is detected in the survey, what happens? (line 117)
- Who must pay for the various closing costs associated with the deed? (line 139)

- What happens to this agreement if the property is destroyed by fire or other casualty before the closing? (line 171)
- What actions can one party take if the other party breaches the contract? (line 198)

OPTION-TO-BUY CONTRACTS

Another type of contract that is often useful in real estate transactions is the **option-to-buy contract.** Sometimes a party is interested in buying a specific property, but is not yet ready to sign a sales contract. The option-to-buy contract is one way to ensure at the property will not be sold to another party before the person who holds the option to buy has made a final decision.

The option-to-buy contract is an agreement between a property owner and a potential buyer that states that the property owner agrees to keep an offer open for acceptance during a stated period of time. If the buyer decides to exercise the option before it expires, the owner must sell the property at the specified price. For example, an owner may state that he or she will sell the property to the option holder for $75,000, and will allow the holder to accept this offer at any time within the next six months. To ensure that the option is binding, it must be in writing and contain all of the necessary elements of a valid contract: offer, acceptance, consideration, parties with capacity, and lawful purpose.

The amount of consideration for the option depends on the circumstances. Suppose, for example, that Broker Judy Michaud is trying to assemble six properties as a tract for a shopping center. She offers Blanche, the owner of one of the six properties, an option-to-buy contract to purchase her house for $110,000, even though the property is worth only $90,000 as a residence. Blanche's property is worth the larger amount only if it can be used for the shopping center, and to achieve this, Judy must both obtain contracts from the other property owners and secure rezoning of the entire tract.

Thus, Judy offers Blanche an option contract that gives Judy the right to purchase the property for $110,000 any time in the next six months. Blanche might be happy to accept consideration of $1,000 or even less for agreeing to this arrangement because she will receive a very good price for her house if Judy is successful in putting the deal together. The consideration received by Blanche for the option granted to Judy is hers to keep, regardless of whether Judy exercises her option to buy. Thus, the consideration received by Blanche is her compensation for giving up the right to sell the property to anyone other than Judy for the next six months.

CONTRACT FOR DEED

In addition to the contracts discussed thus far, real estate transactions are sometimes arranged as "installment sales," using a **contract for deed.** This arrangement stretches out the payments to the seller over time, but allows the seller to retain legal title to the property until the agreed-on amount is paid. While making payments to the seller, the buyer has possession of the property as the "equitable" owner. Contracts for deed are sometimes called **land contracts** or **agreements for deed.**

The obvious question you might be asking is: How does a contract for deed differ from a mortgage? The answer is that the seller's collateral interest in the property is better protected in the event the buyer defaults on the agreement. If the buyer stops making payments, the seller is already (still) the legal owner of the property and thus can simply assert his or her ownership rights and sell the property to another buyer or keep it. Most states, however, recognize the possibility of a buyer losing any equity he or she might have acquired in the property while making payments over time. In these states, buyers who breach a contract for deed are entitled to a refund of their equity (if any) in the property, but not interest paid. This requirement makes the contract for deed even more similar to a mortgage in these states. Regardless of whether default on the contract for deed requires that the seller refund any of the buyer's equity, buyers should realize that the seller is the legal owner of the property while a contract for deed is in place and could possibly cause other liens to be placed on the property prior to transferring title to the buyer.

Recall from the sales contract example we reviewed earlier in this chapter, the buyer, Clay Williams, is acquiring a property from Sarah Howell, the seller, in exchange for $189,000. Sarah will get all of her money at the closing and will simultaneously transfer title to Clay. At the same time, Clay will receive title from Sarah, then immediately pledge the property to the lender as collateral for the mortgage loan. If Clay and Sarah had agreed to use a contract for deed instead of the contract for sale and purchase, Sarah would hold the title to the property in her name while receiving payments over time from Clay. If Clay defaulted on the payments, Sarah's ownership rights would be clear and could easily be defended. Because the property in our example is in Florida (a state that treats contracts for deed as a mortgage document and sales contract combined), Sarah would have to foreclose on Clay just as if she held a mortgage lien on Clay's property if he should ever default on the contract terms.

■ SOME BASIC NEGOTIATION STRATEGIES

Many novice negotiators mistakenly approach a negotiation as if there were one pie that had to be somehow divided among the parties involved, and that every bite one party got was one less bite another party could get. In other words, some negotiators approach a negotiation as if it were a "zero-sum" game with the parties being classified as either "winner" or "loser" when the game is over. In most situations, however, the size of the pie, so to speak, is not nearly as fixed as we might assume and all parties can ultimately benefit if the right solution can be found.

There is an old saying in real estate: "You can name the price if I can name the terms." This saying goes to the heart of what good negotiation is all about. Be willing to let the people who are most concerned about certain slices of the pie grab what they think they want, but look for creative ways to make the total pie bigger, thus ensuring yourself a sufficient slice, too!

In a typical real estate transaction, price is often viewed as the single most important factor to be resolved. Suppose a seller wants to get $1 million for the property and adamantly refuses to take one cent less. While some buyers might be discouraged by the seller's stubbornness, an astute buyer might think of another issue that can be added to the negotiation to "sweeten the deal." Perhaps the buyer will agree to the full asking price if the seller will agree to allow the buyer to pay only $850,000 immediately and make annual payments of $50,000 each for the next three years (a total of $1 million, but an interest free loan for part of this amount). Or perhaps the seller will agree to take part of the $1 million in the form of another parcel of real estate the buyer owns and the remainder in cash or cash and a note. The potential for finding a creative solution is limitless in real estate negotiations and those who seek solutions that make "winners" out of all parties to the negotiation are more likely to enjoy sustained success.

An important step in becoming a successful negotiator is to keep an open mind so you can better understand the other party's position. Find out what is important to the parties and try to ensure that they get what they want, while you get something you want (which may not be the same something you thought you wanted when the negotiation began). Search for common ground early in the negotiation process. With this accomplished, the remaining contentious issues may not appear nearly so large, and both parties may ultimately benefit. One of the worst mistakes a novice negotiator can make is to ignore the possibility of other ways to structure a deal that would benefit all parties involved.

■ CHAPTER REVIEW

- ■ A contract is a legal document that represents an agreement between two or more parties. The essential elements required before any contract is binding include (a) an offer, (b) an acceptance, (c) consideration, (d) parties with legal capacity, and (e) a lawful purpose. In addition, all states require that contracts involving any interest in land must be in writing and signed by the party against whom enforcement is sought.

- ■ Failure to perform contractual duties is a breach of contract. Remedies available to a buyer for the seller's breach include an order for specific performance, monetary damages, or the return of the earnest money. A seller generally cannot seek the specific performance of a buyer who has breached the contract, but will probably be able to retain any earnest money paid by the buyer and may be able to seek additional damage compensation through the courts.

■ Most contracts include various contingency clauses that specify that the contract may be voided in the event of certain conditions. Common examples in real estate contracts include financing contingencies, title contingencies, and inspection and repair contingencies.

■ Real estate sales contracts are, in essence, gap fillers. Such contracts must govern the parties' rights between the time an agreement is reached to transfer property from one party to another and the time the transaction is formally completed, or closed.

■ Several kinds of contracts may be used in a real estate transaction. Among the common types are the sales contract, the option-to-buy contract, and the contract for deed.

■ The traditional real estate sales contract should consist of provisions specifying (a) the property description, (b) the purchase price and the way it is to be paid, (c) the escrow arrangement, (d) the effect on the contract of the destruction of improvements, (e) the pest-free warranty, (f) the closing date, and (g) the broker's commission, if any.

■ The option-to-buy contract gives the holder the right, but not an obligation, to purchase the property at an agreed-on price on or before a specified date. While the optionee is not obligated to perform, the optionor is obligated to honor the contract terms.

■ Contracts for deed are a combination of a sales contract and a financing arrangement. The seller holds title to the property while the buyer makes payments over time. On paying the agreed-on amount, the seller will transfer title to the buyer.

■ Skilled negotiators realize that successful negotiations are not "zero-sum" games in which the parties attempt to capture all they can grab of the same pie. Keeping an open mind and looking for ways to create win-win situations are important keys for becoming a better negotiator.

■ KEY TERMS

acceptance	contract for deed	option-to-buy contract
agreement for deed	counteroffer	partial performance
bilateral	FSBO	real estate sales contract
capacity	land contract	specific performance
consideration	offer	statute of frauds
contingency	offeree	title
contract	offeror	unilateral

■ STUDY EXERCISES

1. List and explain the six essential elements of a valid real estate sales contract.

2. In a contract, what is meant by capacity? By consideration?

3. Mark offered to buy Charlie's four-acre tract for $200,000, and they shook hands on the deal. Both men went to an attorney to draft the formal contract. The next day, Mark signed the written contract, but Charlie refused to do so because he had received a higher offer. What recourse, if any, does Mark have against Charlie for failing to abide by their oral agreement?

4. Suppose instead that Mark and Charlie had agreed on the deal and Mark wrote the terms of the sale on the back of an envelope, which both signed. They planned on hiring an attorney to "flesh out" the agreement and draft a more formal contract. Charlie refused to sign the formal contract, having received a higher offer. Could Mark force Charlie to carry out the contract?

5. Nell and Edward agreed that Nell would purchase Edward's house and lot. Because both parties wanted to avoid the expense of having a formal contract drafted, they signed their names below the following handwritten statement: "Nell hereby agrees to buy from Edward the house at 1023 Washington Avenue for $65,000. Closing to be within sixty days from today: September 13, 2002." Nell had planned to borrow 90 percent of the purchase price but failed to qualify for this loan. Does Nell's inability to obtain a loan excuse her from performance of the agreement as written?

6. After Kristy finished college and started working, she found a small house that she wanted to buy but could not afford. As an alternative, she agreed to lease the house with an option to buy it. To be valid, what must the option agreement include?

7. Answer the following questions based on the real estate sales contract depicted in Figure 6.1.

    ■ When does the buyer get occupancy of the premises?

    ■ What actions can the buyer take if the seller's title proves to be unmarketable?

    ■ Whose responsibility is it to obtain and pay for a survey to detect any encroachments?

    ■ If an encroachment is detected in the survey, what happens?

    ■ Who must pay for the various closing costs associated with the deed?

■ What happens to this agreement if the property is destroyed by fire or other casualty before the closing?

■ What actions can the parties take if the other party breaches the contract?

8. From the buyer's perspective, what advantage does traditional mortgage financing offer in comparison to agreement for deed financing, even in states that treat these arrangements similarly?

9. Why might a buyer elect to use agreement for deed financing instead of traditional mortgage financing?

■ FURTHER READINGS

de Heer, R., *Realty Bluebook,* 31st ed. Chicago: Real Estate Education Company, 1996.

Nierenberg, Gerald I., *The Art of Negotiating,* New York: The Negotiation Institute, 1988.

Werner, R. J., and Kravotil, R., *Real Estate Law,* 10th ed. Englewood Cliffs, N.J.: Prentice-Hall, 1993.89

7

Title Examination and the Closing Process

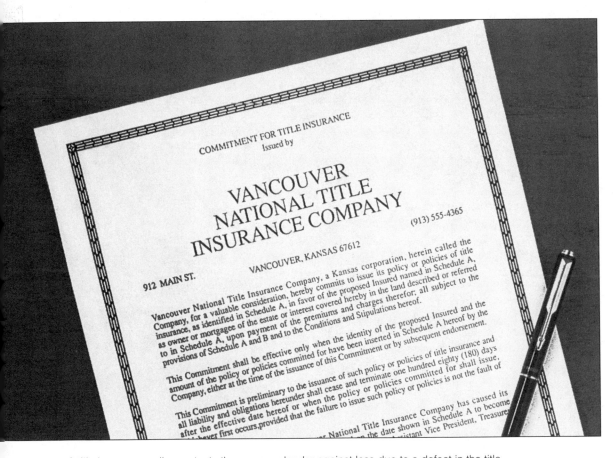

A title insurance policy protects the owner or lender against loss due to a defect in the title.

CHAPTER PREVIEW

As we saw in the previous chapter, the typical real estate transaction involves a sales contract between the buyer and seller that indicates the agreement to transfer the property and specifies the conditions by which that transfer will occur. The transfer of ownership will usually occur only when these conditions are satisfied. Before accepting ownership, the buyer or the buyer's representative must examine the title to the property to verify its validity. The objectives of this chapter are to consider the processes of (1) examining the title to the property and (2) the closing, or settlement, of the transaction.

Under the topic of title examination, we consider

■ transfer of title,

■ acquiring good title,

■ title insurance, and

■ the Torrens system.

Under the topic of closing we will study

■ the buyer's responsibilities,

■ the seller's responsibilities,

■ closing costs and the closing statement,

■ events at closing, and

■ escrow closing.

REAL ESTATE TODAY FEATURES

Legal Highlight
Title Examination Through the Grantor and Grantee Indexes

Legal Highlight
The Case of the Disappearing Island

Legal Highlight
Necessity To Meet "Concurrent Conditions" by Date of Closing

■ TITLE EXAMINATION

In the typical real estate transaction, the buyer's chief desire is to acquire *title,* or ownership, to the property involved. More specifically, the buyer wants "good title" from the seller. The phrase **good title** usually is used in conjunction with some combination of the words *marketable, insurable,* or *perfect of record.*

Sales contracts usually require that the seller furnish "good and marketable title" to the buyer. A **marketable title** is one that is free and clear of all past, present or future claims that would cause a reasonable purchaser to reject such title. An **insurable title** is one that a reputable title insurance company is willing to insure. And **title perfect of record** means that the public records related to the particular title involved show no defects whatsoever. This last condition usually provides the buyer with the most protection. Suppose, for example, that inspection of the seller's title reveals that years ago a deed was signed improperly by a previous title holder. A reasonable buyer might not hesitate to accept the title, and a title insurance company might be willing to insure it, but the seller's title still is not perfect of record.

Any prospective buyer of real estate must discover all possible defects in the seller's title. This responsibility generally is satisfied by means of a lawyer's title opinion or by title insurance. A **title opinion** is a statement by a lawyer that summarizes the findings disclosed by a search through all public documents that may relate to the title. **Title insurance** is a policy that insures the title received by the grantee against any deficiencies that may have been in existence at the time title was transferred. Before a title insurance policy or title opinion can be given concerning a particular property, a search of the title will be performed.

Title Search

A **title search** reveals the ownership history, or **chain of title,** of a property. An examination of the chain of title might show that the seller has good title, or it could show that the seller is only one of several parties claiming to own the real estate being sold. The title search is made possible by the recording system provided by each state.

Recording System

Each state's recording statute provides that any document affecting title to real estate must be recorded. Although recording systems vary from state to state, the purpose of all such systems is to protect the potential interest holder, including the fee simple owner, the tenant, and the mortgagee. The documents related to those interests are, of course, the deed, the lease, and the mortgage. As a result of the recording requirement, anyone concerned with the validity of a real estate title can determine that validity by means of a title search.

Most states require that the recorded document be signed by the grantor. To be filed in the public record, the instrument must be witnessed and acknowledged by a notary public or another person authorized to acknowledge such documents. If this formality is not satisfied, the document cannot be recorded.

The location for the recording of real estate documents varies from state to state. State law generally creates a recorder's office in the local courthouse. The official in charge of that office may be called the clerk of the court, county clerk, recorder, or registrar of deeds.

Because the public has constructive notice of all interests that are properly recorded, any buyer or lender can determine easily whether the seller or borrower has title to the real estate he or she claims. Failure to record an interest may cause the holder to lose that interest to a subsequent good-faith purchaser because that purchaser would have no notice of unrecorded interests.

The recording requirement is the key element that creates an efficient method of transferring title to real estate. Without public records, the confusion that existed in England centuries ago still would occur. Prospective buyers or mortgagees can gain near certainty as to their predecessors' titles because of public records. To reach any level of certainty about the validity of a real estate title, the method of conducting a title search must be understood.

Although real estate title records are public and open to inspection by any interested person, real estate title searches normally should be conducted by an attorney or title examiner (sometimes called an *abstractor*) who is trained specifically in this field. A title examiner must trace the grantor's chain of title to be sure that no defects exist from previous transactions. For example, in a previous transaction involving the property, a spouse may not have signed the deed, even though both the husband and wife jointly owned the property. This type of title defect raises the possibility that the spouse who did not sign still has a legal interest in the property. This defect should be corrected before the new buyer accepts the current grantor's deed.

Assume, for example, that Otis had good and marketable title to a parcel of land. Assume further that Otis sold the parcel to Bill, but Bill failed to record the deed he received. Between the two, Bill has the superior title to the property. Assume, however, that Otis has wrongfully deeded the lot to George, who is unaware of Bill's interest. When George searches Otis's title, he will find no record that Otis previously sold the lot to Bill. Therefore, as far as George can ascertain, Bill has no right to the lot. Because George had no notice of Bill's interest and because George recorded his deed before Bill did, all states would say that George, as a good-faith purchaser, has title to the property.

Grantor and Grantee Indexes

The chain of title can be followed through grantor and grantee indexes. Each county in the United States maintains indexes of people or entities (**grantors**) who have given any interest in real estate to another and people or entities who have received such interests (**grantees**). For a particular property, the current owner will be listed in the grantee index. When ownership of the property is transferred, the previous owner's name will be added to the grantee index, and the new owner's name will be entered into the grantee index. The title examiner begins by tracing the property involved back through the grantee indexes to verify that the seller is, in fact, the current owner of record. Then the examiner searches the applicable grantor indexes to verify that the current owner has not granted any interest in the property to another person. Generally, a title search covers a period of 40 to 60 years.

Completing the Records Search

Merely examining the grantor and grantee indexes is not enough to ensure an accurate title search. The examiner also must check the tax records to discover whether any tax payments are delinquent. Furthermore, the examiner must search the local court records to determine whether any judgment has been awarded or any lien has been filed against the property. Only after these additional factors have been researched can the title be considered insurable or good and marketable. Of course, any recorded document that appears to relate to the property at issue must be checked for its legal description. Only if a tax lien or an attempted transfer by an owner concerns part or all of the property under contract does that record have to be examined.

Title Abstract

In some states, a title examination is made much easier by the use of title abstracts. A **title abstract** is a written summary of the chain of title for a given piece of real estate. Generally, such abstracts are prepared by employees of an abstract company who are not licensed lawyers but are trained specifically to search titles. When an abstract is readily available, the buyer's attorney does not have to go through the detailed search of the grantor and grantee indexes. The attorney obtains the proper abstract, studies it, and issues a *title opinion,* an opinion to the buyer on the validity or defectiveness of the title. When abstracts are used widely, the attorney's fees in a real estate transaction may be much lower than they are when the attorney must perform the entire title examination. Title abstracting is declining in popularity, partially due to the costs of storing and maintaining the documents involved. Title insurance has supplanted the title opinion as a means of title examination in most areas of the country.

Title Insurance

The lawyer's title opinion is not the only type of protection a buyer can obtain to ensure that the seller can deliver marketable title. In many parts of the country, title insurance, which grew out of the expanded function of abstract companies or a group of lawyers, is purchased to provide protection in case the acquired title is defective. In addition to preparing abstracts or writing opinion letters, these companies or associations began to issue insurance that the title to a parcel of real estate was "good and marketable."

On receiving a request for title insurance, the title insurance company conducts its own search of the grantor's title, using public records. The company then evaluates the validity of this title and determines the risk it must take to ensure the title's marketability. The title insurance policy includes a schedule of exceptions, which might list liens, easements, or other encumbrances that appear in an examination of the public record. Often, the policy will state that all restrictions of record are excluded from coverage. In addition, the policy can exclude those defects created by any party who possesses the property at the time the policy is delivered. Other risks excluded might include defects revealed by an accurate survey of the property or defects not recorded as required. The insureds under a title insurance policy must be certain what defects are excepted from the policy and either have the seller-grantor clear the title of these defects or encumbrances or protect themselves by receiving credit from the seller for existing financial liens and paying off such liens thereafter.

In a real estate transaction, title insurance may be purchased for the buyer-grantee or for the institution (mortgagee) financing the transaction and taking a security interest in the real estate. In the typical transaction, the policy is paid for by the buyer, or mortgagor, as a condition of obtaining financing. Title insurance differs from liability, life, or property-hazard insurance in several important ways. First, the insured is charged a premium only once, and it is payable when the policy is delivered. Second, a title insurance policy protects only the named insured; therefore, when the insured transfers the title that is covered, the insurance does not protect the new owner. Third, in contrast with most types of insurance (which protect against future events), title insurance protects against past events only. The schedule of exceptions normally exempts from coverage any liens, encumbrances, or other defects that arise after the title is insured.

A title insurance policy may act as a substitute for the lawyer's title opinion letter. Indeed, the practice in many states is to purchase a title policy rather than obtain a title opinion because some people feel the title policy provides more protection at a better price. Alternatively, a title policy may be purchased as supplemental protection to the lawyer's opinion, although most would consider this redundant and a waste of money.

In essence, a title insurance company provides protection to the insured to the extent that the title was free from unknown defects when the insured acquired title. Primarily, this protection covers the possibility that the recording system has failed to disclose a proper claim to the property. For example, if a previous owner received title through a forged deed, and later the true owner appears, the title insurance company would be obligated to defend the insured's title in court, reach a monetary settlement with the lawful owner, or make good the insured's loss. In such a situation, title insurance can provide very valuable protection.

Mortgage companies usually require a title insurance policy before they will loan money to purchase the property. Although the buyer will normally have to pay for this policy as part of the costs of obtaining the loan, the policy protects only the lender. If the property owners also want title insurance to protect their interest, they must purchase a separate policy. In any case, the buyer can file suit against the seller for breach of warranty if the title turns out to be defective. The seller, however, may be insolvent and unable to pay any judgment the buyer might obtain. Legal action also involves attorney's and other expenses, as well as considerable time and inconvenience.

If a lawyer for a title abstract company has given an opinion on a title that later turns out to be defective and the defect was overlooked because of the negligence of the abstractor or the attorney, the title holder has a cause of action against the negligent party. Here again, however, recovering from a title insurance company normally will be much cheaper and less time-consuming than having to pursue a lawsuit for negligence.

The Legal Highlight on page 135 demonstrates the use of the grantor and grantee indexes in title searches.

The Torrens System

The **Torrens system** of land registration provides the landowner with a title certificate similar to that used to show title to a car. To obtain the Torrens certificate of title, the purported owner must be willing to go through a legal registration proceeding. After reviewing all potential interests in the land, the judge issues a decree naming the true owner of the land and any valid claims, such as mortgages, easements, or other restrictions, against the land. The judge's decree is entered on the court's records, an original certificate of title is recorded, and a duplicate certificate is given to the landowner. To transfer title under the Torrens system, the old certificate of title is returned to the registrar, who then issues a new certificate to the new owner.

Although the Torrens system simplifies the real estate transfer process, it is permitted as an optional method of land transfer in only 11 states (Colorado, Georgia, Hawaii, Massachusetts, Minnesota, New York, North Carolina, Ohio, Oregon, Virginia, and Washington), and even in those areas, it has been applied on a very limited basis.

There are two main reasons for this. First, the high initial cost of the proceeding discourages owners from having their land registered. Second, and perhaps most important, lawyers, abstractors, and title insurance companies have fought against the use of the Torrens system because land transfers under this system eliminate or greatly diminish the need for their services.

■ TITLE CLOSINGS

When all the conditions of the sales contract have been met, the last step in the transaction process is to "close" or "settle" the transaction. In fact, a real estate transaction may involve several types of closings. The borrower and the lending institution must close the loan; the escrow agent, if one is employed, must close the escrow arrangement; and the grantor and grantee must close or transfer the title to the property involved. Generally, but not always, the various closings occur at the same meeting. Therefore, the word *closing* can refer to the conclusion to several different relationships. Remember that the ultimate purpose of the real estate sales process is to transfer title from the seller to the buyer. To look at closing properly, we must first examine each party's prior responsibilities.

REAL ESTATE TODAY

Title Examination Through the Grantor and Grantee Indexes

In the previous chapter, we reviewed a real estate sales contract involving a transaction between Clay Williams, the buyer, and Sarah Howell, the seller. The sales contract has an effective date of June 11, 2001, and a closing date of August 4, 2001. In this contract, the seller is required to obtain a title insurance commitment on behalf of the buyer and, after closing, a title insurance policy. The title commitment must be delivered to the buyer or the buyer's attorney at least five days prior to the closing. The commitment will list any information revealed in the title search that the title insurance underwriter is not willing to cover in the title insurance policy. The buyer, Clay Williams, or his representative must review these exceptions (if any) to determine if they constitute a title defect.

By using the grantor and grantee indexes, the title examiner (the person who searches the public records and evaluates the risk of the insurance policy) finds the following information. First, by looking through the grantee index, the examiner discovers that the seller, Sarah Williams, bought the house now being sold on March 28, 1984, from Charles Edwards. Again via the grantee index, the examiner finds that Edwards purchased the land on which the house sits on June 17, 1965, from J. William Martin. The examiner learns that Martin had owned the property since November 12, 1916, after inheriting it from his mother, Edith Martin. Having determined that the chain of title can be traced back more than 80 years (some states require only a 30-year **root of**

Legal Highlight

title, the time period that must be examined to ensure full legal protection), the examiner must "come forward" with the title to make sure that each grantor had the right and power to transfer title. Beginning with the grantor index, the examiner searches the grantor index to see whether Mrs. Martin's executor deeded the land involved to anyone other than J. William Martin on November 12, 1916. The examiner must take similar measures to learn what Martin did with the property between November 12, 1916, and June 17, 1965.

When the examiner is satisfied that Charles Edwards received good title on June 17, 1965, she finds next that Edwards mortgaged the land to finance the construction of the house Clay Williams now wants to buy. A satisfaction of that mortgage—that is, a discharge of the obligation—was filed when Edwards sold the house and lot to Sarah Howell in 1984. Therefore, it appears that as of the date of her purchase, Sarah Howell had good, clear, marketable title. To complete the job, the examiner must check the grantor index under the name Sarah Howell from March 28, 1984, to the present. Again, the land and house were mortgaged when Sarah bought the property. Because she has not yet paid off that mortgage, at the closing the buyer will insist that a document be recorded showing that the seller has totally paid the mortgage. A mortgage satisfaction generally is filed at the same time as the deed conveying the property from the seller to the buyer.

REAL ESTATE TODAY

The Case of the Disappearing Island

The power of "Old Man River" can result in some confusing land titles. Consider the case of Stack Island, a six-mile-long finger of land separated by a levee and a narrow channel of the Mississippi River from downtown Lake Providence, Louisiana, about 50 miles north of Vicksburg, Mississippi. Who owns Stack Island? Does it still exist? If so, what state is it in? This is a bizarre tale of accretions, thalwegs, and riparian rights.

Legal Highlight

Much of Stack Island is submerged for part of the year, but the river channel between the island and the Louisiana shore is dry during other seasons. The island is uninhabitable and has value only for growing timber and for selling hunting leases. In 1881, the island was separated from the Mississippi shoreline by a 100- to 200-foot-wide channel. Although narrow, this channel was the main navigable thread or thalweg. (I bet that's a new word for you, and probably one you will never hear again.) Because the thalweg of the river fixes the boundary between the two states, this would seem to place the island in Louisiana. However, when dikes were constructed in 1882, there was a sudden shift of the main channel, an avulsive change, to the west side of the island. About 1912, the thalweg shifted again to the east side. Where was the state line? Was Stack Island in Mississippi or Louisiana? All this was further complicated by the island's gradual erosion; it migrated downstream and across the river.

The Houston family gained title to Stack Island in 1938 "with all the accretions or additions thereto." By the 1950s, the island was located almost entirely in a new location, and a dispute arose over whether it was still the Houstons' property or whether the accretions belonged to the landowner on the Louisiana side whose deed also included "all accretions adjoining or in any way connected with the above described land . . . and any islands located between the above described lands and the Louisiana-Mississippi state line." This issue of ownership was finally settled in 1981 when the courts ruled that the Houstons had gained title by virtue of adverse possession because for many years they had sold grazing leases, planted tree seedlings, and hunted on the property.

When the Houstons later attempted to clear up the title so they could sell the land, Louisiana officials jumped into the fray, contending that Stack Island was really located in their state, not in Mississippi. They argued that the original Stack Island had disappeared and that what is now called Stack Island is just sediment from upriver. This sediment, the state of Louisiana maintained, belonged to the riparian owners, or those who own the land on the Louisiana side of the river.

The central issue in this dispute was the historical location of the thalweg. The Federal Circuit Court of Appeals ruled that the 1881 location east of the island established the boundary, placing Stack Island in Louisiana. Even though the thalweg shifted to the west side between 1882 and 1912, the court held that the sudden shift, or avulsive change, did not alter the legal boundary. The U.S. Supreme Court eventually upheld the lower court's ruling.

Yes, the power of the mighty Mississippi River can certainly create some interesting legal property title questions.

Source: *Houston v. United States Gypsum Company,* 652 F.2d 467, 1981; Houston v. Thomas, 937 F.2d 247, 1991; Lousiana v. Mississippi, 116 S.Ct. 290, 1995.

Buyer's Responsibilities

Once the right property is located and a sales contract is signed, the real estate transaction begins. Indeed, during the time period (usually 60 days) between the signing of a contract and the closing of the transaction, buyers often take on many new responsibilities, including

- obtaining financing,
- examining the title evidence,
- having the property surveyed,
- obtaining property insurance, and
- having the property inspected.

Financing the Purchase

A house is the largest financial investment the average American family makes. Very few families are able to pay cash for a home; indeed, even those who have such large amounts of cash are encouraged to borrow money because the interest paid on the loan is deductible from income taxes, and the money otherwise spent on the house is available for other forms of investment. Typically, buyers of residential real estate finance 70, 80, 90, or even 95 percent of the total purchase price. The use of borrowed funds is not limited, of course, to residential real estate. Even large corporations with access to international capital markets may choose to use significant portions of borrowed funds to acquire real estate.

Buyers' reliance on borrowed money requires that they insist on a financing contingency, as discussed in the previous chapter. A buyer who, after a good-faith effort, is unable to secure the specified financing may cancel the sales contract and have the earnest money refunded.

Under a clause conditioning the sale on the buyers' ability to obtain adequate financing, the buyers must use good faith and honesty in all attempts to borrow the required amount. They must apply for the loan within a short time after the contract is signed. They cannot delay such an attempt until there is not enough time for the lending institution to approve the loan before the closing date. If the buyers' failure to secure adequate financing is a result of their lack of good faith, the sellers can sue for damages as a consequence of the buyers' inability to close the transaction. If the money market is exceedingly tight, however, or if lenders are unwilling to risk the loan because they doubt the buyers' ability to pay, or if the loan is not approved for some reason over which the potential borrowers have no direct control, the buyers are relieved of their contractual obligation.

Failure to include in the sales contract the clause conditioning the sale on the buyers' ability to obtain financing can cause great hardship to the buyers. In that case, failure to secure adequate financing does not relieve the buyers of their contractual duties; therefore, buyers who cannot pay the purchase price at closing have breached the contract and are liable for the sellers' damages.

Examining the Title Evidence

Another principal responsibility of the buyer before closing is to examine the title evidence. Even though a seller may agree to pass title by general warranty deed, the buyer must check on the state of the seller's title for at least two important reasons. First, the seller's deed usually promises that there are no encumbrances other than "restrictions of record." It then becomes the buyer's responsibility to learn of any restrictions of record. Second, the sales contract normally requires that the buyer inform the seller of any defects found in the seller's title and give the seller the opportunity to correct them. As discussed above, title defects are discovered through a title examination.

Having the Property Surveyed

An actual survey of the property's boundaries is not always required before title can be transferred, particularly in subdivisions that have been platted. The plat in the public records normally will suffice in lieu of a survey. If there is some confusion as to the actual property lines, however, or if the lending institution requires that a survey be made, the buyer usually must pay for it. Of course, the sales contract can provide that the seller bear the cost of any survey if the buyer and seller agree to this arrangement.

Obtaining Property Insurance

Again, because of the magnitude of real estate costs, most people cannot bear the risk of losing the property's value as a result of fire, vandalism, or other potential hazards. When a buyer is borrowing money to purchase real estate, the lender will require that the buyer purchase property insurance. Indeed, the lending institution will refuse to close the loan unless the borrower has given proof that the property is insured for at least the amount of the loan.

Such proof typically is provided by a letter from the insurance company to the lender, a document often referred to as an *insurance binder.* Property insurance is indirectly vital to the title closing because the property insurance must be obtained before the loan can be completed, and the loan is crucial to the overall perform-ance of the sales contract. Property insurance is considered in a later chapter.

Inspecting the Property

Except in the most unusual circumstances, a buyer will have visited the real estate once or twice, or perhaps many times, before the sales contract is signed. Despite numerous visits to view the property, the prospective buyer seldom investigates thoroughly the property's mechanical systems such as the plumbing, wiring or heating systems. At times, a buyer feels great pressure to sign a sales contract so that he or she will not lose the opportunity to buy a particular property the buyers have selected. The major utilities and appliances, if included, often remain uninspected as well.

The high cost associated with repairing any structural problems, mechanical systems, or appliances makes it extremely important that these items be in good working order. If any of these components of the property are damaged or not working properly, the buyer should know so that the offer to purchase can be adjusted accordingly.

The real estate sales contract we reviewed in the previous chapter included two specific inspection and repair clauses: termite/wood-destroying organisms and functional/mechanical defects. The buyer should inspect the premises during the time period before the closing. The seller must cooperate in allowing access to the buyer for this purpose. Although it does cost money to have someone knowledgeable inspect the major items of concern, the expense is far smaller than that of replacing the heating unit two weeks after the transaction is closed. If the inspections reveal repairs needed up to the agreed-on limit, the seller must correct the problems. Otherwise, the buyer can elect to cancel the contract.

Other Responsibilities

A buyer who is purchasing land for development purposes should investigate the zoning restrictions on the parcel involved. A sales contract for commercial land should contain a provision permitting the buyer to cancel the contract if the zoning regulations do not permit the intended use or cannot be changed to permit it by the stipulated closing date. A buyer of rental property should study the current lease's terms and conditions, as well as the schedule of rental payments. Of course, because the parties are the masters of their contracts, a sales agreement may include other duties owed by the buyer before the closing of the transaction.

Seller's Responsibilities

A seller's work, like a buyer's, really begins when a sales contract is signed. Before actually going to the closing, a seller must do the following:

- Prepare the required deed
- Remove all encumbrances
- Prepare papers with respect to the seller's loan
- Cooperate with inspectors

Preparing the Deed

As we discussed in a previous chapter, various types of deeds can be used to transfer title, depending on the circumstances of the transaction. The sales contract always should specify the kind of deed that is to be delivered by the seller. The typical sales transaction involves a general or special warranty deed. For example, the sales contract between Clay Williams and Sarah Howell in the previous chapter requires that Sarah furnish a general warranty deed to Clay at closing.

Removing Encumbrances

Assuming that a seller is required to present a warranty deed, he or she will covenant that the real estate is free of encumbrances other than those specified in the deed. Encumbrances that the seller may have to remove could include unrecorded claims of ownership, easements, covenants, and liens. One of the most frequently filed liens is the tax lien, resulting from the owner's failure to pay state, county, or city property taxes. Therefore, before the closing, a seller must have paid all taxes that are then due on the property.

Paying the Seller's Loan

Loans for the purchase of residential property usually are to be paid back over a period of 20 to 30 years. Because of the longevity of such loans, most owners do not complete their mortgage payments before they sell the property. Therefore, a major encumbrance on the real estate being purchased is the seller's mortgage. From the title search described earlier, we saw that Sarah Howell bought the house she is now selling on March 28, 1984. If her loan was for the usual 25 or 30 years, then she probably has not yet paid it off.

One of two things can happen with respect to the seller's loan at closing. It will be satisfied out of the sale's proceeds or it will be taken over by the buyer. Whichever event occurs, the seller must have the proper papers ready at the closing. With the aid of the seller's lender and lawyer, either a certificate of satisfaction or the loan assumption papers must be prepared.

Cooperating with Inspectors

As mentioned earlier, the seller may be obligated to cooperate with the various inspectors a buyer may hire to inspect the property for termite damage or structural/functional defects in the property. Cooperation includes making the property available to the inspector and having utilities available to fully test the mechanical systems.

Other Responsibilities

If the property being sold is for a development project, the seller may have contractual duties to assist the buyer in changing the zoning restrictions. On closing a transaction involving rental property, the seller must turn over all valid leases to the buyer. In addition, the rent schedules and copies of letters to all tenants informing them of the change of ownership must be provided.

Once again, a sales contract can place special duties on both the buyer and seller, and generally, these contractual obligations must be performed before the transaction is closed. Failure to do so may void the contract, as the buyer in the Legal Highlight on page 141 discovered.

REAL ESTATE TODAY

Necessity To Meet "Concurrent Conditions" by Date of Closing

As illustrated in our discussion of the sale of Sarah Howell's home to Clay Williams, a real estate sales contract usually creates conditions that both parties must fulfill by the closing date. These are called *concurrent conditions.* Failure to do so can void the contract, as one purchaser found to his sorrow.

Legal Highlight

On November 24, 85-year-old Lily Canham agreed to sell a 56-acre parcel of land in San Luis Obispo County, California, to real estate broker Jeffrey Pittman for $250,000. The contract called for an initial deposit of $1,000 and a further deposit of $24,000 before closing. The balance of the purchase price was to be paid by a note secured by a deed of trust on the property. The closing of escrow was to be within 30 days, and the contract provided that "time is of the essence."

About the second week of December, Canham sent a signed copy of the deed to the escrow agent, which—he pointed out—had not been notarized. When broker Pittman contacted Canham, she told him she would have the deed notarized at an escrow agent near her home. By the closing date of December 24, Canham still had not sent the signed deed to the escrow agent, nor had Pittman tendered the $24,000, promissory note or deed of trust. There

the matter rested until the following May, when Canham told Pittman she had entered into a contract with other purchasers to buy her property for $600,000. Pittman wrote her a letter demanding she sell the property to him as agreed in the earlier contract, but she refused and sold it to the other buyers. Pittman sued for breach of contract. He lost.

Under the contract, Canham was supposed to tender a signed and notarized deed by the closing date of December 24; Pittman was supposed to tender a $24,000 deposit, note, and deed of trust. The court ruled that neither party had fulfilled the concurrent conditions called for in the contract by the closing date, resulting in a "discharge of both parties' duty to perform."

> We appreciate the reluctance of a buyer to act first by placing money into escrow. But in a contract with concurrent conditions, the buyer and seller cannot keep saying to one another, "NO, you first." Ultimately, in such a case the buyer seeking enforcement comes in second; he loses.

Source: *Pittman v. Canham,* 3 Cal. Rptr. 2d 340 (1992).

Costs at Closing

A prospective purchaser of real estate may save up money for the down payment only to learn that he or she needs more cash to cover the closing costs. The elements of closing costs vary from time to time and from location to location, but generally the buyer must pay for the following items in cash:

- Loan origination fee
- Loan discounts, or points
- Appraisal fee
- Credit-report fee
- Lender's inspection fee

- Mortgage insurance premium
- Attorney fees
- Hazard-insurance premium
- Recording fees for the mortgage he or she gives

The loan origination fee, the points, and the mortgage-guarantee insurance premium usually are based on a percentage of the loan. For example, the loan origination fee—the fee charged by the bank to process the loan—may be 1 to 3 percent of the amount of the loan. *Points* are an extra charge made by the bank; each point is 1 percent of the amount of the loan. (Points and other financing charges are discussed in a later chapter.) The typical mortgage insurance premium is 2 percent of the amount of the loan, of which 0.5 percent is due at the closing. The other 1.5 percent is paid over a ten-year period. These types of closing costs generally total 2 to 6 percent of the money borrowed.

The seller also has to pay closing costs, which may include the

- real estate brokerage commission;
- attorney's fees for preparing the deed or other documents;
- documentary stamp taxes, where required; and
- recording fees for the certificate of satisfaction of the seller's mortgage.

A seller, however, generally does not have to worry about coming up with the cash to pay for these items. Such costs simply are subtracted from the proceeds of the sale. We will examine the breakdown of the buyer's and seller's closing costs in detail in Figure 7.1.

Proration of Homeowner's Costs

Certain homeowner's costs must be prorated or shared by the buyer and seller. Such costs normally include state and local taxes, the hazard-insurance premium if that insurance policy is to be assigned to the buyer, and the monthly mortgage payment, should the buyer assume the seller's loan.

The costs of any other contracts that exist during the seller's and buyer's ownership should be prorated. For example, the cost of a pest extermination contract purchased by the seller and not canceled by the buyer must be shared. Whether this proration will appear as a credit to the seller or to the buyer depends on which party pays the amount owed. In commercial sales, the collection or payment of rents also must be prorated equitably. If the house is heated by oil, the buyer must pay the seller for the oil remaining in the storage tank, usually at the current price per gallon.

Understanding the Settlement Statement

In residential transactions involving mortgage loans, the Real Estate Settlement Procedures Act of 1974 requires that lenders fully disclose the financial details of

FIGURE 7.1   Uniform Settlement Statement

A. **Settlement Statement**	U.S. Department of Housing and Urban Development		OMB Approval No. 2502-0265

B. Type of Loan

1. ☐ FHA 2. ☐ FmHA 3. ☒ Conv. Unins. 4. ☐ VA 5. ☐ Conv. Ins.	6. File Number: 01-4569b	7. Loan Number: 78-999034	8. Mortgage Insurance Case Number:

C. Note: This form is furnished to give you a statement of actual settlement costs. Amounts paid to and by the settlement agent are shown. Items marked "(p.o.c.)" were paid outside the closing; they are shown here for informational purposes and are not included in the totals.

D. Name & Address of Borrower:	E. Name & Address of Seller:	F. Name & Address of Lender:
CLAY WILLIAMS 1000 BANYAN STREET SUBURB, FLORIDA 33323	SARAH HOWELL 501 SE 1ST STREET FORT LAUDERDALE FL 33301	REALTY MORTGAGE CO. 101 MAIN ST. FORT LAUDERDALE FL 33301

G. Property Location:	H. Settlement Agent: B.A. SETTLER, INC. FORT LAUDERALE FL	
501 SE 1ST STREET FORT LAUDERDALE FL 33301	Place of Settlement: BROWARD COUNTY	I. Settlement Date: AUGUST 4, 2001

J. **Summary of Borrower's Transaction**		K. **Summary of Seller's Transaction**	
100. Gross Amount Due From Borrower		**400. Gross Amount Due To Seller**	
101. Contract sales price	189,000.00	401. Contract sales price	189,000.00
102. Personal property		402. Personal property	
103. Settlement charges to borrower (line 1400)	6,600.82	403.	
104.		404.	
105.		405.	
Adjustments for items paid by seller in advance		Adjustments for items paid by seller in advance	
106. City/town taxes to		406. City/town taxes to	
107. County taxes to		407. County taxes to	
108. Assessments to		408. Assessments to	
109.		409.	
110.		410.	
111.		411.	
112.		412.	
120. Gross Amount Due From Borrower	195,600.82	**420. Gross Amount Due To Seller**	189,000.00
200. Amounts Paid By Or In Behalf Of Borrower		**500. Reductions In Amount Due To Seller**	
201. Deposit or earnest money	5,000.00	501. Excess deposit (see instructions)	
202. Principal amount of new loan(s)	150,000.00	502. Settlement charges to seller (line 1400)	13,848.50
203. Existing loan(s) taken subject to		503. Existing loan(s) taken subject to	
204.		504. Payoff of first mortgage loan	113,245.00
205.		505. Payoff of second mortgage loan	
206.		506.	
207.		507.	
208.		508.	
209.		509.	
Adjustments for items unpaid by seller		Adjustments for items unpaid by seller	
210. City/town taxes to	1,943.84	510. City/town taxes to	1,943.84
211. County taxes to	1,413.70	511. County taxes to	1,413.70
212. Assessments to		512. Assessments to	
213.		513.	
214.		514.	
215.		515.	
216.		516.	
217.		517.	
218.		518.	
219.		519.	
220. Total Paid By/For Borrower	158,357.54	**520. Total Reduction Amount Due Seller**	130,451.04
300. Cash At Settlement From/To Borrower		**600. Cash At Settlement To/From Seller**	
301. Gross amount due from borrower (line 120)	195,600.82	601. Gross amount due to seller (line 420)	189,000.00
302. Less amounts paid by/for borrower (line 220)	(158,357.54)	602. Less reductions in amt. due seller (line 520)	(130,451.04)
303. Cash ☒ From ☐ To Borrower	37,243.28	**603. Cash ☒ To ☐ From Seller**	58,548.96

Section 5 of the Real Estate Settlement Procedures Act (RESPA) requires the following: • HUD must develop a Special Information Booklet to help persons borrowing money to finance the purchase of residential real estate to better understand the nature and costs of real estate settlement services; • Each lender must provide the booklet to all applicants from whom it receives or for whom it prepares a written application to borrow money to finance the purchase of residential real estate; • Lenders must prepare and distribute with the Booklet a Good Faith Estimate of the settlement costs that the borrower is likely to incur in connection with the settlement. These disclosures are manadatory.

Section 4(a) of RESPA mandates that HUD develop and prescribe this standard form to be used at the time of loan settlement to provide full disclosure of all charges imposed upon the borrower and seller. These are third party disclosures that are designed to provide the borrower with pertinent information during the settlement process in order to be a better shopper.

The Public Reporting Burden for this collection of information is estimated to average one hour per response, including the time for reviewing instructions, searching existing data sources, gathering and maintaining the data needed, and completing and reviewing the collection of information.

This agency may not collect this information, and you are not required to complete this form, unless it displays a currently valid OMB control number. The information requested does not lend itself to confidentiality.

Previous editions are obsolete   Page 1 of 2   form **HUD-1** (3/86) ref Handbook 4305.2

FIGURE 7.1   Uniform Settlement Statement (continued)

L. Settlement Charges

			Paid From Borrowers Funds at Settlement	Paid From Seller's Funds at Settlement
700. Total Sales/Broker's Commission based on price $ 189,000 @ 6 % = 11,340				
Division of Commission (line 700) as follows:				
701. $ 11,340 to Julio Rodriguez				
702. $ to				
703. Commission paid at Settlement				11,340.00
704.				
800. Items Payable In Connection With Loan				
801. Loan Origination Fee %				
802. Loan Discount 2.0 %			3,000.00	
803. Appraisal Fee to Harry Newstreet, Certified General Appraiser			300.00	
804. Credit Report to				
805. Lender's Inspection Fee				
806. Mortgage Insurance Application Fee to				
807. Assumption Fee				
808.				
809.				
810.				
811.				
900. Items Required By Lender To Be Paid In Advance				
901. Interest from 8/4 to 8/31 @$ 36.29 /day			915.32	
902. Mortgage Insurance Premium for months to				
903. Hazard Insurance Premium for years to				
904. years to				
905.				
1000. Reserves Deposited With Lender				
1001. Hazard insurance 2 months@$ 100 per month			200.00	
1002. Mortgage insurance months@$ per month			550.00	
1003. City property taxes 2 months@$ 275 per month			200.00	
1004. County property taxes 2 months@$ 200 per month				
1005. Annual assessments months@$ per month				
1006. months@$ per month				
1007. months@$ per month				
1008. months@$ per month				
1100. Title Charges				
1101. Settlement or closing fee to B.A. Settler, Inc.				300.00
1102. Abstract or title search to				
1103. Title examination to				
1104. Title insurance binder to				
1105. Document preparation to				
1106. Notary fees to				
1107. Attorney's fees to				
(includes above items numbers:)				
1108. Title insurance to B.A. Settler, Inc.			100.00	865.00
(includes above items numbers: 1101, 1102, 1103)				
1109. Lender's coverage $ 150,000.00				
1110. Owner's coverage $ 189,000.00				
1111.				
1112.				
1113.				
1200. Government Recording and Transfer Charges				
1201. Recording fees: Deed $ 10.50 ; Mortgage $ 10.50 ; Releases $ 10.00			10.50	20.50
1202. City/county tax/stamps: Deed $; Mortgage $				
1203. State tax/stamps: Deed $ 1,230.00 ; Mortgage $ 825.00			825.00	1,323.00
1204.				
1205.				
1300. Additional Settlement Charges				
1301. Survey to J. Almond PSM			425.00	
1302. Pest inspection to Trusty Termite Man, Inc.			75.00	
1303.				
1304.				
1305.				
1400. Total Settlement Charges (enter on lines 103, Section J and 502, Section K)			6,600.82	13,848.50

the transaction to the buyer and seller in writing using the uniform **settlement statement** approved by the U.S. Department of Housing and Urban Development. At the closing, the buyer and seller sign this statement, and each receives a copy. The settlement statement shown in Figure 7.1 is completed in accordance with the Howell-Williams transaction in Chapter 6.

Although the settlement statement may appear rather complex at first glance, its purpose is to simplify and summarize the financial transactions. Page 2 of the form is a worksheet designed to help determine the seller's and buyer's closing costs. Let's use this statement to "close" the deal between Sarah Howell and Clay Williams. Sections A through I on page 1 of the statement are self-explanatory, but the other sections require a closer examination.

The first step is to enter the contract sales price on lines 101 and 401. We then turn to the "Settlement Charges" section of the statement beginning at the top of page 2 and calculate the broker's commission in lines 700–704. The broker in this transaction is entitled to $11,340 (6% of the $189,000). The seller is paying the commission in this transaction.

On line 802, we see that the buyer's lender is charging the buyer a 2% loan discount fee (2 percent of the loan amount) for originating the loan. In addition, the lender required that the buyer obtain an appraisal of the property from Harry Newstreet, a State-Certified General Appraiser, who charged $300 for his services.

Lines 901–1008 are often confusing the first time students see the HUD settlement statement, so let's make sure we understand these items before moving on. The topic for lines 900-905 of the settlement statement is "Items Required by Lender to be Paid in Advance." The lender in question is the buyer's lender. This lender is funding the loan for the buyer on the day of closing (August 4), but will not expect the first payment on the loan from the buyer until *the first day of the first full month after origination.* Thus, the first loan payment paid by Clay Williams will occur on October 1. Because Clay will not make a payment on September 1, the lender requires him to "prepay" the interest he will owe for the use of the lender's money during the month of August. (The payment on October 1 will cover the interest charges for the month of September.) The amount of interest due for the period August 4 through August 31 is $915.32. This amount is calculated by multiplying the loan amount by the annual interest rate, dividing the result by 12, then dividing that result by 31 (number of days in August) to get the daily interest amount. We then multiply the daily interest amount by 28 (the number of days Clay uses the lender's money in August) to get the prepaid interest amount for line 901.

Similarly, the lender requires that Clay deposit two months "reserve" of hazard insurance premiums and property taxes into an escrow account. This requirement ensures that when the bills from the insurance company and tax collector are received, the buyer will have the money on hand to pay these bills. The lender estimates the amount of the insurance premium using the first year's policy (which the buyer will have to purchase before the closing directly from the insurance company) and current year's property tax assessments ($2,400 for the county and $3,300 for the city). Two months' reserve of each is entered on lines 1001–1008 as appropriate.

On line 1101, we see that the seller is being charged a $300 fee by the title agent for preparing the closing. On line 1108, we see that the title charges to the buyer and seller are $100 and $865, respectively. The buyer has purchased a title insurance policy to protect the lender (lender's coverage), and the seller has purchased a title insurance policy (as agreed to in the sales contract) to protect the buyer (owner's coverage).

On lines 1201–1203, the buyer and seller have each been charged $10.50 for recording fees: The buyer must pay this fee to record the mortgage for his lender and the seller is paying the fee to record the deed she is giving to the buyer. The seller is also paying the documentary stamp tax on the deed ($1,323), and the buyer is paying the documentary stamps and taxes on the mortgage. The seller must also pay a fee to record the satisfaction of her existing mortgage.

The final section shows any additional settlement charges paid by the parties. In this example, the buyer is charged with the cost of a property survey and a pest inspection.

Line 1400 shows the Total Settlement Charges for the buyer and the seller. These amounts must be posted to line 103 for the buyer and line 502 for the seller on page 1 of the settlement statement.

After entering the settlement charges to the buyer and seller, the next step is to calculate the gross amount due from the borrower, as shown on line 120. We then add up any amounts paid by or on behalf of the borrower. On line 201 we see the $5,000 earnest deposit paid by Clay, and on line 202 we see the loan proceeds he is expecting from his lender. Lines 210 and 211 are another area of some initial confusion for students, so we will consider this section in detail.

Many taxing authorities collect their taxes annually "in arrears," which simply means they collect the money after the services have been provided. In Florida, where our example property is located, city and county governments expect to be paid at the first of each calendar year for services they provided to property owners in the prior calendar year. Because the tax bills will be addressed to Clay Williams (the buyer in our transaction) when they are sent out next year, Clay is entitled to collect from Sarah (the seller) an amount equal to the expected property taxes for the period she owned the property (January 1 through August 3 of the current tax year). The title agent simply calculates the daily tax rate based on the current year's tax bill and then prorates the amount due from the seller based on the number of days of ownership in the current tax year. In this case, the county tax for this property this year was $2,400, and the city tax was $3,300. Dividing each of these amounts by 365 days gives the daily property tax amounts for the county and city, respectively. Multiplying these amounts by 215 (the actual days Sarah was the owner of the property) gives the county and city tax amounts for which the seller should be held responsible. These amounts are entered as adjustments on lines 210 and 211 for the buyer and on lines 510 and 511 for the seller (think double-entry accounting).

The total amount paid by/for the buyer is the sum of lines 201 through 219 and the total reduction amount due the seller is the sum of lines 501 through 519. Subtracting the total amount paid by/for the borrower from the Gross Amount Due from Borrower gives the cash due from (or to, in certain cases) the borrower on line 303. Subtracting the reductions in the amount due the seller from the Gross Amount Due to Seller gives the cash to (or from, in certain cases) the seller on line 603.

To summarize what this statement says, the buyer and seller agreed to transact for $189,000. The seller has an outstanding loan for $113,245 on the property that must be paid off to give the buyer good title. The buyer is borrowing $150,000 from his lender. The seller must pay certain closing expenses (title insurance coverage for the buyer, deed recording fees, deed documentary stamp taxes, the broker's commission, recording fees for the mortgage satisfaction document), and the buyer must pay certain closing expenses (appraisal fee, lender's title insurance coverage, recording fees on his new mortgage, taxes and stamps on his new mortgage, the survey fee, a pest inspection fee, and some prepaid items required by his lender). In addition, the buyer and seller have agreed to prorate the property taxes so both parties will pay the taxes for the time period during which each owned the property. The buyer must bring $37,243.28 to the closing, and the seller will leave the closing with $58,548.96. When the monies are distributed properly to all involved parties and the documents are recorded, the deal is officially closed.

Parties Present at the Closing

Although closings can be handled through the mail without ever having a group meeting of interested parties, the closing of a real estate sale normally is held at the offices of one of the people involved in the transaction: the real estate broker, the lending institution, the title insurance company, seller's attorney, or the buyer's attorney. Obviously, the seller wants to be there to get his or her money, the buyer wants the deed and the keys to the doors, the broker wants the commission, the lender's representative (who may be the title company) wants signatures on the mortgage documents, and the title company and attorneys want to be paid. Usually, the appraiser, pest inspector, and surveyor are content to get their money from the closing agent after the deal is closed.

Escrow Closing

Instead of the conventional closing described above, *escrow closings* are practiced in some communities in the eastern United States and in the majority of western states. Instead of the buyer and seller coming face to face, a third party called an *escrow agent* acts as an intermediary to facilitate the closing. The escrow agent is usually an attorney, a title company, a trust company, an escrow company, or the escrow department of a lending institution.

The seller deposits a fully executed deed with the escrow agent, who then delivers the deed to the purchaser after the receipt of the purchase price. The agent then delivers the deed to the purchaser and the purchase price to the seller.

Some of the advantages of the escrow closing are (1) the seller is assured of receiving the buyer's money before title passes because the check must clear before this occurs, (2) the buyer's money will not be paid until the seller's title is acceptable and free from liens, and (3) the parties need not be present. The last is particularly advantageous if one or both of the parties reside in other areas.

■ CHAPTER REVIEW

- ■ Title to land signifies the legal right to ownership. A buyer of real estate is concerned fundamentally with acquiring "good title." Good title is title that is specified as marketable, insurable, perfect of record, or any combination thereof. To protect themselves against inadvertent acceptance of defective titles, all buyers should obtain a title opinion or title insurance. Title opinions are written by lawyers after they have searched the applicable title or examined the title abstracts. Title insurance provides protection from defects in title that might be discovered after the grantee receives the property from the grantor.

- ■ A title search is conducted by trained personnel who examine the grantor and grantee indexes, the tax records, and the judgment records to determine whether the grantor has the right and power to grant the stated interest. An abstractor searches a title and compiles all records applicable to a piece of real estate; the resulting compilation is called an *abstract*.

- ■ Title insurance can be beneficial in conjunction with or in lieu of a title opinion. In essence, a title policy insures the title against any defects or claims that exist as of the date title is acquired. Title insurance does not cover potential defects or claims that come into existence after the policy is issued. Although title insurance is important in some situations, it should not be purchased automatically when a title opinion is obtained because that opinion may provide sufficient protection.

- ■ The Torrens system of land registration provides an alternative to the more traditional method of exchanging title to real estate by delivery of a deed. Through a legal action to register the land, the judge determines the true owner of the land and the valid claims that exist. A certificate of title is issued then, and new certificates are issued when the property is sold in the future. This registration system has not gained wide acceptance in the United States because of the high cost of the required legal proceeding and the opposition of lawyers and abstractors.

- ■ The real estate transaction is "closed" when title to real property passes from the seller to the buyer. In essence, a closing—or *settlement,* as it is sometimes called—includes the closing of the loan, of the escrow arrangement, and of the title.

■ Between the signing of the sales contract and the closing of the deal, both seller and buyer have certain responsibilities that must be completed. The buyer must obtain an opinion about the status of the title and attempt in good faith to secure the needed financing. Among other obligations, the seller must make sure that all encumbrances are removed and obtain the type of written deed the contract requires.

■ Closing costs are the charges incurred by the buyer and seller at the close of the transaction. Such costs to the buyer include the loan origination fee, the loan discount points, and attorney's fees. Costs to the seller may consist of the real estate brokerage commission and various recording fees. The buyer's closing costs and the down payment must be paid in cash. The seller's closing costs are deducted from the amount due to the seller.

■ At the closing, many papers are examined, signed, and exchanged by the parties. A successful closing of the transaction results in the transfer of the seller's title to the buyer. Thereafter, all necessary papers should be taken to the courthouse and filed in the public record.

■ KEY TERMS

chain of title	insurable title	title insurance
closing costs	marketable title	title opinion
good title	root of title	title perfect of record
grantee	settlement statement	title search
grantor	title abstract	Torrens system

■ STUDY EXERCISES

1. Attorney James Hudson has been retained to search the title of a house owned by Bobby Newton at 1024 College Station Road. Mr. Newton, who purchased the property in 1988, is selling the house to John and Karen Gillespie. Describe the process that Mr. Hudson would go through in searching this title.

2. Define the following terms: marketable title, insurable title, title perfect of record.

3. Karen's offer to purchase Scott's house was accepted on August 17, and a contract was signed by both parties on that day, with closing scheduled for October 4. It was Karen's responsibility to check the marketability of Scott's title. Karen hired an attorney, who said the title was free from all defects on September 23. Before the scheduled closing of the transaction on October 4, Karen's attorney updated his title search and found that a tax lien had been filed against the property because Scott had failed to pay last year's proper-

ty taxes. Does this lien's existence make Scott's title defective? Does Karen have the right to complain about this lien, as it did not appear in the first title search?

4. Suppose that in the situation in question 3, Karen had employed a title insurance company to check Scott's title. If the company had delivered on September 23 a policy exempting from coverage all future liens, would Karen be protected from the tax lien filed on October 2?

5. How does the Torrens system work? Why is it not used more widely?

6. The Hoods and the Wakeleys entered into a formal contract whereby the Hoods agreed to buy the Wakeleys' partially restored 80-year-old house. During the time period between the signing of the contract and the closing of the transaction, what things should the Hoods accomplish? What responsibilities do the Wakeleys have?

7. In a typical residential transaction, what closing costs must the buyer normally pay? Which are usually paid by the seller?

8. Property taxes for the 2002 year are due on March 31, 2003, and will be $1,875 for a property being sold on July 1, 2002. Using a 365-day year, how much should the sellers be responsible for?

9. As a part of a purchase transaction, the buyers have taken out a loan for $75,000 at 10.5 percent annual interest with monthly payments of $702. The closing date is to be March 16, but the first loan payment will not be made until May 1. At the closing, how much interest must the buyers "prepay" for the month of March?

 Go to the Student Study Guide CD-ROM and work through Case 2.

■ FURTHER READINGS

WWW.HUD.GOV

PART TWO

Real Estate Market Analysis

8 Understanding Real Estate Markets

In many urban markets, demand for property exceeds the existing supply. In response, developers are converting abandoned warehouses and factories into residential lofts or upscale commercial space.

CHAPTER PREVIEW

A key requirement for making effective real estate decisions is having a clear understanding of how real estate prices (values) are determined in real estate markets. This understanding is central to all aspects of real estate, including consumption and investment decisions, mortgage lending and borrowing, appraisal, brokerage, land-use policy, and, of course, development. Although we often think of *the* real estate market, there really is no such thing. Real estate market analysts find it much more useful to think of two different types of real estate markets: real estate *space* markets and real estate *asset* markets. Although these two types of markets are definitely interrelated, separating them in this manner will help us understand how the forces of supply and demand interact to determine prices in both types of markets.

The objectives of this chapter are to

■ define the concept of real estate space markets,

■ use the supply and demand model to forecast price changes in space markets,

■ define the concept of real estate asset markets,

■ examine how prices are determined in real estate asset markets,

■ consider how the development industry ties these markets together, and

■ review the procedures for conducting a real estate market analysis.

REAL ESTATE
TODAY
FEATURES

Close-Up
The Rockefeller
Center Saga

153

■ REAL ESTATE SPACE MARKETS

By definition, a *market* is the mechanism or arrangements through which goods and services are traded between market participants. Applying this concept to land and buildings, we can classify real estate transactions into either real estate space markets or real estate asset markets. We first consider space markets; then we will examine asset markets.[1]

Real estate space markets involve transactions for the rights to use land and buildings. On the demand side of this market are people, firms, and other entities that are willing to pay to use space for consumption or production purposes. The supply side of this market consists of property owners who are willing to sell such space to users. The price of use in the space market is often called *rent,* even if the user is the owner/occupant of the space.

Users of space often have specific requirements for the type of space they demand and the locations of that space. A family, for example, wants comfortable, attractive living space near shopping, education, and entertainment resources, but a manufacturing firm is likely to be more concerned with functionality and proximity to its customers or raw materials suppliers. *Suppliers* in the space market have buildings that were designed for specific uses and are fixed in their locations.

Because supply and demand is location- and type-specific, real estate space markets are highly segmented. Office space in Los Angeles is clearly a different market from the warehouse space market in Texas. Prices (rents) for one type of space may be very different from rents for a different type of space in the same geographic area, and prices for the same type of space in two different geographic areas may differ dramatically.

Categories of the Real Estate Space Market

Real estate space markets can be categorized by property usage and by geographic boundaries. The major segments of the real estate space market include residential, industrial, retail, office, agricultural, and lodging. Each of these segments can be further categorized as shown in Figure 8.1. Adding geographic dimensions to these categories allows us to discuss the "highway motel market in the southeastern United States," "warehouse market in Chicago," "class B office market in San Antonio," or almost any other reasonable combination of location and use. Accurate analysis of a real estate space market requires an accurate market definition. Let's consider how each of the major market segments can be further subdivided in terms of property usage. As you read through these categories, keep in mind that the objective for identifying the specific market segment is to be able to analyze the factors that affect activity in that market segment.

---

[1] For a more detailed discussion of real estate market dynamics, we recommend that readers consult Chapter 1 and 2 of *Commercial Real Estate Investment Analysis* by David M. Geltner and Normal G. Miller (Englewood Cliffs, N.J.: Prentice-Hall, 2001). Targeted at graduate students, their text provides a detailed, lucid discussion of real estate market dynamics that incorporates the latest financial and urban economic theories.

FIGURE 8.1   Theoretical Price-Distance Relationships

OFFICE
- Class A
- Class B
- Class C
- Class D

LODGING
- Resort Hotel
- Business/ Convention
- Extended Stay Motel/Apartments
- Highway Motel

RETAIL
- Regional Centers
- Super Regional Centers
- Community Centers
- Neighborhood Centers

INDUSTRIAL
- Warehouse/ Distribution
- Manufacturers
- Material Processing

RESIDENTIAL
- Single Family Detached
- Zero Lot Line
- Single Family Attached
- Manufactured Homes

AGRICULTURE
- Annual Crops
- Perennial Crops
- Livestock Grazing

Office Space Market

The office market is commonly divided into four subcategories: Class A, Class B, Class C, and Class D. The following distinctions are common:

- **Class A**—Buildings that will generate the highest rents per square foot due to their high-quality and/or superior location.
- **Class B**—Buildings that most tenants would find desirable, but lacking certain attributes that would permit owners to charge top dollar.
- **Class C**—Buildings that offer few amenities but are otherwise in physically acceptable condition and provide cost-effective space to tenants who are not particularly image-conscious.
- **Class D**—Buildings with few amenities and poor locations and/or physical condition.

Retail Space Market

Retail space is commonly divided into five subcategories: freestanding retail, neighborhood centers, community centers, regional centers, and superregional centers. These subcategories are generally defined as follows:

- **Freestanding retail**—single tenant buildings.

- **Neighborhood center**—sometimes called a *convenience center,* designed to serve a relatively small trade area (1.5-mile radius) with a population of between 2,500 and 40,000 people. Its anchor tenant (primary tenant) often is a supermarket, with other stores providing convenience goods and personal services (hardware, pharmacy, hair salon, etc.). These centers usually are built in strip style—that is, stores placed side-by-side in a straight line or an L-shape with a covered walkway along the front for pedestrians. The neighborhood center usually is separated from the street by a customer parking area.

- **Community center**—designed to serve a larger trade area than a neighborhood center (35-mile radius), it includes a wider variety of merchandise. Its anchor tenant is usually a discount store, or junior department store. When the anchor tenant is a discount store, the center is sometimes called a *Discount Center.* These centers are usually built in strip style with large customer parking areas in front.

- **Regional center**—designed to serve a primary trade area within a radius of 7 to 12 miles, these centers offer a full range of goods and services. Regional centers are usually designed as enclosed malls with at least one, and sometimes several, full-line department stores serving as the anchor tenants.

- **Superregional center**—designed to serve trade areas with a radius of more than 50 miles, these centers often exceed 1 million square feet of space and offer a tremendous range of products and services. One example of a superregional center is the Sawgrass Mills Mall in south Florida. This mall attracts customers from all over southern Florida and also from Latin America, the Caribbean, and parts of Europe. Billed as one of the world's most popular shopping destinations and Florida's largest retail and entertainment center, Sawgrass Mills Mall features almost 2 miles of enclosed shopping space with more than 400 name-brand stores, pushcarts and kiosks, more than 30 restaurants, several entertainment clubs, and more than 20 movie screens.

Industrial Space Market

Industrial space is commonly divided into three categories: warehouse, manufacturing/production, and materials processing.

Agricultural Space Market

Agricultural space (mostly land) is commonly divided into three categories: annual (seasonal) cropland, perennial cropland, and livestock facilities and grazing land.

Lodging Space Market

Lodging space can be divided into the following categories: highway motels, convention/business hotels, luxury hotels, resort (destination) hotels, and extended stay hotels/motels.

| **FIGURE 8.2** | Supply and Demand in a Real Estate Space Market |

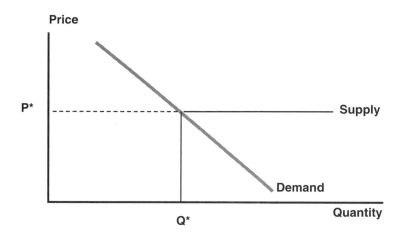

Residential Space Market

Residential space can be divided into single-family detached homes, single-family attached homes (condos, co-ops, townhouses, etc.), manufactured homes, and multifamily apartments.

Price Movements in Segmented Real Estate Space Markets

The basic supply and demand model from an introductory economics course can be quite useful in understanding price movements in real estate space markets, with only a few modifications. The demand function for real estate space looks very much like the demand function for most other goods and services, as shown in Figure 8.2. The demand curve is downward sloping, suggesting that the quantity demanded falls as prices increase. The supply function, however, has an unusual shape because real estate space is a long-lived item whose quantity cannot be reduced quickly in response to changes in demand. The supply curve is depicted as vertical at the current quantity of space in the market and approximately horizontal at all higher quantities. The vertical portion reflects the inability of suppliers to adjust the quantity of space in the market quickly. The horizontal portion reflects the notion that long-run marginal cost of developing new space does not vary as space increases. That is, the cost of constructing the next building is not affected by the amount of space already in existence in the market. Most space market segments around the United States have a long-run supply function that is nearly level, but there are some exceptions.

| FIGURE 8.3 | Impact of Demand Changes in a Real Estate Market |

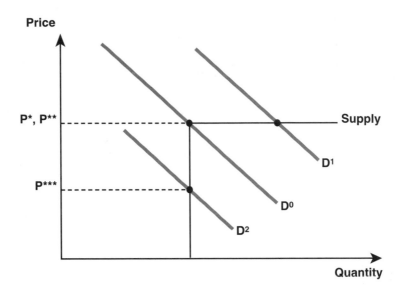

To use this framework to understand long-run price movements in a real estate space market, think of how an increase in demand would move the equilibrium price level from P^* to P^{**}. As shown in Figure 8.3, the model suggests that prices are largely unchanged by increases in demand because developers can simply build more space. Any short-run price increases will dissolve as more space becomes available in the market. On the other hand, the model indicates that decreases in demand will be met with rather dramatic price decreases (P^{***}). This makes sense when you consider the notion that few property owners would immediately tear down their buildings if demand decreased. Instead, we would expect the buildings to exhibit lower occupancy rates and lower rents (prices) until demand conditions improve.

Let's apply this framework to a unique, upscale housing market to see how the model explains current price trends and predicts future prices. Fort Lauderdale, Florida, is an internationally renowned tourist destination. Miles of sandy beaches along the Atlantic Ocean and perpetual sunshine make this city a favorite spot for beach lovers. In addition, much of the eastern portion of the city is criss-crossed by a series of ocean-accessible canals that connect to the Intracoastal Waterway and make it possible to dock oceangoing motor yachts and sailboats in the backyards of many single-family homes. For this reason, Fort Lauderdale is often called the "Venice of America."

REAL ESTATE TODAY

The Rockefeller Center Saga

Close-Up

Rockefeller Center is an almost legendary real estate development. Built during the worst of the Great Depression of the 1930s by John D. Rockefeller, Jr., it represented a great leap of faith even for one of the then most-wealthy individuals in the United States. This faith was amply rewarded, however, as Rockefeller Center became one of the most desired business addresses in New York City.

In 1989 the family sold 80 percent of Rockefeller Center to a Japanese company, Mitsubishi Estate Company, for $1.4 billion. Mitsubishi, which had been counting on significant rent increases when existing leases expired, received a rude shock when the real estate recession shortly thereafter instead caused rents to actually fall. In 1995, after absorbing a $1.3 billion loss, the bankrupt center was taken over by the mortgage holder, which then sold it to an investor group led by Tishman Speyer properties and Goldman Sachs for $1.2 billion.

Since much of the office space had been locked into long-term leases, the new owners realized that the opportunity for the upside in their purchase lay mostly in the chance to improve the return on the center's languishing retail space. Because Rockefeller Center is a designated historical landmark, it would be difficult to make any changes in its Art Deco exterior appearance. Instead, they planned to carve out several two-story anchor sites ranging from 12,000 to 50,000 square feet to be leased to high-profile American brand stores such as Nautica, Brooks Brothers, and Saks Fifth Avenue. On the strength of that presence, they expected to draw tenants for the smaller spaces at rents as high as $500 a square foot. If this plan succeeds, and it probably will have by the time you read this, then Rockefeller Center will become more of a commercial and tourist magnet than ever and also return to its former status as a resounding commercial success.

To apply the supply and demand model discussed above to the market for new, luxury homes on ocean-accessible lots in Fort Lauderdale, let's first consider the supply side of the market. The city's amenities have long been popular with wealthy retirees who were willing to pay top dollar to enjoy the Florida sun, and the city has experienced persistent population growth for most of the last 50 years. Thus, almost all ocean-accessible lots have an existing home on them, with ery few vacant lots available. The supply side consists of mostly older single-family homes that are smaller than the luxury homes of today's standards and are approaching the end of their useful lives (the houses, not the owners).

Because there are no new canals anticipated in this market, the long-run marginal cost of adding additional homes is upward sloping, reflecting the increasing cost of adding a new home to this market as the total number of luxury homes increases. The shape of this curve is distinctly different from the supply curve in most housing markets around the United States and we should explain it carefully to truly understand the price determination process in this market. Consider this: Unless the supply of land is constrained geographically, housing developers in most markets around the United States simply build their projects on the outer edges of the currently developed area on formerly vacant land (the suburbs). Where this strategy is dominant, the marginal cost (land cost) of building the next house is about the same as the marginal cost of building the previous house. In the Fort Lauderdale ocean-accessible home market, however, no new canals are feasible, thus constraining the number of ocean-accessible lots. Therefore, the cost of each new luxury home includes the cost of demolition of an existing home. As more and more luxury homes are built to replace the existing homes, the cost of building the next luxury home increases even more. Over the long run, this market has an upward-sloping supply curve beyond the current inventory because the amount of land with ocean access cannot be increased.

On the demand side of this market are full- and part-time residents who have high disposable income levels or significant wealth portfolios and wish to maintain a permanent residence or vacation home in the area. Many of these full- and part-time residents are quite willing to spend several million dollars for an existing older home that they will demolish and replace with an even more luxurious home where they can dock their multimillion-dollar motor yacht or sailboat in the backyard.

The City of Fort Lauderdale recognizes the importance of attracting these big spenders and works hard to maintain the "Venice of America" image with infrastructure improvements and international marketing campaigns. The price of luxury, ocean-accessible homes in this market depends, at least to some degree, on the success of the city's efforts to maintain this image. When the number of wealthy people (full- and part-time) increases, the demand for such homes increases. Given the shape of the supply curve, the price of such homes increases. As the value of the homes increases, the city's property tax base increases, enabling the city to spend even more money to attract more wealthy residents to the area (see Figure 8.4).

When the city's marketing efforts are not as persuasive, perhaps due to general wealth dissipation attributable to national or international economic declines, demand for luxury, ocean-accessible housing will fall. Given a vertical supply curve at the current inventory level, the prices of such housing would experience dramatic declines.

Between 1999 and 2002, the price of ocean-accessible homes in Fort Lauderdale skyrocketed, and the number of "teardowns" increased dramatically. Developers typically purchase two or three existing homes, tear down the structures, then combine the lots into one large lot and build a single luxury home on the combined parcels. As long as the demand continues to increase, we would expect continued price increases for homes in this market. Should demand start to decline, however, the price decrease may be rather dramatic.

■ REAL ESTATE ASSET MARKETS

Whereas the real estate space market reflects transactions involving the use of space, the **real estate asset market** reflects transactions involving cash-flow rights to real estate. The term *cash-flow rights* refers to the claims to the future cash

| FIGURE 8.4 | A Simple Model of Fort Lauderdale, Florida's Luxury, Ocean-Accessible Housing Market |

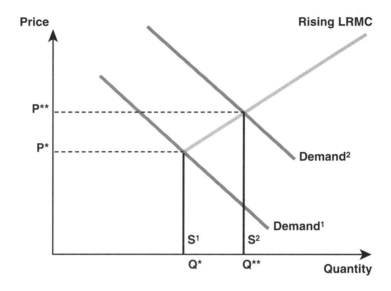

flows the buildings and land are expected to generate. The participants in this market are concerned with the amount and timing of the cash flows a building is capable of producing rather than the building's configuration for a particular use. These market participants make their decisions about buying and selling by comparing real estate assets with other capital market assets such as stocks and bonds. As such, the real estate asset market must be regarded as part of the larger **capital market,** the market for capital assets of all types.

To understand how real estate assets compete with other capital assets, consider the chart provided in Figure 8.5. This chart divides the capital asset market into four broad categories: publicly traded equity assets, publicly traded debt assets, privately traded equity assets, and privately traded debt assets.

Public markets transactions typically involve relatively small portions of ownership rights to various capital assets. The stock market is the most obvious example of a public market. Shares of corporations trade in huge volume on any given trading day, and observed prices reflect all currently available information about the assets.

Private markets involve transactions between individual buyers and sellers without the aid of a formal market mechanism. Private markets usually involve the sale of whole assets rather than shares of assets. Because such transactions happen less frequently than public market transactions and because the parties to

| FIGURE 8.5 | Major Types of Capital Asset Markets and Investment Products |

	Public Markets	Private Markets
Equity Assets	Stocks	Real Property
	REITs	Private Firms
	Mutual Funds	Oil and Gas Partnerships
Debt Assets	Bonds	Bank Loans
	MBS	Whole Mortgages
	Money Instruments	Venture Debt

the transaction may keep information private, it is generally more difficult for private market participants to determine the value of assets traded in these markets. Furthermore, the transaction costs of trading these assets are likely to be much higher than the costs of trading in the public markets.

The chart also divides the capital market into debt and equity categories. Debt assets can be thought of as rights to the future cash flows paid by a borrower on a loan. These cash flows are contractually specified according to the details of the loan agreement. As such, the debt holder is entitled to be paid before the borrower gets any cash flow from the underlying asset (the source of the cash flow). Debt assets typically have a specified maturity date.

Equity assets refer to assets that entitle their owners to the residual cash flow generated by an underlying asset (after the debt holders have been paid). Equity assets are more risky than debt assets, in general, because of their "second" priority behind debt assets. Of course, the riskier the asset, the higher the expected return.

Capital asset vehicles based on real estate as the underlying asset take a variety of forms. In the public equity market, shares of publicly traded real estate investment trusts (REITs, pronounced "reets") trade with a volume comparable to that of shares of industrial corporations. REITs raise money from the sale of shares to investors and then use the proceeds to acquire properties and mortgages. They then manage the portfolios to maximize the return to their shareholders.

In the public debt market, investors can purchase derivative products such as mortgage backed securities (MBSs), whose underlying assets are pools of mortgages on residential and commercial properties. As mortgage payments are made to the pool by borrowers, the money is distributed to the various investors according to the type of security they bought from the pool. In the private debt market, investors and institutions buy and sell mortgage loans that are secured by individual buildings.

Most people who think of the real estate asset market think about the private equity market that involves ownership of whole properties. The lack of complete information and infrequency of trades in the private equity real estate market make this market one of the most dynamic and interesting capital markets. Even so, the different categories of real estate asset markets are well integrated with each other and the markets for other capital assets. The prices of real estate assets in the private equity market reflect the integration of all capital markets and the competition between asset markets for investors' dollars.

Price Determinants in the Real Estate Assets Market

Real estate asset market prices are determined by three main factors: opportunity cost of capital, growth expectations, and risk. Investors make their buy/sell decisions about real estate assets by comparing the return they expect to get from real estate assets with alternative rates of return they could earn from other capital assets in the capital market. As the opportunity cost of capital goes down, investors are generally willing to put more money into real estate assets, thus driving up their prices.

Investors are also concerned with the likely amount of growth (or decline) they expect from a property's cash flow. The cash flow a property can generate is, of course, determined in the real estate space market, as we previously discussed. The higher the expected growth rate in the space market, the more money investors will be willing to pay for property in the asset market.

Finally, the third determinant of prices in the real estate asset market is risk. Investors will evaluate how certain (or uncertain) they feel about a property's future cash flows and will prefer to pay less for a property with higher risk. Paying lower prices allows the investor to have a higher expected return for a given level of risk.

■ TYING TOGETHER THE SPACE AND ASSET MARKETS

So far in this chapter we have discussed the distinctions real estate analysts make between the real estate space market and the real estate asset market. Now our task is to show how these markets are interrelated. Figure 8.6 shows a simple model of "the real estate system" in terms of the development industry, the real estate asset market, and the real estate space market.

In this visual model of the real estate system, activity in the space market, the asset market, and the development industry are simultaneously determined. Influenced primarily by local economic conditions, owners/users and landlords/tenants negotiate over price (rent) levels in the space market. When demand conditions warrant, the owner/users and landlords purchase additional properties from the development industry and make them part of the available supply. At the same time, landlords and the owner/users negotiate in the capital market with potential tenants/buyers who are attracted to real estate assets by attractive risk/return combinations relative to other assets in the national or even international capital market. Potential buyers who become owners then enter the space market as landlords or owner/users, thus completing the "system."

FIGURE 8.6   The Real Estate System

Visualizing the real estate system in this manner can help us see how the three major components of the real estate system (development, space market, asset market) are tied together. Relatively small changes in any one component may flow through the system to the other components and can cause dramatic impacts on them. A prudent real estate market participant is well advised to keep this visual image in mind, especially when analyzing a real estate deal that looks much too good to be true!

■ PREPARING A REAL ESTATE MARKET ANALYSIS

While all of the preceding theoretical discussion is crucial to the understanding of real estate markets, how can we apply these theories to real world situations? This section of the chapter describes how to prepare a structural analysis of a real estate market. By definition, a **market analysis** is an examination of the supply and demand sides of a real estate space market segment and the balance (equilibrium) between these two sides. The goal of market analysis is to assist real estate market participants in making effective real estate decisions. Market analysis can be used to answer such questions as the following:

■ How much rent should I charge tenants in this building?

■ How many new units should I build this year?

■ Where should I locate a new branch office for my business?

■ What type of building should I build on this site?

■ What are the growth prospects for this market segment?

Basic Inputs to Market Analysis

As identified by Geltner and Miller, in *Commerical Real Estate Investment Analysis,* the typical real estate market analysis focuses on a few carefully chosen variables that are designed to characterize the supply and demand sides of the market segment as well as the balance between these two sides. Five of the most common inputs to a real estate market analysis are

1. vacancy rate,

2. rent or price level,

3. quantity of new construction started,

4. quantity of new construction completed, and

5. absorption of new space.

We will consider each of these variables in turn.

Vacancy rate is the measure of the amount of unoccupied space as a percentage of the total amount of space in the market. For example, a community with 50 empty rental apartments and 1,500 total rental apartments has a vacancy rate of about 3.3 percent (50 ÷ 1,500). The vacancy rate is an indicator of the balance between the supply and demand sides of the market segment. The unit of measurement used in calculating vacancy rates varies by market segment. For apartments, the typical unit of measure is "number of units," as we just demonstrated. For commercial and industrial space, the typical unit of measure is "square feet of space."

Another important indicator of the balance between supply and demand in a market segment is the rent or price level. Changes in the market rent or market price of space indicates changes in the balance between supply and demand. In residential markets, rents are often expressed as monthly rents per dwelling unit. In commercial and industrial markets, the unit of measure is more commonly the annual rent per square foot of space.

Two good indicators of the supply side conditions of a real estate space market include construction starts and completions. In residential markets, these variables are measured by the number of new homes or apartments. In commercial and industrial markets, these variables are measured in square feet of space. Construction starts and completions indicate the amount of new supply "in the pipeline" and the amount of new supply "flowing out of the pipeline," respectively. In some markets, a thorough market analysis would also need to address the amount of space being demolished to make room for new construction and the renovation of existing space.

Finally, one of the best indicators of the demand side conditions of a real estate space market is **absorption. Gross absorption** refers to the total amount of new space that became occupied during a specified time period. **Net absorption** is defined as the net change in the amount of occupied space in the market segment during a specified time period.

Using Market Analysis to Look Forward

These five indicators of a space market give a good overview of the supply and demand conditions in a market and the direction of change for both the supply and demand. These five variables can be combined in some creative ways to develop a forecast for future market conditions. For example, many real estate market analysts use the concept of "months supply" to look into the future of a real estate space market. **Months supply** is calculated by the following formula:

$$\text{Months Supply} = \text{(Vacant Space} + \text{Space in Construction)/Net Absorption per Month}$$

The months supply indicator tells us how long it will take (in months) for all the vacant space in the market to be absorbed at the current rate of absorption. A housing developer, for example, can use this measure along with an estimate of the average time it takes to complete new units to determine whether the market can support another project. In a market that is absorbing 30 housing units per month and has 30 currently vacant units and 90 units under construction, the "months supply" is 4. If the developer's construction time is 2 months, it is likely that a new project will hit the market at a time when there is excess supply. The months supply indicator is a simple measure for looking forward in a real estate space market segment.

Professional Market Analysis Reports

Performing a thorough market analysis can be very expensive and time consuming and may require the skills of a professional market analyst. Numerous market research firms around the world offer their services to investors and consumers for a fee. Some of the big names in real estate market research include Torto Wheaton Research, Lasalle Investment Advisors, and RREEF Research. To formulate their market analysis reports, research firms examine the key "drivers" for each market segment. Examples of these drivers for various segments are described below:

- *Office:* employment in office occupations
- *Lodging:* air passenger volume, highway traffic counts, tourism receipts, number of visitors
- *Retail:* per capita income, aggregate income, wealth measures

- *Industrial:* manufacturing employment, transportation employment, shipping volume
- *Apartments:* population, household formation, local housing affordability, employment growth (blue and white collar)
- *Owner-occupied residential:* population, household formation, interest rates, employment growth, income growth

Combining the information on these key drivers with the previously described indicators allows these firms to predict future market conditions and identify investment opportunities for their clients.

Figure 8.7 shows an example of a Market Analysis Report prepared by Torto Wheaton Research, a major real estate consulting firm headed by two highly respected economists, Raymond Torto and William Wheaton. Their firm provides analysis reports for all major space market segments at the local and national level. Figure 8.7 is a page image from *Real Estate Outlook 2001,* published by Torto Wheaton Research, 2001. Figure 8.8 shows an exhibit from RREEF Research's publication *Strategic Outlook,* dated January 2001. Figure 8.9 is a graphic from RREEF Research's website that shows some of the major trends and issues in real estate markets around the United States as of December 2000.

■ CHAPTER REVIEW

- The notion that there is a single "real estate market" is inherently false. Instead, we can better understand real estate market dynamics if we identify two types of real estate markets: the real estate space market and the real estate asset market.
- The real estate space market is concerned with transactions that involve owners/users and landlords/tenants. This market is highly segmented along lines govered by use and location.
- Prices in the real estate space market are determined by the interaction of supply and demand. The demand curve is downward sloping, similar to the demand curve for other goods and services. The supply curve is vertical at the current inventory level and generally horizontal at quantities higher than the current inventory level.
- The shapes of the supply and demand curves suggest that long-run prices in the real estate space market are not very sensitive to demand increases but may be highly sensitive to demand decreases.
- The real estate asset market involves transactions regarding rights to the cash flows generated by real estate assets. Participants in this market are primarily concerned with cash-flow generating ability of a property rather than its configuration for a particular use.
- The real estate asset market is a component in the larger market for all capital assets.

FIGURE 8.7   The Multi-Housing Outlook

The Multi-Housing Outlook

With the economy moving into its tenth year of expansion, the outlook for the multi-housing market is quite promising. Multi-housing construction has recently begun to pick up, with demographic trends remaining quite favorable. The population age group of 18 to 25 years is increasing after many years of decline, as is the large baby boomer group aged 55 and over. Both provide demand for multi-housing. With pent-up demand already existing in many markets, these demographic trends are expected to sustain strong demand for new construction in many markets for several more years.

Nationally, the muti-housing market continues through the expansion phase of its cycle. Demand in 2001 is forecast to remain robust, despite the slowdown in national employment growth. Atlanta, Las Vegas, and Raleigh all have strong growth in employment, population, and personal income resulting in demand exceeding supply in 2001.

More than 310,000 units are projected to be delivered in 2001. While this is a higher completion rate than in 2000 (23,000 more units), the increase is not dramatic, and is still significantly less than the multi-housing building boom of the early 1970s.

The growth of demand relative to supply will increase real (inflation-adjusted) rents and decrease vacancy rates through 2001. Vacancy rates will decline to 7.0 percent in 2001. Rent growth will remain roughly 2 to 3 percent above the rate of inflation, and continue rising in real terms. Several markets with lower than average vacancy a year ago are expected to go even lower. San Francisco, Oakland, and San Jose will continue to see vacancies at 5 percent and lower. In turn, these markets, plus San Diego, Indianapolis, Orange County, and Salt Lake City, where vacancies are yet not as low, should expect to see rent growth between 5.5 percent and 7.5 percent per year through 2001.

The Multi-Housing Outlook
National Vacancy Rate (%)

Torta Wheaton Research

The Multi-Housing Market
National Rent Growth (%)

Torta Wheaton Research

- Prices in the real estate asset market are primarily determined by the opportunity cost of capital, growth expectations, and risk.

- The space and asset markets are tied together by the development industry. When participants in the asset market expect high returns from real estate assets relative to other capital assets, they will purchase new construction from the development industry. The new buildings become part of the available supply in the space market. Together, the real estate space market, the real estate asset market, and the development industry form a "real estate system."

| FIGURE 8.8 | Apartment Absorption, Construction and Vacancy |

U.S. Apartment Vacancy		Forecasted Vacancy Rates in 2001 in Select Metro Areas			
		Highest		Lowest	
YE 2001	**4.5%**	Orlando	9.3%	San Francisco	1.3%
YE 2000	**4.1%**	Houston	8.8%	Chicago	2.2%
3Q 2000	3.0%	West Palm Beach	8.7%	Oakland	2.2%
YE 1999	3.8%	Raleigh	8.6%	Los Angeles	2.4%
YE1998	3.9%	Indianapolis	7.5%	Philadelphia	2.7%
		Phoenix	7.5%	Sacramento	2.7%
		Tampa	7.5%	Washington, DC	2.7%

Forecast

■ KEY TERMS

absorption	market analysis	real estate asset market
capital market	months supply	real estate space market
gross absorption	net absorption	vacancy rate
market		

■ STUDY EXERCISES

1. Why is a portion of the supply curve in the real estate space market depicted as "vertical" at the current inventory level?

2. Why is the supply curve for most real estate space markets depicted as "horizontal" beyond the current inventory level?

3. If demand in the space market declines, what is the predicted impact on prices?

4. If demand in the space market increases, what is the predicted impact on prices in markets with increasing supply curves?

5. What are the three main determinants of prices in the real estate asset market?

6. If price levels in the space market increase significantly, will that entice investors to purchase more real estate in the asset market?

7. How will the asset market and the development industry respond to an increase in demand in a space market with a horizontal supply curve beyond the current inventory level?

FIGURE 8.9   "New Economy" Loses Momentum

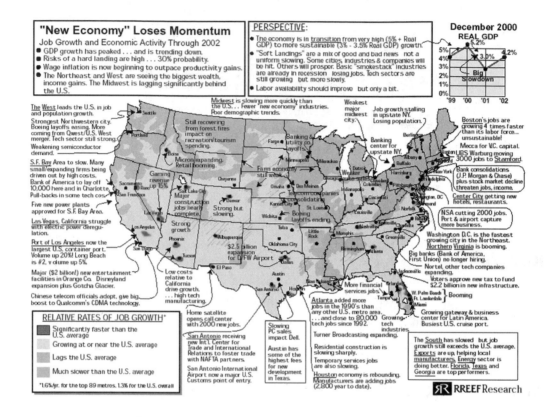

8. What are the three major components of the "real estate system"?

9. Define the terms *net absorption* and *gross absorption*.

10. Calculate the months supply of warehouse space in a market that absorbed 10,000 square feet last year, has 6,000 vacant square feet, and 3,000 square feet under construction. Would this be a good time to start a new warehouse project in this market? Why or why not?

11. Visit the website of a major real estate research firm and compare the multifamily apartment market in your community to the national multifamily apartment market. Does the outlook for this market segment in your community look brighter or dimmer than the national outlook? Why?

■ FURTHER READINGS

Geltner, David M. and Miller, Norman G. Commercial Real Estate Investment Analysis. Englewod Cliffs, N.J.: Prentice-Hall, 2001.

9 Urban and Regional Economics

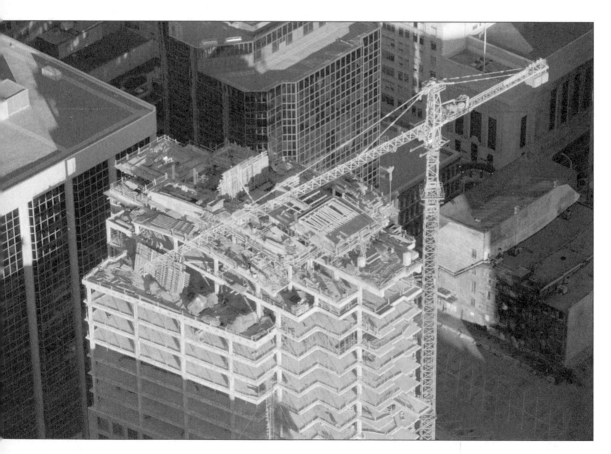

The shift of urban populations throughout a metropolitan area results in new commercial and residential construction projects.

CHAPTER PREVIEW

As we discussed in the previous chapter, the real estate space market is highly segmented because real estate space is "use and location specific." The discipline of studying real estate space markets at the urban and regional level is called *urban and regional economics.* In this chapter we consider some of the concepts and tools that urban and regional economists have developed for evaluating real estate space markets. These tools help explain how cities grow and change and how land uses and values vary within and among urban areas. Because real estate space markets are an integral component of the overall real estate system, the better we understand space market dynamics, the better we can understand the overall system.

The objectives of this chapter are to define various theories and concepts from the urban economics discipline, including

■ the concept of comparative advantage,

■ economic base theory,

■ the bid-rent curve and the concept of highest and best use,

■ the concentric circle model of urban form,

■ the sector growth model,

■ the axial growth model,

■ the multiple-nuclei growth model, and

■ the neighborhood life cycle model.

REAL ESTATE
TODAY
FEATURES

Close-Up
The Piedmont
Crescent of
North Carolina

Close-Up
A Tale of Two
Cities: The Effects
of Public
Expenditure on
the Development
of Boston and
Los Angeles

■ ECONOMIC FACTORS INFLUENCING THE GROWTH AND DECLINE OF CITIES

Why does one region or locality develop into a center of trade or industry while others do not? Why does the economy and population of a city or region grow or decline? What factors determine the economic growth rate of an area? The answers to these questions are closely linked to the concepts of comparative advantage and economic base.

Determinants of a Community's Comparative Advantage

Rapid economic and population growth generally results because one locale has a **comparative advantage** over another. This advantage may result from several factors. A city may grow because it has advantages in transportation facilities, advantages in the quality or quantity of other factors in the created environment, or because of natural resources, a favorable climate, or the quality or quantity of its labor force.

Transportation Facilities

Perhaps the most important factor that gives a community comparative advantage is transportation facilities. Almost all colonial cities in the United States developed around ports, either on natural harbors or along rivers. Most of the latter ports were located at important river junctions or at the fall line (the point at which the rivers cease to be navigable because their waters, descending from the uplands to the lowlands, form rapids and falls).

These initial natural advantages often were aided by further transportation improvements. For example, New York became the dominant port on the eastern seaboard and a world city largely because of the initial advantage it enjoyed after the completion of the Erie Canal in 1825, which provided easy access to the developing West.

Later, the advent of the railroad led to the "railroad town." A community located on a railroad enjoyed a distinct economic advantage over a town that was not, and communities at important rail junctions gained an even greater comparative advantage. The best example is Chicago, which developed into one of the nation's largest cities primarily because of its dominance as a rail center between East and West. Another example is discussed in the Closeup on page 175.

Because major highways have tended to follow the paths of major railroads, rail centers have also become highway centers. Similarly, many have become major air-traffic transfer points. Two of the busiest airports in the United States are those in Chicago and Atlanta, two cities that serve as transfer points, one between East and West and the other for the Southeast.

Educational Facilities

In today's technological and service-oriented economy, the quality of educational facilities is of great importance, both in providing centers for technological development and in increasing the educational quality of the labor force. These factors undoubtedly will become even more important in future years.

REAL ESTATE TODAY

The Piedmont Crescent of North Carolina

Access to improved transportation facilities was particularly important in the development of the Piedmont Crescent of North Carolina, an area that now contains nearly half of the state's urban population. Because there are no distinct geographic differences between the Crescent area and the remainder of the Piedmont, what caused this pattern of urban development?

Close-Up

Because North Carolina has a somewhat treacherous coastline, no major ports, and no rivers flowing from west to east, the state's Piedmont region was populated in colonial days largely by settlers who traveled overland along an Indian trading path. Several small towns, including Hillsborough, Salisbury, and Charlotte, grew up near Indian villages along the path. Other towns and villages sprang up in the region, but by the 1840s, the area still was very poor, its economy committed almost wholly to subsistence agriculture. Governor William A. Graham lamented the lack of adequate transportation:

> The man who is obliged to transport on wagons over no better roads than ours, a distance varying from 60 to 250 miles, at a speed of 25 miles per day,

can no more contend for profits with him who has the advantage of railroads or good navigation, than can the spinning wheel with the cotton mill.

Railroads had been built from the seaport of Wilmington to the small town of Weldon and from the state capital of Raleigh (located, like Washington, D.C., by a political decision) to connect with Virginia railroads. There was a great clamor for a railroad to aid development in the Piedmont, and the North Carolina Railroad Company finally was chartered by the legislature in 1849, funded with $3 million in state funds and $1 million of required private stock subscriptions. This last feature was introduced by legislators from eastern North Carolina in the hope that it would block the construction of the project, but it had some unforeseen consequences.

The charter had specified that the railroad would begin at a junction with the Wilmington & Weldon Railroad, near the present-day city of Goldsboro, and proceed westward to Raleigh, Salisbury, and Charlotte. It did not specify the route between Raleigh and Salisbury but simply stated it should be the "most practical."

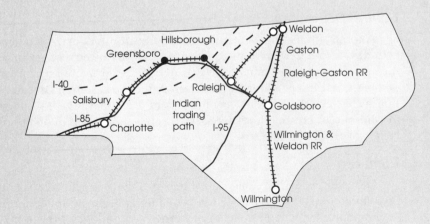

The Piedmont Crescent of North Carolina (continued)

Former governors John M. Morehead of Greensboro and William A. Graham of Hillsborough were convinced that the "most practical" route was by way of their own towns. They led a group that purchased most of the stock, hired a surveyor, and directed him to determine whether the longer route by way of Hillsborough and Greensboro, "all things considered, is not the most practical." To no one's surprise, he decided that it was, and the railroad was built along that somewhat circular path.

The railroad gave the Crescent an initial competitive advantage over the remainder of the Piedmont that it has retained to this day, even though railroads were extended to other portions of the Piedmont within a few years. Towns and cities

Close-Up

whose economies were based primarily on industrial development sprang up along the North Carolina Railroad. In the automobile era, the main highways were built in the same general locations, often alongside the railroad. Today, I-85 and I-40 traverse the same general path.

Because of its excellent access to transportation, Charlotte became a distribution center and one of the leading cities of the Southeast; Greensboro is the second largest city in the state and boasts a viable and diversified economy. Hillsborough, whose people had little desire to encourage growth, remains a rather sleepy but pleasant town of approximately 1,500 population.

Created Environment

The created environment consists of such things as utilities, public services and tax levels, housing, cultural activities, and transportation and educational facilities. The quality and quantity of such factors may give a region or community a comparative advantage or disadvantage. If a community has an industrial park, for instance, it may attract additional industrial employment. Conversely, an industrial firm will not locate where adequate utilities and other services are not available.

Natural Resources

Another important factor in the location of cities is the existence of various natural resources. Denver owes its origins to the discovery of gold and silver in the nearby mountains; ample deposits of coal and iron ore greatly aided the development of Birmingham and Pittsburgh. After the resources that led to its formation have been depleted or become less of a comparative advantage, and if it is to continue to prosper, a resource-based city must develop other advantages as a center of trade and industry.

Climate

Other cities and regions owe much of their comparative advantage to their favorable climate; for those whose economy is based on tourism, this factor may be dominant. Climate has been an extremely important factor in the development of cities in Florida and California and is cited as one of the major comparative advantages of the Sunbelt. As a greater percentage of the population reaches retirement age over the coming decades, the advantage of these communities as retirement locations will also rise in significance.

Labor Force

Another important factor that may give an area a comparative advantage is the quality or quantity of the labor force. For example, the textile industry, for the most part, deserted the cities of New England for those of the Southeast following World War II, largely because the Southeast offered an ample supply of labor that was willing to work for relatively low wages. Conversely, New England cities—particularly those in Massachusetts—were able to attract a substantial portion of the expanding electronics industry because their labor forces possessed a relatively high level of education and skill.

Leadership

An intangible but critical factor in community growth and in a community's becoming a quality place to live is community leadership. In fact, many feel this is *the* most important factor in regional and area growth and quality development. Some communities have many comparative advantages, but languish; others prosper, though they possess few natural advantages. The difference, in most cases, is the caliber of local leadership.

The Concept of an Economic Base

Specialization is both a fundamental economic concept and the primary reason for the existence of cities. In a developed economy, and even in most primitive societies, neither the individual nor the family nor the community can be wholly self-sufficient. Even solitary trappers occasionally must emerge from the wilds to sell pelts and purchase necessary supplies. Similarly, a community or region is not self-sufficient but must sell goods and services outside its borders to pay for the imports it needs.

The pelts Trapper Joe sells are "exports" for his economy, and the proceeds can be used to purchase needed supplies ("imports"). Similarly, a community tends to specialize in certain activities in which it has a comparative advantage and to sell those goods and services to the rest of the world. The income from those exports can be used to import goods and services from outside the community.

In examining local economies, analysts often classify employment into two general categories: (1) **export activities,** also called *basic activities,* which produce goods and services for sale or consumption outside the area's borders, and (2) **population-serving activities,** also called *nonbasic activities,* which produce goods and services for sale or consumption within the community itself. Although it is difficult to determine with any exactness which of a community's activities are for export, they usually include most of those in the fields of agriculture, mining, manufacturing, and wholesale trade.

The population-serving activities generally include those undertaken by the construction industry, public utilities, the retail trade, finance, service industries, and government. Sometimes, however, population-serving activities are also export in nature. A regional shopping center may draw customers from far beyond the local area, a city may serve as headquarters for financial institutions serving a large region, and a large university usually attracts students far from the local area.

If export activity in a region or city expands, so will employment in the population-serving industries. Suppose that Amalgamated Whitzadidle opens a new manufacturing plant in Lower Swampville that employs 500 workers. The economic impact of the new plant will go far beyond this direct employment increase. Construction workers will be needed to build the facility and homes and apartments for individuals and families who may move to the area. Purchases of various goods and services by the manufacturing workers will give rise to additional employment in the trade and service industries. The new residents also will be purchasing and financing homes and buying insurance, thereby creating new jobs in those fields. In the same fashion, the impact of the new plant will spread throughout the local economy so that the total employment and income created will be far greater than the direct impact.

In the past, many regional analysts, planners, and appraisers have tried to quantify the relationship between changes in employment in industries that bring income into a region from beyond its borders—that is, changes in the **economic base**—and changes in total employment, income, and population. Although the use of these models as precise, predictive tools generally has been discredited, the concept of an economic base is still valid. To understand the potential market for real property in a community, it is essential to understand the community's industrial structure and the probable changes that will occur. If the economic base is likely to expand, demand for real property also is likely to expand. Conversely, of course, if the economic base is expected to contract, the demand for real estate also is likely to contract.

■ THE LOCATION OF PEOPLE

Cities tend to develop in places that offer firms a comparative advantage, and exploitation of that advantage leads to growth of the economic base. People also tend to locate where they can achieve a comparative advantage, and although there are exceptions, most people live where they do because of economic opportunities. When jobs are plentiful, other factors come into play as well—personal preferences for a particular type of climate or landscape, big-city attractions or small-town tranquility, and closeness to or distance from relatives. When jobs become more scarce, such considerations tend to lose their force; people go where they can find work.

The growth of Social Security and other retirement benefits in recent years has created a large group of retirees who are relatively free to follow their locational preferences. This group has been a major factor in the population growth of such warm-weather states as Florida and Arizona. Most interstate migrants in this age group move for family or retirement reasons. Even in this age group, however, nearly 14 percent of the moves in a recent census study were made for reasons of employment.

It follows that demand for housing in a locality is very closely related to employment demand—that is, to the community's economic base. Indeed, most real estate activity occurs as a result of changes in the economic base. For example, industrial construction is a direct result of such changes. And indirectly—through increases in the demand for population-related activities—changes in the economic base lead to the development of shopping centers, construction of schools, and the like.

ANALYZING LOCAL REAL ESTATE DEMAND

How do these regional and community growth factors influence the local demand for real estate? The real estate analyst must have an understanding of both the current changes in the industrial structure of the community and the factors that might lead to economic changes that attract new people or cause residents to leave. Demand for existing properties is tied to the current industry mix and expected short-run changes. Long-term demand for existing properties and for new developments is related to the long-run vitality of the community's economy, which can be assessed only by an analysis of potential change.

Analysis of Short-Run Demand

In the previous chapter we saw that although completion of new construction may add to the supply of real property improvements, the supply is largely fixed in the short run. Changes in demand in the short run largely affect vacancy rates, sales of existing properties, prices, and lease rates.

The real estate analyst attempting to ascertain possible short-term changes in local real estate markets must ask the following questions:

- What is the current supply of various types of real estate improvements?
- What is the industrial structure of the community?
- What changes have occurred in the local economy in the recent past?
- What is likely to happen to the economy in the near future?

Suppose, for example, that a city's economy is heavily dependent on the automotive industry. A decrease in demand for automobiles would have an immediate impact on employment, which would lead in turn to a decrease in consumer spending. If these conditions persist, and particularly if a major firm closes its local manufacturing facility, then housing and other real estate markets would be quite adversely affected.

Analysis of Long-Run Demand

Suppose a potential investor is considering building a new resort facility in a community or that a developer is considering building a shopping center in a city whose dominant manufacturing employer has been forced to begin massive layoffs. In these situations, the prospects obviously would be poor in the short run. But the proposed improvements would not actually come onto the market for some time, and demand could then be quite different and favorable for the new project. In this situation, the analyst must examine additional questions:

■ What are the long-run prospects for the economy of the community?

■ What national or regional trends are likely to affect employment in the area?

■ Are new firms likely to locate in the area, bringing additional employment?

Projecting and forecasting future employment trends is an interesting exercise that often involves sophisticated modeling techniques. In the final analysis, however, the real estate investor must carefully evaluate the assumptions that lie behind population and employment projections. Sophisticated techniques are no substitute for informed judgment. While most of our discussion thus far has been targeted at how entire urban areas grow and change, the next several sections of this chapter examine land-use patterns within urban areas.

■ THE BID-RENT CURVE AND THE CONCEPT OF HIGHEST AND BEST USE

Why is a certain parcel of land used for a particular purpose? Why are certain parcels of land worth more than others? The answer to these questions lies in the concept of land rent. The classical economists included land as one of the three elements of production, land, labor, and capital, and rent is the return on or price of land. In theory, a particular parcel will be used in the way that yields the highest return to the owner. **Land rent** is the return that a particular parcel of land will bring in the open market.

Land rent, of course, differs from one parcel to another because the highest and best use of each parcel differs. By definition, *highest and best* use is that use of a parcel that will produce the highest return or price to the owner. Highest and best use is constrained by legal restrictions and the physical characteristics of the parcel. Over time, the highest and best use of a parcel of land may change, but the process by which one land use gives way to another is not rapid. Rather, the existing improvements will be converted to a new use over a period of time; the final conversion occurs only when the value of the land in an alternate use is great enough to pay for the site, the existing building, and its demolition.

To understand how location and use affect price, let's examine one of the classic concepts from the urban economic discipline: the **bid-rent curve.** *Bid-rent* refers to the maximum rent that a potential real estate space user would be willing to pay, or "bid," for a specified location.

| FIGURE 9.1 | Theoretical Price-Distance Relationships |

Consider a simple community that consists of three different types of space users: commercial, residential, and agricultural. Each of these potential users in this community space market has its own bid-rent function that can be expressed as the relationship between the price they would be willing to pay for locations as the distance from the center of the community increases.

Figure 9.1 shows the bid-rent functions for each of the three space users in our community. Notice that the commercial users are willing to pay the highest prices for locations closest to the center of the city. But the commercial users are not willing to pay any price for locations at distances greater than point A from the community center. Similarly, we see that residential users are willing to pay the second highest prices for locations at the center of the community, but not as much as the commercial users are willing to pay. At distances beyond the first vertical dashed line, however, the residential users are the high bidders for space. Beyond the second vertical dashed line, agricultural users are the high bidders. Looking at the "outer edge" of the curve formed by the combination of the three users' bid-rent functions gives the bid-rent curve for this community. We can see the land prices fall as distance from the city center increases, quickly at first, but more slowly as the distance increases more and more.

This model shows that each location has a highest and best use that is determined by its land rent. We will see this concept again in the appraisal chapter of this text.

■ MODELS OF URBAN GROWTH PATTERNS

A city may grow in several ways: vertically, by replacement of smaller structures with taller ones and by use of air rights to construct new buildings over existing ones; by **in-filling** of open spaces between existing structures; and horizontally, by extension of settled areas.

Of these forms of growth, the first two are applicable to already established urban areas, while the last describes the process of urban expansion. Several models have been used to explain these growth patterns, including the concentric-circle, axial, sector, and multiple-nuclei models of growth. Each model describes aspects of modern urban growth in simplified model form, and most observed growth patterns contain elements from several models.

Concentric-Circle Growth

One model of urban growth patterns resulted from the 1920s study of land uses by Ernest Burgess in Chicago.[1] The **concentric-circle model** postulates that from a central business district, several concentric zones radiate outward. (See Figure 9.2.) In this model, zone 2, immediately bordering the central business district, was one of transition, consisting primarily of slums occupied by recent immigrants, who remained there until they were financially and socially prepared to move to better quality residences farther from the center. The study found that this zone also contained widely contrasting development, including luxury apartment buildings, elegant restaurants, nightclubs, and theaters. Light-manufacturing facilities were located at its outer edge.

The next zone was occupied mostly by workers employed in the manufacturing activities located in zone 2. Most housing consisted of older single-family dwellings converted into multifamily use. The passage of older housing to less-affluent families as it ages is referred to as **filtering**, and it is an important element in neighborhood change.

Higher-income families who could afford better housing on larger lots occupied zone 4. This zone also contained specialized commercial activities serving the affluent group. Still farther out was the limit of the commuter zone,

---

[1] Ernest W. Burgess, "The Determinants of Gradients in the Growth of the City," *Publications of the America Sociological Society*, 21 (1927): 178–84.

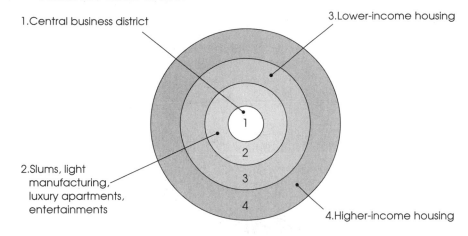

Concentric-Circle Growth

1.Central business district

3.Lower-income housing

2.Slums, light manufacturing, luxury apartments, entertainments

4.Higher-income housing

consisting of satellite cities and suburban developments. The area beyond was given over to agricultural activities.

The concentric-circle model basically follows rent-bid theory. Users who are able to pay higher rents are located closer to the center. When considering the realism of the concentric model, we must remember that it was developed in the 1920s, when the central business district was *the* business district because the automobile had not yet influenced the creation of alternate shopping nodes. The model is also more realistic when its assumption of uniform topography is dropped.

Rivers, lakes, mountains, and other geographic features may constrain growth or make it impossible in certain directions. For example, Chicago cannot grow to the east because of Lake Michigan; and the growth of Colorado Springs to the west is constrained by Pikes Peak. Growth in the San Francisco area has been southward, down the peninsula, and largely restricted to the east because of the coastal mountain range. Urban development in the East Bay area is constrained by San Francisco Bay on the west and the Diablo Range on the east. Similarly, the form of most other urban areas has been shaped by geographic features and barriers.

Axial Growth

Transportation is a critical factor not only in the location of cities but also in the way they develop. We know that cities are often located at transportation nodes—that is, at the junctions of major transportation routes. They may originate near ocean or river ports, at junctions of major railroads or highways, or where various modes of transportation interconnect. These cities have a competitive edge over communities that do not enjoy such transportation advantages.

| FIGURE 9.3 | Axial Growth |

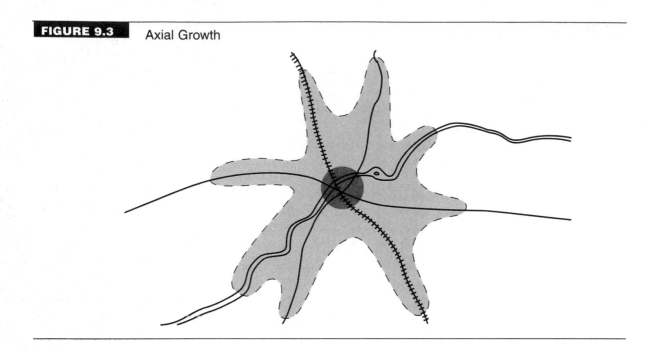

Similarly, land within an urban area that is well served by transportation facilities has a comparative advantage over land that is not. Thus, land tends to develop along major transportation routes. The result, according to the **axial model** of growth, is a star-shaped city with growth extending outward along transportation lines. (See Figure 9.3.)

The axial growth model was developed in the 1930s, before most workers had automobiles to commute to work and before trucks freed industrial facilities from dependence on railroads. These factors, plus the construction of major beltway highways, have reduced the impact of radial transportation routes on urbanization, but they are still an important factor in urban development.

Sector Growth

Extensive studies in the 1930's of residential neighborhood change also led to the development of the **sector model** theory of urban growth by a famous geographer and real estate investor named Homer Hoyt.[2] Hoyt found that particular types of development tended to extend in wedge-shaped sectors from the center

---

[2] Homer Hoyt, *The Sructure and Growth of Residential Neighborhoods in American Cities* (Washington, D.C.: 1939); "Structure of American Cities in the Post-War Era," *American Journal of Sociology,* 48, no. (1943): 475–92.

| FIGURE 9.4 | Sector Growth |

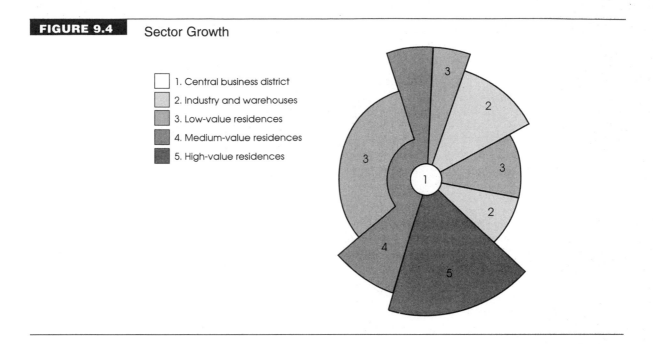

1. Central business district
2. Industry and warehouses
3. Low-value residences
4. Medium-value residences
5. High-value residences

of the city, as illustrated in Figure 9.4. For example, if expensive homes were first built in the western sector of a city, their development tended to continue outward in the same direction. The older houses in the sector would be occupied by successively lower-income groups through the filtering process and eventually might be converted into multifamily dwellings. Lower-income groups were not able to commute long distances and tended to live near their work. Thus, lower-income housing usually was located near manufacturing activities but also tended to develop in wedge-shaped patterns.

Most people's experience verifies the sector model. Consider your own hometown and how it has developed. While it won't follow the model precisely, you probably will be able to identify a number of sectors that conform to this model of urban growth.

Multiple-Nuclei Growth

The **multiple-nuclei model** of city growth takes the sector theory another step toward describing the actual growth process. It emphasizes that many commercial activities occur in clusters and that, in most cities, there is more than one center of commercial activity (see Figure 9.5). This theory of urban growth was formulated in the 1940s by researchers Harris and Ullman, after the automobile's impact on land-use dispersion had more fully developed.[3] This theory maintains that these clusters developed because (1) certain activities require specialized facilities, (2)

Multiple-Nuclei Growth

1. Shopping and offices
2. Industry and warehouses
3. Low-value residences
4. Medium-value residences
5. High-value residences

many similar activities benefit from close proximity to one another, (3) certain dissimilar activities are detrimental to each other, and (4) some activities must seek less desirable, lower-priced sites.

Many factors, particularly highway and communications improvement, have led to the further fragmentation of most cities' commercial activities in recent decades. Generally, the importance of the central business district has greatly declined with the growth of major suburban shopping centers and office parks. The development of such subcenters has led to a serious deterioration in the central business districts of many communities, and the question "What can we do to save downtown?" has occupied the attention of many planners and public officials.

Some downtowns, however, have experienced a revival recently as a result of concern with urban sprawl, a lessening of inner-city tensions and public policies designed to encourage such development.

---

3 Chauncey D. Harris and E. L. Ullman, "The Nature of Cities," *Annals of the American Academy of Political and Social Science,* 242 (1945); 12.

FIGURE 9.6   The Impact of Freeway Construction on Urban Development

■ THE IMPORTANCE OF PUBLIC FACILITIES IN THE GROWTH PROCESS

Investments in public facilities, often called **infrastructure,** play a critical role in the local development process. Transportation improvements figure prominently in the theories of urban form, but other public investments in such facilities as sewerage and water lines also are important in the local development process. Infrastructure development or the lack of it is often used as a policy tool to encourage or discourage growth. The effects of public investments in infrastructure are clearly seen in the development of Boston and Los Angeles, discussed in the Close-Up on pages 188-189.

Transportation Facilities

Until about 1870, urbanized areas were almost exclusively pedestrian cities, with commuting limited to the distance one could travel on foot or in a horse-drawn vehicle. The introduction of the streetcar and electric rail transit greatly extended commuting ranges during the next 50 years and led to axial-type development along the transit lines. The automobile era (which began around 1920), when cheap, mass-produced cars became available, expanded the size of the city even more. The automobile tended to bring more concentric-type growth, for it was not limited to a few axial routes. Freeways and other highways, however, did promote development along their routes.

Figure 9.6 illustrates the process of development that often occurs when a major freeway is constructed at the rural fringe of an urban area. In the first drawing, the land is used primarily for farming, but there are scattered residences and some minor commercial activity at one road junction. In the second stage, the highway is under construction, and developers have recognized the area's heightened potential. Much of the farming activity has ceased, and this land has been purchased for possible future development. In the third picture, intense development is occurring.

A Tale of Two Cities: The Effects of Public Expenditures on the Development of Boston and Los Angeles

Boston and Los Angeles offer the extremes of urban form in the United States. Boston's core dates back to the early colonial period; it later expanded along streetcar lines but remains an area of relatively high population density. Los Angeles developed in the interurban and automobile eras and has a relatively low population density.

Close-Up

Boston

In 1630, the Massachusetts Bay Company established a new town as capital of the colony of Massachusetts Bay on the Shawmut Peninsula, a hilly area barely connected to the mainland by a marshy, narrow neck of land. By 1722, when the map shown here was drawn, the city had a population of 15,000 and had become the center of trade for the New England area. Later, textile and footwear manufacturing became the dominant regional industries. In recent years, these activities have declined and been replaced by electronics firms and various types of service and finance activities.

The colonial city developed a medieval type of street pattern that still confounds drivers in the older section of town. As it grew, Boston expanded outward but also in-filled to create a tighter urban mass. Much of the in-filling required that the swampy areas be drained and filled to create more usable land. (See map below.)

By 1850, the city's population of 200,000 was located almost entirely within a two-mile radius of City Hall, that is, within pedestrian range. During the next 30 years, streetcars pulled by horses stretched out the existing city to an approximate four-mile radius. The 20-year period between 1880 and 1900 was a period of rapid growth in the Boston area. Electric street railroads extended the city dramatically, and subways also were developed. By 1990,

Miles
0   0.25   0.5
0   0.4   0.8
Kilometers

Boston Harbor

In-Filled Land

Charles River

In-Filled Land

In-Filled Land

Fort Point Channel

— Shoreline in Colonial Times

— Modern Streets of Colonial Vintage

— Modern Streets of Later Creation

— Water Bodies

REAL ESTATE TODAY

A Tale of Two Cities: The Effects of Public Expenditures on the Development of Boston and Los Angeles (continued)

the population of approximately 1 million stretched in a ten-mile radius from the center of town. Boston had developed into two distinct sections: an industrial, commercial, and communications center packed tightly against the port and an outer suburban ring of residential, commercial, and industrial subcenters.

Close-Up

During this century, commuter railroads, heavy-rail transit, and highways have extended the urbanized area almost to the semicircular I-495, approximately 25 miles from the old port. The 46 square miles contained in the city of Boston now constitute only 7 percent of the total urbanized area.

Los Angeles

Los Angeles was founded in 1781 by Spanish priests as part of their effort to colonize California. With water for irrigation available from the Los Angeles River, the settlement was to serve as an agricultural village (pueblo) to furnish food to other missions and fortified settlements (presidios). The community retained its primarily agricultural orientation for more than 100 years; by 1850, it had a population of only 1,600.

The next 30 years saw Los Angeles transformed from a Mexican pueblo to a U.S. town and trade center with a population exceeding 11,000. The transcontinental railroads reached the city in the 1880s, bringing thousands of migrants and an economic boom. Population totaled more than 50,000 in 1890 and 102,000 in 1900.

There are several reasons for the subsequent geographic expansion of Los Angeles as the city's population grew. Although ringed by mountains, the Los Angeles basin is essentially flat, with few natural barriers to expansion. The Los Angeles River provided an adequate source of water for the early settlement, but by the turn of the century it proved inadequate, and an aqueduct was built to the Owens Valley, 250 miles to the north. The availability of this water enabled the city to grow from 107 square miles to 440 square miles within the next 15 years.

More recently, southern California has tapped the Colorado River and the northern California area for water to serve its burgeoning population.

The city's period of rapid population growth following the arrival of the steam railroads coincided with the beginning of the trolley age. The first interurban line was built to Pasadena in 1895, and over the next two decades, the Pacific Electric Railway Company built a system of more than 1,000 miles of track that covered the entire basin. The Big Red Cars made it possible to commute long distances and helped create a metropolis of numerous communities and single-family detached homes. New lines, sometimes subsidized by land developers or by the development activities of the transit company, were often built in advance of population—a classic example of axial growth.

The process of population dispersion was furthered by the automobile. The number of automobiles registered in the Los Angeles area mushroomed from fewer than 20,000 in 1910 to more than 800,000 in 1930. In the 1940s, freeways began to replace the interurban railroads, and by 1965, the transit system had been abandoned completely. The freeway system soon grew to more than 600 miles of roadway, and the Los Angeles urban area population totaled more than 8 million.

Los Angeles sometimes is described as a collection of suburbs in search of a city, and one observer commented, "There's no there there." Fear of earthquakes restricted building heights to 150 feet until 1957 (the only exception was the City Hall), but in recent years, a "there" has developed in the central city, which serves as a center of finance and commerce. Population densities also are increasing, with much of the recent residential construction consisting of multifamily dwellings. Los Angeles has also begun a new transit system, but it remains to be seen whether it can be successful in a city with such low population densities.

FIGURE 9.7	Location of Major Shopping Centers in Atlanta and Houston

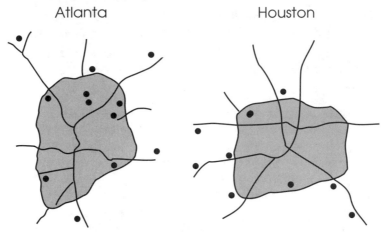

In addition to several subdivisions, commercial strips have formed along the road near the freeway interchange. Some apartments have been constructed, and still another tract awaits development.

The beltways constructed around many large cities as part of the interstate highway program have also had a great effect on urban form. Beltways have reduced the star-shaped growth tendencies of their cities, making many areas more accessible, and have encouraged large amounts of residential and industrial development. They have also served as the sites of many shopping malls and office parks, thereby furthering the development of multiple nuclei and greatly weakening the importance of the central business district. Figure 9.7 shows the influence of freeways and beltways on the development of major shopping centers in Atlanta and Houston.

Water and Sewer Facilities

Water and sewer facilities are not glamorous, but they are essential to urban growth. Even in areas that have ample water, access to a municipal water system is still necessary for any type of concentrated growth. In the more arid regions, where wells are often impractical, almost any type of urban development is impossible without access to a municipal water system. Similarly, if soil and other conditions are adequate, it may be possible to serve low-density developments with septic tanks, but public sewerage is essential to high-density developments. The growth potential of a particular parcel can be influenced dramatically by its access to such facilities.

Figure 9.8 shows how the construction of a major sewer line can enhance the development potential of a particular site. The first drawing shows scattered

FIGURE 9.8   The Impact of a Major Sewer Line on Urban Development

residences along rural roads in the watershed of a creek at the edge of an urban region. The building of the sewerage system paralleling the stream enables subdivisions to be built within this area. Because there are no sewers in the adjoining areas, intensive development cannot occur there.

URBAN FORM: A SYNTHESIS

The development of urban form may, at first, appear of interest only to city planners and public officials. To the contrary, the real estate investor or analyst must understand the factors that direct city growth in order to assess the potential development of a certain piece of real estate. The various theorics of urban growth describe particular aspects of the growth process. Let us synthesize and summarize some of the critical growth factors so we can better understand the impact of potential urban change on the economics of the individual parcel.

Commercial Growth

Because access is so important to commercial developments, major commercial projects such as regional shopping centers are usually located near freeway interchange nodes or other major road junctions. Smaller commercial developments are also dependent on transportation access and the customer traffic it brings; therefore, they usually are located along heavily traveled roads and streets.

Because of improvements in transportation, particularly the development of the automobile and the attendant growth of highways, cities have spread out, and many commercial subcenters have been created. As a result, the central business district has declined in importance and, in many communities, has become a blighted area. Office buildings have also been moving from the central city to outlying subcenters, often in suburban office parks.

Industrial Growth

Like commercial development, industrial growth has tended to move away from the central city to the suburbs or to rural areas. Most small and medium-sized plants, along with warehousing and other distribution facilities, are often found in industrial parks where transportation and other necessary public facilities are available. Major manufacturing facilities often locate in more rural areas, where land for expansion is more readily available but major highways or railroads provide accessible transportation.

Residential Growth

Residential development is also strongly influenced by the location of public facilities. High-density development is impossible without the provision of public water and sewerage facilities. Commuting access is important, but individuals have demonstrated that they will endure long commutes to enjoy a suburban or rural lifestyle and to escape some of the central city problems. In addition, the dispersion of employment to suburban locations in recent years has also encouraged the dispersion of residential development to these areas.

■ THE DYNAMICS OF NEIGHBORHOOD CHANGE

Thus far, we have seen that the value of individual parcels of real estate depends, to a large extent, on national changes in demand, regional and community growth, and urban growth patterns. The final factor that influences property values is neighborhood change.

What Is a Neighborhood?

Location is perhaps the most important single factor in determining the value of real property. The selling prices of identical houses built in different locations within an urban area almost always vary with the character of the surrounding neighborhood.

A **neighborhood** can be defined in several ways: as an area in which types of property are similar; as a distinct geographic area or one distinguished by a conspicuous physical feature; as a social unit—that is, a community with religious or ethnic ties; and as a group of people with the same general level of income. All these factors work to create housing submarkets in which the values of properties are influenced by the same general set of outside influences.

Neighborhood Change

As do humans, neighborhoods go through a life cycle consisting of several stages: (1) gestation, (2) youth, (3) maturity, (4) incipient decline, (5) clear decline, (6) accelerating decline, and (7) death or abandonment. Unlike the human situation, however, the process of change in neighborhoods is not inevitable. It can be arrested or reversed, and a declining neighborhood can be restored to vigorous health.

Gestation, Youth, and Maturity

In the early stages of a neighborhood's life cycle, both property values and residents' incomes generally are rising. Turnover usually is relatively low, and new residents are economically and socially similar to those already living in the neighborhood.

Incipient Decline

At some point in the process of neighborhood change, those who leave the neighborhood are replaced by less affluent families and individuals, and over time, the housing may filter down to still less affluent groups. In this stage of the life cycle, housing prices and rentals decline as more affluent families leave the neighborhood.

The process of decline may be caused by several factors. The houses simply may have reached an age where the costs of maintenance are greater than the residents can afford. There may be outside influences, such as construction of a new freeway, which make living conditions in the area less desirable and competing areas more accessible. The decline of the neighborhood may be caused by various changes in the socioeconomic characteristics of its residents or by their aging and death. Likewise, construction of more desirable dwellings in other neighborhoods may lead to a drop in demand for property in a certain area.

Clear Decline

As the housing in a neighborhood ceases to provide a reasonable return to the owners and becomes substandard by most definitions, the neighborhood enters a period of clear decline. Owners make only minimal repairs, and properties deteriorate noticeably. Financial institutions may avoid investing in the area, making rehabilitation and the introduction of new owners even more difficult. As owners try to squeeze additional income from their declining investments, housing densities and the consequent need for public services increase dramatically, though those services (schools, police protection, sanitation) may not be provided.

Accelerating Decline and Abandonment

The demise of a neighborhood often occurs quickly. Those who are able to move elsewhere do so. Only the lowest-income residents remain, and unemployment rates and the percentage of families on welfare are high. Landlords cease making repairs and often abandon their buildings when they are no longer profitable. At the terminal stage, the neighborhood may be virtually abandoned—as are portions of the South Bronx in New York City—or the buildings may be demolished, allowing the neighborhood to enter a new cycle.

Neighborhood Stabilization and Rehabilitation

It must be emphasized that the process of neighborhood deterioration and decline is not inevitable. Values in many mature neighborhoods remain strong over long periods of time if the area remains competitive in housing markets. Other neighborhoods may, as a result of a conscious public policy effort or natural market forces, reverse their decline and become healthy once again.

The first people who attempt to renovate deteriorated dwellings usually are young, middle-income individuals or families who desire to live in town; cannot afford housing in the established, higher-income neighborhoods; and are willing to spend the time and effort to rebuild the dwellings and social fabric of the declining neighborhood. If the process is successful, values may rise dramatically as the neighborhood becomes a desirable location for middle- or upper-income groups. This process is known as **gentrification.**

A negative aspect is the displacement of low-income families, who often can no longer afford to live in their neighborhood.

■ CHAPTER REVIEW

- ■ The reason why one locality rather than another will develop into a center of trade or industry is because that community enjoys a comparative advantage, which can result from transportation facilities or other factors of the created environment, natural resources, climate, or the quality and quantity of the local labor force.

- ■ A community's export activity produces goods and services for sale outside its borders. Population-serving activities produce goods and services sold within the community itself.

- ■ Almost all real estate market activity and development depends directly or indirectly on the location of people, and the location of people depends largely on the location of employment.

- ■ Because the supply of real estate is largely fixed in the short run, changes in demand largely affect vacancy rates, sales of existing property, prices, and lease rates. Over the long run, the supply can, of course, be increased, and the potential investor in a new development must carefully analyze the long-run prospects for the community's economic base.

- ■ Nothing is more essential to the determination of real estate values than the process of community development and neighborhood change.

- ■ A city may grow in several ways: (1) vertically, by replacement of smaller structures with taller ones and by use of air rights to construct new buildings over existing ones; (2) by in-filling of open spaces between existing structures; and (3) by extension of settled areas.

- Some models that have been used to explain the peripheral growth patterns of urban areas are (a) concentric-circle growth, (b) axial growth, (c) sector growth, and (d) multiple-nuclei growth.

- Investments in public facilities, often called the *infrastructure,* play a critical role in local development. The infrastructure includes transportation improvements, sewer systems, and water lines.

- Because access is so important, major commercial growth tends to occur near transportation nodes, such as freeway interchanges and junctions of other major roads.

- Industrial growth tends to occur along major highways, railroads, or both.

- A neighborhood can be defined in several ways: (1) as an area in which types of property are similar; (2) as a distinct geographic area or one that is distinguished by a conspicuous physical feature; (3) as a social unit—that is, as a community with religious or ethnic ties; and (4) as a group of people with the same general level of income.

- Neighborhoods tend to go through a life cycle, from gestation to maturity to decline, but this process can be arrested or reversed, and a declining neighborhood may be restored to economic health.

■ KEY TERMS

axial model	filtering	multiple-nuclei model
bid-rent curve	gentrification	neighborhood
comparative advantage	in-filling	population-serving
concentric-circle model	infrastructure	activities
economic base	land rent	sector model
export activities		

■ STUDY EXERCISES

1. What is meant by the concept of comparative advantage?
2. What are some of the factors that may give a community a comparative advantage in attracting new employment?
3. Why do people locate where they do?
4. Discuss the concept of an economic base. What are export activities, and what are population-serving activities?
5. How do local real estate markets react to changes in short-run demand? To changes in long-run demand?

6. What steps might a community take when faced with declining industry or a plant that closes?

7. Discuss the concept of land rent, and explain how it tends to allocate land resources.

8. Why would we not expect to find someone growing corn on a lot in Midtown Manhattan in New York City?

9. Discuss some of the models that have been used to explain growth patterns in urban areas.

10. What is meant by *infrastructure?*

11. Suppose a new freeway is completed in a relatively undeveloped suburban area. What would be some of the probable developmental impacts?

12. A new interceptor sewerage line is completed in an area that previously could be served only by septic tanks. How would this likely change residential development?

13. Discuss how improvements in public facilities influence the local development process.

14. Why have American cities tended to develop in a more multinucleated form during the past several decades?

15. Where does major commercial growth tend to occur within a community?

16. Where does industrial growth tend to occur within a community?

17. Describe the life cycle of neighborhoods.

 Go to the Student Study Guide CD-ROM and work through Case 3.

PART THREE

Real Estate
Service Industries

10 Real Estate Brokerage

Online search tools, such as this one at Realtor.com, are changing the way real estate brokerage firms operate.

CHAPTER PREVIEW

Real estate brokers are trained specialists who assist individuals, firms, and other entities in their real estate transactions for compensation. A real estate broker's specialized knowledge is extremely valuable to those who purchase and sell real property infrequently and may not be familiar with the complexities of real estate transactions. To ensure that those who call themselves real estate brokers are competent to perform the task, each state has adopted professional licensing laws that regulate the real estate brokerage profession.

The objective of this chapter is to describe the typical real estate sales process, then consider numerous aspects of the real estate brokerage business, including

■ the difference between real estate brokers and salespersons;

■ state licensing and regulation of brokers and salespersons;

■ the legal nature of agency relationships;

■ the role of real estate brokers in real estate transactions;

■ types of listing agreements, namely the (1) open listing, (2) exclusive-agency listing, (3) exclusive-right-to-sell listing, and (4) net listing;

■ the buyer representation agreement;

■ duties and rights of brokers, sellers, and buyers;

■ termination of agency relationships;

■ types of real estate brokerage firms and their characteristics; and

■ issues relating to broker and salesperson compensation.

REAL ESTATE TODAY FEATURES

Close-Up
Marketing Real Estate on the World Wide Web

Legal Highlight
The Seller's Agent's Obligations to the Buyer

Legal Highlight
Enforcement of Fair Housing Laws

■ THE REAL ESTATE SALES PROCESS

When a property owner decides to sell a property or a potential buyer decides to purchase one, real estate brokers can often provide useful assistance. The primary functions of the real estate brokerage industry are to match properties and customers and guide the buyer and seller through the complexities of real estate transactions. Both buyers and sellers of real estate need to understand the sales process, which typically involves the following steps: (1) listing, (2) marketing the property and qualifying buyers, (3) presentation and negotiations, (4) contracts, and (5) settlement or closing.

Listing Agreement

The listing agreement is the contract that defines the relationship between the property owner and the real estate broker. This agreement authorizes the broker to begin searching for a buyer for the specified property. Perhaps the most critical point in the listing agreement is the determination of an offering (or listing) price. Most sellers do not have adequate market information to determine the value of their property. If the offering price is priced too high, the property probably will not sell within a reasonable period of time, if at all; if it is too low, the owners will not receive as much as they should. In addition to specifying the offering price, the listing agreement usually defines the amount of compensation due to the broker for finding a buyer, how long the broker has to search for a buyer before the relationship ends, and any other details of the relationship between the property owner and the broker.

Marketing the Property and Qualifying Buyers

With the listing agreement in place, the broker will then begin marketing the property to potential buyers. Marketing techniques include a "for sale" sign on the lawn, newspaper advertisements, special television advertisements, open houses, and even a "home page" on the World Wide Web (see the Real Estate Today Feature on page 201). As responses to these advertisements are received, the broker will then deal with potential prospects directly.

In the process of searching for a buyer, the broker provides an important service for the seller: separating true prospects from casual shoppers or those who really do not have adequate financial resources to buy the property. For example, a couple earning $30,000 a year and having little available equity may be quite ready and willing to buy a $175,000 house, but they probably will be unable to pay for it. The process of examining buyers' ability to purchase the property is known as *qualifying the buyer.* Mortgage lenders also use this phrase when they determine a borrower's creditworthiness.

REAL ESTATE TODAY

Marketing Real Estate on the World Wide Web

Close-Up

The World Wide Web has proven itself to be a valuable resource for the real estate industry. A search on the words *real estate* using any of the popular search engines (Infoseek, Lycos, etc.) or a web browser such as Netscape will result in thousands of websites to explore. Many of these sites allow real estate brokers from across the country and around the world to use the web to market all types of properties. Potential homebuyers, apartment renters, and investors can use the web to search for the properties that match their criteria, then view photographs of the properties or take a virtual tour of the property. These sites also make it simple to contact the listing broker via electronic mail.

One popular site with an emphasis on "residential property is located at http://www.america-homes.com/. This address will take you to the home page of the World-Wide Real Estate Network. This site permits licensed real estate brokers to include their current listings in the database, complete with photographs and a text-based description of the home. Potential buyers can search the database for their dream home by browsing the listings or by specifying the features they desire in a home. If a particular home catches your eye, a click of the mouse sends an electronic mail request for the listing broker to provide you with more information. The World Wide Web has become an important marketing tool for real estate brokers and a great time-saver for potential buyers.

Presentation and Negotiations

After the broker has found a qualified and interested buyer, a period of presentation and negotiation begins. This period can last for a few hours or many months, depending on such factors as the complexity of the transaction, the extent to which the property actually meets the potential buyer's perceived needs, and, of course, price. The buyer should remember that in these negotiations the broker generally is employed by the seller and is obligated to represent the seller's interests. Accordingly, in any complicated transaction, buyers may want to employ the services of a broker to represent their interests.

Contracts and Closing

If the parties agree, a contract that spells out the details of the agreement is drawn up and signed by both seller and buyer, a process discussed in a previous chapter. Though the broker cannot provide legal advice unless he or she is a licensed attorney, the broker can assist the parties in negotiating an agreement and committing that agreement to paper. After insurance is obtained, financing is arranged, and the deed and other necessary legal papers are prepared, the transaction can be closed. At the closing, or settlement of the transaction, ownership is formally transferred to the buyer. Real estate closings were discussed in a previous chapter. With this general discussion of the real estate sales process in mind, we now turn our attention to more specific aspects of the real estate brokerage business.

■ REAL ESTATE BROKERS AND SALESPERSONS

In general terms, a **broker** is an intermediary who brings together buyers and sellers, assists in negotiating agreements between them, executes their orders and receives a **commission** (or brokerage) in compensation for services rendered. The broker does not take ownership of the item being transferred from seller to buyer but merely negotiates a transaction between the parties to the transaction. A **real estate broker** is a specialized type of broker—an intermediary licensed by the state in which he or she operates—who arranges real estate sale or lease transactions for a fee or commission. A real estate salesperson is also a broker in the general sense but, under the laws of the state, is authorized to act only under the direction of a licensed real estate broker. In other words, salespersons can carry out only those responsibilities assigned to them by their supervising broker.

■ LICENSING OF SALESPEOPLE AND BROKERS

Although you need not hold a real estate license to conduct real estate transactions on your own behalf, a license is required if you engage in real estate activities on behalf of someone else. The license and educational requirements imposed by states generally do not constitute serious obstacles to most people who want to enter the field, and the number of brokers and salespersons in the industry tends to expand or contract with swings in demand for real estate.

All states and the District of Columbia require that real estate salespeople and brokers obtain a license. The license requirements vary from state to state and also depend on whether the applicant wishes to become a salesperson or a broker. Typically, an applicant for a salesperson's license must have completed high school and a basic real estate course. The most common educational requirement is a 40-hour classroom course or the college equivalent. In addition, the applicant must pass a written test given by the state real estate commission. The prospective salesperson usually needs no previous experience if educational requirements have been satisfactorily met. To obtain a brokerage license, however, the applicant usually must work for several years as a licensed salesperson, complete additional real estate educational courses, and pass a more comprehensive written test.

About half of the states now have continuing education requirements for both salespeople and brokers. The intent of these requirements is to ensure that those involved in real estate brokerage keep abreast of current developments in the field. Successful completion of the required course is a prerequisite for license renewal.

Because real estate licensing laws and regulations change from time to time, readers interested in obtaining a real estate license should contact their local realty board or state real estate commission for full details on current licensing requirements.

■ REAL ESTATE BROKERAGE REGULATION

In addition to licensing salespeople and brokers, the state real estate commission or a similar body is responsible for ensuring that licensees obey laws designed to protect the public from unscrupulous business practices. These include misrepresentation, fraud, and failure to comply with fair housing laws. If the commission finds a licensee guilty of an infraction, it may revoke or suspend that person's license or invoke similar penalties.

In more severe cases, a legal judgment may be brought through a lawsuit by the injured party against a licensee or firm. Because these judgments sometimes are uncollectible due to the defendant's poor financial status, roughly 40 states either require that real estate brokers be bonded or, more commonly, maintain a state-sponsored recovery fund. A portion of each real estate license fee goes into the recovery fund, available to pay uncollectible judgments against licensees.

■ LEGAL ASPECTS OF THE BROKER-CLIENT RELATIONSHIP

Because people have neither the time nor the knowledge to accomplish everything they want or need to do, they hire other people to assist them. This certainly is true in real estate transactions, where a specialized knowledge of markets, law, and financing is vital to the success of the transaction.

The law recognizes the relationship between an employer and an employee as that of principal and agent. The **principal** (employer) is the person who authorizes the **agent** (employee) to act on his or her behalf. The agent is a **fiduciary** of the principal, which means the agent is in a position of confidence and must perform his or her duties in the best interest of the principal. In addition to fair dealings, the principal owes the agent compensation for services, and the agent owes the principal the duties of good faith, diligence, and loyalty.

The legal relationship known as **agency** is applicable to real estate transactions in several ways. First, a seller of real estate may authorize a broker to help locate a buyer. Second, a potential buyer may engage the services of a broker to search for available properties. Third, many brokers hire salespersons to assist in locating buyers and properties. These three relationships are created from written or oral contracts. In each case, one party is the principal, and the other is the agent. The broker is the agent in the relationship with the client (either seller or buyer), and the broker is the principal in the relationship with a salesperson. The salesperson is an agent of the broker and a **subagent** of the broker's principal.

■ THE ROLE OF REAL ESTATE BROKERS

Real estate brokers and salespersons play an important role in many real estate transactions. Traditionally, real estate brokers have been hired by property owners to help locate buyers for their property. The broker's role is to advertise and market the property and assist the seller in finalizing the transaction once a buyer is found. In this situation, the broker is an agent of the seller. Brokers may also represent property owners who wish to lease their properties to tenants. Property management and leasing are discussed in Chapter 12.

Many real estate transactions involve more than one broker. Frequently, one broker (called the **listing broker**) obtains a listing agreement with the property owner, while another broker (called the **selling broker**) actually locates a buyer. The selling broker in such a transaction may represent either the buyer or the seller. If the selling broker represents the seller, he or she is an agent (subagent) of the seller. If the selling broker represents the buyer, the broker is an agent of the buyer.

Increasingly, potential buyers are hiring brokers to assist them in locating a property for purchase. As a buyer's agent, the broker's role is to identify properties that meet the buyer's specifications, then assist the buyer in negotiating a transaction for the desired property.

In some cases, a single broker is employed by both the seller and the buyer to assist in the completion of a transaction. When this broker has fiduciary duties to both parties simultaneously, the broker is known as a **dual agent.** Many states recognize the problems inherent in this type of agency relationship and have declared it illegal for a broker to attempt to work as a dual agent. To overcome this situation, some states recognize that brokers may act as a **transaction broker** in the negotiations between the buyer and seller to help them close their deal.

Most states' laws require that the broker disclose the nature of his or her agency relationship to all parties involved in the negotiations prior to entering into meaningful negotiations to avoid confusion and possible violations of the fiduciary responsibilities. The next section examines the creation of agency relationships between (1) sellers and brokers and (2) buyers and brokers.

■ THE CREATION OF AGENCY RELATIONSHIPS

Before a principal is bound by the acts of an agent, the agent must have actual or apparent authority to transact business on the principal's behalf. In other words, there must be evidence that the principal has authorized the agent to perform in some capacity on behalf of the principal. Real estate brokers can act as agents for either sellers or buyers because a broker may be employed by either. Listing agreements refer to the agreement between the seller and the broker when the broker is a **seller's agent.** Buyer representation agreements define the agency relationship between the buyer and the broker when the broker is a **buyer's agent.** We will examine each of these agency relationships in turn.

The Broker-Seller Relationship (Seller's Agent)

Property owners generally give real estate brokers authority to sell their property using a written document called a **listing agreement.** Because listing agreements are contractual in nature, the essential elements of a binding contract must be present. These elements are discussed more fully in Chapter 6. Only about 20 states actually require listing agreements to be in writing, but as in any transaction, a written contract always is preferable to an oral agreement to clarify the relationship established and the duties owed.

A listing agreement describes the property and states the asking price, the duties of the broker, the extent of authority granted, the duration of the agreement, and the rights of the broker to a commission. There are various forms of listing agreements and each has its own legal impact. The more common types of agreements are the open listing, the exclusive-agency listing, and the exclusive-right-to-sell listing. These listing agreements create certain obligations between the broker and the seller, and the extent of the obligation depends on the type of agreement.

Suppose, for example, that Harold and Gladys Stewart are being transferred and want to sell their home in St. Joseph, Missouri. They have decided to hire the Smith & Smyth Realty Company to assist them in this sale. The following paragraphs outline how the various types of listing agreements would affect the terms of this agency relationship.

Open Listing

If the Stewarts sign the document that appears in Figure 10.1, they grant an **open listing** to the Smith & Smyth Realty Company. Such a listing begins with a paragraph identifying the parties to the agreement and their relationship as owner and broker. Section I describes the property to be sold. The description must be precise enough to precisely identify the property involved. Section II establishes the sales price for the property. Section III sets forth the broker's commission as a percentage of the purchase price. Section IV specifies the type of listing agreement and the conditions under which the broker is entitled to collect the commission.

By signing an open listing, the Stewarts authorize Smith & Smyth to find a willing buyer. Nevertheless, it is clear that the owner reserves the right to authorize another broker to locate a potential buyer. In addition, the Stewarts may sell their property without the aid of any broker. Under the open-listing agreement, Smith & Smyth Realty is entitled to the stated commission only if it successfully brings a buyer to the Stewarts. Smith & Smyth will not receive any commission if either another broker or the Stewarts themselves sell the property.

The open listing has both advantages and disadvantages for the sellers. Because they are not limited to one broker, they have greater flexibility. On the other hand, the broker does not have as much incentive to concentrate on selling their property because there is no assurance of actually earning a commission. For this reason, the open-listing agreement is seldom encouraged by brokers.

Exclusive-Agency Listing

If Mr. and Mrs. Stewart had signed an **exclusive-agency listing** agreement, the contract would be similar to the one in Figure 10.1 except that Section IV would be replaced with the language shown in Figure 10.2. This listing differs from the open listing in that the Stewarts cannot authorize another broker to find a buyer

---

FIGURE 10.1   Open Listing Agreement*

Agreement made this *3rd* day of *October, 2001,* between *Harold and Gladys Stewart, of 1097 Timbers Crossing, St. Joseph, Missouri,* herein referred to jointly as "Owner," and *Smith & Smyth Realty Company of 243 South Thompson Street, St. Joseph, Missouri,* herein referred to as "Broker."

I. This listing agreement is for the real estate described as follows: *That lot and two-story, single-family residence located at 1097 Timbers Crossing in St. Joseph, Missouri. Such property is more accurately described as Lot 3, Block G, of the Harris Billups Estate, as recorded in Plat Book 8, page 37, in the Office of the Clerk of the Circuit Court of Buchanan County, Missouri.*

II. The selling price on the above-described property, herein referred to as the "property," shall be *One Hundred Twenty-Five Thousand Dollars ($125,000),* or such other price as Owner may agree to accept.

III. In consideration for the services provided by Broker, Owner agrees to pay Broker a commission equal to *seven percent (7%) of the purchase price of the property* as long as all the duties and conditions of this agreement are satisfied.

IV. Owner and Broker understand and agree that this is an open-listing agreement and Owner reserves the right to sell the property himself or through any other broker without payment to Broker of the commission established herein. Broker shall be entitled to such commission only in the event that

(a) Broker procures a prospect ready, willing, and able to purchase the property on the terms established herein:

(b) Broker procures a buyer who does in fact purchase the property; or

(c) The property is sold, by Owner or any other person, at any time during this listing agreement or within two (2) months after its termination, to a prospect first submitted, directly or indirectly, to Owner by Broker.

Owner and Broker understand this agreement is to continue from noon on *October 3, 2001,* until noon on *January 4, 2002.*

IN WITNESS WHEREOF, the parties execute this agreement on the day and year first written above.

_____   _____
Smith & Smyth Realty Company   Harold C. Stewart, Owner

BY: _____   _____
     Thomas F. Smith, Broker   Gladys Q. Stewart, Owner

* This example and those following are intended solely for instructional purposes and should not be relied on in practice, as they may not meet all particular circumstances. The portions printed in italics are left blank in the printed form, to be filled in at the time the agreement is made with the seller.

---

as long as the exclusive-agency agreement is effective. Despite the limit placed on the Stewarts' use of brokers, they reserve the right to sell their property without becoming liable to pay Smith & Smyth a commission. This type of agreement may seem most beneficial to the sellers because they have one broker acting as their exclusive agent and can sell their property themselves without becoming liable for the commission. The broker may not be totally dedicated to marketing the property, however, because he or she could lose all rights to the commission on a sale-by-owner transaction.

| FIGURE 10.2 | Exclusive-Agency Listing Agreement |

IV. Owner and Broker understand and agree that this is an exclusive-agency listing and Owner reserves the right to sell the property personally without payment to Broker of the commission established herein. Broker shall be entitled to such commission in the event that

(a) Broker procures a prospect ready, willing, and able to purchase the property on the terms established herein;

(b) Broker procures a buyer who does in fact purchase the property:

(c) The property is sold by any broker during the term of this agreement; or

(d) The property is sold, by Owner or any other person, at any time during this listing agreement or within *two (2) months* after its termination, to a prospect first submitted, directly or indirectly, to Owner by Broker.

Multiple-Listing Service Clause

Frequently, an exclusive-right-to-sell listing will be obtained by a broker who is a member of a **multiple-listing service** or MLS, an arrangement in which participating brokers make their listings available to all other members. If the Smith & Smyth Realty Company were a member of the St. Joseph, Missouri MLS, the language of the exclusive-right-to-sell agreement of Figure 10.3 would be followed by that in Figure 10.4. Under the *multiple-listing service clause,* Smith & Smyth typically must make the Stewarts' listing available to all other MLS members within a specified period from the time the listing agreement is signed. (This time period ranges from 48 hours to one week.) Through an MLS, sellers' properties get the greatest exposure, and potential buyers usually have access to the bulk of properties for sale.

Under an exclusive-right-to-sell listing, distributed through the local MLS, Smith & Smyth, as listing agent, typically will receive 50 percent of the total sales commission. If a broker other than Smith & Smyth assists the buyer, that broker receives the remainder of the commission. Suppose the agreed-on commission is 7 percent of the property's sales price. Thus, if the "commission split" is 50-50 and the seller and the buyer have different agents, each will receive 3.5 percent

| FIGURE 10.3 | Exclusive-Right-to-Sell Listing Agreement |

IV. Owner and Broker understand that this is an exclusive-right-to-sell listing. Broker shall be entitled to the commission established herein in the event that

(a) Broker procures a prospect ready, willing, and able to purchase the property on the terms established herein;

(b) Broker procures a buyer who does in fact purchase the property:

(c) The property is sold by anyone, including Owner, during the term of this listing; or

(d) The property is sold, by Owner or any other person, at any time during this listing agreement or within *two (2) months* after its termination, to a prospect first submitted, directly or indirectly, to Owner by Broker.

| FIGURE 10.4 | Multiple-Listing Service Clause |

V. It is understood that Broker is a member of the *St. Joseph Board of Realtors' multiple-listing service,* and it is understood further that Broker shall file this listing with the multiple-listing system to be referred to its members. Such member will act as subagent in procuring or attempting to procure a purchaser in accordance with this agreement. If a sale or exchange shall be made through any subagent, all the terms of this agreement shall apply to such transaction.

of the selling price. For example, if the Acme Realty Company finds a buyer for the Stewarts' house at the asking price of $125,000, Smith & Smyth—as the listing agent—and Acme—as the selling agent—would receive $4,375 each of the $8,750 total commission.

Of course, Smith & Smyth may find a buyer for the Stewarts' property. In that case, Smith & Smyth would be the listing agent and the selling agent at the same time and would receive the entire 7 percent commission.

Net Listing

A type of listing used very infrequently today, and illegal in many states, is the **net listing.** In this agreement, the seller is guaranteed a specified amount of money, while the broker receives the remainder of the sales price. This type of listing obviously invites fraud because there is an incentive for the broker to deceive the seller about the fair-market value of the property and thus obtain a larger commission.

The Broker's Right to a Commission

To be eligible to collect a commission, a broker must be hired by a principal. As discussed earlier, the seller's broker usually is hired when a written listing agreement is executed. An important purpose of the listing agreement is to make clear when a broker has earned a commission. Typically, a commission is payable to the broker when he or she either (1) procures a ready, willing, and able buyer or (2) sells the property. (Section IV in Figures 10.1 through 10.3 demonstrates these conditions.)

Listing agreements also usually contain a clause protecting the broker from losing the commission when the buyer waits to purchase until the listing agreement expires. Under this clause, the broker is entitled to a commission if the property is sold within some reasonable time period, usually two to six months, after the expiration of the agreement to a prospect introduced to the property by the broker.

Thus, if the Stewarts were to sell their home on March 15 to a buyer who was shown the property by a salesperson from Smith & Smyth Realty (termination of the listing agreement was January 4), the real estate brokerage firm would be entitled to the 7 percent commission. If, however, the same person bought the property two years later, no commission would be due.

The Broker-Buyer Relationship (Buyer's Agent)

When a potential buyer hires a broker to assist in locating a property for purchase, the relationship between the broker and the potential buyer should be clearly specified in a written document referred to as a **buyer representation agreement.** As in the case of listing agreements, buyer representation agreements must contain the essential elements of a contract. In addition, the document should specify the type of property desired, the duties and obligations of the buyer and seller, and the terms by which the broker will be paid for services rendered. A sample buyer representation agreement is provided in Figure 10.5.

Types of Buyer Representation Agreements

Similar to the different types of listing agreements discussed earlier, buyer representation agreements may specify that the broker has an exclusive-right-to-represent or that the arrangement is an "open" one. Under an exclusive right to represent, as in Figure 10.5, the broker is entitled to a commission if the potential buyer purchases a property with or without the assistance of the broker. In an open arrangement, the broker is entitled to a commission only if the buyer purchases a property identified and suggested by the broker. If the buyer finds a property without the broker's assistance, no commission is due.

Compensating the Buyer's Broker

Structuring the compensation to a buyer's broker properly is an important aspect of the buyer representation agreement. In many cases, the agreement calls for a retainer fee at the time the contract is signed, with a commission due if a property is purchased. The commission is either a fixed fee or is calculated as a percentage of the transaction amount. If the property is identified through the MLS, the buyer's broker will receive a "commission split" from the listing agent. Typically, the compensation due from the buyer is reduced by this amount. Because the compensation due the broker is calculated as a percentage of the purchase price, one might question whether the broker will negotiate aggressively for the lowest price possible on behalf of the buyer. Fortunately, the fiduciary responsibility owed to the principal precludes the agent from engaging in this type of behavior.

■ DUTIES AND RIGHTS UNDER AGENCY RELATIONSHIPS

Once any principal-agent relationship is established, each party owes the other the duties of loyalty, good faith, and diligence in fulfilling the conditions promised. These duties are not a matter of choice, but are created by state laws that govern the agency relationship. In addition to their legal responsibilities, successful real estate brokers and salespersons know that ethical business practices are critical to continued professional success. For example, the National Association of REALTORS®, the largest trade organization for real estate brokers and salespersons, holds its members to high ethical standards. In general, these

---

FIGURE 10.5   Buyer Representation Agreement*

I.   Parties: _____ ("Buyer")
     appoints _____("Broker") as
     Buyer's exclusive agent and grants Broker the exclusive right to represent and assist Buyer in locating and negoti-
     ating the acquisition of suitable real property as described in part III below.

II. Term: This agreement will begin on the _____ day of _____, 20___ and will terminate at noon on the
     _____ day of _____, 20___. If the Buyer enters into an agreement to acquire property which is
     pending on the termination date, this agreement will be in effect until the transaction has closed or otherwise termi
     nated.

III. Property: Buyer desires to acquire real property described as follows, or as otherwise acceptable to Buyer.

     (a) Type of property _____

     (b) Location _____

     (c) Price range _____

     (d) Terms and conditions _____

IV. Broker's Obligations: Broker will use his or her best efforts to (a) identify suitable properties, (b) assist Buyer in nego-
     tiating a contract for the chosen property, and (c) monitor the transaction through the closing.

V.   Buyer's Obligations: Buyer agrees to cooperate with the Broker in accomplishing the objective of this agreement,
     including (a) conducting all negotiations through Broker and (b) being available to meet with Broker at reasonable
     times to view properties recommended by broker.

VI. Retainer: Upon execution of this agreement, Buyer will pay to Broker a nonrefundable retainer fee of
     $_____. This fee will be credited to Buyer in the event compensation is earned by Broker as defined in the
     following paragraph.

VII. Compensation: Broker's compensation is earned when Buyer contracts to acquire real property meeting the require-
     ments of paragraph III above and will be responsible for paying Broker $ _____ or _____ percent of the
     total purchase price for the acquired property. The Buyer will be credited with any amount paid to Broker by seller or
     seller's agent.

VIII. Early Termination: Buyer may terminate this agreement at any time, but will be held responsible for Broker's com-
     pensation until the original termination date if the Buyer contracts to acquire any property which, prior to early ter-
     mination, was found by Buyer or submitted to Buyer by Broker or any other person. Broker may terminate this agree-
     ment at any time, in which event the Buyer will be released from all further obligations.

IX. Acknowledgment: The parties execute this agreement on the _____ day of _____ , 20___.

_____   _____
Broker   Buyer

                                                       _____
                                                       Buyer

* This example is intended solely for instructional purposes and should not be relied on in practice, as it may not meet all
  particular circumstances.

standards require fair dealings with clients, customers, and the public. The following sections examine the broker's, seller's and buyer's legal duties to one another in detail.

The Broker's Duties

Real estate brokers and salespeople assume a fiduciary role when they are hired by either a seller or a buyer. A *fiduciary* occupies a position of trust and confidence in relation to another person or his or her property. Therefore, brokers must protect their clients' best interests at all times. A breach of a fiduciary's duties may occur as a result of negligence, fraud, misrepresentation, or failure to follow instructions. **Fraud** is present if a broker, (1) with the intention to mislead, (2) makes a false statement material to a transaction that (3) is justifiably relied on by a client, resulting in (4) injury to the client. The elements of **misrepresentation** are the same as for fraud except that the *intention* to mislead need not be present.

Seller's Agent's Duties to Seller

After a listing agreement is signed, the broker's job is to locate a willing and able buyer. In doing so, of course, the broker must do so honestly, diligently, and in good faith while following any instructions given by the owner and looking out for the owner's interests. The broker must also keep the seller informed at all times and communicate any and all offers received to the seller.

Seller's Agent's Duties to Buyers

When the broker is an agent of the seller, the broker must look out for the seller's best interests. Even so, the broker must be careful not to misrepresent the property to a potential buyer. Courts are increasingly holding that the broker must go farther, having a responsibility to disclose any negative factors that might adversely affect the property's value. Suppose, for example, that the foundation of the house has settled, necessitating repairs. In addition, the basement has been subject to flooding in extremely wet weather. The broker has the responsibility to inform any interested buyer that these problems exist and that additional repairs to correct them may be necessary in the future. The Legal Highlight on page 212 illustrates the liability brokers may face if they do not furnish adequate information to a prospective buyer.

If a buyer gives a broker any money as deposit on a potential purchase, these funds must be kept separate from the broker's personal and other business funds and cannot be used for the broker's benefit. For example, any use of "earnest money" by the broker for anything other than the buyer's instructed purposes is improper and illegal. The money must be deposited in an escrow account and must not be "commingled" with the broker's personal or other business funds.

The Seller's Agent's Obligations to the Buyer

The Strassburgers owned a 3,000-square-foot home in Diablo, California, located on a one-acre lot and complete with a swimming pool and large guest house. They listed their home with Valley Realty, which sold the property to the Eastons for $170,000. Unfortunately for the Eastons, however, they were not aware that part of the property was on filled land that already had been subject to earth slides.

Legal Highlight

Shortly after moving in, the Eastons became painfully aware of this fact when massive earth movement cost them a portion of their driveway and caused the foundation of the house to settle, the walls to crack, and the doorways to warp. Estimates to repair the damage and avoid recurrence ranged as high as $213,000. The Eastons sued the Strassburgers and Valley Realty for damages, charging misrepresentation. In a landmark decision that has had lasting implications for the real estate brokerage industry, they won.

The court held that although there was no evidence that the broker intentionally misled the buyers by deliberately giving false information, he had an "affirmative duty" to the buyers to conduct "a reasonably competent and diligent inspection of the property listed for sale and to disclose to prospective purchasers all facts materially affecting the value or desirability of the property that such an investigation would reveal." Because the broker did not do this, he was liable for part of the assessed damages of $197,000. As a result of this case, brokers are held responsible for disclosing information about the condition of the property to buyers.

Source: *Easton v. Strassburger,* 199 Cal. Rptr. 383 (Cal. App. 1 Dist., 1984).

Buyer's Agent's Duties to Buyers

When a buyer representation agreement is in place, the broker is a fiduciary of the buyer. The broker must act diligently and in good faith to find a property that matches the buyer's criteria. Failure to attempt to locate a property for the buyer would violate the terms of the buyer representation agreement. Although normally still splitting a commission paid by the seller, the buyer's broker's loyalties must lie with the buyer. The broker has the responsibility of advising the buyer, negotiating the lowest price, and otherwise assisting the buyer in closing the transaction.

Buyer's Agent's Duties to Sellers

Even though a buyer's broker is a fiduciary of the buyer, the broker must treat sellers fairly, honestly, and with due care. Failure to do so is a violation of the "fair dealings" requirement imposed on state-licensed real estate agents.

Fair Housing

In all situations, the broker also must be careful not to violate federal **fair housing laws,** which prohibit housing discrimination based on sex, race, color, religion, national origin, disabilities, or familial status. In the past, some brokers have engaged in the practice of **steering**—that is, channeling minority prospects only to minority neighborhoods. Other unscrupulous brokers have engaged in **blockbusting**—using scare tactics to drive down home prices when minority owners begin moving into an area.

The Civil Rights Act of 1866 provides that "All citizens of the United States shall have the same right, in every State and Territory, as is enjoyed by white citizens thereof to inherit, purchase, lease, sell, hold and convey real and personal property." In 1968, the U.S. Supreme Court ruled that this law prohibits "all racial discrimination, private as well as public, in the sale or rental of property." More recently, the Fair Housing Act of 1988, enforced by the U.S. Department of Housing and Urban Development, was enacted to, among other things, provide civil penalties ranging from $10,000 to $50,000 plus actual and compensatory damages against individuals who engage in discriminatory practices. Americans who feel their rights have been violated should file a complaint immediately with the Office of Fair Housing and Equal Opportunity at HUD. The law means what it says, as the broker in the Legal Highlight on page 214 discovered. Most states have similar laws.

Disclosure of Agency Relationship

Most states have enacted laws and regulations that require that real estate brokers and salespersons disclose the nature of any agency relationships at the first substantive contact with clients and customers. In many states, this disclosure must be made in writing and acknowledged by the parties involved. In the past, many buyers have purchased property with the mistaken belief that one of the brokers involved in the transaction represented their best interests. Unless a buyer representation agreement is executed, buyers should not assume that the broker is working exclusively to benefit them.

■ TERMINATION OF AGENCY RELATIONSHIPS

In the typical agency relationship in real estate, the relationship ends when a transaction occurs as specified in the listing agreement or buyer representation agreement. For example, if an open listing created the relationship, the relationship terminates on a sale, whether that sale is completed by the listing broker, another broker or the owner. In an exclusive-agency listing, it is understood that the agreement ends with the sale, whether the real estate is sold by the listing broker, or by the owner.

If a transaction does not occur, the time period provided in the listing agreement governs the duration of the agency relationship. At the expiration of that term, the relationship terminates. Some states do not require a stated termination date for a listing agreement. In such cases, the agency relationship lasts for a reasonable time. A "reasonable" time is generally considered to be three months for residential property and six months for commercial property. The determination of a reasonable time period often must be made by a court; therefore, absence of a specific term in the agency agreement may result in expensive litigation.

REAL ESTATE TODAY

Enforcement of Fair Housing Laws

Gordon Blackwell, a licensed real estate broker, owned a rental house, which he listed for sale with another real estate agent. An African-American couple, the Herrons, were shown the house by their broker. They liked the house, and after offer and counteroffer, a contract for sale was signed by both parties. Later, however, after Blackwell learned that the Herrons were black, he refused to close on the property. He changed the locks and refused to discuss the matter with his broker. He also signed a lease on the property with an option to purchase to the Coopers, whom Blackwell described as "some really good white tenants."

The Herrons filed a housing discrimination complaint with the U.S. Department of Housing and Urban Development (HUD), alleging that Blackwell had discriminated against them because of their race, in violation of the Fair Housing Act. After an investigation by HUD, a federal district court issued an injunction restraining Blackwell from selling or leasing the property except to the Herrons and requiring him to notify the Coopers that they would have to vacate the property. Blackwell still failed to

Legal Highlight

close on the property, and eventually, the Herrons decided they no longer wanted the house.

An appeals court found that the record supported the determination that

■ the Herrons were qualified buyers,

■ they had obtained a mortgage loan commitment,

■ Blackwell rejected the Herrons on the basis of race, and

■ Blackwell made the property available to others after he repudiated his contract with the Herrons.

The court ordered Blackwell to pay the Herrons $4,592 for economic losses and $40,000 for "embarrassment, humiliation and emotional distress." It awarded the Coopers $594 in damages and $20,000 for their emotional distress. Blackwell was also assessed a civil penalty of $10,000.

Source: *Herron v. Blackwell*, 908 F.2d 864 (U.S. Court of Appeals, 11th Circuit, 1990).

A third way the agency relationship between a broker and owner ends is by mutual agreement. Some circumstances make it more beneficial to all parties to relieve the broker of his or her duties to locate a buyer and to relieve the owner of his or her duties to the broker. Such an agreement may occur before the expiration of the agency agreement's term. Provisions for early termination should be specified in the agreement.

Even without the consent of the agent, many states allow the principal to revoke at any time the listing agreement that established the agency relationship. Revocation of an open or exclusive-agency listing is looked upon less harshly than revocation of an exclusive-right-to-sell listing. Of course, the principal who breaches the agreement is liable to the broker for damages, although the determination of an agent's damages may be difficult.

Of course, if either party to the agency relationship breaches his or her duties, the other party is relieved of further liability under the listing agreement. For example, if a broker fails to keep the seller fully informed of negotiations, the seller can list the property with another broker or sell it without a broker even if the original listing agreement was an exclusive right to sell. The owner's revocation of the listing agreement releases the broker from all duties to locate a buyer.

Because the agreement that created the principal-agent relationship is a contract between the parties, loss of contractual capacity by either party terminates the relationship. Such loss of capacity may occur as the result of the death or insanity of either the principal or the agent. Destruction of improvements on the listed property or the property's seizure by the government under the power of eminent domain also terminates the agency relationship. A broker is under no obligation to seek a buyer for a house that has been destroyed in a hurricane, for example, and a seller is not obligated to pay a commission for one that has been condemned for a highway right-of-way.

In summary, there are several means by which the broker-owner agency relationship can be terminated:

- A transaction occurs.
- The term of the agreement expires.
- The parties agree to termination.
- One party breaches his or her duties.
- One party becomes contractually incapacitated.
- A listed property's improvements are destroyed.
- A listed property is taken by the government under the power of eminent domain.

■ TYPES OF BROKERAGE FIRMS

Real estate markets, particularly markets for single-family homes, are local in nature, and real estate brokerage firms traditionally have been small, one-office businesses that operated only in their local markets. For the most part, the real estate brokerage industry is still made up of small firms. Increasingly, however, the real estate brokerage market in most larger communities is dominated by large, multioffice firms, often part of regional or national organizations.

Many real estate brokers and brokerage firms specialize in one type of real estate transaction. Some brokers, for example, act only as buyer's brokers, while others serve only as seller's brokers. Many brokers limit their activities to the owner-occupied residential market; apartment leasing; vacant land sales; or commercial, industrial, or retail properties. Concentrating one's efforts on a smaller market segment allows some brokers to finely tune their skills to the needs of their clients and customers, and ultimately increase their productivity.

Franchises

One way the smaller real estate brokers compete with the large regional and national firms is by becoming part of a franchise chain, such as Century 21 or Better Homes & Gardens. Franchisees pay an initial fee plus a percentage of their annual gross. For this, they receive the advantages of sales and management training programs, a referral network, and, perhaps of most importance, name recognition. Just as families moving to an area recognize McDonald's and Kentucky Fried Chicken, they also often recognize real estate franchise chains. Consumers should recognize, however, that most of these firms are independently owned and operated, and the quality of service can vary.

Desk Fee Arrangements

Increasingly, brokerage firms are organizing the brokers and salespersons who work in the firm in a "desk fee" arrangement. Brokers who wish to work with other members of the firm pay a monthly fee for the right to occupy space in the office. The firm provides phone service, cooperative advertising, and other resources that are shared by the members of the firm. In some cases, the members must also share a portion of their commissions earned with the other members of the firm.

Multiple-Listing Services

Another way the smaller broker is able to compete with larger firms is by becoming part of an MLS. If another broker sells the property, the listing broker still receives a portion of the commission. While the MLS is particularly valuable to the small broker, who otherwise might not have enough properties to sell, the service is also usually an advantage to the seller because all members of the MLS offer the property for sale and may reach many more potential buyers.

■ BROKER AND SALESPERSON COMPENSATION

As discussed above, a real estate broker or salesperson receives a commission for services rendered in connection with the transaction. Normally, the commission is determined by a percentage of the gross transaction amount, though it can also be a flat fee. Usually, no commission is paid until the transaction is completed. In some cases, however, the broker may receive an advance fee, or a fee may be paid for performance of specific services, such as consultation and advice or appraisal of property. The commission amount varies with the type of property sold. Commissions on single-family homes typically range from 5 to 8 percent. Large commercial properties usually carry a lower percentage commission, in the range of 3 to 6 percent, while commissions on unimproved land generally range from 6 to 10 percent.

Of course, real estate brokerage commissions cannot be set by agreement among brokers but must be negotiated between broker and client. Even discussion between brokers concerning the level of commissions is an antitrust violation and a criminal offense. Even so, like other prices, commission rates tend to be relatively uniform, although lower rates can be negotiated, particularly in a "sellers market."

When more than one broker is involved in a transaction, the commission usually will be split among the selling broker, the listing broker, and the firms that employ the brokers. Each broker typically receives half of the commission amount specified in the listing agreement. The brokers may then be obligated to split their commissions with their respective firms, and possibly their salespersons. Of course, if the selling and listing agent were the same person, he or she would collect both commissions.

Compensation for Salespersons

As discussed above, state laws require that salespersons must work under the direction of a broker. Compensation for salespersons is based on a percentage of the commissions earned for the broker. The actual percentage will vary from firm to firm and from salesperson to salesperson on the basis of such factors as the prevailing practice in the area, the degree of advertising and other support provided by the broker, and the sales record of the agent. In general, the portion of the total commission going to the salesperson will increase with his or her level of sales.

■ CHAPTER REVIEW

- Two characteristics of real estate markets—the complexity of transactions and buyers' limited knowledge of the markets—have led to the establishment of various real estate service activities, including real estate brokerage, property management, and appraisal.

- The steps in the real estate sales process are (a) listing, (b) marketing the property and qualifying buyers, (c) presentation and negotiations, (d) contracts, and (e) settlement or closing.

- A real estate broker is an intermediary who arranges real estate sale or lease transactions for a fee or commission. A real estate salesperson must work through a broker and can carry out only those responsibilities assigned by the broker.

- All states and the District of Columbia require that brokers and salespeople be licensed and meet mandatory education or experience requirements. Failure to obtain the proper license prohibits the collection of any commission.

- The primary functions of the real estate brokerage industry are to match properties with buyers and to guide the buyer and seller through the complexities of real estate transactions.

- Real estate brokers' relationships with sellers and buyers are governed by the law of agency. The broker or salesperson serves as an agent for the seller or buyer, who is the principal. A principal authorizes his or her agent to perform certain functions on behalf of the principal. In a typical real estate transaction, the principal (seller) grants the agent (broker) express authority as stated in the listing agreement.

- The broker-seller relationship is created on the establishment of a listing agreement, usually written. Such an agreement specifies the parties, describes the property, states the asking price, and provides the governing terms. The traditional types of listing agreements include (a) the open listing, (b) the exclusive-agency listing, and (c) the exclusive-right-to-sell listing. Net listing agreements are used infrequently today because of the possibility of fraud.

- The broker-buyer relationship is created on the establishment of a buyer representation agreement, usually written. Such an agreement identifies the parties, describes the property desired, and establishes the broker's right to compensation. These agreements can be open or exclusive.

- A broker or salesperson has the duty to act honestly and diligently on the principal's behalf. Complete loyalty is owed to the party the agent represents.

- Federal fair housing laws prohibit housing discrimination based on a buyer's or (lessee's) sex, race, color, religion, national origin, disabilities, or familial status.

- A commission is earned when the conditions of the agreement have been satisfied. In a listing agreement, the commission is due when the broker procures a ready, willing, and able buyer or when the transaction is actually completed. In a buyer representation agreement, the commission is due when the buyer contracts to purchase a property.

- The agency relationship terminates when a transaction occurs, when the term provided in the agreement expires, when both parties consent to termination, when either party breaches its conditions, when either party becomes incapacitated, when the property is destroyed or heavily damaged, or when the property is condemned by the government under the power of eminent domain.

- A real estate broker or salesperson normally receives a commission when the transaction is completed successfully but no salary or other fee until that time. The commission normally is stated as a percentage of the gross sales price, and it varies with the type of property sold.

■ KEY TERMS

agency

agent

blockbusting

broker

buyer representation
   agreement

buyer's agent

commission

dual agency

exclusive-agency listing

exclusive-right-to-sell
   listing

fair housing laws

fiduciary

fraud

listing agreement

listing broker

misrepresentation

multiple-listing service

net listing

open listing

principal

real estate broker

real estate salesperson

seller's agent

selling broker

steering

subagent

transaction broker

■ STUDY EXERCISES

1. What characteristics of real estate have led to the establishment of the real estate brokerage industry?

2. Discuss the difference between the function of a real estate broker and that of a real estate salesperson.

3. What is the difference between an open listing and exclusive-agency listing? How does an exclusive-agency listing differ from an exclusive-right-to-sell listing?

4. What is a net listing? Why is it illegal in most states?

5. What is the difference between fraud and misrepresentation?

6. What are "blockbusting" and "steering"? Why are these practices illegal?

7. What are the advantages of a multiple-listing service to real estate brokers? Are there any advantages for sellers?

8. Joe desires to sell his house. He lists the property with Johnny White, a real estate broker. In this case, who is "principal" and who is the "agent"? What duties does Johnny owe to Joe? What duties does he owe to any potential buyer?

9. Suppose that Johnny shows the house to Janice, who asks him to negotiate on her behalf with Joe. If he does so, what is he guilty of? What must he do to protect his right to a commission on this sale if he grants her request?

10. Sylvia listed her house for sale at $105,000 with the Keg Realty Company, and Keg began to show the property. A prospective buyer looked at Sylvia's house, liked it and gave a written offer for her asking price—$105,000. Having some second thoughts about selling, Sylvia claimed that this particu-

lar buyer could not afford her house, and refused to accept the offer. If there is no evidence that the buyer is in financial difficulty, does Keg Realty have any claim against Sylvia?

11. Real estate broker Molly Smith has listed a house for sale that is located in a floodplain and has been flooded on several occasions. Does Molly have an obligation to make these facts known to prospective buyers?

12. Suppose that Molly knows about the potential floodplain problem, but tells a potential purchaser that the house is not in the floodplain. Of what is she guilty? Would the buyer have a claim against her?

13. Suppose that Molly fully informs the potential buyer about the floodplain problem, but he still buys the house. Later his house is flooded, and he sues Molly for not telling him that houses in floodplains can be flooded. Does he have a legitimate claim?

■ FURTHER READINGS

de Heer, R., *Realty Bluebook,* 31st ed. Chicago: Real Estate Education Company, 1996.

11 Real Estate Appraisal

Because the factors that determine value vary so widely, appraisers tend to specialize in particular types of markets: commercial, residential or agricultural.

CHAPTER PREVIEW

What is the property worth? This question is central to decision making in almost every aspect of real estate. Sellers want to know what their properties should bring in the marketplace, and buyers want to know what their potential purchases are worth in comparison with other properties in the market. Mortgage lenders want to know that the value of a property being pledged as security for a debt is at least as much as the loan amount. Tax assessors, insurance adjusters, and right-of-way agents also must obtain estimates of value in order to collect property taxes, pay insurance claims, and compensate landowners for eminent domain takings.

Arriving at reliable estimates of property values requires an in-depth understanding of the factors that influence value, as well as the methods available for estimating value. A thorough understanding of the process appraisers use to estimate value is beneficial to all real estate market participants, and it is absolutely necessary for anyone who hopes to make a career in the appraisal profession. The objectives of this chapter are to

- discuss the regulatory environment surrounding the appraisal profession,

- define the concept of value,

- define some of the basic principles underlying the appraisal process,

- describe the steps in the appraisal process,

- review the basic techniques appraisers use to arrive at value estimates, and

- demonstrate the appraisal process for a single-family home.

Case Study
Applying the Appraisal Process in a Single-Family Home Appraisal

■ UNDERSTANDING THE APPRAISAL PROCESS

Even though almost all individuals, businesses, and other organizations use real estate in their normal activities, few have the expertise necessary to evaluate real estate market conditions and arrive at sound estimates of property value. As a result, many real estate decision makers often must seek the services of real estate appraisers who possess the skills and knowledge necessary to accurately estimate property value. To ensure that people engaged in appraisal services do so in a competent and professional manner, all states have established minimum education and experience requirements for obtaining an appraisal license or certification.

Prior to 1989, few states regulated the appraisal industry and no specific license was required to perform appraisals. In that year, Congress passed the Financial Institutions Recovery and Reform Act (FIRREA). Among other things, FIRREA established a federal regulatory hierarchy for the appraisal industry in an attempt to improve the reliability of appraisals in the loan approval process. Under FIRREA, appraisals for properties involved in "federally related" transactions must be performed by state-licensed or -certified appraisers. Federally related transactions include those involving certain federal government agencies, as well as those involving institutions that are regulated or insured by federal agencies. Because most banks, savings institutions, and credit unions are federally regulated, virtually all appraisal assignments must be completed by a state-licensed or -certified appraiser.

The Appraisal Foundation establishes minimum guidelines that states must use to issue appraisal licenses and certifications. The guidelines establish three different appraiser categories that permit the license or certificate holder to perform appraisal services in federally related transactions. These categories distinguish between residential and nonresidential assignments and the size of the transactions. Generally, **licensed appraisers** are authorized to perform appraisals for commercial properties in transactions of less than $250,000 and for one- to four-unit residential properties for transactions less than $1 million. **Certified residential appraisers** may perform appraisals on residential property for transactions of any amount and number of units. **Certified general appraisers** are permitted to appraise residential and nonresidential properties, regardless of the transaction amount. The education and experience requirements increase for each category.

■ WHAT IS VALUE?

The concept of *value* is a topic that has been dear to philosophers and economists for centuries, and the debate over a proper definition of value is frequently revisited in the real estate appraisal literature. Some of the questions considered by researchers include—What constitutes value? Is it the worth of a property to society in general or to an individual investor? Is it price in terms of money or some intrinsic characteristic of the property? Is it value in exchange, value in use, or perhaps the cost to produce? For our purposes, we limit our concern to the question—What is it that real estate appraisers are trying to estimate? As we will see, the answer to this question is carefully defined.

Market Value

The type of value that real estate appraisers generally attempt to estimate is **market value.** The following definition, taken from the Uniform Standards of Professional Appraisal Practice, is the most widely accepted definition of market value and is the basis for most appraisal reports.

Market value: The most probable price which a property should bring in a competitive and open market under all conditions requisite to a fair sale, the buyer and seller each acting prudently and knowledgeably, and assuming the price is not affected by undue stimulus. Implicit in this definition is the consummation of a sale as of a specified date and the passing of title from seller to buyer under conditions whereby:

1. buyer and seller are typically motivated;
2. both parties are well informed or well advised, and acting in what they consider their best interests;
3. a reasonable time is allowed for exposure in the open market;
4. payment is made in terms of cash in United States dollars or in terms of financial arrangements comparable thereto; and
5. the price represents the normal consideration for the property sold unaffected by special or creative financing or sales concessions by anyone association with the sale.

Though lengthy, each portion of this definition is important to the appraiser's estimate of value. For example, the price for which one family member might sell a particular property to another could be very different from the price that could be received if the property were offered to all prospective buyers. Similarly, because the financing terms of a transaction may affect the price, the definition of market value refers to the most probable cash or cash equivalent price. Furthermore, this definition assumes that all market participants have an opportunity to consider the property and make an informed and voluntary decision about whether to purchase it. While the implications of the above definition should be always kept in mind, we will simply refer to a property's market value as its most probable selling price.

Investment Value

Market value is what the classical economists called "value in exchange," that is, the consensus price that would be reached in a market with many buyers and sellers. Another classical value concept is "value in use," which has a modern real estate application in the concept of investment value. **Investment value** is defined as the worth of a property to a particular investor, based on that investor's personal standards of investment acceptability. Investment value refers to the value of a property to a specific buyer, while market value refers to the value of a property to the typical, but unspecified, buyer in the market. We will consider the topic of investment analysis in a subsequent chapter.

Price Versus Market Value

As opposed to market value, which is an estimate of the most probable selling price, **price** is the amount actually paid for a property in a particular transaction. It is an historical fact, not a prospective concept. Because the buyer or seller may not be well informed, may not be acting prudently or may not be free from undue pressure, or may not be engaged in an "arm's length" transaction, the price actually paid for a property may not be the same as the market value estimated by an appraiser. On the other hand, price is an accurate indicator of market value if the transaction matches the conditions described in the definition of market value.

Market Value Versus Cost of Production

One of the factors influencing market value is cost of production. No rational entrepreneur will keep producing a product unless it is expected to sell for a price that is high enough to cover costs and provide a profit. Unfortunately, however, this does not mean that an entrepreneur will not make a mistake and produce a product that the market will value at less than the cost of production. Real estate developers occasionally make mistakes by misjudging markets and developing projects that will not sell at their desired price. Although costs are one indication of value, market value actually may be higher or lower than cost of production.

Other Types of Value

Although appraisers usually estimate market value, they may be asked to estimate other measures of value as well. Among these are assessed value and insurable value. **Assessed value** is the value placed on a property for property tax assessment purposes. As already has been shown in the discussion of the property tax, even though assessed value is based on market value, it is seldom a valid estimate of current market value. Property taxation is considered in Chapter 4.

Insurable value represents the amount of insurance that should be carried on the destructible portion of the real estate to compensate the owner adequately in case of loss. Because insurable value is measured using the concepts of actual cash value and replacement cost, it often differs from current market value. The principles of real property insurance are considered in Chapter 19.

■ SOME KEY APPRAISAL PRINCIPLES

A number of basic principles drawn primarily from economic thought are essential to the practice of appraisal, and they apply to every type of real estate appraisal assignment. Among them are the principles of anticipation, change, substitution, and contribution.

Anticipation

The current value of a property depends on the anticipated utility or income that will accrue to the property owner in the future. This is the principle of **anticipation.** Because the present value of a property depends on the expected future benefits of ownership, the appraiser must be skilled in analyzing national, regional, local, and neighborhood trends that will influence future income or utility. For example, a motel may have been very profitable in the past, but changing road patterns and other neighborhood factors may considerably reduce the property's income and, hence, its value in the future.

Change

The principle of anticipation is closely related to the principle of **change,** the notion that economic, social, political, and environmental forces are constantly causing changes that affect the value of real property. Real estate markets are dynamic rather than static, and appraisers must carefully analyze the direction and degree of change in factors affecting market values. For this reason, every value estimate must be made as of a specified date.

Substitution

The principle of **substitution** holds that a prudent buyer will pay no more for a property than the cost of acquiring an equally desirable substitute in the open market. This principle is fundamental to all three traditional approaches to real estate valuation, the sales comparison, income, and cost approaches. It supports the premise that a buyer will not pay any more for a home or other real estate improvement than the cost of reproducing the improvement on a similar site. Suppose, for example, that a lot can be purchased in a particular subdivision and a certain size and type of house constructed for a total cost of $300,000. This will tend to set the upper limit of value for existing houses of similar size and type in the subdivision unless they have some distinguishing locational feature such as an exceptional view or nearness to a golf course or lake.

Contribution

The principles of diminishing marginal utility and diminishing returns as factors of production are fundamental to economic theory. Their application in real estate appraisal is closely related to the principle of **contribution,** which states that the value of a component part of a property depends on the amount it contributes to the value of the whole. For example, tasteful landscaping may increase the value of a home much more than the cost of the improvement. An expenditure for extensive plantings of exotic shrubs, however, probably will not be recovered if the property is sold. In fact, certain improvements to a property can actually have a negative effect on value.

Suppose a homeowner builds an elaborate shrine in the dining room honoring a major league baseball team. Because the typical buyer prefers that such an item not be a part of the property, the "value" of the shrine is negative and equal to the cost of removing it, less any salvage value. The principle of contribution is an especially important consideration for real estate appraisers. Even though a property may have an expensive feature or characteristic, the contribution to market value is often less than the cost of the feature (or perhaps even negative) because the typical buyer in the market does not desire that feature in the property.

■ THE APPRAISAL PROCESS

Over the years, appraisers have developed a formal process to collect data, analyze them to arrive at an estimate of value, and present their findings. The **appraisal process** is a systematic procedure employed to arrive at an estimate of value and convey that estimate to the appraisal user. Although we present the steps of this process in their general chronological order, it is important to realize that in practice, the order of consideration of these steps may need to be adjusted to match the conditions of a specific appraisal assignment. Careful consideration of each of the following steps will lead to sound estimates of value.

1. Definition of the problem
2. Data selection and collection
3. Highest and best use analysis
4. Application of the three approaches to value
5. Reconciliation of value indications into a final value estimate
6. Report of defined value

Step 1: Definition of the Problem

The first step in the appraisal process is to define the problem at hand. The accuracy of the value estimate provided by the appraiser depends on careful specification of the appraisal assignment. The appraiser and the client must be in accord as to

- the type of value to be estimated,
- the property involved,
- the specific property rights being appraised,
- the use of the appraisal, and
- the effective date of the appraisal.

The most common purpose of an appraisal is to estimate market value, but appraisers may be asked to estimate rental value, insurable value, assessed value, or investment value. The type of value to be estimated will largely dictate the type of data that must be collected and the way they should be analyzed. It is essential, therefore, that the purpose of the appraisal and the definition of value be stated clearly.

The identification of the property to be appraised must include the location of the property, usually provided by both its street address and legal description. This description must also include any easements or encroachments that might affect value. Obviously, the physical characteristics of the property must be identified, including buildings and other improvements, the size of the parcel, its topography, soil conditions, elevation, and other physical features.

Not only the physical property but the specific property rights to be appraised must be clearly identified. These rights may be complete, as in a fee simple estate, or partial, including only such interests as air rights, the reversionary right in a leased fee, an easement, or some other type of limited property interest. The description should include limitations on these property rights, such as restrictive covenants and land-use controls.

The appraiser usually is called on to make an estimate of the current value of the property, although in some cases an appraisal is required for some date in the past. Retrospective appraisals may be required for many reasons, including a determination of inheritance taxes and insurance claims. Because the value of property changes over time, specification of an effective date for an appraisal is a necessary part of defining the problem.

Step 2: Data Selection and Collection

After defining the problem, the appraiser must identify and collect data that will permit an accurate estimate of property value. In addition to general information regarding economic, social, political, and environmental factors that may affect the value of the property being appraised, the appraiser must collect specific information regarding recent sales prices of similar properties, construction cost data, and income and expense information for the subject property and comparable properties in the market. As we will see in the remaining steps of the appraisal process, the accuracy and appropriateness of data collected for analysis are critical to the validity of the value estimate. Estimates of value based on inaccurate or inappropriate data are not reliable.

Step 3: Highest and Best Use Analysis

After determining the data requirements for an appraisal assignment and collecting the data for analysis, the next step is to analyze the property's highest and best use. **Highest and best use** is defined as that use that is found to be legally permissible, physically possible, financially feasible, and *maximally productive.* We first considered the concept of highest and best use in Chapter 9, "Urban and Regional Economics." We used this concept to discuss how property value is determined by the "land rent" a property can command in a market as a function of its location and use. As we noted earlier, market value refers to the most probable price a property would bring in an open market transaction. Because the typical buyer in such a transaction would most probably use the property in its highest and best use, value estimates are based on the assumption that the highest and best use of the property has been identified. This follows from the recognition that competition among market participants will result in the most efficient and appropriate use of a property, even if that means changing its current use. Any estimate of market value must include a determination of the property's highest and best use.

The determination of the highest and best use of a property is of primary importance in any appraisal, although in many cases it is readily apparent. For example, if the property to be appraised is a five-year-old house in an established single-family neighborhood, the highest and best use of the property is most likely a single-family home. In other cases, however, the highest and best use of a property may be dramatically different from its current use.

Highest and best use of a property is affected by many factors, including its past and present use, land-use controls, nearby land uses, the availability or absence of utilities and transportation facilities, and recent or anticipated economic growth in the area. Analysis of highest and best use generally is easier for vacant land than for land with improvements that might require removal, so we will consider each in turn.

Highest and Best Use of Vacant Land

Suppose that a 50-acre tract of land has been planted in soybeans for some years. The value of the land in this agricultural use is $2,500 per acre. In the past, farming represented the highest and best use of the tract because the site was located several miles from a small city. More recently, the city has begun expanding because increased business and manufacturing activity there has led to population growth. These factors, combined with road improvements and the extension of water and sewer lines, have led to a change in the highest and best use of the site. In fact, there may be several legally permissible and financially feasible uses for it. One developer believes there is sufficient demand for a low-density, single-family residential subdivision and is willing to pay $30,000 per acre. Another developer wishes to build an apartment complex and is willing to pay $120,000 per acre. The second developer must believe that using the land for an apartment complex is more profitable than using it for single-family homes. Assuming both of these uses are legally permissible and physically possible, the highest and best use of this parcel is for an apartment complex because it results in the highest land value.

Highest and Best Use of Land with Improvements

In the example above, the determination of highest and best use was simplified by the fact that the land was vacant. Suppose, however, that a one-acre lot and the house on it are worth $175,000 as a single-family home. Under the current zoning ordinances, if the land was vacant, it could be sold for $80,000 as a single-family homesite, or for $150,000 for a commercial activity. If vacant, the highest and best use of the site is clearly commercial, but because the property is worth more in its current use, its highest and best use still is residential. If the value of the site for commercial use increases above its value in residential use, however, it would be advantageous to tear down the existing house and change the use to commercial. The highest and best use of this property may change quickly if the existing improvements begin to deteriorate rapidly as a result of age or other factors. Although identifying a property's highest and best use can be a difficult task, appraisers must understand the manner in which the property would be used by the typical buyer in order to estimate its most probable selling price.

Step 4: Application of the Three Approaches to Value

In the traditional appraisal process, the appraiser normally considers three approaches to value. Each of these approaches is intended to replicate the thought processes of the typical buyer in order to estimate a property's most probable selling price in an open market transaction. Because we will consider the details of each of these approaches in the following sections of this chapter, we provide only brief descriptions here.

In the **sales comparison approach,** appraisers compare similar properties that have been sold recently in open market transactions with the subject property. The prices of these comparable properties provide an indication of the value of the subject property. Of course, every property is unique, and any differences between the comparable properties and the subject property must be taken into consideration.

In the **cost approach,** appraisers arrive at an estimate of the market value of a property by estimating its cost of production. Estimating value using this approach involves (1) estimating the value of the site as though it was vacant, (2) estimating the cost to produce the improvements, (3) subtracting depreciation, and (4) adding site value. There are numerous techniques for estimating the value of vacant land, with the most preferred method being the sales comparison approach. Estimating production cost requires knowledge of construction methods and current prices of materials and labor. The estimate of production cost is based on constructing a new structure, so the appraiser must subtract any depreciation that exists in the subject property. Adding the site value to the depreciated cost of the improvements provides an indication of market value.

In the **income approach,** appraisers estimate market value by estimating the income that the property is expected to generate, then converting the income stream into a present value estimate. The techniques used to relate income expectations to market value estimates include gross income multiplier analysis, net income capitalization, and discounted cash-flow analysis.

Step 5: Reconciliation of Value Indications into a Final Value Estimate

Although the three approaches described above should theoretically lead to identical value estimates, the realities of real estate markets usually result in a different estimate of value from each approach. Large differences between the value indications suggest that one or more of the approaches may not be appropriate for estimating a particular property's market value. To arrive at a final estimate of value, appraisers must reconcile the estimates obtained from each approach. Reconciliation of the three approaches requires considerable judgment on the part of the appraiser.

In most appraisal situations, the appraiser may feel that one of the approaches provides a better indication of value than the others, and will therefore give more emphasis to that approach in the reconciliation step. For example, if an appraiser is estimating the market value of a church building, the sales comparison approach might not be appropriate if sales of church buildings are infrequent in the market. Similarly, the income approach may not be appropriate because such properties are not considered income producing. The lack of data required to implement these approaches in this situation may lead the appraiser to place more emphasis on the value estimate provided by the cost approach. In all cases, the appraiser must determine the weight given to the value indicated by each approach using his or her professional judgment. The appropriate weight depends on the amount and quality of available data, as well as the relevance of the approach to the problem at hand. When all of the approaches are relevant to some degree, appraisers often use a weighted average of the three value estimates to arrive at a final value estimate.

Step 6: Report of Defined Value

After reaching an estimate of value, the appraiser must convey the information to the client, normally in a written report. This report describes the data considered as well as the methods and reasoning used in arriving at the final value estimate. Any assumptions used in the analysis must be clearly stated and defended.

When the property involved is a single-family home and the function of the appraiser is to verify property value for loan approval purposes, the appraiser's analysis and conclusion must be reported in a format acceptable to the lender. Because lenders often sell their loans in the secondary mortgage market, the secondary market participants dictate the format of the appraisal report. Fannie Mae and Freddie Mac have jointly approved a Uniform Residential Appraisal Report Form for loans sold in the secondary mortgage market. (An example of the URAR is shown in the case study at the end of this chapter.) Similar forms are used for other types of property, including vacant land and small income properties. For more complex appraisal assignments, the analysis and conclusions are usually presented in a narrative report format. Narrative appraisal reports often exceed several hundred pages for large-scale income properties.

Now that we understand the general process appraisers use to estimate property value, we can take a closer look at the specific techniques used in each of the three approaches to value: the sales comparison approach, the cost approach, and the income approach.

THE SALES COMPARISON APPROACH

Perhaps the best single indication of the value of any good is the price that similar goods are selling for in the marketplace. This is the basis of the sales comparison approach to the valuation of real property. This technique has tremendous intuitive appeal because it closely resembles the process most buyers go through when selecting a property for purchase. The procedure involves comparing the subject property with similar properties that have sold relatively recently or are currently offered for sale, then using the sale prices of these properties to gain insight into the market value of the subject property.

Because individual parcels of real estate all have unique characteristics, close comparisons are difficult. In addition, sales data may be very sketchy or nonexistent for specialized properties. Nevertheless, when data are available, the sales comparison approach generally is considered the best method for estimating the value of real property. It is particularly valuable in appraising single-family homes in active markets.

The sales comparison approach involves two steps: (1) collection of data on sales of similar properties and (2) adjustment of the sales data to make them reflect the subject property as accurately as possible in regard to physical and locational characteristics, financing arrangements, conditions of the sale, and market conditions at the time of the sale.

Comparable Sales Data

The selection of "comparables," recent sales of properties that are roughly the same as the subject property, is critical to the market value estimate. The appraiser must take great care that the sales selected are truly representative and not distorted in some way. For example, the price that results from a voluntary sale to a mortgage lender in lieu of foreclosure probably would not be representative of the property's market value, nor would the price that results from a sale from one family member to another.

Generally, three to six comparable sales are considered adequate. The information on each transaction should include the date of sale, price, financing terms, location of the property, and a description of its physical characteristics and improvements. Deed records can provide information regarding location and date of sale, and where available, deed tax stamps may also give some indication of sales price. More definitive price and property characteristics may be provided by the buyer or seller, brokers, title and abstract companies, multiple-listing services, or specialized financial report services.

Adjustment of Sales Data

After data on comparable sales have been gathered, they must be adjusted to make them reflect the subject property as accurately as possible. The appraiser may make lump-sum adjustments by evaluating all of the differences between the comparable sale and the subject property that are considered important. For example, the appraiser may conclude that on the basis of a comparable sale of $75,000, the subject property should sell for $80,000 because of its more desirable location and better quality construction. A refinement of this lump-sum approach is to evaluate the individual elements that may affect value. In any case, the following elements of comparison must be evaluated for potential differences between the subject property and the comparable properties.

Elements of Comparison

Six different elements of comparison must be considered in the sales comparison approach. The first two elements of comparison are *property rights conveyed* and *conditions of sale.* If analysis of these two elements identifies significant differences between the subject property and any potentially comparable property, the sale price of such a comparable provides little insight into the market value of the subject property and it should be eliminated from further consideration.

For example, if the subject property involves a fee simple absolute estate and a comparable property was sold as a life estate, the subject property is almost certainly worth more than the comparable. Therefore, the sale price of the comparable property will not give a reliable indication of the value of the subject property. In most cases, appraisers prefer to eliminate properties with inconsistent property rights from further analysis. Similarly, if a potentially comparable property's transaction price is not the result of arm's-length negotiation between informed parties, the sale price of the comparable property will not provide a valid indication of the market value of the subject property. The definition of market value is explicit in defining the conditions of sale for the subject property. In general, appraisers assume that the subject property will be sold in a competitive and open market under all conditions necessary for a fair sale.

Another element of comparison addresses the *financing terms* in a comparable sale. As required by the definition of market value, the market value of the subject property is estimated in terms of cash or financial arrangements comparable to cash. If the transaction of a comparable property involves unique financial arrangements that may have affected the sale price, the sale price of the comparable must be adjusted to reflect this difference. For example, if a seller provides a mortgage loan with a below-market interest rate to the buyer, it is likely that the buyer would pay a higher price for the property. Because the financing terms in this transaction are more favorable than those generally available in the market, the price of the comparable must be adjusted downward to accurately reflect the value of the subject property. The amount of adjustment primarily depends on the interest savings provided to the buyer by the below-market financing.

Another important consideration is the fact that local market conditions are subject to change over time as a result of changing economic, political, social, and environmental factors. This element of comparison is frequently referred to as *market conditions.* A property that sold four months ago or even a week ago may sell for more or less today as a result of changing market conditions. Therefore, appraisers must adjust the sales prices of comparable properties to reflect differences in market conditions between the time of sale and the effective date of the appraisal. If conditions have improved such that a sale of a comparable property in today's market would result in a higher price, then the price of the comparable should be adjusted upward to provide a valid indication of the subject property's current market value.

Yet another element of comparison involves differences in the *locational characteristics* of the subject and comparable properties. Most people are familiar with the old saying among real estate investors that the three most important factors affecting real estate values are "location, location, and location." Though simplistic, this statement embodies a certain amount of wisdom. Because real estate values are dramatically influenced by local market factors, properties located in the same neighborhood are considered the most comparable to each other. A *neighborhood* can be defined as a geographic area containing complementary land uses. For some properties, the boundaries that define a neighborhood are quite expansive, while others are more compact. Even within the same neighborhood, one site may be preferable to another due to access and proximity to shopping and schools, traffic volume on the surrounding streets, and numerous other factors. Consideration of locational characteristics is a critical step in the adjustment process.

The final element of comparison reflects differences in *physical characteristics* between the subject property and the comparable properties. Though the possibilities are endless, some commonly encountered differences include the size of the property (land area and improvements), number and size of the rooms, type of construction, quality of construction, interior design, architectural style, and numerous special features. If the comparable properties possess physical characteristics that differ from the subject property, appropriate adjustments must be made to the sale prices of the comparable properties to ensure that the price is indicative of the subject property's market value.

When the adjustments for each of these elements of comparison are complete, the adjusted sales prices for the comparables give an indication of the value of the subject property. Again, the steps involved in this approach mirror the steps a potential buyer might go through when comparing alternative properties and making a purchase decision. The example presented below demonstrates the logic behind the sales comparison approach using "matched pair analysis" to determine the appropriate adjustment amounts.

Applying the Sales Comparison Approach

Consider the problem of estimating the value of a vacant lakefront lot in a residential subdivision. The lot under consideration measures 80 by 120 feet. Three similar vacant lots in this subdivision have sold recently in transactions resulting from arm's-length negotiations for the transfer of fee simple absolute estates, and all sale prices reflect cash-equivalent financing terms. The significant differences between these properties are date of sale, lot size, and location of the lot relative to the lake. Comparable number one measures 85 by 120 feet and is also located on the lake. It sold for $30,100 two weeks ago. Comparable number two is a lakefront lot measuring 85 by 140 feet. This lot sold one year ago for $32,500. Comparable number three sold six months ago for $21,600. It is an interior lot measuring 80 by 120 feet.

A good way to organize and analyze sales comparison data is through a market data grid such as the one shown in Table 11.1. Because the lots differ in terms of size, we can simplify our analysis by first calculating the sale price per square foot. After adjusting the sale prices of each comparable for differences in market conditions since the sale date, we can then multiply the adjusted price per square foot by the size of the subject property to arrive at an estimate of value for the subject property.

To determine the adjustment necessary to account for changing market conditions, notice that comparables 1 and 2 are both lakefront properties, but comparable 2 sold approximately one year later than comparable 1. Because we eliminated the size difference by calculating price per square foot, the only difference between comparables 1 and 2 is the date of sale. The difference in price for these properties suggests that property values have increased by approximately $.22 per square foot over the past year. Because the effective date of the appraisal is today, we must estimate the price the comparables would bring if offered for sale under current market conditions. Thus, we adjust the price per square foot of comparable 2 upward by $.22. Assuming the change in property

TABLE 11.1	Sales Comparison Market Data Grid

	Subject	Comparables #1	Comparables #2	Comparables #3
Sales price	—	$30,100	$32,500	$21,600
Size in square feet	9,600	10,200	$11,900	9,600
Price per square foot	—	$2.95	$2.73	$2.25
Date of sale	Current	– 2 weeks	– 1 year	– 6 months
Adjustment for changing market conditions	—	+$0	+$.22	+$.11
Adjusted price per square foot	—	$2.95	$2.95	$2.36
Location	Lake	Lake	Lake	Interior
Adjustment for location	—	+$0	+$0	+$.59
Adjusted price per square foot	—	$2.95	$2.95	$2.95

Indicated value of subject property: 9,600 square feet × $2.95 = $28,320

values has been constant over the past year, we can also adjust the sale price of comparable 3 upward by half of this amount, or $.11, to account for changing market conditions over the past six months.

After adjusting for changing market conditions, the only remaining difference between the subject property and any of the comparables is location of the lots relative to the lake. Our subject property is a lakefront lot, as are comparables 1 and 2. Comparable 3, however, is an interior lot. Just as we determined the adjustment for changing market conditions by comparing the sale prices of two of the comparables that differed only in terms of their sale date, we can determine the appropriate adjustment for location by comparing the sale price of comparable 3 with the sale prices of the other comparables. The higher sale prices of the first two comparables suggest that lake frontage adds approximately $.59 per square foot to property values in this neighborhood. Adding this amount to the price per square foot of comparable 3 results in a value indication from each of the comparables of $2.95. Multiplying this amount by 9,600 square feet yields $28,320. Thus, we conclude that this amount is an estimate of the current market value of the subject property, after adjustments for differences in market conditions, lot size, and location.

Although this example refers to vacant land, the same procedure can be applied to improved residential and nonresidential properties. We will apply this approach to a single-family home in the case study at the end of the chapter. Of course, it is unlikely that all of the comparable properties will provide an identical indication of value. Also, the appropriate unit of comparison is not always price per square foot. The primary consideration in this approach to value is to correctly determine the appropriate amount and direction of adjustments for each element of comparison. In most situations, the adjustments are much more detailed than those described here. Furthermore, the data available from sales of comparable properties may be insufficient to provide a valid value estimate. Without adequate data, the sales comparison approach is not reliable.

■ THE COST APPROACH

In addition to existing properties to choose from, a potential buyer of a home or other real property improvement usually has the alternative of buying a similar site and constructing a new building. Generally, therefore, site value plus production costs of the improvements tend to set the upper limit to value. In this sense, the principle of substitution is the basis of the cost approach to value. There are four key steps in the cost approach, including (1) estimating the value of the site as though it were vacant, (2) estimating the cost to produce the improvements, (3) subtracting depreciation, and (4) adding site value.

The indicated value of the property is the cost to produce the building, less the estimated accrued depreciation, plus the value of the site and site improvements. Subtracting accrued depreciation is necessary because the cost estimate is based on constructing a new, identically designed building using current prices for materials and labor. The subject property is most likely not new, and if it were constructed new, any design flaws would be corrected. Estimating the accrued depreciation for a property is often the most difficult step of the cost approach.

Estimating Site Value

The first step in the cost approach is to estimate the value of the site. Land values are usually estimated by the sales comparison approach, as demonstrated above, though other techniques are sometimes used. The cost of site improvements such as grading, landscaping, and paving must be added to arrive at a total value for the site.

Estimating Production Cost

The second step in the cost approach is to estimate the production cost of the improvements. Production cost estimates are based on either *reproduction cost* or *replacement cost*. Reproduction cost refers to the cost of constructing an exact replica of the subject property's improvements, while replacement cost refers to the cost of constructing an equally functional improvement, rather than an exact duplicate. Using replacement cost as the basis for this approach simplifies the cost-estimating procedure when the property being appraised contains design elements or materials that are out-of-date and would, therefore, not be included if the building was constructed today.

Estimating production cost requires specialized knowledge regarding construction methods, so appraisers frequently rely on engineering and architectural experts for accurate cost estimates. Professional cost-estimating companies such as *Marshall Valuation* publish cost manuals or provide computerized cost programs that assist appraisers in this task. In practice, construction costs can be estimated by obtaining actual expenditure data on the subject property, by collecting data on other similar projects in the area, or through data services that collect and distribute cost data on various types of construction. Methods used in estimating production costs include the comparative-unit method, the segregated-cost method, and the quantity-survey method. Of these methods, the quantity-survey method is the most detailed.

The comparative-unit method employs the known costs of similar structures, typically measured in dollars per square foot, to derive an estimate of the cost to produce a subject property's improvements. For example, a typical warehouse might cost $32.15 per square foot to construct. If the subject property contains 50,000 square feet, its cost is estimated at $1,607,500. This approach does not separately identify the individual components that make up the building, but it can be fairly accurate for properties with uniform construction.

In the segregated-cost method, the unit costs for various building components are used to arrive at a cost estimate. If the cost of building finished exterior walls on a warehouse is $5.52 per square foot, and the subject property has 10,700 square feet of exterior walls, then the cost of this component would be approximately $59,000. The cost of each major component of the building (walls, roof, flooring, plumbing, etc.) is estimated separately, then all costs are added together for a final cost estimate. This method is more comprehensive than the comparative-unit method, but less detailed than the quantity-survey method.

The quantity-survey method is the most comprehensive method, and is therefore more accurate. In this method, the quantity and quality of all materials and all categories of labor are identified separately, then costs for each of these items are totaled to arrive at a final cost estimate. For example, the number of sheets of plywood, gallons of paint, the amount of piping, hours of electricians' labor, and all other materials or labor needed to construct the building must be identified and the costs of each estimated. The quantity-survey method provides the most detailed cost estimate, but it is time-consuming and not used frequently in the appraisal process.

Estimating Accrued Depreciation

Structures wear out over time. They also may become obsolete or unprofitable because of technological innovation or economic change. Therefore, unless the ubject property's improvements are new, appraisers must estimate **accrued depreciation**—the amount by which the value of a building has declined since it was built, as a consequence of physical deterioration, functional obsolescence, and economic obsolescence.

Physical deterioration may result from ordinary wear and tear, weathering from the elements, vandalism, or neglect. Physical deterioration should be minimal in new buildings and can be prevented or minimized by proper maintenance and quality construction. Appraisers often estimate the effective age of the improvements, then use the ratio of effective age to useful life to measure physical deterioration. For example, a 15-year-old house with normal maintenance might exhibit 25 percent physical deterioration if its useful life is 60 years.

Many properties suffer their greatest loss in value from the effects of obsolescence, both functional and economic. **Functional obsolescence** is a loss in value that occurs because the property has less utility or ability to generate income than a new property designed for the same use. This sort of depreciation results from factors inherent in the property itself. It may occur because of changes in technology or in tastes, which would cause a new building to be constructed quite differently from the way the existing structure was built. For example, buildings using asbestos insulation now suffer a large penalty. To a lesser extent, so do outmoded, multistory factory buildings and poorly designed houses with small, dark rooms. An increasingly important issue faced by appraisers is the difficulty of estimating the value of environmentally contaminated parcels.

Economic (or external) **obsolescence** is a loss in value resulting from factors outside the property that affect its income-producing ability or other degree of use. For example, suppose that a well-designed and well-constructed motel in good physical condition is located in an area that is bypassed by a new highway. The resulting decline in traffic may greatly decrease the income-producing ability of the property and hence its value. Economic obsolescence also may occur because of changes in consumer expenditure patterns, population movements, adverse legislation, or neighborhood change.

Applying the Cost Approach

To demonstrate the steps involved in the cost approach, consider a two-year-old apartment building. To estimate its value by this approach, we must estimate the value of the site, the production cost of the improvements, and the accrued depreciation resulting from physical deterioration and economic and functional obsolescence. Suppose the appraiser estimates these items as shown in Table 11.2. The land value is estimated as $150,000 using the sales comparison approach. Estimated production cost for the 2-year-old building is $594,000.

Even though the buildings are almost new, the appraiser still determines that there should be some allowance for depreciation. A minor roof repair is necessary ($4,680), and there is some miscellaneous physical deterioration that requires attention ($17,820). In addition, the appraiser judges that the swimming pool has been placed too close to apartment number 11, resulting in some minor functional obsolescence that could be eliminated by building an appropriate screening wall ($4,000). Because the property is relatively new, the appraiser determines that no allowance is necessary for economic obsolescence. Depreciation from all causes in

TABLE 11.2	Summary of Cost Valuation of an Apartment Property		
Estimated production cost			$594,000
Depreciation			
Physical deterioration: cost of repairs (roof repair, painting, exterior caulking)		$ 4,680	
Miscellaneous physical deterioration (3% of reproduction costs)		17,820	
Functional obsolescence (screen between swimming pool and apartment to reduce noise from pool)		4,000	
Economic obsolescence		0	
Production cost less depreciation			567,500
Estimated site value			150,000
Total value indicated by cost approach			$717,500
Rounded			$718,000

the amount of $26,500 is subtracted from the estimated reproduction costs to yield a depreciated building value of $567,500. Adding this amount to the site value provides an indication of value by the cost approach of $717,500, which the appraiser rounds to $718,000.

The Income Approach

The income approach to value is based on the principle of anticipation, which implies that purchasers buy properties in expectation of receiving future benefits. In general, the value of any income-earning asset can be thought of as the sum of the present value of the expected future returns to the owner, including both periodic cash flows from operations and cash flows from the eventual sale of the asset. The same logic is valid for any income-producing asset, whether it be the goose that lays golden eggs, a savings certificate from a financial institution, common stock, or such income-producing real estate as an apartment complex, a shopping mall, an office complex, or an industrial building. The income approach in real estate appraisal involves two basic steps: estimating future income and converting the income estimate into a present value estimate.

Appraisers employ many different techniques to convert future income into present value estimates. Each of these techniques has been developed to replicate the thought processes of the typical buyer in a market. We consider three of these techniques here: gross income multiplier analysis, net income capitalization, and discounted cash-flow analysis.

Gross Income Multiplier

All techniques used in the income approach to value are based on the idea that market participants demand investment returns in exchange for purchasing income properties. Furthermore, competition between market participants results in a relatively stable relationship between income and value in most real estate markets. When this relationship can be measured or quantified, appraisers can use it to estimate market values. One rule-of-thumb measure of the relationship between gross income and market value is the **gross income multiplier,** or GIM.

$$Gross\ Income\ Multiplier\ =\ \frac{Value}{Gross\ Income}$$

The GIM is an estimate of the prevailing relationship between prices investors are willing to pay for properties and the gross income the properties are expected to produce. To calculate the GIM for a market, appraisers collect information about properties that have recently sold in the market, then divide the price of each property by its gross income. Of course, the properties used to estimate the GIM for a market must truly be comparable to the subject property. Gross income is defined as the total amount of revenue the property is expected to generate annually.

For example, consider a property that is expected to generate $10,000 per year in gross income. If that property is sold in an arm's-length transaction for $100,000, the GIM for this property is 10: 100,000 ÷ 10,000. To use this measure to estimate the value of a similar property that is expected to generate $9,000 per year in gross income, we multiply $9,000 by 10 to get a market value estimate of $90,000. By observing market transactions, appraisers can measure the relationship between income and value using GIM, then use the multiplier to estimate market value of the subject property.

Because the GIM technique ignores the expenses of operating an income property, it is most appropriate when the expenses of the comparable sales are similar to the expenses of the subject property. When expenses differ across properties, a more detailed technique is required. The net income capitalization technique described below is an alternative technique that recognizes the variability in operating expenses across similar properties.

Net Income Capitalization

The net income capitalization technique recognizes that the value of an income property depends on "net" rather than "gross" income as discussed above. In this technique, net income is converted into a present value estimate using a **capitalization rate** rather than a multiplier. The relationship between value and net income is measured as shown below:

$$Capitalization\ Rate\ =\frac{Net\ Income}{Value}$$

For example, consider a property that recently sold in an arm's-length transaction for $1 million. If this property is expected to generate net income of $100,000 annually, the implied **capitalization rate** for this property is 10 percent. To estimate the value of a similar property that is expected to generate $105,000 in net income (gross income minus expenses), we can rearrange the capitalization rate formula as follows:

$$Value = \frac{Net\ Income}{Capitalization\ Rate}$$

$$Value = \frac{\$105,000}{.10}$$

$$Value = \$1,050,000$$

Dividing net income by 10 percent provides a market value estimate of $1,050,000 for this property. By observing market transactions, appraisers can determine the capitalization rate that best represents the relationship between net income and value, then use this measure to estimate the value of a subject property based on its net income. The accuracy of this technique, of course, depends on accurate estimates of the subject property's net income and the capitalization rate.

Discounted Cash-Flow Analysis

A third technique appraisers use in the income approach is *discounted cash-flow analysis*. Unlike the previous two methods, which focus on a single year's income estimate to arrive at a value estimate, this technique involves forecasting the future benefits the property is expected to generate in each year of the expected holding period. The benefits are classified in two categories: annual expected net income over the holding period and expected net selling price at the end of the holding period. Once estimated, the appraiser then converts these cash flows into a present value estimate by discounting them at the appropriate discount rate. The following example demonstrates this technique.

Consider an appraisal assignment involving a new warehouse with 50,000 square feet of rentable area. After evaluating competing warehouses in this market, the appraiser estimates market rent for this space at $12.50 per square foot in the first year, with annual increases of 3 percent per year. The vacancy rate for this property is expected to be 25 percent in the first year, and 5 percent thereafter. The appraiser estimates operating expenses (utilities, management fees, property taxes, maintenance, etc.) at 20 percent of effective gross income. There is an outstanding mortgage on this property with a balance of $2,200,000. The loan requires annual payments of $224,000 for the next 20 years. Discussions with local real estate investors suggest that the typical buyer for this property would have an expected holding period of 10 years. The appraiser believes that the selling price at the end of year 10 can be forecast by applying an overall

TABLE 11.3   Applying the Discounted Cash-Flow Technique

	Year 1	Year 2	Year 3	Year 4	Year 5	Year 6	Year 7	Year 8	Year 9	Year 10	Year 11
Potential gross income	$625,000	$643,750	$663,063	$682,954	$703,443	$724,546	$746,283	$768,671	$791,731	$815,483	$839,948
– Vacancy losses	–156,250	–32,188	–33,153	–34,148	–35,172	–36,227	–37,314	–38,434	–39,587	–40,774	–41,997
Effective gross income	$468,750	$611,562	$629,910	$648,806	$668,271	$688,319	$708,969	$730,237	$752,144	$774,709	$797,951
– Operating expenses	–93,750	–122,313	–125,982	–129,761	–133,654	–137,664	–141,794	–146,048	–150,429	–154,942	–159,590
Net operating income	$375,000	$489,249	$503,928	$519,045	$534,617	$550,655	$567,175	$584,189	$601,715	$619,767	$638,361

Year 11 net operating income	$638,361
Overall capitalization rate	.10
Gross sale prices (NOI/R)	$6,383,610
– Selling expenses	–319,180
Net sales price	$6,064,430

Present value of cash flows at 13 percent: $2,909,233.

REAL ESTATE TODAY

Applying the Appraisal Process in a Single-Family Home Appraisal

Consider a hypothetical single-family home owned by Harold and Gladys Stewart. Suppose that an agreement has been reached between the Stewarts and Frank and Elizabeth Barr. The Barrs have agreed to purchase the property for $120,000. The Barrs plan on borrowing 90 percent of the purchase price, using a mortgage loan from a local lender. As part of the loan approval process, the lender requires that an appraisal be performed by a qualified real estate appraiser to verify that the property value supports the requested loan amount. The following discussion describes the steps the appraiser will take to apply the appraisal process to this property.

Case Study

Defining the Problem

The appraiser selected to perform the assignment for the Barrs' lender is Michelle Tipton, a state-certified appraiser. Michelle has ten years' experience in the appraisal industry and is qualified to perform appraisals on all types of properties. Her fee for this appraisal assignment is $250. The cost of hiring the appraiser will be paid by the Barrs, even though the appraiser is performing the appraisal on behalf of the lender.

The Barrs and their lender will provide Michelle with the basic information she needs to begin the appraisal process. To define the appraisal problem at hand, the appraiser must know what type of value she is trying to estimate, the property rights being appraised, and the legal description of the property that is the subject of the appraisal. In this case, the purpose of the appraisal is to estimate the current market value of the property described as

> All that tract or parcel of land, situated in St. Joseph, Buchanan County, Missouri, together with all improvements thereon, known as 1097 Timbers Crossing. Such property is more accurately described as Lot 3, Block G, of the Harris Billups Estate,

as recorded in Plat Book 8, page 37, in the Office of the Clerk of the Circuit Court of Buchanan County, Missouri.

The property rights being appraised are those that comprise a fee simple absolute ownership interest in the subject property. All of this information will be entered in the "Subject" section of the URAR as shown in Figure 11.1.

Selecting and Collecting the Data

After defining the appraisal problem, the appraiser begins selecting and collecting the data she will need to estimate the value of the subject property. She begins by personally inspecting the property to familiarize herself with its neighborhood, as well as the physical characteristics of the site and improvements.

As indicated in the "Neighborhood" section of Figure 11.1, the property is located in an urban area that is over 75 percent developed, has a stable growth rate, stable property values, and with supply and demand conditions that appear to be in balance. In addition, Michelle notes that the age of homes in this neighborhood ranges from new to 50 years old, and that prices range from $70,000 to $155,000. Single-family homes make up approximately 85 percent of all properties in this area, with 2-4-family structures, 4-or-more-family structures, and commercial uses accounting for 5 percent each. Michelle believes that a change in land use in this neighborhood is not likely in the near future. Michelle also defines the boundaries of the neighborhood and its characteristics, and provides additional comments about the market conditions in the subject neighborhood as shown on the Report.

In the "Site" section of the URAR, the appraiser reports the site dimensions, the size of the site, whether the property is a corner lot, the zoning classification, zoning compliance, utilities available to the site, off-site improvements, and other site-related information. Notice that this section requires

REAL ESTATE TODAY

Applying the Appraisal Process in a Single-Family Home Appraisal (continued)

FIGURE 11.1   Uniform Residential Appraisal Report

File No. 96-100 Page # 1

Summary Appraisal Report
Property Description

UNIFORM RESIDENTIAL APPRAISAL REPORT   File No. 96-100

Field	Value
Property Address	1097 Timbers Crossing City St. Joseph State MO Zip Code 94334
Legal Description	Lot 3, Block G, Harris Billups Estate, Plat Book 8, P. 37 County Buchanan
Assessor's Parcel No.	9223-03-0471 Tax Year 1994 R.E. Taxes $ 1,207.10 Special Assessments $ N/A
Borrower	Barr, Frank & Elizabeth Current Owner Stewart Occupant [X] Owner [ ] Tenant [ ] Vacant
Property rights appraised	[X] Fee Simple [ ] Leasehold Project Type [ ] PUD [ ] Condominium (HUD/VA only) HOA $ N/A /Mo.
Neighborhood or Project Name	Harris Billups Estate Map Reference Census Tract
Sale Price $	120,000 Date of Sale Description and $ amount of loan charges/concessions to be paid by seller None
Lender/Client	Barber Savings Association Address 4390 N. Main St., St. Joseph MO 94330
Appraiser	Michelle Tipton Address 2125 S. Main St., St. Joseph MO 94330

Location [X] Urban [ ] Suburban [ ] Rural
Built up [X] Over 75% [ ] 25-75% [ ] Under 25%
Growth rate [ ] Rapid [X] Stable [ ] Slow
Property values [ ] Increasing [X] Stable [ ] Declining
Demand/supply [ ] Shortage [X] In balance [ ] Over supply
Marketing time [ ] Under 3 mos. [X] 3-6 mos. [ ] Over 6 mos.

Predominant occupancy [X] Owner [ ] Tenant [X] Vacant (0-5%) [ ] Vac.(over 5%)

Single family housing

	PRICE $(000)	AGE (yrs)
Low	70	00
High	155	50
Predominant	120	20

Present land use %
One family 85
2-4 family 5
Multi-family 5
Commercial 5

Land use change [X] Not likely [ ] Likely [ ] In process   To:

Note: Race and the racial composition of the neighborhood are not appraisal factors.

Neighborhood boundaries and characteristics: Area of mostly single family homes located north of Oak Park Blvd., west of Highway 60, South of Floral Road and east of Dixie Drive.

Factors that affect the marketability of the properties in the neighborhood (proximity to employment and amenities, employment stability, appeal to market, etc.): The subject is located close to neighborhood shopping, parks, public schools and employment centers. The subject's neighborhood exhibits the typical appeal and condition for the area. The presence of 5% commercial utilization is limited to the main thoroughfares and does not adversely affect the subject's value or marketability.

Market conditions in the subject neighborhood (including support for the above conclusions related to the trend of property values, demand/supply, and marketing time -- such as data on competitive properties for sale in the neighborhood, description of the prevalence of sales and financing concessions, etc.): Mortgage money is readily available in the St. Joseph market. Any loan discounts, interest buydowns or concessions do not adversely affect the subject. The subject is located in a family oriented neighborhood whose supply and demand appear to be in balance.

Project Information for PUDs   (If applicable) -- Is the developer/builder in control of the Home Owners' Association (HOA)? [ ] Yes [ ] No
Approximate total number of units in the subject project _____   Approximate total number of units for sale in the subject project _____
Describe common elements and recreational facilities: N/A

Field	Value	Field	Value
Dimensions	80 x 120 (Subject to survey)	Topography	Typical Level
Site area	9600	Size	Typical
	Corner Lot [ ] Yes [X] No	Shape	Rectangular
Specific zoning classification and description	Residential (RM-25)	Drainage	Apparently Adequate
Zoning compliance [X] Legal [ ] Legal nonconforming (Grandfathered use) [ ] Illegal [ ] No zoning		View	Residential
Highest & best use as improved: [X] Present use [ ] Other use (explain)		Landscaping	Adequate/ Typical

Utilities Public / Other
Electricity [X]
Gas
Water [X]
Sanitary sewer [X]
Storm sewer

Off-site improvements Type / Public / Private
Street Asphalt [X]
Curb/gutter None
Sidewalk None
Street lights [X]
Alley None

Driveway Surface Asphalt
Apparent easements None observed
FEMA Special Flood Hazard Area [ ] Yes [X] No
FEMA Zone   Map Date
FEMA Map No.

Comments (apparent adverse easements, encroachments, special assessments, slide areas, illegal or legal nonconforming zoning use, etc.): No apparent adverse easements, encroachments or conditions observed.

GENERAL DESCRIPTION		EXTERIOR DESCRIPTION		FOUNDATION		BASEMENT		INSULATION	
No. of Units	1	Foundation	Concrete	Slab	Yes	Area Sq. Ft.	N/A	Roof	[ ]
No. of Stories	1	Exterior Walls	CBS	Crawl Space	No	% Finished		Ceiling	[ ]
Type (Det./Att.)	Detached	Roof Surface	Shingle	Basement	No	Ceiling		Walls	[ ]
Design (Style)	Ranch	Gutters & Dwnspts.	Typical	Sump Pump	N/A	Walls		Floor	[ ]
Existing/Proposed	Yes/No	Window Type	Awning	Dampness	N/A	Floor		None	[ ]
Age (Yrs.)	15	Storm/Screens	No/Yes	Settlement	N/A	Outside Entry		Unknown	[X]
Effective Age (Yrs.)	14 - 17	Manufactured House	No	Infestation	N/A				

ROOMS	Foyer	Living	Dining	Kitchen	Den	Family Rm.	Rec. Rm.	Bedrooms	# Baths	Laundry	Other	Area Sq. Ft.
Basement												N/A
Level 1		X	X	X		X		3	2	X		1950
Level 2												

Finished area above grade contains: 7 Rooms;   3 Bedroom(s);   2 Bath(s);   1,950 Square Feet of Gross Living Area

INTERIOR	Materials/Condition	HEATING		KITCHEN EQUIP.		ATTIC		AMENITIES		CAR STORAGE: 2	
Floors	Carpet/Vinyl/*	Type	Centrl	Refrigerator	[X]	None	[X]	Fireplace(s) #		None	[ ]
Walls	Plaster/Avg	Fuel	Electr	Range/Oven	[X]	Stairs		Patio Concrete	[X]	Garage	# of cars
Trim/Finish	Wood/Average	Condition Avg		Disposal		Drop Stair		Deck		Attached	
Bath Floor	Vinyl/Average	COOLING		Dishwasher		Scuttle	[X]	Porch Open	[X]	Detached	
Bath Wainscot	Ceramic/Avg	Central	X	Fan/Hood		Floor		Fence		Built-In	
Doors	Wood/Average	Other		Microwave		Heated		Pool		Carport	2
* Average		Condition Avg		Washer/Dryer	[X]	Finished				Driveway	Single

Additional features (special energy efficient items, etc.): Typical, ceiling fans (4).

Condition of the improvements, depreciation (physical, functional, and external), repairs needed, quality of construction, remodeling/additions, etc.: The subject shows average condition on the interior and exterior and exhibits the typical appeal for the area. No functional or external obsolescence observed.

Adverse environmental conditions (such as, but not limited to, hazardous wastes, toxic substances, etc.) present in the improvements, on the site, or in the immediate vicinity of the subject property.: No apparent adverse environmental conditions were observed.

Freddie Mac Form 70 6/93   PAGE 1 OF 2   Fannie Mae Form 1004 6/93

REAL ESTATE TODAY

Applying the Appraisal Process in a Single-Family Home Appraisal (continued)

FIGURE 11.1   Uniform Residential Appraisal Report (continued)

File No. 96-100 Page # 2

UNIFORM RESIDENTIAL APPRAISAL REPORT

Valuation Section   File No. 96-100

COST APPROACH			
ESTIMATED SITE VALUE 32,000	= $ 32,000	Comments on Cost Approach (such as, source of cost estimate, site value, square foot calculation and for HUD, VA and FmHA, the estimated remaining economic life of the property): Cost estimates derived from Marshall Valuation Services publications.	
ESTIMATED REPRODUCTION COST-NEW-OF IMPROVEMENTS:			
Dwelling 1,950 Sq. Ft. @$ 58.00 = $ 113,100			
N/A Sq. Ft. @$ =			
Appliances/Patio/Porch = 2,500			
Garage/Carport 430 Sq. Ft. @$ 11.00 = 4,730			
Total Estimated Cost New = $ 120,330			
Less Physical Functional External		The subject's land to building ratio is typical for the area and does not adversely affect the subject value or marketability.	
Depreciation 30,083 =$ 30,083			
Depreciated Value of Improvements =$ 90,247			
As-is Value of Site Improvements drive, landscp. =$ 2,200			
INDICATED VALUE BY COST APPROACH =$ 124,447		Est. remaining economic life: 40-45 years	

ITEM	SUBJECT	COMPARABLE NO. 1		COMPARABLE NO. 2		COMPARABLE NO. 3	
Address	1097 Timbers Crossin St. Joseph	1255 NE 34 Street		1297 NE 34 Street		1539 NE 38 Street	
Proximity to Subject		1 Block Southwest		1 Block South		5 Blocks Northeast	
Sales Price	$ 120,000	$ 119,000		$ 126,500		$ 121,000	
Price/Gross Living Area	$ 61.54	$ 63.47		$ 65.89		$ 61.58	
Data and/or Verification Source	Inspection	MLS		MLS		MLS	
VALUE ADJUSTMENTS	DESCRIPTION	DESCRIPTION	+(−)$ Adjust.	DESCRIPTION	+(−)$ Adjust.	DESCRIPTION	+(−)$ Adjust.
Sales or Financing Concessions		VA	-1,000	Conventional		Conventional	
Date of Sale/Time		8/96		9/96		7/96	
Location	Average	Average		Average		Average	
Leasehold/Fee Simple	Fee Simple	Fee Simple		Fee Simple		Fee Simple	
Site	9600	Corner/Avg		Corner/Avg		Inside/Avg	
View	Residential	Commercial	+2,000	Residential		Residential	
Design and Appeal	Ranch	Ranch/Avg		Ranch/Avg		Ranch/Avg	
Quality of Construction	CBS	CBS		CBS		CBS	
Age	15	16		14		16	
Condition	Average	Average		Average		Average	
Above Grade Room Count	Total 7 Bdrms 3 Baths 2	Total 7 Bdrms 3 Baths 2		Total 7 Bdrms 3 Baths 2		Total 7 Bdrms 3 Baths 2	
Gross Living Area	1,950 Sq. Ft.	1,875 Sq. Ft.	+1,125	1,920 Sq. Ft.		1,965 Sq. Ft.	
Basement & Finished Rooms Below Grade	N/A	None		None		None	
Functional Utility	Average	Average		Average		Average	
Heating/Cooling	Central	Central		Central		Central	
Energy Efficient Items	Typical	Typical		Typical		Typical	
Garage/Carport		Carport (2)		Garage (2)	-5,000	Carport (2)	
Porch, Patio, Deck,	Porch	Porch		Porch		Porch	
Fireplace(s), etc.	Patio	Patio		Patio		Patio	
Fence, Pool, etc.	Average	Average		Fence	-1,000	Average	
Net Adj. (total)		[X]+ □− $ 2,125		□+ [X]− $ 6,000		[X]+ □− $ 0	
Adjusted Sales Price of Comparable		$ 121,125		$ 120,500		$ 121,000	

Comments on Sales Comparison (including the subject property's compatibility to the neighborhood, etc.): All comparables utilized are of similar single family homes located in the same neighborhood as the subject with a range from $120,500 to $121,125. A time adjustment could not be supported by the market.

ITEM	SUBJECT	COMPARABLE NO. 1	COMPARABLE NO. 2	COMPARABLE NO. 3
Date, Price and Data Source, for prior sales within year of appraisal	N/A	N/A	N/A	N/A

Analysis of any current agreement of sale, option, or listing of subject property and analysis of any prior sales of subject and comparables within one year of the date of appraisal: The subject was not listed for sale on the open market.

INDICATED VALUE BY SALES COMPARISON APPROACH		$ 121,000
INDICATED VALUE BY INCOME APPROACH (If Applicable) Estimated Market Rent $ 1275 /Mo. x Gross Rent Multiplier 95 = $		121,125

This appraisal is made [X] *as is* □ subject to the repairs, alterations, inspections or conditions listed below □ subject to completion per plans & specifications.
Conditions of Appraisal: No personal property was included in the estimate of value.

Final Reconciliation: Weight was given to all three approaches, with the most weight given to the market data approach as it best reflects the action of the buyers and sellers.

The purpose of this appraisal is to estimate the market value of the real property that is the subject of this report, based on the above conditions and the certification, contingent and limiting conditions, and market value definition that are stated in the attached Freddie Mac Form 439/FNMA form 1004B (Revised 6/93).
I (WE) ESTIMATE THE MARKET VALUE, AS DEFINED, OF THE REAL PROPERTY THAT IS THE SUBJECT OF THIS REPORT, AS OF September 4, 1996 (WHICH IS THE DATE OF INSPECTION AND THE EFFECTIVE DATE OF THIS REPORT) TO BE $ 121,000

APPRAISER: Michelle Tipton	SUPERVISORY APPRAISER (ONLY IF REQUIRED):	
Signature	Signature	□ Did □ Did Not
Name Michelle Tipton	Name	Inspect Property
Date Report Signed September 4, 1996	Date Report Signed	
State Certification # St.Cert.Res.REA RD 010092 State MO	State Certification #	State
Or State License # State MO	Or State License #	State

Freddie Mac Form 70 6/93   PAGE 2 OF 2   Fannie Mae Form 1004 6-93

REAL ESTATE TODAY

Applying the Appraisal Process in a Single-Family Home Appraisal (continued)

that the appraiser identify the highest and best use of the site. Of course, if the appraiser determines that the highest and best use of the site is not single-family residential, then the URAR form should not be used to report the value estimate.

Case Study

The site in this example is rectangular (80 feet by 120 feet), is zoned for residential use, and has access to public electricity, water, and sewer. The property is not on a corner, and the street is asphalt. The site appears to be well-drained, has adequate landscaping, and has an asphalt driveway. The property is not located in a flood zone as defined by the Federal Emergency Management Agency (FEMA).

The appraiser will also note the major characteristics of the improvements on the site as shown in the "Description of Improvements" section of Figure 11.1. The single-family detached house located on this site is a one-story, ranch-style home built with concrete block and stucco (CBS) on a concrete slab foundation. The roof is asphalt shingles, with typical gutters and downspouts. The windows are awning type with screens. The house consists of a living room, dining room, kitchen, a family room, three bedrooms, two bathrooms, and a laundry room. The size of the home is 1,950 square feet. The interior walls are plaster, with wooden doors and trim. The floors are covered in carpet and vinyl tile. The house is served by a central heating and cooling unit that operates on electricity. The house has no attic storage, but it does have a small concrete patio and an open porch. As is typical in this market, kitchen equipment includes a refrigerator, range, and washer/dryer. The house has a two-car carport of 430 square feet.

The URAR also has a designated section for the appraiser to comment on any additional features of the property, the overall condition of the improvements, and any adverse environmental conditions that might affect property value. In this example, the appraiser finds no unusual factors that should be noted.

Now that the appraiser is familiar with the property, she must now collect the specific information she will need to apply the three approaches to value. For the cost approach, the information required includes construction cost data and a site value estimate. For the sales comparison approach, she must identify comparable properties that have sold recently in the subject property's neighborhood. For the income approach, she must obtain information about the income-earning ability of the subject property and the relationship between income and value that prevails in the market. We will consider each of these approaches in detail.

Applying the Cost Approach

To complete the first step in the cost approach, Michelle uses the sales comparison approach to estimate the value of the site as if it were vacant. Her estimate of the site value is $32,000. Second, Michelle consults a residential construction cost-estimating guide and finds that this type of dwelling costs approximately $58 per square foot to produce. The appliances, porch, and patio cost approximately $2,500, and the carport costs $11 per square foot. Because the house is 15 years old, Michelle determines that depreciation from all sources is approximately 25 percent of the total production cost. Finally, she estimates the value of site improvements (asphalt driveway and average landscaping) at approximately $2,200. All of this information is summarized in the "Cost Approach" section of the URAR.

Applying the Sales Comparison Approach

The approach that receives the most emphasis in the URAR is the sales comparison approach. In this case, Michelle has identified three comparable properties that have sold recently in the subject property's market area. The address of each com-

REAL ESTATE TODAY

Applying the Appraisal Process in a Single-Family Home Appraisal (continued)

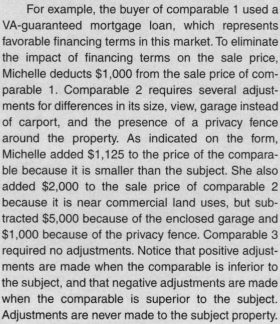

Case Study

parable, its proximity to the subject, and its recent sales price is entered into the "Sales Comparison Analysis" section of the URAR. Michelle then considers each of the elements of comparison discussed in this chapter to determine if adjustments are necessary to account for differences between the subject property transaction and the comparables.

For example, the buyer of comparable 1 used a VA-guaranteed mortgage loan, which represents favorable financing terms in this market. To eliminate the impact of financing terms on the sale price, Michelle deducts $1,000 from the sale price of comparable 1. Comparable 2 requires several adjustments for differences in its size, view, garage instead of carport, and the presence of a privacy fence around the property. As indicated on the form, Michelle added $1,125 to the price of the comparable because it is smaller than the subject. She also added $2,000 to the sale price of comparable 2 because it is near commercial land uses, but subtracted $5,000 because of the enclosed garage and $1,000 because of the privacy fence. Comparable 3 required no adjustments. Notice that positive adjustments are made when the comparable is inferior to the subject, and that negative adjustments are made when the comparable is superior to the subject. Adjustments are never made to the subject property.

The adjusted sales prices of the three comparables suggest that the market value of the subject property by this approach is between $120,500 and $121,125. Michelle concludes that the value indicated by this approach is $121,000.

Applying the Income Approach

The income approach usually receives little emphasis in appraisal assignments involving owner-occupied single-family homes because single-family homes are bought for consumption, rather than purely investment, purposes. The income approach is designed for estimating the value of income-producing investment properties rather than owner-occupied homes. When the income approach is used, a variation of the GIM technique is used to arrive at a value estimate. Known as the **gross rent multiplier** (GRM) technique, the appraiser collects information about the monthly rents and sale prices of homes in the area, then arrives at an estimate of the monthly gross rent multiplier for the market. In this case, Michelle finds two homes in this market that were operated as rental properties and have recently sold. From these transactions, she finds that the monthly market rent for the subject property is approximately $1,275 and the gross rent multiplier is 95. She uses this information to calculate a value estimate using the income approach of $121,125 ($1,275 × 95).

Reconciliation

Now that she has used each of the three approaches, Michelle must reconcile the three value indications into a final estimate of value. Michelle believes that all three approaches to value deserve some consideration, but gives most weight in the reconciliation step to the sales comparison approach. In Michelle's professional judgment, the estimated market value of the property is $121,000.

capitalization rate of 10 percent to year 11's net operating income. Selling expenses are forecast at 5 percent. The appraiser uses this information to forecast the expected net income for each of the next ten years and the expected net selling price at the end of the ten-year holding period as shown in Table 11.3.

The next step in this discounted cash flow method is to select the discount rate. The appropriate discount rate is the rate or "yield" that a knowledgeable investor would expect to receive from competing investment opportunities in the market. Assuming the appraiser in this example determines that investors in this market expect 13 percent yield on their investments, we can discount the cash flows in this example at 13 percent and calculate a present value estimate of $2,909,233, which is then rounded to $2,900,000. (The process of discounting future values into present values is described in detail in a subsequent chapter.)

■ CHAPTER REVIEW

- ■ Real estate appraisers are specialists who possess the skills and knowledge necessary to estimate property value. The appraisal industry is subject to state regulation as a result of the Financial Institutions Recovery and Reform Act of 1989, which requires that appraisals for property involved in "federally related" transactions be performed by state licensed or certified appraisers.

- ■ The type of value that appraisers most often estimate is market value, or a property's most probable selling price in well-defined situations.

- ■ Some of the key principles underlying appraisal practice are (a) anticipation, (b) change, (c) substitution, and (d) contribution.

- ■ The steps in the appraisal process include (a) definition of the problem, (b) data selection and collection, (c) highest and best use analysis, (d) application of the three approaches to value, (e) reconciliation, and (f) reporting the defined value.

- ■ In the sales comparison approach to value, appraisers compare the subject property with similar properties that have sold recently. After adjusting for differences in the appropriate elements of comparison, the prices of these "comparables" provide an indication of the value of the subject property.

- ■ In the cost approach, appraisers estimate value by estimating a property's cost of production. The steps in the cost approach are (a) estimate the value of the site (b) estimate the cost to produce the improvements, (c) estimate accrued depreciation, (d) subtract depreciation from production cost, and (e) add site value.

- ■ In the income approach, appraisers estimate value by forecasting the future income that is expected to be generated by the property, then converting that forecast into a present value. Techniques include gross income multiplier analysis, net income capitalization, and discounted cash-flow analysis.

■ KEY TERMS

accrued depreciation	change	investment value
anticipation	contribution	licensed appraiser
appraisal process	cost approach	market value
assessed value	economic obsolescence	physical deterioration
capitalization rate	functional obsolescence	price
certified residential appraiser	gross income multiplier	sales comparison approach
certified general appraiser	highest and best use	substitution
	income approach	
	insurable value	

■ STUDY EXERCISES

1. Based on the most widely accepted definition, what is market value?
2. Define the following concepts: value in exchange, value in use, investment value.
3. Does the concept of market value reflect the perceptions of the typical buyer in a market or a specific buyer? What is the difference?
4. Under what conditions is price equivalent to market value?
5. In what circumstances is it possible for the production cost of a property to exceed its market value?
6. Define the following terms: assessed value, insurable value.
7. List and define the four key appraisal principles discussed in the chapter.
8. Outline the steps in the appraisal process.
9. What issues must be considered in step 1 of the appraisal process?
10. Define the concept of highest and best use. Why is this an important step in the appraisal process?
11. Consider a property that is worth $45,000 as a vacant commercial site. The property is improved with a single-family residence. As such, the property is worth $35,000. If it costs $5,000 to demolish the structure, what is the value of the site? What is the value of the structure? What is the highest and best use of this property?
12. List the steps involved in each of the three approaches to value.
13. Why is reconciliation a necessary step in the appraisal process?
14. List the six elements of comparison in the sales comparison approach.

15. Consider a vacant lakefront lot measuring 90 by 120 feet in a residential subdivision. Three similar vacant lots have sold recently. Comparable number one measures 85 by 120 feet and is also located on the lake. It sold for $35,000 one week ago. Comparable number two is also on the lake, and it measures 85 by 120. It sold one year ago for $30,000. Comparable number three sold six months ago for $31,000. It is a hillside lot that offers an exceptional view. The lot measures 80 by 120 feet. Complete the market data grid provided above to estimate the value of the subject property.

Sales Comparison Market Data Grid

	Subject	Comparables #1	#2	#3
Sales price	---	$35,000	$30,000	$31,000
Size in square feet	10,800	10,200	10,200	9,600
Price per square foot	---			
Date of sale	Current	– 1 week	– 1 year	– 6 months
Adjustment for changing market conditions		---		
Adjusted price per square foot	---			
Location	Lake	Lake	Lake	Hillside
Adjustment for location	---			
Adjusted price per square foot	---			

Indicated value of subject property:

16. Define the following terms: accrued depreciation, physical deterioration, functional obsolescence, and economic obsolescence.

17 .Consider the example discussed in Table 11.2. If the actual market value of the land was $190,000, and the cost to reproduce the structures was $610,000, what market value would be indicated by the cost approach?

18. Define the following concepts: gross income multiplier, capitalization rate.

19. An investor is considering the purchase of a 11,000 sq. ft. warehouse that is expected to command $8.40 per square foot in annual rents. Two comparable warehouses have recently sold in the market. Comparable 1 measures 12,000 sq. ft. and sold recently for $450,000. Comparable 2 measures 8,600 sq. ft. and sold recently for $322,500. Compute the gross income multiplier that is implied by these transactions and estimate the value of the subject property.

20. Suppose the investor in the previous problem is concerned that the subject property may be more expensive to operate than the comparable properties. Analysis of the operating expenses for each of the properties reveals the following net income estimates:

Subject Property	$52,400
Comparable 1	$65,600
Comparable 2	$47,000

Compute the capitalization rate implied by these transactions to estimate the value of the subject property by the net income capitalization technique.

■ FURTHER READINGS

The Appraisal of Real Estate, 12th ed. Chicago: The Appraisal Institute, 2001.

12 Property Management

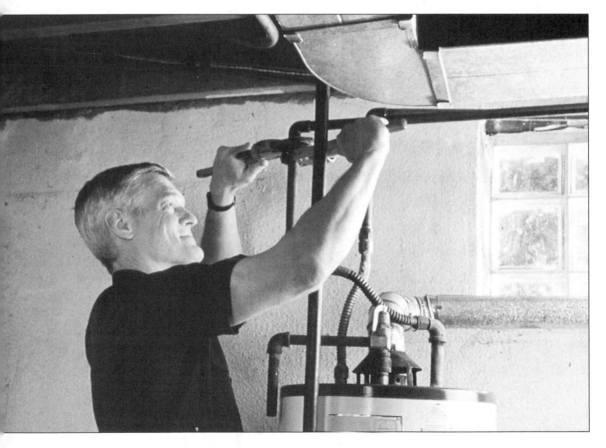

A property manager's responsibilities include selecting tenants, collecting rent, and keeping the building in good repair.

As discussed throughout this text, the characteristics of real estate resources and transactions imply that specialized knowledge is needed for successful decision making regarding real estate. Just as real estate brokers, salespersons, and appraisers provide a valuable service to buyers and sellers, property managers also provide an important service to property owners. This chapter explores several issues related to the business of property management, including

- the role of the property manager in investment real estate;

- the property management agreement and the manager's compensation;

- the functions of the property manager, including

    - administration,

    - marketing and advertising,

    - tenant selection,

    - lease negotiation,

    - move-in inspections,

    - property maintenance,

    - rent collection,

    - move-out inspections, and

    - security deposit returns.

- The role and function of asset managers.

REAL ESTATE TODAY FEATURES

Close-Up
Green Acres
Shopping Center—
A Property
Management Success
Story

Close-Up
The Empire State
Building

■ THE ROLE OF THE PROPERTY MANAGER

While many property owners are quite capable of managing their own properties, others may find they have neither the ability nor the desire to cope with the complexities of managing rental properties. Day-to-day operating decisions for most income-producing properties require specialized skills that many real estate investors do not have. Whether the owner chooses to wear the hat of the property manager or to hire a professional property manager, the goal of the property manager is unchanged: to manage properties efficiently with the objective of securing the highest net return for the property owner over the property's useful life. When an owner hires a professional property manager, the *property manager* acts as an agent for the property owner with respect to the leasing, marketing, and overall operation of the property. In many cases, the property manager is also a licensed real estate broker, though some states issue a separate license to property managers.

Consider an investor who purchases a small shopping center. Unless that investor is experienced in shopping center management, a property manager may be required to handle the center's operations. For example, the property manager will be responsible for marketing space in the center to potential tenants, negotiating the lease agreement, collecting rents, addressing tenant concerns, coordinating the property maintenance program, bookkeeping, and paying the property expenses such as utilities, property insurance, property taxes, and employee salaries. Having a trained professional to handle these tasks improves the likelihood that the investment will prove successful.

Property managers may be hired by the property owner as employees or independent contractors, or property managers may work for a property management firm that has contracted with the property owner to provide management services. Many successful property managers hold designations such as the Institute of Real Estate Management's Certified Property Manager (CPM) or Accredited Resident Manager (ARM) designations. Managers can be awarded these designations only after meeting the education and experience requirements established by the awarding organization. Some states regulate the property management profession by requiring that managers obtain a license from the state after completing educational and experience requirements.

■ THE MANAGEMENT AGREEMENT

The **management agreement** establishes an agency relationship between the owner of a property and the property manager. To clarify each party's duties and responsibilities, this agreement should be written. The document should specify the powers, obligations, and compensation of the manager, and it should set the term of the agreement.

Powers of the Manager

As the agent of the owner, the property manager has the power to set rents; to execute, extend, and cancel leases; to make settlements with tenants; to collect rents; to spend money on behalf of the property (a power generally limited to some maximum dollar amount beyond which the owner's approval is necessary); and to hire, fire, and supervise personnel to operate the property.

Just as the manager has the power to act on behalf of the owner, he or she also has the obligation to carry out those functions in a professional manner. Because the manager has a fiduciary relationship with the owner, many management agreements require that the agent and his or her employees be bonded.

Compensation

If the property manager is employed directly by the property owner, the most common form of compensation is a fee based on a percentage of the property's gross income. The fee ranges from approximately 4 to 10 percent, depending on such factors as the size of the project, the responsibilities of the manager, and the competitiveness of the local market. If the property manager is an employee of a property management firm, the manager's compensation is usually a fixed salary. The management company contracts with the property owner to provide management services for a fee. In the past, fee schedules often were established by the local real estate associations, but this practice now would be considered a violation of the antitrust laws.

When a property owner hires a property manager, the parties should carefully outline their agreement to avoid confusion and disputes. Because property managers serve as a fiduciary of the property owner, the relationship between owners and managers is an agency relationship. We saw the legal issues involved with agency in a previous chapter concerning real estate brokerage. Being a fiduciary means that the manager must always work in the best interest of the principal in the agency relationship. Though some states allow oral management agreements, we recommend, as always, that such an important contract be put into written form. Figure 12.1 shows a typical management agreement document from the Florida Association of REALTORS®.

In the sample property management agreement shown here, the manager (broker) is being authorized to identify a tenant for the property, enter into a lease on the landlord's behalf, manage relations with the tenant (including rent collection and eviction, if necessary), and manage the property repair orders. Additional duties, of course, can be added to the manager's responsibilities. The owner in this agreement is agreeing to compensate the property manager as agreed to in the document. Notice that the compensation is broken down into five major categories: securing a tenant, managing tenant relations, managing the property, supervising property repairs, and other duties as agreed. Compensation may be in the form of a stated dollar amount, an hourly rate, a percentage of the transaction (rent) amount, or any combination of the above.

| FIGURE 12.1 | Exclusive Property Management Agreement |

Exclusive Property Management Agreement
FLORIDA ASSOCIATION OF REALTORS®

This Exclusive Property Management ("Agreement") is between
_____ ("Owner") and
_____ ("Broker")

1. AUTHORITY TO MANAGE PROPERTY: Owner gives **Broker** the EXCLUSIVE RIGHT TO MANAGE the real and personal property (collectively "Property") described below beginning the _____ day of _____ , _____ and ending at 11:59 p.m. the _____ day of _____ , _____, except that either party may terminate this Agreement by giving _____ calendar days written notice to the other party by certified mail. **Owner** certifies and represents that he/she has the legal authority and capacity to lease the Property and improvements.

2. DESCRIPTION OF PROPERTY:
  (a) Real Property: Street Address: _____

  (b) Legal Description: ☐ See **Addendum** _____, Legal Description of Real Property.
    ☐
    _____

  (c) Personal Property, including appliances: ☐ See **Addendum** _____, Inventory.
    ☐
    _____

  (d) Type of Property (single family home, warehouse, etc.): _____.

  (e) Occupancy: Property ☐ is ☐ is not currently occupied by a tenant. If occupied, the lease term expires
    _____.

3. BROKER OBLIGATIONS AND AUTHORITY: Broker will use due diligence to manage, operate and lease the Property in accordance with this Agreement.

  (a) Tenant Matters: Owner authorizes **Broker** to (check if applicable):
    ☐ Secure a tenant for the Property, see **Addendum** _____, Exclusive Right to Lease Agreement.
    ☐ Enter into a lease/contract to lease on **Owner's** behalf (**Owner** must execute special power of attorney).
    ☐ Complete and sign the lead-based paint/hazards certification on **Owner's** behalf (for Property built before 1978).
    ☐ Manage tenant relations, including negotiating renewals of existing leases; collecting, holding and disbursing rents and other amounts due or to become due to **Owner**; handling tenant requests and negotiations; terminating tenancies and signing and serving appropriate notices on behalf of **Owner**; initiating and prosecuting eviction and damages actions on behalf of **Owner;** and procuring legal counsel when necessary to protect **Owner's** interests and rights in connection with the Property.

  (b) Property Maintenance: Owner understands that Florida law requires licensed professionals in the construction trades to perform relevant repairs on rental properties unless the repairs can be made for under $1,000 and are not a life/safety concern. Additionally, **Owner** understands that when **Broker** acts as the **Owner's** agent Florida law provides the **Broker**   may contract for repairs, maintenance, remodeling or improvement of the Property with a certified or registered contractor when labor and materials together do not exceed $5,000. Subject to these limitations set by law, **Owner** authorizes **Broker** to (check if applicable):
    ☐ Maintain and repair interior, exterior and landscaping of Property, including making periodic inspections; purchasing supplies; and supervising alterations, modernization and redecoration of Property. **Broker** will obtain prior approval of **Owner** for any item or service in excess of $_____, except for monthly or recurring expenses and emergency repairs which, in **Broker's** opinion are necessary to prevent the Property from becoming uninhabitable or damaged, to avoid suspension of services required to be provided by law or lease, or to avoid penalties or fines to be imposed by a governmental entity.
    ☐ Enter into contracts on **Owner's** behalf for utilities, public services, maintenance, repairs and other services as **Broker** deems advisable.
    ☐ Hire, discharge and supervise all labor and employees required for the operation and maintenance of the Property, and to arrange for bonding for employees who will handle cash on behalf of **Owner** and **Broker**.

ALTA
STAR
SOFTWARE

FIGURE 12.1   Exclusive Property Management Agreement (continued)

(c) Other Matters: Owner authorizes **Broker** to (check if applicable):
☐ Make payments on **Owner's** behalf, including (check all that apply):
    ☐ mortgage $_____ per _____ to _____
    ☐ insurance $_____ per _____ to _____
    ☐ property taxes $_____ per _____ to _____
    and special assessments as made.
    ☐ condominium or homeowners' association dues $_____ per _____
    to _____ and assessments as made.
    ☐ charges for repairs, materials, equipment, labor and attorneys' fees and costs.
    ☐ state and local sales and service taxes.
☐ Maintain accurate records of receipts, expenses and accruals to **Owner** in connection with managing the Property.
Broker will render to **Owner** itemized financial statements (how often) _____ and will promptly
remit to Owner the balance of receipts less disbursements and accruals for future expenses.
☐ Other Duties: See **Addendum** _____, entitled _____.

4. OWNER OBLIGATIONS: In consideration of the obligations of **Broker, Owner** agrees:
(a) To cooperate with **Broker** in carrying out the purpose of this Agreement.
(b) To provide **Broker** with the following keys to the Property (specify number): unit _____ / building access _____ /
mailbox _____ / pool _____ / garage door/opener _____ / other _____
(c) To provide complete and accurate information to **Broker** including disclosing all known facts that materially affect the value
of the Property (see Addendum _____ , entitled _____). If the Property was built in 1977
or earlier, **Owner** will provide **Broker** with all information **Owner** knows about lead-based paint and lead-based paint hazards in
the Property and with all available documents pertaining to such paint and hazards, as required by federal law. **Owner**
understands that the law requires the provision of this information to **Broker** and to prospective tenants before the tenants
become obligated to lease the Property. **Owner** acknowledges that **Broker** will rely on **Owner's** representations regarding the
Property when dealing with prospective tenants.
(d) To carry, at **Owner's** sole expense, public liability, property damage and worker's compensation insurance adequate to
protect the interests of **Owner** and **Broker.** Said insurance will name both **Broker** and **Owner** as insured parties, and will
specifically cover the indemnity and hold harmless provision of subparagraph 4(h). **Broker** will not be liable for any error of
judgment or mistake of law or fact or for any loss caused by **Broker's** negligence, except when the loss is caused by **Broker's**
willful misconduct or gross negligence. **Owner** will carry insurance as follows:
    (1) Perils of fire, lighting, wind, hail, explosion, smoke, riot, aircraft, vehicles, vandalism, and burglary on the contents of the
    Property in the amount of $_____.
    (2) "At Risk" protection on the building in the amount of $_____, and on rental income in the amount of
    $_____.
    (3) Liability for personal injury and property damage in the amount of $_____ ($500,000 minimum).
(e) To inform **Broker** before conveying or leasing the Property.
(f) Upon termination of this Agreement, to assume obligations of all contracts that **Broker** entered into on **Owner's** behalf.
(g) To pay all amounts billed by **Broker** for authorized expenditures within _____ calendar days after written notice of the
expense is placed in the mail by **Broker.** If **Owner** fails to promptly reimburse **Broker, Owner** authorizes **Broker** to reimburse
itself out of rents collected, if applicable.
(h) To indemnify and hold harmless **Broker** and **Broker's** officers, directors, agents and employees from all claims, demands,
causes of action, costs and expenses, including reasonable attorneys' fees at all levels, and from liability to any person, to the
extent based on **(1) Owner's** misstatement, negligence, action, inaction or failure to perform the obligations of this contract or
any lease or agreement with a vendor; **(2)** the existence of undisclosed material facts about the Property; **(3) Broker's**
performance, at **Owner's** request, of any task beyond the scope of services regulated by Chapter 475, F.S., as amended,
including **Broker's** referral, recommendation or retention of any vendor; or **(4)** services or products provided and expenses
incurred by any vendor. This subparagraph will survive **Broker's** performance and the transfer of title.
(i) To reasonably inspect the Property before allowing the tenant to take possession and to make the repairs necessary to
transfer a reasonably safe dwelling unit to the tenant.
(j) To exercise reasonable care to repair dangerous defective conditions upon notice of their existence by the tenant, after the
tenant takes possession.

5. COMPENSATION: Owner agrees to compensate **Broker** as follows, plus any applicable taxes on **Broker's** services:
(a) For securing a tenant, see **Addendum** _____, Exclusive Right to Lease Agreement.
(b) For managing tenant relations, a fee of:
    ☐ _____% of the gross lease value   ☐ _____% of rent due in each rental period
    ☐ $_____ ☐ other _____
    The above fee is to be paid (when, how) _____
(c) For managing the Property, a fee of:
    ☐ $_____ to be paid (when, how) _____
    ☐ _____% of rent due in each rental period to be paid (when, how) _____
    ☐ other _____
(d) For supervising alterations, modernization, redecorating, or repairs above and beyond normal refurbishment of the Property,
a fee of ☐ $_____ per hour OR ☐ _____ to be paid (when,
how) _____.
(e) Other: ☐ See **Addendum** _____, Attachment to Property Management Agreement.

FIGURE 12.1	Exclusive Property Management Agreement (continued)

6. DISPUTE RESOLUTION: This Agreement will be construed under Florida law. All disputes between **Broker** and **Owner** based on this Agreement or its breach will be mediated under the rules of the American Arbitration Association or other mediator agreed upon by the parties. Mediation is a process in which parties attempt to resolve a dispute by submitting it to an impartial mediator who facilitates the resolution of the dispute but who is not empowered to impose a settlement on the parties. The parties will equally divide the mediation fee, if any. In any litigation based on this Agreement, the prevailing party will be entitled to recover reasonable attorneys' fees and costs at all levels, unless the parties agree that disputes will be settled by arbitration as follows:

    Arbitration: By initialing in the space provided, **Owner** (____) (____), Listing Associate (____) and Listing Broker (____) agree that disputes not resolved by mediation will be settled by neutral binding arbitration in the county in which the Property is located in accordance with the rules of the American Arbitration Association or other arbitrator agreed upon by the parties. The arbitrator may not alter the Contract terms. Each party to any arbitration or litigation (including appeals and interpleaders) will pay its own fees, costs and expenses, including attorneys' fees at all levels, and will equally split the arbitrators' fees and administrative fees of arbitration.

7. ATTORNEYS' FEES: In any action between **Owner** and a tenant in which **Broker** is made a party because of acting as an escrow agent under this Agreement, or if **Broker** interpleads escrowed funds, **Broker** will recover reasonable attorneys' fees and costs, to be paid out of the escrowed funds and charged and awarded as court costs in favor of the prevailing party.

8. MISCELLANEOUS. This Agreement is binding on Broker's and Owner's heirs, personal representatives, administrators, successors and assigns. Signatures, initials, documents referenced in this Agreement, counterparts and modifications communicated electronically or on paper will be acceptable for all purposes and will be binding.

9. ADDITIONAL CLAUSES:

_____
_____
_____
_____
_____
_____
_____
_____
_____
_____

    Broker advises Owner to consult an appropriate professional for related legal, tax, property condition, environmental, foreign reporting requirements and other specialized advice.

Date: _____ **Owner:**_____ Tax ID No: _____

Date: _____ **Owner:**_____ Tax ID No: _____

Home Telephone: _____ Work Telephone: _____ Facsimile: _____

Address: _____
E-mail: _____

Date: _____ **Authorized Licensee or Broker:** _____

Home Telephone: _____ Work Telephone: _____ Facsimile: _____

Address: _____
Email: _____

Copy returned to **Owner** on the _____ day of _____, _____ by: ☐ personal delivery ☐ mail ☐ facsimile.

■ FUNCTIONS OF A PROPERTY MANAGER

The property manager may be involved in virtually all aspects of the operation of a rental property. Whether the property manager is the owner of the property or an agent of the owner, the functions of a property manager include

- administration,
- marketing and advertising,
- tenant selection,
- lease negotiation,
- move-in inspections,
- property maintenance,
- rent collection,
- move-out inspections, and
- security deposit returns.

We will consider each of these functions in turn.

Administration

Part of a property manager's function is to handle the day-to-day administrative concerns of the property. Administration refers to record keeping, report generation, paying the property's bills, monitoring the employees, and generally overseeing the property's operations. The exact administrative activities of the property manager vary with the type of property and the breadth of the property management agreement.

Marketing and Advertising

Leases are perishable commodities: they expire. Rental space, therefore, must be marketed continually so new tenants can be found to take the place of those who leave. Lease periods range from one day for hotel and motel rooms to several years for commercial property. (Apartment complexes may be leased for perhaps six months or a few years.) The general objective of marketing is to maximize income. This usually means to maximize occupancy rates and rental price schedules. The two obviously are in conflict, however, and a balance must be found in order to maximize income. One can ensure a rental unit's occupancy for three years, for example, by granting a three-year lease, but the income derived from the unit may be greater if it is rented to three successive tenants for one year each—if, at the end of each year, market conditions provide a tenant willing and able to pay a higher rent. The property manager must understand the market in which he or she is operating in order to make the right decision.

Choosing the correct marketing strategy is important to the success of any rental project. This is an area where the property manager's experience and expertise can be of tremendous value to the owners. A clear marketing strategy is essential. What types of tenants are sought? Will the project attempt to stress some price advantage, location, design, or other marketing feature? Unless a clear strategy is carried over into tenant selection, rent schedules, and the physical character of the project, it will be impossible for the property to reach its maximum potential.

The purpose of advertising a rental property is to find a tenant, and the type of advertising that is appropriate varies from market segment to market segment. For example, a property manager seeking a tenant for a vacant unit in a trailer park might use very different advertising methods from those secured by a manager seeking a tenant in a Class A office building. The key to "good" advertising is using the advertising tool that will attract the best tenants to that particular property type. Examples of advertising tools include

- signs on the property,
- neighborhood flyers,
- bulletin boards,
- Internet sites,
- listing the property with leasing companies,
- newspaper ads, and
- "open house" days or weekends.

Tenant Selection

If the advertising campaign is effective, potential tenants will respond and express an interest in leasing the property. Property managers must carefully evaluate each tenant to ensure that accepting this tenant is consistent with the overall objective of the manager: maximizing the return to the property owner. Of course, no property manager should discriminate against potential tenants in any way that violates fair housing laws or laws protecting disabled persons, but other tenant characteristics should certainly be used in the tenant selection process.

In the case of residential property, for example, the 1988 Fair Housing Act prohibits anyone from refusing to rent to someone because of their race, color, national origin or ancestry, religion, sex, familial status (including children under the age of 18 living with parents or legal custodians, pregnant women, and people securing custody of children under the age of 18), or physical disability. Discrimination charges under this act are investigated by the U.S. Department of Housing and Urban Development. In addition to this federal requirement, many states and some counties and cities impose additional restrictions on how residential landlords can screen potential tenants. Various state- and city-level antidiscrimination laws address educational status, sexual preference, occupation, medical status, and age.

The tenant mix is also important for nonresidential properties. The objective usually is to achieve a variety of tenants that will complement and enhance the image the project is seeking. For example, a coin-operated laundry would not be a desirable tenant in an upscale shopping center where relatively expensive goods were sold in boutiques, but it might be quite complementary to other stores in a small neighborhood center.

To evaluate prospective tenants on valid grounds, property managers should request from each tenant a completed tenant application that collects information regarding the applicant's financial resources (including employment and income status), credit history, and references from prior landlords. In his book titled *The Landlord's Troubleshooter* (2nd ed., Dearborn Financial Publishing, 1999), Robert Irwin strongly recommends that more emphasis be placed on the reference (or lack thereof) provided by the applicant's landlord before the current one. The current landlord may be anxious for the tenant to leave and may give a glowing recommendation to speed the tenant's departure. The landlord prior to the present one is likely to give a more honest recommendation.

Lease Negotiation

Even before the advertising and tenant selection processes begin, the property manager should decide the acceptable conditions of the lease agreement. Obviously, the rent amount is a key issue, but there are many other factors that should be resolved in a well-written lease. Examples of issues to be addressed include the following:

- What is the amount of the security deposit?
- What day will rent be due each month?
- What day will the rent be considered late each month?
- What is the nature of the tenancy (tenancy for a stated period, tenancy from period to period, or tenancy at will, as discussed in a previous chapter)?
- Is the lease renewable? At what rent level?
- What items will the tenant be responsible for maintaining?
- What is the permitted use of the property?
- How many people may occupy the property?
- Who is responsible for maintaining insurance on the property?
- Can the tenant sublease the property to others?
- Do local laws require that the landlord make any safety or health disclosures to the tenant (asbestos, lead-based paint, radon, etc.)
- Are pets allowed? How many? What kind? How big?

As we discussed in the chapter on contracts, being a good negotiator requires being open to new ways of structuring a deal to benefit all parties. Of course, there are some issues that managers must hold firm to or risk violating their overall objective: maximizing return to the property owner.

Move-in Inspections

When a lease agreement is in place, the next step before turning over the keys to the property is for the manager and tenant to perform a move-in inspection. This inspection is critical because it will be the basis for any claim the manager may make against the tenant's security deposit at the end of the lease. Any existing damage to the property should be carefully documented, and both the manager and the tenant should sign the document. With this strategy, the tenant can be held responsible for any additional damages (beyond normal wear and tear) that might be discovered during the lease period or on termination of the agreement. Some property managers use photographs and videotape to document property condition at the start and finish of a lease agreement.

Property Maintenance

Though some leases require that the tenant take care of any property repairs, the manager is usually responsible for ensuring that the repairs are done promptly and correctly. Some larger properties may have a property maintenance staff, while smaller properties will use local repair contractors (plumbers, roofers, electricians, etc.) on an as-needed basis. The manager must shop for the needed professionals carefully to get the best price and performance for the property owner. Failure to address minor repairs may lead to even more costly repairs in the future.

Physical management is divided into two categories: (1) maintenance designed to conserve the property and (2) rehabilitation and renovation designed to make the project more competitive in a changing market.

A program of continuing maintenance is essential to continued economic viability. Owners and managers who fail to give proper attention to landscaping, redecorating, and other items of general maintenance will soon find their project no longer competitive in the marketplace. Even if a project is well maintained, it may be necessary, after a time, to conduct extensive renovations to keep it viable. For instance, an older shopping center may benefit greatly from a new facade and redesigned landscaping and parking areas. The Real Estate Today Closeup on page 265 gives a vivid example of how good property management can revive an aging shopping center and create value for its owners.

Rent Collection

One of the most arduous tasks facing a property manager is rent collection. Sooner or later, every manager must deal with a tenant who is "late with the rent." If a tenant does not pay the rent on the due date stated in the lease agreement, the manager should take the following actions simultaneously:

■ Discuss the issue with the tenant and determine when the rent will be paid.

■ Begin the eviction process.

REAL ESTATE TODAY

Green Acres Shopping Center—A Property Management Success Story

When Frank Brookins took over the management of the Green Acres Shopping Center, it was in real trouble. Built twenty years earlier in typical neighborhood strip shopping center style, two-thirds of its approximately 60,000 square feet were vacant. The center was showing its age, and the main tenant, a grocery store, had moved out, leaving its 16,000-square-foot space empty. The tenant mix was less than desirable. For example, a "game" room had become well known to local police for the drug activity that allegedly occurred there. The center obviously was not generating an acceptable return for its owners, and its marketability was low.

Frank's first task was to improve the appearance of the center. He was helped by a storm and the local government. The storm tore the outdated turquoise facade off the building, and the insurance settlement provided the monies to replace it and repaint the center. The local government bought right-of-way for widening the road in front of the center, and these monies paid for a new sign with a time and temperature display to give the center some identity. The ugliness of the blacktop parking lot was broken by the construction of islands filled with shrubs and trees. Although these improvements were relatively inexpensive, they vastly improved the attractiveness of the center.

Close-Up

The next task was to improve the tenant mix and to fill the empty spaces. The key was securing a tenant for the black hole formerly occupied by the supermarket. Mr. Brookins learned that the state's nursing school was unhappy with its current location. Although this would be a somewhat unconventional tenant for a neighborhood shopping center, the 100 students would provide a ready market for restaurants and other potential tenants. The catch was that the state required that the owner provide building improvements equal to about three years' rent, although it would sign only a one-year lease. Even so, the owner took the plunge.

With the nursing school as an anchor, two restaurants and other stores soon followed, one replacing the game room whose lease was not renewed. Currently the center is fully leased, and it is generating three times the gross income it did just five years earlier, with consequent increase in value.

"Successful property management depends on constant attention to detail," explains Mr. Brookins. "Every morning I am there making sure the parking lot is clean, the plants maintained, and that the center is ready for customers. That's what keeps tenants happy, creates value for the owners, and provides good commissions for me."

In most cases, tenants will offer an excuse for why they have not paid their rent as required. A "tough" manager will respond that the rent always must be paid on time and that there are no acceptable excuses for late rent. The manager will explain that if the tenant cannot afford to pay the rent on time, then the tenant cannot afford to occupy these premises. What does a "reasonable" manager do? Exactly the same things. If the tenant is persistent in paying rent late, the manager should either renegotiate the lease agreement to change the date rent is due or should evict the tenant for violating the original lease agreement. Of course, if a tenant refuses to pay the rent, the manager has no choice but to evict the tenant.

Most states have landlord/tenant laws that regulate the eviction process. Managers must follow these laws precisely to avoid denying a tenant "due process." Most states require that landlords give tenants a written notice stating that eviction will begin in a certain number of days (usually 3 to 7) if the rent is not paid in full before the time expires. After the time period expires, the landlord must file a lawsuit asking a court for possession of the premises from the tenant. If the landlord prevails in the suit, the tenant is evicted. **Eviction** means the tenant's rights of use and possession are terminated by the court, and the tenant will be forcibly removed (if necessary) from the property by a court officer (sheriff). Managers may not use threats or intimidation tactics to encourage tenants to vacate a property. Managers must follow the process for eviction prescribed by state and local laws.

Move-out Inspections

On termination of the lease agreement, the manager should inspect the premises with the tenant to determine if the tenant is responsible for any damage to the property. As mentioned earlier, having a carefully documented "move-in inspection" makes the "move-out inspection" go more smoothly.

Security Deposit Returns

After the inspection is completed, the manager is legally obligated to return any unused security deposit to the tenant. The **security deposit** is money collected from the tenant prior to granting occupancy that protects the landlord from damages the tenant may cause or from failure to pay rent as agreed. If any of the deposit is retained for damages, most states require that the landlord give the tenant a written explanation of all charges. Most states set a time limit on how long the landlord has after the lease terminates to return any deposits due to the tenant.

Administrative Management

Administrative management—the keeping of records and the preparation of reports—is one of the vital, if not very glamorous, functions of a property manager. Accurate records and accounts are vital to the efficient management of income property. The manager needs such records in order to report receipts and disbursements to the owner, to file tax and other reports required by governmental agencies, and as a source of data on which to base management decisions and reports.

Rent Schedules

The establishment of rent schedules is a continuing function of marketing that requires extensive knowledge of market conditions. If rents are set too low, the project may achieve full occupancy but still not maximize income. If rents are set too high, vacancies may increase to such an extent that total income will be reduced.

■ THE ROLE AND FUNCTION OF ASSET MANAGERS

The preceding discussion has focused on the role of the property manager when the property is operated as income-producing real estate. Another type of property manager, known as the **asset manager,** is increasingly becoming common in the real estate market.

Almost every business firm must own or lease real estate as a part of its operation, even if the firm's primary line of business is not real estate–related. Often, the company's exposure to the real estate market is quite substantial, and a professional real estate manager is needed to manage the company's real estate assets. In this situation, persons assigned to this task are known as *corporate real estate asset managers.* The tasks of an asset manager are often more complicated than those of a traditional property manager because the asset manager must operate within the framework of meeting the company's overall objective in its primary line of business. Corporate real estate asset managers are real estate specialists who provide a wide range of real estate services for their companies, even though the company may not be "in the real estate business."

The asset manager has four major functions, including (1) management, (2) acquisition, (3) financing, and (4) disposition of corporate real estate assets.

Management

The management function of the real estate asset manager goes beyond facility management to include the strategic decisions involving the real estate needs of the firm. The asset manager can aid operating units in planning, acquiring and financing facilities, often improving the return on the firm's real estate that might otherwise be underutilized.

Acquisition

Few top business executives possess the specialized skills needed in planning for their real estate needs or in site selection. A professional real estate asset manager can assist in targeting space requirements and design features. He or she can also aid the site selection process, considering the complex factors involved with locating various types of facilities. The asset manager also serves as the firm's negotiator in reaching a final agreement when it comes to leasing or buying additional space.

Financing

The first issue in financing a new facility is the question of whether it is in the company's best interest to lease or purchase the property. This decision involves many factors, including the general financial status of the firm and whether the facility required is a special-purpose building. The firm might decide to build the structure needed, then immediately sell it to an investor and simultaneously lease it back. This strategy, known as sale-and-leaseback, frees up the firm's capital for use in its primary line of business. If ownership is the chosen alternative, the asset manager assists in deciding what type of financing will best fit the objectives of the firm.

Disposition

Another important part of the corporate asset manager's job is to redeploy or divest property that is no longer needed by the firm. This may occur because of reduced operations and consolidations or because the facilities have become surplus owing to the acquisition of new ones. Disposition may involve the property's sale or lease to another firm, renovation for another use, or exchange for another property. The Close-Up on page 269 describes the role of the corporate asset manager in a modern corporation.

■ CHAPTER REVIEW

- ■ Professional property managers are trained to manage properties efficiently with the objective of securing the highest net return for the property owner over the property's useful life. The property manager acts as an agent for the property owner with respect to the leasing, marketing, and overall operation of the property.

- ■ Property management encompasses several functions: (a) administrative management (the collection of rents, the keeping of records, and the preparation of reports), (b) marketing (the leasing of rental space in the manner most profitable for the owner in the long term), and (c) physical management (maintenance designed to conserve the property and rehabilitation and renovation designed to make the project more competitive in a changing market).

- ■ The management agreement identifies the powers and obligations of the property manager and the compensation he or she is to be paid. The agreement also specifies the time period for which the relationship will exist.

- ■ The usual form of compensation for property managers is a fee based on a percentage of gross income from the property.

- ■ Corporate real estate asset managers are real estate specialists who provide a wide range of real estate services for their company, even though the company may not be "in the real estate business." The asset manager has four major functions, including (1) management, (2) acquisition, (3) financing, and (4) disposition of corporate real estate assets.

REAL ESTATE TODAY

The Empire State Building

Want to buy an historic American icon building cheap? You could have several years ago. The Empire State Building, for four decades the world's tallest, with its 2.24 million square feet of space 95 percent occupied,

Close-Up

is worth somewhere between $600 and $800 million. Why then did the building sell for only $40 million?

Here's a hint. A partnership has a leasehold on the building that controls every aspect of the property through the year 2075. The fee owner receives less than $2 million each year in lease payments, while the owners of the lease-hold currently receive about $35 million in rentals from the firms that actually occupy the space. The lease fee owners will not gain control of the Empire State Building for more than 80 years, when the building will be more than 145 years old. In other words, most of the value of the

building is in the leasehold interest; the leased fee interest is worth comparatively little.

This unusual situation arose when a partnership bought the building in the 1960's for $68 million. The Prudential Insurance Company provided $29 million in financing and was given ownership of the fee interest to transfer tax advantages to Prudential that reduced the cost of financing for the partnership. After these tax advantages were exhausted, the insurance company sold the building, but fee ownership is worth relatively little—unless the lease can be broken. At this writing, a group headed by Donald Trump is trying to do just that, charging that the owners of the lease-hold are not properly maintaining the building, but their chances of success appear less than bright.

■ KEY TERMS

asset manager	management agreement	sale-and-leaseback
eviction	property manager	security deposit

■ STUDY EXERCISES

1. What is the primary objective of a property manager?

2. What are the general functions of a property manager?

3. What is the legal relationship between the property manager and the owner? What document creates this relationship?

4. What purpose do security deposits serve from the lessor's perspective? What does an asset manager do? How do these tasks differ from the traditional property manager's?

5. Describe the strategy known as "sale-and-leaseback."

6. If a tenant fails to pay the rent on time, can the manager or landlord disconnect the utilities to encourage the tenant to cough up the dough?

7. Under what circumstances can a private property owner refuse to accept a tenant because of his or her gender, or race, or religion?

 Go to the Student Study Guide CD-ROM and work through Case 4.

■ FURTHER READINGS

Banning, K. B., *Residential Property Management Handbook,* New York: McGraw-Hill, 1992.

Alexander, A. A., and R. F. Muhlebach, *Managing and Leasing Commercial Properties,* New York: Wiley, 1994.

Lapides, P. D., and E.R. Miller, *Managing and Leasing Residential Properties,* New York: Wiley, 1993.

Brown, R. K., *Managing Corporate Real Estate,* New York: John Wiley, 1994.

PART FOUR

Real Estate Finance and Investment Analysis

13 Residential and Commercial Property Financing

There are many different financing options available to home buyers today, helping everyone from starters to seniors purchase their dream home.

The economic characteristics of real estate make mortgage credit both necessary for most real estate purchasers and attractive to many lenders. The relatively large amounts of money required and the length of time funds must be committed often make it necessary for property owners to borrow the major portion of the purchase price of their properties. Because of the durability of land and improvements, many lenders are willing to provide debt capital for real estate purchases as long as the assets serve as adequate collateral for the loans. As we saw in a previous chapter, a specialized legal framework for real estate financing exists whereby real estate assets can be pledged as security for a debt and, if the borrower should default on the loan, the value of the property can be used to satisfy the debt. Mortgage credit is widely used in the financing of both residential and commercial real estate.

The objectives of this chapter are to describe the processes of obtaining financing for residential and commercial property. With respect to owner-occupied residential properties, we

■ discuss the mortgage concept and U.S. mortgage practice,

■ review the structure of the U.S. housing finance system and its most prominent participants,

■ examine the loan origination process by considering the residential loan application procedure,

■ discuss several federal regulations designed to protect residential mortgage consumers, and

■ outline the underwriting guidelines used by lenders to evaluate residential loan applications.

REAL ESTATE TODAY FEATURES

Close-Up
What is Credit Scoring?

We also consider some important aspects of the commercial property financing system. The commercial property financing system relies on the concept of secured debt just as the housing finance system does, but there are some important differences in the way these two financing systems work. For example, lenders in the commercial property financing system are concerned with the property's income rather than the owner's income as the source for repayment of the debt. In addition, the participants in the commercial property financing system differ from those in the residential financing system, with life insurance companies, pension funds, and real estate investment trusts playing a more prominent role. We address the following topics in the commercial property financing system:

- Sources of debt and equity capital in commercial property markets

- Underwriting criteria used by lenders to evaluate commercial property loan applications

■ UNDERSTANDING THE MORTGAGE CONCEPT

The basic factor that differentiates real estate credit from most other loans is the concept of secured debt. A borrower's promise to repay an **unsecured loan** is not backed by a lien or an encumbrance on a specific property, and if a borrower defaults, the lender's only recourse is to make a claim against the borrower's general assets. The lender's ability to collect depends on the amount and quality of those assets and the debtor's income-earning ability. It is hard to imagine financial institutions making many real estate loans on such a basis because the size of such loans is relatively large, and their duration is so long that the borrower's financial condition could change drastically before the loan is repaid.

In most cases, therefore, borrowers acquire financing for real estate purchases using **secured loans.** In this type of loan, the property being purchased is pledged as security for the debt, and a lien or other encumbrance is created on the title to the property. If the borrower is unable or unwilling to repay the debt as scheduled, the lender can take legal action to sell the specified property to recover the loan funds. This type of credit instrument makes it feasible for lenders to make relatively large, long-term loans for the purchase of real estate.

History of the Mortgage Concept

A **mortgage** is a pledge of property to secure a debt. The concept dates back to early Egyptian, Greek, and Roman times. Under early Roman law, nonpayment of a mortgage loan entitled lenders to make borrowers their slaves. Eventually, Roman law was changed to permit the unpaid debt to be satisfied by the sale of the mortgaged property.

Although the concept of pledging property to secure a debt was widespread in England by the 11th century, the Christian strictures against usury prohibited the charging of interest on loans. Instead of charging interest, Christian lenders simply took over a debtor's property and collected rents until the debt was paid. Jewish lenders, not being bound by Christian precepts, charged interest and left borrowers in possession of their property. By the 14th century, however, the charging of interest to borrowers left in possession of their property, known as **hypothecation,** became universal.

These early mortgages provided that if the borrower met all the terms of the loan and completely repaid the debt, the mortgage was then terminated, and the title was returned to the borrower. If any condition was not met, however, the borrower lost all rights to the property, including all money previously paid, and the property was sold to repay the debt. Gradually, a system developed to more equitably protect the rights of the parties to a loan secured by real estate, and many of these concepts serve as the basis for modern mortgage laws in the United States.

Modern Mortgage Concepts

U.S. courts typically consider a mortgage as a voluntary lien on real estate, given to secure the payment of a debt. Borrowers remain in possession of the property, but some states recognize the lender as the owner of the mortgaged property, while others interpret a mortgage purely as a lien on the property. States that have adopted the concept of **title theory** recognize that the mortgagee (lender) has the right to possession of the mortgaged property immediately on default by the mortgagor (borrower). The property can be sold at this point, with the sale proceeds used to satisfy the debt. In **lien theory** states, however, if the mortgagor defaults, the lender must foreclose on the lien through a court action to acquire possession, then offer the property for sale and apply the funds received from the sale to extinguish the debt. In both title and lien theory states, any proceeds from a foreclosure sale in excess of the loan amount and any costs of sale must be returned to the borrower. In the normal course of a mortgage, the question of title versus lien theory is irrelevant. Only if the borrower defaults will the property be sold to satisfy the debt.

■ U.S. MORTGAGE PRACTICE

Although practice varies somewhat from state to state, the obligation secured by a mortgage generally is acknowledged by a **promissory note**—that is, a written promise to pay money owed. The promissory note document contains the names of the borrower and lender, the amount of the debt, the interest rate and repayment terms, reference to the security instrument, and other details of the loan agreement. The promissory note makes the borrower personally liable for the debt. If the borrower violates the terms of the promissory note, the lender can then take steps to foreclose on the debt. Figure 13.1 contains an example of a promissory note.

■ TYPICAL PROVISIONS OF A PROMISSORY NOTE

While much of the language in this sample promissory note is self-explanatory, a few items deserve special emphasis. Section 4 of the note is a **prepay-**

FIGURE 13.1

Promissory Note

February 5_____ , 2001 _____St. Joseph_____ , _____Missouri__

                                        (City)   (State)

1097 Timbers Crossing_____

                                    (Property Address)

1. Borrower's Promise To Pay

In return for a loan that I have received, I promise to pay U.S. $ 108,000_____ (this amount is called "principal"), plus interest, to the order of the Lender. The Lender is First Savings Bank_____ . I understand that the Lender may transfer this Note. The lender or anyone who takes this Note by transfer and who is entitled to receive payments under this Note is called the "Note Holder."

2. Interest

Interest will be charged on unpaid principal until the full amount of principal has been paid. I will pay interest at a yearly rate of __8.00__ %.

3. Payments

(A) Time and Place of Payments

I will pay principal and interest by making payments every month.

I will make my monthly payments on the __1st__ day of each month beginning on _April 1,_ 2001. I will make these payments every month until I have paid all of the principal and interest and any other charges described below that I may owe under this Note. My monthly payments will be applied to interest before principal. If, on _April 1_ , _2031_, I still owe amounts under this Note, I will pay those amounts in full on that date, which is called the maturity date.

(B) Amount of Monthly Payments

My monthly payment will be in the amount of U.S. __$ 792.47_____ .

4. Borrower's Right To Prepay

I have the right to make payments of principal at any time before they are due. A payment of principal only is known as a "prepayment." When I make a prepayment, I will tell the Note Holder in writing that I am doing so. I may make a full prepayment or partial prepayments without paying any prepayment charge. The Note Holder will use all of my prepayment to reduce the amount of principal that I owe under this Note. If I make a partial prepayment, there will be no changes in the due date or in the amount of my monthly payment unless the Note Holder agrees in writing to those changes.

5. Borrower's Failure To Pay as Required

(A) Late Charge for Overdue Payments

If the Note Holder has not received the full amount of any monthly payment by the end of _five_ calendar days after the date it is due, I will pay a late charge to the Note Holder. The amount of the charge will be _10_ % of my overdue payment of principal and interest. I will pay this late charge promptly, but only once on each late payment.

(B) Default

If I do not pay the full amount of each monthly payment on the date it is due, I will be in default.

FIGURE 13.1   Promissory Note (continued)

(C) Notice of Default

If I am in default, the Note Holder may send me a written notice telling me that if I do not pay the overdue amount by a certain date, the Note Holder may require me to pay immediately the full amount of principal which has not been paid and all the interest that I owe on that amount. That date must be at least 30 days after the date on which the notice is delivered or mailed to me.

(D) No Waiver by Note Holder

Even if, at a time when I am in default, the Note Holder does not require me to pay immediately in full as described above, the Note Holder will still have the right to do so if I am in default at a later time.

(E) Payment of Note Holder's Costs and Expenses

If the Note Holder has required me to pay immediately in full as described above, the Note Holder will have the right to be paid back by me for all of its costs and expenses in enforcing this Note to the extent not prohibited by applicable law. Those expenses include, for example, reasonable attorney's fees.

6. Obligations of Persons under this Note

If more than one person signs this Note, each person is fully and personally obligated to keep all of the promises made in this note, including the promise to pay the full amount owed. The Note Holder may enforce its rights under this Note against each person individually or against all of us together. This means that any one of us may be required to pay all of the amounts owed under this note.

7. Uniform Secured Note

This Note is a uniform instrument with limited variations in some jurisdictions. In addition to the protections given to the Note Holder under this Note, a Mortgage, Deed of Trust, or Security Deed (the "Security Instrument"), dated the same date as this Note, protects the Note Holder from possible losses which might result if I do not keep the promises which I make in this Note. That Security Instrument describes how and under what conditions I may be required to make immediate payment in full of all amounts I owe under this Note. Some of those conditions are described as follows:

Transfer of the Property. If all or any part of the Property or any interest in it is sold or transferred without Lender's prior written consent, Lender may, at its option, require immediate payment in full of all sums secured by the Security Instrument. If Lender exercises this option, Lender shall give Borrower notice of acceleration. The notice shall provide a period of not less than 30 days from the date the notice is delivered or mailed within which Borrower must pay all sums secured by the Security Instrument. If Borrower fails to pay these sums prior to the expiration of the period, Lender may invoke remedies permitted by the Security Instrument.

Witness the Hand(s) and Seal(s) of the Undersigned

_____ (Seal) - Borrower

_____ (Seal) - Borrower

FIGURE 13.2

Mortgage

This Mortgage ("Security Instrument") is given on___February 5___, _2001_. The mortgagor is Frank L. and Elizabeth M. Barr_____ ("Borrower"). This Security Instrument is given to ___First Savings Bank_____ which is organized and existing under the laws of the State of ___Missouri___, and whose address is 220 Las Olas Boulevard, St. Joseph, Missouri___ ("Lender"). Borrower owes Lender the principal sum of U.S.$ 108,000___. This debt is evidenced by Borrower's note dated the same date as this Security Instrument, which provides for monthly payments, with the full debt, if not paid earlier, due and payable on April 1, 2031_____. This Security Instrument secures to the Lender (a) the repayment of the debt, with interest, evidenced by the note, (b) the payment of all other sums necessary to protect the security of this Security Instrument, and (c) the Borrower's covenants and agreements under this Security Instrument and the note. For this purpose, Borrower does hereby mortgage, grant, and convey to Lender the following described property located in Buchanan_____County, in the State of ___Missouri_____:

Lot 3, Block G of the Harris Billups Estate, as recorded in Plat Book 8, page 37, in the Office of the Clerk of the Circuit Court of Buchanan County, Missouri,_____ which has the address of 1097 Timbers Crossing_____ (Property Address); together with all improvements now or hereafter erected on the property, and all easements, appurtenances, and fixtures now or hereafter a part of the property. All replacements and additions shall also be covered by this Security Instrument.

Borrower Covenants that Borrower is lawfully seised of the estate hereby conveyed and has the right to mortgage, grant, and convey the Property and that the Property is unencumbered, except for encumbrances of record. Borrower warrants and will defend generally the title to the Property against all claims and demands, subject to any encumbrances of record.

This Security Instrument implicitly contains all uniform covenants permitted by laws of the applicable jurisdictions to constitute a uniform security interest covering real property.

By signing below, Borrower accepts and agrees to the terms and covenants contained in this Security Instrument and in any rider(s) executed by Borrower and recorded with it.

_____ (Seal) - Borrower

_____ (Seal) - Borrower

---

ment clause. The borrower in this note has the right to prepay any or all of the principal any time before it is due without penalty. Section 5 specifies a late charge for overdue payments, classifies any late payment as a default on the terms of the agreement and, in the event of default, permits the lender to accelerate the full amount of principle that has not been paid and any interest that is owed on that amount. This last item is known as an **acceleration clause.** Section 6 makes all those who sign this note "jointly and severally liable" for the debt. Thus, the lender can demand payment from one or all of the borrowers at its option. Section 7 of this note contains a **due-on-sale clause.** In the event the borrower sells or transfers all or any part of the property secured by the mortgage associated with this note, the lender may, at its option, require immediate payment of all amounts owed.

The promise to repay the debt is secured by a pledge of property as specified in the mortgage document or other security instrument, which typically contains the names of the mortgagor and mortgagee, a description of the property involved, reference to the promissory note, and various provisions common to the mortgage arrangement. Figure 13.2 contains an example of a mortgage document.

Typical Provisions of a Security Instrument

The language of the security instrument, in this case a mortgage, is intended to provide the mortgagee with protection against financial losses resulting from default on the promissory note. The uniform covenants referred to in the security instrument represent promises between the borrower and lender regarding the repayment of the debt, provisions for maintaining the property and keeping insurance premiums and property taxes current, the lender's right to inspect the property, and numerous other issues. If the borrower fails to meet the terms of either the promissory note or the security instrument, the lender may foreclose on the debt, as described below.

■ UNDERSTANDING THE FORECLOSURE PROCESS

When a borrower fails to make payments or defaults on other terms of the mortgage agreement, the mortgagee can begin foreclosure proceedings to enforce its rights. **Foreclosure** refers to the process of seizing control of the collateral for a loan and using the proceeds from its sale to satisfy a defaulted debt. Usually, however, the mortgage holder will attempt to work out some type of alternative payment program to avoid the sale of the collateral. Not only is this practice much better for the lender's community relations efforts, it also avoids the time-consuming, expensive, and generally unprofitable foreclosure process. Foreclosure is, for the most part, an avenue of last resort.

Types of Foreclosure

Specific foreclosure laws vary from state to state, though there are three general types of foreclosure proceedings. In states that recognize **judicial foreclosure,** the mortgagee must request a court-ordered-sale of the property after proving that the borrower has defaulted on the terms of the agreement. Some states allow **nonjudicial foreclosure.** In this situation, the security instrument (either a mortgage or deed of trust) grants the power of sale to the lender should the borrower default. Finally, a few states recognize **strict foreclosure,** whereby the lender receives title to the property immediately on default by the borrower. The lender can then dispose of the property by sale or keep it as satisfaction of the debt.

Regardless of the specific type of foreclosure recognized, most states require the lender to return any proceeds from a foreclosure sale in excess of the loan amount and certain fees to the borrower. On the other hand, some states permit the mortgagee to pursue a **deficiency judgment** against the mortgagor if the proceeds are insufficient to satisfy the debt. If the courts grant the judgment, the borrower is held responsible for the remaining amount of debt after the foreclosure sale. Other states do not allow deficiency judgments, and lenders must accept the proceeds of the sale as satisfaction of the debt.

Alternative Security Instruments

The cumbersome foreclosure process is simplified in many states through the use of a security instrument similar to a mortgage called a **deed of trust** or *trust deed.* The deed of trust is executed at the time the loan is originated to convey title to a third party, called the *trustee.* The trustee's title to the property lies dormant as long as the borrower, or *trustor,* meets the terms of the debt. In the event of default, however, the trustee sells the property to pay off the debt to the lender, who is the *beneficiary* of the trust.

Another financing device that simplifies the foreclosure process is the **land contract,** or contract for a deed. While not a mortgage in the technical sense, land contracts establish an obligation to transfer title from a seller to a buyer at some future date based on an agreed-on payment schedule. The seller retains ownership of the property until the buyer has paid a certain percentage of the purchase price, sometimes 100 percent. The contract gives the buyer equitable ownership, that is, the right to use the property while making payments, but legal ownership is retained by the seller. If the buyer defaults on the contract, the seller already has ownership of the property and no foreclosure is necessary.

Because the buyer has fewer rights under a land contract than under a mortgage or deed of trust, the **land contract** is used almost exclusively when financing cannot be easily obtained in other ways. For example, individual subdivision lots often can be financed through the use of a land contract with a very small down payment paid to the seller. Such loans usually are unobtainable from traditional mortgage lenders. Because the seller is the legal owner until the land contract is satisfied, buyers who use land contracts should make certain that the contract is carefully written to prevent the seller from encumbering the property before legal ownership is transferred.

Some Final Thoughts Related to Foreclosure

If a borrower is unable or unwilling to continue making payments on a mortgage debt and foreclosure is imminent, it may be possible to sell the mortgaged property rather than default. If the loan contains a due-on-sale clause, the mortgagor must repay the debt if the property can be sold. In many cases, the satisfaction of the debt and the sale of the property occur simultaneously, with the proceeds of any sale first being applied to the debt. If no due-on-sale clause is imposed, however, the borrower may sell the property "subject to" the existing mortgage, whereby the buyer begins making the required payments to the lender. In this type of transfer, the original borrower remains personally liable for the debt should the buyer subsequently default on the loan.

Another method of transferring mortgaged property is known as *assumption*. In this situation, the original borrower sells the property and the buyer assumes responsibility for the debt. Whether the original borrower remains personally liable for the debt should the buyer default depends on the terms of the loan. Finally, if foreclosure is imminent and a buyer cannot be found, a borrower who can no longer meet the obligations of a loan may attempt to transfer title to the property to the lender. Lenders may willingly accept a **deed in lieu of foreclosure** to avoid the expenses of a lengthy foreclosure process.

■ STRUCTURE OF THE U.S. HOUSING FINANCE SYSTEM

The residential lending process begins when a potential borrower contacts a mortgage lender in the hopes of acquiring a loan, either to finance the purchase of a property or to refinance property currently owned. The process of creating a new loan agreement between borrower and lender is known as **loan origination.** In essence, the borrower is purchasing the use of the lender's funds over time by paying interest to the lender. Therefore, *loan origination* refers to the transactions that occur between borrower and lender in the **primary mortgage market.** When existing loans are sold by originators to investors or from one investor to another, these transactions are said to occur in the **secondary mortgage market.** This market greatly increases the flow of mortgage funds between regions of the country. In the primary mortgage market, demand for loans depends on potential borrowers' desires and abilities to qualify for a loan, while the supply of loans depends on mortgage lenders' willingness to provide debt capital to the borrowers. As with all markets, the price of mortgage capital (the interest rate) depends on the relative supply and demand for the product at any given point in time. Obviously, these two markets are interdependent with each other, and together serve as the foundation of the U.S. housing finance system.

The **U.S. housing finance system** is defined as the arrangements and institutions that facilitate the financing of residential buildings using the mortgage concepts discussed above. The many facets of our current system evolved over many years, but its roots lie in New Deal legislative actions taken by the federal government in the wake of massive defaults on owner-occupied housing during the Great Depression of the 1930s. During this time period, the stock market and banking industry were in a virtual state of collapse, new construction was at a standstill, and unemployment was rampant.

The housing market was particularly hard hit during the Depression era owing to the reduction in available mortgage credit. As a matter of national policy, the federal government took steps to provide a steady flow of funds to the housing sector and to shield it from future depressions. The results of these and subsequent actions by the federal government have had a tremendous impact on the current status of our nation's housing finance system. To understand this system requires a review of the history of the government's role in the mortgage market. We begin with a discussion of the Federal Housing Administration.

Federal Housing Administration

Prior to 1929, most residential mortgages were short-term, interest-only loans: although the interest rate was fixed, regular payments covered interest only for the term of the loan, and the entire principal was due at the end of the term. During the Depression, many borrowers could not repay their debts when the loans came due, and if lenders refused to refinance the loans, default was almost unavoidable. Without intervention from the federal government, the future of the housing market looked dismal at best. New construction had virtually ceased, and many existing short-term, interest-only mortgages were already in default.

In response to the economic crisis, the Federal Housing Administration (FHA) was created in 1934 to, among other things, restore confidence in the mortgage market. As a federal agency, the FHA had a dramatic impact on the housing finance system. The FHA helped establish rigorous borrowing and lending standards that reduced lenders' risk and promoted the use of long-term, fully amortizing loans that were more consistent with household budgets than the interest-only loans that were prevalent at the time. (The distinction between these loan types is fully explored in Chapter 15.) In addition, the FHA established a mortgage insurance program to cover losses to lenders who originated these loans using the approved borrowing and lending standards.

Instead of lending money directly to borrowers, the primary role of the FHA in the housing finance system is to act as an insurance company for private lenders (banks, mortgage companies, savings associations, etc.) who originate loans for home purchases, repairs, and improvements. To participate in its most popular program today, the 203(b) program, borrowers purchase mortgage insurance from the FHA on behalf of the lender by paying an initial fee of 2.25 percent of the loan amount at the time of origination, followed by an annual fee of ½ of 1 percent of the original loan amount for the full term of the loan, up to 30 years. (Notice that the upfront cost can be added to the loan amount—the borrower need not pay the money in cash to obtain the insurance.) If a borrower defaults on an **FHA-insured loan,** the insurance premiums collected from borrowers are used to protect the lender from losses resulting from foreclosure. In return for reducing the lender's risk in this manner, borrowers can receive a loan for as much as 97 percent of the value of the property at an affordable interest rate. Although anyone is eligible to apply for an FHA-insured loan, the maximum loan amount available depends on the location of the property. In some high-cost areas, the loan limit was approximately $160,950 as of 2001. Loans for larger amounts are not eligible for FHA insurance.

The success of the FHA in the 1930s greatly standardized the mortgage lending process in the United States and reduced lenders' risk exposure from mortgage loans. Life insurance companies with policy reserves to invest were especially attracted to these standardized mortgages, which resulted in much needed capital flows into depressed areas of the country. Many mortgage bankers began actively originating FHA-insured loans in capital-deficit areas and selling them to investors such as life insurance companies who were in search of high-yielding, relatively safe investments. With the help of other government and nongovernment initiatives in the mortgage industry, the secondary mortgage market expanded rapidly as many other types of investors were attracted to mortgage investments.

Private Mortgage Insurance

Insurance against mortgage default was not unheard of in the mortgage market even before 1929. In fact, numerous **private mortgage insurance** companies existed in the United States prior to the collapse of the real estate market. The high number of loan defaults, however, caused a complete failure of the private mortgage insurance industry during the Depression. Not until the establishment of the Mortgage Guaranty Insurance Corporation (MGIC) in 1957 would PMI reappear in the U.S. mortgage market. Since then numerous PMI companies have been established, and PMI is once again an important aspect of the mortgage industry.

There are several reasons borrowers may choose to use PMI rather than FHA insurance. First, PMI is available for loan amounts much larger than the maximum FHA-insured loan. Second, the cost of PMI is generally less than the cost of FHA mortgage insurance because the annual premiums are based on the current loan balance. Third, many lenders allow the borrower to cancel the PMI when the balance on the loan falls below 80 percent of the value of the property. Only FHA-insured loans originated after January 1, 2001, allow borrowers to cancel the mortgage insurance premium when the loan balance falls below 78 percent of the price of the home at origination.

Federal National Mortgage Association

To increase liquidity in mortgage investments and further stimulate the flow of funds between geographic areas with excess capital and areas with excess demand, Congress decided that a formal secondary market was needed in which mortgages originated in one area could easily be sold to investors in other areas. Only by attracting sufficient capital from the investment community would mortgage markets be able to meet the demand for mortgage funds at prices borrowers could afford. Congress created the Federal National Mortgage Association (FNMA) in 1938 to buy mortgages from lenders and to serve as a clearinghouse for the secondary mortgage market. **Fannie Mae,** as the agency became known, was originally established as a government agency to (1) operate a secondary market for FHA-insured loans and (2) to provide FHA-insured loans to low-income borrowers in remote areas who would not otherwise have access to the mortgage market.

Over time, Congress altered the role of Fannie Mae, and in 1968, the agency was converted into a private corporation, wholly owned by investors. As of 2001, the company is traded on the New York Stock Exchange under the symbol FNM and has more than 250,000 shareholders. Fannie Mae is the third largest corporation in the United States in terms of total assets. Fannie Mae has two primary lines of business. First, the company buys residential mortgages from loan originators (up to $275,000 each), earning a spread between the yield on the mortgages and the company's cost of debt. Second, Fannie Mae also receives pools of mortgage loans from lenders and exchanges them for *mortgage-backed securities* which the company guarantees. These securities are very liquid (much more liquid than whole mortgage loans) and are traded through securities dealers on Wall Street. The company earns a fee for guaranteeing the mortgage-backed securities it sells to investors.

Even though Fannie Mae is a private entity, the federal government continues to influence its operations. Today, one-third of the board of directors of the corporation are appointed by the president of the United States, and the U.S. Treasury is authorized to lend the corporation money if necessary to ensure its smooth operation in the secondary mortgage market. Fannie Mae serves as a clearinghouse for FHA-insured loans, as well as loans guaranteed by the Department of Veterans Affairs and PMI companies.

Department of Veterans Affairs Loan Guarantee Program

Another important government agency in the development of the housing finance system has been the Veterans Administration, now the Department of Veterans Affairs. Immediately after World War II, the Veterans Administration (VA) began to guarantee mortgage loans on a large scale as part of the so-called GI Bill of Rights. Congress passed legislation at the end of the war that allowed veterans to obtain mortgage loans for home purchases with little or no down payment and low interest rates. The VA loan program guarantees the payment of a mortgage loan made by a private lender to a qualified veteran should the borrower default. Unlike FHA-insured loans, however, **VA-guaranteed loans** do not require that the borrower pay premiums for the insurance. Much of the housing boom that occurred during the postwar period is attributed to the tremendous number of VA-guaranteed loans originated to provide housing for returning veterans. Although the program has changed in many respects since its inception, the VA-loan guarantee program continues to account for approximately 10 percent of new loans originated each year. As of 2001, VA loan guarantees are available for loans up to $203,000 with no down payment required from the borrower.

To be eligible for a VA-guaranteed loan today, the applicant must be a veteran who served on active duty and was discharged under conditions other than dishonorable during World War II and later periods. World War II (September 16,

1940, to July 25, 1947), Korean conflict (June 27, 1950, to January 31, 1955), and Vietnam era (August 5, 1964, to May 7, 1975) veterans must have at least 90 days' service. Veterans with service only during peacetime periods and active duty military personnel must have had more than 180 days' active service. Veterans of enlisted service that began after September 7, 1980, or officers with service beginning after October 16, 1981, must in most cases have served at least 2 years. Reservists and National Guard members who were activated on or after August 2, 1990 (during the Persian Gulf Conflict), served at least 90 days, and received honorable discharge are eligible. Members of the Selected Reserve, including National Guard, who are not otherwise eligible and who have completed 6 years of service and have been honorably discharged or have completed 6 years of service and are still serving may be eligible. The expanded eligibility for Reserves and National Guard individuals will expire September 30, 2003.

The cost of obtaining a VA-guaranteed loan varies according the borrower's status as a veteran and the amount of down payment the borrower is making to the lender. A basic funding fee of 2 percent must be paid to VA by all but certain exempt veterans. A down payment of 5 percent or more will reduce the fee to 1.5 percent, and a 10 percent down payment will reduce it to 1.25 percent. A funding fee of 2.75 percent must be paid by all eligible Reserve/National Guard individuals. A down payment of 5 percent or more will reduce the fee to 2.25 percent, and a 10 percent down payment will reduce it to 2 percent. The funding fee for loans to refinance an existing VA home loan with a new VA home loan to lower the existing interest rate is 0.5 percent. Veterans who are using entitlement for a second or subsequent time who do not make a down payment of at least 5 percent are charged a funding fee of 3 percent. For all VA home loans, the funding fee may be paid in cash or it may be included in the loan.

Government National Mortgage Association

The reorganization of Fannie Mae in 1968 led to the creation of a new federal agency, the Government National Mortgage Association (GNMA), now known as **Ginnie Mae.** When Fannie Mae became a privately owned corporation, it no longer provided special assistance loans directly to borrowers. To fill this void, Ginnie Mae was organized as a vehicle for providing subsidized loans to borrowers through various FHA loan programs. For example, a lender can originate a home mortgage for a lower-income borrower at a below-market interest rate, then sell that loan to Ginnie Mae for full market value. After purchasing the loans, Ginnie Mae can either sell them for a loss or hold them in its own portfolio. Losses are paid for by funds appropriated by the Department of Housing and Urban Development, Ginnie Mae's primary agency.

In 1970, Ginnie Mae introduced a payment guarantee program aimed at expanding the supply of funds for the mortgage market. Under this program, which was (and is) backed by the full faith and credit of the U.S. government, Ginnie Mae guaranteed the timely payment of principal and interest on mortgages insured by other federal agencies. That is, if an investor bought mortgages insured by FHA, Ginnie Mae guaranteed that payments from the borrowers would occur as scheduled. This guarantee, combined with the insurance against default provided by FHA, made mortgages a very attractive investment for investors who did not wish to be concerned with late payments from borrowers. Thanks to this program, many new types of financial instruments were developed that allowed investors to invest in the mortgage market without directly holding mortgages. Referred to collectively as *mortgage-backed securities,* these instruments have proven to be highly effective at attracting investment funds to the mortgage market.

Mortgage-backed securities (MBS) are securities issued by mortgage holders to investors who wish to invest indirectly in the mortgage market. The mortgage holders combine loans made to many different borrowers into "mortgage pools," then sell securities that are backed by the underlying mortgages. Proceeds from the sale of these securities allow mortgage holders to originate new mortgages to borrowers. Investors who wish to commit their funds to the mortgage market can do so by purchasing a variety of MBS, including securities known as *pass-through certificates, mortgage-backed bonds, pay-through bonds,* and *collateralized mortgage obligations.* Although the specific details of these securities are beyond the scope of this text, it is important to note that the creation of MBS is often credited with the dramatic inflow of capital to the mortgage market that occurred in the 1970s.

Federal Home Loan Mortgage Corporation (Freddie Mac)

Another important action taken by the federal government designed to increase the flow of funds to the mortgage market was the creation of the Federal Home Loan Mortgage Corporation (FHLMC) in 1970. At this time, the secondary market was well established for FHA-insured and VA-guaranteed loans, but no secondary market was in place for **conventional loans.** Conventional loans are those that are not insured by government agencies, either because their loan to value ratio is lower than 80 percent or because they carry private mortgage insurance. Congress authorized the FHLMC, or **Freddie Mac,** as it is now called, to operate a secondary market for conventional loans similar to the one provided by Fannie Mae and Ginnie Mae for FHA and VA mortgages. Freddie Mac is now a major player in the market for all types of mortgages and competes directly with Fannie Mae to purchase mortgages and sell mortgage-backed securities.

Now that we understand the basic structure of the housing finance system of the United States, we can begin a closer look at the participants who operate within it and account for the tremendous volume of mortgage market activity.

■ MORTGAGE MARKET PARTICIPANTS

In the second quarter of 2000, mortgage debt outstanding in the United States totaled more than $6.6 trillion, with about 75 percent of that amount secured by one- to four-family structures. The system by which this large amount of capital

TABLE 13.1	Mortgage Debt Outstanding (millions of $)						
	1994	1995	1996	1997	1998	1999	2000*
Total Outstanding	4,392,794	4,603,981	4,877,536	5,211,286	5,736,638	6,387,651	6,659,097
By Type of Mortgage							
1-4 Family	3,355,485	3,510,319	3,718,723	3,970,848	4,355,376	4,788,204	4,982,853
Multifamily	271,748	277,002	289,186	302,517	330,551	373,514	392,919
Commercial	682,590	732,100	782,493	847,623	954,205	1,122,968	1,175,641
Farm	82,971	84,561	87,134	90,299	96,506	102,965	107,685
By Holder							
Commercial Banks	1,012,711	1,090,189	1,145,389	1,245,315	1,337,217	1,495,717	1,614,307
Savings Institutions	596,191	596,763	628,335	631,826	643,957	668,634	701,992
Life Insurance Cos.	210,904	213,137	208,162	206,840	213,640	229,333	235,452
Federal/Agency	315,580	308,757	295,192	286,167	292,636	320,105	334,715
Mortgage Pools / Trusts	1,730,004	1,863,210	2,040,848	2,239,350	2,589,764	2,954,836	3,041,396
Individuals/Others	527,404	531,926	559,609	601,788	659,425	719,026	731,235

* Second quarter preliminary.

Source: *Federal Reserve Bulletin*

is committed to mortgage loans on the national level involves numerous government and quasi-government agencies. While these agencies serve as the backbone of the housing finance system, many other participants are required to put this capital in the hands of borrowers. These participants can be categorized into two groups: investors and originators. In practice, many participants in the system belong to both groups simultaneously. Table 13.1 shows mortgage debt outstanding by type of mortgage and by type of holder in the United States from 1994 through the second quarter of 2000.

Mortgage Originators and Investors

Who are the mortgage originators? The most visible suppliers in the primary mortgage market include mortgage bankers, mortgage brokers, commercial banks, savings associations, and credit unions. **Mortgage bankers** originate about half of all residential mortgage loans in the United States each year. Although we typically think of a banker as someone who accepts deposits from savers and then lends that money to borrowers, mortgage bankers do not accept deposits from savers. Instead, they borrow money from commercial banks, then use these funds to originate new loans to mortgage borrowers. Mortgage bankers then sell the loans they originate to investors in the secondary market, but may continue to service the loan (collect and process payments) for a fee on behalf of the investor. The revenues to mortgage bankers include origination fees charged to applicants, servicing fees paid by investors, and the spread between the price of borrowed funds and loaned funds.

Closely related to mortgage bankers are **mortgage brokers.** Mortgage brokers typically do not lend funds directly to borrowers, but simply act as brokers between loan applicants and lenders. Unlike bankers, brokers typically do not continue to service the loans they sell. Mortgage brokers' revenues are dependent on the origination fees charged to borrowers. In general, neither mortgage bankers nor mortgage brokers intentionally hold mortgage loans in a portfolio for their own benefit.

Commercial banks are private financial institutions that are organized to accept deposits from individuals and businesses and to loan these funds to all types of borrowers. Although residential mortgage lending is a small part of most commercial banks' business, commercial banks held approximately 24 percent of all outstanding mortgage debt in the United States as of the second quarter of 2000. Commercial banks use their own funds to originate mortgage loans in the primary market and to buy loans in the secondary mortgage market. They provide mortgages on residential and income-producing properties, as well as construction loans for developers and lines of credit for mortgage bankers.

Savings associations have a long history of providing capital for housing purchases. The first savings institution (thrift) was founded in 1831 with the goal of accepting deposits from savers and loaning those funds to residential borrowers. Since that time, the original intent behind these institutions has remained largely unchanged, but the thrift industry has undergone dramatic cycles of growth and decline. Even after the collapse of many thrifts during the 1980s, these institutions continue to play a major role in the housing finance system. Thrifts continue to originate many new loans, both for their own portfolios and for sale in the secondary market. In 2000, savings associations held approximately 10.5 percent of all outstanding mortgage debt in the United States.

Credit unions are an important source of consumer loans and a savings institution for many Americans. Members of a specific industry or community can join a credit union and enjoy access to their deposits through checking or savings accounts. Because profits are returned to the members, the yield available to credit union members on their deposits is slightly higher than that of other thrift institutions. Most credit unions originate mortgages only for their own portfolios, though some do sell their loans in the secondary mortgage market.

Although the participants discussed above originate the bulk of all new mortgage loans, many of them do not hold all of the loans in their own portfolios, but instead sell them to other investors in secondary mortgage market transactions. As shown in Table 13.1, about half of all mortgage debt in the United States is held by mortgage pools and trusts.

■ UNDERSTANDING THE MORTGAGE LOAN ORIGINATION PROCESS

Now that we understand the legal and institutional characteristics of the mortgage market, we turn our attention to the mortgage loan origination process. We begin by reviewing the Fannie Mae/Freddie Mac Uniform Residential Loan Application, then consider borrower and property qualification criteria as well as various federal laws and rules that regulate the mortgage lending industry.

Fannie Mae/Freddie Mac Uniform Residential Loan Application

Because most of the mortgage loan originators we discussed above want to have the option of selling their loans in the secondary market, the origination process is fairly standardized throughout the United States. In fact, the two principal secondary market participants, Fannie Mae and Freddie Mac, have jointly approved an application form to be used with any loan that may eventually wind up in their secondary markets. The information solicited from the applicant by this form is then evaluated by the lender to reach a decision regarding loan approval or denial. A sample Uniform Residential Loan Application form is shown in Figure 13.3.

Information Required from Borrower

The information required to complete the Uniform Residential Loan Application is divided into various categories. Section 1 of the form asks the borrower to describe the type of mortgage requested, including the loan amount, interest rate, and term. Section 3 requests information on the borrower(s). Because most residential loans are made to married couples, both husband and wife must disclose their names, ages, Social Security numbers, present addresses, and former addresses for the past two years. In Section 4, applicants are required to disclose information regarding their employment history, including employer names, addresses, and telephone numbers. Proof of this information may be required in the form of check stubs, W-2 forms, and other documents. For self-employed borrowers, applicants must submit tax returns for at least two years prior to the application, as well as profit and loss statements prepared by an accountant.

Section 5 contains various questions about facts that may affect the borrowers' creditworthiness. Applicants must disclose information regarding their present and proposed monthly housing expenses. Section 6 requires borrowers to fully disclose their assets and liabilities, including real estate owned, stocks, bonds, life insurance policies, checking and savings accounts, credit cards, other outstanding loans, and alimony and child support obligations. In Section 7, the borrowers must disclose the details of the real estate transaction for which the loan will be used, including the purchase price of the property. By signing the application, the borrowers acknowledge that the purpose of the application is to acquire a loan to be secured by the real estate described in the application. In addition, the borrowers promise that the information provided in the application is true, and authorize the lender to

FIGURE 13.3   Uniform Residential Loan Application

Uniform Residential Loan Application

This application is designed to be completed by the applicant(s) with the lender's assistance. Applicants should complete this form as "Borrower" or "Co-Borrower", as applicable. Co-Borrower information must also be provided (and the appropriate box checked) when ☐ the income or assets of a person other than the "Borrower" (including the Borrower's spouse) will be used as a basis for loan qualification or ☐ the income or assets of the Borrower's spouse will not be used as a basis for loan qualification, but his or her liabilities must be considered because the Borrower resides in a community property state, the security property is located in a community property state, or the Borrower is relying on other property located in a community property state as a basis for repayment of the loan.

I. TYPE OF MORTGAGE AND TERMS OF LOAN

Mortgage Applied for:	☐ V.A. ☒ Conventional ☐ Other: ☐ FHA ☐ FmHA	Agency Case Number	Lender Case Number

Amount $ 108,000	Interest Rate 8 %	No. of Months 360	Amortization Type:	☒ Fixed Rate ☐ GPM	☐ Other (explain): ☐ ARM (type):

II. PROPERTY INFORMATION AND PURPOSE OF LOAN

Subject Property Address (street, city, state, ZIP) 1097 Timber Crossing St.Joseph Missouri	No. of Units 1

Legal Description of Subject Property (attach description if necessary) Lot 3 Block G of the Harris Billups Estate Plat Book 8 p.37	Year Built 1983

Purpose of Loan	☒ Purchase ☐ Construction ☐ Other (explain): ☐ Refinance ☐ Construction-Permanent	Property will be: ☒ Primary Residence ☐ Secondary Residence ☐ Investment

Complete this line if construction or construction-permanent loan.

Year Lot Acquired	Original Cost $	Amount Existing Liens $	(a) Present Value of Lot $	(b) Cost of Improvements $	Total (a + b) $

Complete this line if this is a refinance loan.

Year Acquired	Original Cost $	Amount Existing Liens $	Purpose of Refinance	Describe Improvements ☐ made ☐ to be made Cost: $

Title will be held in what Name(s)	Manner in which Title will be held	Estate will be held in: ☐ Fee Simple ☐ Leasehold (show expiration date)

Source of Down Payment, Settlement Charges and/or Subordinate Financing (explain)	

III. BORROWER INFORMATION

Borrower	Co-Borrower
Borrower's Name (include Jr. or Sr. if applicable) Frank L. Barr	Co-Borrower's Name (include Jr. or Sr. if applicable) Elizabeth M. Barr

Social Security Number 000-00-000	Home Phone (incl. area code) 791-954-0723	Age 32	Yrs. School 16	Social Security Number 000-00-000	Home Phone (incl. area code) 791-954-0723	Age 31	Yrs. School 16

☒ Married ☐ Unmarried (include single, divorced, widowed) ☐ Separated	Dependents (not listed by Co-Borrower) no. 0 ages	☒ Married ☐ Unmarried (include single, divorced, widowed) ☐ Separated	Dependents (not listed by Borrower) no. 0 ages

Present Address (street, city, state, ZIP) ☐ Own ☒ Rent 4 No. Yrs. 103 Wilson Street St. Joseph Missouri	Present Address (street, city, state, ZIP) ☐ Own ☒ Rent 4 No. Yrs. 103 Wilson Street St. Joseph Missouri

If residing at present address for less than two years, complete the following:

Former Address (street, city, state, ZIP) ☐ Own ☐ Rent ____ No. Yrs.	Former Address (street, city, state, ZIP) ☐ Own ☐ Rent ____ No. Yrs.

Former Address (street, city, state, ZIP) ☐ Own ☐ Rent ____ No. Yrs.	Former Address (street, city, state, ZIP) ☐ Own ☐ Rent ____ No. Yrs.

IV. EMPLOYMENT INFORMATION

Borrower	Co-Borrower
Name & Address of Employer ☐ Self Employed ABC Corp. 444 A Street St. Joseph Missouri	Yrs. on this job 5 Yrs. employed in this line of work/profession 8	Name & Address of Employer ☐ Self Employed Intense Corp. 1301 Walker Drive St. Joseph Missouri	Yrs. on this job 4 Yrs. employed in this line of work/profession 7

Position/Title/Type of Business Manager, Human Resources	Business Phone (incl. area code) 791-838-2591	Position/Title/Type of Business Consultant, Advertising	Business Phone (incl. area code) 791-847-3965

If employed in current position for less than two years or if currently employed in more than one position, complete the following:

Name & Address of Employer ☐ Self Employed	Dates (from - to)	Name & Address of Employer ☐ Self Employed	Dates (from - to)
	Monthly Income $		Monthly Income $
Position/Title/Type of Business	Business Phone (incl. area code)	Position/Title/Type of Business	Business Phone (incl. area code)

Name & Address of Employer ☐ Self Employed	Dates (from - to)	Name & Address of Employer ☐ Self Employed	Dates (from - to)
	Monthly Income $		Monthly Income $
Position/Title/Type of Business	Business Phone (incl. area code)	Position/Title/Type of Business	Business Phone (incl. area code)

Freddie Mac Form 65 10/92   Fannie Mae Form 1003 10/92

FIGURE 13.3

Uniform Residential Loan Application (continued)

V. MONTHLY INCOME AND COMBINED HOUSING EXPENSE INFORMATION

Gross Monthly Income	Borrower	Co-Borrower	Total	Combined Monthly Housing Expense	Present	Proposed
Base Empl. Income *	$ 3,100	$ 2,500	$ 5,600	Rent	$ 600	
Overtime	200	325	525	First Mortgage (P&I)		$ 793
Bonuses				Other Financing (P&I)		
Commissions				Hazard Insurance		50
Dividends/Interest				Real Estate Taxes		90
Net Rental Income				Mortgage Insurance		45
Other (before completing, see the notice in "describe other income," below)				Homeowner Assn. Dues		0
				Other:		
Total	$ 3,300	$ 2,825	$ 6,125	Total	$ 600	$ 978

* Self Employed Borrower(s) may be required to provide additional documentation such as tax returns and financial statements.

B/C	Describe Other Income Notice: Alimony, child support, or separate maintenance income need not be revealed if the Borrower (B) or Co-Borrower (C) does not choose to have it considered for repaying this loan.	Monthly Amount
		$

VI. ASSETS AND LIABILITIES

This Statement and any applicable supporting schedules may be completed jointly by both married and unmarried Co-Borrowers if their assets and liabilities are sufficiently joined so that the Statement can be meaningfully and fairly presented on a combined basis; otherwise separate Statements and Schedules are required. If the Co-Borrower section was completed about a spouse, this Statement and supporting schedules must be completed about that spouse also.

Completed [XX] Jointly [ ] Not Jointly

ASSETS Description	Cash or Market Value	Liabilities and Pledged Assets. List the creditor's name, address and account number for all outstanding debts, including automobile loans, revolving charge accounts, real estate loans, alimony, child support, stock pledges, etc. Use continuation sheet, if necessary. Indicate by (*) those liabilities which will be satisfied upon sale of real estate owned or upon refinancing of the subject property.		
Cash deposit toward purchase held by:	$	LIABILITIES	Monthly Pmt. & Mos. Left to Pay	Unpaid Balance
R.E. Broker	4,000	Name and address of Company	$ Pmt./Mos.	$
List checking and savings accounts below		Hardy Credit 3423 S. 3rd Street San Jose CA	$120/11	1,200
Name and address of Bank, S&L, or Credit Union First Bank - Checking 123 Elm Street St. Joseph Missouri				
		Acct. no.		
Acct. no. 222222	$ 3,300	Name and address of Company	$ Pmt./Mos.	$
Name and address of Bank, S&L, or Credit Union First Bank - Savings 123 Elm Street St. Joseph Missouri		Proposed Loan	978/360	108,000
Acct. no. 27328	$ 21,800	Acct. no.		
Name and address of Bank, S&L, or Credit Union		Name and address of Company	$ Pmt./Mos.	$
		Acct. no.		
		Name and address of Company	$ Pmt./Mos.	$
Acct. no.	$			
Name and address of Bank, S&L, or Credit Union				
		Acct. no.		
		Name and address of Company	$ Pmt./Mos.	$
Acct. no. 35358	$			
Stocks & Bonds (Company name/number & description)	$			
Olde Discount	18,300	Acct. no.		
		Name and address of Company	$ Pmt./Mos.	$
Life insurance net cash value	$			
Face amount: $		Acct. no.		
Subtotal Liquid Assets	$ 47,400			
Real estate owned (enter market value from schedule of real estate owned)	$ 20,000	Acct. no.		
Vested interest in retirement fund	$	Name and address of Company	$ Pmt./Mos.	$
Net worth of business(es) owned (attach financial statement)	$			
Automobiles owned (make and year)	$			
Ford '92	4,000	Acct. no.		
Nissan '97	11,000	Alimony/Child Support/Separate Maintenance Payments Owed to:	$	
Other Assets (itemize)	$	Job Related Expense (child care, union dues, etc.)	$	
		Total Monthly Payments	$ 1,098	
Total Assets a.	$ 82,400	Net Worth (a minus b) ▶ $ -26,800	Total Liabilities b.	$ 109,200

Freddie Mac Form 65 10/92   Page 2 of 4   Fannie Mae Form 1003 10/92

FIGURE 13.3   Uniform Residential Loan Application (continued)

VI. ASSETS AND LIABILITIES (cont.)

Schedule of Real Estate Owned (If additional properties are owned, use continuation sheet.)

Property Address (enter S if sold, PS if pending sale or R if rental being held for income)	Type of Property	Present Market Value	Amount of Mortgages & Liens	Gross Rental Income	Mortgage Payments	Insurance, Maintenance, Taxes & Misc.	Net Rental Income
Lot 7, Becker Drive	land	$ 20,000	$ 0	$ 0	$ 0	$ 0	$ 0
Totals		$	$	$	$	$	$

List any additional names under which credit has previously been received and indicate appropriate creditor name(s) and account number(s):

Alternate Name	Creditor Name	Account Number

VII. DETAILS OF TRANSACTION

a. Purchase price	$ 120,000
b. Alterations, improvements, repairs	0
c. Land (if acquired separately)	0
d. Refinance (incl. debts to be paid off)	0
e. Estimated prepaid items	1,200
f. Estimated closing costs	5,000
g. PMI, MIP, Funding Fee	
h. Discount (if Borrower will pay)	
i. Total Costs (add items a through h)	126,200
j. Subordinate financing	
k. Borrower's closing costs paid by Seller	
l. Other Credits (explain)	
m. Loan amount (exclude PMI, MIP, Funding Fee financed)	108,000
n. PMI, MIP, Funding Fee financed	
o. Loan amount (add m & n)	108,000
p. Cash from/to Borrower (subtract j, k, l & o from i)	18,200

VIII. DECLARATIONS

If you answer "Yes" to any questions a through i, please use continuation sheet for explanation.

	Borrower Yes	Borrower No	Co-Borrower Yes	Co-Borrower No
a. Are there any outstanding judgments against you?		X		X
b. Have you been declared bankrupt within the past 7 years?		X		X
c. Have you had property foreclosed upon or given title or deed in lieu thereof in the last 7 years?		X		X
d. Are you a party to a lawsuit?		X		X
e. Have you directly or indirectly been obligated on any loan which resulted in foreclosure, transfer of title in lieu of foreclosure, or judgment? (This would include such loans as home mortgage loans, SBA loans, home improvement loans, educational loans, manufactured (mobile) home loans, any mortgage, financial obligation, bond, or loan guarantee. If "Yes," provide details, including date, name and address of Lender, FHA or V.A. case number, if any, and reasons for the action.)		X		X
f. Are you presently delinquent or in default on any Federal debt or any other loan, mortgage, financial obligation, bond, or loan guarantee? If "Yes," give details as described in the preceding question.		X		X
g. Are you obligated to pay alimony, child support, or separate maintenance?		X		X
h. Is any part of the down payment borrowed?		X		X
i. Are you a co-maker or endorser on a note?		X		X
j. Are you a U.S. citizen?	X		X	
k. Are you a permanent resident alien?		X		X
l. Do you intend to occupy the property as your primary residence? If "Yes," complete question m below.	X		X	
m. Have you had an ownership interest in a property in the last three years?	X		X	
(1) What type of property did you own—principal residence (PR), second home (SH), or investment property (IP)?	IP		IP	
(2) How did you hold title to the home—solely by yourself (S), jointly with your spouse (SP), or jointly with another person (O)?	SP		SP	

IX. ACKNOWLEDGMENT AND AGREEMENT

The undersigned specifically acknowledge(s) and agree(s) that: (1) the loan requested by this application will be secured by a first mortgage or deed of trust on the property described herein; (2) the property will not be used for any illegal or prohibited purpose or use; (3) all statements made in this application are made for the purpose of obtaining the loan indicated herein; (4) occupation of the property will be as indicated above; (5) verification or reverification of any information contained in the application may be made at any time by the Lender, its agents, successors and assigns, either directly or through a credit reporting agency, from any source named in this application, and the original copy of this application will be retained by the Lender, even if the loan is not approved; (6) the Lender, its agents, successors and assigns will rely on the information contained in the application and I/we have a continuing obligation to amend and/or supplement the information provided in this application if any of the material facts which I/we have represented herein should change prior to closing; (7) in the event my/our payments on the loan indicated in this application become delinquent, the Lender, its agents, successors and assigns, may, in addition to all their other rights and remedies, report my/our name(s) and account information to a credit reporting agency; (8) ownership of the loan may be transferred to successor or assign of the Lender without notice to me and/or the administration of the loan account may be transferred to an agent, successor or assign of the Lender with prior notice to me; (9) the Lender, its agents, successors and assigns make no representations or warranties, express or implied, to the Borrower(s) regarding the property, the condition of the property, or the value of the property.

Certification: I/We certify that the information provided in this application is true and correct as of the date set forth opposite my/our signature(s) on this application and acknowledge my/our understanding that any intentional or negligent misrepresentation(s) of the information contained in this application may result in civil liability and/or criminal penalties including, but not limited to, fine or imprisonment or both under the provisions of Title 18, United States Code, Section 1001, et seq. and liability for monetary damages to the Lender, its agents, successors and assigns, insurers and any other person who may suffer any loss due to reliance upon any misrepresentation which I/we have made on this application.

Borrower's Signature	Date	Co-Borrower's Signature	Date
X		X	

X. INFORMATION FOR GOVERNMENT MONITORING PURPOSES

The following information is requested by the Federal Government for certain types of loans related to a dwelling, in order to monitor the Lender's compliance with equal credit opportunity, fair housing and home mortgage disclosure laws. You are not required to furnish this information, but are encouraged to do so. The law provides that a Lender may neither discriminate on the basis of this information, nor on whether you choose to furnish it. However, if you choose not to furnish it, under Federal regulations this Lender is required to note race and sex on the basis of visual observation or surname. If you do not wish to furnish the above information, please check the box below. (Lender must review the above material to assure that the disclosures satisfy all requirements to which the Lender is subject under applicable state law for the particular type of loan applied for.)

BORROWER   ☐ I do not wish to furnish this information

Race/National Origin: ☐ American Indian or Alaskan Native   ☐ Asian or Pacific Islander   ☐ White, not of Hispanic Origin   X Black, not of Hispanic origin   ☐ Hispanic   ☐ Other (specify) _____

Sex: ☐ Female   X Male

CO-BORROWER   ☐ I do not wish to furnish this information

Race/National Origin: ☐ American Indian or Alaskan Native   ☐ Asian or Pacific Islander   ☐ White, not of Hispanic Origin   X Black, not of Hispanic origin   ☐ Hispanic   ☐ Other (specify) _____

Sex: X Female   ☐ Male

To be Completed by Interviewer

This application was taken by:
X face-to-face interview
☐ by mail
☐ by telephone

Interviewer's Name (print or type): **Bob Interviewer**

Interviewer's Signature ___ Date ___

Interviewer's Phone Number (incl. area code): **954-761-0264**

Name and Address of Interviewer's Employer: **First Savings Bank St. Joseph Missouri** verify its accuracy. The application also requests certain information that is used by the government to monitor lender activities, and requires that the lender's representative sign the application.

Duties of the Originator

Upon receiving a completed Uniform Residential Loan Application, the lender has various duties to the borrower as determined by federal lending regulations. These regulations are intended to provide protection to mortgage consumers. Important federal legislation to participants in the mortgage lending industry includes the Equal Credit Opportunity Act (Regulation B), the Consumer Protection Act (Regulation Z), the Real Estate Settlement Procedures Act, the Flood Disaster Protection Act, and the Fair Credit Reporting Act.

Equal Credit Opportunity Act

The Equal Credit Opportunity Act has influenced the mortgage lending industry since 1974. Under this act, applicants must be notified within 30 days of application that their loan request has either been approved, denied, or determined to be incomplete. In addition, the act prohibits lenders from discriminating against borrowers on the following basis: race, color, religion, national origin, sex, marital status, age, whether all or part of an applicant's income is derived from public assistance programs, or whether the applicant has exercised any right under the Consumer Credit Protection Act.

Consumer Credit Protection Act

Title I of the Consumer Credit Protection Act is frequently referred to as Regulation Z, or the Truth-in-Lending law. Under this regulation, lenders are required to disclose the full details of the loan to the applicant within three business days of application, including exactly how much the loan will cost. The goal of the Truth-in-Lending requirement is to permit borrowers to shop for the best deal among competing lenders. Specifically, lenders are required to inform applicants of the total finance charges associated with the loan and the annual percentage rate (APR) of interest. In the event the loan is to be used to refinance a property already owned by the applicant, Regulation Z requires that the lender inform the borrower of the right to rescind the loan within three business days of origination. The APR is the effective annual interest rate that the borrower will pay after all fees and charges are taken into consideration. The APR is often quite different from the stated interest rate used to determine the payments on the loan. By comparing the APRs of various lenders, a consumer can determine which lender is offering the best deal and thereby make an informed decision about the loan.

Real Estate Settlement Procedures Act

The Real Estate Settlement Procedures Act (RESPA) is another important source of regulation in the mortgage lending industry. This act applies to federally related mortgage loans, and creates several different duties for mortgage lenders following a residential mortgage loan application. First, RESPA requires that lenders provide borrowers with a copy of a special information booklet prepared by the U.S. Department of Housing and Urban Development (HUD). The information contained in *Settlement Costs and You: A HUD Guide for Home Buyers* is designed to describe and explain the settlement costs borrowers are likely to incur when purchasing a home using mortgage financing.

Second, RESPA requires that lenders provide borrowers with a "good faith estimate" of the settlement costs associated with the loan within three business days of the application. We examined these costs and the loan "closing" process in detail in a previous chapter. Third, the act prohibits kickbacks or referral fees paid to parties who refer a borrower to the lender. Fourth, the act gives the applicant the right to request and receive a copy of any appraisal report used to evaluate the property that serves as security for the debt. Although the borrower is typically charged a fee for the appraisal, the report technically belongs to the lender, not the borrower.

Fifth, RESPA requires the use of the HUD-1 Uniform Settlement Statement by the settlement agent at the loan closing. As we saw in a previous chapter, this settlement statement shows line-by-line costs that will be incurred as a result of the pending real estate transaction, and a copy of this completed form must be made available to both the buyer and seller. Furthermore, the act establishes the borrower's right to inspect this statement one day prior to the actual closing. At that time, the lender must accurately disclose all known closing costs and must provide a good-faith estimate of all uncertain closing costs that will be charged to the borrower. To enforce this right, the borrower must make a written request to the lender on or before the business day prior to settlement.

Sixth, RESPA requires that lenders disclose whether the loan is expected to be sold in the secondary market. If the loan is sold, the lender is required to disclose this information to the borrower within 15 days of transfer. While borrowers can do little to stop the transfer of their loan, it is important that they know who their loan servicer is and how to contact the new servicer after a transfer.

Finally, RESPA limits the amount of money a lender can require the borrower to deposit to cover such recurring expenses as property taxes, hazard-insurance premiums, and other periodic assessments. In addition to the principal and interest payments due from a borrower each month, lenders may also require that a borrower's loan payment include reserve payments to be deposited into an escrow account. As the property tax bill or insurance premiums come due, the lender simply pays the bill from the funds in the escrow account. Having the money on deposit ensures that payment will be made promptly, thus protecting the lender's interest in the collateral for the loan. If these bills are not paid, the property could be destroyed without a current insurance policy, or a tax lien that has priority over the lender's lien or encumbrance could be placed on the property. Both of these events could significantly diminish the protection provided to the lender by the mortgage concept. RESPA limits the amount of reserves that the lender can collect at closing to one-sixth of the annual property taxes and insurance.

Flood Disaster Protection Act

The remaining federal legislation that regulates the mortgage lending industry includes the Flood Disaster Protection Act and the Fair Credit Reporting Act. The Flood Disaster Protection Act requires that lenders disclose to borrowers whether the property they are purchasing lies within a flood hazard area. If so, the lender must require that the borrower to obtain flood insurance if it is available. Flood insurance is generally only available through the Federal Emergency Management Administration's (FEMA) National Flood Insurance Program. This act puts the burden of notifying borrowers that their properties are subject to damage from flooding squarely on the shoulders of the lenders.

Fair Credit Reporting Act

The Fair Credit Reporting Act primarily affects credit reporting agencies, but it also affects the users of information obtained from these agencies. The act requires that lenders obtain permission before investigating an applicant's credit history and handle the applicant's credit information with due care. If an applicant's loan request is denied based on information contained in a credit report, the lender must notify the applicant of this fact and provide the borrower with the name, address, and telephone number of the credit agency that supplied the information.

Mortgage Underwriting

Once the application for a mortgage loan has been received from the applicant, the lender must evaluate the applicant's creditworthiness as well as the suitability of the property as security for the debt. From the lender's perspective, lending money to a borrower is an investment in the borrower's willingness and ability to repay the debt under the terms of the agreement. As discussed earlier, the property can be used to satisfy the debt (through the foreclosure process) if the borrower is unable or unwilling to abide by the terms of the loan. The process of evaluating the risk of an applicant and a property in order to make a decision regarding a loan application is known as **underwriting.** We consider the underwriting process for borrowers and properties separately.

Qualifying an Applicant

To evaluate an applicant's creditworthiness, lenders typically examine the applicant's sources of income, net worth, and credit history, then perform a risk assessment. The sources of income that are considered relevant include wages or salary, self-employment, rent, interest, investment, and commission, as well as child support, alimony, separate maintenance income, retirement, pension, disability, and welfare benefits. Note that disclosure of information regarding child support, separate maintenance income, and alimony is not required if the applicant does not wish for this information to be considered as an income source. The Uniform Residential Loan Application described previously is used to provide information on these sources of income to the lender, and the lender must verify the accuracy of this information. Similarly, the application provides information regarding assets and liabilities that determine the applicant's net worth which can be verified with permission of the applicant. Lenders also obtain permission to request an up-to-date **residential mortgage credit report**. This report, which is required if the lender intends on selling the loan in the secondary market, contains information about outstanding judgments, liens, or divorce proceedings; a list of similar credit inquiries within the previous 90 days; and all available credit information for the past seven years from at least one national credit reporting agency. If any of this information reasonably suggests that the borrower will not be able or willing to repay the proposed debt, the lender can deny the loan application subject to the regulations imposed by the Fair Credit Reporting Act.

Qualifying the Property

In addition to collecting and verifying information on the borrower's creditworthiness, the lender must also collect and verify information regarding the property being pledged as security for the debt. First, the person pledging the property must in fact be the legal owner of the property. As we discussed in a previous chapter, verifying the ownership or title to real estate requires careful inspection of the public records. If there are defects or "clouds" on the title to the property involved, the lender will reject the loan application. To protect their interests in the property, lenders typically require that borrowers purchase title insurance or obtain a title opinion from an attorney. In general, loans originated without title insurance cannot be sold in the secondary mortgage market.

In addition to verifying the applicant's right to pledge the property as security, the lender also has incentive to verify that the value of the property supports the requested loan amount. If the value of the property is less than the amount of the debt, borrowers may be unwilling to meet their obligations. If the lender is faced with foreclosing on the loan in this situation, the sale of the property will not likely result in sufficient proceeds to satisfy the debt. Therefore, the lender may require an appraisal of the property's value before granting final approval for the requested loan amount. After receiving the appraisal report from a qualified appraiser, the lender must review the appraisal report to verify its acceptability. If the loan involved will be sold in the secondary mortgage market, the appraiser's conclusions must be presented on the Uniform Residential Appraisal Report form that is accepted by Fannie Mae and Freddie Mac. We examined the topic of real estate appraisal in a previous chapter.

Risk Assessment

In addition to evaluating a borrower's residential mortgage credit report and the title and value of the pledged property, the lender must consider other factors when making the underwriting decision. Although no absolute rules exist to determine whether a borrower will be able to meet the obligations of a requested loan, there are guidelines that lenders use in the underwriting process. While each lender establishes its own guidelines, the secondary market participants (primarily Fannie Mae and Freddie Mac) provide general guidelines for loans they are willing to buy from loan originators. Because most lenders want to be able to sell their loans in this market, these guidelines are well-accepted in the lending industry. Fannie Mae and Freddie Mac guidelines fall into three categories: loan-to-value ratios, down payment sources, and income ratios.

Loan-to-Value Ratio Guidelines

The **loan-to-value ratio,** or LTV ratio, is determined by dividing the requested loan amount by the lesser of the sale price or the appraised value of the property. Generally expressed as a percentage amount, higher LTV ratios imply greater risk. For example, suppose a lender provides $95,000 to a borrower who purchases a $100,000 house (LTV ratio of 95 percent). Because the borrower has little equity in the property, default is more likely if the value of the property should fall below the loan amount. If default does occur and the property is sold through the foreclosure process, it is doubtful that the proceeds of the sale will be sufficient to cover the loan balance, past due interest, and the expenses of sale. If the LTV ratio was only 50 percent, however, there is a much lower probability of default. If the borrower should default, the proceeds from the property sale should be sufficient to protect the lender. As a general guideline, all loans with an LTV ratio of 80 percent or higher must carry PMI, FHA mortgage insurance, or a VA loan guarantee to be acceptable in the secondary mortgage markets. While most conventional loans have a maximum LTV ratio of 95 percent even with PMI, some FHA-insured loans may have LTV ratios of up to 98.75 percent, and VA-guaranteed loan LTV ratios may be as high as 100 percent.

Downpayment Source Guidelines

The second category of guidelines refers to sources for the borrower's down payment or equity for a home purchase. In general, secondary market guidelines require that funds used for the down payment be provided primarily by the borrower rather than from outside sources. By requiring that borrowers use their own personal funds for the down payment, the borrower is likely to be more diligent in meeting the obligations of the loan. In most conventional loans with LTV ratios above 80 percent, at least 5 percent of the purchase price must represent the borrower's personal investment in the property. The remaining 15 percent could be a gift from an outside source, such as a family member or employer, but never a loan. If the LTV ratio is less than 80 percent, however, the entire down payment amount can be a gift from an outside source. Lenders who intend to sell a loan in the secondary market must verify that the down payment meets or exceeds this requirement by documenting its sources.

The down payment source requirements are applied differently for FHA and VA loans. Some FHA loan programs permit the borrower to contribute only 3 percent of the purchase price from personal savings, with the other 2 percent in the form of a gift from an outside source. Other FHA loan programs allow the entire down payment amount to be a gift to the borrower from outside sources. Many VA-guaranteed loans do not require a down payment at all, but the borrower is required to pay a funding fee that decreases as the down payment amount increases.

Income Ratio Guidelines

Income ratios comprise the third category of underwriting guidelines. These ratios are designed to assess borrowers' abilities to repay the mortgage as specified in the loan documents. Two income ratios that are considered by secondary market participants and the various guaranteeing and insuring entities are the **mortgage debt ratio** (front-end ratio) and the **total debt ratio** (back-end ratio).

The mortgage debt ratio (MDR) is defined as the percentage of a borrower's gross monthly income that is required to meet monthly housing expenses. *Monthly housing expenses* refers to principal and interest payments, hazard insurance, property taxes, mortgage insurance, homeowners' association fees, and any payments on existing or proposed second mortgages on the property. In general, the MDR must not exceed 28 percent on a conventional loan. For example, consider a loan applicant whose gross monthly income is $5,000. The applicant is applying for a loan with monthly payments of $965. Monthly payments for hazard insurance, property taxes, and mortgage insurance total $210. No second mortgages exist, and the home is not part of a homeowners association. The MDR for this applicant is 23.5 percent ($1,175 \div 5,000 \times 100$), which is well below the maximum ratio allowed.

The total debt ratio (TDR) is defined as the percentage of a borrower's gross monthly income that is required to meet monthly contractual expenses. Contractual expenses include housing expenses as defined above, any revolving credit payments, payments on any installment loans with more than 10 remaining payments, and any alimony or child support. Notice that while applicants are not required to provide information regarding alimony and child support as an *income source,* they must disclose this information if it represents an *expense.* As a guideline for conventional loans, total payments for all of the items listed above must not exceed 36 percent of a borrower's gross income. Continuing the example discussed above, if the applicant has an outstanding car loan that requires monthly payments of $280 and child support payments of $500 per month, the TDR would be 39.1 percent ($1,995 \div 5,000 \times 100$). In this case, the applicant would not qualify for the loan under this guideline.

When assessing the risk of a mortgage loan application, lenders calculate both of these ratios to verify that the borrower is capable of repaying the debt and meeting other contractual obligations. Borrowers must qualify under both ratios simultaneously to receive approval. While these ratios have evolved from years of experience with millions of loans, there are possible mitigating circumstances that will allow a lender to deviate from these guidelines. Such circumstances include a demonstrated ability to allocate a higher percentage of income to housing expenses, a low LTV ratio, a spotless credit report, large net worth, or other similar factors. In addition, the ratio limits specified above apply to conventional loans only. For FHA-insured loans, the ratio limits are 29 percent for the front-end ratio, and 41 percent for the back-end ratio. VA-guaranteed loans use a more detailed income standard, and sometimes allow back-end ratios as high as 45 percent.

The Underwriting Decision

The final step in the loan origination process is for the lender to render an underwriting decision. As mentioned above, the Equal Credit Opportunity Act requires that lenders reach their decision for completed applications within 30 days. With modern technology, most underwriting decisions can be made in minutes instead of days. If the loan is approved, the lender notifies the borrower of acceptance and, in most cases, issues a letter of commitment. If the loan is for home purchase rather than a refinancing, then the real estate closing process can occur as planned. If the lender denies the credit application, the lender must notify the applicant, give the reason for the credit denial, and provide a statement of nondiscrimination that is consistent with the provisions of the Equal Credit Opportunity Act.

■ SOURCES OF CAPITAL IN COMMERCIAL PROPERTY MARKETS

Who are the debt and equity investors in commercial property markets? Unlike residential markets, in which most equity capital is provided by households who are seeking a place to live, capital in commercial property markets is provided by investors who are seeking investment returns rather than personal use of the properties. Some of these investors provide equity capital to the market (through their down payments), and other investors provide debt capital by lending money to equity investors. The returns available through debt and equity investments in commercial properties attract individuals, pension funds, life insurance companies, commercial banks, and investment companies that are formed specifically to invest in commercial real estate.

Individual Investors

Many commercial properties are owned by individual investors (sometimes called *"mom and pop" investors)* who invest in relatively small-scale commercial properties as a means of diversifying their investment portfolios, which often include a variety of other asset classes (stocks, bonds, insurance policies, etc.). Individual investors often use a portion of their total wealth portfolio in conjunction with money borrowed from commercial property lenders to purchase properties that are expected to provide investment returns through property value appreciation and cash flow from rental operations to tenants. In addition to direct

REAL ESTATE TODAY

What Is Credit Scoring?

While most of us are aware that our credit history is a critical consideration when we apply for a loan, many people may not realize how their credit history is evaluated by a potential lender. Credit bureaus maintain surprisingly detailed databases regarding our financial affairs, including loan and account balances, payment activity, bankruptcy filings and even denied credit and life insurance applications. Potential lenders review these records before approving loan requests in an effort to assess how likely applicants are to pay their obligations.

Close-Up

Many lenders place significant emphasis on an applicant's "credit score." Credit scores are calculated by the major credit bureaus for everyone with a credit history in an effort to simplify detailed credit history records. The formulas used in calculating the scores are intended to rank credit histories in terms of the probability that borrowers will be delinquent with their payments. Loan applicants with higher credit scores are viewed more favorably than those with lower scores. For example, scores calculated using one popular formula range from 300 to 900, with most consumers falling between 500 and 800. Scores above 700 are considered good, while scores in the 600 range are considered marginal.

The exact details of the formulas used to calculate credit scores are proprietary and are not released to the public. The scores used by the three main credit bureaus (Equifax, Experian, and Trans Union) are calculated using a system developed by Fair, Isaac & Co., a California data-management and consulting firm. Scores calculated using this system are determined by 30 different factors available in a standard credit report. The factors relate to the applicant's delinquency history, the level of indebtedness, the length of the applicant's credit history, the number of recent inquiries regarding the credit history and the types of credit the applicant has outstanding. Through years of research, these factors have proven to be very predictive when it comes to evaluating whether an applicant will repay the debt according to the terms of the loan agreement. Credit scores make it easier and faster to evaluate loan requests, and they are growing in popularity with mortgage lenders.

Because lenders rely heavily on credit bureau reports when evaluating loan applications, it is important that your credit record is accurate and up to date. Many financial planners recommend that consumers check their credit records annually by calling the three main credit bureaus and requesting a credit report. For a nominal fee, you can review your reports for errors and omissions and ensure that your credit history is accurate. In addition to correcting errors, you can enter in your credit record a statement of up to 100 words explaining the circumstances of any negative information.

ownership, mom and pop investors may "hold a mortgage" on a property (provide debt capital) to other equity investors. Mom and pop investors are an important source of capital in many local real estate markets and should not be ignored as a critical component of such markets. We will consider how these investors approach the investment decision and evaluate potential investment opportunities in a subsequent chapter.

Life Insurance Companies

Life insurance companies also invest debt and equity capital in commercial properties. A typical life insurance company sells insurance policies that have expected payouts (on death of the customers) many years into the future. The insurance company invests the proceeds from the policy sales to ensure that funds will be available to pay the eventual policy claims. Commercial real estate is an attractive investment vehicle for many life insurance companies because the assets are durable, long-lived, and provide an acceptable expected rate of return. Insurance companies invest in commercial properties by purchasing properties directly (as equity investors) and also by providing mortgage funds to borrowers seeking to purchase properties.

Pension Funds

Pension funds represent another important participant in the equity and debt capital markets. Pension funds accumulate contributions made by the fund participants over their working lives. As the contributions are received, the fund managers invest the money with the objective of increasing the income stream that will be available to the fund participant when the participant retires. Some examples of large pension funds in the United States include those operated by labor unions, private corporations, and state and local employment systems such as CALSTERS (the California State Teachers Retirement System), CALPERS (California Public Employees Retirement System), and TIAA (Teachers Insurance Annuity Association).

Since the 1980s, pension funds have increased their involvement in commercial property markets and now are a major source of capital in both the debt and equity markets. With plenty of cash on hand, many pension funds invest directly in commercial properties, often on an all-cash basis, while others prefer to underwrite mortgage loans on commercial properties for equity investors. In either case, the investment horizon for pension funds is quite long (the working life of the participants) and thus well matched to the relatively long and durable nature of commercial real estate investment opportunities. In general, investment returns to pension funds are not subject to federal income taxes at the fund level, though the participants may be taxed on the income they receive during their retirement years.

Pension funds may manage their own investments in commercial properties and mortgages, but they often seek the services of an investment management firm to identify properties for investment and to provide portfolio and property management services. In some cases, several different pension funds will combine their money into a commingled real estate fund, or CREF, that is managed by a professional management company. In some cases, these individual CREF participants may sell or buy additional shares of the CREFs as needed to adjust the proportion of real estate held in their total investment portfolios.

Real Estate Investment Trusts

Real estate investment trusts (REITs) are another increasingly important participant in the commercial property equity and debt capital markets. REITs sell shares of stock (units) to investors through public and private markets, then use the proceeds to invest in commercial properties, either as equity or debt investors. In 1990, the total amount of capital invested in publicly traded REITs was approximately $8.7 billion. By the end of 2000, that amount had increased by almost 15-fold, to approximately $138.7 billion. Publicly traded REITs provide an opportunity for even the smallest investors to participate in commercial real estate markets.

REITs are not subject to firm-level taxation as long as the firm meets certain Internal Revenue Service requirements. Most important, the firm must distribute at least 95 percent of its taxable income each year to its shareholders (who are then taxed on this income as dividends). Because of this requirement, REITs have little opportunity to grow through the use of retained earnings. Instead, REITs must issue additional shares of stock or borrow from lenders to significantly increase their holdings.

Commercial Banks

Commercial banks are another important source of capital in commercial property markets. Commercial banks are divided into three broad categories: community banks (less than $500 million in assets), regional banks (more than $500 million in assets), and money center banks (the ten largest banks in the United States) Most banks attempt to match the maturity structure of their liabilities (deposits that could be withdrawn) with their assets (loans and investments). The spread between the interest rate paid on deposits and the yields earned on loans and investments represents profit to the bank. Because their investment funds are subject to withdrawal by the bank's customers, commercial banks tend to be more involved in development and construction financing and less involved in long-term mortgage lending or direct property ownership.

CMBS

An important recent advance in the commercial property financing system has been the increase in securitization of commercial mortgages. As discussed previously in this chapter regarding residential mortgages, commercial mortgages can be divided into financial securities that represent claims on the cash flows to the mortgage holder. These financial securities are called *commercial mortgage-backed securities* **(CMBS).**

To understand how CMBS work, consider a commercial bank or investment banking firm that has expertise in evaluating commercial property mortgage applications but does not wish to tie up its money in long-term mortgage loans. That bank may be able to originate several loans to commercial property investors, then pool those loans together and sell "shares" of the pool to other investors who want to invest in mortgage loans but do not have expertise in originating these loans. The bank that puts the pool together creates different types of securities that entitle the security purchasers to different components of the cash flow coming into the pool over time from the mortgage borrowers. One security class, for example, might be entitled to all of the cash flows for the first 5 years of the life of the loans, at which time this security class will be retired and the next class will be entitled to the cash-flow stream. Investors who might otherwise not have been interested in purchasing mortgage investments will be attracted to the different CMBS that match their investment preferences and horizons. Given the dramatic increase in residential mortgage securitization that occurred during the 1980s and 1990s, CMBS are expected to become an increasingly important component of the commercial financing system over the next several years.

■ COMMERCIAL FINANCING UNDERWRITING CRITERIA

Unlike residential mortgage underwriting criteria that rely heavily on the borrower's personal ability to earn sufficient income to repay the debt, commercial property lenders are much more concerned with the property's ability to generate sufficient income to repay the debt. Lenders typically require that a property's expected net operating income (NOI), defined as gross income less operating expenses, be 15 percent to 20 percent higher than the payments required to service the debt. This underwriting criterion is often called the **debt coverage ratio,** or DCR. The DCR is calculated by dividing the NOI by DS, where NOI represents the expected net operating income to the property (rent collections less operating expenses) and DS represents the debt service (payments on the mortgage). A lender who requires a DCR of 1.2 is, in essence, requiring that the property's expected net operating income be 20 percent larger than its mortgage payments. The lender can be fairly confident that mortgage payments will be made as scheduled as long as the actual NOI is at least 80 percent of the expected amount.

In addition to the DCR, commercial property lenders also look closely at the LTV. As we saw in our discussion of residential mortgages, the larger the LTV ratio, the riskier the loan is from the lender's perspective. In residential mortgages, FHA insurance, VA guarantees, and PMI allow the borrower to purchase residential property with high LTV ratios and relatively small down payment amounts. Because no such mortgage insurance or guarantees are typically available for commercial property mortgages, the LTV ratios on commercial loans are much lower (70 percent is common) than the LTV ratios for residential mortgages (where 95 percent or more is quite common). Lower LTV ratios imply that larger down payment percentages are necessary for commercial property purchases.

■ CHAPTER REVIEW

■ A specialized legal framework has evolved for loans in which real estate is pledged as security for a debt, though the details of the mortgage concept vary slightly from state to state. Most real estate loans involve a promissory note, which makes the borrower personally liable for the debt, and a security instrument, such as a mortgage or deed of trust, which enables the lender to foreclose on the property if the borrower defaults on the loan.

■ Loans are originated to borrowers in primary mortgage markets, and many loans are subsequently sold to investors in secondary mortgage market transactions. The primary and secondary mortgage markets, and the participants in those markets, have evolved into an efficient system for providing housing financing in the United States.

■ Some of the more prominent participants in the housing finance system include the Federal Housing Administration, the Veterans Administration, Ginnie Mae, Fannie Mae, Freddie Mac, private mortgage insurers, mortgage bankers, mortgage brokers, commercial banks, savings associations, and credit unions.

■ To ensure that investors are willing to accept such loans, lenders employ a standardized loan application process and rigorous underwriting criteria. Fannie Mae and Freddie Mac have jointly approved an application form to be used with any loan that may eventually wind up in their secondary markets. This form solicits information about the borrower, the property, and the details of the transaction.

■ The underwriting decision involves careful consideration of the borrower's ability and willingness to repay the debt, as well as the suitability of the property as collateral. Lenders evaluate applicant's employment history, income sources, net worth, and previous credit history to assess the risk of the loan application.

■ Using the general guidelines for risk assessment proposed by Fannie Mae and Freddie Mac, lenders can screen out high risk applicants and feel confident that their lending decisions are made on a sound basis. These guidelines fall into three categories: loan-to-value ratios, down payment sources, and income ratios.

■ Mortgage market consumers are protected against discrimination, fraud, and misrepresentation by various federal regulations that govern lender activity, including the Equal Credit Opportunity Act (Regulation B), the Consumer Protection Act (Regulation Z), the Real Estate Settlement Procedures Act, the Flood Disaster Protection Act, and the Fair Credit Reporting Act.

■ The participants in the commercial property financing system include individual investors, life insurance companies, pension funds, real estate investment trusts, commercial banks, and commercial mortgage-backed securities investors.

■ Commercial property lenders look closely at the debt coverage and the LTV ratios when evaluating the risk of a commercial property loan application.

■ KEY TERMS

acceleration clause

CMBS

commercial banks

conventional loans

credit unions

debt coverage ratio

deed in lieu of
  foreclosure

deed of trust

deficiency judgment

due-on-sale clause

Fannie Mae

FHA-insured loans

foreclosure

Freddie Mac

Ginnie Mae

housing finance system

hypothecation

judicial foreclosure

land contract

lien theory

loan origination

loan-to-value ratio

mortgage

mortgage debt ratio

mortgage-backed
  securities

mortgage bankers

mortgage brokers

nonjudicial foreclosure

pension fund

prepayment clause

primary mortgage market

private mortgage
  insurance

promissory note

real estate investment
  trust (REIT)

residential mortgage
  credit report

savings associations

secondary mortgage
  market

secured loan

strict foreclosure

title theory

total debt ratio

underwriting

unsecured loan

VA-guaranteed loans

■ STUDY EXERCISES

1. Define the following terms: secured loan, unsecured loan, mortgage, hypothecation, promissory note, due-on-sale clause, prepayment clause, and acceleration clause.

2. In what manner can a land contract simplify the foreclosure process?

3. Identify the parties involved in a deed of trust.

4. In states that permit their use, when would a deficiency judgment be in order?

5. Why is PMI generally less expensive than FHA insurance?

6. How does FHA mortgage insurance differ from VA loan guarantees?

7. What is meant by the term "conventional loan"?

8. List the five major types of mortgage originators.

9. List the nine factors that mortgage lenders may *not* use to discriminate against loan applicants as defined by the Equal Credit Opportunity Act.

10. Under the Equal Credit Opportunity Act, how long does a lender have to either accept or reject a completed loan application?

11. What is the general intention behind the Truth-in-Lending law? List three requirements under this regulation.

12. Why does the APR not equal the stated interest rate on a loan? Which rate is usually higher?

13. List seven requirements lenders must observe in conjunction with RESPA.

14. What requirement is imposed on mortgage lenders by the Flood Disaster Protection Act?

15. List three requirements imposed on mortgage lenders by the Fair Credit Reporting Act.

16. What is contained in a residential mortgage credit report?

17. List the three categories of risk assessment guidelines used by mortgage lenders.

18. Consider a borrower who has gross annual income of $48,000 and is applying for a mortgage that requires monthly payments of $1,040. Taxes and insurance premiums for the pledged property total $1,200 per year. The borrower has no other outstanding loans on the property, but she has 24 monthly payments of $260 on her car loan. Based on the MDR and TDR limits for a conventional loan, does she qualify for the loan? Could she qualify for an FHA-insured loan based on the appropriate MDR and TDR guidelines?

19. What is the maximum LTV ratio permitted by secondary mortgage markets on conventional mortgages that do not carry PMI?

20. Why do commercial banks typically limit their involvement in the commercial property financing system to short-term loans?

21. Has the total capitalization of REITs increased or decreased in recent years? Why?

22. Suppose a commercial property loan application has a debt coverage ratio of 0.95. What does this say about the property's ability to cover its debt service payments?

■ FURTHER READINGS

Brueggeman, William B., and Jeffrey D. Fisher. *Real Estate Finance and Investments,* 11th ed., Irwin McGraw Hill, 2001.

Dennis, Marshall W., and Michael J. Robertson. *Residential Mortgage Lending,* 4th ed., Englewood Cliffs, N. J.: Prentice Hall, 1995.

14 Risk, Return and the Time Value of Money

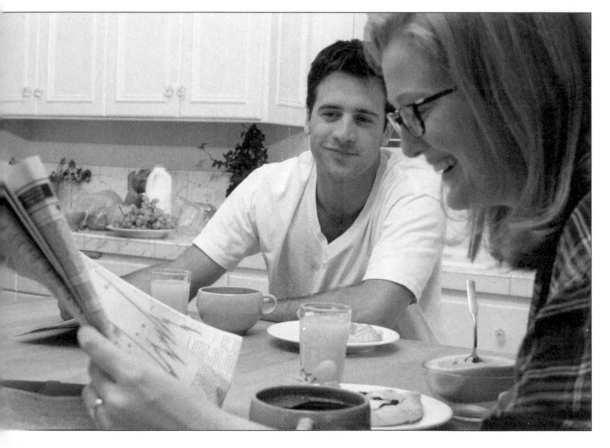

Before potential homebuyers begin looking at specific properties, they need to have thoroughly analyzed their financial position to determine how much money they can afford to spend.

An understanding of basic financial concepts is essential for all real estate market participants. Real estate lending and borrowing decisions, value estimation, and investment analysis all require knowledge of the relationship between risk and return, "time value of money" principles, and financial decision rules. The purpose of this chapter is to consider each of these concepts and demonstrate their role in the financial framework of real estate. Some readers are already familiar with these concepts, but for others they represent an unexplored frontier. For the first group, many topics considered in this chapter will serve as a review. The second group will want to study the material quite carefully and make certain they master the concepts before moving on to subsequent topics. In all cases, it is helpful to think of the topics discussed in this chapter as tools that market participants should have at their disposal as they engage in real estate decision-making situations.

The topics considered in this chapter include

■ the relationship between risk and return,

■ the six time value of money formulas, and

■ the net present value and internal rate of return financial decision rules.

FIGURE 14.1	Relationship Between Risk and Return

■ THE RELATIONSHIP BETWEEN RISK AND RETURN

Financial decision making is defined as the process of comparing the expected benefits from a proposed course of action with the expected costs arising from that course of action. In the case of real estate investment decisions, for example, investors must compare the purchase price of the property with profits (total revenues minus total costs) they expect to receive over the holding period.

Rather than dollar amounts, investment returns are frequently expressed as a percentage **rate of return.** That is, $100 profit on an investment of $1,000 represents a 10 percent rate of return. Because the returns from an investment opportunity are expected to be realized in future time periods, and because the future is uncertain, it would be imprudent for an investor to make decisions without recognizing that the actual rate of return from a particular investment may vary significantly from initial expectations. Uncertainty about the actual rate of return an investment will provide over the holding period is known as **risk.** Because most of us are risk-averse rather than risk-seeking (we view higher levels of risk negatively), risk is an additional cost that must be considered when evaluating an investment opportunity.

For financial decision makers to accept an investment, they must expect to receive a sufficient return to justify its cost. Thus, in addition to considering the revenues and operating expenses resulting from a property investment, real estate investors must consider the risk that the expected rate of return from pursuing that investment may deviate from initial expectations. A riskier investment must promise a higher rate of return than less risky investment opportunities. If not, prudent decision makers would prefer a less risky investment that earns the same level of return. Therefore, a positive relationship exists between risk and investors' required rates of return. This general relationship is depicted graphically in Figure 14.1.

The upward sloping line in the figure illustrates the required rate of return demanded by investors at various levels of risk. As the level of risk increases, so does the required rate of return. The point at which the risk/return line intersects the vertical axis is known as the *risk-free rate.* This point indicates the rate of return that investors are willing to accept for investments that pose no risk. Although one can argue that there is no such thing as a perfectly risk-free investment, the return available from investing in U.S. government securities, such as Treasury bills, is generally considered the risk-free rate because there is virtually no danger that the federal government will default on its obligation to pay its debts. Even though an investment is risk-free, investors require a return that compensates them for giving up use of their funds over time. As we proceed to the right along the risk/return line, it is immediately apparent that higher risk implies higher required rates of return.

Types of Risk

Uncertainty about future returns from an investment opportunity arises from a variety of factors, but most risk can be characterized as business risk, financial risk, purchasing power risk, or liquidity risk. **Business risk** is the uncertainty arising from changing economic conditions that affect an investment's ability to generate returns. **Financial risk** is uncertainty associated with the possibility of defaulting on borrowed funds used to finance an investment. **Purchasing power risk** (inflation risk) arises from the possibility that the amount of goods and services that can be acquired with a given amount of money will decline. Thus, returns from an investment may be less valuable in real terms when they are received. **Liquidity risk** is the possibility of loss resulting from not being able to convert an asset into cash quickly should the need arise. Real estate is often considered to be less liquid than other investment assets such as stocks or bonds, which can be traded almost immediately at the current market price. In general, investors' required rates of return are a combination of the returns required for each of these risk types *and* the risk-free rate of return.

The Time Value of Money

Another important consideration in financial decision making is the "timing" of the expected benefits and costs associated with investment opportunities. Even if risk is minimal, decision makers must recognize that delaying returns until some future time represents an added cost of an investment. As we saw above, investors require a rate of return for any investment whose benefits are expected to occur in the future, even if there is no risk. In other words, a dollar in the hand today is worth more than a dollar to be received in the future because it can either be consumed immediately or put to work earning a return in another investment opportunity. This is known as the **time value of money principle.** To use this principle effectively in decision-making situations, investors must be able to convert future values into present values and present values into future values. The next section of this chapter presents six techniques for accomplishing these conversions while simultaneously accounting for the risk associated with an investment choice.

■ TIME VALUE OF MONEY FORMULAS

There is an old saying that "a bird in the hand is worth two in the bush," and a dollar in the hand is certainly worth more than one to be received sometime in the future. Thus, if given a choice today between receiving $5 immediately or $5 one year from now, we would choose the first option. If the choice were between $5 immediately or $15 one year from now, however, the decision becomes more complicated. Which of these options is the better one *right now?* The answer depends on two issues: risk and the time value of money. As we discussed above, both of these issues are incorporated into the decision-making process by specifying an appropriate required rate of return. A variety of time value of money formulas exist that allow us to address the choices described above, as well as more involved investment decisions. After we consider the intuition behind the first two formulas, we will describe how two popular models of financial calculators (Hewlett Packard 10B and Texas Instruments BAII PLUS) can be used to conduct time value of money analysis.

The first formula we will consider is used to find the future value of a lump sum. This formula allows decision makers to determine what an amount of money in hand today will be worth some time in the future if it increases at a constant rate each period.

Future Value of a Lump Sum

Suppose an investor buys 10 acres of vacant land today for $70,000. If land values are expected to increase at the rate of 10 percent per year, what will the land be worth at the end of three years? In one year, the land is worth $70,000 plus 10 percent of $70,000. Written algebraically, the value of the land in one year is

$$\$70,000 + (.10 \times \$70,000) = \$77,000$$

This equation can also be written as

$$\$70,000(1 + .10) = \$77,000$$

In two years, the land is worth $77,000 plus 10 percent of $77,000, or

$$\$77,000(1 + .10) = \$84,700$$

At the end of three years the original investment of $70,000 is worth

$$\$84,700(1 + .10) = \$93,170$$

As shown here and in Table 14.1, the investment has grown from $70,000 to $93,170, for a total increase of $23,170 over three years. The rate of growth is ten percent annually, but the total growth is 33.1 percent ($23,170 ÷ $70,000 = 0.331). This example demonstrates the concept of **compound interest,** which means that during any given period, interest is earned not only on the original investment, but also on the interest previously earned. Thus, as in this example, after

TABLE 14.1

Year	Present Amount	×	(1 + i)	=	Future Amount
0	$70,000		(1.10)		$77,000
1	$77,000		(1.10)		$84,700
2	$84,700		(1.10)		$93,170
3	$93,170				

the first year the value of the land increases by 10 percent of the previous year's value where this value includes the initial investment plus increases during prior years. Note that multiplying the growth rate by the number of periods (10 percent × 3 = 30 percent) does not provide the total percentage change in value because such a calculation ignores interest earned on previously earned interest. The *total* percentage change in value is 33.1 percent.

If the investor is concerned only with the value of the land at the end of three years, as opposed to each year's value, we can simplify this problem greatly. The value of $70,000 invested today at 10 percent interest for three years is worth $93,170.

$$\$70,000(1 + .10)(1 + .10)(1 + .10) = \$93,170$$

Equivalently, we can write the future value of $70,000 invested at 10 percent for three years as follows:

$$\$70,000(1 + .10)^3 = \$93,170$$

Writing the calculation in this manner leads to the formal specification of the concept of the **future value of a lump sum.** Equation (1) below is used to find the future value of a known present value when the future amount is to be received in a lump sum at a particular time n.

$$FV = PV(1 + i)^n \qquad\qquad \textbf{(1)}$$

where FV is the future value we are seeking to determine, PV is the initial value, i is the rate of return per period and n is the number of periods.

Present Value of a Lump Sum

The converse of the above problem requires a present value calculation; that is, what is the value today of a sum to be received some time in the future? Suppose there is a parcel of land that an investor believes will be worth $93,170 in three years. If the investor requires a 10 percent annual rate of return on investments with comparable risk, how much would he or she be willing to pay for the land today? The **present value of a lump sum** is given by solving equation (1) to move PV on the left side of the equality sign as shown in equation (2):

$$PV = FV\left[\frac{1}{(1 + i)^n}\right] \qquad (2)$$

where PV is the present value we are seeking to determine, FV is the known future value, i is the required rate of return per period, or discount rate, and n is the number of periods.

Applying the present value of a lump sum formula to this investment problem reveals that the present value of $93,170 to be received three years in the future is $70,000.

$$PV = \$93,170\left[\frac{1}{(1 + .10)^3}\right] = \$70,000$$

Note that the equations for present value and future value are mathematically reverse operations, the key difference being the variable that we are trying to find. If we know the present amount, we can find the future amount using the future value formula. Conversely, if we know the future amount, we can find the present amount using the present value formula. In solving time value of money problems, it is often helpful to recognize that when calculating present values we are looking "backward" in time, and when calculating future values, we are looking "forward" in time. The process of finding present values is known as **discounting**, and the process of finding future values is known as **compounding.**

Both time and the rate of return enter into present value calculations. The farther into the future the money will be received, the lower the present value. Also, the greater the rate of discount, the lower the present value. The opposite is true for future value calculations. The longer a present amount is allowed to grow, the greater the future value. The greater the rate of growth, the greater the future value.

Using Financial Calculators to Solve for Present and Future Values

While the formulas presented above are relatively simple, we now consider four other formulas that can become quite cumbersome to work with. We believe that students should work through these formulas to establish an understanding of how to use basic financial concepts in real estate decision making, but we also know that more efficient methods exist for working with time value of money factors once a base level of knowledge is established.

For many years, financial analysts used cumbersome tables that listed time value of money factors for various values of i and n. These tables were a grand improvement over pencil and paper, but today such tables have been replaced by relatively inexpensive financial calculators. Instead of laboriously working through these formulas or selecting the appropriate factor from a table and multiplying it by the appropriate present or future amount, we need only understand how to press a few keys on these wonderful devices. Spending time memorizing the formulas is not necessary for most readers of this text, but learning how to use a financial calculator is a worthwhile endeavor.

We encourage you to learn how your calculator works by first solving the problems using the formulas presented here, then by referencing the manual that came with your calculator to "plug in the numbers" and arrive at the answers. Doing so will ultimately give you confidence in your ability to use the calculator in more complex decision-making situations.

Each calculator manufacturer uses slightly different keys to solve time value of money problems, but there is some degree of uniformity. Almost all financial calculators have keys labeled *PV, FV, I/Y* or *I/YR,* and *n* or *N*. These buttons correspond to the notation used in equations (1) and (2) above. All of the problems considered in this chapter require that your calculator be set in "END" mode. If the screen displays the word "BEGIN" or "BGN," you will not be able to calculate the correct answer. To solve the two examples using the Hewlett-Packard Model 10B and the Texas Instruments BAII PLUS, two of the most popular financial calculators, follow the steps listed below for each calculator. Refer to your calculator's manual if you have another brand or model. (Note that all of the keystroke examples in this chapter assume that you clear your calculator's memory before you begin the steps described. Clearing the screen is *not* equivalent to clearing the memory registers. Clearing the memory registers is a second step.)

HP-10B Keystrokes: Future Value of a Lump Sum

(Be sure that your calculator is set in "END MODE." If the screen displays the word "BEGIN," press the shift key, then press the key lableled *BEG/END*.)

1. Set the number of compounding periods per year at 1	1, *shiftkey, P/YR*
2. Enter the present value	70000, *PV*
3. Enter the number of periods	3, *N*
4. Enter the growth rate (interest)	10, *I/YR*
5. Solve for the future value	*FV* (calculator displays −93170.00)

HP-10B Keystrokes: Present Value of a Lump Sum

1. Set the number of discounting periods per year at 1	1, *shiftkey, P/YR*
2. Enter the future value	93170, *FV*
3. Enter the number of periods	3, *N*
4. Enter the growth rate (interest)	10, *I/YR*
5. Solve for the present value	*PV* (calculator displays −70000.00)

BAII PLUS Keystrokes: Future Value of a Lump Sum

(Be sure that your calculator is set in "END MODE." If the screen displays the letters "BGN" in the top right corner, press the 2nd key, followed by the key labeled *BGN*. Press the 2nd key again, then press the key labled *SET*. Finally, press 2nd key once more and then press *QUIT*.)

1. Set the number of compounding periods per year at 1	*2nd, P/Y,* 1, *ENTER, 2nd, QUIT*
2. Enter the present value	70000, *PV*
3. Enter the number of periods	3, *N*
4. Enter the growth rate (interest)	10, *I/Y*
5. Solve for the future value	*CPT, FV* (calculator displays −93170.00)

BAII PLUS Keystrokes: Present Value of a Lump Sum

1. Set the number of discounting periods per year at 1	*2nd, P/Y,* 1, *ENTER, 2nd, QUIT*
2. Enter the future value	93170, *FV*
3. Enter the number of periods	3, *N*
4. Enter the growth rate (interest)	10, *I/Y*
5. Solve for the present value	*CPT, PV* (calculator displays −70000.00)

Notice that when you follow the keystrokes described here, your calculator displays a negative sign in front of the final answer. The negative sign is a result of the algorithm used by the calculator to solve the time value of money formulas, and should not be a great cause for concern. Just remember that if you enter a positive value in your calculator for a present value, then calculate future value, your calculator will always give you a negative future value. Similarly, if you enter a negative present value, the calculator will always give you a positive future value. The same is true for other time value of money calculations we consider next. The negative sign indicates an outflow of money, while the positive sign indicates an inflow.

Applying the Present Value Formula to Cash-Flow Streams

Up to this point we have focused our attention on finding the value of present and future lump sum amounts. In many real estate investments, however, the project generates flows of cash to the investor throughout the life of the investment. Consider an investment that promises to pay $500 in one year, $1,000 in two years, and $1,500 in three years. If your required rate of return is 10 percent, how much would you be willing to pay for this investment? To solve this problem, first recognize that we know three future amounts. Applying the present value formula to each of these amounts with the proper values for the exponent *n,* then adding the three results, yields the total present value of this stream of cash flows. The present value of this stream at a discount rate of ten percent is

$$PV = 500\left[\frac{1}{(1 + .1)^1}\right] + 1,000\left[\frac{1}{(1 + .1)^2}\right] + 1,500\left[\frac{1}{(1 + .1)^3}\right] = \$2,407.96$$

Thus, if we invested $2,407.96 in this project, we would earn exactly our required 10 percent rate of return.

In the event the stream of cash flows extends over many years, calculating the present value by repetition of the present value of a lump sum formula can be time consuming. (We describe how to use the "cash flow" features of financial calculators to solve this type of problem later in this chapter.) If the periodic cash flows are a series of equal amounts, however, the problem is greatly simplified. Such a series of equal cash flows is called an **annuity.**

Present Value of an Annuity

Consider an investment that promises to pay $1,000 at the end of each year for 3 years. The required rate of return is 10 percent. What is the present value of this stream of payments? Applying the present value of a lump sum formula three times and then adding the results yields

$$PV = 1,000\left[\frac{1}{(1.1)^1}\right] + 1,000\left[\frac{1}{(1.1)^2}\right] + 1,500\left[\frac{1}{(1.1)^3}\right] = \$2,486.85$$

While this calculation is certainly valid, it can be cumbersome when a large number of future cash flows are involved. Fortunately, there is a simpler method. Because the amounts in each period are equal, we can use the **present value of an annuity** formula shown in equation (3).

$$PVA = A\left[\frac{1 - \frac{1}{(1 + i)^n}}{i}\right] \qquad (3)$$

where *A* is the amount each period (the annuity), *i* is the discount rate per period, and *n* is the number of periods.

Applying this equation to the present problem yields

$$PVA = 1000\left[\frac{1 - \frac{1}{(1.1)^3}}{.10}\right] = 1,000(2.486852) = \$2,486.85$$

Using a financial calculator to solve this problem is quite simple. Rather than entering a value using the *FV* key, we use the annuity payment key, which is usually labeled *PMT.* The following keystrokes demonstrate the steps required to solve this problem using the HP-10B and BAII PLUS calculators.

The following example demonstrates the importance of the present value of annuity formula in a real estate context: calculating the outstanding balance on a mortgage loan. Suppose you hold an investment that generates an annual cash flow to you of $16,274.54. Your required rate of return on this investment is 10 per-

HP-10B Keystrokes: Present Value of an Annuity

1. Set the number of discounting periods per year at 1	1, *shiftkey, P/YR*
2. Enter the annuity amount	1000, *PMT*
3. Enter the number of periods	3, *N*
4. Enter the discount rate (interest)	10, *I/YR*
5. Solve for the present value of the annuity	*PV* (calculator displays −2486.85)

BAII PLUS Keystrokes: Present Value of an Annuity

1. Set the number of discounting periods per year at 1	*2nd, P/Y,* 1, *ENTER, 2nd, QUIT*
2. Enter the annuity amount	1000, *PMT*
3. Enter the number of periods	3, *N*
4. Enter the discount rate (interest)	10, *I/YR*
5. Solve for the present value of the annuity	*CPT, PV* (calculator displays −2486.85)

cent annually, and there are seven annual cash flows. What is the value of this investment today? In other words, what is the stream of payments (an annuity) worth to you today at a required rate of return of 10 percent? To find the answer, apply the formula to the annuity amount.

$$PVA = \$16{,}274.54 \left[\frac{1 - \dfrac{1}{(1.1)^7}}{.10} \right] = \$79{,}231.28$$

Using the HP-10B financial calculator, the entries are $PMT = 16274.54$, $I/YR = 10$, $N = 7$. Pressing the PV key yields −79,231.28. Using the BAII PLUS calculator, the entries are $PMT = 16274.54$, $I/Y = 10$, $N = 7$. Pressing CPT, then PV, will yield −79,231.28.

Future Value of an Annuity

In some instances, particularly in personal finance, we are interested in finding the future value of equal payments received over time. In this type of problem, we could apply the future value formula described above to each pay-ment individually using the proper exponent n and then add the results of each calculation, but this can be simplified by using the future value of an annuity formula.

Consider the following example. Suppose you invest $100 at the end of each year for the next five years in an interest-earning bank account paying 10 percent interest per year. How much money would you have in the account at the end of five years?

The first payment will be deposited one year from today and will earn interest for four years. The second deposit will earn interest over three years, and so on for the third and fourth deposits. Note that the fifth payment will not earn any interest, because it will only be deposited at the end of the fifth year. We can solve for the future value at the end of five years using the future value fac-tor for each of the five deposits:

$$FV = 100(1.1)^4 + 100(1.1)^3 + 100(1.1)^2 + 100(1.1)^1 + 100(1.1)^0 = \$610.51$$

To solve this problem quickly, however, we can use the **future value of an annuity** formula given in equation (4).

$$FVA = A\left[\frac{(1 + i)^n - 1}{i}\right] \qquad (4)$$

In this example,

$$FVA = 100\left[\frac{(1 + 1)^5 - 1}{.10}\right] = \$610.51$$

$$FVA = 100(6.105100) = \$610.51$$

Our trusty financial calculators are useful in this type of problem as well. To solve for the future value of this annuity, enter 100 for PMT, 5 for number of years, and 10 for the interest rate. Solving for the future value yields –610.51.

Sinking Fund Payments

The next time value of money principle, the sinking fund payment formula, is algebraically equivalent to the future value of an annuity formula. The important difference is that the unknown variable is not the future value of the stream of payments, but the amount of each payment required to accumulate the future amount.

Suppose, for example, that you wish to buy a home, but do not have the required down payment of $20,000. You decide that you will save that much over the next five years by making equal, annual deposits into a savings account pay-ing 10 percent annually. How much must you deposit each year to accumulate $20,000? This type of problem is known as a *sinking fund problem.* That is, how much must you must "sink" into the account each year to accumulate the desired amount in the future? Just as we solved the future value formula [equation (1)] to get present value on the left side of the equality sign in equation (2), we can also solve equation (4) for the annuity A. To avoid possible confusion, we replace the variable A with the symbol SFP to represent "sinking fund payment." These manipulations of the FVA formula provide equation 5, the formula for finding **sinking fund payments.**

$$SFP = FVA \left[\frac{i}{(1 + i)^n - 1} \right]$$

Applying the sinking fund formula to this problem shows you must deposit $3,275.94 into the account each year for five years to accumulate $20,000 at ten percent interest.

$$SFP = 20,000 \left[\frac{.10}{(1 + .1)^5 - 1} \right] = \$3,275.94$$

$$SFP = 20,000(.163797) = \$3,275.94$$

Using a financial calculator, the entries are as follows: FV = 20000, I/YR (or I/Y) = 10, and N = 5. Solving for the payment (PMT) yields –3,275.94.

Mortgage Payments

The sixth and final time value of money formula to be considered is the mortgage payment formula. This formula is used to calculate payments due on a "fully-amortizing" loan. We will consider the concept of amortization in greater detail in Chapter 15, so our discussion here is limited to using this formula to calculate mortgage payments.

Suppose you wish to borrow $100,000 to buy a parcel of real estate. The bank is willing to lend the money at 10 percent interest, provided that you amortize the debt with annual payments over the next ten years. How much will your payments be? Notice the similarity between this problem and the one we examined during our discussion of the present value of annuities. In both examples, we know the interest rate and the number of periods. In the present value of annuity problem, we know the amount of the annuity, but we do not know the present value. In this problem, we know the present amount, but we do not know the amount of the payment or, in other words, the annuity. Because the problems are identical except for the unknown variable, we can solve equation (3) to move the annuity (variable A) to the left side of the equality sign. To avoid confusion, we then rename A to PMT to represent mortgage payment. This results in the **mortgage payment** formula:

$$PMT = PVA \left[\frac{i}{1 - \dfrac{1}{(1 + i)^n}} \right]$$

Why does the symbol PVA appear in the formula for mortgage payments? The answer to this question is simple, but very important. From the lender's point of view, a mortgage is an investment in the borrower's ability to repay the debt. In return for giving the borrower cash today, the lender will receive an annuity for n periods into the future. The lender is willing to give the borrower the present value of that annuity today in the form of a loan. To the borrower, the present value of the series of future payments represents the loan amount. Thus, the loan amount, or the remaining amount outstanding, can always be thought of as the present value of an annuity, where the annuity is the future mortgage payments. Applying equation (6) to the problem at hand shows the annual mortgage payment the lender will require for a ten-year loan of $100,000 at 10 percent interest.

$$PMT = \$100,000 \left[\frac{\frac{.1}{1}}{1 - \frac{1}{(1.1)^{10}}} \right] = \$16,274.54$$

Using a financial calculator, the entries are as follows: PV = 100000, I/YR (or I/Y) = 10, and N = 10. Solving for the payment (PMT) yields –16,274.54.

Monthly Compounding

We now have developed the six time value of money formulas, but in each of the examples used thus far we have dealt with annual time periods. In many instances, however, the compounding and discounting periods in real estate problems are semiannually, quarterly, or even monthly. For example, almost all residential mortgage loans call for monthly payments. The preceding analysis remains valid for periods of any length, but with one word of caution: Time and interest must always be measured in the same unit. That is, if we wish to solve for a monthly mortgage payment, we must use a monthly interest rate.

Suppose, for example, we wish to calculate the monthly payment required to amortize a $100,000 loan at 12 percent annual interest for 30 years. The number of compounding periods becomes 360 (12 times 30), and the periodic interest rate becomes 1 percent (12 percent divided by 12). Substituting these numbers into the formula for finding the mortgage payment yields a monthly payment of $1,028.61.

We can generalize each of the six formulas to account for any compounding period by "dividing I by m and multiplying n by m," where m is simply the number of compounding or discounting periods per year, i is the annual interest or discount rate, and n is the number of years. Applying this rule restates the six time value of money formulas as follows:

$$FV = PV \left[(1 + \frac{i}{m})^{nm} \right]$$

$$PV = FV \left[\frac{1}{(1 + \frac{i}{m})^{nm}} \right]$$

$$SFP = FVA \left[\frac{1 - \frac{1}{(1 + \frac{i}{m})^{nm}}}{\frac{i}{m}} \right]$$

$$FVA = A \left[\frac{(1 + \frac{i}{m})^{nm}}{\frac{i}{m}} \right]$$

$$SFP = FVA \left[\frac{\frac{i}{m}}{(1 + \frac{i}{m})^{nm} - 1} \right]$$

$$PMT = PVA \left[\frac{\frac{i}{m}}{1 - \frac{1}{(1 + \frac{i}{m})^{nm}}} \right]$$

Most financial calculators can be set to automatically convert the time value of money formulas for any compounding or discounting frequency. Of course, you can do this manually by dividing the interest rate and multiplying the number of years by the number of compounding or discounting periods per year before pressing the appropriate keys, but you must enter all the decimal places (without rounding) to avoid getting the wrong answer. (Dividing 10 percent by 12, for example, will yield 0.01 if your calculator is set to display only two decimal places, but the value to eight decimal places is 0.00833333, which is a very different number from 0.01!) If you wish to take advantage of your calculator's built-in features, the following steps show how to use the HP-10B and BAII PLUS to calculate monthly mortgage payments on a $100,000 loan amount for 30 years at 12 percent interest.

■ FINANCIAL DECISION RULES: NPV AND IRR

Now that we understand the concept of risk and the time value of money formulas, we will examine a framework for making decisions concerning investment

HP-10B Keystrokes: Monthly Mortgage Payments

1. Set the number of discounting periods per year at 12	12, *shiftkey, P/YR*
2. Enter the loan amount	100000, *PV*
3. Enter the number of months	30, *shiftkey, N*
4. Enter the interest rate (calculator divides by *P/YR*)	12, *I/YR*
5. Solve for the monthly payment	*PMT* (calculator displays −1028.61)

BAII PLUS Keystrokes: Monthly Mortgage Payments

1. Set the number of periods per year at 12	*2nd, P/Y,* 12, *ENTER, 2nd, QUIT*
2. Enter the loan amount	100000, *PV*
3. Enter the number of months	30, *2nd, xP/Y, N*
4. Enter the interest rate (calculator divides by *P/Y*)	12, *I/Y*
5. Solve for the monthly payment	*CPT, PMT* (calculator displays −1028.61)

choices. This framework compares the benefits of an investment to its costs, including risk and the time value of money. The key concept is **net present value** (NPV), which is the difference between how much an investment is worth to an investor and how much it costs. Suppose an investment promises to pay you a stream of cash flows that has a present value of $10,000. If the asking price of this investment is $9,000, the investor obviously would decide to buy it. In this case, the net present value is $1,000 ($10,000 − $9,000).

The question is, how do we determine the present value of the stream of cash flows? We discount the cash flows at the proper discount rate, which is the rate of return we require to compensate for the riskiness of the investment. If the stream occurs in uneven amounts, we use the present value of a lump sum formula to discount each cash flow. If the stream is an annuity, we can simplify the calculations by using the present value of an annuity formula. The appropriate discount rate to use is one that accounts for the risk of the investment opportunity, usually determined by comparing the rates of return on alternative investment choices of similar risk. Formally, we can define net present value as follows:

NPV = present value of cash inflows − present value of cash outflows

In decision-making situations, we use the NPV concept as part of the following **NPV decision rule.** If the NPV of an investment is greater than or equal to zero, we choose to invest because the investment is worth at least as much as it costs, given our required rate of return. If NPV is less than zero, we choose not to invest because we would not be earning our required rate of return. Remember that the required rate of return reflects both the time value of money and the riskiness of the investment opportunity. We can take this rule a step farther and say that if faced with several alternative investment choices, we should accept the one with the highest positive NPV, because it will increase our wealth more than the others.

This leads us to another important concept in financial decision making. If the net present value of an investment is greater than or equal to zero, we must be earning at least our required rate of return. In fact, if NPV equals zero, the rate of return on the investment is exactly equal to the required rate. If NPV is not zero, what rate are we earning? We can define the **internal rate of return** (IRR) of an investment as the discount rate which makes NPV exactly equal to zero. To determine an investment's IRR, we can search a variety of discount rates by trial-and-error until we find one that makes NPV equal zero. This rate will be the internal rate of return on the investment. Fortunately, most financial calculators have a feature that allows automatic searches for the internal rate of return for a series of cash flows.

The definition of IRR provides another rule for financial decision making that states that if the IRR is greater than or equal to our required rate of return, we choose to invest: otherwise, we forgo the investment opportunity. While the IRR rule and the NPV rule are based on the same principles, the NPV rule is generally the best choice to use because IRR calculations may yield multiple discount rates that set NPV equal to zero. When our objective is to determine the rate of return provided by an investment, however, the IRR calculation is extremely useful. The following example demonstrates the NPV rule and the IRR rule using both the present value formula approach and financial calculators.

NPV and IRR Decision Rule Example

Suppose you are faced with making a decision about whether to invest $10,000 today in a risky real estate investment. In return for your investment, you expect to receive the following stream of cash flows: year one, $100; year two, $1,600; year three, $1,800; year four, $450; year five, $12,500. You believe other investment opportunities with similar risk offer a 12 percent rate of return. What are the NPV and IRR of this investment? Should you invest?

We can find the NPV of this investment by applying the NPV definition: *NPV = PV of cash inflows – PV of cash outflows.* Table 14.2 shows the intermediate results from the calculation presented below:

$$NPV = \frac{100}{1.12^1} + \frac{1{,}600}{1.12^2} + \frac{1{,}800}{1.12^3} + \frac{450}{1.12^4} + \frac{12{,}500}{1.12^5} - 10{,}000 = 24.82$$

TABLE 14.2

Year	Cash Flow		Present Value	Discounted Cash Flow at 12%
zero	−$10,000	outflow	$-10000/1.12^0$	−$10,000.00
one	100	inflow	$100/1.12^1$	89.29
two	1,600	inflow	$1600/1.12^2$	1,275.51
three	1,800	inflow	$1800/1.12^3$	1,281.20
four	450	inflow	$450/1.12^4$	285.98
five	12,500	inflow	$12500/1.12^5$	7,092.84,

NPV = PV of inflows − PV of outflows
NPV = 89.29 + 1,275.51 + 1,281.20 + 285.98 + 7,092.84 − 10,000
NPV = 24.82
IRR = 12.0646%

Because the NPV is greater than zero, the investment is worth more than it costs and we should choose to accept this opportunity. Likewise, we know that the IRR must be greater than our required rate of return, simply because NPV is positive. To determine the IRR of this investment, we could apply different dis-

HP-10B Keystrokes: NPV and IRR Calculations for Unequal Cash Flows

1. Set the number of periods per year at 1	1, *shiftkey, P/YR*
2. Enter initial cash outflow (a negative amount)	−10000, +/−, *CFj*
3. Enter cash flow for year one	100, *CFj*
4. Enter cash flow for year two	1600, *CFj*
5. Enter cash flow for year three	1800, *CFj*
6. Enter cash flow for year four	450, *CFj*
7. Enter cash flow for year five	12500, *CFj*
8. Enter required rate of return	12, *I/YR*
9. Solve for NPV	*shiftkey, NPV* (calculator displays 24.82)
10. Solve for IRR	*shiftkey, IRR/YR* (calculator displays 12.0646)

BAII PLUS Keystrokes: NPV and IRR Calculations for Unequal Cash Flows

1. Set the number of periods per year at 1	*2nd, P/Y,* 1, *ENTER, 2nd, QUIT*
2. Enter initial cash outflow (a negative amount)	*CF,* −10000, +/-, *ENTER*
3. Enter cash flow for year one	↓, 100, *ENTER*
4. Enter cash flow for year two	↓, ↓, 1600, *ENTER*
5. Enter cash flow for year three	↓ ↓ 1800, *ENTER*
6. Enter cash flow for year four	↓ ↓ 450, *ENTER*
7. Enter cash flow for year five	↓ ↓ 12500, *ENTER*
8. Enter required rate of return	*NPV,* 12, ENTER , ↓
9. Solve for NPV	*CPT* (calculator displays 24.82)
10. Solve for IRR	*IRR , CPT* (calculator displays 12.0646)

count rates in the above calculation until NPV becomes exactly zero, but this process is greatly simplified by a financial calculator. To find NPV and IRR using a financial calculator, follow the steps outlined below. You should find that the IRR of this investment is 12.0646 percent.

■ CHAPTER REVIEW

- ■ All financial decisions can be thought of as a comparison of the expected benefits from a particular course of action and the costs of pursuing it. In addition to the purchase price, however, prudent investors consider the costs of an investment resulting from uncertainty about those future benefits and forgoing the use of the investment capital over time (risk and the time value of money).

- ■ Because most people are risk-averse rather than risk-seeking, there is a positive relationship between risk and return. The greater the risk of an investment, the greater the investor's required rate of return.

- ■ The six time value of money formulas are useful tools for evaluating financial choices whose risky cash flows are distributed over time. These formulas allow calculation of the present value of a lump sum, the future value of a lump sum, the present value of an annuity, the future value of an annuity, sinking fund payments, and mortgage payments.

- ■ By definition, net present value is the present value of cash inflows minus the present value of cash outflows. If the net present value of an investment opportunity is negative, the investment is not worth its cost and should therefore be rejected by the investor.

- ■ The internal rate of return is defined as that discount rate which sets net present value equal to zero. This is the actual return that is provided by an investment opportunity. If the IRR is less than the investor's required rate of return, the investment should be rejected by the investor.

■ KEY TERMS

annuity	future value of an annuity	present value of an annuity
business risk	internal rate of return	purchasing power risk
compound interest	liquidity risk	rate of return
compounding	mortgage payment	risk
discounting	net present value	sinking fund payment
financial risk	NPV decision rule	time value of money principle
future value of a lump sum	present value of a lump sum	

■ STUDY EXERCISES

1. Define the following concepts: risk, business risk, financial risk, purchasing power risk, liquidity risk.

2. Describe the "risk/return relationship."

3. What is the time value of money principle?

4. Joe Saver deposits $1,000 in the Granite City Savings and Loan. To what value will his money accumulate in five years if the account pays 5 percent interest compounded annually? (Future Value of a Lump Sum)

5. How much should Joe be willing to pay today for an investment that is expected to pay $1,000 ten years in the future if he requires a 10 percent rate of return? (Present Value of a Lump Sum)

6. Define the following terms: compound interest, compounding, discounting.

7. Joe is offered the opportunity to receive $1,000 each year for ten years. How much would he be willing to pay for this future income stream if he desires a 10 percent return? (Present Value of an Annuity)

8. Joe expects to receive $1,000 each year for the next ten years beginning one year from today. If he deposits each payment into an account earning 8 percent interest annually, what will the balance of the account be when the last payment is deposited? (Future Value of an Annuity)

9. Joe hopes to accumulate $20,000 with ten annual deposits into a savings account earning 6 percent interest annually. What amount must Joe deposit each year to achieve his objective? (Sinking Fund Payment)

10. Harold and Helen purchase a $150,000 house using a down payment of $15,000 and a fixed rate mortgage for $135,000. The annual interest rate on the loan is 10 percent and the term is 30 years. What monthly payment is necessary to amortize this loan?

11. Define the following terms: net present value, internal rate of return, NPV decision rule, IRR decision rule.

12. An investor is considering purchasing a small retail property at a price of $82,000. The investor has established a required rate of return of 14 percent. Based on the following cash flow forecast, what is the NPV of this investment opportunity? Cash flows: year 1 = 10,000; year 2 = 12,000; year 3 = 11,000; year 4 = 14,000; year 5 = 95,000. Should the investor purchase this property?

13. What is the internal rate of return for the investment in question 12?

14 Bill and Ami borrowed $120,000 at 9 percent interest using a fixed rate mortgage with a maturity of 25 years. Answer the following questions about their loan.

   (a) What is the monthly payment necessary to amortize this loan?

   (b) If the loan required annual payments instead of monthly, what would the annual payment be?

   (c) Multiply the answer in part (a) by 12. Why does this amount not equal the answer in part b?

15 Mortgage Mechanics

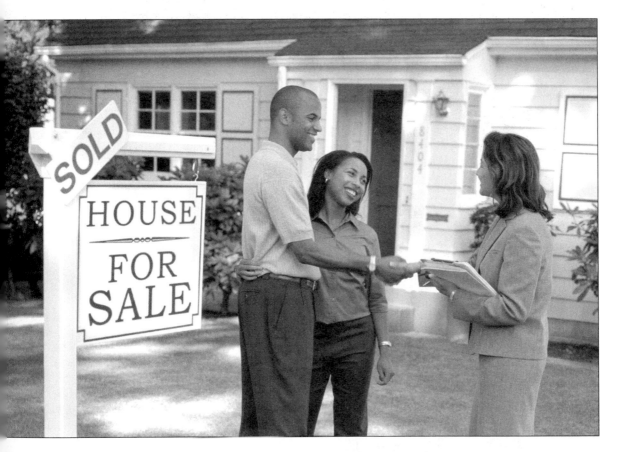

A basic knowledge of mortgages is necessary to purchase real estate in today's real estate market.

Now that we have a basic understanding of the time value of money, we can turn our attention to the mechanics of mortgage loans. In this chapter, we investigate the process of amortization in contrast to "interest-only" loans. We also consider how the internal rate of return can be used to determine the effective interest rate on a mortgage loan. Finally, we examine several alternatives to the fixed-rate mortgage that may be encountered in today's mortgage market, including the two-step mortgage and the adjustable rate mortgage.

■ MORTGAGE MECHANICS

Because most real estate investments involve long-term commitments of relatively large amounts of money, most real estate transactions involve long-term mortgage financing from a third party. Understanding the mechanics of mortgage financing is an important financial concept for students of real estate and real estate practitioners. In this section of the chapter, we explore mortgage mechanics in detail. Our first tasks are to distinguish between amortizing loans and interest-only loans and to fully explore the concept of amortization.

Interest-Only versus Amortizing Loans

As we discussed in Chapter 13, most loans used to finance real estate purchases prior to the 1930s were short-term, interest-only loans. In these loans, the borrower must pay interest on the full loan amount each period, and when the loan term expires, the borrower must repay the loan in one lump sum. During the Depression era, many borrowers could barely afford to make the required interest payments on these loans, much less repay the loan balance when the loan matured. One of the most successful activities of the Federal Housing Administration was the promotion of long-term, amortizing loans for home financing rather than short-term, interest-only loans. Amortizing loans are much easier to budget for most borrowers, and when combined with mortgage insurance, they are much less risky for most lenders. Amortizing loans are the dominant loan type in the housing finance industry. To fully understand the process of amortization, it is often useful to first understand how the payment streams differ between interest-only loans and amortizing loans.

Interest-only loans require that the borrower pay interest each period during the loan term, then repay the full loan amount in one lump sum at the end of the loan term. In contrast, **amortizing loans** require equal periodic payments composed of both interest and principal. As payments in this type of loan are made, the balance of the loan is gradually reduced to zero by the end of the loan term. Interest-only loan payments are calculated by multiplying the periodic interest rate by the loan amount. Amortizing loan payments are calculated using the mortgage payment formula, one of the six time value of money formulas discussed in the previous chapter.

The difference in payment streams between an amortizing loan and an interest-only loan is illustrated in Figure 15.1. Repayment of a five-year, $1,000 interest-only loan carrying a 10 percent interest rate requires a $100 interest payment for each of the first four years. At the end of the fifth year the entire principal amount of $1,000 is due plus $100 interest. (This much larger final payment is often referred to as a **balloon payment.**) The same $1,000 loan can be amortized by five annual payments of $263.80. Notice that although the periodic payments are higher for the amortizing loan, the payment is the same in each period. There is no balloon payment at the end of the loan because the loan balance is gradually reduced by the periodic payments. Also, notice that the total amount of interest paid to the lender ($500) is higher in the interest-only loan, because none of the principal is repaid until the final payment. In the amortizing loan, part of the principal is repaid with each payment, so the total interest paid is less ($319).

Understanding the Amortization Process for an Annual Payment Loan

An **amortization schedule** can be developed for any amortizing loan. A loan amortization schedule describes the payments in each period, the interest and principal contained in each payment, and the amount outstanding in each period. Table 15.1 shows an amortization schedule for a $100,000, ten-year, annual payment loan at 10 percent interest. Figure 15.2 plots the periodic payments and the interest and principal components of each payment. Note that while the payment amount is constant over the life of the loan, the portion going to interest decreases with each payment as the balance owed falls. Conversely, the portion going to payment of

| **FIGURE 15.1** | Repayment of Five Year, $1,000 Interest-Only Term and Fully Amortizing Loans. Each Carrying 10 Percent Annual Interest |

Fully Amortizing Loan

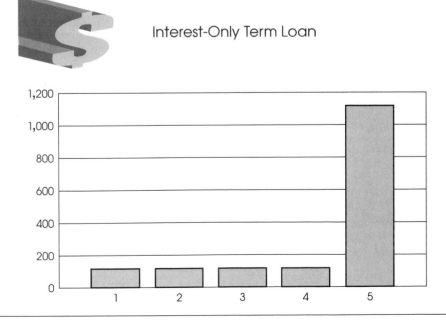

Interest-Only Term Loan

TABLE 15.1 Amortization Schedule for a $100,000 Loan at 10 Percent Annual Interest for Ten Years

Year	Payment PMT	Interest I_t	Principle P_t	Amount Outstanding AO_t
0	–	–	–	
1	$16,274.54	$10,000.00	$6,274.54	$100,000.00
2	16,274.54	9,372.55	6,901.99	93,725.46
3	16,274.54	8,682.35	7,592.19	86,823.47
4	16,274.54	7,923.13	8,351.41	79,231.28
5	16,274.54	7,087.99	9,186.55	70,879.87
6	16,274.54	6,169.33	10,105.21	61,693.32
7	16,274.54	5,158.81	11,115.73	51,588.11
8	16,274.54	4,047.24	12,227.30	40,472.38
9	16,274.54	2,824.51	13.450.03	28,245.08
10	16,274.54	1,479.40	14,795.05	14,795.05
Total	$162,745.40	$62,745.40	$100,000.0	00.00

Note: Component items may not add to totals due to rounding error.

principal increases at an increasing rate over the life of the loan. Also, the loan balance decreases slowly in the earlier years of the loan and more rapidly as the loan approaches maturity.

Understanding the amortization process requires careful consideration of the principal and interest components of each payment as well as the changing loan balance over time. Table 15.1 shows that $10,000 of the first year's payment on the above loan goes for interest, while only $6,274.54 is used to reduce the principal owed. With the loan balance reduced to $93,725.46, interest for the second year drops to $9,372.55, while the principal component of the payment rises to $6,901.99. The process continues until the last year, when interest is only $1,479.51 and principal is $14,795.05. The total amount of principal repaid equals the original loan amount, $100,000, and the total interest paid is $62,745.40. If the loan had been an interest-only loan, the borrower would have paid a total of $200,000 to the lender: $100,000 interest and $100,000 principal.

From this example we can establish several principles regarding the amortization of real estate mortgage loans:

- With a level, constant payment, the portions of each payment going to interest and principal vary greatly over time.
- The interest portion of each payment decreases over time.
- The principal portion of each payment increases over time.
- The amount outstanding declines to zero at the end of the loan term.

FIGURE 15.2 Amortization of a $100,000 Loan over Ten Years at 10 Percent

Being able to construct an amortization table is a valuable tool in many real estate decisions. While most financial calculators have built-in amortization functions, we believe it is instructive for students to construct a simple table manually. To construct an amortization table, begin by calculating the periodic payment required to amortize the loan using the mortgage payment formula (equation [6] in Chapter 14). Rather than solving the equation directly, enter the necessary information into your financial calculator, using the steps outlined there. Because the payments on this type of loan are the same in each period, this calculation need only be done once. To complete the amortization schedule, proceed down the rows of the table, one row at a time, by calculating the interest due, subtracting interest from the payment to get principal for the period, and then subtracting the principal paid in the period from the previous year's balance to get the new balance for the period.

These steps, for the first two years of the loan in Table 15.1, are summarized below. As you can see, each year's principal, interest, and amount outstanding are found in the same manner. The following notation will prove useful as we consider more complicated aspects of mortgage mechanics: PMT = mortgage payment, I_t = interest due in period t, i = periodic interest rate, P_t = principal paid in period t, and AO_t = amount outstanding at the end of period t.

Amortization: Period One

1. $I_t = AO_{t-1} \times i$ $10{,}000.00 = 100{,}000 \times .10$
2. $P_t = PMT - I_t$ $6{,}274.54 = 16{,}274.54 - 10{,}000$
3. $AO_t = AO_{t-1} - P_t$ $93{,}725.46 = 100{,}000 - 6{,}274.54$

TABLE 15.2

First 12 Months of the Amortization Schedule for a $100,000 Loan at Ten Percent Annual Interest for 10 Years

Month	Payment	Interest	Principle	Amount Outstanding
0	0	0	0	$100,000.00
1	$1,321.51	$833.33	$488.17	99,511.83
2	$1,321.51	829.27	492.24	99,019.58
3	$1,321.51	825.16	496.34	98,523.24
4	$1,321.51	821.03	500.48	98,022.76
5	$1,321.51	816.86	504.65	97,518.11
6	$1,321.51	812.65	508.86	97,009.25
7	$1,321.51	808.41	513.10	96,496.15
8	$1,321.51	804.13	517.37	95,978.78
9	$1,321.51	799.82	521.68	94,457.10
10	$1,321.51	795.48	526.03	94,931.07
11	$1,321.51	791.09	530.42	94,400.65
12	$1,321.51	786.67	534.84	93,865.82

Amortization: Period Two

1. $I_t = AO_{t-1} \times i$ $\qquad$ $9{,}372.55 = 93{,}725.46 \times .10$
2. $P_t = PMT - I_t$ $\qquad$ $6{,}901.99 = 16{,}274.54 - 9{,}372.55$
3. $AO_t = AO_{t-1} - P_t$ $\qquad$ $86{,}823.47 = 93{,}725.46 - 6{,}901.99$

Understanding the Amortization Process for a Monthly Payment Loan

At the risk of beating the proverbial dead horse, let's see how the amortization process works for a monthly payment loan. Table 15.2 shows the first two years of an amortization schedule for a $100,000, 10-year, monthly payment loan at 10 percent annual interest. Figure 15.3 plots the periodic payments, and the interest and principal components of each payment. Just as we saw with the annual payment loan, the payment amount is constant over the life of the monthly payment loan, but the portion going to interest decreases with each payment as the balance owed falls. Conversely, the portion going to payment of principal increases at an increasing rate over the life of the loan. Also, the loan balance decreases slowly in the earlier years of the loan and more rapidly as the loan approaches maturity.

■ UNDERSTANDING THE FIXED-RATE MORTGAGE: PREPAYMENT

Now that we have explored the concept of amortization, we can take a clos-

FIGURE 15.3   Dollars/Months

er look at other mechanics of mortgage loans. The most common mortgage loan is the **fixed-rate mortgage,** in which the interest rate is fixed at the time of origination. We have already seen how this type of loan is amortized by the payment calculated using the mortgage payment formula, and we now examine the concepts of prepayment, refinancing, discount points, origination fees, and effective interest rates.

For a variety of reasons, borrowers may decide to extinguish an outstanding mortgage loan by repaying the loan balance before the end of the loan term. Because all loans require "repayment," we use the word **prepayment** to indicate that the loan is repaid before its full term has expired. Based on historical evidence, many residential borrowers "prepay" their loans after 5 to 7 years. Because the loan balance declines with each payment due to amortization, it is important that we be able to calculate the amount outstanding on a loan at any point in time. To simplify the calculations, we assume that all prepayments occur on a payment date, rather than between payment dates.

Consider a fixed-rate mortgage with the following characteristics: loan amount of $133,000, 30 years to maturity, monthly payments, and an annual interest rate of 7.5 percent. Assume the borrower decides to sell the collateral and buy a new property. The loan contract contains a due-on-sale clause, so the borrower must "prepay" the loan if the property is sold. If the borrower prepays at the end of month 60, what is the amount outstanding on this loan at the time of prepayment?

To answer this question, we could construct an amortization schedule for the first 60 months of this loan. Fortunately, there is a less time-consuming method that uses the "annuity" concept to answer this question. Recall that an annuity is a series of equal payments over time. Obviously, the remaining payments on a mortgage meet our definition of an annuity. If we want to find the amount outstanding on a mortgage loan on any payment date, we simply need to calculate the present value of the remaining payments by discounting them at the interest rate on the loan. We can find the present value of an annuity (or amount outstanding at month 60, AO_{60}) using the appropriate formula or calculator keystrokes. First, find the monthly payment amount, then calculate the present value of the 300 payments remaining at the end of month 60. In this example, AO_{60} = $125,841.19. The steps for solving this problem using financial calculators are given below.

Using the present value of an annuity formula (see equation [3] in Chapter 14) to determine the amount outstanding on a loan is useful in many different situations. For example, how can we determine the amount of principal repaid during the sixth year of a loan? First, find the amount outstanding at the end of month 60 (300 payments remaining). Second, find the amount outstanding at the end of month 72 (288 payments remaining). Then, subtract AO_{72} from AO_{60} to

HP-10B Keystrokes: Monthly Mortgage Payments and Amount Outstanding at Time t

1. Set the number of discouting periods per year at 12	12, *shiftkey, P/YR*
2. Enter the loan amount	133000, *PV*
3. Enter the number of months	30, *shiftkey, n*
4. Enter the interest rate (calculator divides by *P/YR*)	7.5, *I/YR*
5. Solve for the monthly payment	*PMT* (calculator displays –929.96)
5. Enter the number of remaining payments	300, *n*
6. Solve for the amount outstanding (AO_{60})	*PV* (calculator displays 125841.19)

BAII PLUS Keystrokes: Monthly Mortgage Payments and Amount Outstanding at Time t

1. Set the number of discounting periods per year at 12	*2nd, P/Y,* 1, *ENTER, 2nd, QUIT*
2. Enter the loan amount	133000, *PV*
3. Enter the number of months	30, *2nd, xP/Y, N*
4. Enter the interest rate (calculator divides by *P/YR*)	7.5, *I/Y*
5. Solve for the monthly payment	*CPT, PMT* (calculator displays –929.96)
5. Enter the number of remaining payments	300, N
6. Solve for the amount outstanding (AO_{60})	*CPT, PV* (calculator displays 125841.19

get $1,781.80. Taking this idea a step farther, we can also find the amount of interest paid in the sixth year by subtracting the principal paid in that year from total payments. In the example above, total payments in any one year amount to $11,159.52. Subtracting the principal amount of $1,781.80 leaves $9,377.72 as interest paid in payments 63 through 72.

This technique of finding the amount outstanding is also useful when we are interested in determining the amount of interest or principal contained in any one monthly payment. How much interest is contained in payment number 61? We know that interest is paid on the outstanding balance after the last payment was made, so we multiply AO_{60} by .075 ÷ 12 (the monthly interest rate) to determine the interest contained in payment number 61. Just as we saw in the amortization table, $I_t = AO_{t-1} \times I \div m$. In this case, $I_{61} = 125,841.19 \times .075 \div 12 = \$786.51$. To find the principal contained in payment 61, we use the following relationship: $P_t = PMT - I_t$. In this case, $P_{61} = 929.96 - 786.51 = \$143.45$.

■ UNDERSTANDING THE FIXED-RATE MORTGAGE: REFINANCING

In many cases, borrowers may find that the interest rate on an outstanding loan is substantially higher than rates available on new mortgages in the market. If the rate on the existing loan is higher than the market interest rate, the borrower can reduce total borrowing costs by refinancing the loan amount at the prevailing market rate. **Refinancing** involves retiring the existing loan with the proceeds of a new loan for the same property. The borrower may obtain the new loan from the same or a different lender. A reduction in borrowing cost can be obtained by either reducing the payment amount or reducing the number of payments required to amortize the loan.

Consider the loan described in the previous example. At the end of 60 months, suppose that current interest rates are at 6 percent. If the borrower obtains a new loan for the same amount for 25 years, the monthly payments will be $810.80, which results in payment reduction of $119.16. Over the remaining 25 years of the loan, refinancing this loan will provide interest savings of $35,748.00.

On the other hand, if the borrower wishes to take advantage of the lower interest rates available in the market and is comfortable making the larger payments, refinancing can reduce the remaining term of the loan. In this case, if the borrower refinances the loan amount of $125,841.19 at 6 percent annual interest, but continues making payments of $929.96 each month, the number of monthly payments required to repay this debt falls from 300 to 227. (The last payment made will be for less than the full amount.) Thus, refinancing the loan at a lower interest rate, but keeping the payments at the same level, reduces the time required to retire the debt by 6 years and 1 month. To reach these conclusions using the HP-10B or BAII PLUS financial calculator, follow the steps outlined on the following page.

HP-10B Keystrokes: Mortgage Refinancing When Interest Rates Decline

1. Set the number of discounting periods per year at 12	12, *shiftkey, P/YR*
2. Enter the loan amount	133000, *PV*
3. Enter the number of months	30, shiftkey, *n*
4. Enter the interest rate (calculator divides by *P/YR*)	7.5, *I/YR*
5. Solve for the monthly payment	*PMT* (calculator displays −929.96)
6. Enter the number of remaining months	300, *n*
7. Solve for the present value of the annuity (AO_t)	*PV* (calculator displays 125841.19)
8. Enter the new interest rate	6, *I/YR*
9. Calculate the payment on the new loan	*PMT* (calculator displays −810.80)

To determine the number of months remaining if the payment is left at $929.96 per month:

10. Enter the original payment amount (negative)	−929.96, *PMT*
11. Solve for the new number of months remaining	*N* (calculator displays 227)

BAII PLUS Keystrokes: Mortgage Refinancing When Interest Rates Decline

1. Set the number of periods per year at 12	*2nd, P/Y,* 12, *ENTER, 2nd, QUIT*
2. Enter the loan amount	133000, *PV*
3. Enter the number of months	30, *2nd, xP/Y, N*
4. Enter the interest rate *(calculator divides by* P/YR*)*	7.5, *I/Y*
5. Solve for monthly payment	*CPT, PMT* (calculator displays −929.96)
6. Enter the number of remaining months	300, *N*
7. Solve for the present value of the annuity (AO^t)	*CPT, PV* (calculator displays −125841.19)
8. Enter the new interest rate	6, *I/Y*
9. Calculate the payment on the new loan	*CPT, PMT* (calculator displays −810.80)

To determine the number of months remaining if the payment is left at $929.96 per month:

10. Enter the original payment amount (negative)	−929.96, *PMT*
11. Solve for the new number of months remaining	*CPT, N* (calculator displays 226.33)

■ UNDERSTANDING THE FIXED-RATE MORTGAGE: DISCOUNT POINTS AND EFFECTIVE INTEREST RATES

Another important aspect of mortgage financing is the use of discount points and origination fees to increase the lender's yield on the loan. The charges represent additional income to the lender and, therefore, additional cost of borrowing to the borrower. When expressed as a percentage of the loan amount, the charges are called **discount points.** One discount point is equal to 1 percent of the loan amount. When expressed as a dollar amount, the charges are generally classified as **origination fees.** These charges cover the lender's cost of processing the loan application, obtaining credit reports, and other costs associated with loan origination. Of course, the lender could simply increase the interest rate on the loan, but many choose to charge these fees at the time of origination rather than throughout the term of the loan.

From the borrower's perspective, discount points and other fees result in an effective interest rate that may be substantially higher than the stated interest rate on the loan. The term **effective interest rate** refers to the actual cost of borrowing funds from a lender, expressed as an annual rate, after consideration of discount points and origination fees. Comparing one loan with another requires careful consideration of the effective interest rate. The calculations presented here are similar to those used by lenders to calculate the annualized percentage rate, or APR, which must be disclosed to all loan applicants under Regulation Z (see Chapter 13).

The table below shows a sample of interest rates and discount points offered by competing lenders. The quotes are based on a $100,000, 30-year loan for an owner-occupied, single-family home. Which loan provides the lowest effective interest rate? The answer to this question requires use of the internal rate of return (IRR) concept discussed previously in Chapter 14.

Lender	Interest Rate	Points
Loan Shack	7.875	0.50%
Marley Lenders	7.625	1.00
First Bank	8.000	0.00
Spider Savings	7.250	3.50

To determine which loan provides the lowest effective interest rate, we first must calculate the payments required under each loan. Notice that payments are based on the full loan amount of $100,000. In three of these loans, borrowers must pay "points" to the lender at the time of origination. Therefore, the net amount disbursed by the lender at origination is determined by subtracting the fee from the loan amount. Using the definition of discount points and the mortgage payment calculations described earlier, the cash flows for each loan are

Lender	Cash Flow at Origination	Cash Flow in Periods 1-360
Loan Shack	−$99,500	$725.07
Marley Lenders	−99,000	707.79
First Bank	−100,000	733.76
Spider Savings	−96,500	682.18

The effective interest rate for each of these loans is equivalent to the IRR of the cash flow stream. We can find the IRR of the cash flows in each loan using our financial calculators. The keystrokes for finding the effective interest rate for the first loan using the HP-10B and BAII Plus are described below.

HP-10B Keystrokes: IRR Calculations for Effective Interest Rates

Note that this problem requires the use of the *Nj* key. This key allows us to tell the calculator that a cash flow will occur for a specified number of periods. The largest value that can be entered with the *Nj* key is 99. Therefore, we must use it several times to enter all 360 monthly loan payments.

1. Set number of compounding periods at 12 per year	12, *shiftkey, P/YR*
2. Enter initial cash outflow (a negative amount)	99500, +/-, *CFj*
3. Enter cash flow one	725.07, *CFj*
4. Enter 99 for the number times cash flow one will occur	99, *shiftkey, Nj*
5. Enter cash flow two	725.07, *CFj*
6. Enter 99 for the number times cash flow two will occur	99, *shiftkey, Nj*
7. Enter cash flow three	725.07, *CFj*
8. Enter 99 for the number times cash flow three will occur	99, *shiftkey, Nj*
9. Enter cash flow four	725.07, *CFj*
10. Enter 63 for the number times cash flow four will occur	63, *shiftkey, Nj*
11. Solve for IRR	*shiftkey, IRR/YR* (calculator displays 7.9275)

BAII PLUS Keystrokes: IRR Calculations for Effective Interest Rates

Note that this problem requires the use of the "cash flow frequency" function of the calculator. This function allows us to tell the calculator that a cash flow will occur for a specified number of periods.

1. Set the number of periods per year at 12	*2nd, P/Y,* 12, *ENTER, 2nd, QUIT*
2. Enter initial cash outflow (a negative amount)	*CF,* 99500, +/-, *ENTER*
3. Enter cash flow amount	↓, 725.07, *ENTER*
4. Enter number of months (frequency)	↓, 360, *ENTER*
5. Solve for monthly IRR	*IRR, CPT* (calculator displays .66)
6. Calculate annual IRR	*X,* 12, = (calculator displays 7.9275)

Repeating this calculation for each of the loans provides the effective interest rates shown below. Notice that the effective interest rate on the loan from First Bank is the same as the stated interest rate because there are no points involved. The answer from our calculators (7.9999 percent) is slightly less than the stated rate because we rounded the payment amount to the nearest penny. Of all four loans, the loan from Spider Savings provides the lowest effective interest rate, in spite of the large amount of points charged at origination.

Lender	Stated Interest Rate	Points	Effective Interest Rate
Loan Shack	7.875	0.50%	7.9275
Marley Lenders	7.625	1.00%	7.7287
First Bank	8.000	0.00%	7.9999
Spider Savings	7.250	3.50%	7.6123

Discount points and origination fees can have a dramatic impact on effective interest rates if the borrower prepays the loan. As we mentioned earlier, most loans are prepaid within five to seven years. To determine the effective interest rate when a loan is prepaid, we must calculate the amount outstanding on the loan at the time of prepayment. To demonstrate the effect of discount points and prepayment on effective interest rates, assume that the loan from Spider Savings is prepaid at the end of month 60. What is the effective interest rate on the loan? To answer this question, first find AO_{60} as described above, then enter the cash flows into your financial calculator as shown below.

HP-10B Keystrokes: Effective Interest Rates with Discount Points and Prepayment

1. Set number of periods at 12 per year	12, *shiftkey, P/YR*
2. Enter initial cash outflow (a negative amount)	96500, +/–, *CFj*
3. Enter cash flow one	682.18, *CFj*
4. Enter 59 for the number times cash flow one will occur	*59, shiftkey, Nj*
5. Enter cash flow two (payment 60 + AO_{60})	95060.96, *CFj*
6. Solve for IRR	*shiftkey, IRR/YR* (calculator displays 8.1252)

BAII Plus Keystrokes: Effective Interest Rates with Discount Points and Prepayment

1. Set the number of periods per year at 12	*2nd, P/Y,* 12, *ENTER, 2nd, QUIT*
2. Enter initial cash outflow (a negative amount)	*CF,* 96500, +/–, *ENTER*
3. Enter cash flow one amount	↓, 682.18, *ENTER*
4. Enter number of months (frequency)	↓, 59, *ENTER*
5. Enter cash flow two amount	↓, 95060.96, *ENTER*
5. Solve for monthly IRR	*IRR, CPT* (calculator displays 0.6771)
6. Calculate annual IRR	*X,* 12, = (calculator displays 8.1252)

As you can see, prepaying a loan with high origination costs can increase the effective interest rate considerably. Prepaying the Spider Savings loan at the end of 5 years raises the effective interest rate to 8.1252 percent, which is significantly above the stated interest rate of 7.250 percent. Notice that the loan from First Bank has an effective interest rate of 8 percent, regardless of prepayment. Furthermore, you should also realize that the earlier you prepay a loan with discount points, the greater the effective interest rate. When shopping for a new mortgage among competing lenders, you should consider how long you expect to keep the loan before making a final choice.

■ ALTERNATIVES TO THE FIXED-RATE MORTGAGE

In addition to shopping for the best deal on a mortgage by comparing effective interest rates resulting from discount points or origination fees, borrowers may also wish to consider various alternatives to the fixed-rate mortgage. Several alternative mortgage types are available, including *two-step mortgages* and *adjustable rate mortgages*. The distinguishing feature of each of these loans is that the payments are not necessarily the same in each period. In the two-step mortgage, the payment amount is reestablished once during the life of the loan, usually at the end of year five or year seven. Payments in an adjustable rate mortgage change more frequently, usually at the end of each year. Lenders are able to offer these loans at lower initial interest rates because the borrower is assuming some of the risk of future interest rate increases. If the general interest rate in the economy increases, the lender's yield on the outstanding loan amount increases as well. Borrowers who are willing to accept this additional risk enjoy a lower initial interest rate. Borrowers who plan on prepaying the loan before it matures find this type of loan, as well as the adjustable rate loan discussed below, especially attractive. The tools we have developed in earlier sections help us understand the mechanics of these alternative loan types.

Understanding the Mechanics of Two-Step Mortgages

Two-step mortgages (also known as *reset mortgages*) are a relatively new type of loan in the residential lending market. Initial payments on this type of loan are calculated using the mortgage payment formula (equation [6] in Chapter 14). At the end of five or seven years, depending on the contract terms, the payment is recalculated for the remaining balance and term of the loan based on the prevailing interest rate. The prevailing interest rate is usually defined as the yield on ten-year Treasury bonds plus 2 percentage points. In other words, the interest rate is "indexed" to the Treasury bond yield with a "margin" of 2 percent. Because the new interest rate may be higher or lower than the original interest rate, the payment amount changes accordingly.

This loan is advantageous to borrowers because the interest rate used to determine the initial payments is lower than the interest rate on a fixed-rate mortgage.

Borrowers who do not expect to hold their loans for the full term find the two-step mortgage especially attractive. Even if the loan is held to maturity, the borrower is protected against large payment changes by an interest rate "cap" which limits the increase in the interest rate to a maximum of 5 percentage points. The following example demonstrates the payment stream required in a typical two-step mortgage.

Two-Step Mortgage Example

Consider a 30-year, two-step mortgage for $110,000. The initial interest rate is 6 percent, but the loan contract requires that the interest rate be adjusted at the end of year seven to 2 percentage points above the ten-year Treasury bond yield. The maximum increase in the interest rate is capped at a 5 percentage point increase over the initial rate. At the end of year seven, the ten-year Treasury yield is 6.9 percent. Assuming the loan is held to maturity, monthly payments are determined as follows.

First, calculate the payment due in months 1 through 84 using the loan amount of $110,000, 6 percent interest, and 30 years. The payment amount is $659.51. Second, find the amount outstanding at the end of month 84 ($98,603.32). Third, determine the new interest rate of 8.9 percent by adding the margin and the current Treasury yield. Notice that the new interest rate is 2.9 percentage points above the initial rate, which is well within the limits of the interest rate cap. Finally, calculate the payment due in months 84 through 360 using the current loan balance, 23 years, and the new interest rate of 8.9 percent. The new payment is $840.68. The financial calculator keystrokes necessary to find the payment amounts are outlined below.

HP-10B Keystrokes: Two-Step Mortgage Payments

1. Set the number of periods per year at 12	12, *shiftkey, P/YR*
2. Enter the loan amount	110000, *PV*
3. Enter the number of months	30, shiftkey, *N*
4. Enter the interest rate (calculator divides by *P/YR*)	6, *I/YR*
5. Solve for the monthly payment	*PMT* (calculator displays –659.51)
6. Enter the number of remaining months	276, *N*
7. Solve for the present value of the annuity (AO_{84})	*PV* (calculator displays 98603.32)
8. Enter the new interest rate	8.9, *I/YR*
9. Calculate the new payment	*PMT* (calculator displays –840.68)

BAII PLUS Keystrokes: Two-Step Mortgage Payments

1. Set the number of periods per year at 12	*2nd, P/Y,* 12, *ENTER, 2nd, QUIT*
2. Enter the loan amount	110000, *PV*
3. Enter the number of months	30, *2nd, xP/Y, N*
4. Enter the interest rate (calculator divides by *P/Y*)	6, *I/Y*
5. Solve for the monthly payment	*CPT, PMT* (calculator displays −659.51)
6. Enter the number of remaining months	276, *N*
7. Solve for the present value of the annuity (AO_{84})	*CPT, PV* (calculator displays 98603.32)
8. Enter the new interest rate	8.9, *I/Y*
9. Calculate the new payment	*CPT, PMT* (calculator displays −840.68)

Understanding the Mechanics of Adjustable Rate Mortgages

Adjustable rate mortgages are a common type of loan in both residential and commercial lending. As with two-step mortgages, the interest rate on an adjustable rate mortgage (ARM) is subject to change as the general interest rate level in the economy changes. The key difference is that the rate changes more than once during the term of the mortgage. In fact, most ARMs require annual rate adjustments, though some require adjustments every three or five years. In general, the initial interest rate on an ARM is lower than the rate on fixed-rate or two-step mortgages, which makes this an attractive loan type for many borrowers. Of course, ARM borrowers must be confident that they can afford the payment increases that are likely to occur over the life of the mortgage.

ARM interest rates are indexed to some general interest rate in the capital market. The most common index for residential ARMs is the one-year Treasury bill. The contract interest rate in any year of an ARM is defined as the index rate plus a margin of 2 or 3 percentage points. In the first year of an ARM, some lenders offer a "teaser" that reduces the margin by 1 or 2 percentage points. At each adjustment period, the contract interest rate is adjusted and the payments are recalculated. To protect borrowers (and lenders) against large payment changes, most ARMs have two types of interest rate caps. Annual caps limit the change in the contract interest rate to 2 percentage points above the prior year's contract rate, and lifetime caps establish a maximum and minimum contract rate that is within 5 percentage points of the initial contract rate. The calculations required to determine the payment stream for a residential ARM with known T-bill rates are demonstrated on the following page.

ARM Example

Consider a 30-year ARM loan for $110,000. The interest rate is indexed to the one-year Treasury bill yield, with a margin of 2 percentage points. The lender offers a teaser of 1 percentage point for the first year. The loan requires annual rate adjustments, with an annual cap of 2 percentage points and a lifetime cap of 5 percentage points. We can use the following assumptions regarding the T-bill yield to determine the payment stream for the first four years of this loan.

Time	T-Bill Yield	Margin	Teaser	Contract Rate	Payment
At origination	4%	2%	-1%	5%	$590.50
At end of first year	5	2	0	7	$728.44
At end of second year	3	2	0	5	$593.35
At end of third year	6	2	0	7	$724.84

For each year, calculate the monthly payment using the current loan amount, remaining years, and the contract interest rate. Finding the current loan amount is accomplished by finding the amount outstanding at the end of each year. Notice that the teaser rate reduces the contract rate in the first year to 5 percent, and that the annual cap limits the contract rate at the end of the third year to 7 percent. The financial calculator keystrokes necessary to find the payment amounts for the first four years are outlined below.

HP-10B Keystrokes: ARM Payments

1. Set the number of discounting periods per year at 12	12, *shiftkey, P/YR*
2. Enter the loan amount	110000, *PV*
3. Enter the number of months	30, *shiftkey, N*
4. Enter the interest rate (calculator divides by *P/YR*)	5, *I/YR*
5. Solve for the monthly payment	*PMT* (calculator displays −590.50)
6. Enter the remaining number of months	348, *N*
7. Solve for the loan balance (AO_{12}) 108,377.10)	*PV* (calculator displays
8. Enter the new interest rate	7, *I/YR*
9. Calculate the new payment	*PMT* (calculator displays −728.44)
10. Enter the number of remaining months	336, *N*
11. Solve for the loan balance (AO_{24})	*PV* (calculator displays 107184.49)
12. Enter the new interest rate	5, *I/YR*
13. Calculate the new payment	*PMT* (calculator displays −593.35)
14. Enter the number of remaining months	324, *N*
15. Solve for the loan balance (AO_{36})	*PV* (calculator displays 105382.65)
16. Enter the new interest rate	7, *I/YR*
17. Calculate the new payment	*PMT* (calculator displays −724.84)

BAII PLUS Keystrokes: Two-Step Mortgage Payments

1. Set the number of periods per year at 12	*2nd, P/Y,* 12, *ENTER, 2nd, QUIT*
2. Enter the loan amount	110000, *PV*
3. Enter the number of months	30, *2nd, xP/Y, N*
4. Enter the interest rate (calculator divides by *P/Y*)	5, *I/Y*
5. Solve for the monthly payment	*CPT, PMT* (calculator displays −590.50)
6. Enter the remaining number of months	348, *N*
7. Solve for the loan balance (AO_{12})	*CPT, PV* (calculator displays 108,377.10)
8. Enter the new interest rate	7, *I/Y*
9. Calculate the new payment	*CPT, PMT* (calculator displays −728.44)
10. Enter the number of remaining months	336, *N*
11. Solve for the loan balance (AO_{24})	*CPT, PV* (calculator displays 107,184.49)
12. Enter the new interest rate	5, *I/Y*
13. Calculate the new payment	*CPT, PMT* (calculator displays -593.35)
14. Enter the number of remaining months	324, *N*
15. Solve for the loan balance (AO_{36})	*CPT, PV* (calculator displays 105,382.65)
16. Enter the new interest rate	7, *I/Y*
17. Calculate the new payment	*CPT, PMT* (calculator displays −724.84)

■ CHAPTER REVIEW

- ■ In contrast to interest-only loans, amortizing loans require the periodic payment of both principal and interest. The balance outstanding on the loan decreases gradually through amortization of the principal.

- ■ The amount outstanding on an amortizing loan at any regular payment date can be determined by finding the present value of the remaining payments. This rule is useful when faced with prepayment and refinancing decisions.

- ■ The effective interest rate on a loan can be much higher than the stated contract rate, especially if the lender charges discount points or origination fees. One discount point means that the borrower must pay one percent of the loan amount at the time of origination. The internal rate of return provides a measure of the effective interest rate for loans that charge discount points or origination fees.

■ Alternatives to the fixed-rate mortgage include two-step mortgages and adjustable rate mortgages. In both of these types of loans, the interest rate is subject to change over time which can cause adjustments in the payment amount. The borrower accepts some of the risk of future interest rate changes in exchange for a lower initial interest rate.

■ KEY TERMS

adjustable rate mortgage	discount point	origination fees
amortization schedule	effective interest rate	prepayment
amortizing loan	fixed rate mortgage	refinance
balloon payment	interest-only loan	two-step mortgage

■ STUDY EXERCISES

1. Define the following terms: interest-only loan, amortizing loan, balloon payment.

2. Construct an amortization schedule for a loan with the following characteristics. Loan amount = $10,000; term = 5 years; interest rate = 8 percent; annual payments.

3. Ron borrows $300,000 to purchase a warehouse. The annual interest rate on the loan is 10.25 percent, and the term of the loan is 15 years. Answer the following questions about this loan:

    (a) What is the monthly payment necessary to amortize this loan?

    (b) What is the balance on the loan at the end of month 36?

    (c) How much interest will Ron pay in month 37?

    (d) How much principal will Ron pay in month 37?

    (e) How much principal will Ron pay in the fourth year of this loan (payments 37 through 48)?

4. Suppose the loan in question 3 required 2 discount points at the time of origination.

    (a) If Ron keeps this loan for the full term, 180 months, what is his effective interest rate?

    (b) If Ron prepays the loan at the end of month 48, what is his effective interest rate?

5. Suppose Ron refinances the loan at the end of month 48 at the prevailing interest rate in the market (8 percent). Rather than reducing his monthly payment, however, Ron decides to keep making the same monthly payments.

   (a) How many months must Ron continue to make the payments on this new loan?

   (b) By how many months has Ron shortened the term of the loan with this strategy?

6. Consider a 30-year, two-step mortgage for $135,000. The initial interest rate is 5.5 percent, but the loan contract calls for a rate adjustment at the end of year 5. The new rate will be 2 percentage points above the 10-year Treasury bond yield. The interest rate is capped at 5 percentage points above the initial interest rate. If the T-bond yield is 7.5 percent at the time of the adjustment, what will the payments be for the last 25 years of this loan?

7. Consider a 30-year ARM for $135,000. The loan is indexed to the one-year T-bill yield, which is currently at 5.25 percent. The margin is 2 percentage points, and the teaser is 1.5 percent. The contract rate adjusts once at the end of each year, but the loan has annual and lifetime interest rate caps of 2 and 5 percentage points, respectively. Answer the following questions assuming that the actual T-bill yields for the first four years of this loan are the same as those shown below.

Time	T-Bill Yield	Margin	Teaser	Contract Rate
At origination	5.25%	2%	−1.5%	?
At end of first year	6.50	2	0.0	?
At end of second year	7.75	2	0.0	?
At end of third year	4.25	2	0.0	?

   (a) What is the monthly payment during months 1 through 12?

   (b) What is the amount outstanding at the end of month 12?

   (c) What is the monthly payment during months 13 through 24?

   (d) What is the amount outstanding at the end of month 24?

   (e) What is the monthly payment during months 25 through 36?

   (f) What is the amount outstanding at the end of month 36?

   (g) What is the monthly payment during months 37 through 48?

8. A prospective home buyer can afford to make monthly loan payments of no more than $475. If the best rate she can obtain on a mortgage is 10 percent (for a 25-year term), what is the maximum amount she can borrow?

9. Congratulations! You won the sweepstakes. The sweepstakes rules entitle you to a choice of one of the following prizes. Using the concept of present value, which choice is the most valuable to you if your opportunity rate is 8 percent?

   Choice A: $40,000 per year for the next 20 years

   Choice B: $25,000 today, plus $35,000 per year for the next 25 years

   Choice C: $200,000 today, plus $12,000 per year for the next 40 years

10. Nikki's mortgage requires her to pay $1,230 per month for the next 180 months. The balance on her loan is $130,000. What is the annual interest rate on Nikki's loan?

 Go to the Student Study Guide CD-ROM and work through Case 5.

CHAPTER

16 Analyzing Income-Producing Properties

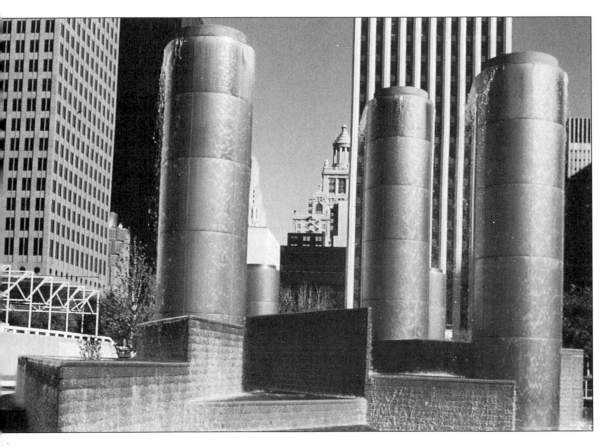

Investment income-producing property, such as an office building, requires a very different set of considerations from an investment in owner-occupied real estate.

One of the most exciting aspects of the real estate industry is investment in income-producing properties. History is filled with the names of people who have made, and sometimes lost, fortunes through real estate investments. The primary question to be considered in this chapter is "How do investors decide whether to invest in a particular project?" Successful investment decision making requires careful analysis of the risks and returns offered by an investment opportunity.

The objective of this chapter is to describe the analysis methods successful investors use to make real estate investment decisions. In general, this process involves (1) evaluating a project's competitive environment, (2) forecasting the cash flows that are expected to accrue to the investor, and (3) making a final decision about whether to proceed with the project. Our focus throughout this chapter is on decision-making situations facing equity investors who are considering investing in existing income properties. In this chapter we

■ discuss the advantages and disadvantages of real estate investment;

■ review the concepts of investment and wealth maximization; and

■ discuss how investors compare the costs and benefits of investment opportunities using net present value, the internal rate of return, and the discounted cash flow model.

REAL ESTATE
TODAY
FEATURES

Close-Up
Renaissance Center:
The Story of an
Investment Failure

■ ADVANTATES OF REAL ESTATE INVESTMENT

What makes real estate an attractive investment category? While there are numerous motivations for pursuing real estate investments, investors often cite cash flow from operations, the possibility of value appreciation, portfolio diversification, and financial leverage as the major incentives for pursuing real estate projects.

Cash Flow from Operations

For many investors, the primary attraction to real estate investments is the operating cash flows generated by income-producing properties. The source of this cash flow is the rent paid by tenants for the use of space in the property. Because real estate is a durable asset, most properties are capable of generating rental revenue for many years into the future. From this revenue, the investor must pay the property's operating expenses, debt service, and income taxes. Operating expenses typically include utilities, maintenance, property management, insurance, and property taxes. Debt service includes principal and interest payments on any outstanding mortgage debt. Income taxes are due on any taxable income generated by the property. Investors refer to the annual operating cash flow that remains after these items are paid as *after-tax cash flow from operations*. Often referred to by its acronym, ATCF, this cash flow represents the money the investor puts in his or her pocket at the end of each year of the investment holding period.

Appreciation

Another motivation for investing in income-producing real estate is the possibility of appreciation in property value over the investment holding period. While investment properties do not always increase in value, investors generally choose properties whose values are expected to grow at the rate of inflation or greater. Furthermore, changing market conditions can improve a property's competitive position in a market, allowing it to command higher rents and thereby increase its value to investors. When an investor sells an income-producing property, the proceeds from the sale, less selling expenses, are used to retire any outstanding mortgage debt and to pay any income taxes due as a result of the sale. To the investor, the sum of money that is generated by the sale of an investment is known as **after-tax equity reversion,** or ATER. The term "equity reversion" refers to the return of funds originally invested in the property, plus any change in the value of the investor's investment in the property.

Portfolio Diversification

Another important motivation for investing in real estate is the diversification real estate adds to a portfolio. Combining real estate investments with investments in stocks and bonds allows investors to develop a diversified portfolio. Diversification allows investors to maximize their investment returns while spreading their risk exposure across different types of investments. Such a strategy provides protection against an economic downturn in any one sector of the economy. In addition, many people are attracted to the security offered by investments in tangible assets that are under their personal control.

Financial Leverage

Real estate investors are also attracted to real estate because it allows the use of **financial leverage,** or "other people's money." The real estate finance industry makes debt capital readily available to most investors, with many lenders willing to provide 70 percent or more of the funds necessary to purchase investment properties. By borrowing additional investment funds from lenders, investors can control more real estate with less of their own funds. The use of borrowed funds has the effect of leveraging, or magnifying, the returns on funds invested by the investor. The benefits of leverage come at a price, however, because investors face increased risk. If the project fails to generate sufficient revenue to satisfy the debt service payments, the project may be forced into foreclosure.

Example of Financial Leverage

To understand the impact of leverage on an equity investor's rate of return, consider the following example. Lou Lever has $100,000 to invest. He can (1) purchase a $100,000 property without using any borrowed funds or (2) use the $100,000 to make a 10 percent down payment on a $1,000,000 property and borrow $900,000 at 11 percent annual interest on an interest-only loan. If each of the two properties provides a 15 percent return before debt service and income taxes are considered, the second is clearly more advantageous owing to the effects of financial leverage. To see why, calculate Lou's rate of return on his equity investment for both properties.

If Lou follows the first strategy, he would earn $15,000, or 15 percent, on his equity investment of $100,000. If he follows the second strategy, Lou would earn $51,000. This amount is calculated by first determining the total return on the investment (.15 × $1,000,000 = $150,000), then subtracting the interest due on the borrowed funds (.11 × $900,000 = $99,000). As a percentage of his equity investment of $100,000, the $51,000 ($150,000 − $99,000) reflects 51 percent rate of return.

As you can see, financial leverage can greatly magnify the rate of return on equity. If the property in the second strategy provides an overall return of 18 percent instead of 15 percent, Lou's rate of return on equity would jump to 81 percent; an overall return of 20 percent would balloon Lou's return to 101 percent.

Of course, the magnification of the return on equity also works in the opposite direction. If, for example, the property provides a return of only 5 percent overall, then Lou would suffer a negative rate of return on equity of

49 percent. (.05 × $1,000,000 – .11 × $900,000 = –$49,000). The ability of leverage to magnify returns on equity implies that leverage increases risk. The additional risk comes from the fact that Lou has a fixed liability (interest on the debt) that he must satisfy each year. If the property's earnings are insufficient to cover the debt service, Lou stands to lose cash out of his pocket to keep the investment alive.

As a rule, financial leverage will increase the investor's return on equity as long as the cost (interest rate) of the borrowed funds is less than the overall return on the investment. If the interest rate exceeds the overall return, then financial leverage will reduce the return on the investor's return on equity, possibly causing it to be negative.

Disadvantages of Real Estate Investment

Though there are numerous advantages to investing in real estate, the disadvantages must not be ignored. For example, even with borrowed funds, real estate investments often require relatively large capital requirements. Large-scale properties such as office buildings and shopping centers are often beyond the resources of individual investors. In addition, investing in real estate is risky, and the risk exposure may not be suitable for every investor.

In the preceding discussion we saw how financial leverage could increase the risk of an investment. Another aspect of real estate risk comes from the lack of liquidity that real estate investments have in comparison with other types of investments. Liquidity refers to the ability to convert an asset into cash quickly without having to accept a low price. For example, stocks are considered a liquid asset because an investor who wishes to sell a portfolio of common stocks can do so by simply calling a stockbroker. The broker will immediately sell the shares at the current market price. Real estate investors should anticipate that selling a property quickly may mean that the property will sell at a lower price than could otherwise be obtained.

Real estate investors also face the risk of changing economic conditions that may affect the rents they are able to charge to tenants and the value of investment properties. Successful investors spend considerable time and effort evaluating the markets in which their properties compete to understand how changing market conditions affect the risk exposure of their portfolios.

Weighing the benefits and costs of a real estate investment opportunity requires a high degree of knowledge about the characteristics of real estate markets and transactions, as well as careful consideration of the risks involved in real estate investment. The next section takes a closer look at the process real estate investors use when making the investment decision.

■ FINANCIAL DECISION MAKING

As we discussed in Chapter 14, all financial decisions involve a comparison of the expected benefits from a proposed course of action with the expected costs arising from that course of action. In this context, **investment** is defined as present sacrifice in anticipation of expected future benefit. Based on this definition, the decision to continue your education is an investment, as is a decision to place money in a savings account for future use. If you do not expect the benefits of these activities to be greater than the sacrifices you must make, you would choose not to engage in them. Similarly, real estate investment decisions require a comparison of the benefits a project is expected to generate with the sacrifices one must make in order to engage in the project.

The Wealth Maximization Objective

In order to make investment decisions, investors must define their criteria for determining the acceptability of alternative projects. Some investors pursue projects that will generate income, while others are more interested in the appreciation potential that real estate offers. Other investors are in search of projects that provide tax-sheltering benefits, or those that have minimum management concerns. Although each investor has different interests, tastes, and preferences, the ultimate goal of all investors is to accept those projects that will maximize their wealth. Wealth maximizing investors will choose only those projects that offer expected benefits in excess of the costs of pursuing them and, if faced with a choice between two or more projects that increase wealth, wealth-maximizing investors will choose the project in which benefits exceed costs by the largest amount.

The NPV Rule

To evaluate the impact a project will have on wealth, investors use the net present value decision rule and the internal rate of return decision rule discussed in Chapter 14. We will review each of these rules in turn.

Recall that **net present value (NPV)** is defined as the present value of cash inflows less the present value of cash outflows. The conversion of future cash flows into present values is accomplished by discounting the future cash flows at the investor's required rate of return. The **required rate of return** reflects both the time value of money and the riskiness of the investment opportunity.

Investors use the NPV of a particular project as a decision rule by evaluating its sign (positive or negative). If the NPV of an investment is greater than or equal to zero, the investor should choose to invest because the investment is worth at least as much as it costs, given the investor's required rate of return. If NPV is less than zero, the investor should choose not to invest.

Taking this rule one step further, if we are faced with several alternative investment choices, we should accept the one with the highest positive NPV because it will increase our wealth more than the others. To use this rule in investment analysis, we must estimate the cash flows associated with an investment opportunity, then convert the cash flows into present values using the appropriate discount rate. The following example demonstrates the NPV decision rule.

Using the NPV Rule

Consider an investor who is facing a choice between two alternative investments. The investor has performed a detailed analysis of both projects' competitive environments and has developed the cash-flow forecasts shown below. He believes that both projects are equally risky, and that the level of risk of the projects suggests an annual required rate of return of 15 percent for both projects. Which project should the investor choose?

	Project A	Project B
Initial investment	$ 90,000	$ 80,000
Cash flow in year one	10,000	9,100
Cash flow in year two	11,100	10,000
Cash flow in year three	12,000	11,000
Cash flow in year four	12,000	11,000
Cash flow in year five	120,000	104,000

Given that the investor's objective is to choose the project that increases his wealth by the greatest amount, he should calculate the NPV of each project and choose the one with the highest NPV. These calculations are shown below:

Project A

$$NPV = \frac{10,000}{(1.15)^1} + \frac{11,100}{(1.15)^2} + \frac{12,000}{(1.15)^3} + \frac{12,000}{(1.15)^4} + \frac{120,000}{(1.15)^5} - 90,000 = \$1,501$$

Project B

$$NPV = \frac{9,100}{(1.15)^1} + \frac{10,000}{(1.15)^2} + \frac{11,000}{(1.15)^3} + \frac{11,000}{(1.15)^4} + \frac{104,000}{(1.15)^5} - 80,000 = \$703$$

Both projects result in a positive NPV, which suggests that both are good projects that will result in a wealth increase to the investor above and beyond the cost of pursuing them. Because the NPV of project A is greater than the NPV of project B, the investor should choose A. By doing so, the investor expects to receive a return of 15 percent, plus a wealth increase of $1,501.

Using the IRR Rule

The internal rate of return decision rule also provides us with a "yes or no" decision about whether to proceed with an investment opportunity. Notice that in project A, above, the investor's required rate of return was 15 percent. Because the net present value is greater than zero, and because its NPV is larger than project B's NPV, the investor should choose to accept this project. But what rate of return does the investor expect to earn? Obviously, the investor expects to earn some rate above 15 percent. To find the exact return the investor expects to earn, we can define the **internal rate of return** (IRR) of an investment as the discount rate that makes NPV exactly equal to zero. To determine an investment's IRR, we can search a variety of discount rates by trial-and-error until we find one that makes NPV equal zero. This rate will be the internal rate of return on the investment. Fortunately, most financial calculators have a feature that allows automatic searches for the internal rate of return for a series of cash flows.

The steps outlined below show how to use a financial calculator to determine NPV and IRR for the series of cash flows forecast for project A.

HP-10B Keystrokes: NPV and IRR Calculations for Project A

1. Enter initial cash outflow (a negative amount)	90000, +/–, *CFj*
2. Enter cash flow for year one	10000, *CFj*
3. Enter cash flow for year two	11100, *CFj*
4. Enter cash flow for year three	12000, *CFj*
5. Enter cash flow for year four	12000, *CFj*
6. Enter cash flow for year five	120000, *CFj*
7. Enter required rate of return	15, *I/YR*
8. Solve for NPV	*shiftkey, NPV* (calculator displays 1501.29)
9. Solve for IRR	*shiftkey, IRR/YR* (calculator displays 15.47)

To use the IRR as a financial decision-making rule, we simply compare the IRR of an investment opportunity with our required rate of return. If the IRR is greater than or equal to our required rate of return, we choose to invest; otherwise, we forgo the investment opportunity. While the IRR rule and the NPV rule are based on the same principles, the NPV rule is generally the best choice to use because IRR calculations may yield multiple discount rates that set NPV equal to zero. Furthermore, the NPV rule should be used when forced to choose between mutually exclusive projects such as those described above. When our objective is to determine the rate of return provided by an investment, however, the IRR calculation is extremely useful.

Real estate investors can use these decision rules to evaluate individual projects and to decide whether to pursue them. Applying the rules, however, requires a forecast of the cash flows that the investor expects to receive during the investment holding period. The discounted cash flow model described below provides a systematic framework for calculating the expected net present value and internal rate of return of real estate investment opportunities on an "after-tax" basis.

■ THE DISCOUNTED CASH FLOW MODEL

The NPV and IRR decision rules provide a sound basis for defining the suitability of an investment opportunity by identifying its impact on the investor's wealth. Using these rules, we know that a "good" investment is one that is worth more than it costs, assuming all benefits and sacrifices are identified correctly. To put the decision rules into practice, real estate investors often rely on the following discounted cash flow model.

$$NPV = \sum_{t=1}^{T} + \frac{ATCF_t}{(1+i)^t} + \frac{ATER_T}{(1.i)^T} - \text{initial equity}$$

In this model, *ATCF* is the annual after-tax cash flow from operations, *ATER* is the after-tax equity reversion realized on the sale of the property at the end of the holding period, i is the investor's required rate of return, T is the expected number of years the property will be held, and *initial equity* is the difference between the purchase price and any debt used to finance the purchase. Understanding the model requires careful consideration of the components of ATCF and ATER. The following example describes each of these concepts in detail.

Applying the Discounted Cash Flow Model

To illustrate some of the issues involved in real estate investment analysis, consider the decision facing Susan Adrep, an advertising account executive who is considering adding real estate to her investment portfolio. Susan became interested in buying an income-producing property several months ago. She has discussed her interests with her accountant, local lenders, other real estate investors, and several different real estate brokers. Because this is her first real estate investment, she has decided to focus on smaller residential properties located in her neighborhood. After looking at several properties that are currently available in the market, Susan feels that one property, a four-unit apartment building, deserves further consideration.

The property is located on a quiet street between a commercial district and an area containing single-family homes. Property values in this area have been increasing at approximately 5 percent per year over the past ten years. The eight-year-old building was well-constructed and the owner has maintained the property in excellent condition. The owner is moving to another city and has decided to sell the property rather than manage it as an absentee owner.

John Block, a local real estate broker, has agreed to market the property for the owner at a firm asking price of $255,000. John provides Susan with a summary of the rental income and operating expenses for the past two years. In addition, Susan talks with several lenders and learns that a 25-year, monthly payment mortgage loan can be obtained at 9 percent interest for 70 percent of the property value. Based on this information, as well as her own analysis of local market conditions, Susan develops the following forecast for income and expenses for the property.

	Year 1
Rent ($725 per unit per month)	$34,800
Annual rent increases	5 percent
Operating expenses	
Lawn service	800
Maintenance and repairs	4,000
Property taxes	2,100
Insurance	900
Property management services	2,100
Total	$9,900
Annual operating expense increase	3 percent

The question Susan faces is whether this property is a suitable investment for her portfolio. To make a decision about buying the property, Susan must identify the sacrifices she must make to acquire the property and compare those sacrifices with the benefits she expects to receive from this investment.

The sacrifices facing Susan Adrep in this project include the initial equity contribution she must make at the time of purchase and the risk she will be exposed to as a result of her decision to invest. *Initial equity* is the purchase price of a project less any debt that is used to complete the purchase. *Risk* is defined as the possibility that the actual benefits provided by the investment will deviate from the investor's initial expectations. The benefits Susan expects to receive from pursuing this opportunity include the net cash flows that will occur during the investment holding period.

Expected benefits from real estate investments are typically divided into two categories: after-tax cash flows from operations and after-tax equity reversion. The first category refers to income received each year of the investment holding period, and the second category refers to income that is realized when the property is sold. Because income taxes are an important consideration in any investment strategy, Susan must consider their impact on the income she expects to receive from this investment.

Forecasting ATCF

To forecast the after-tax cash flows from operations for the investment opportunity under consideration by Susan, we use the relationships shown in Table 16.1. We will consider the second category of cash flows in real estate investments, after-tax equity reversion, in the next section.

The starting point for estimating annual cash flows from operations in a real estate investment is **potential gross income** (PGI). PGI is the total income potential of the investment, assuming all leasable space is rented and all rents are

TABLE 16.1	After-Tax Cash Flow from Operations for Year 1		
Potential gross income	PGI	34,800
– Vacancy and credit losses	–VCL	1,392
Effective gross income	EGI	33,408
– Operating expenses	–OE	9,900
Net operating income	NOI	23,508
– Annual Debt Service	–ADS	17,976
Before-tax cash flow	BTCF	5,532
– Taxes (determined below)	–Taxes	302
After-tax cash flow	ATCF	5,230
Determining Taxes from Operations		
Net operating income	NOI	23,508
– Interest expense	–Int.	15,984
– Depreciation deduction	–Dep.	6,447
Taxable income	TI	1,077
× Marginal tax rate	× MTR	x.28
Taxes from operations	Taxes	302

collected. Investors must have knowledge of the expected rent for the space in the property to estimate PGI. The source of this knowledge is usually a survey of rental rates for similar space in other properties in the marketplace. For the property Susan is considering, the PGI in the first year of her holding period is expected to be $38,400 ($725 rent per unit × 12 months × 4 units). Susan also believes that rents will increase at 5 percent per year for the next 5 years, which is her anticipated holding period.

Calculating Net Operating Income

Because some of the PGI may not be received as a result of vacancies or uncollected rents, an allowance for these items should be deducted from PGI in the form of **vacancy and credit losses** (VCL). The forecasted allowance of VCL (often expressed as a percentage of PGI) depends on observations of historic data, comparable properties, and general market conditions. For new properties, the vacancy rate may be quite high during the initial leasing period, and older properties in declining areas may experience high credit losses from faltering tenants. Susan believes that 4 percent of PGI is a reasonable allowance for the property she is considering, so the VCL in year one is expected to be $1,392 (34,800 × .04). Subtracting VCL from PGI results in **effective gross income** (EGI), or the actual amount of rental revenue expected to be received each year.

With revenues accounted for, the next step is to subtract operating expenses (OE) from EGI to determine **net operating income** (NOI). OE includes any expenditures made in the operation of the investment property such as maintenance costs, management fees, property taxes, insurance premiums, and utility fees. NOI is the amount of revenue left after paying the expenses of operation, but before paying the mortgage payments and income taxes on the investment. In this case, Susan feels that OE for year one will be $9,900, resulting in NOI of $23,508. She also believes that these expenses will increase by 3 percent each year.

Annual Debt Service

Susan now must consider the impact of financing on this investment opportunity. Using the mortgage payment formula described in Chapter 14, Susan calculates the monthly payment required to amortize a 25-year loan for $178,500 ($255,000 times 0.70) at 9 percent annual interest. Multiplying this amount, $1,497.97 times 12 gives annual **debt service** (ADS) of $17,976. Subtracting ADS from NOI results in the **before-tax cash flow** (BTCF) of $5,532. Because taxes are a real expense, however, the analysis must be based on **after-tax cash flow** (ATCF). To calculate the annual income tax consequence of Susan's investment, we must first determine the *taxable income* (TI) generated by this project.

Taxable Income

Two items that require careful consideration when determining TI in most real estate investments are (1) interest expense and (2) depreciation deduction. Considering interest expense (Int) first, notice that we subtracted the annual debt service from NOI to get BTCF. ADS, however, also includes principal repayments, which are not tax-deductible. Therefore, BTCF is not the same as TI. To determine TI, we subtract only the interest component of ADS from NOI. Recall from the discussion of amortizing loans in Chapter 15 that the amount of interest in each payment is reduced as the loan balance declines. Developing an amortization schedule for the loan used to finance a property investment allows us to determine the amount of interest paid each year. To construct an amortization schedule, the mortgage payment is calculated by the mortgage payment formula, then each payment is separated into interest and principal components. If payments are made more frequently than once each year, annual totals are necessary. An amortization schedule for Susan's loan is shown in Table 16.2. Interest in year one totals $15,984.

The second item to consider when calculating taxable income is the amount of the depreciation deduction (Dep). Income tax laws allow depreciation deductions (also known as *cost recovery allowances*), which provide investors with a means of recovering their original capital investment without paying taxes on this amount until the property is sold. Nonresidential and residential property improvements have depreciable lives of 39 and 27.5 years, respectively. Land is not depreciable under current tax laws, so the amount of the purchase price attributable to improvements must be identified separately.

To determine the annual **depreciation deduction,** we divide the value of the improvements by the appropriate depreciable life. Assuming that the value of the

TABLE 16.2 Amortization Schedule (Annual Summary)

Year	PMT	Int	Prin	AO*
0	0	0	0	$178,500
1	$17,976	$15,984	$1,991	176,509
2	17,976	15,797	2,178	174,330
3	17,976	15,593	2,383	171,948
4	17,976	15,370	2,606	169,342
5	17,976	15,125	2,851	166,491

*Amount outstanding

building alone is $185,000, the annual depreciation deduction is $6,727 ($185,000 divided by 27.5). Under current tax laws, however, an investor must make some additional calculations to determine the depreciation deduction during the first and last years of ownership. As a rule, the investor is presumed to have purchased the property in the middle of the month in which the property was purchased or sold, regardless of the actual day of the month the transaction occurs. For example, if an investor buys a property in January, the depreciation deduction for the first year of ownership is $11.5 \div 12$ of the annual amount. Similarly, if the investor sells the property in July of a later year, the depreciation deduction is $5.5 \div 12$ of the annual amount for the last year of ownership.

In the example being considered here, we can assume that Susan buys the property in January of year 1, and sells the property in December of year 5. The depreciation deductions in those two years will be $6,447 ($6,727 times $11.5 \div 12$). For years 2, 3 and 4, the full deduction of $6,727 is used. In this example, subtracting interest and depreciation from NOI yields TI in year 1 of $933.

Income Taxes

Annual *income taxes* are calculated by multiplying taxable income by the investors' marginal tax rate (MTR). Susan faces am MTR of 28 percent, which means that any additional income she earns will be subject to a tax of 28 percent. Therefore, the taxes from operations in year one are $261 ($933 × .28). (In the event that taxable income is a negative number, which is sometimes the case in real estate investments, the tax loss may be used to offset taxable income from other investments in the investor's portfolio. A full discussion of the tax implications of real estate investment is beyond the scope of this text.) Subtracting taxes from BTCF yields ATCF in year one of $5,127.

These calculations are repeated for each year of the investment holding period as shown in Table 16.3 Thus far in her analysis of this property, Susan knows that she must invest $76,500 ($255,000 minus $178,500) in return for annual cash flows from operations shown in the table for years 1 through 5. Susan must now forecast the cash flow she will receive at the end of year 5 from the sale of the property.

TABLE 16.3	After-Tax Cash Flow Estimates, Years 1–5				
	Year 1	Year 2	Year 3	Year 4	Year 5
Forecasting After-Tax Cash Flows					
PGI	$34,800	$36,540	$38,367	$40,285	$42,300
–VCL	1,392	1,462	1,535	1,611	1,692
EGI	33,408	35,078	36,832	38,674	40,608
–OE	9,900	10,197	10,503	10,818	11,143
NOI	23,508	24,881	26,329	27,856	29,465
–ADS	17,976	17,976	17,976	17,976	17,976
BTCG	5,632	6,906	8,354	9,880	11,490
–Taxes	302	660	1,123	1,613	2,210
ATCF	5,230	6,246	7,231	8,268	9,279
Forecasting Taxes from Operations					
EGI	$33,408	$35,078	$36,832	$38,674	$40,608
–OE	9,900	10,197	10,503	10,818	11,143
NOI	23,508	24,881	26,329	27,856	29,465
–Int.	15,984	15,797	15,593	15,370	15,125
–Dep.	6,447	6,727	6,727	6,727	6,447
TI	1,077	2,357	4,009	5,759	7,893
*MTR	0.28	0.28	0.28	0.28	0.28
Taxes	$302	$660	$1,123	$1,613	$2,210

Forecasting ATER

The second source of cash flow in real estate investments to be considered comes from the sale of the property at the end of the holding period. *after-tax equity reversion* (ATER) is the term used to represent the after-tax cash flow to the investor when the property is sold. The relationships involved in the calculation of ATER for Susan's investment opportunity are presented in Table 16.4.

The starting point in determining the ATER is forecasting a future sale price. *Sale price* is the estimated transaction price that will be negotiated between the buyer and the seller at the time of the transaction. To estimate sale price, Susan assumes that the value of her property will increase by about 5 percent each year. If it is worth $255,000 at the time of purchase, and increases in value by 5 percent annually, it will sell for approximately $325,450 at the end of five years.

From this amount, Susan subtracts $16,500 for expenses she expects to incur during the sale, including such items as brokerage commissions and attorney fees. The difference between the sale price and selling expenses gives **net sale proceeds** of $308,950. Subtracting *amount outstanding* ($166,491) on the mortgage from net sale proceeds, where the amount outstanding on the loan is determined by the amortization schedule, gives the *before-tax equity reversion* (BTER) of $142,459.

The next step is to calculate the taxable gain on the sale for tax purposes. The *taxable gain* on an investment is defined as net sale proceeds less original

TABLE 16.4	After-Tax Equity Reversion	
	Sale price	325,450
	−Selling expenses	−16,500
	Net Sale srice	308,950
	−Amount outstanding	−166,491
	Before-tax equity reversion	142,459
	−Taxes (determined below)	−24,367
	After-tax equity reversion	118,092
	Determining Taxes Due on Sale	
	Net sale price	308,950
	− Purchase price	−255,000
	+ Accumulated depreciation	+ 33,075
	Taxable gain	87,025
	× MTR	× .28
	Taxes	24,367

purchase price plus all depreciation deductions taken in previous years. (Notice that the depreciation deduction used in determining cash flows from operations only defers income tax payments until the sale of the asset.) In this example, the accumulated depreciation is $33,075. Therefore, the taxable gain is $87,025 (or $308,950 minus $255,000 plus $33,075). Taxes due on sale are calculated by multiplying the taxable gain by the investor's marginal income tax rate. In this case, $24,367 (or $87,025 times .28). (We have assumed for simplicity that capital gains are taxed at the same marginal rate as ordinary income.) *ATER* is determined by subtracting taxes due on sale and from the BTER. Based on these calculations, Susan expects to receive an ATER of $118,092.

Now that we have carefully estimated ATCF and ATER for Susan's investment opportunity, we can apply the *discounted cash flow model* and decide whether she should proceed with this project. Given a loan amount of $178,500 and a purchase price of $255,000, the equity required to buy this property is $76,500. Assume that Susan believes a required rate of return of 16 percent reflects the riskiness of the investment as well as the time value of money over the holding period. Using the estimated ATCF for each year of the holding period and the estimated ATER, Susan calculates NPV as follows:

$$NPV = \frac{5,230}{(1+.16)^1} + \frac{6,246}{(1+.16)^2} + \frac{7,231}{(1+.16)^3} + \frac{8,268}{(1+.16)^4} + \frac{9,279}{(1+.16)^5} + \frac{118,092}{(1+.16)^6} - \$76,500 = \$2,493$$

$$IRR = 16.85\%$$

Based on the NPV and IRR decision rules, Susan should choose to purchase this property. While there is no guarantee that this property will be a profitable investment, the discounted cash flow model provides a systematic process for analyzing investment choices and evaluating them with the objective of maximizing investor wealth. The accuracy of the technique depends on the quality of the information used to develop the cash-flow forecasts and on the appropriate evaluation of the risk of the investment when formulating a required rate of return.

■ CHAPTER REVIEW

- ■ Investing in real estate is one of the most exciting aspects of the real estate industry. To be a successful real estate investor requires considerable knowledge about all of the topics addressed in this text. In addition, investors must have a clear understanding of the criteria they should use when evaluating an investment opportunity.

- ■ Advantages of investing in income-producing properties include cash flow from operations, appreciation in property value, portfolio diversification, and financial leverage. Disadvantages include relatively large capital requirements, risk, and the lack of liquidity of real estate investments.

■ The net present value decision rule provides a basis for sound financial decision making that is consistent with the objective of wealth maximization. To apply this rule to real estate investment opportunities, we must develop a forecast of the expected cash flows the projects are likely to generate.

■ The discounted cash flow model is the recommended framework for making real estate investment decisions. By forecasting the cash flows that are likely to result from operating the property during each year of the holding period and the cash flow that will result when the property is sold, we can calculate the expected net present value of an investment opportunity. Using the net present value rule, we can then make a decision about whether the project is expected to increase our wealth.

■ Estimating after-tax cash flow requires estimates of potential gross income, vacancy and credit losses, operating expenses, mortgage amortization, and a thorough understanding of income tax rules regarding real estate investment. Estimates of after-tax equity reversion are obtained by subtracting selling expenses, taxes due on sale, and the amount outstanding on any loans from the sale price of the property. Converting these cash flows into present value is accomplished by discounting them at the rate of return that reflects the time value of money and the riskiness of the investment opportunity.

■ If the present value of after-tax cash flow and equity reversion exceed the equity required, then the net present value is positive, and the investor should choose to accept the project.

■ KEY TERMS

after-tax cash flow	effective gross income	net present value
after-tax equity reversion	financial leverage	net sale proceeds
before-tax cash flow	internal rate of return	potential gross income
debt service	investment	required rate of return
depreciation deduction	net operating income	vacancy and credit losses

■ STUDY EXERCISES

1. What are the attractions of real estate as an investment?

2. What are the disadvantages of real estate as an investment?

3. Explain the logic behind the net present value decision rule and the internal rate of return decision rule.

4. Why do you suppose the depreciable life for residential investment properties is shorter than that of nonresidential properties? How does this fact influence investor's decisions?

5. A real estate broker is offering an apartment building for sale that has the following characteristics:

    a. Asking price: $3,500,000, with the land valued at $500,000.

    b. 160 apartment units that rent for $450 per month with rent expected to increase by 4 percent per year starting in year 2.

    c. Vacancy and bad debt allowance is 6 percent of the potential gross income.

    d. Property taxes and insurance are expected to be constant over the investment horizon at $60,000 per year. Utilities, maintenance, management, and other operating expenses are expected to be 25 percent of the annual effective gross income.

    e. The real estate agent estimates that the value of the property will be $4.4 million at the end of the five-year investment horizon

    f. A 12 percent, 20-year mortgage for $2,400,000 is available with annual payments.

    g. The investment horizon is five years, beginning January 1997 and ending December 2001. Your marginal tax rate is 28 percent. The investor has several profitable real estate investments and can utilize any tax losses. The appropriate discount rate for this investment (the required rate of return) is 18 percent.

    Calculate the relevant cash flows for this investment and apply the NPV and IRR rules to decide whether to pursue this project.

■ FURTHER READINGS

Jaffe, A.J. and C.F. Sirmans, *Fundamentals of Real Estate Investment,* 3rd ed., Englewood Cliffs, N.J.: Prentice-Hall, 1995.

Hoven, V., *The Real Estate Investor's Tax Guide,* 2nd ed., Chicago: Real Estate Education Company, 1996.

Greer, G.E., *Investment Analysis for Real Estate Decisions,* 4th ed., Chicago: Dearborn Financial Publishing, Inc., 1997.

CHAPTER

17 Residential Land Uses

With land and other development costs escalating, single-family attached houses, such as these duplexes, are quickly becoming a popular residential alternative to the more traditional detached home.

CHAPTER PREVIEW

The process of real estate development is one that requires extensive knowledge and practice of all aspects of real estate: legal, financial, and markets. Because of the special characteristics of real estate improvements—large size, long life, and long gestation period—success in real estate development is in large part determined by the accuracy of forecasts of long-term market potential for the project.

This chapter and Chapter 18 examine the real estate development process. In this chapter, we focus on residential land development, while Chapter 18 deals with various types of commercial development.

Residential development takes various forms: single-family and multi-family dwellings, primary and secondary homes, custom-built and factory-built houses. Whatever form a development is to take, successful developers must study carefully the market for the type of housing they contemplate and analyze carefully the financial feasibility of the proposed project.

The topics to be covered in this chapter are

■ types of residential development, including (1) single-family detached houses, (2) single-family attached houses, (3) multifamily residences, (4) manufactured homes, and (5) second homes;

■ time-sharing;

■ market and feasibility analysis; and

■ financial feasibility analysis.

REAL ESTATE TODAY FEATURES

Close-Up
Summit Place—An
Infill Example

Close-Up
Cheyenne
Quadruplexes

Close-Up
Fairview Village

Close-Up
Highlands Falls
Country Club

Case Study
Market and
Feasibility for the
Millford Hills
Subdivision

■ TYPES OF RESIDENTIAL DEVELOPMENT

Although the single-family home on its own lot remains the ideal of most American families, other forms of single-family dwellings are becoming increasingly popular. Multifamily residences, too, take various forms. The five principal types of residential development are

1. single-family detached houses,
2. single-family attached houses,
3. multifamily residences,
4. manufactured homes, and
5. second homes.

Single-Family Detached Houses

The single-family house separated from any adjoining house with at least some open land on all four sides remains the dwelling type most sought after by American families. Many will accept a very basic house on a very small lot simply to attain this goal. The reason often given is that the detached house provides more privacy than an attached dwelling, though this is not always the case, especially if lots are small. Nevertheless, because of this perception, detached houses often have the best resale value.

In the years following World War II, the single-family detached dwelling overwhelmingly dominated housing markets in the United States. Land was cheap on the urban fringe, and large investments in public facilities such as roads, schools, and sewer and water extensions made this type of horizontal sprawl feasible.

In more recent years, however, land and other developmental costs have escalated, making detached housing too expensive for many potential buyers. Design modifications, such as the clustering of such houses, help conserve open space and reduce costs.

Single-Family Attached Houses

The attached row house is a form of housing that goes back to colonial times. This type of dwelling, on its own fee simple lot but sharing common walls with its neighbors, was quite common in cities of the East and in San Francisco.

The first association of homeowners who owned streets and parkland in common was founded in Boston in 1826. Louisburg Square, which contains 18 row houses and a common park on a 2.3-acre site on Beacon Hill, remains a very desirable residential area even today.

The rise of the suburbs shortly after the turn of this century led to the domination of the detached house. The suburban form of the row house, the town house (see page 371), was a rarity until the 1960s; the overwhelming majority of such dwellings have been built since 1970. For projects that are owner-occupied, almost all have used the condominium form of ownership, with a community association managing common areas.

REAL ESTATE TODAY

Summit Place—An Infill Example

One of the biggest problems facing American cities is the rehabilitation of older declining neighborhoods. Summit Place, an urban infill development in St. Paul, Minnesota, is a successful project that has helped revitalize the neighborhood, even beyond its boundaries. It also illustrates some of the difficulties faced by this type of project.

Close-Up

The St. Paul Housing and Redevelopment Authority purchased the 5.5-acre site comprising two and a half blocks in the Ramsey Hill neighborhood, a historic early residential development a mile from downtown St. Paul. It partially cleared the site and arranged for a developer to build "suburban-type" townhouses. When the developer withdrew after vigorous neighborhood opposition to the plan, a new developer took over with a greatly revised plan that rehabilitated the existing historic structures from the Victorian era and added new ones that were similar in character and designed to blend in with the neighborhood fabric.

The city's cooperation was essential to the success of the project. First, of course, the city provided below-market-rate permanent financing and additional funds from HUD grants, a critical element. Second, it closed two alleys, which enhanced security and enabled the developers to locate usable open space in the middle of the block. It also granted zoning variances to allow reduced front-yard setbacks and additional building heights to make the new buildings conform more closely to the existing structures.

The single-family attached dwelling has several advantages over the detached project. Clustering requires less road frontage and shorter utility lines resulting in lower development costs per unit. The higher density of houses also permits lower land costs, further reducing cost per unit. This type of development also can result in less adverse ecological impact, with more of the site being left in its natural state and with more useful open space. A frequent complaint in conventional subdivisions is "I have to spend my weekends cutting all that grass, but there's no place for the kids to play." In a well-designed single-family attached project, yard maintenance by the homeowner is reduced greatly or eliminated, and there is a place for the children to play.

Single-family attached housing can be of several types, including the town house, the plex, and the patio house.

Town Houses

The **town house** is similar to the old row house. Each unit has its own front door that opens to the outdoors, but it shares one or both side walls with adjacent houses. Although the town house has no side yards, it may have front and rear yards. Town houses may front on the street or may be built in a series of five to ten units fronting on a common area.

Plexes

The **plex** shares the characteristics of the town house and the single-family detached house. Each building in a plex contains two or more units, each with

Cheyenne Quadraplexes

As buildable land in our urban areas becomes more and more expensive, higher density housing is essential in providing affordable housing for the middle income market. Because of its identification with nondescript rental housing, one almost overlooked type of residential development is the plex. The Cheyenne quadruplex development in Henderson, Nevada, illustrates that this type of housing can provide quite desirable and affordable living.

Close-Up

The Cheyenne development offers condominium ownership units in buildings that contain four units sharing a common roof. The buildings are of Southwest style, with stucco walls and concrete tile roofs. The individual units have two or three bedrooms, with 1,266 to 1,728 square feet of living area, plus a one- or two-car garage. Each also contains a walled side yard for outdoor privacy. Common areas include a club house with swimming pool, a fitness center and parks, including a barbecue area. The Cheyenne homes are priced at $100,000 to $120,000.

its own outside entrance. A duplex is for two families; a triplex, for three families; a quadruplex, for four families; and so on.

Patio or Zero-Lot-Line Houses

The **patio house,** or zero-lot-line house, is very similar to the detached house except that construction is from lot line to lot line, with an outdoor living area in an interior garden court.

The garden court is normally enclosed by the house or by the house and walls. Although small compared to the yard of the usual single-family detached house, the secluded area provides a great deal of privacy. The houses are usually one story, are often L-shaped and may have one small side yard to provide passage to the rear court area.

Multifamily Residences

Although the single-family home is still preferred by most families, it is too expensive for an increasing portion of the population. Multifamily housing may be the best alternative for such families, as well as for young couples who lack the down payments necessary to purchase their own homes, "empty nesters" who no longer need or desire as large a home as they did when their children lived with them, and single-person households. Where land prices are extremely high, rental or owner-occupied apartments may be the only feasible type of new housing available. Multifamily housing can take the form of garden apartments and midrise or highrise apartments.

A **garden apartment** generally is a two- or three-story building with a density of 10 to 20 units per acre, with open space between the buildings and convenient parking. They generally are built in suburban locations.

REAL ESTATE TODAY

Fairview Village

Close-Up

Urban planners, policy makers, environmentalists, and developers are engaged in a very contentious debate regarding the desirability of the automobile-oriented suburban development that has dominated urban development in the United States for most of the 20th Century, and particularly since World War II. Combined with typical suburban zoning, which segregates retail and office space from residences and different residential types from each other, the result has been what is derisively referred to as "sprawl." While critics decry this type of development, examples of economically viable alternatives have been rare. Fairview Village is one such development.

Rick Holt is an experienced developer who had a vision and a mission—to demonstrate that it was financially feasible to build an "urban village" rather than a typical suburban subdivision. He bought 96 acres of land previously zoned industrial located in Fairview, a small city located on the eastern edge of the Portland, Oregon, metropolitan area. The city

had no "center"— for example, the city hall was located in an old Grange hall—so Holt worked with the city to incorporate a new city hall, branch library, post office, community church, and pedestrian-oriented shopping area into the plan for his village. It also included an office building, day care center, and gym, as well as 600 residential units. The residences encompass single-family detached homes ranging from $150,000 to $300,000, attached town homes, duplexes, and apartments, some above the retail shops. Although the residential density is much higher than in a traditional subdivision, the inclusion of miniparks and walking trails creates a feeling of ample open space and a sense of community. The trails also make it feasible to walk to shopping and other community activities.

Fairview Village is not complete at this writing, but it certainly appears to be headed to a successful completion that will yield both a community of outstanding livability and a considerable profit for the developer.

1 VILLAGE RETAIL
2 FAIRVIEW POST OFFICE
3 VILLAGE OFFICE
4 LIBRARY/MARKET SQUARE
5 TOWNHOME APARTMENTS
6 GOLD'S GYM
7 ROWHOUSES
8 LIVE-WORK BROWNSTONES
9 VILLAGE DUPLEXES
10 TOWNHOMES
11 VILLAGE CHURCH
12 WOODLAND ELEMENTARY
13 SINGLE FAMILY HOMES
14 MEDICAL/OFFICE BUILDING
15 LA PETITE ACADEMY
16 FAIRVIEW CITY HALL

Many garden-apartment projects contain precious little "garden," consisting only of buildings separated by slivers of grass surrounded by a sea of asphalt paving. Good design and careful use of open space, however, can produce a very pleasant housing environment.

A **midrise apartment** building consists of four to eight stories with one or more apartments per floor. Elevators almost always are found in this type of development, and the eight-story maximum height is set by the capacity of a single residential elevator.

Most **highrise apartment** buildings contain more than eight stories and sometimes rise to nearly 100 stories, as in the case of the John Hancock Building in Chicago. The highrise apartment project is more expensive to construct than the garden-apartment project and, typically, contains only luxury apartments. Until recently, almost all highrise apartments were rental units, but condominium ownership has grown rapidly in the past few years.

Ownership Alternatives: Condominiums and Cooperatives

As noted in Chapter 2, many potential homeowners look to condominiums and cooperatives as ownership alternatives. To review these concepts very briefly, the owner of a condominium (condo) holds title in fee simple to the particular unit occupied and shares ownership in common areas such as recreational facilities, lobbies, and parking lots. The owner of a cooperative (co-op) owns stock in a corporation that actually holds title to the property, but the individual has the right to live in a particular apartment. The condominium, which in the United States is a relatively recent development, is far more common than the older cooperative form; most cooperatives are located in New York City. Almost all condos and co-ops are attached or multifamily units.

Condominiums and cooperatives offer several economic advantages to the buyer when contrasted with renting. Like other homeowners, the owner of a condo or co-op can deduct property taxes and mortgage interest from taxable income for income tax purposes. Second, and perhaps of even greater importance, condominium or cooperative ownership serves as a hedge against potential inflation, enabling the owner to accumulate an equity position. Conversely, of course, it also exposes the owner to potential declines in housing prices.

The demand for condos and co-ops has increased during the past several decades, primarily in response to demographic trends and rapidly rising home prices. Many first-time buyers were forced out of the single-family detached market, but they still could afford a condominium or cooperative. The market was also helped by the growth in the number of households, by the smaller size of families and the increase in single-member households, by growing preference for in-town living, and by increasing commuting costs.

Besides these demographic trends, economic factors affecting the rental market have also helped increase the popularity of condos and co-ops. Owners of rental property have been caught in a serious cost squeeze. Operating costs in many cities have increased far more rapidly than rents, and in cities with rent controls, the squeeze has been much worse. This has led to a large number of conversions from rental units to condominiums and cooperatives. The large-scale trend began in Chicago, then spread rapidly across the country.

Manufactured Homes

A **manufactured home,** or *mobile home,* is a dwelling that is manufactured in a factory and then moved to a particular site. The traditional image of mobile homes has been that of cheap, tacky, and high-density housing in sleazy "shantytown" trailer parks. Unfortunately, in the past, much of this reputation was richly deserved. In contrast to the resale value of conventional site-built houses, which has generally appreciated, that of a mobile home generally fell each year. This caused many lenders to treat mobile homes as personal property, much like automobiles, and to provide only relatively short-term, high-interest installment loans. In many areas, it was impossible to obtain a single mortgage that would cover the purchase of both a mobile home and its site. Opposition to mobile-home developments led many communities either to zone them out completely or to limit them to generally undesirable or rural areas.

The image is changing, however, because the design and construction of manufactured homes has been greatly improved. With the introduction of new materials and designs, the "oversized aluminum shoebox" has been replaced by a structure much closer to a conventional house in appearance. Part of this process has been the trend toward wider units and the double-wide and triple-wide units that are assembled on site into 24- to 36-foot-wide homes. Construction quality also has improved tremendously with the introduction of required national construction standards.

These factors, plus the trend toward owner-occupied manufactured-home subdivisions instead of rental parks, have led lenders to liberalize financing and make it more comparable to that for conventional homes. In the past, mobile homes were considered personal property and were financed with 10- to 15-year consumer installment loans that generally carried an interest rate approximately 2 percentage points above conventional mortgage rates. Today, however, owners of manufactured homes located permanently on their lots can obtain 30-year, FHA-insured mortgages.

The rising absolute and relative cost of conventional "stick-built" housing and increasing rents in apartments have increased manufactured housing's share of the market. It now accounts for about 25 percent of new single-family home sales and for more than 35 percent of home sales of less than $50,000.

Second Homes

By their very nature, second homes are very different from primary homes, and second-home markets are quite different from primary-home markets. The principal reason for owning a second home is the desire to use it for leisure-time enjoyment, and certain amenities are ordinarily the main factors in its location: beaches, mountains, golf courses, tennis courts, ski lifts, and so on.

Most second-home owners occupy their dwellings for only a small portion of the year, often because of the seasonal nature of many resorts but also because the owners are unable to get away from their jobs or other responsibilities for extended periods. Hence, many units are bought at least partially for their investment potential and rented for much of the year. As landlords, owners enjoy various tax benefits, including depreciation allowances and deduction of maintenance costs, but changes in tax laws and regulations have greatly reduced potential tax advantages in recent years. For example, there are limits on the time the owner can occupy the dwelling and still claim it as rental property.

Because ownership of a second home is so expensive, many buyers in recent years have turned to resort **time-sharing,** a concept discussed in Chapter 2. Under time-sharing, a single dwelling is sold to a number of buyers, each of whom receives exclusive ownership of the dwelling for a specified time period each year. Like other forms of fee simple ownership, this ownership interest can be willed, leased, or sold.

The time-sharing concept of vacation property first appeared in the 1960s, grew rapidly with the collapse of the resort condominium market in the 1970s, and peaked during the early years of the 1980s. Since that time, many buyers have turned away from the concept as the disadvantages of time-sharing have become apparent, particularly the questionable values offered by many projects and the slow appreciation or actual decline in price of existing time-share units.

■ MARKET AND FEASIBILITY ANALYSIS

We have covered in previous chapters some of the factors that determine the demand for housing at the national, regional, and neighborhood levels. All such factors must be considered when analyzing the market for a particular project. Both developers and lenders need to know what the market will be for a project in order to determine its feasibility. Essentially, they must determine what market conditions have been in the recent past and which factors that would affect the market for the project are likely to change in the near future. The steps in such a market analysis are

1. delineation of the market area;

2. analysis of recent economic trends in the local market area;

3. determination of possible changes in demand factors, such as employment, disposable income, population, household characteristics, and the **absorption rate** (the number of units that are being absorbed by the market); and

4. analysis of the potential supply, including other possible competing projects.

REAL ESTATE TODAY

Highland Falls Country Club

Close-Up

It was not an outstanding golf club community or real estate development. In fact, the Highlands Falls Country Club was a failure. Located near the western North Carolina mountain resort town of Highlands, the club was first opened as the nine-hole Skylake golf course in the 1960s. It was a shoestring operation, with golfers depositing their greens fees in an honor box, where the money was picked up at the end of the day. Several developers worked on the project, the last adding nine more holes and a clubhouse. By 1980, there were about 85 homes, but the sales were slow and the project's mortgage was foreclosed.

The mortgage on the Highlands Falls Country Club was held by two real estate investment trusts. They had to decide whether the development could be made economically viable.

Not only was Highlands Falls Country Club a failed project with a poor reputation, it also came with about 85 very disgruntled and suspicious existing homeowners. Thus, the new development firm was faced with the daunting task of not only developing a high-quality golf club that could yield a development profit but also handling a near revolt of existing club members. It was no small task.

Noted golf architect Joe Lee completely redesigned the golf course, building several new holes and combining others to create longer ones, and the entire course was refurbished. While this made Highlands Falls a much better and more challenging golf course, it also made some of the old club members unhappy because they preferred the shorter course. A tennis and swim center were added, and extensive additions and renovations were made to the clubhouse.

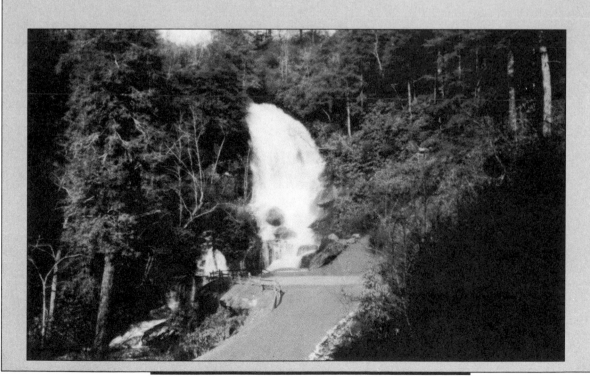

Highland Falls Country Club (continued)

The developer worked very hard to upgrade the image of Highlands Falls, but this was a slow, uphill process. Both the members and the community had seen too much mediocre development and failure in the past. Rumors persisted that the club would soon be foreclosed again. Gradually, however, the sweeping physical facility improvements, increasing lot and home sales, and small but important touches such as extensive landscaping and masses of flowers turned the country club's image around.

Today, Highlands Falls Country Club has a deserved reputation as one of the premier clubs in an area of very exclusive golf courses. Lots, which in 1980 ranged in price from $10,000 to $15,000, have

Close-Up

sold for up to $250,000 for view lots. There are more than 300 homes in the development, with only a few lots available. Club memberships, which in 1984 sold for only $1,100, now sell for $38,000. Home prices range from about $190,000 for some of the older homes to well over $1 million for a few of the newer ones.

The story of the Highlands Falls Country Club shows that even a failed development can be turned into an outstanding and profitable one if the basic elements for success are present and the project is managed by a knowledgeable developer with sufficient resources and a sincere desire to create a quality development.

Delineation of the Market Area

To begin with, the project's market area—that is, the extent of the housing submarket in which it will compete—must be described. The market area is determined largely by employment opportunities and commuting ranges. In smaller communities, of course, all of the local employers will be within the market area, but local workers also may commute to jobs in nearby communities.

In larger urban areas, the analyst must determine the extent of employment available within relevant commuting ranges. Public transportation facilities can extend the commuting range and expand the market area.

Analysis of Recent Trends

What has been the demand for housing within the market area during the past few years, and what economic factors lie behind recent trends? What are the vacancy rates for local rental housing and the absorption rates for new owner-occupied units? Such data usually are available and are essential for an analysis of the market potential of a new project.

Determination of Future Demand

After past and present housing market conditions have been determined, the most important part of the analysis remains—the estimation of future demand. How much unfulfilled demand remains in the market? What changes in the economic base or in national or regional economic conditions will affect demand in the local area? Are new transportation facilities or other public facilities being completed that will influence demand? The developer must analyze such factors carefully to make a reasonably accurate estimation of potential demand for the project.

Of course, not even the most keen and careful analyst can always accurately prophesy the future. Indeed, one would need almost supernatural powers to totally forecast the impact on real estate of the interactions of international political and economic intrigues, tax changes coming from Congress or state and local governments, the expansion or contraction plans of large corporations, and the complexity of business locational decisions.

Analysis of Future Supply

Many developers correctly analyze demand factors but then court disaster by ignoring competitive projects. One of the primary characteristics of real estate improvements is their long gestation period, and developers must estimate both demand and supply conditions during that period.

Suppose, for example, there is a potential demand for 500 new apartment units in a community within the next two years. If three developers respond to this potential demand by constructing three 500-unit complexes, it is impossible that each will be successful in the short run unless the market expands more than anticipated. At best, vacancy rates in the local market probably will rise to a high level, and the general profitability of all complexes will be reduced, or perhaps will be nonexistent, resulting in foreclosure and failure.

The second step in the analysis—determining what lies behind recent trends—sometimes is not given enough emphasis, much to the subsequent regret of the developer. Suppose that housing markets in a particular community have been very tight during the past five years; that is, there has been excess demand. Without proper analysis, this might indicate a continuing strong demand for housing in the next few years.

On more thorough investigation, however, the developer might determine that the tight market conditions resulted from an influx of workers to a major new manufacturing plant, which now operates at its designed level. Unless growth occurs in either the plant or some other part of the community's economic base, the absorption rate—and, therefore, absolute demand for new housing—will decline.

The analyst also must carefully evaluate potential demand in the particular submarket at which the project is aimed. For example, it may be that the new plant mentioned above caused a significant expansion in demand for rental housing. The future demand for this segment of the market may decline, even though demand in other segments may expand, if the new workers move out of the rental units to owner-occupied houses.

■ FINANCIAL FEASIBILITY ANALYSIS

In addition to a market analysis, the developer should conduct a financial feasibility analysis of the proposed project. Such an analysis may be quite sophisticated in the case of a large and complicated development or relatively simple for a small one. In either case, the purpose is to determine—on paper, at least—the probable success of the project.

Finally, bank financing, which is usually essential, also helps to reduce the developer's risk because a large amount of the developer's own or company funds are not involved. On the other hand, any delays can be quite expensive when the interest-rate meter is running. For example, if the site improvements cannot be constructed as rapidly as the developer anticipates or if the houses do not sell as rapidly as expected, the result could be a greatly reduced profit or even default on the loan.

■ THE IMPORTANCE OF MARKET ANALYSIS

If the three most important factors in real estate are "location, location, and location," it should be clear to the readers of this book that the three most important factors in real estate development are "the market, the market, and the market." Real estate developers who forget this lesson usually fail; those who carefully and correctly analyze the market usually succeed.

■ CHAPTER REVIEW

■ The five principal types of residential development are (1) single-family detached houses, (2) single-family attached houses, (3) multifamily residences, (4) mobile homes, and (5) second homes.

■ The single-family detached home has dominated the housing markets for the past 50 years and remains the most sought after type of dwelling. Escalating land costs and growing environmental and energy concerns have made this type of housing less attractive than it once was, however.

■ Types of attached housing include (a) the town house, (b) the plex, and (c) the patio house.

■ Multifamily residential projects are of three types: (1) garden apartments, which are generally two- or three-story buildings; (2) the midrise, consisting of four to eight stories, usually with an elevator; and (3) the highrise, which contains more than eight stories and multiple elevators.

■ Condominium and cooperative ownership of multifamily and attached housing is increasing because of the economic benefits of such ownership, favorable demographic trends, and the declining profitability of rental housing.

■ Manufactured or mobile homes gradually are moving toward greater acceptance by consumers, financial institutions, and communities. As a result of improvements in design and quality, the availability of financing and the rising cost of conventional housing, manufactured homes probably will capture an increasing share of the single-family market.

■ Amenities are the primary factors leading to the purchase of a second home. Because most buyers cannot occupy their units for much of the year, many units are purchased for their investment potential.

■ Time-sharing enables buyers to purchase the use of a second home for a specific time period each year. Buyers thus protect a large portion of their future vacation costs from inflation and benefit from any appreciation in the value of their interest.

■ The steps in analyzing the market for a residential project are (1) delineation of the market area, (2) analysis of recent trends in the local market area, (3) determination of possible changes in the demand factor of the project, and (4) analysis of the potential supply, including other possible competing projects.

■ The market area is determined largely by employment opportunities within the relevant commuting range.

■ The market analyst essentially determines what market conditions have been in the recent past and which factors that would affect the market for the project are likely to change in the near future.

■ The developer should conduct a financial feasibility analysis that projects the probable cash flow and profit or loss of a proposed project.

FIGURE 17.1   Location Map of Milford Hills Subdivision

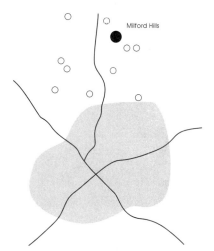

REAL ESTATE TODAY

Market and Feasibility for the Milford Hills Subdivision

Developer Angus Talberson was considering developing a 19.5-acre tract into a subdivision of 30 single-family attached houses that would sell for approximately $95,000 each. Even though Talberson was well acquainted with the local market, he performed a careful analysis of the potential demand for the proposed project.

Close-Up

The subdivision site was located in northern Rowan County, a desirable residential section of a metropolitan area containing a population of approximately 800,000. Talberson compared Milford Hills with ten existing subdivisions located in the same general area. As the map in Figure 17.1 shows, all of the subdivisions were located north of the beltway surrounding the city and had reasonable access to the freeway system. Milford Hills was farther from the beltway and the office-park employment located there than most of the other subdivisions, but the site was near a freeway interchange and still within relatively easy commuting range.

Talberson obtained the sales figures for the existing subdivisions during the previous year, data that are presented in Table 17.1. Nearly 150 homes were sold in the price range that Talberson had proposed for Milford Hills, meaning that if the size of the market remained the same, in order to sell 30 homes in 15 months he would have to capture approximately 16 percent of total sales in this category, certainly not an unreasonable expectation. Because the subdivision could not be developed and placed on the market for more than two years, Talberson also tried to determine any changes that might influence the size of the market two or three years into the future. The economy of the metropolitan area was widely diversified, with no dominant industry or employer. Hence, it seemed logical to assume that there would be no dramatic shifts in employment that would greatly affect the local housing market.

On the contrary, the absorption of new housing units had been increasing at approximately 10 percent annually in this price bracket, and it seemed probable that this trend would continue, further reducing the market penetration needed to make Milford Hills a success.

Talberson also analyzed the supply of homes currently on the market in the price range of his proposed project and tried to find out whether other new projects were in the planning stage. From these studies, he determined that there was no large supply of competing homes either currently on the market or planned that would create an excess supply in his market segment.

In summary, Talberson's analysis led to the conclusion that the market for the proposed project was adequate to support it and that he could proceed to determine its financial feasibility.

In analyzing the financial feasibility of Milford Hills, Talberson made several assumptions:

■ The land would be purchased in quarter 1 of the development process for $136,500 with 10 percent in cash, balance due in quarter 6. (The project was divided into 14 quarters over a three-and-one-half-year period.) The land acquisition would be financed by the seller, with a 9 percent rate of interest on the mortgage.

■ Planning, engineering, and subdivision approval would require 15 months.

■ A development loan could be secured from a commercial bank at the following terms:
  a. Line of credit up to $1,300,000;
  b. Loan to be repaid within 36 months;
  c. Nine percent annual interest, payable quarterly on the average funds outstanding the previous quarter; and
  d. Three points ($39,000) payable to the bank at closing as an additional inducement to make the loan.

REAL ESTATE TODAY

Market and Feasibility for the Milford Hills Subdivision (continued)

■ The houses could be started six months after site improvements had been begun. Six houses could be finished and sold in each of quarters 10 to 14. All would be sold and the project completed by the end of quarter 14.

Close-Up

■ Any increases in costs resulting from inflation would be reflected in the prices of the houses sold.

From these assumptions, Talberson constructed the cash-flow statement shown in Table 17.2 on pages 383 and 384.

Two characteristics of subdivision development are apparent here. First, development requires a large negative cash flow for a long period before any positive cash flow occurs. For the Milford Hills project, no cash inflow would be received until quarter 10. By that time, the project would have recorded a total negative cash outflow of $1,280,000 because funds would have to be used for land acquisition, planning and engineering, site improvements, house construction, financing and administration. Milford Hills would not develop a positive cash flow until quarter 13.

Second, development loans are usually needed to absorb large negative cash flows during the early months of such projects. After Talberson secured a development loan from a commercial bank at the terms enumerated above, he constructed a revised cash-flow statement to show the impact of the financing costs. The profit and loss statement shown in Table 17.3, developed from these data, shows an expected profit of $541,000.

TABLE 17.1   Sales in Selected Rowan County Subdivisions

Subdivision	Up to $70,000	$71,000-$85,000	$86,000-$100,000	$101,000-$115,000	$116,000-$130,000	More than $130,000
Brookwood		10	15	5		
Chimney Springs			4	13	10	
Hollyberry		2	23	11	1	
Huntcliffe				10	15	15
Lost Forest			5	7	11	
River Chase		22	48	24	1	
Rivermont			10	19	16	1
Saddle Creek			26	9	2	
Terramont	36	5				
Woodland Hills			16	10	2	
Total	36	39	147	108	58	16

TABLE 17.2 Cash Flow Statement, Milford Hills Subdivision

| | Quarter | | | | | |
	1	2	3	4	5	6
Sources of Funds:						
Sales						
Less cost of sales						
Net receipts						
Uses of Funds:						
Land acquisition	13,650					122,850
Planning and engineering site	9,375	9,375	9,375	9,375	9,375	9,375
Improvements						110,000
Home construction						
Administration and other	15,000	15,000	15,000	15,000	15,000	15,000
Total	38,025	24,375	24,375	24,375	24,375	257,225
Net cash flow	(38,025)	(24,375)	(24,375)	(24,375)	(24,375)	(257,225)
Cumulative cash flow	(38,025)	(62,400)	(86,775)	(111,150)	(135,525)	(352,750)
Borrowings	122,850 (land)		85,000	25,000	24,000	351,000
Repayments						475,000
Cumulative borrowings			85,000	110,000	134,000	

TABLE 17.3 Pro Forma Profit and Loss Statement, Milford Hills Subdivision

Revenue	
Sale of houses: 30 × $95,000	$2,850,000
Less selling cost (3.5%)	99,750
	$2,750,250
Costs	
Land acquisition: 19.5 acres × $7,000 per acre	$136,500
Planning and engineering	75,000
Site improvements	350,000
House construction	1,250,000
Estimated financing costs	187,650
Administration and other costs	210,000
	$2,209,150
Expected profit	$541,100

| TABLE 17.2 | Cash Flow Statement, Milford Hills Subdivision (continued) | | | | | | | |

	Quarter							
7	8	9	10	11	12	13	14
			$570,000	$570,000	$570,000	$570,000	$570,000
			19,950	19,950	19,950	19,950	19,950
			550,050	550,050	550,050	550,050	550,050
9,375	9,375						
140,000	100,000						
125,000	125,000	250,000	250,000	250,000	125,000	125,000	
15,000	15,000	15,000	15,000	15,000	15,000	15,000	15,000
289,375	249,375	265,000	265,000	265,000	140,00	140,000	15,000
(289,375)	(249,375)	(265,000)	285,000	285,050	410,050	410,050	535,050
(642,125)	(1,156,500)	(1,280,000)	(995,000)	(586,400)	(176,350)	233,700	768,850
290,000	250,000	265,000					
			285,000	285,000	410,000	300,000	
765,000	1,015,000	1,280,000	995,000	710,000	310,000		

■ KEY TERMS

absorption rate	manufactured home	plex
garden apartment	midrise apartment	time-sharing
highrise apartment	patio house	town house

■ REVIEW QUESTIONS

1. What are the five principal types of residential developments?

2. What are the differences between condominium and cooperative ownership? What are some of the advantages of these types of ownership over renting?

3. What are the three types of single-family attached housing? What are the differences among the three?

4. What are the three types of multifamily residential housing? What are the differences among the three?

5. Discuss some of the factors that are leading to greater acceptance of manufactured or mobile homes.

6. What are the principal reasons for owning a vacation home, and how do they differ from the reasons for owning a principal residence?

7. Discuss the use of time-sharing in the marketing of vacation homes.

8. Describe the steps in analyzing the market for a residential project.

9. What factors determine the market for a residential project?

10. Describe the process of financial feasibility analysis for a proposed residential project.

■ FURTHER READINGS

Arendt, Randall G., *Conservation Design for Subdivisions: A Practical Guide to Creating Open Space Networks.* Washington, D.C.: Island Press, 1996.

Bookout, Lloyd W., *Value by Design: Landscape, Site Planning, and Amenities.* Washington, D.C.: Urban Land Institute, 1994.

Ewing, Reid, *Best Development Practices: Doing the Right Thing and Making Money at the Same Time.* Chicago: Planners Press, 1996.

Katz, Peter, *The New Urbanism: Toward an Architecture of Community.* New York: McGraw-Hill, 1994.

Langdon, Philip, *A Better Place to Live.* Amherst, Mass.: University of Massachusetts Press, 1994.

Muirhead, Desmond, and Guy L. Rando, *Golf Course Development and Real Estate.* Washington, D.C.: Urban Land Institute, 1994.

Petit, Jack, Debra L. Bassert, and Cheryl Kollin, *Building Greener Neighborhoods: Trees as Part of the Plan.* Washington, D.C.: National Association of Home Builders, 1995.

American Society of Civil Engineers, National Association of Home Builders, and Urban Land Institute. *Residential Streets,* 2nd ed. Washington, D.C.: Urban Land Institute, 1990.

18 Commercial and Industrial Development

The Nichols Memorial Fountain serves as a focal point for the Country Plaza, which has the distinction of being known as the first suburban shopping center. For a complete description of the evolution of the shopping center, turn to to the Close-Up on page 394.

Shopping Centers and other buildings for retail trade, office buildings, hotels and motels, and restaurants are examples of income-producing commercial properties. Industrial property includes factory buildings and warehouses. The development of these types of properties is the focus of this chapter.

Specific topics to be discussed are

- shopping center development;

- evolution of the shopping center;

- the development process of commercial properties, including (1) market and feasibility analysis, (2) site location, (3) tenant selection, and (4) financial feasibility analysis;

- office buildings;

- industrial parks and distribution facilities; and

- hotels and motels.

SHOPPING CENTER DEVELOPMENT

The suburban shopping center is a creature of the automobile and is both a result and a cause of the suburban explosion that has taken place since World War II. As shopping centers have proliferated in suburban areas, the older **central business districts** of many cities have

| FIGURE 18.1 | Types of Shopping Centers |

become economic backwaters. Others have been redeveloped, some as specialized shopping areas.

The traditional American shopping area was the central business district, an unplanned series of buildings constructed along major streets in the center of town. The modern shopping center is distinguished from the traditional commercial district by the following characteristics:

- One or more structures of unified architecture housing firms that are selected and managed as a unit for the benefit of all tenants
- A site that serves a particular trade area
- On-site parking
- Facilities for deliveries separated from the shopping area
- Single ownership and management

Although all shopping centers share these characteristics, not all shopping centers are alike. In fact, there are four major types, classified on the basis of type of tenants, size, and function: the neighborhood center, the community center, the regional center, and the superregional center. The types of shopping centers and their characteristics are shown in Figure 18.1 and listed in Table 18.1.

The **neighborhood shopping center,** sometimes called a *convenience center,* is designed to serve an area within a radius of approximately 1.5 miles and a population of 2,500 to 40,000. Its principal tenant usually is a supermarket, while the other stores largely provide convenience and shopping goods, such as pharmaceuticals, housewares, and personal services. Its **gross leasable area**—that is, the total floor area designed for the tenants' use—ranges from 30,000 to 100,000 square feet, with 50,000 square feet typical. It usually is located on about three acres of land. Generally, the neighborhood center is built in the strip style—that is, in basically a straight line, with stores tied together by a canopy over a pedestrian walk. Parking space is provided adjacent to the stores and off the public street.

The **community shopping center** provides a wider range of merchandise and usually is built around a junior department store, variety store, or discount store. It is designed to serve an area with a radius of approximately three to five miles and has a gross leasable area of 100,000 to 300,000 square feet located on from 10 to 30 acres.

When a discount store is the main tenant, the community shopping center sometimes is known as a **discount shopping center.**

The **regional shopping center** offers a full range of goods and services, usually has between 300,000 and 750,000 square feet of gross leasable area, and occupies between 30 and 50 acres. It is anchored by at least one full-line department store but usually has two or more. These shopping centers almost always are built as open or enclosed pedestrian malls, with the closed mall the overwhelming choice in recent years.

TABLE 18.1   Characteristics of Shopping Center, by Type

Type	Leasing Tenant	Typical Leasable Area (Square Feet)	Range of Gross Leasable Area (Square Feet)	Typical Site Area (Acres)	Minimum Support Required (Number of People)
Neighborhood or convenience center	Supermarket or drugstore	50,000	30,000 – 100,000	3	2,500 - 40,000
Community center	Variety, discount, or junior department store	150,000	100,000 – 300,000	10 - 30	40,000 - 100,000
Regional center	One or more full-line department stores	400,000	300,000 – 750,000	30 - 50	150,000 or more
Superregional center	Three or more full-line department stores	1,000,000	750,000 – 1,500,000	100 or more	200,000 or more

A **superregional shopping center** exceeds 750,000 square feet in gross leasable area, occupies 100 acres or more, and includes at least three department stores. Most centers exceed 1 million square feet and may draw customers from more than 50 miles. Most superregional centers are built with multiple levels to reduce walking distances for shoppers.

Variations on the major types of shopping centers include the superstore, the power center, the specialty shopping center, and the factory outlet center. The **superstore** is a very large discount store with between 60,000 and 150,000 square feet under one roof. Such stores, which are found more often in Europe than in the United States, typically offer foodstuffs, general merchandise, and hard lines such as appliances in a warehouse atmosphere. The **power center** is a large strip type shopping center that is anchored by one or more "big box" retailers, along with smaller shops. The **specialty shopping center** focuses on unusual market segments, usually offering high-quality and high-priced merchandise in boutique-type stores, although a number of new specialty centers focus only on discount stores.

Another type of specialty center is the **factory outlet center,** which consists of manufacturers' retail outlet facilities, where goods are sold directly to the public in stores owned and operated by manufacturers. These centers began a decade or so ago when manufacturers opened factory-owned stores near their plants to sell off seconds, outdated or overproduced goods or goods, sent back unsold by retailers. Then, in the 1980s, developers began constructing shopping malls catering specifically to outlet stores. Now there are more than 300 outlet malls. These malls bear little resemblance to the often dingy original stores and carry top-quality merchandise with extensive size and selection.

The locational requirements of outlet malls are similar to those of full-price centers, with the exception that factory outlet malls generally must be located on the outskirts of large market areas or major tourist resorts. This requirement appeases major retailers, which are not happy to have factory stores in their markets selling the same merchandise at cheaper prices.

■ EVOLUTION OF THE SHOPPING CENTER

The tremendous rise in automobile ownership during the 1920s put a strain on downtown shopping areas, designed for pedestrians and public transportation. Congested streets, parking meters, and the limited curbside areas available for parking in most cities encouraged a shift to new concentrations of shopping facilities with adequate provisions for parking.

The automobile also encouraged population movement to the suburbs, and these areas on the outskirts of cities became the logical sites for the new shopping facilities. A few developers built the first true suburban shopping centers with unified architecture, a planned mix of tenants, and the essential ingredient—off-street parking. The surge in the number of centers came after World War II, with the explosion of residential suburbs.

The first suburban shopping center was Country Club Plaza in Kansas City, profiled on page 394. The first regional shopping center to contain a major full-line department store as the leading tenant was the Northgate Shopping Center in Seattle, constructed in 1950. The center contains several features that soon became familiar, including a central pedestrian mall, a truck tunnel to separate deliveries from the shopping areas, and vast seas of parking spaces surrounding the central building.

In the late 1950s, a design breakthrough was achieved when developers began to construct completely enclosed malls so that the interior climate could be controlled with air-conditioning and heating. Developers also began to expand centers vertically instead of horizontally to conserve land and protect the environment. The first enclosed mall, which also initiated the multilevel concept, was the Southdale Center near Minneapolis, opened in 1956. In the 1960s and 1970s, the enclosed multilevel mall became the dominant form of regional shopping center. There also was a trend toward larger complexes, with three or more full-line department stores.

The building of large, multilevel regional shopping centers continued in the 1980s, but at a reduced pace. Major activity centered on the expansion, redesign and refurbishment of earlier centers, including older strip centers. One recent development is the mega mall, as typified by the Mall of America in Minneapolis-St. Paul, a 4.2-million-square-foot development, containing a 2.5-million-square-foot shopping mall with more than 350 stores, a seven-acre amusement park with a roller coaster, and a two-level miniature golf course.

■ THE SHOPPING CENTER DEVELOPMENT PROCESS

A developer who contemplates the construction of a shopping center must undertake several exhaustive studies if the proposed project is to have any hope of succeeding. The first task is to analyze the market to determine whether the proposed project is economically feasible. If it is, the developer then must determine the precise site that will be most likely to ensure the project's success. Having settled on a site, the developer then must secure the commitments of the key anchor tenants and the proper supplementary tenants to ensure a complementary mix of shopping facilities.

Market and Feasibility Analysis

Before a developer will build a shopping center, before a lender will make a mortgage loan, and before potential anchor tenants will consider signing leases, several questions need to be answered regarding the proposed center's market and economic feasibility. Can the proposed center generate enough sales volume—and, therefore, rental income—to justify its development? Can the community absorb the proposed new retailing space? Are the population and purchasing power of the potential trade area expanding? If the market is not expanding, can the proposed center and its particular merchandising mix succeed in taking business away from existing stores or shopping centers?

REAL ESTATE TODAY

The First Suburban Shopping Center: Country Club Plaza

The first suburban shopping center generally is considered to be Country Club Plaza in Kansas City, although strictly speaking, it is a shopping district rather than a shopping center. At any rate, it was the first suburban shopping area to incorporate unified architecture, common management, tenant selection, and off-street parking. It remains one of the premier urban spaces in the country, although its owners realized that a $240 million expansion and renovation project was necessary to keep it competitive with rapid shopping center development in the city's newer suburbs.

Close-Up

The J. C. Nichols Company began to develop the Country Club district shortly after the turn of the century, when it was the extreme southern suburb of Kansas City. To the north of this area and between it and the developed portion of the city was Brush Creek Valley, a largely overgrown area that was occupied by a brick kiln, several trash dumps, and an old goat farm. In these unpromising surroundings, Nichols developed a new shopping center that featured off-street parking in what he termed "parking stations" and architecture reminiscent of that of Seville, Spain.

The first building was completed in 1923, and the center has been under almost continuous development and redevelopment since that time. It expanded greatly after World War II into a prestige shopping area containing more than 180 retail and service shops. Over the years the center has changed from a shopping center catering to general needs to a specialty center catering to high-income shoppers. The last drugstore closed in late 1996.

In order to remain competitive, the Plaza's owner, the J. C. Nichols Company, is in the midst of a $240 million expansion and renovation project that will add 780,000 square feet of new retail and office space to the 2.8 million square feet of existing space. It will partially be financed with $55 million in tax increment financing extended by the city. Under this arrangement, 100 percent of property taxes on the new buildings and 50 percent of sales and other taxes generated by the expansion will be rebated to the developer until the total reaches $55 million.

Country Club Plaza pioneered many of the concepts that are commonplace in suburban shopping centers today. Because of the high quality of its design and architecture and continuing good management that has successfully adapted the center's facilities to keep abreast of evolving marketing trends, Country Club Plaza has retained its rank as a prestige shopping center for more over 75 years.

A new center can do little to create business; basically, it must take business away from other retailers or capture expanded trade in a growing area. It is essential, therefore, that the developer also carefully analyze the status of the competition and the future prospects of the trade area.

Defining the Trade Area

The first step in a feasibility and market analysis is to define the **trade area**— that is, the geographic area from which the major portion of the patronage necessary to support the shopping center is to be drawn. This area will vary with the types and quality of merchandise offered. For example, families generally purchase food and sundries close to their homes, but for more expensive items, such as clothing, furniture, and major appliances, they often will drive long distances to secure a better selection or lower prices. Similarly, those seeking specialty items, such as sports equipment or high-quality cameras, also will travel longer distances to shop.

These factors are reflected in the trade areas for the various types of centers. The **primary trade area**—that is, the area that accounts for 60 to 70 percent of the center's sales—will have a radius of approximately 1.5 miles for a neighborhood shopping center, 3 to 5 miles for a community shopping center, and 8 to 10 miles for a regional shopping center. Additional shoppers may come from the **secondary trade area**—the area for a regional center that is 15 to 20 minutes' driving time from the primary trade area and that normally accounts for 15 to 20 percent of sales.

Besides the types of goods desired, the main factors that determine the size and shape of the trade area are the nature and location of competitive centers, the location of major transportation facilities, and natural barriers. For example, the defined trade area for the proposed center shown in Figure 18.2 is skewed toward the east and north because there is little or no competition in those directions.

A lake forms a natural barrier in the southeast, and competitive facilities in the south and particularly the west greatly reduce the radius of the trade area in those directions.

Determining the Size of the Market

After the extent of the trade area has been determined, the next step is to calculate the size of the potential market within the trade area. Basic data can be obtained from the Census of Population and Housing and the Census of Retail Trade. They can be supplemented by other public and private data sources, such as the annual estimates of personal income by county supplied by the Bureau of Economic Analysis and the *Survey of Buying Power,* published annually by *Sales and Marketing Management* magazine.

Analyzing the Competition

After the current size and characteristics of the trade area's population have been determined, these data must be projected into the future. Projections are

FIGURE 18.2   Primary Trade Area of a Proposed Shopping Center, Skewed by a
Natural Barrier and Competitive Facilities

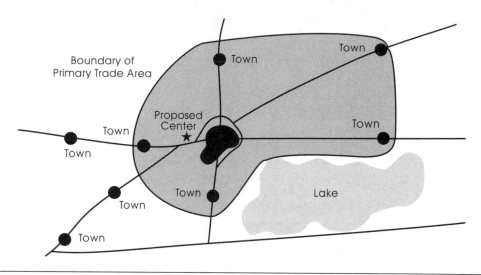

critical to the center's potential success because it is in the future that the center
must compete in the marketplace.

It often is tempting simply to extrapolate recent trends into the future, but
this method will provide a very poor basis for decision making unless the best
evidence indicates that a recent trend *will* continue. The experienced analyst or
investor goes behind recent trends to find their causes and then attempts to project those trends on the basis of his or her findings.

Competitive Survey

After the probable future purchasing power and retail purchases of the defined
trade area have been estimated, the analyst must estimate the percentage of the
total that can be captured by the proposed development.

One obvious step is to make a competitive survey to determine the extent and
strength of existing centers in the market. It also is essential to find out what
other potential competitors are planned. A market study that indicates a potential
demand sufficient to support a new shopping center probably will lead to a very
unsuccessful project if the developer fails to take into account another proposed
new center.

Site Location

The market and feasibility analysis can substantiate the practicability of a center within the defined trade area, but it does not pinpoint the exact site, and site
selection is a crucial factor in the success of a shopping center.

Several factors are important in the selection of the shopping center site, including size, shape, topography, drainage, utilities, and zoning. The most important considerations by far, however, are location and access. The neighborhood or convenience shopping center requires easy access from the supporting residential area. It usually is located on a connector street, and in a planned community, it also may be located to encourage pedestrian access. The community center normally is located along a major thoroughfare, while the principal location requirement for regional and superregional centers is easy access to major freeways and, increasingly, mass-transit facilities.

It is not necessary for shopping centers to be located far from other centers; in fact, centers located across the street from or adjacent to each other may be complementary. For example, a specialty fashion center may draw customers to an adjacent regional shopping center from competing centers in the area because the specialty center enhances the general location for shoppers. Alternatively, one center may not compete with another nearby because it handles different types of goods. For example, a convenience or neighborhood shopping center may be located near a regional center and actually benefit from this location.

There is a saying among developers that there are only three important considerations in real estate development: "location, location, and location." The maxim is especially applicable in choosing a shopping center site. Selection of any but the best site not only will mean a less successful center initially; it usually will mean that a competing center eventually will be built on the best site and will use this advantage to secure the lion's share of the business.

Tenant Selection

The success of most shopping centers is contingent upon the securing of key anchor tenants. For regional and superregional centers, the anchors are major department stores; for community centers, they are junior department stores or discount stores; and for neighborhood centers, they are supermarkets or drugstores. Consequently, the negotiating strength of such firms is great, and they usually secure very favorable lease terms. Often, the major tenants in a regional center purchase land from the developer and construct their own buildings.

The major tenants are expected to attract shoppers to the supplementary tenants. These tenants must be chosen carefully to be complementary to each other and to the anchor stores. For example, men's stores—shoes, clothing, and sporting goods—tend to reinforce each other. The same principle holds for women's clothing and related shops, including food products and personal services. To yield the highest return, continuing careful attention is also crucial to ensure that the tenant mix changes when necessary to reflect new trends.

■ OFFICE BUILDINGS

The demand for office space in a community depends on the level of certain types of business activity and government employment. Nationally, the increasing percentage of the work force in white-collar occupations and the growth in service industries in the past several decades have added to the demand for additional office space. Increased business activity in expanding areas, particularly in the Sunbelt region, has also fueled the demand for additional office space. Within cities, the growth of suburban office parks has greatly expanded the supply of office buildings in these locations.

Location of Office Activity

Office buildings traditionally have been located in downtown business districts, and in recent years, they have become the dominant form of land use in many city centers. Downtown office buildings most likely are to be used as main offices of financial institutions, corporate headquarters, attorneys' offices, and government facilities.

Most cities also have at least one secondary "uptown" office node, usually located along a major thoroughfare leading to the suburbs. Other specialized nodes may develop near governmental installations, shopping centers, hospitals, and universities.

Another more recent type of development is the **office park,** a community of office structures under central management and administration, usually located in the suburbs and adjacent to a major freeway. Such parks generally consist of lowrise buildings in a campuslike setting. They attract tenants in sales, manufacturing, and similar activities that do not need downtown locations. The office park's advantages are its location near suburban residential areas, with resultant reduction in commuting time, ease of parking, and a pleasant environment.

Types of Office Products

Office buildings can be classified in several ways. Building location, discussed above, is one way. Another is by number of tenants. Single-tenant buildings are very common. They range in size from a 1,000 square-foot suburban structure for a small firm or physical to a one-million-square-foot skyscraper for a large corporation. They may be owner-occupied or leased from an investor.

Many office buildings, particularly the larger ones, are built by investors on a speculative basis for lease to multiple tenants. Sometimes a large company will lease a major portion of the building, which then will be named for the firm. In other cases, ownership is organized on a condominium basis, with the individual firms owning their office space and sharing ownership of the common areas.

REAL ESTATE TODAY

The Development of Willow Springs Center

Case Study

Cindy Owensby and Carlos Slawson had taken an option on a three-acre site and were considering developing a small shopping center called the Willow Springs Center. Before they could proceed, they had to answer the following questions:

■ Was there sufficient market demand to support a new center at the proposed location?

■ What type of center should be built?

The site was located just off a heavily traveled arterial street in a rapidly growing high-income suburb of a major city. A recent study conducted by a consulting firm indicated that the general area had great potential for retail stores. The population of the primary trade area (approximately a two-mile radius) was 45,000 and was forecast to increase to 65,000 in 15 years. The secondary trade area (the fan-shaped area shown in Figure 18.3, lying principally to the north of the proposed center and away from the central city) had a population of 70,000 and a projected population in 15 years of 95,000. The

area's population was relatively young and affluent; only 6 percent were over 65, and the average household income was 75 percent higher than the average for the entire metropolitan area. Even though these data indicated a strong market potential, it was still not clear whether that side would be viable for a new shopping center.

Specifically, the site for the Willow Springs Center lay on the northern edge of a shopping district that had developed along Salisbury Road. (See Figure 18.4.) There were several neighborhood specialty store centers in the district, but none contained a major department store. The only large discount department store in the area was located in a new center across from the subject property.

Slawson and Owensby realized that the discount department store and large supermarket in this center provided a major attraction for shoppers that could benefit their proposed center as well. Accordingly, they reasoned that a strip center containing specialty and local service shops would have the greatest probability of success.

TABLE 18.2   Estimated First-Year Expenses, Willow Springs Center

Expense	Amount
Property taxes	
32,500 sq. ft. × 61 cents per sq. ft.	$ 19,856
Insurance	
32,500 sq. ft. × 13.3 cents per sq. ft.	4,329
Utilities	
32,500 sq. ft. × 19.5 cents per sq. ft.	6,347
Maintenance	
32,500 sq. ft. × 21 cents per sq. ft.	6,836
Reserves	
32,500 sq. ft. × 8 cents per sq. ft.	2,604
Management	
4% of gross income ($546,840)	21,874
Leasing commissions	
2% of gross income	10,937
TOTAL	$72,783

The Development of Willow Springs Center (Continued)

Working with an architect and site planner, Slawson and Owensby developed a plan for a 32,550-square-foot center with 12 shops ranging in size from 1,200 to 6,500 square feet. From their knowledge of the local market, the two developers felt that these shops could be leased for an average annual rental of approximately $16.80 per square foot, with escalation clauses raising the rates in future years.

Case Study

An insurance company agreed to finance 75 percent of the estimated value of the center ($3,840,000) at 9 percent interest provided the developers secured an adequate number of tenants approved by the lender. Expenses the first year, excluding debt service on the line, were estimated at $72,783. (See Table 18.2.)

From the data in this table, an income and expense statement was prepared, which is shown in Table 18.3. It indicated a $173,092 cash flow the first year, a return that would make the project financially feasible—if the market assumptions were correct.

The next step was to secure tenants. Jolly Charlie's, a branch of a prominent local liquor and wine store, signed a 20-year lease at $15.40 per square foot that provided for escalation based on the consumer price index. A textile mill outlet was a second major tenant, signing a ten-year lease for 35,800 square feet at an annual rental of $16 per square foot. Other tenants included a furniture and decorating shop, a drugstore, a children's clothing shop, a ladies high-fashion clothing store, a sporting goods shop, an arts and crafts shop, a florist, a dry cleaner, a beauty shop, and an ice cream parlor.

Rents for these firms ranged from $16.40 to $19.70 a square foot, with lease terms ranging from three to ten years. Most of the leases provided for percentage rents in addition to the base rates; the others contained escalation clauses.

Despite inflationary pressures, Willow Springs was completed within its budget. Sales during the first 18 months were quite good, and actual rents the first year averaged $17 per square foot.

TABLE 18.3	Income and Expense Statement, Willow Springs Center

First-year income	$546,840
Less vacancy, 2%	10,937
Effective income	535,903
Less expenses	72,783
Net operating income	463,120
Less debt service	290,028
Cash flow	$173,092

Mortgage Data

Amount	$2,880,000
Rate	9%
Monthly debt service	$24,169

FIGURE 18.3 Trade Area for Willow Springs Center

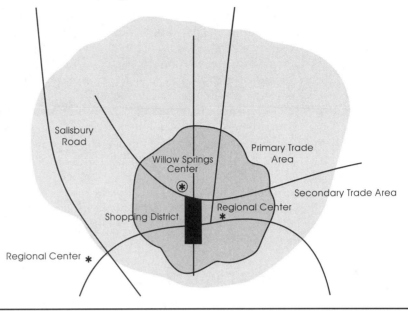

FIGURE 18.4 Willow Springs Center Site

■ INDUSTRIAL PARKS AND DISTRIBUTION FACILITIES

Early industrial facilities were located wherever transportation facilities, water, power, and other such features were adequate. Around the turn of the century, however, **industrial parks**—controlled, parklike developments designed to accommodate specific types of industry and providing all necessary utilities—came into existence. These parks provided location advantages and also avoided conflicts with other land uses.

Several planned industrial districts were pioneered in Chicago, beginning with the Original East District in 1902. These districts were served by railroads, and their success led to the establishment of other railroad-sponsored industrial districts in other parts of the country. Following World War II, the industrial-park concept spread widely. Most recent parks depend primarily on road access, but most also are served by rail facilities.

Some industrial parks contain manufacturing plants, but many allow only light manufacturing activities. Others are devoted exclusively to warehousing and distribution activities.

■ ANALYSIS OF INDUSTRIAL SITES

The task of determining the feasibility of developing a site for industrial use is much like that of analyzing other types of property. The basic technique is to

- determine the amount of existing or potential supply,
- forecast the demand for additional developed industrial acreage or building space in the general area,
- estimate the absorption rate during the analysis period, and
- compare the competitiveness of the subject site with that of other properties.

■ HOTEL, MOTEL, AND RESORT DEVELOPMENTS

The demand for lodging services comes from several sources, including pleasure travelers, business travelers, and conventioneers. The various types of lodging customers necessitate different types of facilities, although there often is considerable overlap. For example, many pleasure travelers seek easy access to and from major highways, and so do many business travelers. Pleasure travelers seek resort locations, and so do many convention groups.

The distinction between motels and hotels was quite marked in the early days of the motel. Motels usually were small structures of one or two stories offering parking space adjacent to rooms and a minimum of services. Today, many motels are almost indistinguishable from hotels, the primary distinction being that hotels generally offer a wider range of services.

Lodging facilities usually are classified as commercial hotels, highway or airport hotels, and resort hotels.

Commercial hotels cater primarily to businesspeople and conventioneers. Their occupancy is usually relatively stable throughout the year but often drops to low levels on weekends. Many depend heavily on convention trade and have extensive facilities to attract this type of business.

A **highway,** or *airport,* **hotel** caters primarily to businesspeople or vacationers who are in transit. Such facilities range from the small highway motel that offers little more than a sparsely furnished room to elaborate facilities with extensive amenities.

Resort hotels, which are also known as *destination* or *seasonal hotels,* cater to individuals or families on vacation. By definition, the hotels must be located near scenic, historic, or other attractions that appeal to pleasure travelers. To enhance their appeal further, most offer extensive facilities—golf courses, tennis courts, swimming pools, and the like. Many are seasonal, often closing completely in the off-season or catering to convention groups.

Lodging facilities differ in several ways from other types of real estate. Their revenues are very susceptible to changes in business activity or pleasure travel, as rentals usually are from night to night rather than on the basis of the long-term leases used for other types of rental property. Conversely, rates can be adjusted quickly in periods of rapid inflation, a desirable characteristic for investors. Management is of critical importance to the success of such facilities, usually making the difference between a successful and an unsuccessful project. Even a well-designed and well-located lodging facility will have difficulty overcoming inadequate management.

■ CHAPTER REVIEW

- ■ The shopping center is distinguished from the traditional commercial district by the following characteristics: (a) one or more structures of unified architecture housing firms that are selected and managed as a unit, (b) a site that serves a particular trade area, (c) on-site parking, (d) facilities for deliveries separated from the shopping area, and (e) single ownership and management.

- ■ There are four major types of shopping centers, classified on the basis of type of tenants and functions: (1) the neighborhood or convenience center, with a typical gross leasable area of 50,000 square feet and a supermarket or drugstore as leading tenant; (2) the community center, with a typical gross leasable area of 150,000 square feet and a variety, discount, or junior department store as leading tenant; (3) the regional center, with one or more full-line department stores and 400,000 square feet of gross leasable area; and (4) the superregional center, with three or more full-line department stores and 1 million square feet of gross leasable area.

- ■ The factory outlet center was a development of the 1980s. These centers contain stores where goods are sold directly to the public by manufacturers.

- ■ The steps involved in a feasibility and market analysis for a shopping center are (1) define the trade area—that is, the geographic area from which the major portion of the center's patronage will be drawn; the primary trade area (the area from which 60 to 70 percent of sales are expected to come) will have a radius of approximately 1.5 miles for a neighborhood shopping center, 3 to 5 miles for a community shopping center and 8 to 10 miles for a regional shopping center; (2) determine the size of the market in terms of population, purchasing power, and expected sales; (3) analyze existing and potential competition; and (4) estimate the percentage of sales of the total trade area that can be captured by the proposed center.

■ Several factors are important in the selection of the shopping center site, including size, shape, topography, drainage, utilities, and zoning. Most important is location.

■ The demand for office space in a community depends on business activity and government employment.

■ Office buildings generally are located in downtown business districts, in office nodes along major thoroughfares leading to the suburbs, and in office parks.

■ A firm's selection of an industrial site is influenced by many factors, including (a) the availability of land, (b) the availability of utilities, and (c) access to major transportation facilities.

■ The steps in determining the feasibility of developing a site for industrial use are (1) determining the amount of existing or potential supply, (2) forecasting the demand for additional developed industrial acreage or building space in the general area, (3) estimating the absorption rate during the analysis period, and (4) comparing the competitiveness of the subject site with that of other properties.

■ Demand for lodging services comes from several sources, including pleasure travelers, business travelers, and conventioneers.

■ Transient hotels and motels usually are classified as (a) commercial hotels, which cater primarily to businesspeople and conventioneers; (b) highway or airport hotels, which cater primarily to businesspeople and vacationers who are in transit; and (c) resort hotels, which cater to individuals or families on vacation.

■ KEY TERMS

central business district
commercial hotel
community shopping center
discount shopping center
factory outlet center
gross leasable area
highway hotel

industrial park
neighborhood shopping center
office park
power center
primary trade area
regional shopping center

resort hotel
secondary trade area
specialty shopping center
superregional shopping center
superstore
trade area

■ STUDY EXERCISES

1. What characteristics distinguish a shopping center from the traditional commercial district?

2. What are the four major types of shopping centers?

3. Describe the characteristics of (a) the neighborhood shopping center (b) the community center, (c) the regional center, and (d) the superregional center.

4. Discuss the steps involved in a feasibility and market analysis for a proposed shopping center.

5. Define the primary trade area. What is its typical size for each of the major types of centers?

6. What factors are most important in the selection of a successful shopping center site?

7. What is a specialty shopping center? What is a discount shopping center?

8. What factors determine the demand for office space in a community?

9. What types of firms tend to lease space in downtown office locations? Why do financial institutions and attorneys often choose downtown locations?

10. Where are "office nodes" likely to develop?

11. What factors have led to the growing popularity of the suburban office park?

12. What factors determine a firm's selection of a specific industrial site?

■ FURTHER READINGS

Baltin, B., et al. Hotel Development. Washington, D.C.: Urban Land Institute, 1996.

O'Mara, W. P., M. D. Deyard, and D. M. Casey. *Developing Power Centers*. Washington, D.C.: Urban Land Institute, 1996.

Sabbagh, K., *Skyscraper: The Making of a Building*. New York: Penguin Books, 1989.

Schwanke, D., *Resort Development Handbook*. Washington, D.C.: Urban Land Institute, 1997.

PART FIVE

Special Topics

19 Principles of Real Property Insurance

Farmers often add special provisions for flood coverage to their property insurance policies to protect themselves from weather-related crop failures.

CHAPTER PREVIEW

There are three primary reasons for the inclusion of an overview of real property insurance in this book. First, and of greatest importance, every property owner needs to understand the broad principles of property and liability risk and insurance to purchase coverage wisely to protect against these perils. Second, property insurance coverage is required by mortgage lenders. Unless adequate protection against loss is in place, a lender will not advance the funds needed to purchase a property. Third, real estate property insurance is an important part of the business of many real estate brokerage firms because this activity complements their other activities and adds to the firms' profits.

In addition to discussing various aspects of property ownership, this chapter examines the homeowner's policy, including

- risks covered,
- personal articles floater policies,
- coinsurance,
- renter's and condominium owner's insurance, and
- liability insurance.

We also look at two special types of insurance of interest to homeowners:

- Flood insurance
- Mortgage life insurance

Finally, we examine property insurance for commercial property, particularly the businessowner's policy for small and medium-sized businesses.

■ RISKS OF PROPERTY OWNERSHIP

The ownership and use of real property involve several types of insurable **risk**—the chance of loss. These risks fall into four broad categories:

1. Loss of property because of fire, wind, water, vandalism, or other hazards
2. Loss of the use of property
3. Additional expenses resulting from the loss of use of property
4. Liability losses resulting from negligence in the use of property resulting in bodily injury, property damage, medical expenses, or related costs

In addition to the risk of real property loss, a family may suffer financial loss, particularly the inability to make mortgage payments, because of the death or disability of a wage earner.

All these hazards involve risk to the individual, family, or business. An individual may suffer a catastrophic fire that completely destroys his or her home and its furnishings. A family may lose its home through inability to meet mortgage payments after the head of the household dies. A business may face a large liability payment because a customer is injured in a fall on the premises. The financial consequences of each of these risks can be eliminated or lessened through insurance.

Insurance against risk is possible because of the law of large numbers: what is unpredictable for an individual becomes predictable for a large number of individuals. For example, most families never lose their homes to fire, and the probability that a single family will do so in any particular year is so small as to be unpredictable. But an insurer can predict potential losses from fires among a large group of insured properties with considerable accuracy. Such predictability makes it possible for a company to assume risk for an insured party through a **policy** (contract) on payment of a **premium** (fee).

Unless the company concentrates its coverage too heavily in one area, so that it might be affected very adversely by a natural disaster such as a hurricane or a massive forest fire, it should be able to pay the losses suffered by individual policyholders from policy income.

■ INSURANCE AGAINST PROPERTY LOSSES

Property insurance protects the policyholder against direct and indirect losses on insured risks. **Direct losses** are the costs of replacing or repairing property destroyed or damaged. **Indirect losses** are the additional living expenses or losses of business income suffered before the property can be restored. **Liability insurance** protects the insured against lawsuits brought in response to supposed acts of negligence that result in injury or loss of property to the public.

TABLE 19.1	Coverage under the HO-3 Homeowner's Policy

Coverage	Loss Covered	Amount
A	Dwelling	Minimum of $20,000
B	Other structures	10% of coverage A
C	Personal property	50% of coverage A
D	Loss of use	20% of coverage A
E	Personal liability	$100,000
F	Medical payments to others	$1,000 per person, $25,000 per accident

The Homeowner's Policy

The **homeowner's policy** is designed as a single package to provide coverage of losses from fire and other perils, personal liability, medical payments, and theft. It is required by mortgage lenders and prudent homeowners. Under the most widely used form, HO-3, the homeowner must purchase at least $20,000 coverage on the dwelling, with other coverages as shown in Table 19.1.

These amounts can be modified to meet most needs. For example, a property owner might purchase $100,000 coverage on his or her dwelling (coverage A). In this case, other structures on the residential premises, such as garages or pool houses, are covered for $10,000 (coverage B) and personal property for $50,000 (coverage C). Special limits of liability exist for certain items—for example, $200 for money, bank notes, and precious metals; $2,000 for guns; $2,500 for silverware, goldware, and pewterware; $2,500 for business property on the premises; and only $250 for business property away from the premises. Thus, if you have a $5,000 computer, you should increase coverage on this item. These special limits and the total amount of insurance may be increased by payment of a larger premium.

Some items of personal property are not covered. These include

■ animals, birds, and fish;

■ motorized vehicles, except nonlicensed vehicles such as mowers used in the maintenance of the premises or electric wheelchairs (Motorized vehicles are insured under automobile policies.);

■ aircraft;

■ property of unrelated roomers;

■ business property;

■ sound equipment such as tape players and tapes used in motor vehicles; and

■ separately described property specifically insured. (This exclusion prevents the insured from collecting twice for a loss on the same item.)

Coverage D provides payment for additional living expenses if the residence is made uninhabitable by one of the covered perils. If the home in our example was damaged by a runaway truck or a fire and could not be occupied for two months while repairs were being made, the insurer would pay the necessary increased living expenses for the family up to $10,000.

Personal liability (coverage E) and medical payments to others (coverage F) will be discussed later in this chapter, when we consider liability insurance.

Replacement Cost Coverage

In the homeowner's policy, payment for loss or damage to personal property normally is limited to **actual cash value,** generally interpreted to mean the cost of replacing the destroyed or damaged property minus the amount by which the property had fallen in value as a result of normal wear and tear since it was new. Thus, a six-year-old television set originally costing $450 that would cost $500 to replace today might have an actual cash value of only $200. In other words, it would have a market value of $200. Unless the household furnishings, clothing, and other personal property in a home are virtually new, the difference between replacement cost and actual cash value could be financially devastating, even if the peril was covered by insurance.

Fortunately, the homeowner can purchase a **personal property replacement cost endorsement,** which allows the policyholder to recoup the full replacement cost of stolen or damaged goods. Replacement cost is limited to 400 percent of the actual cash value at the time of loss and excludes art, antiques, stamps, coins, and other collectibles, as these items often are difficult or impossible to replace. Coverage of such special items requires a separate floater rider.

Personal Articles Floater Policies

Suppose a family collects antique porcelains, guns, or coins; or perhaps Great-Aunt Mabel left the family several pieces of valuable heirloom jewelry. Because of the limitations in the homeowner's policy, these items probably are not fully covered. For this protection, a **personal articles floater policy** can be obtained. This insures specific scheduled (listed) property for specific amounts. It usually is necessary to be able to establish the value of articles that are insured, sometimes through a qualified appraisal.

Credit Card Forgery and Counterfeit Money Losses

The personal property portion of the homeowner's policy also covers losses of up to $1,000 from the unauthorized use of a policyholder's credit card. In addition, it covers losses that might occur when the policyholder accepts counterfeit money or when someone forges the policyholder's name on a check.

Factors Influencing Rates

Homeowner's insurance rates are influenced by a number of factors, including location, type of construction, and amount of deductibles. A house located in a community that has a highly rated fire department and an adequate water supply is much less likely to suffer a severe fire loss than a house located in a rural area with no fire department. Thus, the owner of the house in the urban area will pay a lower insurance rate per $1,000 of coverage than the owner of the house in the unprotected rural area. Other rate classifications fall in between these extremes. A suburban house located more than five miles from a fire station will pay a higher rate than one located near a fire station, as will the house located more than 1,000 feet from a fire hydrant.

Type of construction also affects insurance rates. Whatever its other virtues, a wooden house is more susceptible to fire than a masonry house; a wooden roof catches fire more easily than one covered with fiberglass shingles. In general, the more fire-resistant the construction of a home, the lower its insurance rates.

Whatever the type of construction, it is possible to reduce insurance rates by reducing the chance of loss. For example, many companies offer discounts for the installation of burglar and fire alarm systems, sprinkler systems, or smoke alarms.

Another way to reduce premiums is to increase the amount of deductibles. The homeowner's policy is written with a deductible, usually $250, for any one occurrence. If lightning strikes the house and destroys a new $700 television, for example, the insurance company would pay $450 ($700 minus the $250 deductible). Increasing the deductible will reduce the premium, but the homeowner then becomes a self-insurer for the deductible and must be prepared to cover this additional loss.

Coinsurance

Actual cash value (replacement cost less depreciation) is paid for losses to personal property under the homeowner's policy. Replacement cost without deduction for depreciation up to the face value of the policy is paid for losses to the building under coverages A and B, however.

Full payment for partial losses to buildings under the homeowner's policy is made only if insurance equal to 80 percent of the replacement cost of the building was carried at the time of loss. If not, the policyholder becomes a coinsurer with the company. **Coinsurance** is the joint assumption of risk by two or more parties. In that case, the policy pays only (1) the actual cash value of the loss or (2) "that proportion of the cost to repair or replace, without deduction for depreciation, of that part of the building damaged, which the total amount of insurance in [the] policy on the damaged building bears to 80% of the replacement cost of the building."

Let us illustrate with a simple example. Suppose that Roger and Laura Whitaker's house has a replacement cost of $100,000, and they carry $80,000 in insurance. The Whitakers suffer $20,000 in damages to the home when a portion of the roof collapses after a record snow and sleet storm. How much would they recover from the insurance company? The percentage of recovery is determined by the following formula:

$$\frac{\text{Amount of insurance coverage}}{80\% \text{ of replacement cost of the building}} = \text{Percentage}$$

In this case, all of the loss will be paid by the company:

$$\frac{\$80,000}{\$80,000} = 1, \text{ or } 100 \text{ percent}$$

Suppose, however, that the Whitakers carried only $60,000 worth of insurance on the building. In that case, the Whitakers would recover only 75 percent ($7,500) of the loss:

$$\frac{\$60,000}{\$80,000} = .75 \text{ or } 75 \text{ percent}$$

Why do companies include a coinsurance clause? Most insurance claims do not involve a total loss. Consequently, in the absence of the coinsurance clause, the policyholder who carried insurance covering only partial value would receive greater relative benefits than one who carried full coverage. Suppose, for example, that the Springers and the Michauds each live in a ten-year-old house having a $100,000 replacement value. The Springers carry $100,000 worth of insurance on their home, while the Michauds carry only $60,000. In case of total loss, the Springers' insurance proceeds would be adequate to replace their house, while the Michauds would receive only $60,000. Suppose, however, that each suffered a $20,000 loss. Again, the Springers would be fully compensated, but if the Michauds also were paid $20,000, they obviously would be receiving much more for their insurance dollar. Under the coinsurance clause, however, the Michauds would recover only 75 percent of their loss:

$$\frac{\$60,000}{\$80,000} = .75 \text{ or } 75 \text{ percent}$$

As inflation boosts replacement costs, it becomes increasingly important to evaluate the amount of coverage on one's home, as the subjects of the Case Study on page 415 discovered. An alternative is to include a replacement cost endorsement, a common feature in homeowner's policies.

Renter's and Condominium Owner's Insurance

Renters and condominium or cooperative owners do not need insurance on their dwelling units because this coverage is provided by the landlord or the condominium or cooperative association. However, they do need coverage for their personal property and personal liability. Consequently, special versions of the homeowner's policy are designed for renters and condominium owners.

Form HO-4 covers a tenant's personal property against loss or damage and also provides personal liability insurance. If the insured makes any alterations or additions to the dwelling, losses of this property are covered for up to 10 percent of the amount of personal property coverage.

Form HO-6 is designed for the owners of condominium units and cooperative apartments. In addition to coverage for personal property and personal liability, the policy provides a minimum of $1,000 of insurance for alterations, appliances, fixtures, and other improvements that are not covered by the condominium or cooperative association's insurance on the dwelling.

The Impact of Inflation on Adequacy of Insurance Coverage

Jim and Joan Foil insured their home in suburban Birmingham, Alabama, for $70,000 when they bought it about nine years ago. Even though they paid $90,000 for the property, Jim considered the amount of insurance adequate because the lot represented $15,000 of the total cost. Furthermore, even a disastrous fire would not destroy the driveway, foundation, and water and sewer lines.

Case Study

One night, Jim poured vegetable oil in his popcorn popper, plugged it in, and then forgot it. When he remembered and removed the lid, the hot oil blazed up fiercely. By the time the firefighters left four hours later, the house and furnishings had suffered $35,000 in fire, smoke, and water damage.

The next day, the Foils got another shock. Because they had ignored their insurance agent's advice to add coverage as inflation increased building costs, the loss was not fully covered. The Foils were considered coinsurers.

For the loss to be fully covered, the Foils would have needed to carry approximately $98,000 in insurance, 80 percent of the estimated replacement cost of $122,500. Because they had only $70,000 in coverage, the insurance company would pay only 71 percent of the loss ($70,000 ÷ $98,000). The family had to dig into its savings for $10,150 to complete the repairs. Previous plans for a European vacation and new furniture had to be forgotten.

Suppose that events had taken another turn. When the oil blazed up, Jim had the presence of mind to put the top back on the popper and smother the fire. The kitchen suffered only minor smoke damage. But Jim did some hard thinking about what might have happened, and the next day, he phoned his insurance agent, Judy Akers, and asked about increasing the coverage. Judy estimated replacement cost for the Foils' home at approximately $126,566, using the simplified cost guide shown on the following pages.

The Foils raised the amount of their insurance to $115,000, considerably above the 80 percent required but still less than full coverage. They again reasoned that the chances of a total loss were small and that, in any case, the foundation and other such improvements would not be destroyed. They resolved, however, to carefully check their coverage each year to make sure they were keeping up with the inflation in replacement costs.

The Modified Coverage Form HO-8

Owners of older homes (usually those located in urban neighborhoods) often have a problem because the replacement cost of their properties is considerably greater than the market value. For example, a house may have a replacement cost of $100,000, but a market value of only $60,000. So that he or she does not become a coinsurer under a standard homeowner's policy, the owner would have to carry at least $80,000 in coverage on the dwelling. The owner may be quite reluctant to do this on a house worth only $60,000, and the insurer may also be reluctant to insure the house for that amount. Thus, to provide homeowner's insurance for these properties, the HO-8 form was developed.

Under the HO-8 form, losses are paid based on the amount required to repair or replace a property using common construction materials and methods, not on replacement cost. In addition, theft coverage is limited to $1,000 per occurrence

Home Cost Estimator

61 74091-20 S

You need 80% of replacement cost to cover partial dwelling losses without depreciation. You should have 100% of replacement cost to cover a TOTAL loss (if eligible, a special endorsement can be added to maintain 100% replacement). The intent of this ESTIMATOR is to furnish an easy method for <u>approximating</u> the cost to rebuild under AVERAGE circumstances. Higher valued homes or unique construction might require a different approach. In either case, get in touch with us. WE CAN HELP.

NAME _Jim and Joan Foil_   POLICY # _AX53B2_
ADDRESS _1653 Wiltshire Rd, Birmingham Alabama_   ZIP _35263_
STREET   CITY   STATE

STEP 1   CONSTRUCTION YEAR CLASSES

Read the following class descriptions and select the one that **most nearly** applies to your home.

1980 TO PRESENT / PRE-1980 CLASSES

Class A/AA
- simple rectangular shape
- one-foot roof overhang
- inexpensive floor coverings
- painted or simulated wood-grain softwood cabinets

CLASS A

Class B/BB
- rectangular or L-shaped
- one-and-one-half-foot roof overhang
- basic grade floor coverings
- moderate hardwood kitchen cabinetry
- average materials and quality

CLASS B

Class C/CC
- larger L-shape or rectangle
- one-and-one-half-foot roof overhang
- above-average hardwood cabinets
- carpeting, vinyl, hardwood, and ceramic tile floors
- average to above-average materials and quality

CLASS C

Class D/DD
- two-foot roof overhang
- carpeting, hardwood, slate and ceramic tile floors
- extra baths are common and adjoin bedrooms
- large rooms and special purpose rooms
- usually custom designed by architect for owner
- above-average materials and quality

CLASS D

PRE-1940 CLASSES

Class X
- similar to Basic Class A
- plain box-shaped design
- one-foot roof overhang
- minimal softwood cabinetry
- hardwood and linoleum floors

CLASS X

Class Y
- similar to Basic Class B
- one-and-one-half-foot roof overhang
- adequate hardwood cabinetry and trim
- dining room and porches common
- plaster walls and ceilings
- hardwood, linoleum and ceramic tile floors
- average materials and quality

CLASS Y

Class Z
- similar to Basic Class C
- large rectangular shaped design
- one-and-one-half-foot roof overhang
- ample hardwood cabinetry
- large dining room, foyer and porch common
- plaster walls and ceilings
- hardwood, vinyl and ceramic tile, and slate floors
- average to above-average materials and quality

CLASS Z

STEP 2   UNIT COUNT

Enter number of units

Count	Unit
1	Living Room
3	Bedrooms
2	Bathrooms (3 or more fixtures)
1	Kitchen
1	Dining Room
1	Family and/or Recreation Room
	Den, Study, or Office
	Unfinished Attic (not crawl space)
	Unfinished Basement
	Stone Exterior Walls
	Clay Tile or Slate Roof
1	Two-Car Attached Garage
	Two-Car Built-in Garage
	Three-Car Carport
	Double-Size Rooms (over 300 sq. ft.)
10	Total multiplied by 3 = 30 (a)
	Dinette or Breakfast Nook
1	Half Baths (2 or less fixtures)
1	Laundry Room with Adjacent Half Bath
	Brick Exterior Walls
1	Central Air Conditioning
	Enclosed Porch
	One-Car Attached Garage
	One-Car Built-in Garage
	One or Two-Car Carport
	Large Rooms (200 to 300 sq. ft.)
3	Total multiplied by 2 = 6 (b)
	Foyer or Entrance Hall
	Walk-in Closet or Dressing room
1	Work, Storage, or Laundry Room
	Open Porch, Breezeway, or Large Deck
1	Fireplace
2	Total — Repeat here = 2 (c)

ADD a + b + c for UNIT COUNT	38

STEP 3   BASE COSTS

Locate the construction year class column below (from Step 1). In the class columns find the Base Cost opposite the unit count (from Step 2).

UNIT COUNT	1980 TO PRESENT CLASSES A	B	C	D	PRE-1980 CLASSES AA	BB	CC	DD	PRE-1940 CLASSES X	Y	Z
25	$ 37,400	$ 49,200	$ 64,500	$ 79,700	$ 42,800	$ 55,100	$ 68,900	$ 84,600	$ 53,100	$ 64,000	$ 74,800
26	38,800	51,100	66,900	82,800	44,500	57,200	71,500	87,900	55,200	66,400	77,700
27	40,400	53,100	69,600	86,000	46,200	59,500	74,300	91,300	57,300	69,000	80,700
28	41,900	55,100	72,200	89,300	47,900	61,700	77,100	94,800	59,500	71,600	83,800
29	43,300	57,000	74,700	92,300	49,600	63,800	79,800	98,000	61,600	74,100	86,600
30	44,800	59,000	77,300	95,600	51,300	66,100	82,600	101,500	63,700	76,700	89,700
31	46,400	61,000	79,900	98,800	53,100	68,300	85,400	104,900	65,900	79,300	92,700
32	47,800	62,900	82,400	101,900	54,700	70,400	88,100	108,200	67,900	81,800	95,600
33	49,300	64,900	85,000	105,100	56,500	72,700	90,900	111,600	70,100	84,400	98,600
34	50,800	66,900	87,600	108,400	58,200	74,900	93,700	115,100	72,300	87,000	101,700
35	52,300	68,800	90,100	111,500	59,900	77,100	96,300	118,300	74,300	89,400	104,600
36	53,800	70,800	92,700	114,700	61,600	79,300	99,100	121,800	76,500	92,000	107,600
37	55,300	72,800	95,400	117,900	63,300	81,500	101,900	125,200	78,600	94,600	110,700
38	56,800	74,700	97,900	121,000	65,000	83,700	104,600	128,500	80,700	97,100	113,500
39	58,300	76,700	100,500	124,300	66,700	85,900	107,400	131,900	82,800	99,700	116,600
40	59,800	78,700	103,100	127,500	68,500	88,100	110,200	135,400	85,000	102,300	119,600
41	61,300	80,600	105,600	130,600	70,100	90,300	112,800	138,600	87,000	104,800	122,500
42	62,800	82,600	108,200	133,800	71,900	92,500	115,600	142,100	89,200	107,400	125,600
43	64,300	84,600	110,800	137,100	73,600	94,800	118,400	145,500	91,400	110,000	128,600
44	65,700	86,500	113,300	140,100	75,300	96,900	121,100	148,800	93,400	112,500	131,500
45	67,300	88,500	115,900	143,400	77,000	99,100	123,900	152,200	95,600	115,100	134,500
46	68,800	90,500	118,600	146,600	78,700	101,400	126,700	155,700	97,700	117,700	137,600
47	70,200	92,400	121,000	149,700	80,400	103,500	129,400	158,900	99,800	120,100	140,400
48	71,700	94,400	123,700	152,900	82,100	105,700	132,200	162,400	102,000	122,700	143,500
49	73,300	96,400	126,300	156,200	83,900	108,000	135,000	165,800	104,100	125,300	146,500
50	74,800	98,400	128,900	159,400	85,600	110,200	137,800	169,200	106,300	127,900	149,600
51	76,200	100,300	131,400	162,500	87,300	112,300	140,400	172,500	108,300	130,400	152,500
52	77,700	102,300	134,000	165,700	89,000	114,600	143,200	176,000	110,500	133,000	155,500
53	79,300	104,300	136,600	169,000	90,700	116,800	146,000	179,400	112,600	135,600	158,500
54	80,700	106,200	139,100	172,000	92,400	118,900	148,700	182,700	114,700	138,100	161,400
55	82,200	108,200	141,700	175,300	94,100	121,200	151,500	186,100	116,900	140,700	164,500
56	83,800	110,200	144,400	178,500	95,900	123,400	154,300	189,500	119,000	143,300	167,500
57	85,200	112,100	146,900	181,600	97,500	125,600	156,900	192,800	121,100	145,700	170,400
58	86,700	114,100	149,500	184,800	99,300	127,800	159,700	196,300	123,200	148,300	173,400
59	88,200	116,100	152,100	188,100	101,000	130,000	162,500	199,700	125,400	150,900	176,500
60	89,700	118,000	154,600	191,200	102,700	132,200	165,200	203,000	127,400	153,400	179,400
add for each additional unit over 60	+1,500	+2,000	+2,600	+3,200	+1,700	+2,200	+2,800	+3,400	+2,100	+2,600	+3,000

STEP 4   LOCATION MULTIPLIERS

Use your zip code to select a multiplier.

ALABAMA
350-351 . . . . 1.20
352 . . . . 1.21
354 . . . . 1.20
355 . . . . 1.19
356-358 . . . . 1.15
359 . . . . 1.16
360 . . . . 1.15
361, 369 . . . . 1.16
362 . . . . 1.16
363 . . . . 1.13
364-365 . . . . 1.20
366 . . . . 1.22
367 . . . . 1.15
368 . . . . 1.13

FLORIDA
320, 322 . . . . 1.19
321 . . . . 1.20
323 . . . . 1.13
324 . . . . 1.21
325 . . . . 1.22
326 . . . . 1.18
327 . . . . 1.31
328, 347 . . . . 1.31
329 . . . . 1.25
330-331, 333 . . . . 1.41
334 . . . . 1.44
335-337, 346 . . . . 1.27
338 . . . . 1.25
339 . . . . 1.43
342 . . . . 1.29
344 . . . . 1.18
349 . . . . 1.32

GEORGIA
300, 303 . . . . 1.26
301-302 . . . . 1.25
304, 313-314 . . . . 1.16
305-306 . . . . 1.19
307 . . . . 1.18
308-309 . . . . 1.15
310 . . . . 1.13
312 . . . . 1.14
315 . . . . 1.14
316 . . . . 1.13
317 . . . . 1.13
318 . . . . 1.13
319 . . . . 1.12

KENTUCKY
400-402 . . . . 1.27
403-404, 406-409 . . . . 1.22
405 . . . . 1.23
410 . . . . 1.36
411-412 . . . . 1.29
413-414, 417-418 . . . . 1.24
415-416 . . . . 1.27
420 . . . . 1.28
421, 427 . . . . 1.26
422-424 . . . . 1.28
425-426 . . . . 1.26

MICHIGAN
480, 482-483 . . . . 1.57
481 . . . . 1.56
484-485 . . . . 1.43
486-487 . . . . 1.38
488 . . . . 1.40
489, 492 . . . . 1.42

MICHIGAN cont.
490-491 . . . . 1.36
493-495 . . . . 1.32
496-497 . . . . 1.29
498 . . . . 1.39
499 . . . . 1.33

NORTH CAROLINA
270 . . . . 1.36
271 . . . . 1.38
272-273 . . . . 1.38
274 . . . . 1.38
275 . . . . 1.46
276-277 . . . . 1.49
278 . . . . 1.26
279 . . . . 1.26
280-281 . . . . 1.38
282 . . . . 1.42
283 . . . . 1.28
284 . . . . 1.26
285 . . . . 1.20
286 . . . . 1.19
287-289 . . . . 1.19

OHIO
430-431 . . . . 1.34
432 . . . . 1.36
433 . . . . 1.35
434, 436 . . . . 1.43
435 . . . . 1.38
437-438 . . . . 1.34
439 . . . . 1.38
440 . . . . 1.47
441 . . . . 1.51
442-443 . . . . 1.46

OHIO cont.
444-445 . . . . 1.39
446-447 . . . . 1.39
448 . . . . 1.37
449 . . . . 1.36
450 . . . . 1.34
451 . . . . 1.34
452 . . . . 1.34
453-455 . . . . 1.37
456 . . . . 1.34
457 . . . . 1.34
458 . . . . 1.36

SOUTH CAROLINA
290-291 . . . . 1.18
292 . . . . 1.20
293, 296 . . . . 1.17
294 . . . . 1.23
295 . . . . 1.15
297-298 . . . . 1.12
299 . . . . 1.22

TENNESSEE
370-371, 384 . . . . 1.19
372 . . . . 1.20
373 . . . . 1.17
374 . . . . 1.18
376-378 . . . . 1.18
379 . . . . 1.19
380 . . . . 1.18
381 . . . . 1.19
382 . . . . 1.16
383 . . . . 1.18
385 . . . . 1.18

STEP 5   REPLACEMENT COST ESTIMATE

a. Enter the BASE COST from Step 3.

b. Enter the MULTIPLIER from Step 4 and multiply it by the base cost.

c. The result is the estimated replacement cost of your home.

$ 104,600	Base Cost
× 1.21	Location Multiplier
= $ 126,566	Estimated Replacement Cost

Taking Inventory Before the Disaster Occurs

Suppose you come home to find your home's back door forced open and the house ransacked. Or you are awakened by smoke and must flee for your life while fire destroys your home and its furnishings. As horrifying as these events are, they will soon be followed by a new ordeal—proving to the insurance adjuster what items of personal property you lost and their value.

Close-Up

To get a feel for how difficult this might be, try making from memory a complete inventory of all your clothes and kitchen utensils. Even though these items can add up to hundreds and even thousands of dollars, most homeowners would find this to be an extremely difficult task. They also would have a difficult time proving their loss to an insurance adjuster unless they previously had made an inventory, preferably backed up by a photographic record.

Suppose the burglars took your complete set of silverware for twelve. Could you prove to the adjuster you actually had a set of silverware for twelve? You could if you had a photograph in your bank safe-deposit box showing the silverware laid out on your dining room table. Or suppose the fire destroyed the valuable antique dining table and chairs left to you by Great-Aunt Matilda. When you put in a claim for these items to the insurance company for $10,000, the adjuster might regard you with some skepticism and ask you to prove this high value. Could you? You could if you had in your safe-deposit box an appraisal of your valuable items made by a professional appraiser, preferably backed by photographs, movies or videotapes, and bills of sale for other expensive items you purchased.

Making an Inventory and a Photographic Record

Making your own home inventory takes time and is somewhat tedious, but it is time well spent. Personal property inventory booklets are usually available from an insurance agent or a bookstore. These booklets often list items owned by most families and have spaces to list the year bought, the original cost, and the estimated current value.

Photographs are an excellent, and even essential, backup to the written inventory. Each room should be photographed from several angles to include all the furnishings, and separate photos should be taken of closets, cabinets, and drawers. It is also desirable to take individual photos of valuable items, including closeups of details. These photographs can be taken as slides (which take up little space and can be projected to help pick out details), as color prints (which can be included along with the written inventory in some inventory albums), as movies, or on videotape.

In addition to the inventory list and photographs, it is wise to include detailed descriptions of expensive items, along with sales receipts. For things such as stereos, televisions, and cameras, list the manufacturer, serial number, model, year of purchase, and original cost of each. For antiques or other collectibles, give descriptions and list such items as size, material, style, country of origin, inscriptions, where and when bought, and price paid. It may also be desirable to obtain professional appraisals of valuable items of this type.

Once the inventory has been completed, it serves two important functions. First, it can be used to check the adequacy of personal property insurance protection. Most people are quite surprised at the total value of their personal possessions, and many need to increase their personal property insurance coverage. Others find they have items such as valuable collections of silver, pewter, or fine art that are not fully covered under their homeowner's policies and require additional coverage.

Taking Inventory Before the Disaster Occurs (continued)

The second use of the inventory is to substantiate claims in the event of loss. The inventory should be stored in a safe place outside the home, preferably in a bank box. A copy might also be kept in an office, with the family lawyer or with the insurance agent. The place the inventory should not be kept is in the home; not only might the inventory be destroyed by fire, but

Clsoe-Up

providing this information to burglars would really help make their day.

An inventory of your possessions involves some cost and time, but it will be invaluable in proving loss to your insurance company. It can also help you check the adequacy of insurance coverage and aid the police in recovering any stolen property.

and applies only to losses that occur on the premises or in a bank or public warehouse.

■ EARTHQUAKE INSURANCE

Losses from earthquakes are not covered under the standard homeowner's policy. Fortunately, the chance of losses from earthquakes is very rare; however, when they occur, losses can be catastrophic. It is possible to purchase an earthquake endorsement to the homeowner's policy to cover this risk, but the cost is relatively high, and a deductible of up to 10 percent applies separately to coverages A, B, and C. For these reasons and the low probability of loss, few homeowners purchase this coverage. For example, total property losses caused by the 1989 San Francisco earthquake were estimated at more than $10 billion, but only $1 billion was covered by insurance.

■ LIABILITY INSURANCE

Liability insurance protects the insured against lawsuits brought in response to supposed acts of negligence that result in injury or loss of property to the public. For example, someone might be injured in a fall on ice-covered steps and sue for damages, claiming that the owner's failure to remove the ice promptly constituted negligence.

As shown in Table 19.1, coverage E of the homeowner's policy, personal liability, protects the property owner up to the limits of liability from damages for which the insured is legally liable to pay and also pays the cost of legal defense against such claims. Even though the standard homeowner's policy now provides $100,000 in liability protection, this does not provide enough protection for most homeowners, and it is wise to purchase additional coverage, perhaps including an umbrella liability policy (discussed in the following section).

Coverage F, medical payments, pays the necessary medical expenses of people injured on the premises except for residents and residence employees. For example, when Aunt Maude breaks her arm falling over the loose porch boards, she need not sue you to collect the money to pay her doctor's bill; this coverage will provide the money for the medical expenses.

The Personal Excess Liability Policy

A **personal excess liability policy,** or umbrella liability policy, protects you from disastrous liability claims involving a home, an automobile, or a boat. It is combined with liability coverage included under homeowner's and automobile insurance policies and provides no coverage until the maximum limits in these policies have been exceeded. Relatively high limits for these other policies are required, usually $300,000 for the homeowner's and $500,000 for the automobile insurance. Generally, the personal excess liability policy is subject to a $500 deductible for liability exposures not covered by homeowner's and automobile policies, such as lawsuits for libel, slander, and defamation of character. It excludes malpractice, professional liability, and business liability, as well as aircraft liability.

Given the high amounts of coverage, the cost of these policies is surprisingly low. This exact cost depends on a number of factors, but for a qualified person, generally, it is possible to acquire $2 million in coverage for less than $200 annually.

The umbrella policy should be considered essential, particularly in light of its low cost. Not only does the policy protect against large damage claims, it provides for the costs of legal fees in defending against such claims. These are often quite substantial.

■ FLOOD INSURANCE

People have shown their ignorance of nature throughout history by building on floodplains. Periodically, Mother Nature shows her displeasure with this practice by using the floodplains as they were intended to be used—as places to dump excess water. As a result, flood losses in the United States exceed $1 billion annually.

Private insurance companies have been unwilling to insure against flood damage because a major storm could result in financially disastrous losses. The National Flood Insurance Act of 1968 made federally subsidized flood insurance available to property owners in flood-prone areas, and in 1973, such insurance was ruled mandatory on all loans made by federally regulated banks and savings and loan associations in such areas.

The affected communities must enact certain land-use controls to minimize building on the floodplains and require that existing structures be floodproofed by raising them (or through other measures). These controls are designed to reduce the likelihood of flood losses, although critics charge that the subsidized insurance program actually has increased building on environmentally sensitive floodplains by reducing the financial risk of the practice. Whatever the merits of this argument, the homeowner who lives in a flood-prone area is well advised to carry this type of insurance.

■ MORTGAGE LIFE INSURANCE

Almost all younger families require a mortgage to purchase a house. Even in two-income families, the death of either wage earner may make it difficult or impossible for the family to continue to meet the mortgage payments, and thus, the home may be lost.

This risk can be eliminated through **mortgage life insurance,** a diminishing term life insurance policy whose amount is keyed to the outstanding mortgage balance. In case of the death of the insured, the policy proceeds will be available to pay off the mortgage, leaving the family home free of debt. Alternatively, of course, this risk can be covered by adding additional coverage under another life insurance policy. A lender cannot require that a borrower obtain mortgage life insurance as a condition of approving the loan. Note that mortgage *life* insurance and mortgage insurance are different concepts. Mortgage insurance, as discussed in Chapter 13, protects the lender rather than the borrower.

■ BUSINESSOWNER'S POLICY

Commercial property insurance is quite complex and generally beyond the scope of this chapter. However, we will examine the **businessowner's policy** (BOP), a package policy for small and medium-sized retail stores, office buildings, apartment buildings, and similar businesses that is very similar to the homeowner's policy for residences.

The businessowner's policy covers the following:

- ■ Buildings on a replacement cost basis. The amount of coverage is increased by a stated inflationary percentage each quarter.
- ■ Business personal property on a replacement cost basis.
- ■ Additional coverages, including debris removal, fire department service charges, business income losses, extra expenses, and pollutant cleanup and removal.
- ■ Optional coverages, which can cover outdoor signs, the building exterior, grade floor glass, burglary, robbery, and employee dishonesty.
- ■ Business liability insurance.

The standard deductible is $250 per occurrence for all property coverages, as well as for burglary, robbery, and employee dishonesty. The deductible does not apply to business income losses, extra expenses, and fire department service charges.

■ CHAPTER REVIEW

- ■ The three categories of risk associated with the ownership and use of real property are (1) loss of property because of some peril, (2) liability losses resulting from negligence in the use of property, and (3) financial losses because of the death or disability of the owner.

- ■ Insurance of risk is possible because of the law of large numbers: what is unpredictable for an individual becomes predictable for a large number of individuals.

- ■ Two types of property insurance losses exist: (1) direct losses—the costs of replacing or repairing the property destroyed or damaged; (2) indirect losses—the additional living expenses or losses of business income suffered before the property can be restored.

- ■ The homeowner's policy is designed as a single packet to provide coverage of losses from fire and other perils, personal liability, medical payments, and theft.

- ■ Full payment for repair or replacement of buildings damaged under a homeowner's policy is made only if insurance equal to 80 percent of the replacement cost of the building was carried at the time of loss. If not, the policyholder becomes a coinsurer with the company.

- ■ Federally subsidized flood insurance is available to property owners in flood-prone areas, provided that their communities enact certain land-use controls to minimize potential losses.

- ■ The risk that a family will lose its home because its members are unable to continue making mortgage payments following the death of a wage earner can be eliminated through mortgage life insurance.

- ■ The businessowner's policy is a package policy for small businesses that covers real and personal property, business liability, and other business property risks.

■ KEY TERMS

actual cash value	liability insurance	personal property replacement cost endorsement
businessowner's policy	mortgage life insurance	
coinsurance	personal articles floater policy	policy
direct losses		
homeowner's policy	personal excess liability policy	premium
indirect losses		risk

■ STUDY EXERCISES

1. What are the three categories of risk associated with the ownership and use of real property?

2. What is the law of large numbers, and why does it make the insurance of risk possible?

3. What is the difference between direct and indirect property losses?

4. In Table 19.1, which items are direct losses? Which are indirect losses?

5. Use the home cost estimator in this chapter to find the estimated replacement cost for a brick exterior, three-bedroom, two-and-a-half-bath home with living room, kitchen, separate dining room, family room, and laundry. The house also has an attached two-car garage, two fireplaces, and central air-conditioning. The style of this house is Class B, and it is located in the 303 zip code in Georgia.

6. For an identical home (see question 5) located in the 440 zip code in Ohio, how much difference would there be in estimated replacement cost?

7. If the house from question 5 is remodeled by adding another bedroom and enclosing the porch, how much additional replacement value would result?

8. What is replacement cost coverage, and why is it important for both personal property and the dwelling?

9. Define and describe the principle of coinsurance.

10. Joe and Ann Homeowner carry a $70,000 homeowner's policy on their house, which is valued at $100,000. If they suffered a $20,000 fire loss, what percentage of the loss would the insurance company pay?

11. The Owensbys paid $80,000 for their house in 1985 and insured it for that amount. The replacement cost of the house had escalated to $120,000 by 1996, when it was destroyed by fire. How much will the insurance company pay for the total loss?

12. Suppose the Owensbys (see question 11) had damage only to the kitchen that would cost $12,000 to repair. What amount would they be paid by the insurance company for the loss? How much insurance would they have needed to be reimbursed in full for the loss?

13. What is the purpose of liability insurance?

14. Why is it important for the owner of a condominium to carry condominium owner's insurance even though the condominium association carries insurance on the structure?

■ FURTHER READINGS

Baldwin, B. G., *The Complete Book of Insurance: The Consumer's Guide to Insuring Your Life, Health, Property, and Income.* Chicago: Irwin Professional Publishing, 1996.

Sloane, Leonard, *The New York Times Personal Finance Handbook.* New York: Random House, 1995.

20 Home Purchase Decisions

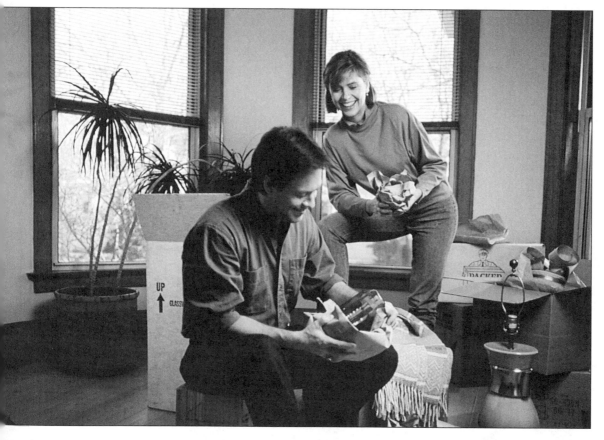

The American dream of home ownership requires thoughtful planning and careful decision making. The information presented in this book should prepare you well for your future real estate decisions.

Buing a home is the most important investment decision that the average U.S. family ever makes. Too often, however, it is made with the buyer at a distinct disadvantage and without the complete information needed to make the best choice at the most favorable terms. By now, you should be far better informed about real estate transactions than the usual homebuyer because you already know the basic principles of real estate.

This chapter covers four topics specifically related to buying a home:

■ The rent or buy decision

■ How much home you can afford

■ Choosing the right property

■ The negotiation, purchase, and closing process

■ THE RENT OR BUY DECISION

Everyone needs a place to live, and housing expense is a dominant portion of most families' budgets. A major question facing these families is the rent or buy decision.

Should you rent, or should you buy? That depends on a great number of factors, many of which are not economic. For example, many families derive great satisfaction from owning their own homes; to others, the responsibility of home ownership is a psychological burden.

To make the correct economic decision, you really need an all-seeing crystal ball that accurately reveals the

REAL ESTATE
TODAY
FEATURES

Case Study
The House that
Came Off the
Mountain

Close-Up
What Will Happen
to Home Prices

future. What will happen to home prices in the future? Will they rise, making your investment in a home more valuable? How much will they rise? Or will home prices fall, making your investment an unwise decision? What will happen to income tax laws that affect the deductions you can take for mortgage interest and property taxes? If these deductions are reduced or eliminated, home owner-ship will be relatively less desirable than renting. How long will you live in the home? Will your work require that you move within a relatively short time, or will you remain in the home for many years? Will you and your spouse contin-ue to live in marital bliss, or will you split, making your home just one more thing to fight over?

We could go on and on conjuring up more and more imponderables, but let's try to analyze the rent or buy decision based on some reasonable assumptions regarding the future. Suppose that Carlos and Mary Mallory, a financially successful young couple, are pondering the purchase of a home. They currently live in an apartment, which costs them $1,000 per month plus utilities, but they have found a $180,000 house they like. They can finance the home with a down payment of $36,000 and a 30-year, 7.5 percent, $144,000 mortgage. In addition to the down payment, closing costs on the loan will add $3,800 to the required investment.

Monthly payments for principal and interest on the mortgage will be $1,006.87, plus another $230 per month for property taxes and $80 for property insurance—a total of $1,316.87. The first year's interest charges will be approx-imately $10,755, and property taxes will total $2,760. These two items are deductible from taxable income, and for their analysis, Carlos and Mary assume a marginal federal and state tax rate of 30 percent. This means they can save $4,055 in income taxes during the coming year, or $337.88 per month, if they purchase the house. This reduces their after-tax monthly payment on the new home to $978.99, approximately the amount they currently pay in rent.

Of course, home ownership also entails additional maintenance expenses, but because the house is new, Carlos and Mary believe these will be relatively minor during the analysis period.

(The amount of income tax savings depends on many factors. With their assumed income of $79,200, the Mallorys are entitled to a standard deduction of $6,000. Until their itemized deductions exceed this amount, they gain no tax advantage. Let us assume that the Mallorys pay $4,000 in state income taxes, but they have no additional deductions other than the $2,760 in property taxes and $10,755 in mortgage interest. Under these assumptions, the tax savings would be only $3,245 annually, not $4,055, as assumed above. If they live in a state with no state income tax, the tax savings would be even less; however, if they have other allowable deductions, such as charitable contributions or unreimbursed employee expenses, their income tax savings from buying the house could equal or exceed the assumed $4,055. Life is not simple!)

Their jobs may require that the Mallorys move sometime in the next several years, but they do not know when that might occur or whether it will be nec-

TABLE 20.1	The Mallorys' Home Ownership Analysis

Assumptions

1. House will cost $180,000. It will appreciate 3 percent annually over five years. House will sell for $208,669 in five years.

2. Real estate sales commission will be 6 percent of sales price.

3. House will be financed by a down payment of $36,000 and a 30-year, 7.5 percent, $144,000 mortgage. Financing costs will be $3,800.

Sales price after five years	$208,669
Sales commission	12,520
Net sales receipts	$196,149
Loan repayment	136,249
Cash to Mallorys	$59,900
Cash after taxes	$55,055
Return on investment of $39,800 = 8.6% annually	
After-tax return on alternative investment = 4.3% annually	

essary or desirable at all. This is one of the uncertainties that make the rent or buy decision difficult. For this analysis, however, the Mallorys assume they will move after five years.

The next question is what will happen to home prices. This, of course, is a critical assumption. Carlos and Mary initially assume a 3 percent annual growth rate, but recognize that they must also analyze other possibilities.

Given these assumptions, the Mallorys arrive at the analysis summarized in Table 20.1. At a 3 percent annual rate of appreciation, the home can be sold for $208,669 in five years, or $196,149 after deducting a 6 percent real estate sales commission. From the mortgage loan repayment schedule in Table 20.2, we find that the principal of the mortgage has been reduced by only 5.4 percent, leaving a balance of $136,249.

After paying off the loan, the Mallorys would be left with $59,900, which would represent a 8.6 percent annual return on their $39,800 initial investment.

The Mallorys also would benefit from another Federal income tax break for homeowners. Profit on the sale of a principal residence up to $250,000 for individuals and $500,000 for married couples filing jointly is excluded from taxable income, and a taxpayer can claim this exemption every two years. In our example, Carlos and Mary would have a profit on the sale of their home of $16,149, but no income taxes would be due.

Alternative Investment

We must not forget that if Carlos and Mary do not buy the home, they can invest the $39,800 elsewhere. They might buy Amalgamated Whitzadiddle stock,

| TABLE 20.2 | Mortgage Loan Repayment Schedule |

Year	6%	7.5%	9%
1	1.2	.9	.7
2	2.5	1.9	1.4
3	3.9	3.0	2.2
4	5.4	4.1	3.1
5	6.9	5.4	4.1
6	8.6	6.7	5.2
7	10.4	8.3	6.4
8	12.2	9.7	7.6
9	14.2	11.4	9.0
10	16.3	13.2	10.6
15	28.9	24.6	20.7
20	46.0	41.1	36.5
25	69.0	65.1	61.2
30	100.0	100.0	100.00

which could be worth 100 times their initial investment. But Amalgamated Whitzadiddle might also go bankrupt, leaving their investment worthless. For simplicity, let's suppose the Mallorys invest the money very conservatively in U.S. government savings bonds, an investment that pays 6 percent annually, with income taxes on the interest not due until the bonds are cashed. This investment yields a 4.3 percent after-tax annual rate of return on the Mallorys' $39,800 investment—considerably less than the yield on the investment in the home.

Impact of Inflation or Deflation on Home Prices

Suppose, however, that Carlos and Mary purchase the home just before a period of rapid inflation, during which home prices rise 10 percent annually. Under this assumption, the Mallorys' house could be sold for $289,892 at the end of five years, yielding a profit of $92,498 after the sales commission and giving the Mallorys $136,249 in cash after they repay the loan. This would yield a 27.9 percent annual return on their investment of $39,800.

In this type of inflationary situation, it would be extremely likely that the cost of renting an apartment would also rise rapidly. If the cost of renting their apartment should rise at this assumed 10 percent annual rate, the Mallorys' $1,000-per-month apartment would cost $1,600 per month in five years. On the other hand, if they buy the house and finance the purchase with a fixed-rate mortgage, the mortgage payment would not rise. This is another factor that makes home ownership more advantageous in inflationary times.

Now, let's make the pessimistic but often realistic assumption that home prices decline by 3 percent annually during the five-year analysis period. Under this grim scenario, the Mallorys could sell their house for only $154,572 in five years, leaving them with $9,049 after paying a real estate brokerage commission and repaying the mortgage. This means they would lose $30,751 of their $39,800 investment—a decidedly negative return.

Are Carlos and Mary likely to experience a 10 percent annual increase in the value of their home during the analysis period? Probably not. Are they likely to experience a 3 percent annual decline? Probably not. But these extremes set realistic parameters for their analysis.

Impact of Mortgage Interest Rates

In this evaluation of the rent or buy decision, the Mallorys have benefited from a relatively low mortgage interest rate of 7.5 percent. Suppose, however, that the best rate they can obtain is 9 percent. This would affect the analysis in two principal ways. First, of course, the Mallorys would face much higher monthly payments for principal and interest—$1,158.66 compared with $1,006.87. This would make the total monthly payment $1,468.66, or $1,062 after taxes the first year assuming they benefit from the entire mortgage interest and property tax deduction.

In addition, as indicated in Table 20.2, the mortgage payback is much slower with the higher interest rate. If we assume our initial 3 percent annual rate of appreciation in home prices, the Mallorys will receive a lower cash return because they have a larger mortgage repayment—$138,067 compared with $136,249 with the 7.5 percent mortgage. This reduces their rate of return to only 5.9 percent annually.

Period of Ownership

Generally, because of the inflation in home prices, the longer the period of ownership, the greater the relative advantage of home ownership over renting. For example, let's return to our original assumptions for the Mallorys' rent versus buy analysis, with one exception.

Let's now assume that Carlos and Mary will own the home for ten years rather than five. The results of this analysis are shown in Table 20.3. The sales price of the house would increase to $241,905, leaving the Mallorys with $88,189 in cash after paying the brokerage commission and repaying the mortgage.

This represents a 10 percent after-tax annual rate of return on their original $39,800 investment. We might also note that if apartment rents increase at the same 3 percent annual rate, in ten years, the Mallorys will pay more than $1,345 a month if they stay in their apartment.

TABLE 20.3	The Mallory's Rent versus Buy Analysis—Ten-Year Ownership Period

Assumptions

1. House will cost $180,000. It will appreciate 3 percent annually over ten years. House will sell for $241,905 in ten years.

2. Real estate commission will be 6 percent of sales price.

3. House will be financed by a down payment of $36,000 and a 30-year, 7.5 percent, $144,000 mortgage. Financing costs will be $3,800.

Sales price after ten years	$241,905
Sales commission	14,514
Net sales receipts	$227,391
Loan repayment	124,985
Cash to Mallorys	$102,406

Return on investment of $39,800 in home = 10% annually
After-tax return on alternative investment = 4.3% annually

Some Conclusions

After all this, should Carlos and Mary rent, or should they buy? That depends on what assumptions they make regarding these future imponderables. However, at least we now know the parameters for the decision. Given the history of the past several decades, homeowners have done well compared to renters because their homes have served as hedges against inflation. Although it appears that rates of inflation will be lower in future years, don't count on it.

And what will happen to present income tax breaks enjoyed by homeowners? Will proponents of a flat tax remove the deductions for mortgage interest and property taxes? Will the tax forgiveness on the profit on the sale of a principal residence be done away with? We don't know, although these tax breaks have broad support.

Of course, the Mallorys' decision may well rest on noneconomic factors. Perhaps the intangibles of owning a home are very important to the Mallorys. Perhaps they love to garden and will enjoy working on their home. If so, they may want to buy even if they feel the investment probably will not be economically profitable. Or perhaps they hate yard work and all forms of home maintenance. They might want to be able to simply call the landlord when the heating system conks out, rather than having to deal with it themselves. If so, they may even be willing to pay a premium to live in a rental unit.

■ HOW MUCH CAN YOU AFFORD?

After working through the rent or buy analysis, Carlos and Mary decide that they want to explore the option of buying a house further. The next question is

TABLE 20.4	The Mallorys' Estimated Monthly Income	
	Salary (gross)	$6,200
	Self-employment income	500
	Dividends	300
	Interest on $20,000	100
	Total	$7,100

how much house can they afford? In other words, how big a mortgage can they expect a lender to extend, given their income and financial obligations? First, the Mallorys need to estimate their income, including gross salary, self-employment income, wages from a second job, dividends, interest, pensions, Social Security, rental income, and child support or alimony received, but excluding one-time events, such as inheritances, insurance settlements, and capital gains.

Carlos and Mary have combined gross monthly salaries of $6,200. In addition, Carlos earns an average of $500 monthly in tax work for outside clients and has done so for several years. Mary receives an average of $300 in dividends on some Amalgamated Whitzadiddle stock that she inherited from her uncle. They also receive $300 in monthly interest on $60,000 of savings and Mary's additional inheritance they have in a bank, but they would need to use almost $40,000 of this money for the down payment and closing costs if they buy the home they are considering. See Table 20.4 for a breakdown of the Mallorys' monthly income.

Next, the Mallorys calculate their monthly payments. These include items such as payments on loans for automobiles, furniture, appliances, boats or recreational vehicles, revolving credit, and student loans. Carlos and Mary's monthly payments, shown in Table 20.5, are $1,100: $450 for a car, $200 for furniture, $300 for revolving credit, and $150 for a student loan.

As noted earlier, lenders use qualifying ratios as rules of thumb to estimate maximum mortgage payments. Generally, these ratios range between 25/33 and 28/36. The first figure of both ratios is the percentage of gross income a lender

TABLE 20.5	The Mallorys' Monthly Payments	
	Car	$ 450
	Furniture	200
	Appliances	0
	Boat or recreational vehicle	0
	Revolving credit	300
	Student Loan	150
	Other	0
	Total	$1,100

will allow as a maximum monthly mortgage payment. For the Mallorys' $7,100 monthly gross income, this amount would range from the conservative 25 percent ($1,775) to the more generous 28 percent ($1,988).

The second calculation reduces this amount to account for payments on other indebtedness. Using the 33 percent conservative figure, a lender would calculate the Mallorys' maximum monthly payment as follows:

Monthly gross income	$7,100
Times 33% (one-third)	2,367
Less other monthly payments	1,100
Amount available for payment	$1,267

Using the more liberal 36 percent ratio, the maximum monthly payment could be $1,456. In other words, the Mallorys' maximum monthly payment would be reduced significantly to reflect the impact of their existing debts.

In addition to principal and interest, the typical house payment includes one-twelfth of yearly property taxes and property insurance. Thus, the $1,267 to $1,456 that Carlos and Mary have available for a monthly house payment must be reduced to reflect these items before the Mallorys can estimate the maximum mortgage they can afford. The amount of property taxes depends on several factors, including the value of the home and the community in which it is located. Property taxes for the house the Mallorys are considering would be $280 each month, with another $80 for property insurance. This means they are left with $957 to $1,146 for the actual mortgage payment.

Because the monthly payment for principal and interest on the 7.5 percent, 30-year, $144,000 loan they need to buy the house is $1,007, the Mallorys have adequate income to qualify for this loan. The fact that Mary owns the Amalgamated Whitzadiddle stock and they would still have $20,000 in the bank after expending $39,800 for the down payment and closing costs also makes them a more favorable credit risk.

■ CHOOSING A PROPERTY

Now that Carlos and Mary know the price range of the home they can afford, they need to decide whether their chosen house is really their best buy. The search for a home has two aspects. First, they must decide on a general area in which to look, and second, they must decide on a particular property. While the decision is very important, it is not one they will have to live with forever—the average first-time homebuyer moves after five years—and the decision must be based partly on the Mallorys' desires and preferences and what will appeal to prospective future buyers.

Choosing an Area

If the Mallorys buy in a small or medium-sized town, choosing an area may be quite uncomplicated. But if they live in a large metropolitan area, the choice can be quite complex. Let's suppose the latter is the case. Not only do Carlos and Mary have to decide what type of home they would like and what development they might like to live in, they must also choose a community.

The Mallorys begin their search by deciding how far they want to commute to work. Some people do not like commuting and choose residences that are close to their employment. Others will endure longer commutes to enjoy the suburban lifestyle they prefer. Carlos and Mary decide they will limit their hunt to a maximum commuting distance of 60 minutes during rush hour. Within this area, they concentrate on six basic criteria for choosing one community over another:

1. Property tax base
2. Quality of general public services
3. Available recreational facilities
4. Quality of public school system
5. Crime statistics
6. Overall quality of community

Property Tax Base and Quality of Public Services

In a metropolitan area, property tax rates and the quality of public services can vary considerably from one community to another. Other things equal, a low tax rate is desirable if it is not achieved by cutting necessary services. Both factors are important.

Available Recreational Facilities

Good public recreational facilities and established sports programs may be very important factors in locational decisions for some families. For others, they may not be important at all. Carlos and Mary, who have no children, are much more interested in access to cultural events and good shopping.

Quality of Public School System

Having no children, the Mallorys are not concerned significantly about the local school system, although they know it may be quite important in the future. In addition, they realize that quality of schools probably will be a vital consideration for potential future buyers of their home.

Crime Statistics

Carlos and Mary, like most homebuyers today, are very concerned about their security. Thus, crime statistics and the quality of the local police force are extremely important considerations in their locational decision.

Overall Quality of Community

In the final analysis, the locational decision may come down to what the Mallorys perceive as the overall quality of the community. Is it attractive? Does it control signage, or are its thoroughfares visual litterboxes? Are homes in the community well maintained? And, finally, does the community control its growth and require quality real estate development, or does mediocrity abound? The answers to these questions may be based partly on fact and partly on perception, but the quality of a community is vital to property values.

Many sources of information are available on these community factors, including real estate agents, building and real estate publications, and bankers or lenders. Another extremely good source of information is people in a neighborhood. If they respond favorably to inquiries about their area, this almost certainly indicates a desirable community.

Evaluating the Individual Home

Even more than the selection of a community or housing area, selection of an individual property is governed by personal preferences. Carlos and Mary prefer a home with traditional architecture, for example, and want large, open rooms that are good for entertaining.

If a house has a swimming pool, they will not even consider buying it because neither likes to swim, and they don't want the maintenance burden that goes with a pool. To others, a pool would be a very desirable feature.

Despite these individual preference items, all homebuyers should consider certain basic factors. The first rule is to buy a home that is less expensive than the average for the neighborhood. The more expensive homes will tend to raise its value. Conversely, never buy the most expensive home in a neighborhood. The others will drag down its value.

Also, look carefully at other factors that affect a home's investment potential. Does it have a good exterior design? Is the floor plan well arranged? Does it have convenient traffic flow? Is the home well placed on the lot? Is the lot well drained, with good landscaping?

Finally, the structural integrity of the home is extremely important, as the Case Study on page 437 shows. In fact, even if the home is new, but particularly if it is not, it may be very prudent to have the home inspected by a professional. But there are many items that anyone armed with a flashlight and a bit of common sense can examine. Carlos and Mary did this with several houses they considered, covering the following items:

Attic

Does inspection of the attic reveal water leaks or signs of rodent infestation? Are insulation and ventilation adequate?

Walls and Ceilings

Are there cracks in plaster walls or ceilings? Are seams in wallboard smooth and invisible?

REAL ESTATE TODAY

The House That Came Off the Mountain

Case Study

Why should you obtain a professional home inspection before you purchase a home? Let's look at a dramatic example.

Philip and Phyllis McDonald (not their real name) bought a mountainside house with a spectacular view in an exclusive resort area of western North Carolina. Even though the house had a 40-foot-high concrete block foundation wall on the downhill side, the McDonalds did not have the house inspected before they purchased it for $375,000. They should have!

Less than six years later, the McDonalds came up from Florida to open their summer mountain home. That night, Philip awoke to hear loud cracking noises. The next day, he had the house inspected by a local contractor and later by an engineer. Both informed him that the structure was very unsafe and could collapse at any time. They noted separated and bulging foundation walls, twisted nd leaning deck supports, separation of roof sections and walls, and separation of concrete blocks throughout the basement area. The house was in such dangerous and deteriorated condition that the only practical course of action was to move out immediately and have the house demolished. The demolition cost $25,000.

The McDonalds, sadder but wiser, suffered a loss of more than $400,000. They could not recover anything from their homeowner's insurance policy because no "occurrence" caused the loss. For the same reason, they could not claim a casualty loss on their income tax return. The contractor who built the home had gone out of business, so the McDonalds were advised that legal action against him was not practical. The loss fell on them alone.

This financial tragedy could have been avoided if the McDonalds had only spent perhaps $200 to have the house inspected before they bought it, as any qualified inspector could have spotted the inadequate construction methods and the potential for disaster. This sad tale also points out the need for adequate building codes to protect consumers.

Floors

What is the condition of the flors? Do they show signs of buckling or sagging? What is the condition of any carpets?

Roof

Does the roof show signs of wear? An asphalt roof usually lasts only 15 to 20 years, for example, and bare spots can mean it will have to be replaced soon.

Basement or Crawlspace

Are there signs of water damage under the house? If so, a professional should evaluate the problem. Is there evidence of rot or termites? Almost all lenders require an inspection by a professional from a pest control firm.

Electrical System

A professional should inspect the electrical system, but the potential buyer can check some important things on his or her own. For example, does the home have adequate electrical capacity? A modern home should have at least a 150-ampere entrance. Are there enough outlets throughout the home?

Heating and Cooling System

How old is the heating and air-conditioning system? Older units are less efficient and may need to be replaced soon. Again, the services of a professional may be necessary.

Water Supply and Waste Disposal

If the home is connected to a municipal water and sewerage system, the potential buyer need worry about only the adequacy of the household plumbing. If the home depends on a well, the water should be tested before purchase. Is the supply adequate throughout the year? How old is the pump? If the home uses a septic tank disposal system, this also needs to be checked by a professional. In many states, inspection by the state health department is required before the property can be sold.

Two Final Thoughts

Following these guidelines can help you make an informed decision regarding where and what home to buy. And remember—you can always find a buyer for a good home in a good location. Take the time and effort to do the job right.

Finally, remember that this home is probably not your last. Consider your future needs, but unless you are an extremely unusual buyer, you will move in a few years.

■ MAKING AND CLOSING THE DEAL

Carlos and Mary have now completed the preliminary steps to buying a home. They have determined how much home they can afford. They have researched communities and specific neighborhoods and developments to determine where they might like to locate. They also have learned some of the factors they should look for in a home and have thought carefully about what features are important to them.

Now they are ready to choose a property, negotiate its purchase, obtain financing, and close the deal.

In this process, always remember one thing: in the normal sales transaction, no one works for you. The real estate broker works for the seller (unless you have hired a buyer's broker); the lender works for the mortgage company; even the closing attorney, whose fee you pay, does not really look out for your interests. This does not mean that these people are dishonest or out to cheat you, but *they do not work for you.* It is not their job to look out for your interests.

The Real Estate Agent

A real estate broker or salesperson can be a valuable source of information on neighborhoods and homes for sale. He or she can also save you considerable time by narrowing your search to properties that might really fit your needs and desires. But remember, unless you hire an agent specifically to represent you, the real estate broker does not work for you. The broker works for the seller and is legally bound to represent the seller's interests, not yours. Even though the salesperson spends long hours showing you around town, taking you to lunch and, in general, being a wonderful person, don't forget that simple fact. For example, you certainly shouldn't tell the agent that you probably would be willing to make a higher offer on a particular house. The agent is duty bound to take that information to the seller, thereby weakening your position.

As discussed earlier in this book, buyers are increasingly being represented by buyer's brokers. This may be a very good idea, particularly when you move to a community that you do not know thoroughly.

The Negotiating Process

Suppose you have found a home that fits your needs. Now comes the tricky part—negotiating a price and terms. In this process, there are two rules:

1. Set a top limit above which you will not go.
2. Be prepared to walk away from the deal.

If you fall in love with a home and just have to have it, you are in a very poor bargaining position. Be prepared to walk away. On the other hand, if you really have found the home of your dreams, it may be worth spending a little more to get it, rather than going through the time-consuming process of extending the search. But be certain it really is the home you want. Don't fall in love with the first thing you see.

Not everyone, and particularly not a first-time homebuyer, is an experienced and shrewd negotiator. This may be one more reason to engage an agent to represent your interests. For one thing, the buyer's broker probably knows conditions in the market better than you do. Your agent may know that the house you are considering has been on the market for some time, and the owners are eager to sell. This information may place you in position to obtain a much better deal, which may more than pay for your representative's fee.

Finally, don't forget a fundamental rule of contracts: Verbal agreements are not worth the paper they are written on. Unless something is written down as part of a contract, it is *not* part of the contract. If promises or agreements are made, be certain they are contained in the written contract. If not, they are worthless.

What Will Happen to Home Prices?

Perhaps the most critical element in the rent or buy decision is the question of future home prices. Thus, let us examine the question of what is likely to happen to home prices in the United States over the next two decades.

Close-Up

The change in home prices depends on many factors, particularly changes in population, the level of general inflation, general economic growth, and growth or decline in the local economy. During the 1960s, for example, there was great upward pressure on home prices because of the large expansion in the number of households—the Baby Boom effect. General inflation in the 1970s was the primary factor causing home prices to rise more than 10 percent annually in some years of that decade, but increases in other demand factors caused home prices to rise 50 percent faster than the general level of inflation.

The increase in home prices moderated during most of the 1980s, but some areas such as Southern California and Boston experienced large increases, partially fueled by speculative fever. Conversely, local economic factors caused declines in other markets. For example, the drop in oil prices caused a bust in the Houston market.

The general economic recession of the early 1990s triggered a decline in home prices in many areas, particularly those that had experienced speculative run-ups in earlier years. Some homeowners in Southern California and the Northeast were faced with ugly financial leverage and saddled with mortgages greater than the values of their homes. Finally, with the return of general prosperity in the later years of the 1990s, home prices rose in almost all areas of the country.

But all that is in the past. What of the future? Let us examine some of the factors that will influence the general level of home prices in the future, always recognizing that real estate markets are local in nature and heavily influenced by local economic conditions.

In contrast to earlier periods, the number of Americans in the age 25 to 34 first-time homebuyers group is declining and will be through about 2005. Only about 27 million of the possible 40 million Baby Boomers will want to sell their homes over the next few years. This has led some economists to predict an absolute decline in home prices over this analysis period.

Recent population estimates by the Census Bureau contradict this gloomy prediction, however. The current forecast predicts a population increase of 27 million for the 1990s, resulting in a total household formation about the same as that of the 1980s. A major factor in this estimate of increase is the large number of immigrants. Studies show that immigrants, particularly those coming from Asian countries, highly value home ownership.

The large group of aging Baby Boomers with accumulated home equity and relatively large disposable income bodes well for both the trade-up market for more expensive homes and the second home market for vacation homes. Preferred retirement areas should also benefit from the existence of this group.

Rapid inflation is the friend of debtors, particularly heavily leveraged homeowners. Thus, the greatly reduced rates of inflation in recent years have made home ownership somewhat less attractive, while also making it more affordable. Slow growth in home prices and relatively low interest rates combined to make housing more affordable in 1998 than at any time in the past 20 years. These factors have also increased the home ownership rate to its highest level in many years.

What Will Happen to Home Prices? (continued)

A big unknown is the future of the mortgage interest deduction from taxable income. This deduction now costs the Treasury about $50 billion annually, and many, particularly those advocating a flat tax, are calling for its repeal. If this were to occur, many feel that the negative impact on home prices would be severe, a factor that makes the deduction's repeal unlikely.

So, what's likely to happen to home prices during the time when most readers of this book will be faced with the rent or buy decision? The most likely scenario appears to be that prices will keep up with, or possibly slightly exceed, the rate of general inflation. But that is also the general outlook; home prices where you might buy a home also depend heavily on what happens in the local economy.

Close-Up

Dealing with the Lender

Lenders sell money, and naturally, they want to get the highest price (the interest rate) they can. You should shop as carefully for a mortgage loan as you do for a home. Don't take the first offer, and check with several lenders to find the best deal.

Also, remember that any appraisal and inspections required by the lender are to protect the lender, not necessarily you. For example, the purpose of the appraisal, which you normally pay for, is to ensure that the home has value high enough to enable the lender to be able to recover its money in case of foreclosure. The appraisal does not tell you whether the home is a good investment for you, although it certainly should help in this determination. (It is amazing how many appraisals for lending purposes arrive at values that are almost exactly the selling prices.)

The Closing Attorney or Escrow Agent

The closing attorney's or escrow agent's job is to prepare the necessary documents relating to the sale and loan and to make sure the title is in order, the requirements of the lender and the title insurance company have been met, all funds have been collected and properly disbursed, and the necessary documents have been recorded. All of this is important to the buyer, but again, the closing agent is not paid to look after the buyer's interests. The agent does not negotiate for you, draft a purchase contract favorable to you, make certain the contract has no clauses that are unfavorable to your interests, help arrange favorable financing, or make sure that the seller fully honors his or her agreement with you. To the contrary, the closing agent's job is to see that the transaction meets legal requirements and is closed.

Perhaps we have been too forceful in warning you of the pitfalls in the sales, lending, and closing transactions when buying a home. Certainly, the intention is not to convey that real estate brokers, lenders, and attorneys are dishonest or unethical. But do remember whom they work for. If you feel you need someone to represent your interests, don't depend on these individuals; hire your own representative.

■ CHAPTER REVIEW

- Important factors in the rent or buy decision are (1) the future of home prices, (2) the probable period of ownership, (3) the mortgage interest rate, and (4) noneconomic factors.

- Lenders will normally make a mortgage loan with a monthly payment equal to between 25 and 28 percent of monthly gross income or, if the payment is less, an amount equal to 33 to 36 percent of monthly gross income reduced by the amount of existing monthly debt payments.

- Important factors in choosing a community in which to buy a home are (1) commuting distance to work, (2) property tax base, (3) quality of general public services, (4) available recreational facilities, (5) quality of the public school system, (6) crime statistics, and (7) overall quality of the community.

- In choosing a home, it is a good rule to buy one priced lower than the average for the neighborhood. Also, the buyer should consider a home that has a good design and should carefully check the home's structural integrity.

- In the negotiating, lending and closing process, always remember that in the normal sales transaction, no one works for the buyer, and therefore, no one really looks out for the buyer's interests.

■ STUDY EXERCISES

1. What are some of the important factors to consider in the rent or buy decision?

2. Jack and Jill Jolly are thinking about buying a home. Their combined monthly income is $5,000, and they have $30,000 savings in a bank. They also have existing debt that requires monthly payments of $350 for a car, $200 for furniture, and $250 for revolving credit. How large a mortgage loan could they expect to get if the current interest rate is 8.5 percent? How expensive a home could they buy?

3. In choosing a location and home, what factors should Jack and Jill consider?

4. Is the assertion really true that in the negotiating, lending, and closing process, no one works for the buyer? Why or why not?

GLOSSARY

A

absorption rate   the number of units capable of being absorbed by the market over a given time period.

acceleration clause   clause in a promissory note that permits the lender to demand payment in full of any unpaid principal and any interest due in the event of default.

acceptance   an expression of satisfaction with an offer.

accrued depreciation   loss in value from any cause.

actual cash value   the cost of replacing an insured item minus the amount by which the item has depreciated in value since it was new.

adaptive use   use of a building in a manner different from the use for which it was originally designed.

adjustable-rate mortgage   a loan whose interest rate is periodically adjusted based on the current interest rate environment.

ad valorem tax   a tax levied as a percentage of the value of the taxed item.

adverse possession   the acquisition of property as a result of "actual and exclusive, open and notorious, hostile and continuous" possession under a claim of right for a statutory period of time.

after-tax cash flow   annual operating cash flow that remains after expenses, debt service and taxes have been paid.

after-tax equity reversion   the amount of money generated by the sale of an investment after taxes have been paid and any debts extinguished.

agency   a legal relationship between a principal and an agent.

agent   the party authorized to conduct business on the principal's behalf.

airport hotel   a hotel near an airport that caters to business travelers.

air rights   property rights associated with the space above the surface of the earth.

alienable   a property owner's right to transfer interests owned in a property during his or her lifetime.

amortization   the process of gradually retiring a loan or other asset; also, the requirement that a nonconforming use be discontinued after a stated period of time.

amortization schedule   a table showing the breakdown of principal and interest paid over the life of a mortgage.

amortizing loan   a loan whose balance is gradually retired by periodic payments.

annuity   a series of equal amounts, received one at the end of each period, for a specified number of periods.

anticipation   the idea that the current value of a property depends on the anticipated utility or income that will accrue to the property owner in the future.

appraisal   an estimate of value.

appraisal process   a systematic procedure employed to arrive at an estimate of value and convey that estimate to the appraisal user.

assessed value   the estimated value of a property for tax purposes.

asset manager   a company executive charged with management of the firm's real estate facilities and activities.

assignment   the act of passing all of one's rights and responsibilities under a legal agreement to a third party.

axial model   a model of urban growth patterns based on transportation routes.

B

balloon payment   a lump sum payment due on a specified date in the future.

bargain and sale deed   a deed that simply states that the grantor has title to the property and the right to convey it but does not contain any express covenants or warranties to the title's validity.

base lines   east-west lines used as reference points in the rectangular survey system.

before-tax cash flow   annual operating cash flow that remains after expenses and debt service have been paid.

before-tax equity reversion   the amount of money generated by the sale of an investment before taxes have been paid.

blockbusting   the illegal practice of encouraging property owners to sell their homes when minorities begin moving into an area.

broker   an intermediary who brings together buyers and sellers, assists in negotiating agreements between them, executes their orders, and receives compensation for services rendered.

building codes   regulations that establish standards for the construction of new buildings and the alteration of existing ones.

bulk regulations   regulations that control the percentage of the lot area that may be occupied by buildings on a site.

businessowner's policy   an insurance policy for small and medium-sized businesses.

business risk   uncertainty arising from changing economic conditions that affect an investment's ability to generate returns.

buyer representation agreement   the legal agreement between a buyer and a broker hired to represent the buyer's interests.

buyer's agent   a broker who is legally obligated to represent a buyer's interests.

C

capacity   legal ability to understand and accept the terms of a contract.

capital gain   the amount calculated as net sale proceeds less original purchase price plus all depreciation deductions taken in previous years.

capitalization rate   the relationship between income and value, where the capitalization rate equals net operating income divided by property value.

cash on cash return   the amount calculated by dividing the amount of equity invested in a property by an estimate of annual before-tax cash flow (BTCF ÷ equity).

central business district   an unplanned series of buildings constructed along major streets in the center of town.

certified general appraiser   an appraiser who is certified by the state to perform appraisals on all property types.

certified residential appraiser   an appraiser who is certified by the state to perform residential appraisals regardless of complexity.

chain of title   ownership history of a specific property.

change   the idea that economic, social, political, and environmental forces are constantly causing changes that affect the value of real estate.

closing costs   costs associated with closing a real estate transaction.

closing statement   a worksheet showing the sources and uses of funds in a real estate transaction.

coinsurance   the joint assumption of risk by two or more parties.

commercial hotel   a hotel that caters primarily to businesspeople and conventioneers.

commission   the compensation received by a broker for services rendered.

community property   theory under which all property acquired during a marriage is considered to be equally owned by the husband and wife, regardless of the financial contribution each spouse actually made to the property's acquisition.

community shopping center   a shopping center containing between 100,000 and 300,000 square feet of gross leasable area that is designed to serve an area within a radius of three to five miles.

comparative advantage   the advantage one locale has over another because of transportation facilities, created environment, natural resources, or its labor force.

compounding   the process of converting present amounts into future amounts.

compound interest   interest earned on a principal amount plus any interest previously earned.

comprehensive general plan   a statement of land-use policies that shape the future development of a community.

comprehensive zoning   division of a community's land into specific land-use districts to regulate the use of land and buildings and the intensity of various uses.

concentric-circle model   a model of urban growth patterns based on concentric zones surrounding a central business district.

concurrent estate   ownership interests held jointly by two or more owners.

condominium   a form of joint ownership whereby the property owners own their individual units separately but share ownership of common areas; a building owned in this manner.

condominium declaration   legal document that describes the individual units and common areas of a property owned as a condominium, creates an association to govern the property, and sets forth restrictions on use.

consideration   anything that incurs legal detriment or the forgoing of a legal benefit.

contract   a legal device used by two or more persons to indicate they have reached an agreement.

contribution   the idea that the value of a component part of a property depends on the amount it contributes to the value of the whole.

conventional loan   mortgage loans not insured or guaranteed by a government agency but that may carry private mortgage insurance.

cooperative   a form of joint ownership whereby the property owners own shares of stock in a corporation that owns the property and are entitled to occupy space within the building.

cost approach   a method used to estimate value by implementing the following steps: (1) estimate the value of the site as though it were vacant, (2) estimate the cost to produce the improvements, (3) subtract accrued depreciation, and (4) add site value to the estimated depreciated cost of the improvements.

counteroffer   a response to an offer that represents a new offer.

covenant   a promise or guarantee made by a grantor in a deed.

covenant against encumbrances   an assurance made by the grantor that no liens or encumbrances other than those of public record exist against the property.

covenant of further assurances   an assurance made by the grantor that the grantor will execute any future documents needed to perfect the grantee's title.

covenant of quiet enjoyment   an assurance made by the grantor that no other party will disturb the grantee claiming to own the property or to have a lien on it; a promise from the lessor that the tenant has the right of exclusive possession of the property during the term of the lease.

covenant of seisin   an assurance made by the grantor that he or she is in full possession of the interest being conveyed by a deed and thus has the right to convey it.

D

debt coverage ratio   calculated by dividing net operating income by debt service (NOI ÷ DS).

debt service   total amount paid to lenders to service outstanding debt.

deed   a written document that evidences ownership.

deed in lieu of foreclosure   a process by which a borrower transfers ownership of a mortgaged property to the lender rather than face foreclosure.

deed of trust   a security instrument that conveys title to the property pledged as collateral to a trustee until the loan is repaid.

defeasible estate   an estate that can be lost should some event or stated condition come to pass.

deficiency judgment   a judgment against a borrower following a foreclosure that permits the lender to recover any shortfall between the sale price and the balance of the loan.

depreciation deduction   a noncash deduction permitted by the Internal Revenue Service (IRS) for capital recovery.

descendible   a property owner's right to transfer interests owned in a property to legal heirs should the owner die without a valid will.

devisable   a property owner's right to transfer interests owned in a property via a will.

direct losses   costs of replacing or repairing property destroyed or damaged.

discounting   the process of converting future amounts into present amounts.

discount point 1 percent of the loan amount.

discount shopping center a community shopping center that contains a discount store as the main tenant.

dominant estate the property benefited by the existence of an easement appurtenant.

dual agency a legal relationship that exists when an agent is legally obligated to represent the best interests of two competing principals.

due-on-sale clause a clause in a promissory note that requires the borrower to repay all amounts due immediately upon transferring the property to a new owner.

E

easement a right given to another party by a landowner to use a property in a specified manner.

easement appurtenant an easement with clearly identifiable dominant and servient estates.

easement by prescription a method of creating an easement as a result of "actual and exclusive, open and notorious, hostile and continuous" use for a statutory period of time.

easement in gross an easement with only a servient estate.

economic base employment in industries that bring income into a region from beyond its borders.

economic obsolescence loss in value resulting from factors outside the property that affect its income-producing ability or degree of use.

effective gross income potential gross income less vacancy and credit losses.

effective interest rate the actual cost of borrowed funds expressed as an interest rate.

eminent domain the government's power to take private property for public use upon payment of just compensation.

encroachment an unauthorized invasion or intrusion of a fixture, building, or another improvement onto another person's property.

encumbrance restriction or limitation on ownership rights.

escheat the government's right to own real estate following the owner's death in the absence of a valid will or legal heirs.

estate in land ownership interests in real property.

estate in severalty term used to describe ownership interests without regard to the number of owners.

exclusive-agency listing a listing agreement that guarantees the broker's right to a commission if the property is sold by any licensed real estate broker or salesperson.

exclusive-right-to-sell listing a listing agreement that guarantees the broker's right to a commission if the property is sold by the seller or any licensed real estate broker or salesperson.

executor's deed a special use deed used by the executor of an estate to transfer ownership without any assurances regarding the quality of title being transferred.

export activities activities that produce goods and services for sale or consumption outside an area's borders.

express grant method of expressly creating an easement on a grantor's property.

express reservation method of expressly creating an easement on a grantee's property.

F

factory outlet center a shopping center consisting of retail outlet facilities where goods are sold directly to the public in stores owned and operated by the manufacturers.

fair housing laws laws that protect the rights of certain citizens in housing transactions.

Fannie Mae Federal National Mortgage Association.

fee interest time-share a type of concurrent estate that splits ownership of a property over time across joint owners.

fee simple absolute estate the fullest and most complete set of ownership rights one can possess in real property.

FHA-insured loan a loan insured against default by the Federal Housing Administration.

fiduciary   a person who is obligated to act in the best interest of another.

filtering   the passage of housing to less affluent families as the housing ages.

financial leverage   the use of borrowed funds with the intention of magnifying investment returns.

financial risk   uncertainty associated with the possibility of defaulting on borrowed funds used to finance an investment.

fixed-rate mortgage   a loan with a fixed interest rate over the loan term.

fixed-rent lease   a lease contract that stipulates a fixed rent amount for the period of the lease.

fixture   an item that was once personal property but has become part of the real estate.

floor-area ratio   relationship between the total floor area of a building and the total area of a site.

foreclosure   the process of seizing control of the collateral for a loan and using the proceeds from its sale to satisfy a defaulted debt.

fraud   a false statement made with the intention to mislead, that is material to a transaction, that is justifiably relied on by a client, and that results in injury to the client.

Freddie Mac   Federal Home Loan Mortgage Corporation.

freehold estate   ownership interests in real property.

functional obsolescence   loss in value that occurs because a property has less utility or ability to generate income than a new property designed for the same use.

future value of a lump sum $FV = PV(1 + i)^n$

future value of an annuity

$$FVA = A \left[\frac{1 + i^n - 1}{i} \right]$$

G

garden apartment   a two-story or three-story building with a density of 10 to 20 units per acre.

general lien   a security interest on all property owned by an individual.

general warranty deed   the deed that offers the most protection to the grantee, complete with all relevant covenants and warranties.

gestation period   the time between conception of the idea for a development project and its completion and entry into the available supply.

Ginnie Mae   Government National Mortgage Association.

graduated-rent lease   a lease contract that stipulates scheduled rent increases over the period of the lease.

grantee   the party who receives a freehold estate in real property from a grantor.

grantor   the party who transfers a freehold estate in real property to a grantee.

gross income multiplier   the relationship between income and value, where the gross income multiplier equals value divided by gross income.

gross leasable area   the total floor area of a building designed for the tenants' use.

gross lease   a lease contract stipulating that the landlord will pay all operating expenses, taxes, and insurance for the property during the period of the lease.

gross rent multiplier   the relationship between rent and value, where the gross rent multiplier equals value divided by gross rent.

ground lease   a long-term lease for vacant land.

H

highest and best use   that use, found to be legally permissible, physically possible, and financially feasible, that results in the highest land value; that use of land most likely to result in the greatest long-term economic return to the owner.

highrise apartment   apartment buildings containing more than eight stories.

highway hotel   a motel that caters primarily to businesspeople and vacationers who are in transit.

homeowner's policy   an insurance policy that provides coverage of losses from fire and other perils, personal liability, medical payments, and theft.

housing finance system   the arrangements and institutions that facilitate the financing of residential buildings.

hypothecation   the practice of leaving borrowers in possession of their property while repaying a loan with interest.

I

impact fees   fees charged to developers to raise funds for expansion of public facilities needed as a result of the new development.

implied grant   a method of implicitly creating an easement on a grantor's property.

implied reservation   a method of implicitly creating an easement on a grantee's property.

incentive zoning   a practice used by communities to encourage developers to provide certain publicly desired features in their developments in exchange for relaxed enforcement of the zoning code.

income approach   a method used to estimate value by discounting or capitalizing the expected future income that is expected to accrue to the property owner.

index lease   a lease in which rent payments are adjusted based on changes in the cost of living.

indirect losses   additional living expenses or loss of business income suffered before a damaged property is restored.

industrial park   controlled, parklike developments designed to accommodate specific types of industry.

in-filling   a method of city growth where open spaces between structures are filled in with new structures.

infrastructure   investment in public facilities such as roads, schools, etc.

inheritable freehold estate   an ownership interest that passes to heirs upon the death of the owner.

insurable title   a title in real estate that a reputable title insurance company is willing to insure. An insurable title most frequently is one without major defect.

insurable value   an estimate of value for insurance purposes.

insurance binder   temporary evidence of insurance.

interest-only loan   a nonamortizing loan that requires periodic payments of interest and a single balloon payment of the principal at the end of the loan term.

interim use   temporary use of a property until such time that conditions are favorable to convert it to another use intended to be permanent.

internal rate of return   the discount rate that sets net present value exactly equal to zero.

inverse condemnation   a lawsuit initiated by a property owner to force the government to purchase a property whose value has been diminished by a governmental action.

investment   present sacrifice in anticipation of expected future benefit.

investment value   the worth of a property to a particular investor, based on that investor's personal standards of investment acceptability.

IRR decision rule   if the internal rate of return is greater than or equal to the required rate of return, accept the investment.

J

joint tenancy   joint ownership in which all owners have an equal, but undivided, interest in a property.

judicial foreclosure   a court ordered sale of the property following default by the mortgagor.

L

land contract   a contract that establishes an obligation to transfer title from a seller to a buyer at some future date based on an agreed-upon payment schedule.

land rent   the return that a parcel of land will bring in the open market.

lease   a legal agreement between lessor and lessee.

leasehold estate   a tenant's rights to use and possess (but not own) a property as defined in a lease agreement.

lessee   the person who receives a leasehold interest in a property from the lessor.

lessor   the person who gives a leasehold interest in a property to a lessee.

liability insurance insurance that protects the insured against lawsuits brought in response to supposed acts of negligence that result in injury or loss of property to the public.

license a revocable personal privilege to use land for a particular purpose.

licensed appraiser a person licensed by the state to perform noncomplex residential appraisals.

lien a claim on a property as security for a debt or fulfillment of some monetary charge or obligation.

lien theory a concept adopted by some states that recognizes that the mortgagee must foreclose on the property through a court action to acquire possession in the event of default.

life estate an ownership interest in real property that normally ends upon the death of a named person.

liquidity risk possibility of loss resulting from not being able to convert an asset into cash quickly should the need arise.

listing agreement the legal agreement between a broker and a property owner that authorizes the broker to attempt to sell the property.

listing broker the broker who negotiates the listing agreement with the seller.

littoral proprietor owner of land that adjoins navigable bodies of water.

loan origination the process of creating a new loan agreement between a borrower and a lender.

loan-to-value ratio the ratio obtained by dividing the loan amount by an estimate of property value.

M

management agreement a legal agreement authorizing a property manager to conduct business on behalf of the landlord.

mandatory dedication a requirement that developers donate property to the community for public use as a condition for obtaining development approval.

manufactured home a dwelling unit that is manufactured in a factory and then moved to a particular site.

marketable title a title free and clear of all past, present, and future claims that would cause a reasonable purchaser to reject such title.

market value the most probable price that a property should bring in a competitive and open market under all conditions requisite to a fair sale, the buyer and seller each acting prudently and knowledgeably, and assuming the price is not affected by undue stimulus. Implicit in this definition is the consummation of a sale as of a specified date and the passing of title from seller to buyer under conditions whereby

1. buyer and seller are typically motivated;
2. both parties are well informed or well advised and acting in what they consider their best interests;
3. a reasonable time is allowed for exposure in the open market;
4. payment is made in terms of cash in U.S. dollars or in terms of financial arrangements comparable thereto; and
5. the price represents the normal consideration for the property sold unaffected by special or creative financing or sales concessions by anyone associated with the sale.

mechanic's lien a claim on a property held by a supplier of materials or labor for nonpayment of a debt.

metes and bounds a legal method for describing the exact boundaries of a property; *metes* refers to the distances and *bounds* refers to the directions of the property's boundaries.

midrise apartment apartment building consisting of four to eight stories.

mill one one-thousandth, or 0.001.

millage rate the tax rate imposed on property owners, expressed as the dollars of tax for each $1,000 of property value.

mineral rights ownership rights associated with minerals that may be located below the surface of the earth.

misrepresentation a false statement that is material to a transaction, that is justifiably relied upon by a client, and that results in injury to the client.

monument a visible marker, either a natural or an artificial object used to establish the lines and boundaries of a survey.

mortgage a contract by which real property is pledged as security for a loan.

mortgage-backed securities securities issued by mortgage holders to investors who wish to invest indirectly in the mortgage market.

mortgage debt ratio the percentage of a borrower's gross monthly income that is required to meet housing expenses.

mortgagee the lender in a mortgage loan transaction.

mortgage life insurance a diminishing term life insurance policy whose amount is keyed to the outstanding mortgage balance.

mortgage payment

$$PMT = PVA \left[\frac{i}{1 - \dfrac{1}{1 + i^m}} \right]$$

mortgagor the borrower in a mortgage loan transaction.

multiple-listing service an arrangement in which brokers share their listings with other brokers in exchange for a share of the commission generated by a transaction.

multiple-nuclei model a model of urban growth patterns that emphasizes more than one center of commercial activity.

N

negative renewal clause a clause in a lease contract that automatically renews the lease in the event neither party desires to terminate the agreement.

neighborhood an area containing properties of similar type. It also can be defined by reference to geographical area; to social, religious, or ethnic ties; or to income group.

neighborhood shopping center a shopping center designed to serve an area within a radius of 1.5 miles and a population of 2,500 to 40,000.

net lease a lease that stipulates that the lessee will pay operating expenses for a property during the lease period.

net listing a listing agreement in which the broker is entitled to receive as commission any amount above a base price.

net-net lease a lease that stipulates that the lessee will pay operating expenses and insurance for the property during the lease period.

net-net-net lease a lease that stipulates that the lessee will pay operating expenses, insurance and property taxes for the property during the lease period.

net operating income annual operating cash flow that remains after expenses have been paid.

net present value present value of inflows minus present value of outflows.

net sales proceeds proceeds from sale after selling expenses have been paid.

nonconforming use a use of land that does not conform to the current land-use controls imposed by the government.

nonjudicial foreclosure a situation in which the security instrument grants the lender power of sale should the borrower default.

NPV decision rule if the net present value is greater than or equal to zero, accept the investment.

nuisance the use of property in such a way as to harm the property of others.

O

offer a statement that specifies the position of its maker (offeror) and indicates that the offeror is willing to be bound by the conditions stated.

office park a community of lowrise office structures under central management and administration, usually located in the suburbs and adjacent to a major freeway.

operating expense ratio defined as operating expenses divided by effective gross income (OE ÷ EGI).

open listing a listing agreement in which a broker is entitled to receive a commission only in the event the broker procures a buyer for the property.

option-to-buy contract a contract that gives one party the right, but not an obligation, to purchase a property within a specified time horizon at a specified price.

origination fees fees charged by lenders in the origination process.

P

partial performance fulfillment of the terms of an agreement to such an extent that the existence of the agreement may be reasonably inferred.

patio house a detached house with at least one wall that touches the property line.

percentage lease a lease for a property used for commercial purposes under which the rental payments are based on some percentage of sales made on the premises.

performance zoning regulations that restrict land-use based on the environmental carrying capacity of the site.

personal articles floater policy an insurance policy that insures specific personal property items for specific amounts.

personal excess liability policy an insurance policy that insures against disastrous liability claims involving a home, automobile or boat.

personal property movable items such as cars, clothing, books, etc.

personal property replacement cost endorsement an insurance policy that allows the holder to recoup the full replacement cost of stolen or damaged goods rather than the actual cash value of the goods.

physical deterioration loss in value that occurs from ordinary wear and tear, vandalism, or neglect.

plat a detailed land survey drawing, usually prepared by a professional surveyor, that shows the features of a property and its legal description.

plex a form of attached hous ing containing two or more units, each with its own outside entrance.

police power the government's power to regulate the way private property is used to protect the health, safety, morals, and general welfare of the public.

policy a contract providing insurance coverage.

population-serving activities activities that produce goods and services for sale or consumption within an area's borders.

positive renewal clause a clause on a lease that states that if no notice of renewal is given properly, normally one to two months prior to the expiration of the lease, the lease terminates at the end of the lease period.

possibility of reversion the future interest that follows a qualified fee determinable estate.

potential gross income the total income potential of an investment, assuming all space is leased and all rents are collected.

power center a large strip-style shopping center that is anchored by one or more "big box" retailers, along with smaller shops.

power of termination the future interest that follows a qualified fee conditional estate.

premium the consideration paid for an insurance policy.

prepayment early repayment of principal.

prepayment clause a clause in a promissory note that determines the borrower's right to prepay any or all of the principal before it is due.

prescriptive easement an easement created when someone other than the owner uses the land "openly, hostilely, and continuously" for a statutory time period.

present value of a lump sum

$$PA = FV \left[\frac{1}{(1 + i)^n} \right]$$

present value of an annuity

$$PVA = A \left[\frac{1 - \frac{1}{(1 + i)^n}}{i} \right]$$

price actual amount paid for a property in a particular transaction.

primary mortgage market transactions that occur between a borrower and a lender.

primary trade area the geographic area immediately surrounding a shopping center that typically accounts for 60 percent to 70 percent of the center's sales.

principal the person who authorizes an agent to conduct business on his or her behalf.

principal meridians north-south lines used as reference points in the rectangular survey system.

prior appropriation doctrine theory that states that the first person to use a body of water for some beneficial economic purpose has the right to use all the water needed, even though landowners who later find a use for the water may be precluded from using it.

private mortgage insurance nongovernment insurance that provides protection for the lender against the borrower's default.

profit a prendre a nonpossessory interest in real property that permits the holder to remove specified natural resources from a property.

promissory note a written promise to pay money owed.

property manager a person authorized by a property owner to manage the property on his or her behalf.

purchasing power risk uncertainty associated with the possibility that the amount of goods and services that can be acquired with a given amount of money will decline.

Q

qualified estate an estate that can be lost should an event or stated condition come to pass.

qualified fee conditional estate an estate that a court may rule has been terminated should some condition be violated.

qualified fee determinable estate an estate that terminates automatically should some condition be violated.

quitclaim deed a deed used to transfer any interest a grantor may or may not have in a property, without implying that the grantor has a valid interest to convey.

R

range lines north-south lines that run parallel to principal meridians in the rectangular survey system.

real estate land and structures that are attached to it.

real estate broker an individual licensed by a state to represent others in real estate transactions in exchange for compensation.

real estate investment trusts (REITs) publicly traded companies that own and manage real estate portfolios.

real estate salesperson an individual licensed by a state to assist real estate brokers in arranging real estate transactions in exchange for compensation.

real property the legal interests associated with the ownership of real estate.

reappraisal lease a lease that stipulates that the rent will be adjusted periodically as the value of the building changes, as determined by an appraisal.

rectangular survey system a grid-based system used to legally describe the location of a property.

refinancing the process of obtaining a new loan and using the proceeds to repay an existing loan.

regional shopping center a shopping center that contains between 300,000 and 750,000 square feet in gross leasable area and contains at least one full-line department store.

remainder the future interest associated with a life estate held by someone other than the grantor.

renewal option a clause in a lease agreement that defines the parties' agreement regarding renewal of the lease upon termination.

replacement cost the estimated cost of replacing the property being appraised with a property built at today's prices, by current construction methods, and with the same usefulness as the one being appraised.

reproduction cost the cost of constructing an exact replacement of the property being appraised with the same or similar materials, at today's prices.

required rate of return a minimum acceptable rate of return.

residential mortgage credit report a standardized credit report used in the underwriting process for residential loans.

resort hotel a hotel that caters to individuals or families on vacation.

restrictive covenant limitations placed on a property by a landowner or previous landowner that prevents the property from being used in certain ways.

reversion the future interest associated with a life estate held by the grantor.

right of survivorship the right of surviving joint owners to automatically divide the share owned by a deceased owner.

right-to-use time-share a form of leasehold estate that permits the holder to use a property for a certain period each year.

riparian rights doctrine theory that permits landowners whose land underlies or borders nonnavigable bodies of water to use all the water needed as long as the use does not deprive other landowners who are also entitled to use some of the water.

risk the chance of loss; also, the uncertainty about the actual rate of return an investment will provide over the holding period.

S

sale-leaseback an arrangement whereby a property owner sells the property to an investor and immediately leases the property back from the investor.

sales comparison approach a method used to estimate value by comparing the property to other properties that have recently sold for known prices.

secondary mortgage market transactions involving mortgages that occur between investors.

secondary trade area the area outside the primary trade area that typically accounts for 15 percent to 20 percent of sales at a shopping center.

section 1-square-mile rectangles that divide townships into 36 equal areas of 640 acres each.

sector model a model of urban growth in which types of development tend to extend outward in wedge-shaped sections from the center of the city.

secured loan a loan for which a specific item has been pledged as collateral.

security deposit an amount required by a lessor in advance of occupancy as security against potential damages caused by the lessee.

seller's agent a real estate broker who is obligated to represent the best interest of the seller.

selling broker the broker who actually locates a buyer for a property.

servient estate the property burdened by the existence of an easement appurtenant or easement in gross.

setback a common land-use regulation that requires a certain amount of space between improvements on a property and the property lines.

sinking fund payment

$$SFP = FVA \left[\frac{i}{(1 + i)^n - 1} \right]$$

special lien a security interest that relates only to real estate.

special warranty deed similar to a general warranty deed, except the covenants and warranties apply only to events that occurred during the grantor's period of ownership.

specialty shopping center a shopping center that focuses on unusual market segments and usually offers high-quality, high-priced merchandise in boutique-type stores.

specific performance a requirement that the terms of a contract be exactly complied with.

statute of frauds a law designed to prevent fraudulent practices involving contracts.

steering the illegal practice of steering potential home buyers into certain areas to influence the racial or ethnic composition of the areas.

strip shopping center a neighborhood shopping center built in a straight line, with stores tied together by a canopy over a pedestrian walk.

strict foreclosure a situation in which the lender is entitled to immediate ownership of the property should the borrower default.

subagent an agent of an agent of a principal.

subdivision regulations the standards and procedures that regulate the subdivision of land for development and sale.

subleasing the act of transferring a portion of the leasehold estate to a third party.

substitution the idea that a prudent buyer will pay no more for a property than the cost of acquiring an equally desirable substitute in the open market.

superregional shopping center a shopping center that exceeds 750,000 square feet of gross leasable area and includes at least three department stores.

superstore a very large discount store with between 60,000 and 150,000 square feet under one roof.

T

tenancy at sufferance a leasehold estate that defines a tenant's rights to occupy the property against the wishes of the lessor.

tenancy at will an informal leasehold estate of indeterminable length that may last as long as the parties agree.

tenancy by the entirety a form of concurrent estate in which a husband and wife can own property jointly.

tenancy for a stated period a leasehold estate that has definite starting and ending dates.

tenancy from period to period   a leasehold estate that continues to automatically renew each period unless terminated by either party.

tenancy in common   a form of concurrent estate in which each owner has an undivided interest in the property.

time-sharing   a form of concurrent estate that splits ownership of a property across owners and across time.

time value of money principle   a dollar in hand is worth more than a dollar to be received in the future because it can either be consumed immediately or put to work to earn a return.

title   the legal right to ownership.

title abstract   a written history of a property's chain of title.

title insurance   an insurance policy that protects property owners and lenders against undiscovered defects in a property's chain of title.

title opinion   an attorney's opinion of the quality of title for a specific property.

title perfect of record   a property for which there are no defects.

title search   the process of verifying the quality of title.

title theory   a concept adopted by some states that recognizes that the mortgagee has the right to immediate possession of mortgaged property in the event of default.

Torrens system   a system of land registration used by a few states as an alternative to grantor/grantee indexes.

total debt ratio   the percentage of a borrower's gross monthly income required to meet monthly contractual expenses.

town house   a form of attached housing in which each unit has its own front door but shares one or two walls with adjacent units.

township   a 36-square-mile area formed by township and range lines in the rectangular survey system.

township lines   east-west lines that run parallel to base lines in the rectangular survey system.

trade area   the geographic area from which the major portion of the patronage necessary to support the shopping center is to be drawn.

trade fixture   personal property used in a trade or business.

transfer of development rights   a system whereby landowners can sell their development rights to other property owners so the other property owners can use their property more intensely.

two-step mortgage   a loan whose interest rate is adjusted once during the term of the loan.

U

underwriting   process of evaluating the risk of a loan applicant and the property being pledged in order to make a decision regarding the loan application.

unsecured loan   a loan for which no specific item has been pledged as collateral.

V

vacancy and credit losses   revenues not received due to vacancy in the property or uncollectible rents.

VA-guaranteed loans   a loan in which the lender is protected from the borrower's default by a guarantee of repayment from the Department of Veterans Affairs.

variance   permission granted by a government for a landowner to use the property in a manner not ordinarily permitted.

voidable   capable of being rescinded, as a contract entered into by a minor or by a person who has been declared insane.

W

warranty   a promise or guarantee made by a grantor in a deed.

warranty forever   an assurance made by the grantor to always defend the title conveyed to the grantee.

warranty of habitability   an assurance made by a lessor that the property is fit for its intended use.

A Time Value of Money Tables

This appendix presents time value of money tables (often called *capitalization tables*) for interest rates of 6, 8, 10, 12, and 14 percent. They are adapted from *Financial Compound Interest and Annuity Tables.* Sixth Edition (Boston: financial Publishing Co., 1980). Other rates and other periods can be found in this publication or with the aid of a financial calculator.

Time Value of Money at 6%

Periods	Future Value Factors	Future Value of Annuity Factors	Sinking Fund Factors	Present Value Factors	Present Value of Annuity Factor	Mortgage Constant
1	1.060 000	1.000 000	1.000 000	.943 396	.943 396	1.060 000
2	1.123 600	2.060 000	.485 437	.889 996	1.833 393	.545 437
3	1.191 016	3.183 600	.314 110	.839 619	2.673 012	.374 110
4	1.262 477	4.374 616	.228 591	.792 094	3.465 106	.288 591
5	1.338 226	5.637 093	.177 396	.747 258	4.212 364	.237 396
6	1.418 519	6.975 319	.143 363	.704 961	4.917 324	.203 363
7	1.503 630	8.393 838	.119 135	.665 057	5.582 381	.179 135
8	1.593 848	9.897 468	.101 036	.627 412	6.209 794	.161 036
9	1.689 479	11.491 316	.087 022	.591 898	6.801 692	.147 022
10	1.790 848	13.180 795	.075 868	.558 395	7.360 087	.135 868
11	1.898 299	14.971 643	.066 793	.526 788	7.886 875	.126 793
12	2.012 196	16.869 941	.059 277	.496 969	8.383 844	.119 277
13	2.132 928	18.882 138	.052 960	.468 839	8.852 683	.112 960
14	2.260 904	21.015 066	.047 585	.442 301	9.294 984	.107 585
15	2.396 558	23.275 970	.042 963	.417 265	9.712 249	.102 963
16	2.540 352	25.672 528	.038 952	.393 646	10.105 895	.098 952
17	2.692 773	28.212 880	.035 445	.371 364	10.477 260	.095 445
18	2.854 339	30.905 653	.032 357	.350 344	10.827 603	.092 357
19	3.025 600	33.759 992	.029 621	.330 513	11.158 116	.089 621
20	3.207 135	36.785 591	.027 185	.311 805	11.469 921	.087 185
21	3.399 564	39.992 727	.025 005	.294 155	11.764 077	.085 005
22	3.603 537	43.392 290	.023 046	.277 505	12.041 582	.083 046
23	3.819 750	46.995 828	.021 278	.261 797	12.303 379	.081 278
24	4.048 935	50.815 577	.019 679	.246 979	12.550 358	.079 679
25	4.291 871	54.864 512	.018 227	.232 999	12.783 356	.078 227
26	4.549 383	59.156 383	.016 904	.219 810	13.003 166	.076 904
27	4.822 346	63.705 766	.015 697	.207 368	13.210 534	.075 697
28	5.111 687	68.528 112	.014 593	.195 630	13.406 164	.074 593
29	5.418 388	73.639 798	.013 580	.184 557	13.590 721	.073 580
30	5.743 491	79.058 186	.012 649	.174 110	13.764 831	.072 649
31	6.088 101	84.801 677	.011 792	.164 255	13.929 086	.071 792
32	6.453 387	90.889 778	.011 002	.154 957	14.084 043	.071 002
33	6.840 590	97.343 165	.010 273	.146 186	14.230 230	.070 273
34	7.251 025	104.183 755	.009 598	.137 912	14.368 141	.069 598
35	7.686 087	111.434 780	.008 974	.130 105	14.498 246	.068 974
36	8.147 252	119.120 867	.008 395	.122 741	14.620 987	.068 395
37	8.636 087	127.268 119	.007 857	.115 793	14.736 780	.067 857
38	9.154 252	135.904 206	.007 358	.109 239	14.846 019	.067 358
39	9.703 507	145.058 458	.006 894	.103 056	14.949 075	.066 894
40	10.285 718	154.761 966	.006 462	.097 222	15.046 297	.066 462
41	10.902 861	165.047 684	.006 059	.091 719	15.138 016	.066 059
42	11.557 033	175.950 545	.005 683	.086 527	15.224 543	.065 683
43	12.250 455	187.507 577	.005 333	.081 630	15.306 173	.065 333
44	12.985 482	199.758 032	.005 006	.077 009	15.383 182	.065 006
45	13.764 611	212.743 514	.004 700	.072 650	15.455 832	.064 700
46	14.590 487	226.508 125	.004 415	.068 538	15.524 370	.064 415
47	15.465 917	241.098 612	.004 148	.064 658	15.589 028	.064 148
48	16.393 872	256.564 529	.003 898	.060 998	15.650 027	.063 898
49	17.377 504	272.958 401	.003 664	.057 546	15.707 572	.063 664
50	18.420 154	290.335 905	.003 444	.054 288	15.761 861	.063 444

[1] How $1 left at compound interest will grow
[2] How $1 deposited periodically will grow
[3] Periodic deposit that will grow to $1 at future date

[4] What $1 due in the future is worth today
[5] What $1 payable periodically is worth today
[6] Annuity worth $1 today. Periodic payment necessary to pay off a loan of $1

Time Value of Money at 8%

Periods	Future Value Factors	Future Value of Annuity Factors	Sinking Fund Factors	Present Value Factors	Present Value of Annuity Factor	Mortgage Constant
1	1.080 000	1.000 000	1.000 000	.925 926	.925 926	1.080 000
2	1.166 400	2.080 000	.480 769	.857 339	1.783 265	.560 769
3	1.259 712	3.246 400	.308 034	.793 832	2.577 097	.388 034
4	1.360 489	4.506 112	.221 921	.735 030	3.312 127	.301 921
5	1.469 328	5.866 601	.170 456	.680 583	3.992 710	.250 456
6	1.586 874	7.335 929	.136 315	.630 170	4.622 880	.216 315
7	1.713 824	8.922 803	.112 072	.583 490	5.206 370	.192 072
8	1.850 930	10.636 628	.094 015	.540 269	5.746 639	.174 015
9	1.999 005	12.487 558	.080 080	.500 249	6.246 888	.160 080
10	2.158 925	14.486 562	.069 029	.463 193	6.710 081	.149 029
11	2.331 639	16.645 487	.060 076	.428 883	7.138 964	.140 076
12	2.518 170	18.977 126	.052 695	.397 114	7.536 078	.132 695
13	2.719 624	21.495 297	.046 522	.367 698	7.903 776	.126 522
14	2.937 194	24.214 920	.041 297	.340 461	8.244 237	.121 297
15	3.172 169	27.152 114	.036 830	.315 242	8.559 479	.116 830
16	3.425 943	30.324 283	.032 977	.291 890	8.851 369	.112 977
17	3.700 018	33.750 226	.029 629	.270 269	9.121 638	.109 629
18	3.996 019	37.450 244	.026 702	.250 249	9.371 887	.106 702
19	4.315 701	41.446 263	.024 128	.231 712	9.603 599	.104 128
20	4.660 957	45.761 964	.021 852	.214 548	9.818 147	.101 852
21	5.033 834	50.422 921	.019 832	.198 656	10.016 803	.099 832
22	5.436 540	55.456 755	.018 032	.183 941	10.200 744	.098 032
23	5.871 464	60.893 296	.016 422	.170 315	10.371 059	.096 422
24	6.341 181	66.764 759	.014 978	.157 699	10.528 758	.094 978
25	6.848 475	73.105 940	.013 679	.146 018	10.674 776	.093 679
26	7.396 353	79.954 415	.012 507	.135 202	10.809 978	.092 507
27	7.988 061	87.350 768	.011 448	.125 187	10.935 165	.091 448
28	8.627 106	95.338 830	.010 489	.115 914	11.051 078	.090 489
29	9.317 275	103.965 936	.009 619	.107 328	11.158 406	.089 619
30	10.062 657	113.283 211	.008 827	.099 377	11.257 783	.088 827
31	10.867 669	123.345 868	.008 107	.092 016	11.349 799	.088 107
32	11.737 083	134.213 537	.007 451	.085 200	11.434 999	.087 451
33	12.676 050	145.950 620	.006 852	.078 889	11.513 888	.086 852
34	13.690 134	158.626 670	.006 304	.073 045	11.586 934	.086 304
35	14.785 344	172.316 804	.005 803	.067 635	11.654 568	.085 803
36	15.968 172	187.102 148	.005 345	.062 625	11.717 193	.085 345
37	17.245 626	203.070 320	.004 924	.057 986	11.775 179	.084 924
38	18.625 276	220.315 945	.004 539	.053 690	11.828 869	.084 539
39	20.115 298	238.941 221	.004 185	.049 713	11.878 582	.084 185
40	21.724 521	259.056 519	.003 860	.046 031	11.924 613	.083 860
41	23.462 483	280.781 040	.003 561	.042 621	11.967 235	.083 561
42	25.339 482	304.243 523	.003 287	.039 464	12.006 699	.083 287
43	27.366 640	329.583 005	.003 034	.036 541	12.043 240	.083 034
44	29.555 972	356.949 646	.002 802	.033 834	12.077 074	.082 802
45	31.920 449	386.505 617	.002 587	.031 328	12.108 402	.082 587
46	34.474 085	418.426 067	.002 390	.029 007	12.137 409	.082 390
47	37.232 012	452.900 152	.002 208	.026 859	12.164 267	.082 208
48	40.210 573	490.132 164	.002 040	.024 869	12.189 136	.082 040
49	43.427 419	530.342 737	.001 886	.023 027	12.212 163	.081 886
50	46.901 613	573.770 156	.001 743	.021 321	12.233 485	.081 743

Time Value of Money at 10%

Periods	Future Value Factors	Future Value of Annuity Factors	Sinking Fund Factors	Present Value Factors	Present Value of Annuity Factor	Mortgage Constant
1	1.100 000	1.000 000	1.000 000	.909 091	.909 091	1.100 000
2	1.210 000	2.100 000	.476 190	.826 446	1.735 537	.576 190
3	1.331 000	3.310 000	.302 115	.751 315	2.486 852	.402 115
4	1.464 100	4.641 000	.215 471	.683 013	3.169 865	.315 471
5	1.610 510	6.105 100	.163 797	.620 921	3.790 787	.263 797
6	1.771 561	7.715 610	.129 607	.564 474	4.355 261	.229 607
7	1.948 717	9.487 171	.105 405	.513 158	4.868 419	.205 405
8	2.143 589	11.435 888	.087 444	.466 507	5.334 926	.187 444
9	2.357 948	13.579 477	.073 641	.424 098	5.759 024	.173 641
10	2.593 742	15.937 425	.062 745	.385 543	6.144 567	.162 745
11	2.853 117	18.531 167	.053 963	.350 494	6.495 061	.153 963
12	3.138 428	21.384 284	.046 763	.318 631	6.813 692	.146 763
13	3.452 271	24.522 712	.040 779	.289 664	7.103 356	.140 779
14	3.797 498	27.974 983	.035 746	.263 331	7.366 687	.135 746
15	4.177 248	31.772 482	.031 474	.239 392	7.606 080	.131 474
16	4.594 973	35.949 730	.027 817	.217 629	7.823 709	.127 817
17	5.054 470	40.544 703	.024 664	.197 845	8.021 553	.124 664
18	5.559 917	45.599 173	.021 930	.179 859	8.201 412	.121 930
19	6.115 909	51.159 090	.019 547	.163 508	8.364 920	.119 547
20	6.727 500	57.274 999	.017 460	.148 644	8.513 564	.117 460
21	7.400 250	64.002 499	.015 624	.135 131	8.648 694	.115 624
22	8.140 275	71.402 749	.014 005	.122 846	8.771 540	.114 005
23	8.954 302	79.543 024	.012 572	.111 678	8.883 218	.112 572
24	9.849 733	88.497 327	.011 300	.101 526	8.984 744	.111 300
25	10.834 706	98.347 059	.010 168	.092 296	9.077 040	.110 168
26	11.918 177	109.181 765	.009 159	.083 905	9.160 945	.109 159
27	13.109 994	121.099 942	.008 258	.076 278	9.237 223	.108 258
28	14.420 994	134.209 936	.007 451	.069 343	9.306 567	.107 451
29	15.863 093	148.630 930	.006 728	.063 039	9.369 606	.106 728
30	17.449 402	164.494 023	.006 079	.057 309	9.426 914	.106 079
31	19.194 342	181.943 425	.005 496	.052 099	9.479 013	.105 496
32	21.113 777	201.137 767	.004 972	.047 362	9.526 376	.104 972
33	23.225 154	222.251 544	.004 499	.043 057	9.569 432	.104 499
34	25.547 670	245.476 699	.004 074	.039 143	9.608 575	.104 074
35	28.102 437	271.024 368	.003 690	.035 584	9.644 159	.103 690
36	30.912 681	299.126 805	.003 343	.032 349	9.676 508	.103 343
37	34.003 949	330.039 486	.003 030	.029 408	9.705 917	.103 030
38	37.404 343	364.043 434	.002 747	.026 735	9.732 651	.102 747
39	41.144 778	401.447 778	.002 491	.024 304	9.756 956	.102 491
40	45.259 256	442.592 556	.002 259	.022 095	9.779 051	.102 259
41	49.785 181	487.851 811	.002 050	.020 086	9.799 137	.102 050
42	54.763 699	537.636 992	.001 860	.018 260	9.817 397	.101 860
43	60.240 069	592.400 692	.001 688	.016 600	9.833 998	.101 688
44	66.264 076	652.640 761	.001 532	.015 091	9.849 089	.101 532
45	72.890 484	718.904 837	.001 391	.013 719	9.862 808	.101 391
46	80.179 532	791.795 321	.001 263	.012 472	9.875 280	.101 263
47	88.197 485	871.974 853	.001 147	.011 338	9.886 618	.101 147
48	97.017 234	960.172 338	.001 041	.010 307	9.896 926	.101 041
49	106.718 957	1057.189 572	.000 946	.009 370	9.906 296	.100 946
50	117.390 853	1163.908 529	.000 859	.008 519	9.914 814	.100 859

Time Value of Money at 12%

Periods	Future Value Factors	Future Value of Annuity Factors	Sinking Fund Factors	Present Value Factors	Present Value of Annuity Factor	Mortgage Constant
1	1.120 000	1.000 000	1.000 000	.892 857	.892 857	1.120 000
2	1.254 400	2.120 000	.471 698	.797 194	1.690 051	.591 698
3	1.404 928	3.374 400	.296 349	.711 780	2.401 831	.416 349
4	1.573 519	4.779 328	.209 234	.635 518	3.037 349	.329 234
5	1.762 342	6.352 847	.157 410	.567 427	3.604 776	.277 410
6	1.973 823	8.115 189	.123 226	.506 631	4.111 407	.243 226
7	2.210 681	10.089 012	.099 118	.452 349	4.563 757	.219 118
8	2.475 963	12.299 693	.081 303	.403 883	4.967 640	.201 303
9	2.773 079	14.775 656	.067 679	.360 610	5.328 250	.187 679
10	3.105 848	17.548 735	.056 984	.321 973	5.650 223	.176 984
11	3.478 550	20.654 583	.048 415	.287 476	5.937 699	.168 415
12	3.895 976	24.133 133	.041 437	.256 675	6.194 374	.161 437
13	4.363 493	28.029 109	.035 677	.229 174	6.423 548	.155 677
14	4.887 112	32.392 602	.030 871	.204 620	6.628 168	.150 871
15	5.473 566	37.279 715	.026 824	.182 696	6.810 864	.146 824
16	6.130 394	42.753 280	.023 390	.163 122	6.973 986	.143 390
17	6.866 041	48.883 674	.020 457	.145 644	7.119 630	.140 457
18	7.689 966	55.749 715	.017 937	.130 040	7.249 670	.137 937
19	8.612 762	63.439 681	.015 763	.116 107	7.365 777	.135 763
20	9.646 293	72.052 442	.013 879	.103 667	7.469 444	.133 879
21	10.803 848	81.698 736	.012 240	.092 560	7.562 003	.132 240
22	12.100 310	92.502 584	.010 811	.082 643	7.644 646	.130 811
23	13.552 347	104.602 894	.009 560	.073 788	7.718 434	.129 560
24	15.178 629	118.155 241	.008 463	.065 882	7.784 316	.128 463
25	17.000 064	133.333 870	.007 500	.058 823	7.843 139	.127 500
26	19.040 072	150.333 934	.006 652	.052 521	7.895 660	.126 652
27	21.324 881	169.374 007	.005 904	.046 894	7.942 554	.125 904
28	23.883 866	190.698 887	.005 244	.041 869	7.984 423	.125 244
29	26.749 930	214.582 754	.004 660	.037 383	8.021 806	.124 660
30	29.959 922	241.332 684	.004 144	.033 378	8.055 184	.124 144
31	33.555 113	271.292 606	.003 686	.029 802	8.084 986	.123 686
32	37.581 726	304.847 719	.003 280	.026 609	8.111 594	.123 280
33	42.091 533	342.429 446	.002 920	.023 758	8.135 352	.122 920
34	47.142 517	384.520 979	.002 601	.021 212	8.156 564	.122 601
35	52.799 620	431.663 496	.002 317	.018 940	8.175 504	.122 317
36	59.135 574	484.463 116	.002 064	.016 910	8.192 414	.122 064
37	66.231 843	543.598 690	.001 840	.015 098	8.207 513	.121 840
38	74.179 664	609.830 533	.001 640	.013 481	8.220 993	.121 640
39	83.081 224	684.010 197	.001 462	.012 036	8.233 030	.121 462
40	93.050 970	767.091 420	.001 304	.010 747	8.243 777	.121 304
41	104.217 087	860.142 391	.001 163	.009 595	8.253 372	.121 163
42	116.723 137	964.359 478	.001 037	.008 567	8.261 939	.121 037
43	130.729 914	1081.082 615	.000 925	.007 649	8.269 589	.120 925
44	146.417 503	1211.812 529	.000 825	.006 830	8.276 418	.120 825
45	163.987 604	1358.230 032	.000 736	.006 098	8.282 516	.120 736
46	183.666 116	1522.217 636	.000 657	.005 445	8.287 961	.120 657
47	205.706 050	1705.883 752	.000 586	.004 861	8.292 822	.120 586
48	230.390 776	1911.589 803	.000 523	.004 340	8.297 163	.120 523
49	258.037 669	2141.980 579	.000 467	.003 875	8.301 038	.120 467
50	289.002 190	2400.018 249	.000 417	.003 460	8.304 498	.120 417

Time Value of Money at 14%

Periods	Future Value Factors	Future Value of Annuity Factors	Sinking Fund Factors	Present Value Factors	Present Value of Annuity Factor	Mortgage Constant
1	1.140 000	1.000 000	1.000 000	.877 193	.877 193	1.140 000
2	1.299 600	2.140 000	.467 290	.769 468	1.646 661	.607 290
3	1.481 544	3.439 600	.290 731	.674 972	2.321 632	.430 731
4	1.688 960	4.921 144	.203 205	.592 080	2.913 712	.343 205
5	1.925 415	6.610 104	.151 284	.519 369	3.433 081	.291 284
6	2.194 973	8.535 519	.117 157	.455 587	3.888 668	.257 157
7	2.502 269	10.730 491	.093 192	.399 637	4.288 305	.233 192
8	2.852 586	13.232 760	.075 570	.350 559	4.638 864	.215 570
9	3.251 949	16.085 347	.062 168	.307 508	4.946 372	.202 168
10	3.707 221	19.337 295	.051 714	.269 744	5.216 116	.191 714
11	4.226 232	23.044 516	.043 394	.236 617	5.452 733	.183 394
12	4.817 905	27.270 749	.036 669	.207 559	5.660 292	.176 669
13	5.492 411	32.088 654	.031 164	.182 069	5.842 362	.171 164
14	6.261 349	37.581 065	.026 609	.159 710	6.002 072	.166 609
15	7.137 938	43.842 414	.022 809	.140 096	6.142 168	.162 809
16	8.137 249	50.980 352	.019 615	.122 892	6.265 060	.159 615
17	9.276 464	59.117 601	.016 915	.107 800	6.372 859	.156 915
18	10.575 169	68.394 066	.014 621	.094 561	6.467 420	.154 621
19	12.055 693	78.969 235	.012 663	.082 948	6.550 369	.152 663
20	13.743 490	91.024 928	.010 986	.072 762	6.623 131	.150 986
21	15.667 578	104.768 418	.009 545	.063 826	6.686 957	.149 545
22	17.861 039	120.435 996	.008 303	.055 988	6.742 944	.148 303
23	20.361 585	138.297 035	.007 231	.049 112	6.792 056	.147 231
24	23.212 207	158.658 620	.006 303	.043 081	6.835 137	.146 303
25	26.461 916	181.870 827	.005 498	.037 790	6.872 927	.145 498
26	30.166 584	208.332 743	.004 800	.033 149	6.906 077	.144 800
27	34.389 906	238.499 327	.004 193	.029 078	6.935 155	.144 193
28	39.204 493	272.889 233	.003 664	.025 507	6.960 662	.143 664
29	44.693 122	312.093 725	.003 204	.022 375	6.983 037	.143 204
30	50.950 159	356.786 847	.002 803	.019 627	7.002 664	.142 803
31	58.083 181	407.737 006	.002 453	.017 217	7.019 881	.142 453
32	66.214 826	465.820 186	.002 147	.015 102	7.034 983	.142 147
33	75.484 902	532.035 012	.001 880	.013 248	7.048 231	.141 880
34	86.052 788	607.519 914	.001 646	.011 621	7.059 852	.141 646
35	98.100 178	693.572 702	.001 442	.010 194	7.070 045	.141 442
36	111.834 203	791.672 881	.001 263	.008 942	7.078 987	.141 263
37	127.490 992	903.507 084	.001 107	.007 844	7.086 831	.141 107
38	145.339 731	1030.998 076	.000 970	.006 880	7.093 711	.140 970
39	165.687 293	1176.337 806	.000 850	.006 035	7.099 747	.140 850
40	188.883 514	1342.025 099	.000 745	.005 294	7.105 041	.140 745
41	215.327 206	1530.908 613	.000 653	.004 644	7.109 685	.140 653
42	245.473 015	1746.235 819	.000 573	.004 074	7.113 759	.140 573
43	279.839 237	1991.708 833	.000 502	.003 573	7.117 332	.140 502
44	319.016 730	2271.548 070	.000 440	.003 135	7.120 467	.140 440
45	363.679 072	2590.564 800	.000 386	.002 750	7.123 217	.140 386
46	414.594 142	2954.243 872	.000 338	.002 412	7.125 629	.140 338
47	472.637 322	3368.838 014	.000 297	.002 116	7.127 744	.140 297
48	538.806 547	3841.475 336	.000 260	.001 856	7.129 600	.140 260
49	614.239 464	4380.281 883	.000 228	.001 628	7.131 228	.140 228
50	700.232 988	4994.521 346	.000 200	.001 428	7.132 656	.140 200

B NAR's Code of Ethics and Standards of Practice

Code of Ethics and Standards of Practice
of the NATIONAL ASSOCIATION OF REALTORS®
Effective January 1, 2002

Where the word REALTORS® is used in this Code and Preamble, it shall be deemed to include REALTOR-ASSOCIATE®s.

While the Code of Ethics establishes obligations that may be higher than those mandated by law, in any instance where the Code of Ethics and the law conflict, the obligations of the law must take precedence.

Preamble . . .
Under all is the land. Upon its wise utilization and widely allocated ownership depend the survival and growth of free institutions and of our civilization. REALTORS® should recognize that the interests of the nation and its citizens require the highest and best use of the land and the widest distribution of land ownership. They require the creation of adequate housing, the building of functioning cities, the development of productive industries and farms, and the preservation of a healthful environment.

Such interests impose obligations beyond those of ordinary commerce. They impose grave social responsibility and a patriotic duty to which REALTORS® should dedicate themselves, and for which they should be diligent in preparing themselves. REALTORS®, therefore, are zealous to maintain and improve the standards of their calling and share with their fellow REALTORS® a common responsibility for its integrity and honor.

In recognition and appreciation of their obligations to clients, customers, the public, and each other, REALTORS® continuously strive to become and remain informed on issues affecting real estate and, as knowledgeable professionals, they willingly share the fruit of their experience and study with others. They identify and take steps, through enforcement of this Code of Ethics and by assisting appropriate regulatory bodies, to eliminate practices which may damage the public or which might discredit or bring dishonor to the real estate profession. REALTORS® having direct personal knowledge of conduct that may violate the Code of Ethics involving misappropriation of client or customer funds or property, willful discrimination, or fraud resulting in substantial economic harm, bring such matters to the attention of the appropriate Board or Association of REALTORS®. (Amended 1/00)

Realizing that cooperation with other real estate professionals promotes the best interests of those who utilize their services, REALTORS® urge exclusive representation of clients; do not attempt to gain any unfair advantage over their competitors; and they refrain from making unsolicited comments about other practitioners. In instances where their opinion is sought, or where

REALTORS® believe that comment is necessary, their opinion is offered in an objective, professional manner, uninfluenced by any personal motivation or potential advantage or gain.

The term REALTOR® has come to connote competency, fairness, and high integrity resulting from adherence to a lofty ideal of moral conduct in business relations. No inducement of profit and no instruction from clients ever can justify departure from this ideal.

In the interpretation of this obligation, REALTORS® can take no safer guide than that which has been handed down through the centuries, embodied in the Golden Rule, "Whatsoever ye would that others should do to you, do ye even so to them."

Accepting this standard as their own, REALTORS® pledge to observe its spirit in all of their activities and to conduct their business in accordance with the tenets set forth below.

Duties to Clients and Customers

Article 1
When representing a buyer, seller, landlord, tenant, or other client as an agent, REALTORS® pledge themselves to protect and promote the interests of their client. This obligation to the client is primary, but it does not relieve REALTORS® of their obligation to treat all parties honestly. When serving a buyer, seller, landlord, tenant or other party in a non-agency capacity, REALTORS® remain obligated to treat all parties honestly. (Amended 1/01)

- Standard of Practice 1-1
  REALTORS®, when acting as principals in a real estate transaction, remain obligated by the duties imposed by the Code of Ethics. (Amended 1/93)

- Standard of Practice 1-2
  The duties the Code of Ethics imposes are applicable whether REALTORS® are acting as agents or in legally recognized non-agency capacities except that any duty imposed exclusively on agents by law or regulation shall not be imposed by this Code of Ethics on REALTORS® acting in non-agency capacities.

As used in this Code of Ethics, "client" means the person(s) or entity(ies) with whom a REALTOR® or a REALTOR®'s firm has an agency or legally recognized non-agency relationship; "customer" means a party to a real estate transaction who receives information, services, or benefits but has no contractual

NATIONAL ASSOCIATION OF REALTORS®

The Voice for Real Estate

REALTOR®

NAR ETHICS AND POLICY RESOURCE

relationship with the REALTOR® or the REALTOR®'s firm; "agent" means a real estate licensee (including brokers and sales associates) acting in an agency relationship as defined by state law or regulation; and "broker" means a real estate licensee (including brokers and sales associates) acting as an agent or in a legally recognized non-agency capacity. (Adopted 1/95, Amended 1/99)

- Standard of Practice 1-3
REALTORS®, in attempting to secure a listing, shall not deliberately mislead the owner as to market value.

- Standard of Practice 1-4
REALTORS®, when seeking to become a buyer/tenant representative, shall not mislead buyers or tenants as to savings or other benefits that might be realized through use of the REALTOR®'s services. (Amended 1/93)

- Standard of Practice 1-5
REALTORS® may represent the seller/landlord and buyer/tenant in the same transaction only after full disclosure to and with informed consent of both parties. (Adopted 1/93)

- Standard of Practice 1-6
REALTORS® shall submit offers and counter-offers objectively and as quickly as possible. (Adopted 1/93, Amended 1/95)

- Standard of Practice 1-7
When acting as listing brokers, REALTORS® shall continue to submit to the seller/landlord all offers and counter-offers until closing or execution of a lease unless the seller/landlord has waived this obligation in writing. REALTORS® shall not be obligated to continue to market the property after an offer has been accepted by the seller/landlord. REALTORS® shall recommend that sellers/landlords obtain the advice of legal counsel prior to acceptance of a subsequent offer except where the acceptance is contingent on the termination of the pre-existing purchase contract or lease. (Amended 1/93)

- Standard of Practice 1-8
REALTORS® acting as agents or brokers of buyers/tenants shall submit to buyers/tenants all offers and counter-offers until acceptance but have no obligation to continue to show properties to their clients after an offer has been accepted unless otherwise agreed in writing. REALTORS® acting as agents or brokers of buyers/tenants shall recommend that buyers/tenants obtain the advice of legal counsel if there is a question as to whether a pre-existing contract has been terminated. (Adopted 1/93, Amended 1/99)

- Standard of Practice 1-9
The obligation of REALTORS® to preserve confidential information (as defined by state law) provided by their clients in the course of any agency relationship or non-agency relationship recognized by law continues after termination of agency relationships or any non-agency relationships recognized by law. REALTORS® shall not knowingly, during or following the termination of professional relationships with their clients:

1) reveal confidential information of clients; or
2) use confidential information of clients to the disadvantage of clients; or
3) use confidential information of clients for the REALTOR®'s advantage or the advantage of third parties unless:
    a) clients consent after full disclosure; or
    b) REALTORS® are required by court order; or
    c) it is the intention of a client to commit a crime and the information is necessary to prevent the crime; or
    d) it is necessary to defend a REALTOR® or the REALTOR®'s employees or associates against an accusation of wrongful conduct.

Information concerning latent material defects is not considered confidential information under this Code of Ethics. (Adopted 1/93, Amended 1/01)

- Standard of Practice 1-10
REALTORS® shall, consistent with the terms and conditions of their real estate licensure and their property management agreement, competently manage the property of clients with due regard for the rights, safety and health of tenants and others lawfully on the premises. (Adopted 1/95, Amended 1/00)

- Standard of Practice 1-11
REALTORS® who are employed to maintain or manage a client's property shall exercise due diligence and make reasonable efforts to protect it against reasonably foreseeable contingencies and losses. (Adopted 1/95)

- Standard of Practice 1-12
When entering into listing contracts, REALTORS® must advise sellers/landlords of:
1) the REALTOR®'s general company policies regarding cooperation with and compensation to subagents, buyer/tenant agents and/or brokers acting in legally recognized non-agency capacities;
2) the fact that buyer/tenant agents or brokers, even if compensated by listing brokers, or by sellers/landlords may represent the interests of buyers/tenants; and
3) any potential for listing brokers to act as disclosed dual agents, e.g. buyer/tenant agents. (Adopted 1/93, Renumbered 1/98, Amended 1/99)

- Standard of Practice 1-13
When entering into buyer/tenant agreements, REALTORS® must advise potential clients of:
1) the REALTOR®'s general company policies regarding cooperation and compensation; and
2) any potential for the buyer/tenant representative to act as a disclosed dual agent, e.g. listing broker, subagent, landlord's agent, etc. (Adopted 1/93, Renumbered 1/98, Amended 1/99)

- Standard of Practice 1-14
Fees for preparing appraisals or other valuations shall not be contingent upon the amount of the appraisal or valuation. (Adopted 1/02)

Article 2

REALTORS® shall avoid exaggeration, misrepresentation, or concealment of pertinent facts relating to the property or the transaction. REALTORS® shall not, however, be obligated to discover latent defects in the property, to advise on matters outside the scope of their real estate license, or to disclose facts which are confidential under the scope of agency or non-agency relationships as defined by state law. (Amended 1/00)

- Standard of Practice 2-1
  REALTORS® shall only be obligated to discover and disclose adverse factors reasonably apparent to someone with expertise in those areas required by their real estate licensing authority. Article 2 does not impose upon the REALTOR® the obligation of expertise in other professional or technical disciplines. (Amended 1/96)

- Standard of Practice 2-2
  (Renumbered as Standard of Practice 1-12 1/98)

- Standard of Practice 2-3
  (Renumbered as Standard of Practice 1-13 1/98)

- Standard of Practice 2-4
  REALTORS® shall not be parties to the naming of a false consideration in any document, unless it be the naming of an obviously nominal consideration.

- Standard of Practice 2-5
  Factors defined as "non-material" by law or regulation or which are expressly referenced in law or regulation as not being subject to disclosure are considered not "pertinent" for purposes of Article 2. (Adopted 1/93)

Article 3

REALTORS® shall cooperate with other brokers except when cooperation is not in the client's best interest. The obligation to cooperate does not include the obligation to share commissions, fees, or to otherwise compensate another broker. (Amended 1/95)

- Standard of Practice 3-1
  REALTORS®, acting as exclusive agents or brokers of sellers/ landlords, establish the terms and conditions of offers to cooperate. Unless expressly indicated in offers to cooperate, cooperating brokers may not assume that the offer of cooperation includes an offer of compensation. Terms of compensation, if any, shall be ascertained by cooperating brokers before beginning efforts to accept the offer of cooperation. (Amended 1/99)

- Standard of Practice 3-2
  REALTORS® shall, with respect to offers of compensation to another REALTOR®, timely communicate any change of compensation for cooperative services to the other REALTOR® prior to the time such REALTOR® produces an offer to purchase/lease the property. (Amended 1/94)

- Standard of Practice 3-3
  Standard of Practice 3-2 does not preclude the listing broker and cooperating broker from entering into an agreement to change cooperative compensation. (Adopted 1/94)

- Standard of Practice 3-4
  REALTORS®, acting as listing brokers, have an affirmative obligation to disclose the existence of dual or variable rate commission arrangements (i.e., listings where one amount of commission is payable if the listing broker's firm is the procuring cause of sale/lease and a different amount of commission is payable if the sale/lease results through the efforts of the seller/landlord or a cooperating broker). The listing broker shall, as soon as practical, disclose the existence of such arrangements to potential cooperating brokers and shall, in response to inquiries from cooperating brokers, disclose the differential that would result in a cooperative transaction or in a sale/lease that results through the efforts of the seller/landlord. If the cooperating broker is a buyer/tenant representative, the buyer/tenant representative must disclose such information to their client before the client makes an offer to purchase or lease. (Amended 1/02)

- Standard of Practice 3-5
  It is the obligation of subagents to promptly disclose all pertinent facts to the principal's agent prior to as well as after a purchase or lease agreement is executed. (Amended 1/93)

- Standard of Practice 3-6
  REALTORS® shall disclose the existence of an accepted offer to any broker seeking cooperation. (Adopted 5/86)

- Standard of Practice 3-7
  When seeking information from another REALTOR® concerning property under a management or listing agreement, REALTORS® shall disclose their REALTOR® status and whether their interest is personal or on behalf of a client and, if on behalf of a client, their representational status. (Amended 1/95)

- Standard of Practice 3-8
  REALTORS® shall not misrepresent the availability of access to show or inspect a listed property. (Amended 11/87)

Article 4

REALTORS® shall not acquire an interest in or buy or present offers from themselves, any member of their immediate families, their firms or any member thereof, or any entities in which they have any ownership interest, any real property without making their true position known to the owner or the owner's agent or broker. In selling property they own, or in which they have any interest, REALTORS® shall reveal their ownership or interest in writing to the purchaser or the purchaser's representative. (Amended 1/00)

- Standard of Practice 4-1
  For the protection of all parties, the disclosures required by Article 4 shall be in writing and provided by REALTORS® prior to the signing of any contract. (Adopted 2/86)

Article 5

REALTORS® shall not undertake to provide professional services concerning a property or its value where they have a present or contemplated interest unless such interest is specifically disclosed to all affected parties.

Article 6

REALTORS® shall not accept any commission, rebate, or profit on expenditures made for their client, without the client's knowledge and consent.

When recommending real estate products or services (e.g., homeowner's insurance, warranty programs, mortgage financing, title insurance, etc.), REALTORS® shall disclose to the client or customer to whom the recommendation is made any financial benefits or fees, other than real estate referral fees, the REALTOR® or REALTOR®'s firm may receive as a direct result of such recommendation. (Amended 1/99)

- Standard of Practice 6-1

   REALTORS® shall not recommend or suggest to a client or a customer the use of services of another organization or business entity in which they have a direct interest without disclosing such interest at the time of the recommendation or suggestion. (Amended 5/88)

Article 7

In a transaction, REALTORS® shall not accept compensation from more than one party, even if permitted by law, without disclosure to all parties and the informed consent of the REALTOR®'s client or clients. (Amended 1/93)

Article 8

REALTORS® shall keep in a special account in an appropriate financial institution, separated from their own funds, monies coming into their possession in trust for other persons, such as escrows, trust funds, clients' monies, and other like items.

Article 9

REALTORS®, for the protection of all parties, shall assure whenever possible that agreements shall be in writing, and shall be in clear and understandable language expressing the specific terms, conditions, obligations and commitments of the parties. A copy of each agreement shall be furnished to each party upon their signing or initialing. (Amended 1/95)

- Standard of Practice 9-1

   For the protection of all parties, REALTORS® shall use reasonable care to ensure that documents pertaining to the purchase, sale, or lease of real estate are kept current through the use of written extensions or amendments. (Amended 1/93)

Duties to the Public

Article 10

REALTORS® shall not deny equal professional services to any person for reasons of race, color, religion, sex, handicap, familial status, or national origin. REALTORS® shall not be parties to any plan or agreement to discriminate against a person or persons on the basis of race, color, religion, sex, handicap, familial status, or national origin. (Amended 1/90)

REALTORS®, in their real estate employment practices, shall not discriminate against any person or persons on the basis of race, color, religion, sex, handicap, familial status, or national origin. (Amended 1/00)

- Standard of Practice 10-1

   REALTORS® shall not volunteer information regarding the racial, religious or ethnic composition of any neighborhood and shall not engage in any activity which may result in panic selling. REALTORS® shall not print, display or circulate any statement or advertisement with respect to the selling or renting of a property that indicates any preference, limitations or discrimination based on race, color, religion, sex, handicap, familial status, or national origin. (Adopted 1/94)

- Standard of Practice 10-2

   As used in Article 10 "real estate employment practices" relates to employees and independent contractors providing real-estate related services and the administrative and clerical staff directly supporting those individuals. (Adopted 1/00)

Article 11

The services which REALTORS® provide to their clients and customers shall conform to the standards of practice and competence which are reasonably expected in the specific real estate disciplines in which they engage; specifically, residential real estate brokerage, real property management, commercial and industrial real estate brokerage, real estate appraisal, real estate counseling, real estate syndication, real estate auction, and international real estate.

REALTORS® shall not undertake to provide specialized professional services concerning a type of property or service that is outside their field of competence unless they engage the assistance of one who is competent on such types of property or service, or unless the facts are fully disclosed to the client. Any persons engaged to provide such assistance shall be so identified to the client and their contribution to the assignment should be set forth. (Amended 1/95)

- Standard of Practice 11-1

   When REALTORS® prepare opinions of real property value or price, other than in pursuit of a listing or to assist a potential purchaser in formulating a purchase offer, such opinions shall include the following:
   1) identification of the subject property
   2) date prepared

3) defined value or price
4) limiting conditions, including statements of purpose(s) and intended user(s)
5) any present or contemplated interest, including the possibility of representing the seller/landlord or buyers/tenants
6) basis for the opinion, including applicable market data
7) if the opinion is not an appraisal, a statement to that effect (Amended 1/01)

- Standard of Practice 11-2
The obligations of the Code of Ethics in respect of real estate disciplines other than appraisal shall be interpreted and applied in accordance with the standards of competence and practice which clients and the public reasonably require to protect their rights and interests considering the complexity of the transaction, the availability of expert assistance, and, where the REALTOR® is an agent or subagent, the obligations of a fiduciary. (Adopted 1/95)

- Standard of Practice 11-3
When REALTORS® provide consultive services to clients which involve advice or counsel for a fee (not a commission), such advice shall be rendered in an objective manner and the fee shall not be contingent on the substance of the advice or counsel given. If brokerage or transaction services are to be provided in addition to consultive services, a separate compensation may be paid with prior agreement between the client and REALTOR®. (Adopted 1/96)

- Standard of Practice 11-4
The competency required by Article 11 relates to services contracted for between REALTORS® and their clients or customers; the duties expressly imposed by the Code of Ethics; and the duties imposed by law or regulation. (Adopted 1/02)

Article 12
REALTORS® shall be careful at all times to present a true picture in their advertising and representations to the public. REALTORS® shall also ensure that their professional status (e.g., broker, appraiser, property manager, etc.) or status as REALTORS® is clearly identifiable in any such advertising. (Amended 1/93)

- Standard of Practice 12-1
REALTORS® may use the term "free" and similar terms in their advertising and in other representations provided that all terms governing availability of the offered product or service are clearly disclosed at the same time. (Amended 1/97)

- Standard of Practice 12-2
REALTORS® may represent their services as "free" or without cost even if they expect to receive compensation from a source other than their client provided that the potential for the REALTOR® to obtain a benefit from a third party is clearly disclosed at the same time. (Amended 1/97)

- Standard of Practice 12-3
The offering of premiums, prizes, merchandise discounts or other inducements to list, sell, purchase, or lease is not, in itself, unethical even if receipt of the benefit is contingent on listing, selling, purchasing, or leasing through the REALTOR® making the offer. However, REALTORS® must exercise care and candor in any such advertising or other public or private representations so that any party interested in receiving or otherwise benefiting from the REALTOR®'s offer will have clear, thorough, advance understanding of all the terms and conditions of the offer. The offering of any inducements to do business is subject to the limitations and restrictions of state law and the ethical obligations established by any applicable Standard of Practice. (Amended 1/95)

- Standard of Practice 12-4
REALTORS® shall not offer for sale/lease or advertise property without authority. When acting as listing brokers or as subagents, REALTORS® shall not quote a price different from that agreed upon with the seller/landlord. (Amended 1/93)

- Standard of Practice 12-5
REALTORS® shall not advertise nor permit any person employed by or affiliated with them to advertise listed property without disclosing the name of the firm. (Adopted 11/86)

- Standard of Practice 12-6
REALTORS®, when advertising unlisted real property for sale/lease in which they have an ownership interest, shall disclose their status as both owners/landlords and as REALTORS® or real estate licensees. (Amended 1/93)

- Standard of Practice 12-7
Only REALTORS® who participated in the transaction as the listing broker or cooperating broker (selling broker) may claim to have "sold" the property. Prior to closing, a cooperating broker may post a "sold" sign only with the consent of the listing broker. (Amended 1/96)

Article 13
REALTORS® shall not engage in activities that constitute the unauthorized practice of law and shall recommend that legal counsel be obtained when the interest of any party to the transaction requires it.

Article 14
If charged with unethical practice or asked to present evidence or to cooperate in any other way, in any professional standards proceeding or investigation, REALTORS® shall place all pertinent facts before the proper tribunals of the Member Board or affiliated institute, society, or council in which membership is held and shall take no action to disrupt or obstruct such processes. (Amended 1/99)

- Standard of Practice 14-1
REALTORS® shall not be subject to disciplinary proceedings in more than one Board of REALTORS® or affiliated institute, society or council in which they hold membership with respect to alleged violations of the Code of Ethics relating to the same transaction or event. (Amended 1/95)

- Standard of Practice 14-2
  REALTORS® shall not make any unauthorized disclosure or dissemination of the allegations, findings, or decision developed in connection with an ethics hearing or appeal or in connection with an arbitration hearing or procedural review. (Amended 1/92)

- Standard of Practice 14-3
  REALTORS® shall not obstruct the Board's investigative or professional standards proceedings by instituting or threatening to institute actions for libel, slander or defamation against any party to a professional standards proceeding or their witnesses based on the filing of an arbitration request, an ethics complaint, or testimony given before any tribunal. (Adopted 11/87, Amended 1/99)

- Standard of Practice 14-4
  REALTORS® shall not intentionally impede the Board's investigative or disciplinary proceedings by filing multiple ethics complaints based on the same event or transaction. (Adopted 11/88)

Duties to REALTORS®

Article 15
REALTORS® shall not knowingly or recklessly make false or misleading statements about competitors, their businesses, or their business practices. (Amended 1/92)

- Standard of Practice 15-1
  REALTORS® shall not knowingly or recklessly file false or unfounded ethics complaints. (Adopted 1/00)

Article 16
REALTORS® shall not engage in any practice or take any action inconsistent with the agency or other exclusive relationship recognized by law that other REALTORS® have with clients. (Amended 1/98)

- Standard of Practice 16-1
  Article 16 is not intended to prohibit aggressive or innovative business practices which are otherwise ethical and does not prohibit disagreements with other REALTORS® involving commission, fees, compensation or other forms of payment or expenses. (Adopted 1/93, Amended 1/95)

- Standard of Practice 16-2
  Article 16 does not preclude REALTORS® from making general announcements to prospective clients describing their services and the terms of their availability even though some recipients may have entered into agency agreements or other exclusive relationships with another REALTOR®. A general telephone canvass, general mailing or distribution addressed to all prospective clients in a given geographical area or in a given profession, business, club, or organization, or other classification or group is deemed "general" for purposes of this standard. (Amended 1/98)

Article 16 is intended to recognize as unethical two basic types of solicitations:

First, telephone or personal solicitations of property owners who have been identified by a real estate sign, multiple listing compilation, or other information service as having exclusively listed their property with another REALTOR®; and

Second, mail or other forms of written solicitations of prospective clients whose properties are exclusively listed with another REALTOR® when such solicitations are not part of a general mailing but are directed specifically to property owners identified through compilations of current listings, "for sale" or "for rent" signs, or other sources of information required by Article 3 and Multiple Listing Service rules to be made available to other REALTORS® under offers of subagency or cooperation. (Amended 1/93)

- Standard of Practice 16-3
  Article 16 does not preclude REALTORS® from contacting the client of another broker for the purpose of offering to provide, or entering into a contract to provide, a different type of real estate service unrelated to the type of service currently being provided (e.g., property management as opposed to brokerage). However, information received through a Multiple Listing Service or any other offer of cooperation may not be used to target clients of other REALTORS® to whom such offers to provide services may be made. (Amended 1/93)

- Standard of Practice 16-4
  REALTORS® shall not solicit a listing which is currently listed exclusively with another broker. However, if the listing broker, when asked by the REALTOR®, refuses to disclose the expiration date and nature of such listing; i.e., an exclusive right to sell, an exclusive agency, open listing, or other form of contractual agreement between the listing broker and the client, the REALTOR® may contact the owner to secure such information and may discuss the terms upon which the REALTOR® might take a future listing or, alternatively, may take a listing to become effective upon expiration of any existing exclusive listing. (Amended 1/94)

- Standard of Practice 16-5
  REALTORS® shall not solicit buyer/tenant agreements from buyers/tenants who are subject to exclusive buyer/tenant agreements. However, if asked by a REALTOR®, the broker refuses to disclose the expiration date of the exclusive buyer/tenant agreement, the REALTOR® may contact the buyer/tenant to secure such information and may discuss the terms upon which the REALTOR® might enter into a future buyer/tenant agreement or, alternatively, may enter into a buyer/tenant agreement to become effective upon the expiration of any existing exclusive buyer/tenant agreement. (Adopted 1/94, Amended 1/98)

- Standard of Practice 16-6
  When REALTORS® are contacted by the client of another REALTOR® regarding the creation of an exclusive relationship

to provide the same type of service, and REALTORS® have not directly or indirectly initiated such discussions, they may discuss the terms upon which they might enter into a future agreement or, alternatively, may enter into an agreement which becomes effective upon expiration of any existing exclusive agreement. (Amended 1/98)

- Standard of Practice 16-7
The fact that a client has retained a REALTOR® as an agent or in another exclusive relationship in one or more past transactions does not preclude other REALTORS® from seeking such former client's future business. (Amended 1/98)

- Standard of Practice 16-8
The fact that an exclusive agreement has been entered into with a REALTOR® shall not preclude or inhibit any other REALTOR® from entering into a similar agreement after the expiration of the prior agreement. (Amended 1/98)

- Standard of Practice 16-9
REALTORS®, prior to entering into an agency agreement or other exclusive relationship, have an affirmative obligation to make reasonable efforts to determine whether the client is subject to a current, valid exclusive agreement to provide the same type of real estate service. (Amended 1/98)

- Standard of Practice 16-10
REALTORS®, acting as agents of, or in another relationship with, buyers or tenants, shall disclose that relationship to the seller/landlord's agent or broker at first contact and shall provide written confirmation of that disclosure to the seller/landlord's agent or broker not later than execution of a purchase agreement or lease. (Amended 1/98)

- Standard of Practice 16-11
On unlisted property, REALTORS® acting as buyer/tenant agents or brokers shall disclose that relationship to the seller/landlord at first contact for that client and shall provide written confirmation of such disclosure to the seller/landlord not later than execution of any purchase or lease agreement.

REALTORS® shall make any request for anticipated compensation from the seller/landlord at first contact. (Amended 1/98)

- Standard of Practice 16-12
REALTORS®, acting as agents or brokers of sellers/landlords or as subagents of listing brokers, shall disclose that relationship to buyers/tenants as soon as practicable and shall provide written confirmation of such disclosure to buyers/tenants not later than execution of any purchase or lease agreement. (Amended 1/98)

- Standard of Practice 16-13
All dealings concerning property exclusively listed, or with buyer/tenants who are subject to an exclusive agreement shall be carried on with the client's agent or broker, and not with the client, except with the consent of the client's agent or broker or except where such dealings are initiated by the client. (Adopted 1/93, Amended 1/98)

- Standard of Practice 16-14
REALTORS® are free to enter into contractual relationships or to negotiate with sellers/landlords, buyers/tenants or others who are not subject to an exclusive agreement but shall not knowingly obligate them to pay more than one commission except with their informed consent. (Amended 1/98)

- Standard of Practice 16-15
In cooperative transactions REALTORS® shall compensate cooperating REALTORS® (principal brokers) and shall not compensate nor offer to compensate, directly or indirectly, any of the sales licensees employed by or affiliated with other REALTORS® without the prior express knowledge and consent of the cooperating broker.

- Standard of Practice 16-16
REALTORS®, acting as subagents or buyer/tenant agents or brokers, shall not use the terms of an offer to purchase/lease to attempt to modify the listing broker's offer of compensation to subagents or buyer's agents or brokers nor make the submission of an executed offer to purchase/lease contingent on the listing broker's agreement to modify the offer of compensation. (Amended 1/98)

- Standard of Practice 16-17
REALTORS® acting as subagents or as buyer/tenant agents or brokers, shall not attempt to extend a listing broker's offer of cooperation and/or compensation to other brokers without the consent of the listing broker. (Amended 1/98)

- Standard of Practice 16-18
REALTORS® shall not use information obtained from listing brokers through offers to cooperate made through multiple listing services or through other offers of cooperation to refer listing brokers' clients to other brokers or to create buyer/tenant relationships with listing brokers' clients, unless such use is authorized by listing brokers. (Amended 1/02)

- Standard of Practice 16-19
Signs giving notice of property for sale, rent, lease, or exchange shall not be placed on property without consent of the seller/landlord. (Amended 1/93)

- Standard of Practice 16-20
REALTORS®, prior to or after terminating their relationship with their current firm, shall not induce clients of their current firm to cancel exclusive contractual agreements between the client and that firm. This does not preclude REALTORS® (principals) from establishing agreements with their associated licensees governing assignability of exclusive agreements. (Adopted 1/98)

Article 17
In the event of contractual disputes or specific non-contractual disputes as defined in Standard of Practice 17-4 between REALTORS® (principals) associated with different firms, arising out of their relationship as REALTORS®, the REALTORS® shall submit the dispute to arbitration in accordance with the regulations of their Board or Boards rather than litigate the matter.

In the event clients of REALTORS® wish to arbitrate contractual disputes arising out of real estate transactions, REALTORS® shall arbitrate those disputes in accordance with the regulations of their Board, provided the clients agree to be bound by the decision.

The obligation to participate in arbitration contemplated by this Article includes the obligation of REALTORS® (principals) to cause their firms to arbitrate and be bound by any award. (Amended 1/01)

- Standard of Practice 17-1
  The filing of litigation and refusal to withdraw from it by REALTORS® in an arbitrable matter constitutes a refusal to arbitrate. (Adopted 2/86)

- Standard of Practice 17-2
  Article 17 does not require REALTORS® to arbitrate in those circumstances when all parties to the dispute advise the Board in writing that they choose not to arbitrate before the Board. (Amended 1/93)

- Standard of Practice 17-3
  REALTORS®, when acting solely as principals in a real estate transaction, are not obligated to arbitrate disputes with other REALTORS® absent a specific written agreement to the contrary. (Adopted 1/96)

- Standard of Practice 17-4
  Specific non-contractual disputes that are subject to arbitration pursuant to Article 17 are:

  1) Where a listing broker has compensated a cooperating broker and another cooperating broker subsequently claims to be the procuring cause of the sale or lease. In such cases the complainant may name the first cooperating broker as respondent and arbitration may proceed without the listing broker being named as a respondent. Alternatively, if the complaint is brought against the listing broker, the listing broker may name the first cooperating broker as a third-party respondent. In either instance the decision of the hearing panel as to procuring cause shall be conclusive with respect to all current or subsequent claims of the parties for compensation arising out of the underlying cooperative transaction. (Adopted 1/97)

  2) Where a buyer or tenant representative is compensated by the seller or landlord, and not by the listing broker, and the listing broker, as a result, reduces the commission owed by the seller or landlord and, subsequent to such actions, another cooperating broker claims to be the procuring cause of sale or lease. In such cases the complainant may name the first cooperating broker as respondent and arbitration may proceed without the listing broker being named as a respondent. Alternatively, if the complaint is brought against the listing broker, the listing broker may name the first cooperating broker as a third-party

respondent. In either instance the decision of the hearing panel as to procuring cause shall be conclusive with respect to all current or subsequent claims of the parties for compensation arising out of the underlying cooperative transaction. (Adopted 1/97)

  3) Where a buyer or tenant representative is compensated by the buyer or tenant and, as a result, the listing broker reduces the commission owed by the seller or landlord and, subsequent to such actions, another cooperating broker claims to be the procuring cause of sale or lease. In such cases the complainant may name the first cooperating broker as respondent and arbitration may proceed without the listing broker being named as a respondent. Alternatively, if the complaint is brought against the listing broker, the listing broker may name the first cooperating broker as a third-party respondent. In either instance the decision of the hearing panel as to procuring cause shall be conclusive with respect to all current or subsequent claims of the parties for compensation arising out of the underlying cooperative transaction. (Adopted 1/97)

  4) Where two or more listing brokers claim entitlement to compensation pursuant to open listings with a seller or landlord who agrees to participate in arbitration (or who requests arbitration) and who agrees to be bound by the decision. In cases where one of the listing brokers has been compensated by the seller or landlord, the other listing broker, as complainant, may name the first listing broker as respondent and arbitration may proceed between the brokers. (Adopted 1/97)

The Code of Ethics was adopted in 1913. Amended at the Annual Convention in 1924, 1928, 1950, 1951, 1952, 1955, 1956, 1961, 1962, 1974, 1982, 1986, 1987, 1989, 1990, 1991, 1992, 1993, 1994, 1995, 1996, 1997, 1998, 1999, 2000 and 2001.

Explanatory Notes

The reader should be aware of the following policies which have been approved by the Board of Directors of the National Association:

In filing a charge of an alleged violation of the Code of Ethics by a REALTOR®, the charge must read as an alleged violation of one or more Articles of the Code. Standards of Practice may be cited in support of the charge.

The Standards of Practice serve to clarify the ethical obligations imposed by the various Articles and supplement, and do not substitute for, the Case Interpretations in Interpretations of the Code of Ethics.

Modifications to existing Standards of Practice and additional new Standards of Practice are approved from time to time. Readers are cautioned to ensure that the most recent publications are utilized.

INDEX

CREDITS AND ACKNOWLEDGEMENTS